INTERNATIONAL COURTS
AND TRIBUNALS SERIES

General Editors

RUTH MACKENZIE
CESARE P. R. ROMANO
MIKAEL RASK MADSEN

Hybrid Justice

INTERNATIONAL COURTS AND TRIBUNALS SERIES

A distinctive feature of modern international society is the increase in the number of international judicial bodies and dispute settlement and implementation control bodies; in their case-loads; and in the range and importance of the issues that are called upon to address. These factors reflect a new stage in the delivery of international justice. The International Courts and Tribunals series has been established to encourage the publication of independent and scholarly works which address, in critical and analytical fashion, the legal and policy aspects of the functioning of international courts and tribunals, including their institutional, substantive, and procedural aspects.

Hybrid Justice

Innovation and Impact in the Prosecution of Atrocity Crimes

Edited by

KIRSTEN AINLEY AND MARK KERSTEN

OXFORD
UNIVERSITY PRESS

OXFORD
UNIVERSITY PRESS

Great Clarendon Street, Oxford, OX2 6DP,
United Kingdom

Oxford University Press is a department of the University of Oxford.
It furthers the University's objective of excellence in research, scholarship,
and education by publishing worldwide. Oxford is a registered trade mark of
Oxford University Press in the UK and in certain other countries

Published in the United States of America by Oxford University Press
198 Madison Avenue, New York, NY 10016, United States of America

British Library Cataloguing in Publication Data

Data available

Library of Congress Control Number: 2024945805

ISBN 978–0–19–289375–8

DOI: 10.1093/oso/9780192893758.001.0001

Printed and bound by
CPI Group (UK) Ltd, Croydon, CR0 4YY

MIX
Paper | Supporting responsible forestry
FSC® C013604

The manufacturer's authorised representative in the EU for product safety is
Oxford University Press España S.A. of el Parque Empresarial San Fernando
de Henares, Avenida de Castilla, 2 – 28830 Madrid (www.oup.es/en).

Foreword: The Promise of Hybrid Justice

Beth van Schaack
United States Ambassador-at-Large for Global Criminal Justice

We are at an historic moment for international justice. As we witness atrocity crimes being perpetrated against civilian populations around the world, states, courts, and civil society organizations are mobilizing to deliver justice to victims and survivors in a range of new and emergent accountability mechanisms. Attempts to achieve justice in these varied situations reflect the tremendous legacy of the Nuremburg and Tokyo Tribunals established after World War II, the work of the ad hoc international tribunals dedicated to the conflicts in the former Yugoslavia (ICTY) and Rwanda (ICTR), the establishment of a permanent International Criminal Court (ICC), and the plethora of international justice mechanisms that have followed since. With the international community unwilling or unable to create additional standalone ad hoc tribunals in the ICTY/R model, hybrid, mixed, and internationalized tribunals increasingly play an essential role in the ecosystem of international justice and the imaginations of justice entrepreneurs. As such, this book offers a timely and valuable resource as we seek to strengthen the global justice architecture.

As demonstrated by the contributors to this book, the hybrid model has much to recommend it. Through the integration of international elements into domestic legal systems, hybrid tribunals provide an opportunity to internationalize domestic judicial systems. They can advance the rule of law in keeping with international principles but in ways that are responsive to local and regional norms. They enable greater local ownership of justice processes while also providing an opportunity to (re)build domestic capacity through technology and knowledge transfer. When established according to established best practices, they can be agile, effective, and efficient tools of justice. Hybrids have the potential to enjoy greater cultural and procedural legitimacy than either purely domestic or fully international institutions. This, in turn, builds confidence in the independence and impartiality of the mechanisms—a tall order in low-trust environments where national authorities may be accused of being blind to, or even complicit in, conflict-related crimes or at risk of being co-opted by political forces. In such contexts, the presence of international elements, particularly experienced personnel, can serve to restore legitimacy and popular faith in domestic institutions and insulate justice processes from problematic local dynamics.

It may seem odd to focus on hybrid mechanisms with a fully operational International Criminal Court available in which to try the most egregious breaches of international criminal law. However, the court's jurisdiction remains incomplete and its resources limited. The ICC is plagued by challenges to its legitimacy, erratic state cooperation, and persistent perceptions of inefficacy and inefficiency. As such, the international community must continue to create, enable, and support additional accountability mechanisms to respond to the commission of international crimes when the political will for an ICC referral is lacking, when the ICC is not an appropriate forum, or when only a minority of the abuses or perpetrators in question will find themselves in The Hague.

This reality undergirds US support for the development of an internationalized tribunal dedicated to prosecuting the crime of aggression against Ukraine. A special tribunal is necessary as the ICC does not have jurisdiction over the crime of aggression, the crime from which spring all other horrors suffered by the Ukrainian people. The tribunal as proposed would be deeply rooted in Ukraine's judicial system, but also benefit from significant international investment in the form of substantive law, personnel, information sources, location, and structure. However, the envisioned hybrid institution would do more than just supplement the ICC; it could also facilitate broader cross-regional international support, demonstrate Ukraine's leadership in ensuring accountability for the crime of aggression, enhance the domestic legal system, and further institutionalize the rule of law. Ukraine is not alone in exploring the hybrid model. In my current capacity, I have worked extensively in other societies exploring their own hybrid models, including most recently in The Gambia and Liberia.

This book explores the multifaceted opportunities presented, and challenges faced, in establishing hybrid mechanisms. It offers practical observations about the design, function, and impact of hybrid mechanisms as well as academic evaluations of past precedent. As such, the book offers a valuable toolkit for those designing future hybrid mechanisms and an important record of the achievements and shortcomings of prior efforts. I attended the first workshop of the Hybrid Justice project at the London School of Economics and am delighted to see the steady dissemination of the project's outputs—including this publication—given the enduring relevance of this work to the fields of international criminal law and transitional justice. This book's many contributions to the field will offer inspiration to those innovating and building new institutions to deliver justice to victims and hold perpetrators accountable for the worst crimes known to humankind.

Acknowledgements

This book is the result of many years of work that we completed alongside fantastic colleagues on the Hybrid Justice project https://hybridjustice.com. We are grateful to have had the opportunity to bring most of the authors of the book's chapters together to workshop their contributions at the London School of Economics (LSE) in 2018, funded by the Rockefeller Foundation through the LSE Institute of Global Affairs, and supported by Maddalena Procopio. The Wayamo Foundation is a partner on the project and enabled Mark Kersten's participation in it.

The book was delayed significantly by the onset of the COVID-19 pandemic in 2020 and various crises and commitments downstream of it. The editors are particularly appreciative of Shivangi Seth for her stellar work in reinvigorating the project, conducting additional research, indexing, and copy-editing all chapters to help us, finally, to reach publication. We are grateful to the authors for their patience, but more than that for their outstanding and important chapters. Rizwaan Ahmad, our editor at Oxford University Press, has generously guided us throughout the process and Catherine Hirst stepped in to help index the book at very late notice, producing exceptional work.

The final manuscript of the book was submitted in January 2024, as evidence of war crimes was livestreamed daily from Gaza and as Russia persisted in its illegal war on Ukraine. The International Court of Justice and the International Criminal Court are both operative in addressing alleged violations of international humanitarian and criminal law in each case, but even if these international courts are willing and able to hold states and individuals to account for the most egregious violations of the law, they will never be able to comprehensively address the scale of harms caused. Hybrid tribunals have been proposed in each case to supplement the work of the international courts and we stand in solidarity with the lawyers, civil society organizations, activists, and journalists who continue to fight for justice alongside, and in response to the needs of, those who have faced crimes of appalling gravity.

Finally, we acknowledge the privilege that comes with being able to step away from our work, to spend time with loved ones, or focus on other parts of life. As the wars in Gaza and Ukraine make clear, many do not have that luxury. We thank our friends and families for their love and support, and hope that justice for international crimes, whether achieved through hybrid courts or any other mechanism or process, can play a part in making all families, indeed all civilians, free from fear and safe from attack.

Kirsten Ainley and Mark Kersten

Contents

Abbreviations

ACFODE	Action for Development
ACHPR	African Charter on Human and Peoples Rights
ACJHR	African Court of Justice and Human Rights
ADHOC	Cambodian Human Rights and Development Association
AFRC	Armed Forces Revolutionary Council
AGA	African Governance Architecture
ARCSS	Agreement on the Resolution of the Conflict in the Republic of South Sudan
AU	African Union
AUPD	African Union High Level Panel on Darfur
AUTJF	African Union Transitional Justice Framework
AUTJP	African Union Transitional Justice Policy
BiH	Bosnia and Herzegovina
BIH WCC	The War Crimes Chamber in Bosnia and Herzegovina
CAR	Central African Republic
CAT	Committee Against Torture
CAVR	Commission for Reception Truth and Reconciliation East Timor
CDF	Civil Defence Forces
CEDAW	Convention on the Elimination of Discrimination Against Women
CICC	Coalition for the International Criminal Court
CICIG	Commission against Impunity in Guatemala
CJA	Centre for Justice and Accountability
CPK	Communist Party of Kampuchea
CSO	Civil Society Organisation
Dakar Guidelines	Dakar Guidelines on the Establishment of Hybrid Courts
DLU	Defence Lawyers Unit
DRC	Democratic Republic of the Congo
EAC	Extraordinary African Chambers
ECCC	Extraordinary Chambers in the Courts of Cambodia
ECOWAS	Economic Community of West African States
ECHR	The European Convention on Human Rights and Fundamental Freedoms
ESCR	Economic, social and cultural rights
ETT	East Timor Tribunal
EU	European Union
EU CSFP	European Union Common Foreign and Security Policy
GDP	General Department of Prisons of the Ministry of Interior
HCSS	Hybrid Court for South Sudan

HR	Human resources
HRBH	Human Rights Chamber for Bosnia and Herzegovina
HRW	Human Rights Watch
IACHR	Inter-American Commission on Human Rights
ICC	International Criminal Court
ICCPR	International Covenant on Civil and Political Rights
ICESCR	International Covenant on Economic, Social and Cultural Rights
ICJ	International Court of Justice
ICL	International criminal law
ICRC	International Committee of the Red Cross
ICTJ	International Center for Transitional Justice
ICTR	International Criminal Tribunal for Rwanda
ICTY	International Criminal Tribunal for the Former Yugoslavia
IGAD	Intergovernmental Authority on Development
IGIE	Interdisciplinary Group of Independent Experts
IHT	Iraqi High Tribunal
IIIM Syria	International, Impartial and Independent Mechanism to Assist in the Investigation and Prosecution of Persons Responsible for the Most Serious Crimes Under International Law Committed in the Syrian Arab Republic Since March 2011
ILO	International Labour Organization
ITJRC	International and Transitional Justice Resource Center
IMT	International Military Tribunal at Nuremberg
IMTFE	International Military Tribunal for the Far East
IRMCT	International Residual Mechanism for Criminal Tribunals
ISIS	Islamic State of Iraq and Syria
IT	Information technology
IUC-ICLP	Inter-University Programme-International Criminal Law and Procedure
JIT	Joint Investigation Team
KLA	Kosovo Liberation Army
KPIs	Key performance indicators
KSC	Kosovo Specialist Chambers
Malabo Protocol	Protocol on Amendments to the Protocol on the Statute of the African Court of Justice and Human Rights
MACCIH	Mission to Support the Fight Against Corruption and Impunity in Honduras
MINUSCA	United Nations Multidimensional Integrated Stabilization Mission in the Central African Republic
MoU	Memoranda of understanding
MONUSCO	United Nations Organization Stabilization Mission in the Democratic Republic of the Congo
NCCK	National Council of Churches of Kenya
NGO	Non-governmental organization

NOCEM	National Organization for Civic Education and Election Monitoring
OAS	Organization of American States
ODIHR	Office for Democratic Institutions and Human Rights
OECD	Organisation for Economic Co-operation and Development
OHCHR	United Nations High Commissioner for Human Rights
OHR	Office of the High Representative
OSCE	Organisation for Security and Co-operation in Europe
OSJI	Open Society Justice Initiative
OTP	Office of the Prosecutor
PCRD	African Union Policy Framework on Post Conflict Reconstruction and Development
R-ARCSS	Revitalised Agreement on the Resolution of the Conflict in the Republic of South Sudan
REC	Regional Economic Communities
RPE	Rules of Procedure and Evidence
RPS	Rwandan Prison Services
RSCSL	Residual Mechanism for the Special Court for Sierra Leone
RUF	Revolutionary United Front
SCC	Special Criminal Court in the Central African Republic
SCIT	Serious Crimes Investigation Team
SCSL	Special Court for Sierra Leone
SCU	East Timor Special Panels for Serious Crimes
SGBC	Sexual and gender-based crimes
SITF	Specialist Investigative Task Force
SLPS	Sierra Leone Prison Service
SPDDC	Special Panels of the Dili District Court in East Timor
SPLM	Sudan People's Liberation Movement
SPO	Kosovo Specialist Prosecutor's Office
SPSC	Special Panels for Serious Crimes
STL	Special Tribunal for Lebanon
TFV	Trust Fund for Victims
TJ	Transitional justice
TJWG	South Sudanese Transitional Justice Working Group
TRC	Truth and Reconciliation Commission
UDHR	Universal Declaration of Human Rights
UFECIC	Special Prosecutorial Unit against Corruption and Impunity
UN	United Nations
UNAKRT	United Nations Assistance to the Khmer Rouge Trials
UNAMSIL	United Nations Mission in Sierra Leone
UNCHR	United Nations Commission on Human Rights
UNDP	United Nations Development Programme
UNGA	United Nations General Assembly
UNICRI	United Nations Interregional Crime and Justice Research Institute

UNITAD	UN Investigative Team to Promote Accountability for Crimes Committed by Da'esh/ISIL
UNMIK	United Nations Mission in Kosovo
UNMIT	United Nations Integrated Mission in East Timor
UNPROFOR	United Nations Protection Force
UNSC	United Nations Security Council
UNTAET	United Nations Transitional Administration in East Timor
VSS	Victim Support Section
VWU	Victim and Witness Unit

Contributors

Kirsten Ainley is Professor of International Relations at the Australian National University, a research fellow at the Centre for Women, Peace and Security at the London School of Economics, and the Co-Principal Investigator of the UKRI GCRF Gender, Justice and Security Hub and the Hybrid Justice project. Her research focuses on international policy and practice in military, legal, and development-focused interventions, and the impacts of these interventions, with an increasing focus on their gendered impacts. She has published on international criminal law, transitional justice, the International Criminal Court, and the Responsibility to Protect, and her current work traces funding streams for international courts and transitional justice programmes. She recently co-authored, with Mark Kersten, the Dakar Guidelines on the Establishment of Hybrid Courts, which develop good practice on setting up hybrid criminal tribunals and investigatory mechanisms.

Philipp Ambach is Chief of the Victims Participation and Reparations Section at the International Criminal Court (ICC). He previously served as the ICC President's Special Assistant for over six years. Before that, he worked at the UN ad hoc tribunals ICTY and ICTR as a legal advisor to the judges of the Appeals Chamber. Prior to that, he worked as an associate legal officer in the ICTY Registry. Philipp holds a PhD in international criminal law from Free University of Berlin and has been admitted as prosecutor to the prosecutor's office of Cologne, Germany. He obtained his master's degree in law in 2004 from Humboldt-University of Berlin, Germany. He is a guest lecturer in international criminal and humanitarian law at various legal institutions and has published a number of academic contributions in these fields.

Sareta Ashraph is a barrister specializing in international criminal law, with expertise in the gendered commission and impact of international crimes. She serves as a senior legal consultant to both the Center for Justice and Accountability, where she leads on case-building for crimes committed in Syria and Iraq, and to the US Holocaust Memorial Museum's Simon-Skjodt Center for the Prevention of Genocide, where she supports their intersectional analytical approaches to determinations of genocide and other core international crimes in situations around the world. Sareta has served as the Director of Field Investigations at the UN Investigative Team to promote accountability for the crimes committed by Da'esh/ISIL (UNITAD) (2019–2022), as the Chief Legal Analyst to the UN Commission of Inquiry on Syria (2012–2016) and the Commission of Inquiry on Libya (2012–2012). Prior to this, Sareta was a legal advisor to the Defence Office of the International Criminal Court (2010–2011) and the Defence Co-Counsel before the Special Court for Sierra Leone (2003–2009).

Elena Baylis is a Professor at the University of Pittsburgh School of Law with a joint appointment by courtesy in the Graduate School of Public and International Affairs. She is a graduate of Yale Law School and the University of Oregon Honors College. Elena's scholarship focuses topics that concern the relationships among communities and between domestic and international law, such as protection and repatriation of cultural objects; reconciliation mechanisms; the intersections between international criminal law and rule of law initiatives; and the role of transnational networks. She has written extensively about the new wave of hybrid courts and served as an expert and a primary drafter for the Dakar Guidelines on the Establishment of Hybrid Courts. She also studies the intersections between US and international law, including the risk of crimes against humanity within the United States, as well as issues of US national security and immigration policy. She has conducted field research and worked on legal education/rule of law initiatives in several post-conflict states, including Kosovo, Ethiopia, and the Democratic Republic of Congo. Her research has been commissioned by the International Center for Transitional Justice and the US Institute of Peace.

Erica Bussey is currently working with the United Nations Office of the Ombudsperson to the ISIL (Da'esh) and Al-Qaida Sanctions Committee. She was previously the Deputy Director of the Joint Human Rights Office (JHRO) at MONUSCO, the United Nations peace operation in the Democratic Republic of Congo (DRC), working, inter alia, on accountability and transitional justice. She has previously served as a Judicial Affairs Officer with the UN Justice and Corrections Standing Capacity, where she was deployed to the Central African Republic (CAR), DRC, and Afghanistan, as a Senior Human Rights Advisor with OHCHR in Sierra Leone, and as a Senior Legal Advisor for Amnesty International in Senegal, focusing on the Special Criminal Court for CAR, the proposed Hybrid Court for South Sudan, the Hissène Habré trial, and on ICC–Africa relations. Erica has also worked at several hybrid and ad hoc tribunals, including the Special Court for Sierra Leone (including, inter alia, on the Charles Taylor trial), the Extraordinary Chambers in the Courts of Cambodia and the International Criminal Tribunal for Rwanda. She is qualified to practice law in Ontario (Canada), and holds an LL.M. in International Law from Cambridge and a JD from the University of Toronto. The views expressed herein are those of the author and do not necessarily reflect the views of the United Nations.

Kerstin Bree Carlson is Associate Professor at Roskilde University, where she teaches law and society related topics. She is also affiliated with iCourts at the University of Copenhagen and the American University of Paris. She is the author of *Model(ing) Justice: Perfecting the Promise of International Criminal Law* (Cambridge University Press 2018) and *The Justice Laboratory: International Law in Africa* (Chatham House/Brookings 2022), and co-editor of *The President on Trial: Prosecuting Hissène Habré* (Oxford University Press 2020) and *Transitional Justice in Aparadigmatic Contexts: Accountability, Recognition and Disruption* (Routledge 2023) as well as several articles and book chapters on topics in international criminal law and transitional justice. She writes frequently for *The Conversation* blog. Her current research focuses on terror law in France and Denmark, and Colombia's Special Jurisdiction for Peace.

Alice Dieci currently works as a Human Rights Officer for the National Reporting and Investigation Unit, Joint Human Rights Officeat MONUSCO in the Democratic Republic of the Congo and she previously served as a Human Rights Officer at MINUSCA in the Central African Republic,as well as with the UN Office of the High Commissioner for Human Rights in Colombia, Venezuela and Geneva. She also worked as an expert consultant for the IOM/

UNHCR anti-trafficking task team of the Global Protection Cluster working on Cameroon and Venezuela and for the European Union cooperation in Latin America on technical cooperation projects in Mexico Before joining the UN, she worked with civil society, academia, and law firms and participated in various research projects. She is part of the Justice Rapid Response Roster as a SGBV expert and of the Italian network of experts on trafficking in persons and she is a member of the Spanish Bar Association. In 2024, she founded the NGO 'Artivism and Sport for Human Rights', whose mission is to promote a culture of peace and respect for human rights through art and sport, as forms of activism and resistance. She holds an LLM in international humanitarian law and human rights from the Geneva Academy of International Humanitarian Law and Human Rights in Switzerland and a law degree from the University of Modena in Italy. The views expressed herein are those of the author and do not necessarily reflect the views of the United Nations.

Philippa Greer is an expert in international criminal justice, detention, international human rights, and international humanitarian law. She has over twelve years of experience gained working with the UN, non-governmental organizations (NGOs), courts, and academic institutions, including in challenging contexts in Africa, the Middle East, Southeast Asia and Afghanistan. She currently serves as the Head of the Legal Office of the United Nations Relief and Works Agency for Palestine Refugees in the Near East, based in the Gaza Strip, after spending the past nine years working for the UN in Kabul, East Jerusalem, Gaza, New York, Phnom Penh, Arusha, and the Hague. Prior to joining the UN, Philippa has pursued work on death penalty abolition advocacy, criminal justice, and access to justice issues in various countries, including the United States and Pakistan. She has also served as the Law Clerk to the Chief Justice of the Republic of South Africa. Philippa writes for a variety of publications on international human rights topics and has been featured on CNN, the BBC, and others. She was a John F Kennedy Memorial Scholar at Harvard Law School.

Rosemary Grey is a Senior Lecturer at Sydney Law School, at the University of Sydney. Her research focuses on gender and international criminal law, particularly at the International Criminal Court (ICC) and Extraordinary Chambers in the Courts of Cambodia (ECCC). Her book, *Prosecuting Sexual and Gender-Based Crimes in the International Criminal Court*, was published by Cambridge University Press in 2019. Rosemary has been invited to present her research at international forums including the ICC Assembly of States Parties and the ICC Office of the Prosecutor. Rosemary's current research is funded by two Australian Research Council (ARC) grants for her DECRA project, 'Reproductive Crimes in International Law: Lessons from Cambodia', and a Discovery Project titled 'Reimagining Judging in International Criminal Courts: A Gendered Approach'. She teaches public international law, international criminal law, , and the laws of armed conflict, and has collaborated with several organizations in the international criminal justice field, including Africa Legal Aid, Amnesty International, the Global Justice Center, Women's Initiatives for Gender Justice, , and the ICC.

Ezequiel Jimenez Martinez earned his PhD from Middlesex University (United Kingdom). He currently works at Amnesty International (International Secretariat). Before joining Amnesty International, Ezequiel was the Human Rights Officer in the Province of Salta's House Chamber (Argentina), and later a research adviser at the School of Global Studies at the University of Gothenburg (Sweden). He serves in the Editorial Board of En Letra Penal (University of Buenos Aires). Ezequiel has a BA in Political Science and International Relations from Macalester College (United States), and an MA in Human Rights Policy and Practice as an Erasmus Mundus Scholar (European Union) at the University of Roehampton (UK), Gothenburg (Sweden) and Tromsø (Norway). He is a graduate of the United World Colleges (Red Cross Nordic), and a fellow of the Royal Society for the encouragement of Arts, Manufactures and Commerce (United Kingdom).

Olga Kavran is the Founding Director of IUSTICOM, established in 2021 as the first non-governmental organization dedicated to communicating justice, and a fellow at the Vrije Universiteit Brussel in Belgium completing a PhD on the topic of international criminal courts' obligation to provide information to the public. From 2010–2020, Olga was the Head of Outreach and Legacy at the Special Tribunal for Lebanon (STL). Prior to the STL, she had worked at the International Criminal Tribunal for the former Yugoslavia (ICTY) in various positions—as a translator (1997–2000), Outreach Deputy Coordinator (2000–2006), and Spokesperson for the Prosecutor (2006–2010). Her career began in Saatchi & Saatchi Advertising where she received a number of awards. Olga also has an LLM in public international law with a specialization in international criminal law from Leiden University in The Netherlands; has taught at the American University of Beirut, as well as several other universities in Lebanon, the former Yugoslavia, the United States and the United Kingdom; and has published extensively on international criminal courts and proceedings.

Elise Keppler is executive director of the Global Justice Center, a human rights organization focused on leveraging international law to advance gender equality. Prior to joining Global Justice Center in January 2024, she was associate international justice director and associate general counsel at Human Rights Watch. For twenty years at Human Rights Watch, she worked to advance justice for serious crimes committed in violation of international law before domestic, hybrid, and international courts. She focused on situations in Africa and strengthening prospects for credible accountability at the domestic level, including in the Central African Republic, Guinea, Liberia, Sierra Leone, South Sudan, Sudan, and Uganda. She worked with activists across Africa to counter backlash against the ICC and helped lead campaigns for Darfur's referral to the ICC and for the surrender of the former Liberian president, Charles Taylor, to face justice. In the General Counsel's Office, where she worked part time from November 2020 to January 2024, she assessed and mitigated risk to support the organization carrying out its mandate effectively. In 2012, she was a visiting scholar with the Democratic Governance and Rights Unit at the University of Cape Town's Faculty of Law. She holds a Bachelor of Arts from Brown University and a Juris Doctor from the University of California, Berkeley School of Law. Prior to joining Human Rights Watch she worked as an associate at Schulte Roth & Zabel LLP.

Mark Kersten is an assistant professor in the Criminology and Criminal Justice Department at the University of the Fraser Valley in British Columbia, Canada, and a Senior Consultant at the Wayamo Foundation in Berlin, Germany. Mark is the founder of the blog *Justice in Conflict* and author of the book, published by Oxford University Press, of the same name. He holds an MSc and PhD in International Relations from the London School of Economics and a BA (Hons) from the University of Guelph. Mark has previously been a research associate at the Refugee Law Project in Uganda, and a researcher at Justice Africa and Lawyers for Justice in Libya in London. He has taught courses on genocide studies; the politics of international law; transitional justice; diplomacy; and conflict and peace studies at the London School of Economics, SOAS, and the University of Toronto. Mark's research has appeared in numerous academic fora as well as in media publications such as *The Globe and Mail*, *Al Jazeera*, *BBC*, *Foreign Policy*, the *CBC*, *Toronto Star*, and *The Washington Post*. He has a passion for gardening, reading, hockey (on ice), date nights, late nights, Lego, and creating time for loved ones.

Patryk I. Labuda is an assistant professor of international law and international relations at Central European University in Vienna. He earned his PhD in international law from the Geneva Graduate Institute of International and Development Studies. A lawyer and historian by training, Patryk studies how global governance institutions, in particular international criminal tribunals and UN peace operations, use international norms to achieve public policy aims. His first book, *International Criminal Tribunals and Domestic Accountability: In the Court's Shadow*, was published by Oxford University Press.

Tyanai Masiya is based at the School of Public Management and Administration, University of Pretoria. He has written extensively on issues of citizenship and democracy in Zimbabwe, including constitutionalism, democratization, elections, as well as the transparency and accountability of the state. Some of his articles on Zimbabwe include, 'When the Military Become a Security and Political Threat: Zimbabwean Army Generals in Electoral Politics'; The Use of Heroism in the Zimbabwe African National Union Patriotic Front (ZANU PF) Intra-Party Factional Dynamics, and 'The Security Sector and the Plunder of Zimbabwe's Chiadzwa Alluvial Diamonds: "Goat Mentality" in Practice'. Tyanai has also edited a book on civil society and constitutional reforms in Africa. Beyond issues of the state, his areas of interest include local government management and service delivery.

Shastry Njeru is the Team Leader for Research and Advocacy Unit in Harare, an independent non-governmental organization which was set up in 2006. He has a passion for research on human rights and governance issues, particularly those pertaining to women, children, and state institutions, with a view to bringing about policy changes which promote a democratic culture within Zimbabwe. Shastry has worked extensively in civil society in Zimbabwe, in the academia and in the public sector. His interests include dealing with the past, conflict transformation, evaluation, post conflict recovery, and gender.

Nelson Camilo Sánchez is an associate professor of law at the University of Virginia (UVA) School of Law. He directs the UVA's International Human Rights Law Clinic and co-directs the Center for Comparative and International Law. Sánchez holds an LLB and PhD in Law from the National University of Colombia and an LLM from Harvard Law School. His research focuses on transitional justice processes, examining how societies address human rights violations and work towards reconciliation and accountability. He is formerly research director of the Center for the Study of Law, Justice, and Society (Dejusticia) and associate professor of law at the Universidad Nacional de Colombia, in Bogota, Colombia. Before joining Dejusticia in 2008, he served with the Inter-American Commission on Human Rights and the Colombian Commission of Jurists.

Dennis R. Schmidt is Assistant Professor in International Relations at the School of Government and International Affairs at Durham University. He has held fellowships and visiting posts at the Hamburg Institute for Advanced Studies, George Washington University, the London School of Economics and Political Science, and the University of Tübingen. Interested in the normative dimension of world politics, his research explores how international law and institutions shape, and are shaped by, changing ideas and patterns of global order, and how these changes affect the constitution and morality of global governance. He has published on international norms and institutions, pluralism, global order, and the normative foundations of international law in journals such as *Cambridge Review of International Affairs, International Studies Quarterly, International Theory, Journal on the Use Force and International Law, and Review of International Studies.*

Shannon Maree Torrens is an international and human rights lawyer, admitted in the Supreme Court of New South Wales, Australia. She was awarded a PhD in international criminal law from the University of Sydney Law School. Shannon has worked in international criminal law at the international criminal courts and tribunals for Rwanda (ICTR), the former Yugoslavia (ICTY), Sierra Leone (SCSL), and Cambodia (ECCC). In addition, she has worked as a legal advisor for the Marshall Islands Permanent Mission to the United Nations in New York in the Sixth Committee (Legal) of the UN General Assembly, working on state engagement with the International Criminal Court (ICC) and the Assembly of State Parties to the Rome Statute. Shannon has also worked with the UN Food and Agriculture Organisation (FAO), the United Nations Children's Fund (UNICEF), and at the Australian Embassies to Italy and the Holy See (the Vatican). Shannon has taught international law at the Australian National University (ANU) in Canberra, has served as an editorial advisor for the *Cambodia Law and Policy Journal*, and has lectured, published, and presented papers in the areas of international law and human rights internationally.

Sarah Williams is a professor at the Faculty of Law and Justice at UNSW Sydney, an associate of the Australian Human Rights Institute, and a member of the Centre for Crime, Law and Justice. Sarah was the Dorset Fellow in Public International Law at the British Institute of International and Comparative Law, a senior legal researcher at the UK Foreign and Commonwealth Office, and a lecturer at Durham Law School, University of Durham. She has been a consultant for a range of organizations and civil society actors, including the European Commission, the International Federation of Red Cross and Red Crescent Societies, the British Red Cross, and the Commonwealth Parliamentary Association. Her areas of expertise include international criminal law, international humanitarian law, and disaster law.

1
Hybrid Justice
Innovation and Impact in the Prosecution of Atrocity Crimes

Kirsten Ainley and Mark Kersten

1.1 Introduction

On 30 May 2016, Hissène Habré was convicted for his role in the commission of crimes against humanity, war crimes, and torture during his reign as President of Chad. Habré's trial took place not in N'Djamena, but in Dakar, Senegal, where the Extraordinary African Chambers (EAC) were established, as a joint venture between the African Union (AU) and Senegal, for his prosecution. The EAC's creation represented a return to a model of international criminal justice that many at the time thought was no longer in vogue: the hybrid tribunal, a species of international court that blends together both national and international staff as well as national and international law.

At the EAC, Habré was convicted of numerous crimes, including arbitrary arrest and detention, rape, sexual slavery, as well as ordering the deaths of some 40,000 people between 1982 and 1990. As his trial progressed in the Palace of Justice in Dakar, other hybrid courts were being negotiated and made into reality. This included the proposed hybrid court for South Sudan as well as the hybrid tribunal in the Central African Republic. In The Hague, the Kosovo Specialist Chambers and Specialist Prosecutors Office (KSC), a hybrid court in many senses, is up and running. In the years of the project that produced this edited volume, courts that blend various combinations of international and national law and staff have been proposed to deal with atrocities in Syria, Sri Lanka, Myanmar, The Gambia, Palestine, and Liberia, among other situations. Until Israel's war in Gaza, one of the most pressing conversations in international criminal law was whether, and how, a specialized, hybrid court could be set up to address the crimes of aggression in Ukraine.

In many respects, this re-emergence of the hybrid model was unexpected. The first generation of hybrid tribunals was initiated by the creation of the Regulation 64 Panels in the Courts of Kosovo and the Special Panels for Serious Crimes in East Timor in 2000. These were followed by the Special Court for Sierra Leone (SCSL), the Extraordinary Chambers in the Courts of Cambodia (ECCC), the War Crimes

Kirsten Ainley and Mark Kersten, *Hybrid Justice* In: *Hybrid Justice*. Edited by: Kirsten Ainley and Mark Kersten, Oxford University Press.
DOI: 10.1093/oso/9780192893758.003.0001

Chamber of the Court of Bosnia and Herzegovina (BIH WCC), and the Special Tribunal for Lebanon (STL). This initial series of hybrids was seen as a response to the need to make justice more—albeit not entirely—local. In doing so, hybrids offered a substantive alternative to their predecessors, the International Criminal Tribunals for Rwanda and the former Yugoslavia (ICTR and ICTY). They brought together differing degrees and elements of national and international law and staff. Some held proceedings in the relevant situation country, others in third-party states, and yet others offered a mix of both. All contributed significantly to the broader 'system' of international criminal justice. However, with the creation of the International Criminal Court (ICC) in 2002 and an international community increasingly prioritizing funding for international security and combating terrorism, interest in creating additional hybrid courts waned. From 2007–2014, the hybrid model had seemingly fallen out of favour, with no new hybridized courts created during this time.

Since 2014, however, the hybrid tribunal emerged once more as a popular response to mass atrocities, at least in part due to the real and perceived limitations of the ICC. This book examines the resurgence of hybrids, with its authors offering analysis of the ways in which hybrids succeeded or failed in promoting resilience through resisting political pressure, achieving legitimacy, delivering accountability, and contributing to the resilience of the communities in which they operate.

1.2 The Situation Today

As noted above, the popularity of hybrid tribunals has ebbed and flowed since they were first introduced as a means of mixing and matching national and international law and staff in a single criminal court. While the momentum that saw a number of new hybrid tribunals created after 2014 has not been sustained, hybrids remain of interest to the various actors engaged in addressing mass atrocities: affected communities, legal experts, international organizations, and states.

The renewed interest in hybrids is occurring against a backdrop of unease for international criminal justice. Not only have rising nationalism and populism threatened the multilateral order that underpins the international justice project, but the COVID-19 pandemic disrupted progress in the field as well. With states spending trillions on maintaining their economies and implementing programmes to support citizens adversely affected by the pandemic, financial support for international organizations—including courts—seemed bound to suffer.[1] This

[1] It was made clear to one of the authors, for example, that Canada would push for a reduced budget for the ICC in the wake of the pandemic. See also, Eric Wiebelhaus-Brahm and Kirsten Ainley, 'The Evolution of Funding for the International Criminal Court: Budgets, Donors and Gender Justice' (2023) 22(1) Journal of Human Rights.

is despite the fact that, across the globe, people from Myanmar to Manila, from Caracas to Canada, are agitating for justice and accountability for mass atrocities, a demand that did not ebb during the pandemic and which remains palpable today. But it is not all doom and gloom, and certain significant commitments to international criminal justice have been made in recent years.

Recent years have shown that, when pushed into the proverbial corner, proponents of international criminal justice respond with creative thinking and strategies. Despite a deadlocked United Nations (UN) Security Council and therefore no prospect of a referral of Syria to the ICC, dedicated diplomats established the International, Impartial and Independent Mechanism (IIIM) via the UN General Assembly in 2016. Since then, the IIIM has collected evidence to use in prosecutions of mass atrocities perpetrators in Syria.[2] While work in the area remains contentious among keen observers, the situation in Syria also inspired the creation of private organizations funded by states to investigate atrocities.[3] Further, universal jurisdiction cases relating to atrocities in Syria, The Gambia, Liberia, and elsewhere have produced a trickle of justice and accountability in situations where more coherent and comprehensive processes have been stymied.[4] Sometimes such developments are pursued with the specific aim of creating pressure on states to establish hybrid courts, as has been the case with recent litigation over Liberian war crimes and a civil society-led push to create a hybrid court to deal with atrocities committed in the Liberian civil war.

In response to Russia's invasion of Ukraine in February 2022, states embarked on what may emerge as the most comprehensive legal response to a situation of mass atrocities to date. Not only did dozens of states refer the situation in Ukraine to the ICC and thereby allow the Prosecutor to immediately open an investigation, without judicial approval, but many states sent money and staff to support the Court and national Ukrainian investigators in their efforts to document war crimes and crimes against humanity. In addition, at least a dozen states opened their own national investigations into atrocities committed in the country. Because the ICC does not have jurisdiction over the crime of aggression in Ukraine, numerous states are considering the creation of a new court that would be able to exercise jurisdiction of the crime, with many scholars insisting that any such court should be hybrid.[5]

[2] International, Independent and Impartial Mechanism on Syria, 'Mandate' <https://iiim.un.org/mandate/> accessed 19 March 2024.

[3] See Michelle Burgis-Kasthala, 'Assembling Atrocity Archives for Syria: Assessing the Work of the CIJA and the IIIM' (2021) 19(5) Journal of International Criminal Justice.

[4] See TRIAL, 'Universal Jurisdiction Database' <https://trialinternational.org/resources/universal-jurisdiction-database/> accessed 10 August 2022; Redress and others, 'Universal Jurisdiction: Annual Review 2022' (2022) <https://redress.org/news/universal-jurisdiction-2021-highlights-in-the-2022-universal-jurisdiction-annual-review/> accessed 19 March 2024.

[5] Owiso Owiso, 'An Aggression Chamber for Ukraine Supported by the Council of Europe' (*Opinio Juris*, 30 March 2022) <https://opiniojuris.org/2022/03/30/an-aggression-chamber-for-ukraine-supported-by-the-council-of-europe/> accessed 19 March 2024; Kevin Jon Heller, 'The Best Option: An Extraordinary Ukrainian Chamber for Aggression' (*Opinio Juris*, 16 March 2022) <https://

Among the features that make hybrids unique is the fact that they are created and re-created through time and across different contexts. In permanent tribunals, change and reform can be a cumbersome process, as exemplified by attempts to improve the functioning and efficiency of the ICC.[6] In contrast, the design of hybrid courts can draw on lessons learned from past tribunals and adopt not only features that are context-sensitive but also novel elements that address the shortcomings of past courts or that respond to new trends in addressing mass atrocities and related crimes. In previous work, we have highlighted the 'spectrum' of creative possibilities that exists when creating hybrid tribunals.[7] To name one example, we noted the creativity of the EAC—where former Chadian dictator Hissène Habré was tried—in outsourcing outreach activities to a consortium of expert media groups.[8] The consortium was better placed and able to address the multiple constituencies interested and invested in the EAC's work than any unit entrenched in the tribunal would have been: Chadian citizens, communities in Senegal, where the trial took place, and the broader international community. Hybrids can thus foster and implement creative design elements, set new precedents, streamline tribunal functions, reduce costs and institutional 'red tape', and, most importantly, produce positive results with respect to justice and accountability for affected communities.

At the time of writing, there continues to be significant activity in the hybrid realm. Some existing hybrid courts have experienced turmoil. With Lebanon facing a protracted economic crisis and unable to provide its share of funding, the Special Tribunal for Lebanon, for example, faced a funding emergency in 2021.[9] So severe is the STL's financial situation that, in June 2021, the tribunal announced it would have to close the following month.[10] By contrast, there has been some positive progress on the establishment of the Hybrid Court for South Sudan (HCSS), with the government in Juba finally approving the tribunal in January 2021.[11] To

opiniojuris.org/2022/03/16/the-best-option-an-extraordinary-ukrainian-chamber-for-aggression/> accessed 19 March 2024.

[6] See ICC, 'Review of the International Criminal Court and the Rome Statute System' (30 September 2020) <https://asp.icc-cpi.int/Review-Court> accessed 19 March 2024.

[7] Mark Kersten and Kirsten Ainley, 'Hybridization: A Spectrum of Creative Possibilities' in Sharon Weill, Kim Thuy Seelinger, and Kerstin Bree Carlson (eds), *The President on Trial: Prosecuting Hissène Habré* (Oxford University Press 2020).

[8] ibid.

[9] Maha El Dahan, 'Lebanon asks U.N. to explore ways to fund special tribunal' *Reuters* (4 June 2021) <https://www.reuters.com/world/middle-east/lebanon-asks-un-explore-means-funding-special-tribunal-2021-06-04/> accessed 19 March 2024; David Enders, 'Lebanon's Economic Woes Threaten Terrorism Tribunal' (*Foreign Policy*, 9 June 2021) <https://foreignpolicy.com/2021/06/09/lebanon-economy-terrorism-tribunal-closing/> accessed 19 March 2024.

[10] Janet Anderson, 'The Inglorious End of the Lebanon Tribunal' (*Justice Info*, 4 June 2021) <https://www.justiceinfo.net/en/78159-inglorious-end-lebanon-tribunal.html> accessed 19 March 2024.

[11] Jale Richard, 'Cabinet approves establishment of hybrid court' *Eye Radio* (30 January 2021) https://eyeradio.org/cabinet-approves-establishment-of-hybrid-court/ accessed 19 March 2024; Nyagoah Tut Pur, 'A Glimmer of Hope for South Sudan's Victims' (*Human Rights Watch*, 31 January 2021) <https://www.hrw.org/news/2021/01/31/glimmer-hope-south-sudans-victims> accessed 19 March 2024.

be sure, with alleged perpetrators in the senior-most positions of government, it is hard to imagine the HCSS as a court with much bite, and the institution continues to exist only on paper. Nevertheless, the drive to create the tribunal has shown some staying power and it is possible that political changes in the future will create space for the eventual establishment of the HCSS.

As The Gambia continues its transition away from the autocratic and brutal rule of Yahya Jammeh, major steps have been taken to set up a hybrid court in partnership with the Economic Community of West African States (ECOWAS).[12] The tribunal promises to build on the findings of the Truth, Reconciliation and Reparations Commission and, it is hoped, eventually lead to the prosecution of Jammeh, who remains in exile in Equatorial Guinea. In Kurdistan, there is ongoing support for the creation of a hybrid court to address atrocities committed by the Islamic State (IS), with numerous Western powers expressing support for such a court and a bill being introduced into the Kurdish parliament on the matter.[13] Important criticisms of such a tribunal continue to be voiced, especially around the dangers of setting up a court with a jurisdiction restricted to investigating IS crimes and not atrocities committed by, inter alia, Iraqi, Russian, and pro-Western Syrian forces.

In Sri Lanka, where there was once great hope that an internationalized court might be set up to address atrocities in the conflict between the country's armed forces and the Tamil population, the prospects of a hybrid being established appear to have been extinguished.[14] While there remains some hope among advocates that a hybrid will be set up to investigate and prosecute those responsible for the crime of aggression in Ukraine, it appears just as likely that a fully ad hoc international court will be set up. Hybrids remain relevant but, as ever, interest in their role in delivering accountability is neither stable nor consistent through time and across contexts.

The COVID-19 pandemic and its ongoing reverberations on economic and financial systems is likely to increase pressure on any newly created hybrid tribunals to be funded with voluntary contributions. As a number of the chapters in this book make clear, this is less than ideal. We also note in the *Dakar Guidelines on the*

[12] See Mustapha K Darboe, 'Banjul Working Towards a Hybrid Gambia-ECOWAS Court' (*JusticeInfo*, 23 June 2022) <https://www.justiceinfo.net/en/102524-banjul-working-towards-hybrid-gambia-ecowas-court.html> accessed 19 March 2024.

[13] See Draft Statute of Special Court for ISIS Crimes in KRI (Hawre Ahmed and Zelan Kader trs) (2021) <https://kc-interlaw.org/web/viewer.html?file=https://images.kc-interlaw.org/root/root/images/171352021_Special%20Court%20for%20ISIS%20Crimes.pdf> accessed 19 March 2024.

[14] EIN Presswire, 'Sri Lankan Tamil Political Parties Jointly Write to UN, Ahead of UN Human Rights Council Session, with Six Requests' (16 August 2022) <https://www.einpresswire.com/article/586223772/sri-lankan-tamil-political-parties-jointly-write-to-un-ahead-of-un-human-rights-council-session-with-six-requests> accessed 19 March 2024.

Establishment of Hybrid Courts that the funding of courts via voluntary contributions can create pressure points that political actors take advantage of in order to steer a court's work and thereby undermine its impartiality and independence. It can also lead to significant tribunal staff resources being allotted to fundraising as opposed to achieving accountability.[15]

Responding effectively to such pressures will once again require innovative thinking. As states tighten the purse strings and diminish their funding of international institutions, advocates of international criminal justice will have to harness their creativity in order to deliver meaningful justice and accountability whenever and wherever the opportunity to do so arises. One novel development that proponents might consider is the use of video-conferencing and digital technologies in trial proceedings. Prior to the pandemic, national courts regularly declined to consider e-proceedings, even in those states facing serious access to justice crises and where high numbers of accused persons were required to wait for months and even years for bail hearings or trial dates. The pandemic and the concomitant broad-based shutdown of in-person court hearings, however, resulted in a belated embrace of digital proceedings.[16] While courts—be they national, regional, or international—must avoid exacerbating the global digital divide, the development of e-proceedings may be particularly apt for hybrid courts which, despite assumptions about their local character, regularly prosecute atrocities from outside of affected communities and face the challenge of fostering meaningful access to proceedings for victims and survivors. Put another way, there is space to consider how hybrid courts can hybridize the very space of trial processes. And while technological start-up costs might be high, a move to hybridized proceedings in appropriate cases would also reduce the expense of internationalized courts, surely an appealing prospect for donor states.

The manner in which interested actors navigate the legal and political landscape in the post-pandemic world, in the wake of the Russian invasion of Ukraine, and through the ongoing war in Gaza, will ultimately determine whether hybrid courts remain in vogue and whether new tribunals adapt and learn the lessons of their predecessors. But as the contributions in this book make clear, hybrids will persist as relevant, even if imperfect, tools in the broader struggle to address mass atrocities and rebuild societies after conflict.

[15] Kirsten Ainley and Mark Kersten, 'Dakar Guidelines on the Establishment of Hybrid Courts' LSE and Wayamo Foundation (2019) <https://hybridjustice.com/dakar-guidelines/> accessed 19 March 2024.

[16] See, eg, Christina Piccinin and Sophie Sklar, 'Forced to Adapt: Innovations and best practices regarding access to Justice in Canadian courts and abroad during COVID-19' Winkler Institute for Dispute Resolution (2022) <https://www.osgoode.yorku.ca/wp-content/uploads/2022/09/2022_Forced-to-Adapt-Report-AODA-Version.pdf> accessed 19 March 2024.

1.3 Overview

This book is an output of the Hybrid Justice project, funded by the Rockefeller Foundation through the Institute of Global Affairs at the London School of Economics, as part of their support for research on resilience in general and in post-conflict states in particular.[17] The project was a collaboration between lawyers, academics, and activists to compare and evaluate past hybrids, and to produce academic publications along with a set of guidelines for the establishment of future hybrids.[18] Like this book, the conceptual approach of the project was a product of its members' interest in the intersection between international criminal law and international relations and focused on hybrid courts and resilience: the resilience of hybrid mechanisms to withstand political and other pressures in order to deliver justice and accountability as well as the potential contribution of hybrids to the resilience of affected communities.

Proponents of hybrid justice claim that hybrid courts can underwrite durable and stable peace, strengthen institutions and the rule of law, and enhance human rights protections, that is, increase societal resilience. Critics note the susceptibility of hybrids to political inference if they lack authority and resources, that is, if they are not resilient themselves. Resilience is therefore operationalized in two ways within the book, to cover two conceptually distinct (though in practice interrelated) aspects of hybrid justice: internal resilience is understood to mean the extent to which the design of hybrid mechanisms enables them to function robustly and with legitimacy in the face of external pressures from donors, host states, states which oppose the mechanism, and other interested parties. Societal resilience is the extent to which hybrid mechanisms enable post-conflict societies to heal, reconcile, strengthen, and address the root causes of prior conflict. Societal resilience might include the extent to which hybrids support the embedding and extension of the rule of law, democratization, and the development of a human rights culture. While the authors of the chapters that follow do not always use this framing

[17] The Hybrid Justice project website is available at: Hybrid Justice, 'The Hybrid Justice Project' <https://hybridjustice.com/> accessed 19 March 2024. There are a range of online resources on the project website that complement this book, for instance key facts about each past and present hybrid court, including links to their founding legal documents; lists of the status of cases as of January 2019; literature reviews specific to each court; and diagrams illustrating the organizational structure of each court. The website additionally features a general literature review of the hybrid justice field, available on the Hybrids page.

[18] Outputs of the project include: Kirsten Ainley and Mark Kersten, 'Dakar Guidelines on the Establishment of Hybrid Courts' LSE and Wayamo Foundation (2019) <https://hybridjustice.com/dakar-guidelines/> accessed 19 March 2024; Special Section on 'International Criminal Courts and Tribunals: Symposium on Resilience and the Impacts Of Hybrid Courts' (2020) 33(4) Leiden Journal of International Law; Justice in Conflict, 'Hybrid Justice: A Justice in Conflict Symposium' (2018) <https://justiceinconflict.org/2018/03/12/hybrid-justice-a-justice-in-conflict-symposium/> accessed 19 March 2024.

explicitly, there is much to learn about internal and external resilience from their contributions on the fields, practices, innovations, and impacts of hybrid courts.

Many of the authors in this volume have dedicated their professional lives to situations where hybrids have been established or are being proposed as a mechanism to address atrocity crimes. However, readers will no doubt recognize that the contributors are primarily from outside of conflict-affected contexts. While participation in the London conference and therefore in contributing to this volume was open and we advertised widely, we regret not having greater representation from authors in conflict-affected communities. We nevertheless hope that readers find contributors' insights in this book to be of value and of ongoing relevance in conversations regarding the future of hybrid justice, resilience, and international criminal law.

The first section of the book focuses on the *field* of hybrid courts—the legal, political, and institutional environments in which they are created and must operate.

Dennis Schmidt asks the question: in whose name do hybrid courts act? Hybrids are typically portrayed, Schmidt suggests, as the most advanced version of international criminal law mechanisms, appearing to be the result of a dialectical learning process in which the international community has gradually discovered an enforcement mechanism for international criminal law that can address the drawbacks of both purely international and purely domestic tribunals. Hybrids are argued to have the structural ability to collapse the artificial boundary between the international and the domestic. A court may be hybrid in its origins (created through domestic and international processes), its mandate (splicing together domestic and international law), or its composition (combining domestic and international members). Moreover, the way in which those institutions have collapsed the international–domestic distinction varies significantly in the sense that the institutional structure and operation of particular hybrids never represent a midpoint between the two jurisdictions. Instead, past hybrids and internationalized criminal courts have moved along a spectrum ranging at the one end, from purely international criminal courts, such as the ICC, to purely domestic courts at the other. A critical question then is, what is the ideal weight of each element in the composition and design of a hybrid court? How international or how domestic should a hybrid court be, or should we aim for a 'perfect' merger of the two? In the chapter, Schmidt seeks to address this question by placing the international–domestic distinction within an area in which the hybrid model is claimed to hold significant advantages over alternative international criminal law mechanisms—legitimacy. While the 'legitimacy promise' has seen some evaluation since the completion of the first round of hybrids, there has been little serious theoretically informed engagement with the deeper-seated sources of hybrid court's legitimacy. Schmidt concludes by offering some more general observations about legitimacy and hybrid courts that may help to improve their institutional design and implementation.

Elena Baylis' chapter focuses on regionalized hybrid courts. She describes how international collaboration in the first wave of hybrid courts followed a consistent pattern: the international partner in each instance was the UN. The second wave of hybrid courts indicated a significant change to this configuration. For the first time, two of the three new hybrid courts were structured as partnerships with regional organizations, the AU and the European Union (EU). This pattern is replicated with the proposed hybrid tribunal for South Sudan, which is, on paper, to exist as a regional partnership between South Sudan and the AU. From the perspective of the history of hybrid courts, this marks an abrupt change. However, as Baylis notes, this regional engagement in hybrid tribunals is an expression of a long-term trend towards the development of regional commitments to transitional justice and international criminal law. The EU and the AU, as well as other regional organizations, have supported various transitional justice endeavours. The chapter assesses this trend towards regional commitments to transitional justice and international criminal law as well as the theoretical arguments for regional transitional justice institutions. It then evaluates the engagement of regional actors in the KSC, the EAC, and the proposed Hybrid Court for South Sudan (HCSS) in light of these trends and arguments.

In their chapter on 'Securing Resilient Peace', Shastry Njeru and Tyanai Masiya show how the Africa Union Transitional Justice Framework is conceptualized to 'end violent conflicts and repressive rule, and nurture sustainable development, social justice, human and peoples' rights, democratic rule, and good governance, consolidate peace, reconciliation and justice in Africa, and prevent impunity'. However, instead of consolidating the peace dividend after many years of violent conflict, Njeru and Masiya suggest that many African countries face significant turmoil. Ethnic cleavages, oil spoils, and personal ambitions often drive these relapses into violent conflicts, even when the peace dividend is more valuable. Although institutions such as the African Union and the Intergovernmental Authority on Development argue for the need for hybrid courts to confront the violence in a number of African countries, Njeru and Masiya argue that the complexity and plurality of such conflicts around the continent needs more than court hybridity. It needs localized polyvalence responses to addressing the ever-challenging situations besetting the countries in conflict time and again. The Western neo-liberal peacebuilding and transitional justice models, from which most elements of hybridity are borrowed, are inadequate. They are narrow; focus on retributive outcomes; and have logics of inclusion and exclusion. They are prone to instrumentalization, misappropriation, or co-option by more powerful national or international actors against the interests of local justice and security. This affects peace resilient outcomes in most of the cases. Njeru and Masiya thus advocate for strategic polyvalence approaches as the most appropriate responses to conflict in which they not only consider dominant discourses, but the operant, dormant, challenged, and even strongly negated views within the transitional justice field.

Various manifestations of dissent in international criminal justice are illustrated both in the original establishment and now re-emergence of the hybrid court model. This is the subject of Shannon Torrens' contribution to the volume. Torrens argues that state responses to international criminal justice can be divided into three general categories: support, acquiescence, and dissent. Her chapter looks at the tension between these three viewpoints and modes of action on a historical continuum marking the trajectory of international criminal justice but also as comprising former and current conflicting views on international hybrid justice. Torrens discusses how dissenting responses can be defined, where they are illustrated, and what impact these mentalities and actions have had on the work of international courts and tribunals and in particular on modern hybrid courts, their creation and re-emergence. Whilst the ICC commenced its work with general support for the prosecution of individuals at an international level, as time has progressed, there has been a shift from support to acquiescence and now finally open dissent, such as through the opposition to the Court of numerous African States and the African Union. Torrens' chapter examines how these developments and this dissent has inspired the re-emergence of hybrid justice and how the lessons learned from the ICC and earlier models of hybrid justice may assist these future justice responses. It further analyses how the original dissent which created the earlier hybrid tribunals, namely the SCSL and ECCC, is distinct from the more recent dissent and discusses the reasons for this distinction. In pursuing this line of thought, the notion of dissent is further tied to the internal politics of post conflict states and their both open and veiled responses to hybrid justice.

In his chapter on 'Institutional Design and Complementarity', Patryk Labuda notes how hybrid tribunals sometimes operate alongside other judicial and non-judicial bodies with similar accountability functions. For instance, a hybrid tribunal can share jurisdictional powers with ordinary national courts, an international criminal tribunal, a truth commission, or other investigative and prosecutorial bodies. When the mandates of these different institutions overlap, Labuda argues that relations should be regulated so as to minimize duplication tasks, prevent unnecessary conflict, encourage cooperation to the extent possible, and maximize cross-fertilization. Drawing on examples from several conflict and post-conflict countries, Labuda explores how best to regulate relations between hybrid tribunals and other judicial and non-judicial institutions with overlapping jurisdictional claims. It argues that, while the phrase 'complementarity' is sometimes invoked in institutional design scholarship, the International Criminal Court's logic of apportioning jurisdiction is not a helpful way of thinking about regulating relations between hybrid tribunals and other judicial and non-judicial institutions.

Sareta Ashraph's contribution headlines Part II of the book, which explores the *practices* of hybrid courts. Ashraph's focus is on defence counsel. At the outset of the fledgling systems of the hybrid tribunals, she observes, there often appears to be no proper provision for the defence. Starting with the Special Panels of the

District Courts of Dili, and tracing its way through the Special Court for Sierra Leone (SCSL), the Iraqi High Criminal Court[19] (IHT), the Special Tribunal for Lebanon, to today's Kosovo Specialist Chambers (KSC), Ashraph's chapter looks at the development of the defence within the structures of the hybrid tribunals. It recounts that, while the need for prosecutors, judges, and even prison officers has always been recognized, each iteration of the hybrid courts appears to have been taken by surprise at the need to fund defence counsel, and/or to have an office within the Court's structure dedicated to defence rights. It traces the impulses—ideological, financial, cosmetic—that first motivated the creation of defence offices and other support to defence teams and looks at how the approach to the defence has evolved. Finally, Ashraph examines whether hybrid justice systems have finally learned to value the defence.

Philipp Ambach's chapter explores victim participation in hybrid and international(ized) tribunals. The ICC pioneered a set of new victim-centred features in its normative framework that are unprecedented by the ICC's predecessors. All internationalized ad hoc criminal courts and tribunals established subsequent to the ICC's creation include legal regimes on victim participation and, to some degree, reparations. It would thus appear that such a victim participation/reparations component has become a core feature of any modern international criminal justice mechanism. Yet such victim participation and reparations regimes are not without their challenges. These range from budgetary constraints to the general question of meaningfulness and impact on victims and affected communities. While the ICC promises to be well equipped to face these problems due to its permanent nature and rather secure funding, this appears less likely in some respects for regional ad hoc solutions exercising international criminal justice. A number of key challenges can be identified which may be decisive over the success or failure of meaningful victim participation in criminal proceedings and reparations at the end of the criminal process. Future lawmakers may want to consider, Ambach concludes, how comprehensive a victim regime they want to introduce into future hybrid courts in order not to be set up for failure.

The Special Criminal Court in the Central African Republic and the Kosovo Specialist Chambers are the focus of Erica Bussey's chapter. The Special Criminal Court, a 'hybrid' tribunal wholly grounded within the national justice system, has a majority of national judges and nationals in key staff positions. At the opposite end of the spectrum, the Kosovo Specialist Chambers, by design, has no national judges or staff. In the middle there are uneasy compromises—the proposed Hybrid Court for South Sudan, as well as several of the first-wave of hybrids such as the Special Court for Sierra Leone and the Extraordinary Chambers in the Courts of Cambodia. Against the backdrop of these two opposite models, and by looking at

[19] More commonly referred to as the Iraqi High Tribunal.

case studies from several tribunals, Bussey examines the rationales for including and for excluding national judges and staff in hybrid tribunals, with an emphasis on the question of legitimacy, and the effects of these choices on internal and external resilience. Her chapter also breaks down the national and international components of hybrid tribunals, with an emphasis on the effects of the regionalization of the composition of judges and staff on the legitimacy of recently created tribunals, as well as on other questions relating to personnel who fall between the narrow 'national' and 'international' categories, such as those from the diaspora.

Enforcement practices are the subject of Philippa Greer's chapter in this volume. The enforcement of sentences is an indispensable component of any effective international criminal justice mechanism. The modern international criminal justice system utilizes imprisonment as its primary sanction, yet the issue of sentencing and the implementation of penalties has often been viewed as more of an afterthought, rather than a starting point, when such institutions are established. Hybrid criminal mechanisms, as well as the United Nations ad hoc tribunals and the ICC, enforce sentences by either employing a domestic solution directly in domestic prisons (a model of 'local enforcement'), or by adopting an ad hoc cooperating states model, which utilizes existing prison facilities in third states, relying on the cooperation of those states. Greer's contribution addresses the enforcement practices of several hybrid criminal mechanisms to date, evaluating their ability to function robustly and legitimately in this crucial area, as well as the ability of both local and decentralized models of enforcement to enable post-conflict societies to reconcile, strengthen, and address the root causes of prior conflict. It reflects upon broader questions related to legitimacy, accessibility, capacity-building, strengthening of the domestic rule of law, and the synthetization and intersection of international and domestic legal regimes with respect to sentence enforcement.

Part III of the book delves into *innovation* at hybrid tribunals. Kerstin Bree Carlson's chapter explores the ongoing disagreement in international criminal law regarding sovereign immunity. International humanitarian law takes the possibility of challenging impunity as a central element of its mandate, in part because a fundamental norm of rule of law practice is that none is above the law, and in part because leaders are those who arguably bear the greatest responsibility for the types of collective harms international humanitarian law would criminalize. This norm does not distinguish between sitting and former heads of state. Across Africa, however, there has been significant pushback regarding prosecuting sitting leaders for atrocity crimes. Carlson notes that this has led to what is perhaps the central conflict defining international criminal law discourse today: a plurality of opinions regarding how sovereignty comports with state-sponsored atrocity crimes. Her chapter examines the recent trial of deposed Chadian head of state Hissène Habré to consider questions of pluralism under international criminal law regarding sovereign immunity. Through a detailed analysis of the work and doctrinal content of the Habré trial, Carlson shows that while the Habré trial is celebrated as an example of bringing a former head of state to justice, the experience of the Habré trial does not change the balance as regards an African pluralism on the question of sovereign immunity.

Elise Keppler's chapter delves into innovations at hybrids, with a comparative focus on the Central African Republic's Special Criminal Court and the proposed Hybrid Court for South Sudan. In recent years, Keppler observes, the resurgence of hybrid war crimes courts has engendered innovations in this form of accountability mechanism. Her chapter evaluates the comparative strengths and challenges of two such mechanisms: the Special Criminal Court, which was being established at the time of writing, and the proposed Hybrid Court for South Sudan. Keppler has conducted research in South Sudan and the Central African Republic and is involved in ongoing advocacy to promote the operationalization of these courts. She draws from these experiences to discuss the different approaches these courts are taking, or intend to take, with respect to their creation, governance, staffing, and location. Keppler thus analyses the potential implications of such differences for assuring their effective operations and positive impact.

In her contribution, Rosemary Grey explores the subject of forced marriage and how this crime has been addressed by hybrid courts. When it comes to sexual and gender-based crimes, the hybrids in Sierra Leone and Cambodia have played key roles in setting precedents. Specifically, both tribunals have broken new ground in recognizing 'forced marriage' as a crime against humanity: a precedent which has now been followed in two cases at the ICC. Grey explores differing responses to the SCSL's and ECCC's precedents on forced marriage, seeking to show that this development is not as progressive as it may at first appear. Indeed, some commentators thinking these courts have *under*-emphasized the distinction between forced marriage and traditional marriage customs, and others thinking the opposite. Grey's chapter then considers what these two hybrid tribunals have contributed to understandings of sexual violence during the Sierra Leone war and the Democratic Kampuchea period, respectively. It shows that both tribunals made significant progress is recognizing sexual and gender-based violence against women and girls, but neither tribunal sufficiently acknowledged evidence of sexual and gender-based violence experienced by men, boys, and non-binary people.

Camilo Sánchez explores a blind spot for hybrid courts: Latin America. He observes that hybrid tribunals have not generally been used in the region, with domestic ordinary criminal courts favoured to provide accountability in transitions. However, in recent years, domestic justice systems—especially in Central America—have struggled with successfully linking longstanding contexts of corruption and impunity with macro criminality patterns and specific crimes. Against that backdrop, hybrid investigatory mechanisms and other hybrid justice initiatives have gained regional—and global—attention in the past decade. The International Commission against Impunity in Guatemala—UN-backed commission set up to support, strengthen, and assist Guatemalan institutions in investigating, prosecuting, and dismantling illegal groups and clandestine structures responsible for organized crime and human rights violations—led the way to the creation of a similar commission in Honduras (MACCIH) and a possible twin commission expected to be set up in El Salvador (CICIES). In parallel, the Inter-American Commission on Human Rights launched an 'Interdisciplinary Group of Experts' to assist national authorities with the investigation and search of the disappearance of forty-three students in Ayotzinapa Mexico (Interdisciplinary Group of Independent Experts—IGIE). Sanchez focuses on these new hybrid investigatory mechanisms and other innovative hybrid justice initiatives. In the first part, his chapter summarizes the main traits of modern hybrid justice mechanisms. This assessment includes not only the aforementioned Latin American commissions but also other arrangements of the type such as the International Impartial Independence Mechanism to assist the investigation and prosecution of serious crimes in Syria and the Joint Investigation Team established to conduct the criminal investigation of the Malaysia Airlines flight MH17 brought down over eastern Ukraine, in 2014. In the second part, Sanchez uses the Latin American commissions and the context in which they operate to test some of the main questions of the book: how they are failing/succeeding in resisting political pressure; how they have increased their legitimacy; and how much we can expect their contribution to be to delivering accountability.

Sarah Williams' contribution explores whether hybrids can deliver reparative justice. Earlier international and hybrid tribunals did not have a mandate, or the power, to award reparations to victims. Instead, any reparative potential arose from their trial proceedings. The constituent instruments of more recent tribunals include a reparations function. The Rome Statute of the International Criminal Court enables Chambers to order reparations to assist victims of crimes, while the Extraordinary Chambers in the Courts of Cambodia, and the Extraordinary African Chambers may, and have, issued orders for reparations for victims of crimes. It has become common practice for the constituent instruments of hybrid tribunals to include a provision empowering the tribunal to determine and award appropriate reparations. However, the practice has been mixed in terms of the successful awarding, design, and implementation of appropriate reparations including the limited legal capacity of many institutions to award reparations that challenge underlying social, political, and economic structures. To be effective, reparations orders and projects usually require engagement and support from states to be feasible and effective; yet such support is often absent. Williams explores the reparations mandate and experience of a number of international and hybrid tribunals, including the ICC and the ECCC, to assess whether, and if so under which conditions, a hybrid tribunal is a suitable mechanism for reparative justice. In particular, Williams' chapter considers whether the hybrid model offers better prospects of engaging states in reparative justice.

The final Part of the book focuses on the *impacts* of hybrid courts. Olga Kavran's contribution examines the area of outreach. Twenty years have passed since the first Outreach Programme was established at the International Criminal Tribunal for the former Yugoslavia. At that time, it was an afterthought in what had become an emerging system of international criminal justice. Today, outreach is considered an essential element of the work of any international or hybrid court or tribunal. Yet, despite the prominent role it seems to have been assigned, outreach is still not necessarily seen as a legal obligation of these institutions, as evidenced by both the lack of any reference to outreach in the founding documents of institutions, the absence of guidelines on how to conduct outreach, and, very often, lack of funding for outreach programmes. All this results in different approaches by different institutions, ranging from the very conservative to the very innovative. Kavran's chapter looks at the different approaches taken by hybrid tribunals in respect of their outreach and legacy to identify lessons to be learned for the future.

Ezequiel Jiminez's contribution examines the premise of capacity building within the hybrid tribunal model and analyses the experience of the Special Court for Sierra Leone, the ongoing trials in the Extraordinary Chambers in the Courts of Cambodia, and the unique judicial set up in the Bosnian War Crimes Chamber within the Court of Bosnia Herzegovina, with the backing of the International Tribunal for the Former Yugoslavia. Tasked with prosecuting war crimes, genocide, and crimes against humanity, the hybrid tribunal model contemplates the premise of rebuilding domestic judicial capacity through a mix of applicable domestic and international law, knowledge transfer between local and foreign judicial personal, and infrastructure investment, to bring the judicial process closer to victims in post-conflict situations. However, Jiminez argues that experiences in Sierra Leone, Cambodia, and Bosnia Herzegovina point out dissimilar implementation of the capacity building element of the hybrid tribunal model, uncovering issues of operational clarity in the mandates of hybrid tribunals to rebuild domestic judicial systems as well as the level of impact and resources allocated for this task. Given the re-emergence of the hybrid tribunal model to address situations where an accountability gap persists, strengthening the premise of the capacity building element in the hybrid tribunal model is paramount for processes aimed at developing resilient states based in the rule of law and the right of access to justice.

In her chapter, Alice Dieci explores the potential of hybrid courts in prosecuting economic, social and cultural rights (ESCR) violations amounting to international crimes from a twofold perspective. The first part of her chapter addresses the notion of fragmentation of international criminal law in its positive connotation of legal pluralism and judicial creativity and links it to the marginalization of ESCR in international criminal law. It does so by exploring the limited jurisprudence of some hybrid courts, such as the SCSL, the Extraordinary Chambers for the Court of Cambodia (ECCC), and the East Timor Special Panels for Serious

Crimes (SCU) in relation to prosecution of ESCR, pointing out their limitations and missed opportunities. The second part explores some of the inherent features of hybrid courts and their potential in more effectively addressing ESCR violations, as compared to international, national, or regional courts. It concludes that the inclusion of ESCR in a hybridity framework could positively reconcile the tension between the top down approach of international justice, increasingly perceived as Western-dominated and as disproportionately focusing on civil and political rights, and the bottom up approach of local and regional demands, increasingly pushing for accountability of economic and social violations, such as land grabbing and forced displacement in relation to illegal exploitation of natural resources. Dieci argues that, instead of increasing fragmentation of international criminal law, hybrid courts could provide further legitimacy to international justice and restore trust among affected communities, by better reflecting the extent of victimization on the ground, which inevitably includes ESCR violations. By more comprehensively addressing ESCR violations in their prosecutorial strategy, Dieci finds, hybrid courts could better incorporate the dynamic pluralism of international criminal justice and be better equipped to challenge international power dynamics and increased human rights' politicization.

Finally, Kirsten Ainley and Mark Kersten conclude the book by using the recommendations of the *Dakar Guidelines on the Establishment of Hybrid Courts* in order to draw the volume's chapters into conversation around the design, function, and evaluation of hybrid mechanisms. The conclusion highlights the most important findings of the chapters and considers their implications for hybrid courts now operating and those likely to be established in the future.

PART I

FIELDS

2

In Whose Name? Mapping the Constitutional Legitimacy of Hybrid International Criminal Courts

Dennis R. Schmidt

2.1 Introduction

Hybrid courts have been claimed to be the most advanced version of international criminal law (ICL) mechanisms. As the former International Criminal Tribunal for the Former Yugoslavia (ICTY) Judge Wald once heralded, hybrid tribunals are a 'phenomenal development' in the progressive path of international criminal justice.[1] Much of the hopes and enthusiasm Judge Wald and others have voiced for the hybrid model—if not all—stems from its ability to bridge or collapse the artificial boundary between the international and the domestic—a dichotomy that has penetrated and plagued the international criminal justice discourse since Nuremberg.[2]

Hybrids' joint venture between the international and domestic communities has come in different forms. A court may be hybrid in its origins (created through domestic and international processes), its mandate (splicing together domestic and international law), and/or its composition (combining domestic and international members).[3] Moreover, the ways in which those institutions have collapsed the international–domestic distinction vary significantly in the sense that the institutional structure and operation of particular hybrids never represent a mid-point between the two jurisdictions. Instead, past hybrids and internationalized criminal courts have moved along a spectrum ranging at the one end, from purely international criminal courts, such as the International Criminal Court (ICC), to purely domestic courts at the other. A critical question then is, how should we

[1] Patricia Wald, 'Wald Sees International Tribunals Evolving Toward "Hybrid" Courts' (Remarks made at the award of Thomas Jefferson Foundation Medal in Law from University of Virginia, 15 April 2005).

[2] Frederic Megret, 'In Defence of Hybridity: Towards a Representational Theory of International Criminal Justice' (2005) 38 Cornell International Law Journal 725, 747.

[3] Elizabeth Bruch, 'Hybrid Courts: Examining Hybridity Through a Post-Colonial Lens', (2010) 28 Boston University International Law Journal 1, 6.

Dennis R. Schmidt, *In Whose Name? Mapping the Constitutional Legitimacy of Hybrid International Criminal Courts* In: *Hybrid Justice*. Edited by: Kirsten Ainley and Mark Kersten, Oxford University Press.
 DOI: 10.1093/oso/9780192893758.003.0002

determine the ideal composition of a hybrid court? How international or how domestic should a hybrid court be?

This chapter seeks to address this question by placing the international–domestic distinction within an area in which the hybrid model is claimed to hold significant advantages over alternative ICL mechanisms—legitimacy. After the first iteration of hybrid models were established in or for East Timor, Sierra Leone, Cambodia, Bosnia, and Lebanon, scholars have identified a number of potential benefits of their institutional design, chief among them their enhanced potential for legitimacy. On the one hand, the presence of international elements was said to enhance their legitimacy by ensuring impartiality, competence, due process, and unbiased judgements. On the other hand, securing domestic participation was claimed to alleviate the legitimacy deficit that impaired the reconciliation effects of the purely international ad hoc tribunals for Yugoslavia and Rwanda.[4]

While the 'legitimacy promise' has seen some evaluation since the completion of the first round of hybrids—with the sobering conclusion that it was largely 'overblown'[5]—there has been little serious, theoretically informed engagement with the deeper-seated sources of hybrid courts' legitimacy. This is surprising, given the immense significance attributed to legitimacy in ICL. Absent any enforcement mechanism, the general acceptance of hybrid courts' operation and decisions relies on legitimacy, understood as a quality of 'oughtness' that produces voluntary compliance.[6] Courts will engender greater compliance among stakeholders—with regard to financial contributions, local cooperation, or the execution of international arrest warrants—when actors feel that they ought to follow their mandate and decisions. It is clear also that a legitimate hybrid court is more stable, in the sense that there is likely to be less conflict about its fundamental goals and principles, which would severely weaken the prospect of the acceptance of its authority.

The literature offers different approaches to studying institutional legitimacy. I analyse these approaches in Section 2.3, showing how they can be adapted to shed light on the legitimacy of international(ized) courts. Suggesting that international criminal lawyers have heretofore neglected the deeper-seated sources of courts' legitimacy, Section 2.4 draws on debates in International Relations to develop the concept of constitutional legitimacy. The theoretical assumption here is that a hybrid's ultimate authority rests in the collective subject in whose name it is established and enacted. This collective constitutes the public identity of a hybrid court, grounds its purpose, and thereby grants it legitimacy. Asking the question

[4] Laura Dickinson, 'The Promise of Hybrid Courts' (2003) 97 American Journal of International Law 295.

[5] Padraig McAuliffe, 'Hybrid Tribunals at Ten: How International Criminal Justice's Golden Child Became an Orphan' (2011) 7 Journal of International Law and International Relations 1.

[6] Legitimacy stands alongside coercion and self-interest as one of the three main mechanisms of social-control. Jonathan Symons, 'The Legitimation of International Organisations: Examining the Identity of the Communities That Grant Legitimacy' (2011) 37 Review of International Studies 2559.

of who the constituent power of a hybrid court should be, I provide a theoretically grounded analysis of the way in which authority over a hybrid court is distributed between the international and the domestic communities. To illustrate the analytical potential of this approach, Section 2.5 briefly examines how debates over constituent power have shaped two different hybrid settings. Based on this discussion, I conclude by offering some more general observations about legitimacy and hybrid courts that can help to improve their institutional design and implementation.

2.2 Legitimacy in International Criminal Law: Some Methodological Remarks

Questions about legitimacy have been standard fare in political theory for over two millennia.[7] Whilst the nature and focus of political theorizing about legitimacy has changed over time, authoritative literature tells us that the concept relates to the justification and acceptance of authority.[8] The most widely cited distinction in the conceptual discourse about legitimacy is that between normative and the sociological understandings. Whereas normative theories of legitimacy seek to develop a set of external criteria for assessing *the right to rule*, sociological approaches focus on the empirical question whether someone is *believed* to have the right to rule.[9]

On a cursory inspection, the predominant focus in the ICL literature appears to lie on the sociological dimension, that is, on factors that tend to make the decisions of a judicial body acceptable to the various populations observing its procedures. This focus is echoed in the recent emergence of studies using psychological methods to uncover public opinion about, and perceived legitimacy of, courts through the study of discourse.[10] Interestingly, the results appear to be at odds with theorists' understanding of perceived legitimacy in a number of ways. Looking at both purely international and hybrid courts, Ford, for example, finds that only a 'tiny percentage of the affected population will know how the court was created, the institutional structure it has, or the procedures it uses, and outreach efforts

[7] For a good overview of the historical evolution of the concept of legitimacy, see Shane P Mulligan, 'The Use of Legitimacy in International Relations' (2005) 34 Millennium: Journal of International Studies 356.

[8] See Seymour Martin Lipset, 'Some Social Requisites of Democracy: Economic Development and Political Legitimacy' (1959) 53 American Political Science Review 69; Peter G Stillman, 'The Concept of Legitimacy' (1974) 7 Polity 32; Arthur Isak Applbaum, 'Legitimacy without the Duty to Obey' (2010) 38 Philosophy & Public Affairs 215.

[9] Allen Buchanan and Robert O Keohane, 'The Legitimacy of Global Governance Institutions' (2006) 20 Ethics & International Affairs 405; Ian Clark, *Legitimacy in International Society* (Oxford University Press 2007) 19. The distinction is typically traced back to Max Weber, see Max Weber, *Economy and Society: An Outline of Interpretive Sociology* (University of California Press 1968) 33–38.

[10] See, eg, Stuart Ford, 'A Social Psychology Model of the Perceived Legitimacy of International Criminal Courts: Implications for the Success of Transitional Justice Mechanisms' (2012) 45 Vanderbilt Journal of Transnational Law 405; James Meernik and Kimi King, 'A Psychological Jurisprudence Model of Public Opinion and International Prosecution' (2014) 17 International Area Studies Review 3.

are unlikely to overcome this fundamental ignorance', suggesting that those factors have little impact on the courts' perceived legitimacy.[11]

This points to an important legitimacy problem every transitional justice institution faces, namely the lack of the kind of institutional authority that derives from deeply entrenched legal-cultural traditions.[12] Sociological legitimacy of international(ized) courts has to be understood within the context of post-conflict societies, where pre-existing institutions have typically been corrupted or damaged, and a multitude of authority claims from various national and international actors exist. Generally speaking, 'individuals in post-conflict states lack the long-term exposure and acculturation to almost all of these institutions that would ordinarily form the basis of judgments regarding legitimacy'.[13] So to the extent that people's legitimacy beliefs about transitional justice institutions can be accurately 'measured' at all, they would seem to be based on limited information about the institution in question.

Coming from a more theoretical angle, scholars have also been sceptical of the extent to which the legitimacy of transitional justice institutions should be inferred exclusively from peoples' perceptions. The argument here is that peoples' beliefs, no matter how accurately captured, cannot be self-validating.[14] On this view, the legitimacy of international courts and tribunals does not rest upon peoples' beliefs, perceptions and behaviours. Instead, it is grounded in a justificatory account, derived from a principled conception of the rightfulness of transitional justice mechanisms that can validate its political authority. This raises the familiar question of whether a boundary between sociological and normative conceptions of legitimacy is desirable at all.[15] Without going into the details of this discussion, I will simply assume that we need to interrogate both the normative and sociological dimensions of legitimacy to understand when a hybrid court is understood to be legitimate by a particular group.

2.3 Hybrid Courts, Legitimacy, and the International–Domestic Distinction

The best way to bring legitimacy into the present study is to relate it to the distinction between a court's procedural and substantive legitimacy. This distinction is

[11] Ford (n 10) 409.

[12] Chrisje Brants and Susanne Karstedt (eds), *Transitional Justice and the Public Sphere: Engagement, Legitimacy and Contestation* (Bloomsbury Publishing 2017) 3–4.

[13] Meernik and King (n 10) 8.

[14] Stephen Winter, 'Towards a Unified Theory of Transitional Justice' (2013) 7 International Journal of Transitional Justice 224.

[15] See, eg, Fabienne Peter, 'Political Legitimacy', *The Stanford Encyclopaedia of Philosophy* (Summer edn, 2017); Jürgen Habermas, *Communication and the Evolution of Society* (Thomas McCarthy tr, Beacon Press 1979) 205.

essentially about the 'source' from which an institution's legitimacy is derived. As I will show below, each of the two constitutive collectives of a hybrid court (ie the international and the domestic) is claimed to offer a distinct source of legitimacy. Whereas the international is more closely aligned with the procedural dimension, the incorporation of domestic elements helps to secure substantive legitimacy.

2.3.1 Legitimacy as procedural fairness

The primary legitimacy advantage claimed for the internationalization of hybrid courts is the independence and impartiality provided by foreign judges and prosecutors in relation to their domestic counterparts. As McAuliffe writes:

> the presence of international actors in the units of the hybrid tribunals, especially when in a majority or in leadership positions, would suffice to insulate the court from domestic political factors, the most obvious of which is governmental interference.[16]

Given that hybrid courts try either political opponents or allies of the new domestic authority, the impact of the presence of international actors on perceived impartiality certainly seems significant. The temptation to seek vengeance under the guise of punishment in transitional justice cases is high, and the presence of estranged, impartial international actors can serve to alleviate allegations of ethnic bias or 'victor's justice'. In East Timor and Kosovo, for instance, justice institutions had been dominated by perceived oppressors—Indonesians in East Timor and Serbs in Kosovo. Though in others cases, such as in Sierra Leone, ethnic divisions were not as overt, the fact that the Revolutionary United Front (RUF), the rebel army that fought against the government, retained control over various aspects of the country's governance mechanisms made it unlikely that RUF members would be held accountable by local judges.[17] The appointment of foreign judges in these cases, Dickinson thus concludes, may have helped to 'enhance the perception of the independence of the judiciary and therefore its legitimacy within a broad cross-section of the local population'.[18]

This *procedural* approach to legitimacy has been well established in international jurisprudence, most notably through the widely influential works of Thomas Franck.[19] According to Franck, legitimacy is 'the perception of those

[16] McAuliffe (n 5) 12. See also William W Burke-White, 'Regionalization of International Criminal Law Enforcement: A Preliminary Exploration' (2003) 38 Texas International Law Journal 729, 742.

[17] Dickinson (n 4) 301.

[18] ibid 306.

[19] Thomas M Franck, *The Power of Legitimacy Among Nations* (Oxford University Press 1990). See also Thomas M Frank, *Fairness in International Law and Institutions* (Oxford University Press 1998).

addressed by a rule or a rule-making institution that the rule or institution has come into being and operates in accordance with generally accepted principles of right process'.[20] Indeed, for many international criminal lawyers, the legitimacy of international courts and tribunals is largely, if not exclusively, derived from the fairness of the procedures through which international criminal justice is delivered.[21] David Luban has developed a special version of this approach, which offers a particularly sophisticated elaboration of procedural legitimacy in the context of internationalized criminal courts.[22] As Luban writes:

> The legitimacy of international tribunals comes not from the shaky political authority that creates them, but from the manifested fairness of their procedures and punishments. Tribunals bootstrap themselves into legitimacy by the quality of justice they deliver; their rightness depends on their fairness.[23]

This preoccupation with procedure is based on an interesting assertion about the distinctiveness of *international* criminal law. In contrast to domestic criminal law, international criminal law shifts the principal focus from punishment to trials, making the proceedings rather than their aftermath the centre of gravity. As Luban argues, the classical justifications for ICL such as promoting social reconciliation, giving victims a voice, or making a historical record of mass atrocities to help secure the past against deniers and revisionists are first and foremost goals of trials, not punishments.[24] The degree of an internationalized court's legitimacy thus hinges on the fairness of the trial and the extent to which it meets a number of well-known natural justice requirements, such as right to a speedy, public trial before an impartial tribunal; the right to offer a defence; the right to be informed of the charges; the right of the accused to confront the witnesses against him; the right of the accused to have compulsory process for obtaining witnesses in his favour; the right to counsel; the privilege against self-incrimination; and the ban on double jeopardy.[25]

Meeting those requirements certainly bolsters legitimacy. However, what often gets lost in the discussions about procedural legitimacy in ICL is that legitimacy is a much broader concept than legality. Legitimacy cannot only exist outside a legal system—think, for example, of the UN General Assembly, which exercises some form of rightful authority in the absence of legally binding authority or the famous 'illegal but legitimate' verdict on NATO's Kosovo intervention—, but also relates

[20] Franck, *The Power of Legitimacy Among Nations* (n 19) 19.

[21] Frédéric Mégret, 'What Sort of Global Justice is International Criminal Justice' (2015) 13 Journal of International Criminal Justice 77, 79–80.

[22] David J Luban, 'Fairness to Rightness: Jurisdiction, Legality, and the Legitimacy of International Criminal Law' (2008) Georgetown Public Law Research Paper No 1154117.

[23] ibid 13.

[24] ibid 8.

[25] ibid 14.

to justifications of a court's authority that goes beyond compliance and procedure. The point here is that institutions are accepted, and considered to bear rightful authority 'because of their congruence with fundamental extra-legal values'.[26] Indeed, I as will argue below, much of the legitimacy promise associated with the inclusion of domestic elements in hybrids is of *substantive* rather than procedural nature.

2.3.2 From procedural to substantive legitimacy

The legitimacy promise attached to the inclusion of domestic elements is typically established in relation to the legitimacy deficit that impaired the expected progress of the ICTY and the International Criminal Tribunal for Rwanda (ICTR) in advancing reconciliation in Yugoslavia and Rwanda, respectively. Though significant portions of the Yugoslav and Rwandan societies initially supported the formation of purely international tribunals,[27] much of that support was lost during the trials. A widely cited survey in Croatia, for example, found a high percentage of Croatians believed that the Hague-based tribunal was biased, with 52 per cent believing that 'The Hague wants to criminalize the Homeland War'.[28] Accordingly, it was found that 78 per cent believed that citizens should not be extradited should the ICTY request it.[29] The pollsters concluded that there was 'an express anti-Hague atmosphere in the country'.[30] In other words, there was widespread reluctance on behalf of the affected communities to accept the court's authority.

The most intuitive explanation for the legitimacy deficit of the purely international tribunals concerns the physical and psychological distance between the tribunal and the site of the atrocities. There is ample evidence that remoteness generates negativity and apathy towards a court.[31] Interviews with Bosnian judges and prosecutors from various ethnic groups, for example, revealed that although they were generally supportive of the ICTY's mandate and work, geographical distance engendered suspicion of political biases and ignorance of procedures and rules of evidence.[32] Comparing the ICTY and the ICTR to locally-held criminal trials in Argentina, France, Israel and South Korea, Jenia Turner similarly

[26] Martin E Spencer, 'Weber on Legitimate Norms and Authority' (1970) 21 British Journal of Sociology 123, 133.
[27] McAuliffe (n 5) 10.
[28] Payam Akhavan, 'Beyond Impunity: Can International Criminal Justice Prevent Future Atrocities?' (2001) 95 American Journal of International Law 7, 22, citing Jutarnji List (tr), 'Survey Shows "Anti-Hague Atmosphere" Increasing in Croatia' (2000) FBIS Doc EUP20000823000244.
[29] Akhavan (n 28).
[30] ibid.
[31] McAuliffe (n 5) 12.
[32] Laurel E Fletcher and Harvey M Weinstein, 'Justice, Accountability and Social Reconstruction: An Interview Study of Bosnian Judges and Prosecutors' (2000) 18 Berkeley Journal of International Law 102.

found that the two ad hoc tribunals received relatively little attention from the domestic society.[33]

Conceptually, there are two general sorts of reasons why the inclusion of local communities in criminal trials positively affects their legitimacy. First, if criminal trials in transitional justice societies are supposed to write narratives of truth, justice, and reconciliation in a lasting fashion, then this narrative should be defined by the communities it seeks to address. The importance of entrenched local cultures and expectations in achieving long-term stability in post-conflict rebuilding has been emphasized by numerous transitional justice scholars.[34] Crucially, those who argue for greater local ownership and a greater balancing of local and international forms of justice and accountability in post-conflict societies have explicitly identified legitimacy as measured from the local population as 'the key *jus post bellum* criterion'.[35] The second, and related, reason concerns public compliance with the court. As psychological studies have demonstrated, individuals are more likely to comply with institutions and legal codes if they operate according to their own intuition of what is right and just.[36] It is precisely for these reasons that scholars such as Burke-White suggest that a greater regionalization of international criminal courts could harness legitimacy.[37]

The legitimacy deficit of purely international courts, however, runs much deeper than the psychological distance between the trial and the victim community upon which perceived (sociological) legitimacy necessarily depends. This more fundamental deficit is perhaps best exemplified by the imperialism critique and notions of 'white man's justice' that casts international courts as vehicles of colonialist ideologies and oppressive political agendas. In the last few years, a small group of African leaders have seen an opportunity in the ICC's uneven geographical enforcement of international criminal justice to frame the court as an instrument of big powers precisely on these grounds.[38] The fact that those claims have resonated not only throughout Africa, but also within certain academic circles,[39]

[33] Jenia Iontcheva Turner, 'Nationalizing International Criminal Law: The International Criminal Court as a Roving Mixed Court' (2005) 41 Stanford Journal of International 1.

[34] See, eg, Patricia Lundy and Mark McGovern, 'Whose Justice? Rethinking Transitional Justice from the Bottom Up' (2008) 38 Journal of Law and Society 265.

[35] Michael A Newton, 'Community Based Accountability in Afghanistan: Recommendations to Balance the Interests of Justice' in Larry May and Elizabeth Edenberg (eds), *Just Post Bellum and Transitional Justice* (Cambridge University Press 2013) 76.

[36] See Kevin M Carlsmith, John M Darley, and Paul H Robinson, 'Why Do We Punish? Deterrence and Just Deserts as Motives for Punishment' (2002) 83 Journal of Personality and Social Psychology 284; John M Darley, Kevin M Carlsmith, and Paul H Robinson, 'Ex Ante Function of the Criminal Law' (2001) 35 Law and Society Review 165.

[37] Burke-White (n 16) 737.

[38] Elise Keppler, 'Managing Setbacks for the International Criminal Court' (2012) 56 Journal of African Law 1.

[39] See, eg, Barbara Hudson, 'Beyond White Man's Justice: Race, Gender and Justice in Late Modernity' (2006) 10 Theoretical Criminology 29; Awol K Allo, 'The ICC's problem is not overt racism, it is Eurocentricism' *Aljazeera* (28 July 2018) <https://www.aljazeera.com/indepth/opinion/icc-problem-simple-racism-eurocentricism-180725111213623.html> accessed 11 January 2024.

should not surprise; international law has had an extremely difficult relationship with race and colonial oppression,[40] and there are strong normative and political dimensions to international criminal trials that are only marginal to most domestic criminal justice systems.

Even if we can prove that imperial characterizations are unfounded, it seems hard to quarrel, not least from democratic premises, with the claim that the involvement of those affected by the institution in question is a key requirement for its legitimacy. This is the basic insight of the so-called 'input legitimacy' criterion, which seeks to capture the extent to which citizens are able to participate in the decisions and processes of the institutions that govern their lives, most notably through electoral representation.[41] However, incorporating local communities in international criminal trials through domestic participation is about more than fulfilling democratic requirements for input control and accountability. Consider, for example, Jose Alvarez's claim that: '[i]f Rwandan society shares comparable notions of judicial legitimacy, it stands to reason that having judges who come from the local community may itself be determinative of the legitimacy of these processes.'[42] This is based on his widely invoked observation that:

> [to] many surviving victims of the Rwandan genocide it matters a great deal whether an alleged perpetrator of mass atrocity is paraded before the local press, judged in a local courtroom in a language that they can understand, subjected to local procedures, and given a sentence that accords with local sentiments, including perhaps the death penalty.[43]

If this argument is accepted, then the legitimacy fault-lines of hybrid courts go far beyond procedure and legality. Instead, they touch upon the shared sense of common identity, membership ties, historical experience, and cultural values which local communities share, and the way in which they ought to find expression in the institutions that govern them. International(ized) criminal courts deal with a fundamental tension that arises from an uncertainty about whose interests, identities, and values should be the focus of institutional authority. To better appreciate these tensions and the competing claims over the rightful authority of hybrid courts, the next section turns to the discipline of International Relations and introduces the concept of constitutional legitimacy.

[40] Kimberly J Cook and others, 'Beyond White Man's Justice' (2016) 10 Theoretical Criminology 29.

[41] See Wilhelm Scharpf, *Governing in Europe* (Oxford University Press 1999), who distinguishes between an institution's 'input' and 'output' legitimacy.

[42] Jose E Alvarez, 'Crimes of States/Crimes of Hate: Lessons from Rwanda' (1999) 24 Yale Journal of International Law 365, 403.

[43] ibid 405.

2.4 Constituent Power and Constitutional Legitimacy

As soon as an institution is established and operates outside domestic boundaries, no matter how artificial those boundaries may be drawn, a basic puzzle emerges: whose interests, welfare, and fate are at stake in its establishment and operation? In the domestic context, this collective is typically associated with 'the nation' or 'the people' that constitute the central source of authority for the state and its institutions. With the onset of globalization and the proliferation of supranational institutions, however, questions about the relationship between collectives and institutional authority have become much more complicated. Scholars of International Relations and international law have thus begun to (re)examine the politics of legitimacy surrounding constituent power beyond the state.[44] Focusing on supranational organizations such as the European Union (EU), these writers have sought to better understand the political subjects in whose name specific international institutions are enacted and in whom ultimate authority resides. Crucially for our purpose, studying institutions' constituent power means reaching deeper than merely capturing the interests their decisions and outputs seek to serve. Instead, as Hans Lindahl points out, questions about constituent power are about the processes through which a collective constructs its 'socio-political identity' and their 'collective selfhood', respectively.[45]

It is readily apparent that the notion of constituent power should be of significant concern for the conceptualization and study of international(ized) courts. Because internationalized criminal courts are not part of a legal order that has a central authority that produces laws that are then applied by the courts, questions about constitutional authority and accountability arise naturally: who has the right to establish ICL institutions? Who has the right to refer cases to the ICC—supranational institutions such as the UN Security Council? What should the relationship be between national constitutional traditions and ICL in courts?

Building on the notion of constituent power, John Oates recently provided an account of constituent power that offers a useful path into the legitimacy fault-lines of hybrid courts.[46] Oates takes as the starting point the assumption that an institution's ultimate authority rests in the collective, be it states, cosmopolitan communities, or other social collectives, in whose name it is established and enacted.[47] From here, he develops the notion of constitutional legitimacy, suggesting

[44] For a review of this literature, see Markus Patberg, 'Constituent Power Beyond the State: An Emerging Debate in International Political Theory' (2012) 42 Millennium Journal of International Studies 224.

[45] Hans Lindahl, 'Constituent Power and Reflexive Identity: Towards an Ontology of Collective Selfhood' in Martin Laughlin and Neil Walker (eds), *The Paradox of Constitutionalism: Constituent power and constitutional form* (Oxford University Press 2013).

[46] John Oates, 'The Fourth Face of Legitimacy: Constituent Power and the Constitutional Legitimacy of International Institutions' (2016) 43 Review of International Studies 199.

[47] ibid 208.

that the ideas and beliefs members of an institutional order hold about the constituent power of that order constitute a distinct dimension of its legitimacy. As Oates explains:

> Constitutional legitimacy concerns the constitutive justifications for a particular institutional order and involves two sets of questions: the first order question of *who* the constituent power of that order should be and second order question of *what* the relationship should be between the constituent and constituted powers of that institutional order.[48]

These questions can and should be asked about hybrid courts, whose authority structure is necessarily divided and ambiguous, and whose anterior sources of legitimacy extends beyond those associated with the institutional structure of purely international courts and tribunals.

The *first order question of hybrid courts' constitutional legitimacy* asks whether its authority is grounded in the appropriate constituent subject. The issue here is whether hybrid courts should primarily serve the interests of the international community and its shared collective interests, or whether they should serve the society in which the crimes they address were committed. This is an important question that cuts to the beliefs collectives hold about the purpose and public identity of hybrids. If, for example, we believe that the international community should serve as a constituency for hybrid courts, granting international actors authority over the court—be it through the composition of the bench, or through the applicable law and procedure—would not only be permissible, but also necessary in order to effectively represent the values and interests of the international community.

The *second order question of constitutional legitimacy* concerns the authority relations that specify the distribution of roles, rights, responsibilities, and jurisdictions. Put simply, how should authority within a hybrid court be distributed among the international and the domestic communities? The appropriate distribution of authority within a hybrid court essentially depends on how we answer the first order question; that is, who we see as hybrids' proper constituent subject. This is because beliefs about what the constituent power of an institution should be provide the normative and rhetorical resources needed to legitimize the distribution of authority within them.[49]

Before analysing the politics of legitimacy in particular hybrids, one last theoretical point seems to be in order. While any ICL mechanism that fails to ground its practices in the collective subjects it seeks to serve will see its constitutional legitimacy under strain,[50] the view that legitimacy is required in all subject

[48] ibid.
[49] ibid 210.
[50] ibid 209–10.

constituencies to equal degree is not only empirically infeasible but also inconsistent with the theoretical scholarship on constitutional legitimacy.[51] In global governance, some relationships between the constituency and the institution in question are so indirect, so distant, that little legitimacy is required by each actor. So which constituencies matter?

For International Relations scholars, the constituency an actor ultimately must establish legitimacy in typically largely depends upon where one seeks to act, so that the relevant constituency of an institution will be determined by its realm of political action.[52] In the case of international(ized) criminal courts, however, assigning the relevant constituency is different. Because criminal trials are institutionalized processes in which a public holds its members to account,[53] determining their relevant constituency is first and foremost about identifying the public to whom the perpetrator is answerable. To use the words of Anthony Duff, '[we] must show that the court acts in the name of some group to who the defendant is answerable for his alleged crimes'.[54] For purely international courts such as the ICTY and the ICC, this group has been unequivocally global. This is perhaps most evident in their sentencing judgments, which are replete with cosmopolitan language and references to notions of humanity and global community.[55]

The problem with adjudicating international wrongs exclusively in the name of humanity, however, is that it tends to downplay the dual nature of international crimes. Whilst cosmopolitan notions of humanity have done a variety of work for international lawyers in establishing criminal justice mechanisms beyond the state,[56] international crimes are an assault on both the global public *and* a direct attack on the local society, with the latter being the 'primary victim' that directly suffers the atrocity.[57] This makes domestic actors a key constituent subject whose interests, identities, and claims to authority over the court are necessary resources of its constitutional legitimacy. Conceptually, hybrids' mixed composition thus offers significant advantages over their purely domestic counterparts when it comes to accommodating the twofold public interests international criminal trials seek to serve.

[51] Symons (n 6) 2561.

[52] Christian Reus-Smit, 'International Crisis of Legitimacy' (2007) 44 International Politics 164.

[53] Anthony Duff, 'Authority and Responsibility in International Criminal Law' in Samantha Besson and John Tasioulas (eds), *The Philosophy of International Law* (Oxford University Press 2010).

[54] ibid 598.

[55] See, eg, Luigi DA Corrias and Geoffrey M Gordon, 'Judging in the Name of Humanity: International Criminal Tribunals and the Representation of a Global Public' (2015) 13 Journal of International Criminal Justice 97.

[56] See Antonio Franceschet, 'Four Cosmopolitan Projects: The International Criminal Court in Context' in Steven C Roach (ed), *Governance, Order, and the International Criminal Court: Between Realpolitik and a Cosmopolitan Court* (Oxford University Press 2009).

[57] Harry Hobbs, 'Towards a Principled Justification for the Mixed Composition of Hybrid International Criminal Tribunals' (2017) 30 Leiden Journal of International Law 187. See also Megret (n 2).

2.5 (Re)constructing Constitutional Legitimacy

The above discussion has sought to show that the questions of (a) who the constituent power of a hybrid court should be and (b) how authority within them is distributed among domestic and international actors are theoretically relevant for assessing their legitimacy. This section briefly illustrates how these issues have shaped legitimacy dynamics within two different internationalized courts: the Extraordinary Chambers in the Courts of Cambodia and the Human Rights Chamber for Bosnia and Herzegovina. In each case, I focus on how the court has confronted a competing array of constituent powers and show how different representations thereof have shaped their legitimacy. The principal aim here is to show how the notion of constituent power enables us to analyse the legitimacy dynamics of hybrids rather than evaluating their normative status (though the examples may involve normative considerations).

2.5.1 The Extraordinary Chambers in the Courts of Cambodia

Established in 2004 through an agreement between the United Nations (UN) and the Cambodian government, the Extraordinary Chambers in the Courts of Cambodia (ECCC) was set up to address crimes committed during the Khmer Rouge regime in Cambodia between 1975 and 1979. Based in Cambodia's capital, Phnom Penh, its jurisdiction includes crimes committed by the senior leadership of the Democratic Kampuchea and those most responsible for serious crimes under national and international law. As I will show below, one of the main dividing lines in the establishment of the ECCC concerns the question of authority over the court, and how roles should be distributed among the Cambodian government and the UN.

The question of constitutional legitimacy arose early during the establishment process of the ECCC. In June 1997, after the UN Commission on Human Rights (UNCHR) issued a Resolution that 'called for an examination of any request by Cambodia for assistance in responding to past serious violations of Cambodian and international laws',[58] the UN Special Representative of Human Rights to Cambodia, Thomas Hammarberg, suggested to Cambodian authorities to consider acting upon the opportunity the Resolution presented. Though initially hesitant about the effects of the tribunal, Prince Norodom Ranariddh agreed to submit a formal request to the UN Secretary General, but asked Hammarberg to draft the letter for him.[59] Hammarbarg agreed to draft the letter that subsequently figured in

[58] UNCHR, 'Situation of human rights in Cambodia' (11 April 1997) UN Doc E/CN.4/1997/49.

[59] Thomas Hammarberg, 'How the Khmer Rouge Tribunal was agreed: Discussions between the Cambodian government and the UN' (*Searching for the Truth, Documentation Center of Cambodia,*

every discussion between the UN and the Cambodian government on the Khmer Rouge issue, but emphasized that it would be crucial that Cambodia claimed authority over the request.[60] As Hammarberg recalls: 'I was willing to give him such technical help [drafting the text] but the letter should be considered as his and Hun Sen's.'[61]

It took eight years until the hybrid court became operational in 2005. During that time, intense negotiations and political bargaining between the UN and the Cambodian government took place.

The main issues of disagreement were over the extent of participation by international judges and staff and whether the institution would be integrated into the Cambodian legal system or exist as a separate international entity as in the case of the ICTY and ICTR.[62] Underlying these disagreements were two views on what the court's constituent power should be, and who would hold authority over the trial. Whereas the Cambodian government insisted on 'a strong Cambodian hallmark on the court', the UN sought 'to guarantee international standards by demanding more international influence'.[63] To be sure, the Cambodian government was in principle open to international assistance, but it demanded sufficient control over the process. Deputy Prime-Minister Sok highlighted the point during the adoption speech of the ECCC Law in the National Assembly:

> [During the negotiations] [w]e pointed out that in order to reflect the respect for Cambodian sovereignty, the trial chambers have to [have] a Cambodian majority. (...) [In the past] the majority of criminal tribunals in the world were established by foreign judges, initiated by foreign judges, and imposed into the country. As for our agreement, [...] [it] is a compromise between us, the host, the case owner, and the United Nations.[64]

Note here how Cambodia's constituent power is historically constructed. That is, concerns on behalf of the Cambodian government, and the Cambodian people in general, about an externally imposed trial and the violation of sovereignty not

2001) <https://d.dccam.org/Tribunal/Analysis/How_Khmer_Rouge_Tribunal.htm> accessed 11 January 2024.

60 UNGA and UNSC, 'Identical Letters dated 23 June 1997 from the Secretary-General addressed to the President of the General Assembly and the President of the Security Council' (1997) UN Doc A/51/135-S/1997/488.

61 Hammarberg (n 59).

62 UNGA, 'Report of the Secretary-General on Khmer Rouge trials' (2003) UN Doc A/57/769.

63 Sarah MH Nouwen, 'Hybrid Courts: The Hybrid Category of a New Type of International Crimes Courts' (2006) 2(2) Utrecht Law Review 190, 194.

64 Cited in Hanna Bertelman, 'International Standards and National Ownership—Judicial Independence in Hybrid Courts: The Extraordinary Chambers in the Courts of Cambodia' (2010) 79 Nordic Journal of International Law 341, 363.

only emerged from observations about previous international tribunals, but also reflected the country's past and extremely complicated relationship with the international community. Indeed, it seems impossible to understand the current structure, composition, and jurisdiction of the ECCC without taking into account the political context of the Khmer Rouge regime, including the role of outside powers, and its impact on the negotiation process.[65]

This is an important reminder of how the constitutional legitimacy of an internationalized court is never acontextual in the sense that it can be pre-determined by relying on an objective, one-size-fits-all institutional blueprint that specifies the distribution of roles, responsibilities, and authorities in advance. Instead, the constitutional legitimacy of a hybrid is socially constructed through an intersubjective political process in which actors negotiate constituent power. The establishment of the ECCC may have been overshadowed and prolonged by the political struggle between the Cambodian government and the UN. However, the articulation of actors' historical experiences and cultural narratives about rightful authority and appropriate forms of social control is crucial for shaping the constitutional legitimacy of a court.

The extent to which Cambodia has been able to successfully utilize its constituent power and gain authority over the courts is reflected in the constitutive rules and procedural law of the ECCC. While the court combines Cambodian criminal and civil law with international law, including recognition of international standards of justice, fairness, and due process of law as set out in the 1976 International Covenant of Civil and Political Rights, the ECCC is firmly rooted in the Cambodian legal system and is part of its judicial structure.[66] Following the Cambodian Code of Criminal Procedure, one of the key innovations of the ECCC, for example, is that it allows for civil parties to attend the hearings and intervene in the proceedings by becoming a 'civil party'.[67] However, the main indicator for the way in which Cambodia remains the primary constituent power of the court is the participation of the Cambodian judiciary in the trials. In addition to the guaranteed presence of local judges, Cambodian institutions exercise significant control over judicial appointments.[68] That is, not only are the domestic judges appointed by the Cambodian Supreme Council of the Magistracy, the same body also selects the international judges from a list of candidates submitted by the UN Secretary

65 ibid 343–46.

66 Law on the Establishment of the Extraordinary Chambers in the Courts of Cambodia 2004 article 2 new. For years, concerns have, however, been expressed by local and international observers regarding the state of the Cambodian judiciary, particularly when in it comes to its independence from political interference.

67 Cambodian Code of Criminal Procedure (2007), Article 137.

68 The ECCC is comprised of a Trial Chamber, composed of three domestic and two foreign judges, and one Supreme Court Chamber, composed of four domestic and three foreign judges.

General.[69] By the same procedure the co-prosecutors, co-investigating judges and Pre-Trial Chamber judges are selected.

Through control over the composition of the bench, Cambodia was able to secure significant institutional authority, and to shape the public identity of the trial in an important way. Considering that the absence of guaranteed local judges on the bench of the ICC, as well as the ICTY and ICTR, significantly undermined the courts' legitimacy within the affected state,[70] Cambodia's authority over judicial appointments and the ECCC's strong integration into the Cambodian legal system offer a basis for its constitutional legitimacy. Whether or not the significant influence Cambodia holds over the court and its composition has impeded its procedural legitimacy is a separate consideration from how the distribution of authority affects its constitutional legitimacy. That said, the sustained criticism concerning political interference, judicial bias, and corruption suggest that the tribunal's strong domestic constitution has had negative consequences for its procedural legitimacy.

2.5.2 The Human Rights Chamber for Bosnia and Herzegovina

The Human Rights Chamber for Bosnia and Herzegovina (HRBH) was a hybrid human rights tribunal created by the General Framework Agreement for Peace (the Dayton Peace Agreement) that ended the war in Bosnia and Herzegovina in 1995. In contrast to the ECCC, and most hybrids for that matter, the HRBH was designed to assist a post-war state in honouring its obligations to protect international human rights.[71] It had jurisdiction to investigate and prosecute violations of the European Convention on Human Rights and Fundamental Freedoms (ECHR) and violations of a range of other international human rights treaties. Its broader focus on human rights protection rather than exclusively on war crimes and crimes against humanity, and its close alignment with a specific regional human rights framework, makes the HRBH a somewhat *sui generis* hybrid institution. Because the Chamber applies the jurisprudence of the Council of Europe, it lays bare some of the specific legitimacy problems that arise when a hybrid's normative structure is closely tied to international authority.

The constitutional power of the HRBH was fundamentally defined by the post-war institutional context in which it operated. After the falling of the Yugoslavian federation, the Dayton Peace Agreement constructed a new institutional and legal

[69] Law on the Establishment of Extraordinary Chambers in the Courts of Cambodia for the Prosecution of Crimes Committed During the Period of Democratic Kampuchea (amended and promulgated on 27 October 2004) NS/RKM/1004/006, Articles 18 new and 26.

[70] Harry Hobbs, 'Hybrid Tribunals and the Composition of the Court: In Search of Sociological Legitimacy' (2016) 16 Chicago Journal of International Law 482.

[71] The General Framework Agreement for Peace in Bosnia and Herzegovina (adopted 14 December 1995) (Dayton Agreement) annex 6.

framework for Bosnia. In the absence of any functioning state structures, authority was placed entirely in the hands of international actors and ad hoc institutions. Whereas the UN Protection Force (UNPROFOR) was tasked with overseeing the military aspects of the peace, the Office of the High Representative (OHR) was responsible for the civilian aspects of the peace. The OHR, which included a substantial focus on the rule of law and the protection of human rights,[72] was an international institution staffed primarily by non-Bosnians and endowed with a robust mandate. In addition to having the final say over the interpretation of clauses concerning the peace implementation, the Dayton Peace Agreement gave the High Representative the authority to interpret their own authorities and powers.[73] The consequences of this arrangement for the distribution of constituent power among international and domestic actors were significant. As Niels van Willigen observed:

> whereas the Bosniaks, the Bosnian Serbs, and the Bosnian Croats as the three major ethnic groups in Bosnia, as well as Croatia and Serbia, were bound to the Dayton Agreement, the international administration was not. Consequently, being the highest political authority in Bosnia, the High Representative was formally not subjected to the Bosnian constitution.[74]

The Dayton Peace Agreement thus not only (re)organized relationships between collectives based on their underlying layers of ethnic, national, and religious identities,[75] but also distributed constituent power among them in a way that reaffirmed the hierarchy between international and national actors and institutions.

The unequal distribution of constituent power emanating from the institutional framework superimposed by Dayton Peace Agreement was reflected in various aspects of the HRBH. It was perhaps most visible in the composition of the bench. The majority of judges were internationals, directly appointed by the Committee of Ministers of the Council of Europe. The President of the Chamber was also selected by the Committee of Ministers of the Council of Europe from among the international judges. Of the remaining six judges, four were appointed by the predominantly Muslim and Croat Federation of Bosnia and Herzegovina and two by the predominantly Serb Republika Srpska.[76] The international identity of the

[72] Dayton Agreement, including the provision of a new Bosnian Constitution for Bosnia, a new constitutional court, and a human rights commission consisting of an ombudsperson and the Human Rights Chamber.

[73] Dayton Agreement (n 71) annex 10.

[74] Niels van Willigen, 'International Administration and Institutional Autonomy in Bosnia and Herzegovina and Kosovo' (2012) 28 East European Politics 429, 433.

[75] Elizabeth M Bruch, 'Hybrid Courts: Examining Hybridity through a Post-Colonial Lens' (2010) 28 Boston University International Law Journal 1, 8–10.

[76] David Yeager, 'The Human Rights Chamber for Bosnia and Herzegovina: A Case Study in Transitional Justice' (2004) 14 International Legal Perspectives 44.

HRBH was further reinforced by the fact that although multiple languages were deployed in formal procedures and publications of the Chamber, English was the primary language of interaction among judges and staff.[77] There is good reason to assume that this had a negative impact on the Chamber's legitimacy. The ability of international judges and staff to speak, or at least willingness to learn the language of the affected communities, has been identified as key to gaining sociological legitimacy in the eyes of the people.[78] The constitutional perspective advanced here reinforces this view, for its sees language as an important signifier for culture, identity, and belonging.[79]

That the HRBH represented the interests of the international community rather than those of Bosnian society was also evident in the procedures and substantive law. In order to re-establish the rule of law in Bosnia, the international mission instilled a new legal framework that replaced existing domestic law with a European and international human rights legal regime. Under the new Constitution of Bosnia and Herzegovina, for example, the ECHR was directly incorporated into domestic law and given 'priority over all other law'.[80] In the case of the HRBH, the procedures and substantive law of the European human rights regime were imported without adaption.

While the wholesale importation of international human rights law may seem unproblematic considering its universal status, it has supressed the national and local involvement in the development and application of the law. Elizabeth Bruch's first-hand account of the underlying social-structural dynamics of the internationalization of the Chamber offers some useful insights into the distribution of constituent power. Drawing on post-colonial and critical social theory, Bruch shows how the translation of both law and procedure was essentially a one-way process.[81] She not only highlights how the Chamber repeatedly overturned decisions pronounced during the war by relying exclusively on the European Convention and the case law of the European Court,[82] but also points out how its work was often aimed at training Bosnians as 'a "class of interpreters" to use and participate appropriately'.[83] This kind of unequal hybridity, Bruch concludes, further shifted the balance of power towards international or European dominance while ensuring that Bosnia was always '"not quite" Europe'.[84] It is beyond the scope of the chapter to do full justice to her account here, but the concept of constituent power helps bring

[77] Bruch (n 75) 13. Noting that 'the idea that international judges and staff might use (or learn) the national language(s) was never suggested'.

[78] See Hobbs (n 70) 517–18.

[79] See, eg, Mary Bucholtz and Kira Hall, 'Language and Identity' in Alessandro Duranti (ed), *A Companion to Linguistic Anthropology* (Blackwell Publishing 2004).

[80] UNSC, 'Report to the General Assembly' (4 December 1996) UN Doc A/51/21, annex 4, article II.

[81] Bruch (n 75).

[82] ibid 17–19.

[83] ibid 24.

[84] ibid 21.

these underlying hierarchies and tensions into conceptual relief and suggests that hybrids' legitimacy is contingent upon the ability of *all* actors to exercise effective agency in the interpretation and application of the law and the day-to-day operation of the court. It also feeds directly into the realist perspective on international criminal justice, which sees a court's constitutional basis as a result of great power interests rather than careful negotiation between key stakeholders.

2.6 Conclusions

Hybrids confront an array of competing interests and identities that are typically structured around the domestic–international distinction. This chapter has sought to show how the analysis of the legitimacy of hybrid courts and tribunals would benefit from a more direct engagement with the underlying interests and identities they (seek to) serve and represent. My primary concern was to show that collective judgements and shared beliefs about whose interests and welfare are held to be at stake in the establishment and operation of international(ized) criminal courts are key to understanding their political authority and legitimacy. Given that international crimes affect both the international and the local community, courts addressing them should serve the interests of both constituencies. In this sense, hybrid institutional settings carry a potential legitimacy advantage over purely domestic/international courts.

However, the relationship between international and domestic actors and law within hybrids are often organized hierarchically. Drawing on the concepts of constituent power and constitutional legitimacy, I have therefore provided the contours of framework that turns the spotlight on the distribution of authority within hybrid settings and how this distribution affects the normative status of the court. This framework should be understood as a first attempt to shift the analytical focus away from procedural questions towards the deeper-seated legitimacy dynamics of hybrid courts. To illustrate the potential benefits of such an approach, I have then briefly examined the 'struggle' over constitutional legitimacy within two hybrids. Rather than offering an exhaustive analysis, my principal aim was to demonstrate the analytical potential of the framework, hoping that it will animate researchers and practitioners to think more systematically about the competing constituent powers that shape the legitimacy dynamics of hybrids.

While the empirical analysis offered in this chapter is by no means exhaustive, it nevertheless serves to highlight three issues that are central to the general legitimacy debate about hybrids.

The first concerns the historically contingent nature of legitimacy politics. Like every social construct, constitutional legitimacy does not exist in a vacuum. Instead, the shared beliefs actors, in particular local actors, hold about the legitimacy of a criminal law institution are heavily determined by cultural narratives and historical experiences. Here, notions of hegemonic power and imperial domination play a significant role, because they fundamentally shape the collective judgements about the rightfulness of political and legal authority in post-colonial societies. There is not blueprint for dividing constituent power among international and domestic actors. However, given that most hybrids operate in societies that have experienced periods of foreign occupation or other forms of external intervention, according sufficient constituent power to local actors is a necessary condition for constitutional legitimacy. This means that international actors need to respect, and take seriously, the distinct cultural and historical backgrounds of the affected communities when negotiating the distribution of roles and authority in specific hybrids.

The second issue has to do with balancing different forms of legitimacy concerns. As we have seen, legitimacy has different faces that do not always sit happily within the same institutional setting. The HRBH is a case in point. Whereas the wholesale importation of international human rights law certainly strengthened the rule of law, thereby strengthening the Chamber's procedural legitimacy, it significantly impeded the representation of Bosnian interests and identity in the application and development of law and process. Claims to constitutional legitimacy must thus be weighed against other legitimacy concerns, most notably procedural ones stemming from fairness and impartiality. Theoretically, the concepts of constitutional and procedural legitimacy operate independently from each other: whereas the former flows from the appropriate constituencies in which a court's authority is grounded, the latter has to do with the procedures and processes that underpin the operation of international criminal justice mechanisms. However, because *international* control over transitional justice mechanisms is closely connected to the promise of fair and impartial procedure, the question of how authority over a court should be distributed has both constitutional and procedural consequences. While the case studies in this chapter suggest that there is a trade-off between localized constituent power and impartiality/fair procedure, we should be careful not to deduce a general causal story that places constitutional and procedural forms of legitimacy in a zero-sum, or even negative-sum, relationship. Instead, any fundamental claim about the normative dynamics of internationalized criminal law institutions ought to focus on the specific requirements for different forms of legitimacy within a particular setting.

Thirdly and lastly, the construction of constitutional legitimacy does not end with the establishment of the court. While the distribution of constituent power among international and local actors is fundamentally determined by the legal framework/treaty that establishes the institutional setting, hybridity is (re)constructed during the everyday work of the court. Hybrid structures need to be enacted, which means that judges and staff play an important role in the construction of the public identity of the institution. Developing codes of conduct that allow for a dialectical practice in which actors from different constituent communities engage constructively with each other is most likely to be critical here. Such guidelines could be helpful in promoting an institutional culture based on equality and mutual respect for different identities and cultural backgrounds. If hybridity is to be organic, based on amalgamation rather than imposition, interaction among local and international actors needs to take the form of constructive engagement. The willingness to learn, respect, and understand the interests, values, and organizational approaches of others is likely to be key to effective cross-cultural collaborations within hybrids.

3

Regionalized Hybrid Courts

*Elena Baylis**

3.1 Introduction

International collaboration in the first wave of hybrid courts[1] followed a consistent pattern: the international partner in each instance was the United Nations (UN). The second wave of hybrid courts evinces a significant change in this configuration. For the first time, two of the three new hybrid courts have been structured as partnerships with regional organizations, the African Union (AU) and the European Union (EU). An additional proposed hybrid tribunal for South Sudan is also being developed as a regional partnership with the AU.[2]

From the perspective of the history of hybrid courts, this marks an abrupt change. However, this regional engagement in hybrid tribunals is an expression of a long-term trend towards the development of regional commitments to transitional justice and ICL. The EU and the AU, as well as other regional organizations, have supported various transitional justice endeavours.[3]

This chapter assesses the trend towards regional commitments to transitional justice and ICL and the theoretical arguments for regional transitional justice institutions. It then evaluates the engagement of regional actors in the Kosovo Specialist Chambers and Special Prosecutor's Office (KSC), the Extraordinary

* Professor of Law, University of Pittsburgh School of Law. Thanks to Andrew Boyle, Stuart Ford, James Fry, Allyson Ford Ouoba, Milena Sterio, Susana SáCouto, and Timothy Waters for their comments; to Kirsten Ainley and Mark Kersten for organizing the Hybrid Justice project; and to all of the contributors for their insights.

[1] For the purposes of this chapter, I am including all ad hoc criminal courts and judicial chambers with both international and domestic components as part of the same category of 'hybrid courts' or 'hybrid tribunals' and am using those two terms interchangeably. This is in keeping with the definitions used by the Hybrid Justice project and also with this chapter's focus on the engagement of regional organizations, rather than on comparative degrees of internationalization or on the implications of a hybrid court's international or domestic character. Cf Sarah Williams, *Hybrid and Internationalised Criminal Tribunals* (Hart Publishing 2012) 249–50.

[2] Furthermore, while the new hybrid court for the Central African Republic is not based on a regional partnership, it utilizes substantial regional human resources in its selection of predominantly regional judges and attorneys as its international staff.

[3] See, eg, Eleonora Mesquita Ceia, 'The Contributions of the Inter-American Court of Human Rights to the Development of Transitional Justice' (2015) 14 Law and Practice of International Courts and Tribunals 457.

Elena Baylis, *Regionalized Hybrid Courts* In: *Hybrid Justice*. Edited by: Kirsten Ainley and Mark Kersten, Oxford University Press. © Elena Baylis 2025. DOI: 10.1093/oso/9780192893758.003.0003

African Chambers in the Courts of Senegal (EAC), and the proposed Hybrid Court for South Sudan (HCSS) in light of these trends and arguments.

This new wave of regionalized hybrid courts represents a manifestation of regional interests, with the AU focused on internal regional authority within its borders, and the EU focused on external security and norms, particularly along its borders. Neither the KSC nor the EAC emerges in the forms anticipated by scholars, and accordingly, they do not produce most of the predicted benefits of regionalizing transitional justice institutions. The regionalized hybrid courts do, however, represent viable judicial institutions with jurisdiction to hear otherwise unprosecuted atrocity cases, in addition to enabling the involved regional organizations to pursue their aims. For future hybrid courts, regional involvement could offer advantages in comparison to partnerships with international institutions. However, those regionalized hybrid courts would need to be designed to achieve those benefits; to gain an advantage from regionalization, it is not sufficient to merely substitute regional partners for international ones in a hybrid court framework.

3.2 Theoretical Arguments for Regional Transitional Justice Institutions

Proponents of regional transitional justice institutions focus predominantly on three factors which, they argue, should make regional institutions particularly appropriate and effective transitional justice mechanisms in many instances. First, some regional organizations have authority over and competence in matters relating to transitional justice. Also, many of the concerned conflicts are characterized by regional scope or effects. Finally, regional organizations may be able to offer greater localization, contextualization, and legitimacy than international partners. Notably, this third factor overlaps considerably with the original justifications for establishing hybrid courts rather than purely international tribunals; it thus suggests the possibility of synergies between hybridization and regionalization. In addition, at least one transitional justice scholar argues that regional institutions could advance the development of regional norms, and that this would be constructive for ICL as a field.

Concerning the first factor, the arguments for regional authority to act in the transitional justice sphere are strong. Peace, security, and justice lie squarely within the authority and competence of both the EU and the AU and provide a basis for these entities' engagement in transitional justice.[4] Indeed, where conflicts within

[4] Katy Crossley-Frolick, 'The European Union and Transitional Justice: Human Rights and Post-Conflict Reconciliation in Europe and Beyond' (2011) 1 Contemporary Readings in Law and Social Justice 33, 37–38 <https://www.ceeol.com/search/article-detail?id=56479> accessed 29 December 2023; Matiangai Sirleaf, 'Regionalism, Regime Complexes and the Crisis in International Criminal

their borders are concerned, arguably support for transitional justice is an obligation and not merely an opportunity for the EU and AU. There are also numerous other regional organizations with commitments to ensuring security.[5]

Regarding the regional scope and effect of conflicts, certainly, many conflicts are of a transnational scope or have significant regional effects, including, for example, the conflicts in Sierra Leone, Rwanda, and the former Yugoslavia. In such instances, Amy Ross and Chandra Sriram argue that:

> While many conflicts and attendant human rights abuses are regionalized, involving multiple countries, most peace agreements and accountability processes are developed for single states in isolation, creating a patchwork of accountability, whereby complex regionalized crimes are treated differently by individual countries and/or international processes.[6]

Accordingly, Matiangai Sirleaf advocates establishing regional transitional justice mechanisms that can address the entirety of transnational conflicts.[7]

In addition, regional institutions are perceived as being more closely connected to the concerned states and thus as possessing greater perceived legitimacy with concerned states and communities, as well as an enhanced ability to contextualize transitional justice processes. For example, William Burke-White argues that regional processes offer a balance between the respective benefits and detriments of purely national and purely international processes. Thus, as compared to international processes, regional entities tend to be more physically proximate and thus better able to engage with communities; more closely connected culturally, socially, and politically, and thus possessing greater domestic legitimacy; and potentially less expensive. As compared to domestic courts, regional courts can avail themselves of regional expertise and are more resistant to domestic political influence.[8] Similarly, Sirleaf contends that regional institutions have a greater ability to tailor their procedures and modes of reparation to meet local expectations.[9]

Justice' (2016) 54 Columbia Journal of Transnational Law 699, 731 <http://dx.doi.org/10.2139/ssrn.2293988> accessed 29 December 2023.

[5] Amy Ross and Chandra Sriram, 'Closing Impunity Gaps?: Regional Transitional Justice Processes' (2012) 1 Transitional Justice Review 3, 12–13 <http://dx.doi.org/10.5206/tjr.2012.1.1.2> accessed 29 December 2023.

[6] ibid 5.

[7] Matiangai Sirleaf, 'Regional Approach to Transitional Justice?: Examining the Special Court for Sierra Leone and the Truth and Reconciliation Commission for Liberia' (2009) 21 Florida Journal of International Law 209, 271–80 <https://scholarship.law.ufl.edu/fjil/vol21/iss2/3/> accessed 29 December 2023; Sirleaf, 'Regionalism' (n 4).

[8] William Burke-White, 'Regionalization of International Criminal Law Enforcement: A Preliminary Explanation' (2003) 38 Texas International Law Journal 729, 734–43 <https://scholarship.law.upenn.edu/faculty_scholarship/959> accessed 29 December 2023.

[9] Sirleaf, Regionalism (n 4) 770–71.

Importantly, these arguments in many ways parallel those made in favour of hybrid courts over fully international or national tribunals: that the domestic components of hybrid tribunals will provide greater authenticity and engagement with the concerned communities, while the international components will protect them against undue influence. Hybrid courts have also been expected to contribute to domestic capacity building and norm adoption through dialogue between international and national attorneys and judges within the tribunals; however, in reality, there have been barriers such as language differences and differing legal traditions, as well as unfamiliarity with national law and history on the part of the international participants. If regional attorneys and judges were to share a language, similar legal traditions, or greater awareness of the concerned country's law and history with the national participants, that would promote these original hybrid court goals. Thus, in principle, the inclusion of a regional partner could synergize with the hybrid structure, so that the regional and domestic components enhance and reinforce each other's positive domestic effects.

Furthermore, both Burke-White and Sirleaf argue that states may prefer regional to international institutions because of the nature of states' relationships to regional institutions. Member states typically have more influence in regional than international organizations by virtue of the smaller number of members. The region also may share certain core values or interdependent interests that could be effectively promoted by a regional institution.[10] In addition, in multifaceted organizations like the EU and AU, states that already engage in other aspects of the organization's work may more readily participate in ICL adjudications as well.[11]

One additional argument for regional institutions is comparatively controversial: while many scholars warn against the fragmentation of ICL norms,[12] William Schabas supports the development of regional ICL norms. He argues that the example of the regional human rights systems demonstrates both that regional institutions can effectively implement international norms and that regional variation in definitions of universal standards and their application to particular circumstances does not necessarily undermine their core universality. Indeed, he contends that allowing regional variation could produce a trend towards increasing protections in some regions, rather than promoting a lowest common denominator approach that defines a single universal ICL standard in terms of only those

[10] Burke-White (n 8) 746–47; Sirleaf, 'Regionalism' (n 4) 735, 767.

[11] Sirleaf, 'Regionalism' (n 4) 767.

[12] For overviews of the ICL norm pluralism/fragmentation debate, see, eg, Elies van Sliedregt and Sergey Vasiliev, 'Pluralism: A New Framework for International Criminal Justice' in Elies van Sliedregt and Sergey Vasiliev (eds), *Pluralism in International Criminal Law* (Oxford University Press 2014); Larissa van den Herik and Carsten Stahn, '"Fragmentation", Diversification and "3D" Legal Pluralism: International Criminal Law as the Jack-in-the-Box?' in Larissa van den Herik and Carsten Stahn (eds), *The Diversification and Fragmentation of International Criminal Law* (Martinus Nijhoff 2012).

positions on which all states can agree.[13] However, others argue that regional variation in substantive ICL norms would undermine ICL's universality and legitimacy and thus constitutes a risk of regionalized arrangements.[14]

3.3 A Regional Transitional Justice Trend

Transitional justice includes a wide variety of mechanisms, including processes and institutions aimed at memorialization, education, domestic legal and institutional reforms, and truth-telling, as well as those focused on criminal trials. This section focuses on regional engagement with, and support for, ICL trials, as this is the aspect of transitional justice most closely related to the work of hybrid courts.

Regional engagement has developed in the context of prior and ongoing international engagement in ICL trials. It was the UN that initially carried out international and hybrid trials in the late 1990s and early 2000s, first in the International Criminal Tribunal for the former Yugoslavia and the International Criminal Tribunal for Rwanda, and then as the international partner for hybrid courts such as the Special Court for Sierra Leone. The International Criminal Court (ICC) then became active in investigating and prosecuting violations of ICL.

3.3.1 African Union

The AU's charter establishes its authority over matters of peace and security and provides the foundation for its engagement in transitional justice. The possibility of a regional court with jurisdiction over international crimes was raised in the 1970s during the development of the draft African Charter on Peoples and Human Rights under the auspices of the Organization of African Unity, the AU's predecessor organization. At that time, the proposal for a regional court was dropped in anticipation of the creation of a UN court to prosecute apartheid and other international crimes, however the projected international court was not in fact brought to fruition.[15] The idea of a regional criminal court arose again in 2006 when the Committee of Eminent Jurists appointed by the AU to consider the options for prosecuting Habré recommended that, in the future, criminal jurisdiction over such cases should be conferred on a regional court.[16] In the following years, the AU

13 William Schabas, 'Regions, Regionalism and International Criminal Law' (2007) 4 New Zealand Yearbook of International Law 3 <http://www8.austlii.edu.au/nz/journals/NZYbkIntLaw/2007/2.html> accessed 29 December 2023.

14 See, eg, Burke-White (n 8) 756–57.

15 Ademola Abass, 'Prosecuting International Crimes in Africa: Rationale, Prospects and Challenges' (2013) 24 European Journal of International Law 933, 936–37.

16 ibid 939; African Union 'Report of the Committee of Eminent African Jurists on the Case of Hissene Habré' 5 (2006) <https://thehagueinstituteforglobaljustice.org/files/legacy/justice/habre/ceja_repor0506.pdf> accessed 29 December 2023.

and some of its member states expressed growing dissatisfaction with international engagement in ICL prosecutions of African defendants, including indictments on the basis of universal jurisdiction in European states and the Africa-focused ICC prosecutorial strategy. The history of the AU and its member states' relationships with the ICC and foreign courts has been well documented by others.[17]

For the purposes of this chapter, what is most important is that at the regional level, AU support for regional modes of transitional justice and disillusionment with reliance on international mechanisms have manifested in several ways, including not only political statements of non-cooperation and opposition to international initiatives,[18] but also the development of its own regional transitional justice policies and institutions. The most robust of these is the 2014 Malabo Protocol, which establishes an International Criminal Law Section of the African Court of Justice and Human Rights with jurisdiction over ICL cases.[19] If it becomes active, the International Criminal Law Section would be an unprecedented regional ICL mechanism. However, to date this institution remains nascent. States have been slow to sign the Malabo Protocol, with only fifteen signatures thus far and no ratifications; the Protocol requires fifteen ratifications to take effect.[20]

The AU's most comprehensive statement on transitional justice is its February 2019 Transitional Justice Policy (AUTJP). The AUTJP strongly emphasizes regional authority over transitional justice.[21] The first principle asserted is 'African leadership', and another is 'African shared values'; in addition, the final principle of 'capacity building for sustainability' emphasizes the importance of 'leverag[ing] relevant African capacity' if support is needed for local transitional justice mechanisms .[22] The AUTJP specifically endorses hybrid courts in situations when local

[17] See, eg, Sirleaf, 'Regionalism' (n 4) 709–17; A Dube, 'The AU Model Law on Universal Jurisdiction: An African Response to Western Prosecutions Based on the Universality Principle' (2015) 18 Potchefstroomse Elektroniese Regsblad 449, 457–58 <https://dx.doi.org/10.4314/pelj.v18i3.01> accessed 29 December 2023; Abass (n 15); Charles Chernor Jalloh, 'Regionalizing International Criminal Law' (2009) 9 International Criminal Law Review 445.

[18] See, eg, Jalloh (n 17) 464–65.

[19] Protocol on Amendments to the Protocol on the Statute of the African Court of Justice and Human Rights (14 May 2014) Article 9 (Malabo Protocol) <https://au.int/en/treaties/protocol-amendments-protocol-statute-african-court-justice-and-human-rights> accessed 29 December 2023 (amending Article 19 of the Statute concerning the Chambers of the Court).

[20] AU, 'List of Countries which have signed, ratified/acceded to the Protocol on Amendments to the Protocol on the Statute of the African Court of Justice and Human Rights' (20 May 2019) <https://au.int/sites/default/files/treaties/36398-sl-PROTOCOL%20ON%20AMENDMENTS%20TO%20THE%20PROTOCOL%20ON%20THE%20STATUTE%20OF%20THE%20AFRICAN%20COURT%20OF%20JUSTICE%20AND%20HUMAN%20RIGHTS.pdf> accessed 29 December 2023.

[21] AU, 'Transitional Justice Policy' (2019) iv–vi (AUTJP) <https://au.int/sites/default/files/documents/36541-doc-au_tj_policy_eng_web.pdf> accessed 29 December 2023. This policy builds on a 2006 AU Policy on Post-Conflict Reconstruction and Development and a 2011 report, 'Non-Impunity, Truth, Peace, Justice, and Reconciliation in Africa: Opportunities and Constraints'.

[22] ibid 5–8. Note, however, that the AUTJP refers to AU action as being on a 'continental' level and uses the word 'regional' to denote the multiple regions making up the AU. Eg AUTJP (n 21) 1. For the sake of consistency with the terms used in the transitional justice literature, this chapter uses the word 'regional' in its more general sense to denote the sphere of AU authority vis-à-vis other world regions.

and national courts are unable to conduct transitional justice processes themselves; in keeping with its emphasis on localization, it prioritizes such courts over purely regional or international processes.[23]

The AU has been criticized for taking action on transitional justice in a reactive and protective mode, responsive to immediate threats of international intervention and limited to what is strictly necessary to stave off that intervention. However, an alternative narrative characterizes the AU's movement towards regional mechanisms as a result of disillusionment with flawed international and foreign courts and a bid for genuine self-reliance.[24] In addition, the AU regularly engages with international partners, including the EU, concerning transitional justice; its policy emphasizes that any international engagement should support its member states' understandings of their transitional justice needs. The AU's 2020 Roadmap for the Implementation of the AUTJP prescribes a series of proactive transitional justice measures, including ensuring sufficient financial resources to support transitional justice initiatives, mapping member states' transitional justice needs, and providing technical assistance to member states.[25] Thus, a key question for AU partnerships with hybrid courts is whether they represent part of an independent system that responds effectively to AU states' transitional justice issues on its own initiative.

Relatedly, the AU has been criticized for endorsing certain controversial normative positions, and in particular for backing the immunity of sitting heads of state and other high-ranking state officials to prosecution;[26] the Malabo Protocol ensures such immunity.[27] While this norm appears reactive to ICC indictments and protective in nature, the Malabo Protocol also develops ICL norms in the direction of transnational crimes that are particularly important in the region and not usually included in the jurisdiction of ICL courts, such as trafficking, piracy, and corruption, as well as providing for corporate criminal liability.[28] As noted above, development of regional norms is a predicted output of regional courts, and thus the implementation of the Malabo Protocol would provide the opportunity to assess this expectation.

23 AUTJP (n 21) 16.

24 Abass (n 15).

25 AU, 'Roadmap for the Implementation of the African Union Transitional Justice Policy' (May 2020) <https://au.int/sites/default/files/documents/41242-doc-Roadmap_for_the_Implementation_of_AU_ENGLISH_Sep_091.pdf> accessed 29 December 2023.

26 Jalloh (n 17) 482–85.

27 Malabo Protocol (n 19) Article 46A; Matiangai Sirleaf, 'The African Justice Cascade and the Malabo Protocol' (2017) 11 International Journal of Transitional Justice 71 <https://d-scholarship.pitt.edu/30678/> accessed 29 December 2023.

28 The Malabo Protocol also includes the traditional ICL crimes of genocide, crimes against humanity, and war crimes. Malabo Protocol (n 19) Article 28A, 46C.

3.3.2 European Union

While the AU's transitional justice policy and initiatives are focused internally on conflicts within its borders, the EU's transitional justice policy and initiatives are focused predominantly externally, at candidate and potential candidate countries, as well as worldwide. This manifests primarily in the form of funding and technical support for a wide variety of transitional justice mechanisms, which are channelled through development programmes relating to democracy and human rights issues at the European Commission, as well as through projects relating to peacebuilding and security sector reform under the Common Foreign and Security Policy. Overall, the EU is among the largest donors to transitional justice and related programmes globally.[29]

In keeping with this outward-facing strategy, while the AUTJP treats transitional justice as a matter of regional control, the EU's Policy Framework on Support for Transitional Justice repeatedly refers to transitional justice as an aspect of EU external assistance to national and local transitional justice programmes outside the EU.[30] Its external orientation is underlined by its reference to EU member states' transitional justice mechanisms as being either entirely in the past or, at most, 'still ongoing' modes of dealing with past conflicts.[31] Hence, unlike the AU, it has not thus far undertaken the difficult political task of persuading its own member states to take action on their own conflicts or crimes.

The EU Policy Framework also characterizes the EU as a partner with international organizations. The EU links itself to the UN and international norms, adopting the UN's definition of transitional justice as its own, repeatedly citing UN documents in support of its own policy, and identifying implementation of international standards as one of its guiding principles.[32] It also describes itself as a 'staunch supporter' of the ICC,[33] which has not conducted any preliminary examinations of situations within EU borders thus far.[34] Thus, the EU policy seeks to extend European support for transitional justice beyond its borders, in conjunction with broader international engagement by the ICC and the UN.

Paige Arthur understands the EU's extensive global investment in transitional justice initiatives to serve its cross-cutting interests in security and in promoting core regional values concerning human rights and rule of law.[35] Similarly, Katy

29 Crossley-Frolick (n 4); 'The EU's Policy Framework on Support to Transitional Justice' (2015) (EU Policy Framework) <http://eeas.europa.eu/archives/docs/top_stories/pdf/the_eus_policy_framework_on_support_to_transitional_justice.pdf> accessed 29 December 2023.

30 EU Policy Framework (n 29) 12.

31 ibid 4.

32 ibid 1, 9.

33 ibid 3.

34 ICC, 'Preliminary Examinations' <https://www.icc-cpi.int/pages/pe.aspx> accessed 29 December 2023.

35 Paige Arthur, 'Why do Donors Choose to Fund Transitional Justice?' in Paige Arthur and Christalla Yakinthou (eds), *Transitional Justice, International Assistance and Civil Society: Missed Connections* (Cambridge University Press 2018) 209, 217–21.

Crossley-Frolick argues that the EU's transitional justice policies are focused on a key strategic aim of ensuring Europe's security through global 'human security, the "new" strategic narrative for Europe'.[36] Indeed, these human security goals are prominently highlighted in the Policy Framework document as the context for the EU's transitional justice commitment.[37]

Of particular significance for the EU's hybrid court partnership with Kosovo, the EU Policy Framework emphasizes the importance of transitional justice for states hoping to accede to the EU:

> The EU considers transitional justice to be a priority for candidate countries and potential candidates ... All countries seeking to exceed to the Union must demonstrate a credible commitment to promoting these principles by addressing all relevant aspects where obstacles to justice persist.[38]

By treating transitional justice as a prerequisite for candidate countries, the EU may better ensure not only its internal security, but also a precommitment to EU human rights values and justice systems, both on its borders (before accession) and internally (after accession).

The exclusively external focus of the EU's transitional justice policy has been the subject of critique. Hugo Van der Merwe characterizes the policy as hypocritical, observing:

> The European Union's policy on transitional justice is basically a policy of how the South should deal with their transitional justice. It says absolutely nothing about colonial legacies. It says nothing about what the European powers should do about their responsibility for hundreds of years of abuse.[39]

Similarly, Peter Verovšek describes the EU's 'failure to address the crimes of European colonialism' as 'perhaps the biggest issue with the EU's attempts to address past wrongs'.[40]

In addition, the EU has also been criticized for ineffectiveness in carrying out its transitional justice initiatives; this should be a key factor in assessing its role as

[36] Crossley-Frolick (n 4) 38.
[37] EU Policy Framework (n 29) 1, 9.
[38] ibid (n 29) 17.
[39] Laurel E Fletcher and Harvey Weinstein, '"North-South" Dialogue: Bridging the Gap in Transitional Justice-Workshop Transcript' (2018) 36 Berkeley Journal of International Law 218 <https://doi.org/10.15779/Z38KW57J37> accessed 29 December 2023.
[40] Peter J Verovšek, 'A Burgeoning Community of Justice: The European Union as a Promotor of Transitional Justice' (2021) 15 International Journal of Transitional Justice 351 <https://doi.org/10.1093/ijtj/ijab005> accessed 29 December 2023.

a partner in hybrid courts.[41] In particular, ineffectiveness has been a longstanding concern in the EU's engagement in Kosovo and relates directly to its motivation and justifications for establishing the KSC, as discussed below.

3.4 Regional Partnerships in Hybrid Courts

The original arguments in favour of establishing hybrid courts with both international and national components were centred on the anticipated benefits of a hybrid structure; these included opportunities for capacity building, norm internalization, and improving ICL courts' domestic perceived legitimacy in the concerned state.[42] However, in reality, the first wave of hybrid courts did not emerge from a detached assessment of these potential benefits, but rather, from a perceived immediate need for a tribunal to hear certain cases, the incapacity of existing courts to do so, and a political context that enabled or even demanded that a new tribunal come to fruition.[43] Similarly, the advent of two of the new hybrid courts as regional partnerships is based in a combination of practical need and political impetus, relating more closely to the interests of the EU and AU identified in Section 3.3 than to the theoretical benefits of regionalized institutions discussed in Section 3.2.

3.4.1 African Union

3.4.1.1 Development of Extraordinary African Chambers in the Courts of Senegal

The EAC was established by agreement between Senegal and the AU, primarily in order to prosecute Hissene Habré, the former President of Chad.[44] It was created in Senegal rather than the concerned state of Chad, because Habré was living in Senegal and thus Senegal had the legal responsibility to prosecute him; Chad could have sought to prosecute him but did not request his extradition.[45] The AU

[41] ibid; Laura Davis, 'The European Union and Transitional Justice' (2010) International Center for Transitional Justice 18 <https://www.ictj.org/sites/default/files/ICTJ-IFP-EU-Justice-2010-English.pdf> accessed 29 December 2023.

[42] Laura A Dickinson, 'The Promise of Hybrid Courts' (2003) 97 American Journal of International Law 295 <https://www.cambridge.org/core/journals/american-journal-of-international-law/article/abs/promise-of-hybrid-courts/46149003329C4A71D7C524E6A76E89F6> accessed 29 December 2023.

[43] Elena Baylis, 'Cosmopolitan Pluralist Hybrid Tribunals' in Paul Schiff Berman (ed), *Oxford Research Handbook on Global Legal Pluralism* (Oxford University Press 2020).

[44] Agreement on the Establishment of the Extraordinary African Chambers Within the Senegalese Judicial System Between the Government of the Republic of Senegal and the African Union (2013) 52 International Legal Materials 1020, 1024.

[45] African Union, 'Report of the Committee of Eminent African Jurists on the Case of Hissene Habré' (n 16) 5 <https://thehagueinstituteforglobaljustice.org/files/legacy/justice/habre/ceja_repor0506.pdf> accessed 29 December 2023.

contributed a portion of the Court's funding, as part of a donor group that also included the EU, Chad, and other states.[46] The AU Commission had the responsibility of appointing the judges and prosecutors nominated by Senegal, and the international presidents of the appellate and trial chambers were required to be judges from other AU states.[47] However, the EAC was predominantly a Senegalese court in its structure: the vast majority of its staff were of Senegalese nationality, and the law it applied was primarily the domestic law of Senegal (including, however, international law as domesticated). The EAC held Habré's trial in 2015–2016; he was convicted for his role in crimes against humanity, torture, and war crimes, and his conviction was affirmed on appeal in 2017.

The agreement to establish the EAC and the AU's role in it were the culmination of extensive, multifaceted efforts by victims' groups and non-governmental organizations (NGOs) to compel prosecution of Habré in one of various jurisdictions. These efforts have been well documented by others.[48]

For the purposes of this chapter, what is significant about the long development of the Habré case is that it presented the AU with two key decision points concerning its role. In each instance, the AU chose to assert regional authority over the matter. Specifically, when Senegal was faced with an extradition request from Belgium, and the UN Committee Against Torture concluded that Senegal had violated its obligations under the Convention Against Torture by failing to either prosecute or extradite Habré, the AU determined that Senegal should prosecute Habré rather than extraditing him (or, for that matter, refusing to either prosecute or extradite).[49] In so doing, it explicitly signalled the regional significance that it placed on a trial in an AU state rather than Belgium by noting that the crimes of which Habré was accused fell within the AU's mandate and delegating authority to Senegal to prosecute 'on behalf of Africa'.[50] Next, when the Court of Justice of the Economic Community of West African States held that Senegal could not prosecute Habré in a domestic court due to retroactivity concerns, and the International Court of Justice separately determined that Senegal must either

[46] Roland Adjovi, Introductory Note to the Agreement on the Establishment of the Extraordinary African Chambers within the Senegalese Judicial System between the Government of the Republic of Senegal and the African Union and the Statute of the Chambers (2013) 52 International Legal Materials 1020, 1021.

[47] Statute of the Extraordinary African Chambers within the courts of Senegal created to prosecute international crimes committed in Chad between 7 June 1982 and 1 December 1990 (2013) 52 International Legal Materials 1028, Articles 11, 12 (EAC Statute).

[48] Reed Brody, 'Bringing a Dictator to Justice: The Case of Hissène Habré' (2015) 13 Journal of International Criminal Justice 209 <https://doi.org/10.1093/jicj/mqv005> accessed 29 December 2023; Beth Van Schaack, 'The Building Blocks of Hybrid Justice' (2016) 44 Denver Journal of International Law and Policy 101 <https://core.ac.uk/download/pdf/304688205.pdf> accessed 29 December 2023.

[49] Brody (n 48).

[50] AU, 'Decision on the Hissène Habré Case and the African Union' (2007) DOC ASSEMBLY/AU/3 (VII), Assembly/AU/Dec127 (VII) <http://archives.au.int/handle/123456789/955> accessed 29 December 2023.

prosecute Habré itself or extradite him, the AU reached an agreement with Senegal to form the EAC.[51]

3.4.1.2 Development of the Hybrid Court for South Sudan

The AU Commission has also developed a draft statute for the HCSS; if this court is established, the AU would once again be the regional partner. In 2014, an AU Commission of Inquiry issued an extensive report on atrocities committed in South Sudan and recommended development of a hybrid court, among other transitional justice mechanisms. As with the EAC, the AU couched this recommendation in terms of regional authority: 'the Commission recommends an Africa-led, Africa-owned, Africa-resourced legal mechanism under the aegis of the AU.'[52]

Under the auspices of the 2015 Agreement on the Resolution of the Conflict in the Republic of South Sudan, as reconfirmed by a 2018 Agreement, the AU has responsibility for establishing the key components of a hybrid court and entering a Memorandum of Agreement with South Sudan. However, thus far, South Sudan's parliament has not acted on the AU's 2016 draft Statute and Memorandum of Understanding.[53] Instead, notwithstanding a series of meetings between South Sudanese and AU officials, the only concrete step taken by South Sudan appears to be the Council of Ministers' approval in 2021 of a plan to establish the HCSS; a 2022 roadmap for continuing to implement the 2018 peace agreement once again acknowledges the need for implementing legislation for the HCSS and other transitional justice institutions.[54] At the time of writing, the fate of this endeavour remains uncertain.

3.4.1.3 Manifestation of expected regional benefits and interests

As described in Section 3.2, the arguments for regional engagement include regional authority and impact, as well as the opportunity for greater localization of the court, greater buy-in from the concerned states, and the opportunity to develop

[51] Brody (n 48); Van Schaack (n 48). However, there has been significant criticism of the ECOWAS decision as unfounded. See, eg, Sarah Williams, 'The Extraordinary African Chambers in the Senegalese Courts: An African Solution to an African Problem?' (2013) 11 Journal of International Criminal Justice 1139 <https://academic.oup.com/jicj/article-abstract/11/5/1139/845621> accessed 29 December 2023.

[52] AU, 'Final Report of the African Union Commission of Inquiry on South Sudan' (15 October 2014) 300, para 1148 <http://www.peaceau.org/uploads/auciss.final.report.pdf> accessed 29 December 2023.

[53] Owiso Owiso, 'The Proposed Hybrid Court for South Sudan: Moving South Sudan and the African Union to Action against Impunity' (2018) 18 African Journal on Conflict Resolution 87; Fred Oluoch, 'Justice Close as South Sudan Hybrid Court Gets AU Nod' (*The East African*, 6 July 2019) <https://www.theeastafrican.co.ke/news/ea/Justice-close-as-south-sudan-hybrid-court-gets-au-nod/4552908-5185550-xc16e7/index.html> accessed 29 December 2023.

[54] Amnesty International and Transitional Justice Working Group South Sudan, 'African Union's Abandoned Commitment to Justice in Africa: The Case of the Hybrid Court for South Sudan' (23 November 2022) 8–9, <https://www.amnesty.org/en/documents/afr65/6196/2022/en/> accessed 29 December 2023.

regional norms. These expectations are met only in part in the EAC and HCSS, which are not designed to achieve the aims that many commentators envisioned for regional institutions. The EAC and HCSS do manifest the AU's expressed interests in greater regional involvement in transitional justice and in forestalling international intervention, but do not directly advance its commitments to regional norms.

The AU certainly has the requisite authority over transitional justice. However, looking to regional scope and impact, both the EAC and the HCSS are not designed for regional jurisdiction that would allow them to address transnational events more effectively than a national court. Instead, each focuses on internal matters within one state, although neither limits personal jurisdiction by nationality, allowing for the possibility of prosecuting defendants from other states should the need arise.[55] In this sense, these hybrids are not the kind of regional institutions envisioned by proponents of regionalization, which would represent a transnational authority capable of addressing all components of a transnational conflict; rather, like the previous international, hybrid, and national courts those authors critiqued, their focus is on a particular national setting.

As far as localization, the EAC was a highly national court, in that the vast majority of its personnel, its location, and its applied law were national (albeit including international law as domesticated). Only a few personnel and the Court's funding came from international sources. However, the purpose of localization is to ensure proximity to the concerned communities, enhanced perceived domestic legitimacy and a sense of local ownership within the concerned state, and opportunities for capacity building in the judicial system of the concerned state. Because the EAC was a foreign court, rather than a court of the concerned state of Chad, localizing the proceedings did not serve these intended functions.

In contrast, the proposed HCSS has as its domestic partner the judiciary of South Sudan, which is the concerned state. However, the HCSS would operate in a considerably different context that limits the potential for localization; the South Sudanese judicial system has been ravaged by conflict, and there are risks of political interference and security threats that favour internationalizing the proceedings to a significant extent. The agreement to establish the Court provides for a majority of international judges and a minority of national judges, and also for all other staff to be international, although those international staff are required to be regional personnel from other African states. Hence, in terms of staffing, the HCSS would be less domesticated than many other courts, but its international staff would be more localized than many other hybrid courts in the sense that they

[55] Although both conflicts have some nexus to neighbouring states (Chad's to Libya and South Sudan's to Sudan), that connection is attenuated. The EAC has territorial jurisdiction over crimes and violations of international law only if they were committed within the territory of Chad. EAC Statute (n 47) Article 3. The proposed HCSS would be focused on events within South Sudan. Owiso (n 53).

would be from the same region. The lack of opportunity for interaction among national and international staff except at the judicial level will curtail opportunities for capacity building and dialogue concerning norms, however.[56]

As addressed in Section 3, the EAC and HCSS are being created against the backdrop of increasing AU assertions of regional authority over internal transitional justice matters within its borders. Establishing regional hybrid courts enables the AU to demonstrate that it can perform as a transitional justice actor itself, in lieu of the ICC, the UN, or foreign courts. This is neither a repudiation of transitional justice principles, nor a repudiation of external involvement in transitional justice scenarios, but rather a claiming of those values and that role.[57] It constitutes the assertion that the AU can play the interventionist and supportive roles that international and foreign actors have played in the past; that when AU member states require additional assistance, the AU has both the capability and the commitment to transitional justice to step in itself.

Some have argued that the EAC is an example of the AU's deployment of transitional justice institutions only as part of a 'protectionist stance' against intervention by external actors, rather than as part of a true commitment to transitional justice.[58] If so, one would expect to see a pattern of action only as a reaction to the threat of such intervention. Certainly, in the EAC instance, there was an imminent risk of external intervention in the form of the pending Belgian extradition request, particularly in light of the International Court of Justice judgment.[59] There does not seem to be such an imminent risk of international intervention in the South Sudanese context, however; rather, external international pressure supports the implementation of the proposed AU-backed hybrid court.[60] On the one hand, South Sudan represents an example of the AU engaging in an extensive investigation followed by development of an AU transitional justice mechanism, supporting the narrative of active AU engagement. However, to date that court has not yet come to fruition, providing support for the theory that the AU will not deploy the political capital necessary to gain domestic South Sudanese approval of a transitional justice initiative absent a protectionist motivation.

Thus far, scholars' expectation that pre-existing national commitments of member states to a regional institution would facilitate willingness to engage in transitional justice enterprises holds true in the case of the EAC but not the HCSS. Senegal evinced substantial reluctance to prosecute Habré but acceded at the behest of the AU and with promises of external financial support. However, South

56 ibid.

57 See, eg, Brody (n 48) 216; Van Schaack (n 48) 132.

58 Williams, 'The Extraordinary African Chambers' (n 51) 1148.

59 ibid.

60 See, eg, OHCHR, 'Commission on Human Rights Urges South Sudan to make peace and justice a reality' (17 September 2018) <https://www.ohchr.org/EN/HRBodies/HRC/Pages/NewsDetail.aspx?NewsID=23576&LangID=E> accessed 29 December 2023.

Sudan has not yet taken steps to actualize the proposed HCSS, in spite of the AU's public avowals of support for the initiative and production of a draft statute.

Another incentive for AU engagement might be the development and enforcement of regional ICL norms; this has also been noted as a potential benefit of regional courts, at least in the eyes of some scholars. However, the EAC and HCSS do not seem to have seized the opportunity to advance proposed regional norms. The crimes over which they have jurisdiction are traditional ICL crimes, not the Malabo Protocol's transnational crimes of trafficking, piracy, and corruption. In addition, while the AU has taken the position that immunity should be granted to sitting heads of state and that not to do so undermines peace agreements,[61] neither the EAC Statute nor the proposed HCSS statute provide for such immunity.[62]

Finally, it is important to recognize that while the EAC did not promote the predicted benefits of regionalization or hybridization due to its particular structure, jurisdiction, and location, it did succeed in its core criminal justice and transitional justice aims as an ICL tribunal. It held a trial that has been widely praised as fair and legitimate, and it effectively assessed the culpability of a defendant who had long been living in freedom while accused of atrocity crimes. It created an authoritative historical record of crimes committed in Chad under Habré's rule. It recognized the harm done to victims, by enabling them to observe and to some extent participate, and by ordering reparations for them.

3.4.2 European Union

3.4.2.1 Development of Kosovo Specialist Chambers

The KSC was created by a law passed by Kosovo's parliament, which ratified an agreement formed by an exchange of letters between the EU and Kosovo.[63] While the KSC is formally part of the Kosovo court system and is subject to the Kosovo constitution, it is highly independent of Kosovo's judiciary and in many ways is functionally an EU court. The court is physically located in The Hague; it is run entirely by international judges, prosecutors, and other staff; it has independent legal personality and primacy over other Kosovo courts; and its organizational

[61] Sirleaf, 'Regionalism' (n 4).

[62] EAC Statute (n 55) Article 10; Owiso (n 53). Of course, the AU was not faced with the risk of prosecution of a current president or senior official in the EAC, since Hissene Habré was a former rather than a current head of state at the time of his prosecution. In addition, Chad had waived any residual immunity he might have possessed. It is not yet apparent whether these or other issues touching on potential regional norms will arise in the HCSS context.

[63] Law on Ratification of the International Agreement between the Republic of Kosovo and the European Union on the European Union Rule of Law Mission in Kosovo (23 April 2014) Law No 04/L-274; see also Law on Specialist Chambers and Specialist Prosecutor's Office (3 August 2015) Law No 05/L-053.

structure is parallel to, but independent of, the Kosovo court system.[64] The EU provides most of the funding for the KSC, in addition to some donations from other states.[65] The judges and other staff are primarily from EU member states, with some staff hailing from other contributing states.[66] At the time of writing, the KSC is actively hearing cases, with four matters in the pre-trial, trial, and appeal stages.[67]

The agreement to establish the KSC followed lengthy EU engagement in transitional justice in Kosovo. In 2008, the EULEX mission in Kosovo was established as the largest civilian EU mission. For the following ten years, until its mandate ended in 2018, EULEX was engaged in rule of law initiatives aimed at strengthening the Kosovo legal system.[68] This included significant involvement specifically in war crimes cases. EULEX investigated and assisted in the adjudication of numerous war crimes cases within Kosovo; these cases were specially designated to be heard by hybrid chambers within the domestic court system that included both international and domestic judges, and were tried by international prosecutors.[69]

Despite the lengthy EU intervention focused on rebuilding Kosovo's legal system, which followed a UN effort of the same kind, the risk of intimidation of judges, political interference, and witness tampering had kept war crimes cases under EULEX's authority, rather than devolved to the domestic courts. However,

64 Sarah Williams, 'The Specialist Chambers of Kosovo: The Limits of Internationalization?' (2016) 14 Journal of International Criminal Justice 25, 35–37 <https://doi.org/10.1093/jicj/mqv081> accessed 29 December 2023; Robert Muharremi, 'The Concept of Hybrid Courts Revisited: The Case of the Kosovo Specialist Chambers' (2018) 18 International Criminal Law Review 623, 640 <https://doi.org/10.1163/15718123-01804008> accessed 29 December 2023. However, the significance of the Court being subject to the Kosovo constitution has already become evident in the early stages of the Court's work. Lekë Batalli, 'Parallel Justice: A First Test for Kosovo's Specialist Chambers and Specialist Prosecutor's Office' (*Verfassungsblog*, 4 March 2019) <https://verfassungsblog.de/parallel-justice-a-first-test-for-kosovos-specialist-chambers-and-specialist-prosecutors-office/> accessed 29 December 2023.

65 Council Decision (CFSP) 2018/856 of 8 June 2018 amending Joint Action 2008/124/CFSP on the European Union Rule of Law Mission in Kosovo [2018] OJ L146/5 <https://eur-lex.europa.eu/eli/dec/2018/856/oj> accessed 29 December 2023; Kosovo Specialist Chambers and Specialist Prosecutor's Office, 'First Report' (2018) 47–48 <https://www.scp-ks.org/sites/default/files/public/content/ksc_spo_first_report_en.pdf> accessed 29 December 2023.

66 Kosovo Specialist Chambers and Specialist Prosecutor's Office, 'First Report' (n 65) 16–19 <https://www.scp-ks.org/sites/default/files/public/content/ksc_spo_first_report_en.pdf> accessed 29 December 2023.

67 Kosovo Specialist Chambers and Specialist Prosecutor's Office, 'Cases' <https://www.scp-ks.org/en/cases> accessed 29 December 2023.

68 EULEX Kosovo, 'EU Rule of Law Mission in Kosovo' (2009) <https://www.eulex-kosovo.eu/eul/repository/docs/66653-300909factsheet_eulex_kosovo_2_en.pdf> accessed 29 December 2023; EULEX Kosovo, 'Basic Facts' (2016) <https://www.eulex-kosovo.eu/eul/repository/docs/36165-20161209_EULEX-FactSheet.pdf> accessed 29 December 2023. The EU had previously taken the lead on the reconstruction and economic pillar of the prior UN Mission in Kosovo. Williams, 'Specialist Chambers' (n 64) 27.

69 Gëzim Visoka, 'Assessing the potential impact of the Kosovo Specialist Court' (2017) Impunity Watch/PAX 15 <https://paxforpeace.nl/media/download/paxreport-assessing-the-potential-impact-of-the-kosovo-specialist-court.pdf> accessed 29 December 2023; Williams, 'Specialist Chambers' (n 64) 32.

this did not prevent problems with witness tampering and corruption; there have been numerous criticisms of EULEX's effectiveness in protecting witnesses and accusations of corruption among its international staff. Accordingly, cases of political significance were deemed not capable of being heard within Kosovo; hence the need for a hybrid court, and one with considerable independence and internationalization.[70]

The EU's determination to establish a new hybrid tribunal for Kosovo originated with a claim by former ICTY prosecutor Carla del Ponte that evidence of crimes by Kosovo Albanian leaders against Serbs during the Yugoslav conflict had gone uninvestigated by the ICTY due to lack of jurisdiction. There followed a pair of consecutive Council of Europe and EU investigations, each finding sufficient evidence of such crimes to warrant further steps.[71] While the idea of prosecuting Kosovo's political and social leaders has been highly controversial and met significant resistance within Kosovo, domestic political acquiescence was eventually achieved. This agreement was the result of considerable political pressure by the EU on Kosovo, including the threat of an UN-backed international court should a hybrid court not be established.[72]

3.4.2.2 Manifestation of expected benefits and interests

Even more than the EAC and HCSS, the structure of the KSC and the relationship of Kosovo to the EU do not allow for realization of the theoretical benefits of a regional transitional justice institution, nor, for that matter, of hybridization. Rather, the development of the KSC stems directly from the EU's stated commitment to human security and from its prior engagement in Kosovo, that is, from its own regional interests.

Whereas Senegal, Chad, and South Sudan are all member states of the AU, Kosovo is not a member of the EU. However, it has long been considered a potential candidate, and in 2022, it applied for the status of candidate for membership. As a non-member state, Kosovo does not have the interdependent relationship with the EU or the rights and privileges of membership that commentators anticipated would exist between a regional organization and the concerned state.[73] Furthermore, because Kosovo is not a member state, the EU does not have authority within Kosovo except by agreement. Thus, in both of these senses, the KSC

[70] Visoka (n 69) 17–20; Mathias Holvoet, 'The Continuing Relevance of the Hybrid or Internationalized Justice Model: The Example of the Kosovo Specialist Chambers' (2017) 28 Criminal Law Forum 35; Valerie Hopkins, 'EU Courts Trouble with Kosovo Scandal' (*Politico*, 17 November 2017) <https://www.politico.eu/article/malcolm-simmons-eulex-eu-courts-chaos-with-kosovo-scandal/> accessed 29 December 2023.

[71] Muharremi (n 64) 624; Van Schaack (n 48) 133–35; Visoka (n 69) 17–20; Holvoet (n 35) 41–42.

[72] Muharremi (n 64) 624; Van Schaack (n 48) 133–35; Visoka (n 69) 17–20; Holvoet (n 35) 45–46.

[73] Emanuele Cimiotta, 'The Specialist Chambers and the Specialist Prosecutor's Office in Kosovo: The "Regionalization" of International Criminal Justice in Context' (2016) 14 Journal of International Criminal Justice 53, 69.

is not the kind of regional transitional justice institution advocated by scholars. Rather, the EU's position vis-à-vis Kosovo is more like that of an international organization; it is an external entity. Kosovo and the EU do have a long history of engagement, but that history is one of unidirectional EU power in Kosovo, both in the form of the authority it has exerted in the EULEX mission and in the control it holds over Kosovo's opportunity to accede to membership.

One justification for regional engagement in hybrid courts is that regional organizations will share values and interests with the concerned state, and will thus avoid the taint of foreign intervention.[74] However, while attitudes vary, there seems to be a strongly negative view of the KSC within the Kosovo government, which identifies the EU as an outside, intervening force despite its regional nature.[75] In addition, while scholars anticipated that a regional institution might offer greater localization and contextualization than an international one, the KSC is the most internationalized hybrid court yet to be created. Its only domestic components are its formal place within the Kosovo judicial system and its application of domestic law, in addition to international law. Otherwise, as noted above, it is an international court.

Relatedly, the EU's relatively aggressive approach to achieving Kosovo's agreement and its heavy internationalization of the Court runs the risk of undermining some of the intended benefits of hybridization. A hybrid court sponsored by a regional institution might be expected to be particularly effective at promoting domestic ownership, on the theory noted above that regional institutions are more closely engaged with the national government than remote international institutions, and in keeping with the expectation also noted above that regionalization and hybridization might produce synergistic positive domestic effects. However, domestic ownership requires genuine buy-in from the concerned country, not its mere appearance. Along these lines, Mathias Holvoet argues that 'Kosovo's political, diplomatic, and financial dependency on and the pressure exerted by the EU and the US' undercut its agreement to establish the KSC.[76] In addition, the KSC is not able to promote the capacity building or norm adoption goals of hybridization, due to its lack of national staff; however, given the long engagement of the EU in such efforts within Kosovo, it is unlikely that the KSC could have added value to what had already been done.

One sense in which the KSC meets scholars' expectations for a regional court is that it does address a conflict with regional scope and impact; however, it does

[74] See, eg, Sirleaf, 'Regionalism' (n 4) 771–72 (acknowledging, however, that conflicts and perceptions of external intervention will likely arise when a regional institution is at odds with the concerned state in a particular instance).

[75] Visoka (n 69) 27–29; Holvoet (n 35); European Western Balkans, 'EU: Attempt to Repeal Mandate of Specialist Chambers Would Jeopardise EU-Kosovo Relations' (12 January 2018) <https://europeanwesternbalkans.com/2018/01/12/eu-attempt-repeal-mandate-specialist-chambers-jeopardise-eu-kosovo-relations/> accessed 29 December 2023.

[76] Holvoet (n 35) 46.

not do so in a fully regionalized way. The scope of the conflict is regional in that the crimes at issue are alleged to have occurred within both Kosovo and Albania, and concern Serbian victims; in addition, the broader Yugoslavian conflict encompassed numerous areas that are now independent states and had broader regional impacts. On the one hand, the KSC can exercise territorial, active, and passive personality jurisdiction, allowing for prosecution of crimes commenced or continued in Kosovo, or in which either the defendant or victim held Kosovo or Federal Republic of Yugoslavia citizenship. This should capture most potential cases, although it would exclude crimes committed entirely within Albania against a non-Yugoslavian victim by a non-Yugoslavian defendant. However, the KSC does not address the past and present reality of ongoing transnational crime throughout this region nor the responsibility of Albania and other involved states to respond appropriately, instead focusing attention on a single state and on events with a nexus to that state.[77]

Concerning regional norms, the KSC has provided the EU with the opportunity to demonstrate its support for the norm of non-immunity for heads of state; former President Hashim Thaçi resigned to face trial in the KSC, and among those summoned for questioning by investigators was Kosovo's then-Prime Minister Ramush Hardinaj.[78] On this topic, Sarah Williams contends that it is critically important for the EU to 'use the available political and financial incentives to ensure compliance' with the KSC, so as to demonstrate its commitment to non-impunity and avoid flagrant violation of that principle in Kosovo.[79]

The KSC's establishment does also represent expressed EU interests. It can be understood as an effort to redeem the EULEX mission's rule of law aims, or at least to address a set of alleged crimes that persist as a highly visible manifestation of its limits.[80] Holvoet and Williams both note EULEX's failure to achieve its mission of strengthening the Kosovo legal system and effectively managing war crimes cases, as evidenced by the fact that it was not deemed capable of taking on the Kosovo Liberation Army (KLA) cases.[81] Particularly given the long involvement of the EU in Kosovo and its specific investment in rule of law endeavours, the continued political authority of Kosovo leaders who have been credibly accused of international crimes represented an affront to these EU principles. Continued EU support for such a government would contradict central EU commitments, particularly when the government has aspirations to EU membership.

[77] Williams, 'Specialist Chambers' (n 64) 40.

[78] Isabella Kwai, 'Kosovo President Resigns to Fight War Crimes Case in the Netherlands' (*New York Times*, 5 November 2020) <https://www.nytimes.com/2020/11/05/world/europe/kosovo-hashim-thaci-resigns.html> accessed 29 December 2023; 'Kosovo Leader Resigns After Being Called to War Crimes Court' (*New York Times*, 19 July 2019) <https://www.nytimes.com/2019/07/19/world/europe/kosovo-leader-resigns-after-being-called-to-war-crimes-court.html> accessed 29 December 2023.

[79] Williams, 'Specialist Chambers' (n 64) 51.

[80] Visoka (n 69) 24.

[81] Holvoet (n 35); Williams, 'Specialist Court' (n 64) 51.

To this last point, another significant context for the EU's engagement in the KSC is Kosovo's aim of acceding to the EU, and the EU's corresponding interest in assuring that potential candidate states adopt its values. Gëzim Visoka identifies cooperation with the KSC and development of its own domestic accountability mechanisms as a critical step for Kosovo's perceived identification with European values:

> The Specialist Court represents one of the most challenging tests that Kosovo society must pass to demonstrate that it is an open, democratic society that respects truth, justice and the rule of law. This will be an essential indicator of the Europeanisation of Kosovo society and a collective statement on what direction Kosovo wants to take as a society.[82]

While Visoka focuses on the values nexus, Emanuele Cimiotta notes that the KSC addresses EU security concerns regarding accession:

> The EU's participation [in the KSC] seems aimed at creating the factual and legal pre-conditions for Kosovo's future admission into the EU, namely the restoration and reinforcement of stability and rule of law in Kosovo, with possible positive consequences in the whole region. In this sense, the SC and the SPO may be perceived as a means of ensuring European internal security, given that they are tasked with prosecuting KLA leaders who are allegedly responsible for heinous crimes.[83]

Certainly, Kosovo's own aspirations to EU accession require it to cooperate with the KSC's processes. Thus, the political and economic benefits offered by the EU gave it additional leverage over Kosovo beyond what an international organization might have, and thereby enabled it to pressure Kosovo into acting.

Overall, the KSC's structure and the decision of the EU to serve as its regional partner promote the EU's own perceived security and values interests in Kosovo as a border state, as a potential candidate for EU admission, and as the recipient of significant EU transitional justice resources. The structure of the Court does not match the expectations of scholars for how a regional institution might evolve, and thus does not serve the anticipated purposes of matching regional structures to regional conflicts. Because Kosovo is not an EU member state, the relationship between the EU and Kosovo in this partnership is much more like that of an international partner to a national government than that of a regional organization to one of its member states. However, as with the EAC, it should be acknowledged that the KSC may very well serve its core criminal justice and transitional justice

[82] Visoka (n 69) 24–25.
[83] Cimiotta (n 73) 69–70.

objectives by holding fair trials, establishing an authoritative historical record, and so on; these key functions are separate from the expected advantages of regionalizing the Court.

3.5 Implications

Regional institutions have gradually become more involved in transitional justice, each doing so for their own reasons. This involvement has recently emerged in the form of partnerships in hybrid courts. However, such courts remain constrained in particular ways. Because they are regional partnerships with individual states, they do not offer the more extensive regional jurisdiction that scholars have advocated as more effectively addressing regional conflicts and crimes. And because the EU's partnership with Kosovo is external, the EU is operating in much the same way as an international partner vis-à-vis Kosovo, rather than leveraging a more robust and reciprocal relationship with a member state. Thus far, these courts do not show a distinctive move towards localization beyond what one would typically see in a hybrid court with an international partner, nor do they consistently evince the development of regional legal norms.

Nonetheless, this move towards regional partnerships in hybrid courts offers opportunities that both states and regional organizations could use to their advantage and to the benefit of the cause of transitional justice. In order to achieve the aim of comprehensively addressing regional conflicts with regional impacts, regionalized hybrid courts would have to be organized fundamentally differently. The regional organization would need to reach an agreement with all of the involved states concerning the establishment of the hybrid tribunal, rather than with only one. This would present significant challenges, for example in the applicable law and in the connection of the Court to one or more domestic judicial systems.

Although the current regionalized hybrid courts do not achieve the proposed benefits of regionalization, those aims are achievable. If combined with sufficient domestic personnel, regional staffing may promote capacity building, so long as the regional staff share a common language and similar legal systems with the concerned state. Regionalized hybrids could readily offer the benefits of drawing on member states' pre-existing commitments to regional institutions for their legitimacy, but only in contexts like the AU, where those hybrids concern member states. Regional organizations could also readily integrate regional norms such as immunity (or the lack thereof) and additional transnational crimes into the founding statutes and rules of future regionalized hybrid courts. Finally, regionalized hybrids could choose to promote greater localization, and both the AU and EU have expressed a commitment to this concept in principle. But in implementation, significant localization is possible only where security and local judicial capacity permit; in contexts with dire insecurity, corruption, or judiciaries dramatically weakened by conflict, regional organizations are no more capable than international organizations of remedying those fundamental obstacles to localization.

Finally, on a pragmatic level, regional organizations offer an additional potential conduit for financial and human resources. Hybrid courts often struggle to raise sufficient funds, and if regional organizations were willing to take responsibility for that funding, as the EU has done with the KSC, that would be a significant benefit to such courts, which could then be comparatively well assured of having the opportunity to fulfill their mandates.

Overall, to take advantage of these opportunities would require deliberately structuring regionalized hybrid courts to achieve particular aims. Regardless, regional engagement in transitional justice in general and in hybrid courts in particular is a trend that is likely to continue, given the regional interests in self-governance, security, and regional values that present continuing incentives for regional involvement.

4

Securing Resilient Peace

From Hybridity to Polyvalence

Shastry Njeru and Tyanai Masiya

4.1 Introduction

> A simple white dress, high-waisted and made of sheer muslin, is considered fashion's tribute to the French Revolution. Radically simple by historical standards, the dress is credited with responding sartorially to the demands of *liberté*, *égalité*, and *fraternité*. The dress was *liberating* in a physical sense, doing away with cumbersome corsets and *paniers*. It was *egalitarian*, with its unvarying cut and color. And it was unassuming—*fraternal*—as opposed to individualized rococo ostentation[1].

What is important about this dress is that it was French, not British or German. It identified with everything French at that time. It motivated for the desired change. It was possible to read the dress as a political statement of the time, expressing the democratic aspiration of the French people.[2] It was an answer to the practical questions of the extent of people's devotion to the revolution, which groups claimed it, how and for which purpose, how that revolution was depicted, adapted, and discussed in public.[3] A simple dress carried it all, ideologically and politically—catering for various meanings and sectors of the French society—for the

> revolutionaries, for the aristocratic élite, for Napoléon's imperial agenda, but also for participants in a discussion of social issues, such as women's rights, colonialism, Jewish emancipation, and the abolition of slavery.[4]

[1] Naomi Lubrich, 'The Little White Dress: Politics and Polyvalence in Revolutionary France' (2016) 20 Fashion Theory 273.
[2] ibid 274.
[3] ibid 274.
[4] ibid.

Shastry Njeru and Tyanai Masiya, *Securing Resilient Peace* In: *Hybrid Justice*. Edited by: Kirsten Ainley and Mark Kersten, Oxford University Press. © Shastry Njeru and Tyanai Masiya 2025.
DOI: 10.1093/oso/9780192893758.003.0004

A simple dress carried the enormity of the French Revolution on its threads. This dress metaphor effectively managed to render all sectors of the French population into revolutionary subjects.

This is usually not the case when countries in Africa are faced with conflict—responses are neither African, nor collectivizing. In addressing conflicts and justice seeking, Western models and institutions have been predominant. Why is it that when an African country is faced with challenges of its own, the world quickly intervenes with foreign solutions as if the continent is bereft of its own? After intervention, why do Western models fail to adequately address the core of the issues in African countries bedevilled by conflict? Why do the continent's supra bodies such as the African Union (AU) and individual countries fail to reject such impositions? The reasons are partly that conflicts can easily destroy institutions and working processes capable of dealing with post-conflict situations. In addition, African contact with the West has been essentially tragic, destroying practices and mechanisms that held the continent and nations in Africa together. Africa is left with very limited options.

After the Cold War, many options for peacebuilding, post-conflict transitions, governance, and transitional justice models were suggested for countries with difficult pasts. In Africa, countries such as South Africa, Liberia, Sierra Leone, Ivory Coast, Tunisia, Rwanda, Burundi, Mozambique, Zimbabwe, and many more, have predominantly seen these Western modelled programmes of addressing conflicts and their past as part of the political settlements. For instance, it has been noticed that peacebuilding programmes have been criticized for being 'Western cut and paste exercises'.[5] Western liberal entrepreneurs offered paradigms that overshadowed or simply bypassed local approaches. However, the outcomes have not been as effective as the French Revolution dress, of embracing friends and enemies alike, each making contributions to a better future. A search for alternative responses to problems in post-conflict African states is necessary, and attempted in this chapter.

The disaffection with the inadequacies of the Western justice models or transitional justice paradigms in addressing the complex conflict and post-conflict situations in many parts of the world necessitated a review of new and emerging methods. In many African countries, the local turn has been beckoning, though it has been tempting to try what the liberal entrepreneurs offered, bypassing local approaches. However, scholars and practitioners alike continue to seek 'holistic' post-conflict approaches[6] for transitional justice processes or peacebuilding work.

[5] Ruben Gonzalez-Vicente, 'The Liberal Peace Fallacy: Violent Neoliberalism and the Temporal and Spatial Traps of State-based Approaches to Peace' (2020) 8 Territory, Politics, Governance 100.

[6] Phil Clark, 'Hybridity, Holism and Traditional Justice: The Case of the Gacaca Courts in Post-Genocide Rwanda' (2007) 39 George Washington International Law Review.

4.2 The African Context

Civil wars, genocide, droughts, intractable political violence, resource conflicts, and despicable diseases like Ebola and AIDS—all of which have significant ramifications on the social fibre—have been all too prevalent in Africa. Since the end of colonial rule, very few African states have enjoyed the peace dividend. In many ways, Africa is like a 'punch drunk' boxer, hit by everything, including the ropes. Many countries on the continent, therefore, have vacillated between longer periods of conflict and shorter ones of peace. Many more have been under the violent rule of strong men, ruling without legitimacy. Most of these strong men have been bank rolled by foreign governments to continue to oppress their people, in exchange for resources. Citizens have rebelled in response, often violently, as in the cases of the Democratic Republic of Congo, Kenya, Uganda, Liberia, Zimbabwe, Somalia, to just mention a few. Thus, the African continent has contributed its fair share to global conflicts. Most of these conflicts are not considered high intensity, even though their consequences on social relations, at local levels, have been grave.[7]

As a result of these conflicts, the roads to recovery or peace on the African continent have been characterized as 'political despair and disillusionment'.[8] Peace has been made more difficult by a profound and debilitating failure of development, as well as by dishonest politics. Such politics have included corruption that feeds on weak institutions, presided over by dictatorial leaders, who thrive on non-free media and undemocratic elections. Thus, Africa has been described as a region of 'coups, civil unrests, ethnic violence; and widespread bureaucratic corruption alongside administrative inefficiency, and institutional ineptitude or outright failure'.[9] The impact of these challenges has been social dislocation resulting from displacements, refugees, deaths, destruction of infrastructure, wars, poverty, and, as always, human rights violations. The following section examines ways of approaching these challenges, in particular the utility of the hybridity approach to justice and peace.

In states where violent conflicts have come to an end and peace agreements have been concluded, numerous institutions, organizations, and civil society movements typically converge with the intention of bringing relief and building a lasting peace. Relationships forged at the national level significantly influence the post-conflict processes in the affected country. Some organizations forge relationships with the affected communities directly in an attempt to strengthen local capacities for peace, which builds relationships, with various results for justice and peace.

[7] Phillippe Bocquier and Harve Maupeu, 'Analysing Low Intensity Conflict in Africa Using Press Reports' (2005) 21 European Journal of Population 321.

[8] Sunday Tasen Okune and Alexander Essien Timothy, 'Despair and Disillusionment in Post-Negritude African Literature' (2017) 2 English Language, Literature & Culture 45.

[9] Oluwole Owoye and Nicole Bissessar, 'Bad Governance and Corruption in Africa: Symptoms of Leadership and Institutional Failures' (2009) Commission for Asia & Pacific (UNESCAP).

At the continent level, African leaders and civil society have recently become pre-occupied with the search for home-grown formulae for addressing problems. Some African leaders have started to push for the 'made in Africa initiatives'[10] as a way of addressing accountability and impunity challenges on the continent. In an attempt to find home-grown methods to address the egregious past, civil society in Africa successfully advocated for an African Union Transitional Justice Framework (AUTJF).[11] This was conceived and drafted as a commitment to fight impunity and promote justice in both practical and normative ways. The Framework would complement the African Union's Constitutive Act (Article 4 h) on 'acknowledge[ing] the threat posed by the scourge of conflicts and commit[ing] the AU to the promotion of peace and security, human rights, and the fight against impunity'. In addition to the Constitutive Act, the importance of transitional justice is captured in the African Union Policy Framework on Post Conflict Reconstruction and Development (PCRD), the African Union High Level Panel on Darfur (AUPD), and the AU Panel of the Wise report: 'Peace, Justice, and Reconciliation in Africa: Opportunities and Challenges in the Fight Against Impunity'.

The AUTJF was conceived as a practical and actionable tool to: (a) consolidate peace, reconciliation, and justice in Africa and prevent impunity; (b) help end repressive rule and conflicts and nurture sustainable peace with development, social justice, human and peoples' rights, democratic rule, and good governance; (c) articulate a set of common concepts and principles to constitute a reference point for developing and strengthening peace agreements and transitional justice institutions and initiatives in Africa; and (d) develop African Union benchmarks for assessing compliance with the need to combat impunity.[12]

The Framework supports internal and regional mechanisms to deal with accountability and impunity and it draws lessons from the Inter-American Court of Human Rights, which intervened in the case of Peru's former dictator, Alberto Fujimori, signalling a consistent stance from the greater American region to approach impunity in a strong and uncompromising way. The Framework seeks to deal with impunity in the strongest way possible. The Framework also supports

> innovations in truth-telling processes and inclusion of traditional, informal or community-based justice practices contribute to greater account- ability and the

[10] Bagele Chilisa, 'A Synthesis on the Made in African Evaluation Concept' (2015) University of Botswana.

[11] Niké Wentholt, 'Policy Brief: African Transitional Justice and International Norms A Dynamic Relationship' (2018) Centre for the Study of Violence and Reconciliation, <https://www.csvr.org.za/pdf/African%20Transitional%20Justice%20and%20International%20Norms.pdf> accessed 13 January 2022.

[12] AU, 'The African Union Transitional Justice Policy and Framework' (February 2019) <https://au.int/sites/default/files/documents/36541-doc-au_tj_policy_eng_web.pdf> accessed 21 January 2022.

> establishment of a historical record, opening the door to guarantees of not only civil and political rights but also economic, social and cultural rights.[13]

This is a collective attempt by African people at developing their own 'internal' mechanisms to address post-conflict situations holistically. With these formulae, the AU seeks to deepen the links between transitional justice, governance, human rights, peace and security, and development. It is assumed that by using these tools, the timeliness, effectiveness, and coordination of efforts by states emerging from conflicts and oppressive rule will be improved, thus laying the foundations for accountability, social justice, sustainable peace, healing, and reconciliation.

All post-conflict societies require political reconciliation to find practical ways for restoring divided societies. Reconciliation has implications going 'beyond the relations of formerly hostile individuals, groups, communities, and even states'.[14] The processes leading to such reconciliation need to have local ownership, and have the capacity to breach social, political, ethnic, economic, and religious boundaries that always surface when sensitive issues of addressing the past feature. While the proposed African formulations are good foundations for starting the process of dealing with the past, they are essentially modelled on Western frameworks. This weakens their legitimacy. In Africa, therefore, more is needed to address conflict situations in many countries, as these conflicts have an impact on all aspects of life. In seeking to deal with the challenges of Eurocentric models of post-conflict interventions, hybrid approaches naturally emerge in many countries in Africa.

These approaches seek to cater for the strengths of both European and local ways of knowing and practices. However, hybridization has remained an ineffective solution because of its weak balance of Western and local ingredients. It is briefly discussed below drawing from some of the African experiences in the conflicts in Kenya, South Sudan, Rwanda, Zimbabwe, and South Africa. African ways of knowing emphasize a polycentric or polyvalence approach to dealing with issues, from the individual through to the spiritual realms. Polycentric approaches to justice and peace are therefore an advancement from the general hybridity models, which imbed local experiences and Western jurisprudence, although in a less formalized way and embracing daily models in greater detail when contributing to everyday justice and peace. They are richer than ordinary hybridity, which appear like decentralized Western models and dispense their work beyond the binaries to include:

[13] Jasmina Brankovic, 'African Union Transitional Justice Policy Framework in Practice: Implementing Accountability Measures' (2012) Centre for the Study of Violence and Reconciliation 7 <https://www.files.ethz.ch/isn/167157/accountabilitybriefautransitionaljusticepolicyframeworkinpractice.pdf> accessed 15 February 2022.

[14] Joanne Wallis, Renee Jeffery, and Lia Kent, 'Political Reconciliation in Timor Leste, Solomon Islands and Bougainville: The Dark Side of Hybridity' (2016) 70 Australian Journal of International Affairs 159.

traditional chieftaincies, village and tribal elders and religious figures who preside over customary dispute resolution. A range of civil society organizations, youth and women's groups, guilds or associations, private security companies and vigilante/community watch groups are also important – as are 'secret societies' and those who act as a bridge to the spiritual realm.[15]

4.3 Dealing with the Past

It is imperative to address a post-conflict environment quickly and completely to prevent a relapse into conflict. However, dealing with a legacy of gross human rights violations is one of the greatest challenges facing societies in the aftermath of violent conflict, an authoritarian regime, or occupation. Political settlements are challenging due to the often-continued existence of the historic problems that fed the conflict in the first place. One such enduring problem is how to effect justice for the victims of past human rights violations. Mechanisms available to bring about justice and peace in post-conflict environments are always contestable. But finding a way to deal with a violent past following events such as civil war, or the end of an authoritarian regime or occupation, is often argued to be the basis for lasting peace, democracy, and rule of law.[16] In most cases, the international advocacy networks, norms, and legal frameworks readily kick in to support national and local actors in designing mechanisms and processes like truth commissions, tribunals, or commemorations—ostensibly to deal with the conflict situation and to assist people to move on.

The various models suggested to stabilize post-conflict states differ considerably. It is therefore worth examining the structural and practical strengths and limitations of available models, including international law, and determining whether these models necessitate reform or reconceptualization.[17] The argument has been that external models of dealing with conflicts have largely failed to provide effective and sustainable solutions to post-colonial conflicts in Africa mainly due to the way they are articulated.[18] In its normative and institutional framings, international law is proving incapable of advancing innovative approaches to confronting African conflicts. For instance, the International Criminal Court (ICC), a court that was designed to replace the hybrid court system, has been criticized. The 'ICC is plagued by challenges to its legitimacy, erratic state cooperation, and

[15] Charles T Hunt, 'Beyond the Binaries: Towards a Relational Approach to Peacebuilding' (2017) 29 Global Change, Peace & Security 209 <https://www.tandfonline.com/doi/full/10.1080/14781158.2017.1360855?needAccess = true> accessed 17 February 2022.

[16] Elizabeth Andersen, 'Transitional Justice and the Rule of Law: Lessons from the Field' (2015) 47 Case Western Reserve Journal of International Law 305.

[17] Bonny Ibhawoh, 'Imperial Justice: Africans in Empire's Court' (2013) ASA 2013 Annual Meeting Paper <https://papers.ssrn.com/sol3/papers.cfm?abstract_id=2236831> accessed 10 March 2022.

[18] ibid.

persistent perceptions of inefficacy and inefficiency'.[19] This is corroborated by Mutua who argues that international law is illegitimate and predatory, seeking only to subordinate and sustain the plunder of the Third World by the West.[20] A major reason for this, as Jeng alleges, is that international law and Western tools are 'still overwhelmingly trapped in dialogues of historical contradictions and controversies',[21] such as colonialism and its injustices. This argument is persuasive even though it ignores the good things external approaches have brought with them, such as professionalism, due process, standardization of approaches, measurability, and normativity.

The contradictions we see in international law Western tools arise partly from the Eurocentric historical framework from which contemporary international law is sustained.[22] Dominant advocacy has generally conceptualized justice and peacebuilding in the context of 'Eurocentric thinking'.[23] Given the challenges posed by the Eurocentric models of dealing with post-conflict situations, and alongside the AU values in the Constitutive Act, particularly Article 4, the principle of 'non-indifference' to the conflict situation, we propose the 'polyvalence approach' to address the complexity and nuances of African conflicts. This could be the most 'robust challenge to the dominance of the neoliberal international approaches to peace',[24] marking a profound departure from 'aspects of international law's foundational ethos that have conditioned and constrained postcolonial Africa's peacebuilding initiatives'.[25] This chapter's approach does not seek to homogenize the practices of peacebuilding or dealing with the past, but aims to show the limitations of the neo-liberal template.

4.4 Hybridization

There is a line of scholarship that views hybridization in its current form as a pragmatic innovation in the dispensing of post-conflict justice in that it relates to the creation of new transcultural forms of dealing with the past, involving the integration of Western-oriented principles with indigenous systems. We accept that in the

[19] Beth Van Schaack, 'The Building Blocks of Hybrid Justice' (2016) Stanford Public Law Working Paper No 2705110 101 <https://papers.ssrn.com/sol3/papers.cfm?abstract_id = 2705110> accessed 10 March 2022.

[20] W Mutua Mukau, 'What is Twail?' (2000) American Society of International Law, Proceedings of the 94th Annual Meeting 31 <https://papers.ssrn.com/sol3/papers.cfm?abstract_id = 1533471> accessed 10 March 2022.

[21] Abou Jeng, *Peacebuilding in the African Union: Law, Philosophy and Practice* (Cambridge University Press 2012) 278.

[22] Ibhawoh (n 17).

[23] Jeng (n 21) 6.

[24] ibid 10.

[25] Ibhawoh (n 17).

context of state fragility 'hybridization' of interventions can be the magic wand.[26] However, if one looks at it more closely, it is a form of ruse, a decentralization of the ICC's elements to the local level so that its forms of justice are dispensed more cheaply. This form of hybridization supports the idea that legal approaches should also be hybrid—partnerships between local and international organizations. This has been justified under the concept of 'legal pluralism'.[27] The growing scholarship on legal pluralism has emerged as a response to the limits of the liberal agenda.[28]

The terms 'hybrid,' 'hybridity', or 'hybridization' are commonplace in post-conflict societies. They trace ancestry in post-colonial cultural theory and a search for modern cultural, social, and political relationships.[29] The idea also emerged from the realization that the ICC lacked the capacity to deal with justice demands across the globe.[30] The concept of hybridity has been used in fiction novels such as Timothy Findley's *Not Wanted on the Voyage* (1984) and Zadie Smith's *White Teeth* (2000) to explore post-colonial themes. The work of Homi K Bhabha is also relevant to the concept of hybridity in respect of post-colonialism, which he conceived as 'the sign of the productivity of colonial power, its shifting forces and fixities; it is the name for the strategic reversal of the process of domination through disavowal . . .'.[31] Bhabha further asserted that there is a lot of mimicry resulting in the fixing of 'the colonial subject as a "partial' presence'".[32] The 'partial presence' in peace and justice responses to conflict are local mechanisms. Hybrid arrangements have been seen as the answer to the processes that subordinate local processes and institutions and privilege external or international processes and institutions by virtue of their privileged position in the colonial past, often as colonizers. Therefore, hybrid courts are 'halfway houses' in that they possess the 'qualities of both domestic and international courts'.[33]

[26] Roger Mac Ginty, *International Peacebuilding and Local Resistance: Hybrid Forms of Peace* (Palgrave Macmillan 2011); Edward Newman, Roland Paris, and Oliver Richmond (eds), *New Perspectives on Liberal Peacebuilding* (United Nations University Press 2009); Phil Clark, 'Hybridity, Holism and Traditional Justice: The Case of the Gacaca Courts in Post-Genocide Rwanda' (2007) 39 George Washington International Law Review <https://papers.ssrn.com/sol3/papers.cfm?abstract_id = 1031739> accessed 10 March 2022; Volker Boege and others, 'On Hybrid Political Orders and Emerging States On Hybrid Political Orders and Emerging States: State Formation in the Context of "Fragility"' (2008) Berghof Handbook for Conflict Transformation <https://berghof-foundation.org/library/on-hybrid-political-orders-and-emerging-states-state-formation-in-the-context-of-fragility> accessed 10 March 2022; Briony Jones, 'Understanding Resistance and its Implications for Hybridity' (September 2013) European Consortium for Political Research, Bordeaux.

[27] Clark (n 26).

[28] Jones (n 26).

[29] Jenny H Peterson, 'A Conceptual Unpacking of Hybridity: Accounting for Notions of Power, Politics and Progress in Analyses of Aid-Driven Interfaces' (2012) 7 Journal of Peacebuilding & Development 9.

[30] Van Schaack (n 19).

[31] Homi K Bhabha, 'Signs Taken for Wonders: Questions of Ambivalence and Authority under a Tree outside Delhi' (1985) 12 Critical Inquiry 144.

[32] Homi K Bhabha, *The Location of Culture* (2nd edn, Routledge 1994).

[33] Van Schaack (n 19) 104.

The concept of hybridization or hybridity has been used among scholars as an analytical tool for assessing liberal peacebuilding, justice, and development models. In theoretical terms it 'refers to the creation of new transcultural forms within the contact zone produced by colonisation'.[34] Now it is further used to:

> explore the many varieties and outcomes of externally led interventions, and in some cases are portrayed as desirable political projects that could stimulate alternatives and counter what is perceived to be hegemonic, externally driven liberal programming.[35]

This has led many to understand that the hybrid project is not as benevolent as it appears to be when the relationship between the local and the external is seriously analysed. This realization of the collision course between the 'local' and 'external', the 'traditional, indigenous, and customary', and internationally supported external peace and development operations[36] has led to a rethinking of current forms of hybridity, viewing them as decentralizations or cascading elements of international systems.

This view is noted in peacebuilding, where it is

> increasingly difficult to talk about [peacebuilding] without reference to the wide array of international actors who have come to play an important role in war-affected countries. These actors generally have diverse (and, at times, conflicting) values, interests and mandates which are not necessarily aligned with local realities, needs or goals.[37]

The consequence of international participation in conflict situations has had both intended and unintended results, mainly due to international actors taking too long to understand that conflicts in many African countries 'were not unilinear in nature; nor could they be addressed sequentially'.[38]

The focus of post-conflict interventions is to build and heal relationships and societies and, ultimately, achieve 'positive peace'.[39] Unfortunately, such approaches are ontologically and epistemologically Western in nature. It should be no surprise if very little is achieved even with resources and time invested in the processes.

[34] Bill Ashcroft, Gareth Griffiths, and Helen Tiffin, *Post-Colonial Studies: Key Concepts* (2nd edn, Routledge 2007) 118.

[35] Peterson (n 29).

[36] Mac Ginty (n 26).

[37] Necla Tscirgi, 'Bridging the Chasm between Domestic and International Approaches to Peacebuilding: Conceptual and Institutional Tools' (2015) 7 RCCS Annual Review 74 <https://journals.openedition.org/rccsar/605>.

[38] ibid 76.

[39] John Paul Lederach, *Building Peace: Sustainable Reconciliation in Divided Societies* (US Institute of Peace Press 1997).

The weakness is in the assumptions that local methods are used only to supplement the imported methods to address a local conflict. Moreover, it is believed that through foreign mechanisms it is possible to 'rebuild political relationships'[40] and the 'pervasive and widespread negative attitudes' will be overcome; trust within a polity rebuilt by reinforcing normative expectations, or to reconstitute a political community.[41]

Epistemologically, the concept of peace as we know it is a Western concept. Theories and practices of peace derive from Western ontological claims. The local lens is disqualified for lacking theory and concepts.[42] Viewed through such a lens, the current post-conflict work in general is essentially built as a Western project and 'implemented primarily through the existing system of international organizations, donor agencies, and various governmental and non-government organizations'[43] for the furtherance of Western interests. Such an approach prioritizes:

> policies and programs which reflected a strong commitment to liberal values, including good governance, rule of law, human rights, political participation, free and fair elections, gender equality, free markets, transparency and accountability.[44]

These approaches may appear promising, yet they are resisted or rejected in a majority of the places where they are implemented, particularly for their disregard for the models that traditional societies have spent years perfecting. Rwanda and East Timor are good examples where a return to traditional methods was used to deal with the enormity of the crisis. In Rwanda, the Gacaca system was recalled, but it had to use rules of procedure with elements of Western jurisprudence.[45] It was considered a hybrid system. This route was seen to be compatible with thousands of small-scale conflicts and was hailed by many as successful.[46] The Gacaca system was popular compared with the International Criminal Tribunal for Rwanda due to its efficient handling of the multitudes of alleged genocide cases. Unlike the Western court in Arusha, Gacaca proceedings were conducted in the village, by the people, and in front of victims. However, the rules of procedure were Western.[47]

[40] Colleen Murphy, *A Moral Theory of Political Reconciliation* (Cambridge University Press 2010) 8 <https://www.cambridge.org/core/books/moral-theory-of-political-reconciliation/2263D29F3DC8632A325224DBC7CEA3FB> accessed 13 March 2022.

[41] ibid 10, 13, and 20.

[42] Oldrich Bures, 'Wanted: A Mid-Range Theory of International Peacekeeping' (2007) 9 International Studies Review 407.

[43] Tscirgi (n 37) 76.

[44] ibid 77.

[45] Suthaharan Nadarajah and David Rampton, 'The Limits of Hybridity and the Crisis of Liberal Peace' (2015) 41 Review of International Studies 49.

[46] Mac Ginty (n 26) 181.

[47] Luc Huyse and Mark Salter (eds), 'Traditional Justice and Reconciliation after Violent Conflict: Learning from African Experiences' (2008) International Institute for Democracy and

One-size-fits-all models, whether they are traditional or Western, are rejected due to their attempt at de-contextualizing ways of framing and explaining reality, or making Africa ashamed of its methods—as argued below, there is a need to reclaim the ontological and epistemological foundations of peace that have sustained the continent's different communities. Suthaharan Nadarajah and David Rampton have criticized the liberal approach as having 'narrow ethnocentric boundaries, technocratic tendencies and fixation with the state'[48] and this ignores the local turn that is 'empathetic, responsive, culturally sensitive and ultimately radical peace encompassing the local, indigenous and quotidian experience, especially that of the subaltern categories, within conflict-affected spaces and societies'.[49]

One recurrent criticism of the liberal approach to peacebuilding has been its top-down, mechanistic, and almost prescriptive modelling. It neglects the multilectal character of hybridization by being 'coercive, top-down, technocratic, uncompromising and blind to the local conditions in which it is pursued'.[50] Conversely, the African approaches, just as its culture, are communal and participatory, inclusive, and thus are able to integrate other approaches seamlessly and create plural peace at the intersection of the international and local institutions, practices, and values. Gacaca courts in Rwanda achieved this effectiveness by using local traditional structures blended with Western jurisprudence to deal with thousands of cases, which would have taken a Western court many years to process.[51] Hybrid approaches to addressing conflicts are not essentially framed as scientific endeavours—explained by data, methods, and theories of change. This is in recognition of the fact that resolving conflict and achieving justice cannot be treated as a scientific project or object of inquiry, but rather it is an organic process that must align with people's own ways of life. It is no wonder that the legitimacy of Western approaches is questioned. In reality, it is polyvalent methods, a form of hybridity in dealing with the past or post-conflict situations, that are likely to contribute to lasting peace.

4.5 Polyvalence

Given the limitations of Eurocentric models in addressing post-conflict situations, as well as the African Union's values as outlined in the Constitutive Act—specifically Article 4's principle of 'non-indifference' to conflict—we propose a

Electoral Assistance <https://www.idea.int/sites/default/files/publications/traditional-justice-and-reconciliation-after-violent-conflict-learning-from-african-experiences_0.pdf> accessed 10 March 2022

[48] Nadarajah and Rampton (n 45).
[49] ibid 54.
[50] Ibid 55.
[51] ibid 55.

'polyvalence approach' to managing the complexity of African conflicts.[52] This approach presents a strong challenge to the dominance of neoliberal international peacebuilding strategies and represents a significant shift away from elements of international law that have shaped and restricted postcolonial Africa's peace efforts, while re-embracing African knowledge systems.[53]

Western models alone cannot be appropriate catharsis to the post-conflict challenges in most African countries. Combining Western models with local approaches has the tendency to create binaries, such as Western vs local and traditional vs European. Bifurcation, or even mixing, has its own structural problems that can affect the quality of the results. One such problem is that the models tend to leave out too many stakeholders from the peace process by relying on static templates. We witnessed this in the structure of the Gacaca system, which was organized in the realm of tradition, but dispensing Western justice. Despite its efficiencies, the Gacaca system favoured Western jurisprudence, using it as the basis for documentation even though this created discontent. Although tradition is typically learned naturally through socialization, rather than formal training, the Gacaca system trained more than 160,000 judges,[54] and this blurred the distinction between Western judges in the Rwanda Court and the Gacaca judges on the ground. Therefore, can the context-based mechanisms such as *mat o put* be adequate in themselves to address similar problems? By their nature, conflicts are polyvalent, and so their solutions must be too. The polyvalent approaches to ending conflict and achieving justice need to be naturally inclusive of societal layers and structures in a manner that empowers each actor involved. Timothy Donais suggests that the basis of a lasting solution is 'natural ownership'.[55] This is ownership that stretches from the soil where the ordinary person in the village stands to the person developing polices in government buildings. There must be at least some consonance in the narrative of the violence that occurred and the peace sought after. This ensures that ownership is not entirely limited to technocrats and elites, but also includes women, youth, and the marginalized; those most affected by the conflict and most in need of peace. This understanding of ownership was also referred to by Ban Ki Moon when he said that peace that is not embraced by those who live it will fail.[56]

Michel Foucault concurs in his introduction to the idea of 'polyvalence', which he defined as 'a multiplicity of discursive elements', rather than the division of dominant discourse and 'the dominated one'[57] in addressing issues. This approach

[52] Wallis, Jeffery, and Kent (n 14) 169.

[53] Ibhawoh (n 17).

[54] IRIN, 'Justice for a Lawless World: Rights and Reconciliation in a New Era of International Law (Part I)' (2006) IRIN In-Depth.

[55] Timothy Donais, *Peacebuilding and Local Ownership* (Routledge 2012).

[56] UNGA and UNSC, 'Report of the Secretary General on Peacebuilding in the Immediate Aftermath of Conflict' (2009) UN Doc A/63/881-S/2009/304.

[57] Michel Foucault, *The History of Sexuality Volume I: An Introduction* (Robert Hurley tr, Pantheon Books 1976) 100.

encourages the mutual participation of various layers of actors and avoids dividing the discourse along layers of power and domination. At the community level, where the majority of those who were violated are found, a violation of one is a violation of all. When justice is sought, it is not for the individual to carry the scar alone, but for everyone who is part of their lineage. Therefore, there is a power of transcendence in this model, as it touches a code with all sections of society. As a result, local actors affected by the conflict are allowed to be drawn into the search for solutions using local means and technologies. Even though the French dress's collective action amounted to revolution in France, its strength was in reaching out to the demands of *liberté*, *égalité*, and *fraternité* and finding resonance with the narratives of everyone: the revolutionary, court, imperial, and the activist. Current forms of the hybrid approach, on the contrary, are selective and binary, often subordinating one form of narrative to another.

A closer look at some conflicts shows that they are not as simple as they are initially appear. Therefore, suggested interventions to address these conflicts should cater for their various causes. The depth of the conflicts in Darfur, South Sudan, Liberia, Somalia, and Uganda shows that there cannot be one model, but rather there needs to be diverse ways, which are inclusive, beyond the rigid technical and elitist approaches.

4.5.1 The Polyvalence layers

4.5.1.1 The people: the activist, the victim and the perpetrator

When violent conflicts happen in many African countries, they happen *in*communities. The biggest victim is relationships because of people's strong interconnectedness, even across national borders. Societies, including those in Africa, are value laden and the starting point in dealing with conflicts is to go back to shared values, those that permeate across everyone in the conflict. Though not uniform across Africa, one common value is *Ubuntu* (Humanity). This value embraces the common principles of accountability, justice, life, peace, and reconciliation. These values are reinforcing and interlinked. Such values exist daily in many communities and there is no way they are considered foreign. The concept of *Ubuntu* values humans equally. The inclusivity and recognition of victims, perpetrators, the state, and local institutions in inherently participatory, expressive, and almost religious ways strongly affects the conflict trajectory. This allows the whole community to collectively see the cost of violence, as they are able to count their losses together. State-centric approaches, while they espouse the need to address problems nationally and not just internationally, usually through a national commission or tribunal, are limited to the question of dry accountability and retribution through legal and penal systems.

Because of the religious and moral pillars of *Ubuntu* governing the treatment of individuals, Indigenous systems in many African societies may not consider cases going through the courts as representing complete justice. As in the Shona[58] example, even when a person is tried by the courts and convicted for crimes against humanity, the court's judgment is not 'final in itself', it is only finished when the convicts face the 'moral court' presided by the victims, relatives of the victims, and the community, who serve as powerful judges in the moral realm. This moral court is considered spiritually higher than the secular or civil courts for they address the spiritual aspects of the crime, which the civil court will never attempt to do. In the case of murder, the spirit of the deceased is summoned to 'come and bear witness to the justice process'. In most of the cases, the convicts even 'face' the 'spirit of the dead' when they genuinely admit their crimes. Serving time as prescribed by a national court, therefore, including even the execution of the convicted, does not erase the charges or crimes committed against the people; only pleading guilty to the community and paying reparations as determined by the elders and spiritual leaders, will appease the victims' spirits and grant true freedom to the perpetrators. In particular, crimes that involve the spilling of blood will always have grave consequences and would certainly attract the attention of cosmic forces whose anger would spare no one. Responses to these challenges cannot be left to the technical experts: it is a community responsibility.

The AUTJF realized this critical intervention when it provided for the participation of local processes from the start of the transitional justice process, rather than in the middle or at the end, and maintained this involvement throughout.

> The AU TJ Policy Framework in recognition of this [weakness in the current approaches] sought to cure that deficit by underlining the primacy and centrality of victims and citizens in conceptualization, design, implementation, monitoring and evaluation of transitional justice processes in Africa.[59]

The most pressing challenge is then how to involve all the people when the conflict is ongoing, as, for instance, in South Sudan. How do we involve people that have fled the country other than through their elites who have the privilege of travelling across the world to peace conferences?

[58] The Shona are a Bantu ethnic group native to Southern Africa, primarily the country of Zimbabwe where they form a vast majority. The people are divided into five major clans and are closely related to other groups with very similar cultures and languages. Vincent Mabvurira, George A Muchinako, and Ivy E Smith 'Shona Traditional Religion and Sustainable Environmental Management: An Afrocentric Perspective' (2021) 11 African Journal of Social Work 111.

[59] George M Wachira, 'The African Union Transitional Justice Policy Framework and How it Fits into the African Governance Architecture (AGA): Promise and Prospects for the African Court of Justice and Human Rights' in Charles C Jalloh, Kamari M Clarke, and Vincent O Nmehielle (eds), *The African Court of Justice and Human and People's Rights in Context: Development and Challenges* (Cambridge University Press 2019).

In communal life, where everything is shared, many rituals must be carried out before a person can be fully reintegrated into the society that they spoiled through committing egregious crimes. The people that run the state are fully aware of these processes. While the law makes certain pronouncements about justice, it is left to the perpetrator to undertake the final act. In most cases, the perpetrator is left alone to face the moral consequences of their crime; the court cannot help them at this level. This is the moment of truth that even the court system is unable to extract from the perpetrator, but the community can. Through rituals, the perpetrators admit that they committed the crimes and they want to be cleansed of the spirits of those they killed or witnessed being killed. They must undergo some difficult rituals for their own good, or for the good of their family and their community. In Zimbabwe, some of the post-bush war guerrillas (1964–1980) had to be cleansed of their experiences during the war, and some of those who did not go through this ritual still suffer the hangovers of war and have continued to commit violence in the communities they live in. In Sierra Leone, the communities engaged at the grassroot level to resolve collective madness in what was called *Fambultok* in Creole, translated as 'family talk'. The country was ravaged by a civil war in which countless unspeakable atrocities were inflicted upon the populace, often by individuals (and, in some cases, family members) who knew one another personally. The programme is based on traditional village bonfire gatherings in which victims and perpetrators address one another, not only to make amends, but also to help restore the longstanding Sierra Leonean tradition of 'community' as a way of life. Victims are afforded an opportunity to express their suffering—usually in painfully explicit detail—and in turn perpetrators are subsequently offered the chance to express their remorse, after which victims are asked if they can accept the apologies of their offenders. In some cases, if the victims are offered compensation but appear overly demanding, the community in its collective position can force the victim to accept recompense and this will even be accepted by the spirits. Remarkably, forgiveness is nearly always the result, even in the most egregious cases. While *Fambultok* brings about the mending of relations at the micro level, the justice component of the process has been 'met' following Western models.[60] The question has been whose justice is this?

4.5.1.2 Local civil society

In the modern sense, a new institution has developed to bridge the gap between family and state. Civil society organizations (CSOs) in the Africa region have a role to play in the prevention of conflicts and in post-conflict recovery, including transitional justice. As a bridge between traditional societies and the rest of the world, CSOs have managed to advocate for justice by broadening access to justice

[60] Global Minnesota, 'Learning from Sierra Leone: Fambul Tok and the Power of Forgiveness' (2020) <https://www.youtube.com/watch?v = 0KsmD5p0zgs> accessed 13 March 2022.

for ordinary people who want to engage with all worlds. The International Peace Academy has noted the active CSOs in Uganda, Kenya, Democratic Republic of the Congo, Rwanda and Tanzania making various contributions towards peace.[61] The role of CSOs include democratization and conflict prevention in countries such as Uganda and Kenya. In Uganda, Action for Development (ACFODE), a women's non-governmental organization, and the National Organization for Civic Education and Election Monitoring (NOCEM) conducted public education campaigns countrywide to assess and enlist people's views of inclusion in the constitution. They achieved their goals through the dissemination of information in a publication called *The Link*.

In Kenya, the Green Belt Movement, the Law Society of Kenya, and National Council of Churches of Kenya (NCCK), resisted KANU's one-party dictatorship by mobilizing citizens both in rural and urban areas to demand political reforms. In Rwanda, the religious institutions played an active role in constructing a viable post-conflict environment. For instance, some Muslim groups played crucial roles in saving lives by maintaining peace in their areas and providing humanitarian assistance for escapees.[62] Even in Northern Uganda, organizations such as Refugees Law Project, Church of Uganda, and the Uganda Joint Christian Council were instrumental in the peacemaking efforts between the government and the Lord's Resistance Army of Joseph Kony.[63] However, while CSOs help to create the momentum for justice and peace, statist models that frame these momentums limit their capacity to dispense complete justice. While they can help in bridging societies divided by years of conflict, just as the *Fambultok* has done, they rely on the state to ensure that mechanisms of transitional justice are implemented.

Mbayo outlines the important roles of CSOs during and after conflicts in Africa, including protection of citizens against violence from all parties; monitoring of human rights violations; the implementation of peace agreements; advocacy for accountability and human rights; socialization to promote the values of peace and democracy; fostering intergroup cohesion; facilitation of dialogue on local and international levels between various actors; and service delivery as an entry point to peacebuilding.[64] Civil societies provide the greatest social capital for peacebuilding and transitional justice because these processes are inherently multidimensional and involve relationships. For instance, in Liberia, CSOs touched everyone's lives during the civil war, including on matters related to disarmament, where the Inter-faith Mediation Committee, Liberia Council of

[61] Arthur Bainomugisha and Mashood Issaka, 'The Role of Civil Society in Peacebuilding in the Great Lakes Region' (2004) International Peace Academy 6.

[62] ibid.

[63] ibid.

[64] AS Mbayo, 'Civil Society and Peacebuilding in Africa: An Assessment of the Contribution by Local Women's Civil Society Organisations to Peacebuilding in Sierra Leone' (DPhil thesis, Hiroshima University 2012) 51.

Churches, and the National Muslim Council of Liberia[65] played a pivotal role in bringing sanity to the country.

While these CSOs were involved in developing their societies' peace architecture, others campaigned successfully for the delivery of justice. This process was possible in states that practised what Scheye characterized as 'rule by the intermediaries', when the state depended on a 'series of networks and polities that substitute and compensate for the lack of authority of the central, legally constituted state and its ability to deliver essential public goods and services'.[66] To administer justice, communities had to fall back on local systems and idiosyncrasies to draw individuals to face justice.

4.5.1.3 Governments

Even when they are conflict actors, national governments can still play major roles in securing justice and lasting peace. Governments negotiate deals with belligerents resulting in political settlements[67] and provide institutions and support for transforming armed rebels into political parties. Therefore, the state is preponderant in its role, and post-conflict interventions should be understood as broadly linked to issues of peacebuilding, development, and establishing the rule of law. The complexity of these processes means that they cannot be managed at the community level alone, but require state involvement. The state provides conflict actors space to bargain, and establish the rule of law as the foundation for further negotiations. This will enable what Christine Bell calls 'the transition from authoritarian exclusive political settlements to more inclusive forms of government characterised by the rule of law'.[68] The state also enables political mobilization to continue, not from the theatre of guns and blood, but further up at political levels as politicians jostle for the electoral vote.

In mass-scale violence the state's approach is to build the state[69] as a method of addressing the past. Liberia took this route. It invited the politico-military elites

[65] Augustine Toure, 'The Role of Civil Society in National Reconciliation and Peacebuilding in Liberia' (2002) International Peace Academy.

[66] Eric Scheye, 'State-Provided Service, Contracting Out and Non-State Networks: Justice and Security as Public and Private Goods and Services' (2009) The International Network on Conflict and Fragility and Organisation for Economic Co-operation and Development.

[67] Christine Bell, 'Contending with the Past: Transitional Justice and Political Settlement Processes' in Roger Duthie and Paul Seils (eds), *Justice Mosaics: How Context Shapes Transitional Justice in Fractured Societies* (International Center for Transitional Justice 2017) 85; Kris Brown and Fionnuala Ni Aoláin, 'Good Fences Make Good Neighbours: Assessing the Role of Consociational Politics in Transitional Justice' (2016) Political Settlements Research Programme Working Paper No 3; Catherine O'Rourke, 'Law, Governance and Development: A Case Study of Women's Social Mobilisation and Transitional Justice' (2015) Political Settlements Research Programme Briefing Paper No 5.

[68] Christine Bell, 'What We Talk About When We Talk About Political Settlements: Towards Inclusive And Open Political Settlements in an Era of Disillusionment' (2015) Political Settlements Research Programme Working Paper No 2.

[69] Christine Bell, 'International Law and Processes of Political Settlement' in Aileen McHarg and others (eds), *The Scottish Independence Referendum: Constitutional and Political Implications* (Oxford University Press 2016).

into a public power project, though this also involved international actors. Lessons from Liberia also show that international actors can get involved for strategic instrumentalism, where they use their involvement to influence the balance of power in the conflict.[70] International involvement in Liberia worked to 'punish' the recalcitrant politicians who reneged on peace negotiations, or even remove them from the conflict fray and positions of power.[71]

4.5.1.4 Regional Economic Communities (RECs) and the AU

Regional economic communities play a critical role in resilient peace. The AU and the RECs have together established the African Peace and Security Architecture (APSA) framework to respond to conflicts. The AU has further added the Transitional Justice Framework and Policy as a normative tool to deal with the past and challenges of impunity and rule of law. The APSA Roadmap (2016–2020) demonstrates the important and growing role assigned to RECs by emphasizing enhanced relationships between the AU and RECs as one of its strategic priorities.[72] RECs have a comparative advantage in the African conflict matrix as they can systemize institutional responses to conflicts. These regional arrangements facilitate engagement with traditional authorities, women, youth, and civil society in finding long-term responses to conflict.[73] A good example is the Intergovernmental Authority on Development (IGAD) whose increased focus now includes peace and security. Elevating the role of IGAD to peace and security is based on the argument that it is 'better equipped to deal with the socio-cultural and political intricacies within their respective regions.'[74]

4.5.1.5 Polyvalence Complete

In contrast to hybridization, polyvalence is a comprehensive set of interconnected rings— people, civil society, governments, the AU, and its regional economic commissions. The depth of this approach lies in its embrace of only international practices that matter, particularly where there is reference to crimes against humanity, while emphasizing local ways of knowing. Crimes against humanity invoke international interest, but the affected communities feel them first. Therefore, with the deep involvement of the people affected by the conflict, the use of their practices, the inclusion of civil society, the state, and the collective values of the *Ubuntu* as embodied in the AU, there will be less need for reference to foreign approaches of knowing and justice.

[70] ibid.
[71] ibid 60.
[72] Amanda Lucey and Berouk Mesfin, 'More Than a Chip Off the Block: Strengthening IGAD–AU Peacebuilding Linkages' (2016) Institute for Security Studies Policy Brief 91.
[73] ibid.
[74] ibid 2.

The trial of Hissène Habrè's in Senegal is not the best example of innovative justice. In fact, it is seen as an alternative to the ICC, rather than an innovation. Its major weakness is that it left out the local component, creating a form of distant justice for the people of Chad.[75] While the hybrid court in Senegal marks the beginning of a widened justice process for the those who suffered at the hands of dictators, it is not them who pulled the strings. Because the affected countries still had to work out strategies for addressing the dynamics of handling cases involving former heads of state, their relationship with the ICC mattered more than with the affected people. Now that Habré is locked up in a distant cell in a distant African country, can justice be considered served for the communities that lost their loved ones and suffered so much? This may not be the case. Conversely, would the polyvalence detail have managed the weight of Habré? Possibly not. However, in the African tradition, there exists a rich vein of mechanisms and processes that can work to effectively realize peace and justice. What is important is to create linkages in the African structures existing on the ground, recognize them as fundamental to meeting the justice needs of the people, and integrate them with the regional and continental frameworks.

The African Governance Architecture (AGA), based on the African Charter on Democracy, Elections and Governance, which came into force in 2012 is one additional normative way of addressing conflicts. Its mandate is to provide a 'platform for dialogue between the various stakeholders' in order to promote good governance and democracy, and to strengthen the objectives of the legal and policy pronouncements in the AU Shared Values.[76] Using its clusters on democracy, governance, human rights, and transitional justice, as well as constitutionalism and the rule of law, it can resonate with the AU PCRD pillars of security, political governance and transition; human rights, justice, and reconciliation; humanitarian assistance, reconstruction, and socio-economic development; and gender.[77] This principle, if replicated across Africa, will render it less important to adopt a hybrid approach to justice that involves international partners because what will be available will be sufficient internally within Africa. The case of the Extraordinary African Chambers, which sentenced the former Chadian President Hissène Habrè to life imprisonment, was not a particularly exciting proposition for the victims even though trying the president in Senegal helped to defuse tensions which could have been stoked by trying him in Chad. The weakness of this form of hybridity is that it dispenses distant justice, but it is a starting point and provides useful lessons.

However, it must be noted that the polyvalence approach itself also has some limitations, and research on its improvement is paramount. For instance, layers of

[75] Phil Clark, *Distant Justice: The Impact of the International Criminal Court on African Politics* (University of Cambridge Press 2018).

[76] AU, 'About AGA' <https://au.int/aga/about> accessed 15 January 2024.

[77] Lucey and Mesfin (n 72).

polyvalence may exclude all external actors, including the diaspora and sometimes the donors and partner states and seek to concentrate on everything African, as though this could provide a comprehensive solution to all continental problems. Lumping all African 'people' into one category has weaknesses as this reduces Africa to a continent with no historical, cultural, and economic diversities.

4.6 Conclusion

The hybrid approach to peace and justice is appealing on the surface and there is much support for it. International criminal law is now favouring this approach as a solution to the weaknesses of the traditional neo-liberal models. But African experiences, and the involving nature of the conflicts, require broader, polyvalent, methods that are African in nature and design. Such methods draw from the African values of *Ubuntu*, of an essentially communitarian approach to problems and solutions that address them. This is because conflicts are understood to be a 'bad odour' which spoils the atmosphere for everyone, not just a few—we are all affected by conflict, so must work together to build peace and achieve justice.

5
Dissent in International Criminal Justice and the Creation and Re-emergence of the Hybrid Court

Shannon Maree Torrens

5.1 Introduction

State responses to international criminal justice can be categorized as falling into three general categories: support, acquiescence, and dissent, with some blurring of the boundaries between each of these responses. This chapter looks at the interaction and tension between these three viewpoints, modes of behaviour, and communication styles to better understand hybrid courts and in particular state responses to these justice mechanisms. These three response styles of support, acquiescence, and dissent can be evidenced firstly on a historical continuum marking the trajectory of international criminal justice from the United Nations (UN) ad hoc tribunals of the early 1990s, through to the early hybrid courts, then to the International Criminal Court (ICC), and now in the re-emergence of hybrid courts. In outlining this historical trajectory of support to acquiescence and then dissent, this chapter illustrates how these three responses comprise not only former and current views on international hybrid justice, but also how these responses exist simultaneously within each hybrid court. The range of state responses to hybrid courts from acquiescence to dissent creates tension in the work of these courts, which contributes to challenges with respect to legitimacy and the perceived relevance of these justice responses in the post-conflict state.

Taking a critical and theoretical approach to international criminal justice, this chapter focuses specifically on the notion of state dissent in response to hybrid courts, through defining this behaviour, identifying where it is exhibited, and then assessing its impact on past, present, and future hybrid courts. In doing so, this chapter strives to assess the original creation, subsequent failings, and now re-emergence of hybrid courts through an analysis of state behaviour in response to these justice processes. Through this analysis, the chapter discusses the reasons for the recent re-emergence of hybrid courts, including the relationship of past and present hybrids to one another and then in connection to what was intended to be

Shannon Maree Torrens, *Dissent in International Criminal Justice and the Creation and Re-emergence of the Hybrid Court* In: *Hybrid Justice*. Edited by: Kirsten Ainley and Mark Kersten, Oxford University Press.
 DOI: 10.1093/oso/9780192893758.003.0005

a permanent, overarching response to international crime, the ICC. This will then be contextualized through an examination of the internal resilience of the court and the contribution it makes to the external resilience of the situation state.

5.2 Primary Arguments

This chapter argues that the original dissent which created the first hybrid tribunals, such as the Special Court for Sierra Leone (SCSL) and the Extraordinary Chambers in the Courts of Cambodia (ECCC), is distinct from the more recent dissent which inspired the re-emergence of hybrid justice despite the existence of the ICC. The original dissent, which contributed to the creation of the first wave of hybrid courts, was due to growing criticism of the UN ad hoc tribunals for the former Yugoslavia and Rwanda, namely due to their high cost, restricted mandates, inability to respond to victim needs, and protracted trials.[1] This first wave of hybrid courts included the hybrid courts for Sierra Leone, Cambodia, East Timor, Bosnia, and Lebanon.[2]

The re-emergence of hybrid justice in more recent years through the established or proposed courts for/in Senegal, Kosovo, South Sudan, the Central African Republic (CAR), Ukraine, Sri Lanka, and the Islamic State (ISIS/ISIL/Da'esh/IS) is due to more generalized dissent which has been expressed in recent years over the perceived inadequacy of globalized justice responses such as the ICC and the neo-colonial nature of international intervention. Whilst the original hybrid courts were created in the search for new justice responses, as more efficient and democratic alternatives to the UN ad hoc tribunals for the former Yugoslavia and Rwanda, the re-emergence of hybrid courts in recent years is due to the increasing prioritization of the local over the international and a reclaiming of justice responses by the state.

State dissent in international criminal justice can be either situational or external. For example, the state in which conflict took place (the situation state) can express dissent over the hybrid court. However, states external to the situation, but still involved in some respects such as through being a member of the UN, a funding state, or merely an influential state whose actions impact the

[1] See UNSC Res 827 (25 May 1993) UN Doc S/RES/827; UNSC Res 955 (8 November 1994) UN Doc S/RES/955; Brian Frederking, *The United States and the Security Council: Collective Security since the Cold War* (Routledge 2007) 97.

[2] See, eg, Agreement between the United Nations and the Government of Sierra Leone on the establishment of a Special Court for Sierra Leone (signed 16 January 2002, entered into force 12 April 2002) 2178 UNTS 138 (SCSL Agreement); Agreement between the United Nations and the Royal Government of Cambodia Concerning the Prosecution under Cambodian Law of Crimes Committed During the Period of Democratic Kampuchea (signed 6 June 2003, entered into force 29 April 2005) 2329 UNTS 117 (ECCC Agreement).

international community can also dissent. Both types of dissent are influential on the outcome of the hybrid justice process. This chapter focuses on the behaviour of the host state of the hybrid, whilst also noting the influence of external dissent on the hybrid court (which could include the situation state if the hybrid is not hosted within it).

This chapter also looks at how dissent at other international criminal justice initiatives has affected the hybrid courts. Dissent with regard to the work of the Yugoslav and Rwandan tribunals resulted in the creation of the hybrid courts. Similarly, with dissent from the ICC becoming increasingly vocal, hybrid justice has regained its place in the forefront of responses to international crime despite the fact that none of the original wave of hybrid courts are particularly compelling examples of successful international justice.

An analysis of dissent is a valuable method to better understand not only international criminal justice, but also more specifically the creation of hybrid courts. It also enables the better comprehension of why hybrid courts were established in the first wave and why those original courts faced considerable challenges throughout their mandates. Such an analysis also highlights why there has been a renewed interest in this type of justice response rather than states looking solely towards the ICC to respond to international crimes. These issues will be discussed below with a view to improving and reforming newly emerging hybrid courts.

5.3 Definitions

For something to be described or defined as 'hybrid' means that it is the compilation of two things, a joint effort, a collaboration. The labelling of internationalized courts as hybrid highlights their character as collaborative ventures, usually between an international entity and a host state, rather than as purely domestic or international initiatives. This collaboration is seen as being beneficial to the host state, whilst still being directed to some extent by the international community. In this context, the labelling of a court as 'hybrid' responds to accusations that international courts are neo-colonial. If the court is hybrid, then in theory it is not neo-colonial, as the situation state has a significant role within it as long as it hosts the court. Whilst all of the courts mentioned in the introduction through the first and second waves of internationalized hybrid courts are hybrid in that they are collaborations, the extent of cooperation differs depending on each particular court. Each one is distinct and influenced by the circumstances of the court's establishment, including the political climate, culture, conflict history, time, and logistical support.

The relationship between the court and the host state is particularly influential in the character and outcomes of the hybrid court. As distinct from the creation of the UN ad hoc tribunals, the hybrid courts are established generally through agreements that involve more than one stakeholder. For example, the SCSL and

ECCC were both established pursuant to agreements between the post-conflict state and the UN.[3] The Special Tribunal for Lebanon (STL) was intended to be established pursuant to a similar agreement, however due to government opposition, as will be discussed more fully in this chapter, the Tribunal was established by the UN Security Council.[4] The South Sudan hybrid court was proposed in the 2015 South Sudan peace agreement and 2018 peace accord, to be established by the Sudanese government in collaboration with the African Union (AU).[5] These are all differing paths towards the establishment of hybrid courts, however they all involve the input and cooperation of multiple stakeholders in concert with the host state. The key international stakeholder is often the UN but has also been the AU. This means that it is not a relationship merely between two states, but rather between a state and an entity or arguably an 'authority'. This important relationship comprises the wielding of both state and institutional power and the joining of two authorities with differing levels and types of influence to further a justice goal.

The relationship between the state and the 'authority' in the creation of a hybrid court is highly influential on the character of the court and on the outcomes of the justice process. Such a relationship inspires a situation where historical and current-day power dynamics are played out in the establishment of a hybrid court, where there is a testing of authority and power and a conflict between competing interests, despite the relationship being pursued through intentions to collaborate and facilitate. This makes the relationship between the host state and the 'authority' at times contentious, giving rise to accusations of the potential encroachment on the host state by the authority, leading to the pushing back on that authority by the host state and the resultant conflict and instability at the hybrid court that infringes on the judicial process.

In the context of the establishment of hybrid courts and the difficult position that the host state finds itself in having to negotiate a justice response with an external authority that is in theory a partner in the establishment process, there are a range of responses from the state to the establishment and work of the hybrid court. These responses fall loosely into three categories: support, acquiescence, and dissent. State responses, of course, have far greater nuance than this, however for the purposes of analysis it is useful to look at state behaviour through these three broad categories of response.

[3] SCSL Agreement (n 2); ECCC Agreement (n 2). UN Security Council Resolution 1315 requested that the UN Secretary General commence negotiations with Sierra Leone with a view to establishing the SCSL: UNSC Res 1315 (14 August 2000) UN Doc S/RES/1315. UN Security Council Resolution 57/228 urged the UN Secretary General and Cambodia to implement the draft Agreement following its entry into force to establish the ECCC: UNGA Res 57/228 (18 December 2002) UN Doc A/RES/57/228.

[4] UNSC Res 1757 (30 May 2007) UN Doc S/RES/1757.

[5] Elise Keppler, 'South Sudan's Cynical Bid to Block War Crimes Court' (*Human Rights Watch*, 30 April 2019) <https://www.hrw.org/news/2019/04/30/south-sudans-cynical-bid-block-war-crimes-court> accessed 23 December 2023.

'Support' in the context of hybrid justice encompasses a range of responses from simple agreement to active engagement with the justice process. Support can mean to actively assist something in coming to fruition, whether that is logistically, financially, or politically. It could mean to ensure that the creation and work of the court is not hindered by political interests that are in opposition to the court's work. Acquiescence is the reluctant acceptance of something without actively protesting or objecting to it. It can also mean to comply without creating difficulties or obvious impediments to the process, but in the absence of exhibiting active support. It comprises elements of both support and dissent, because to agree to the establishment of a hybrid court requires a degree of support, whilst the failure to actively engage in the court evidences an element of dissent. A state may exhibit acquiescence with regard to a hybrid justice initiative because they have no other option other than to agree to the creation of the court due to political or economic pressure that is being placed on them by a global authority or another state. In this context they might accept the development and then express dissent following creation.

Finally, dissent is the antithesis of support. To dissent means to disagree and to stand in opposition to something. The dissent of a state in response to the creation of a hybrid court can be both obvious, but also covert. More obviously dissent could be expressed through a state being unwilling to take part in the justice process such as being unwilling to sign the agreement, or even once signing has occurred being unwilling to ratify it. It means being unwilling to implement the terms of the agreement, or even working actively to undermine those terms as an act of dissent in opposition to the justice process. This chapter does not focus on judicial dissent in the legal sense, but rather state dissent.

5.4 Historical Continuum

In assessing state responses to modern international crime since the establishment of the International Criminal Tribunal for the former Yugoslavia (ICTY), support, acquiescence, and dissent can be signposted more broadly on a historical continuum of international justice. In short, modern international criminal justice began in the 1990s with general state support for the project as evidenced through the UN Security Council voting to establish the ad hoc tribunals for the former Yugoslavia and Rwanda.[6] However this support moved onto acquiescence and is currently arguably in the midst of dissent. Assessing this continuum facilitates a

[6] See the discussions and voting records of UN member states on the establishment of the ICTY and ICTR: UNSC Provisional Verbatim Record of the Three Thousand Two Hundred and Seventeenth Meeting (25 May 1993) UN Doc S/PV/3217; UNSC 3453rd meeting (8 November 1994) UN Doc S/PV/3453.

better understanding of hybrid justice because these state responses and in particular state dissent have contributed to the creation, failings, and re-emergence of hybrid courts. This trajectory of international criminal justice also highlights issues with the establishment and work of the ICC and the future of international criminal justice more generally.

Following World War II, the Nuremberg and Tokyo trials were created to respond to the crimes that had been committed, however it was not until the early 1990s when what is understood to be modern international criminal justice came into being.[7] With the creation of the ICTY and the International Criminal Tribunal for Rwanda (ICTR) there was a revival of international criminal justice and an initial lauding of the international criminal justice project.[8] There was limited vocal dissent at this stage from affected states, at least comparatively to more recent dissent that has been evidenced at the ICC, because the ability of situation state governments to push back on these initiatives was limited. To dissent requires at least some degree of autonomy and power, which was lacking following the wars in the former Yugoslavia and the Rwandan genocide.[9]

As time progressed, the international criminal justice project shifted to acquiescence on the part of the situation states, with states agreeing to the justice process in theory whilst in practice exhibiting evidence of veiled opposition to the project. For example, Rwanda's failure to vote for the creation of the ICTR in the UN Security Council and its later challenges to the Tribunal's authority, with the country creating obstacles when the Tribunal required the assistance of Rwanda to transport witnesses to the seat of the Tribunal in Arusha, Tanzania.[10] This shift from support to acquiescence with respect to the UN ad hoc tribunals continued with the creation of the first wave of hybrid courts.

The creation of the original hybrid courts including Sierra Leone and Cambodia sit on the timeline of international justice as arguable acquiescence of situation/host states (which was the same in these cases). Without state and UN collaboration these courts would not have been established due to both the intentions of the international community to create hybrid courts and also the disinclination of these states to be the subject of purely UN ad hoc tribunals in the form of the ICTY and ICTR. During the tense negotiations between Cambodia and the UN,

[7] Yves Beigbeder, *International Justice against Impunity: Progress and New Challenges* (Martinus Nijhoff 2005) 70.

[8] Mark Kersten, *Justice in Conflict: The Effects of the International Criminal Court's Interventions on Ending Wars and Building Peace* (Oxford University Press 2016) 2.

[9] Regarding the destruction of Rwanda following the genocide, see Barbara Oomen, 'Justice Mechanisms and the Question of Legitimacy: The Example of Rwanda's Multi-Layered Justice Mechanisms' in Kai Ambos, Judith Large, and Marieke Wierda (eds), *Building a Future on Peace and Justice: Studies on Transitional Justice, Peace and Development the Nuremberg Declaration on Peace and Justice* (Springer 2008) 175, 192.

[10] LJ van den Herik, *The Contribution of the Rwandan Tribunal to the Development of International Law* (Martinus Nijhoff 2005) 43.

Cambodia had one particular vision for the Court, whilst the UN had another.[11] However, for the Court to be established there needed to be certain concessions on both sides, resulting in a degree of acquiescence that had ramifications for the remainder of the Court's mandate.

With the creation of the ICC, there has been a considerable rise in dissent in response to not only the ICC itself, but also international criminal courts and tribunals more generally.[12] The ICC was established following the creation of the UN ad hoc tribunals and alongside the original hybrid courts, inspired by criticism over the frailties of those original justice initiatives.[13] Initial support for the ICC has ceded to criticism, which has affected the ICC and also trust in global responses to international crime.[14] The ICC has been accused of being anti-African, with allegations that prosecutions are directed towards African states and individuals.[15] The Court has also been accused of failing to act pursuant to the rule of law and for not conducting fair trials.[16] Whilst the ICC was intended to serve as an overarching and primary response to international crime, the Court's frailties have instead contributed to the dispersal of international justice initiatives away from a singular central court to the renewed creation of hybrid courts.

5.5 Concurrent Support, Acquiescence, and Dissent

5.5.1 First wave hybrid courts

Three responses to international criminal justice: support, acquiescence, and dissent, not only exist along a historical continuum showing the path of international criminal justice, they also co-exist concurrently within each justice response. At each hybrid court there is a different expression of state dissent and in some instances a deficit of dissent. A selection of the key issues relating to state dissent at each of the first wave and second wave hybrid courts will be discussed in the following sections.

[11] The Aspen Institute, 'Trying Atrocity Crimes: The Khmer Rouge Trials, Transitional Justice, and the Rule of Law' (7 November 2013) <http://www.aspeninstitute.org/video/trying-atrocity-crimes-khmer-rouge-trials-transitional-justice-rule-law> accessed 23 December 2023.

[12] Solomon A Dersso, 'The ICC's Africa Problem: A Spotight on the Politics and Limits of International Criminal Justice' in Kamari Clarke, Abel S Knottnerus, and Eefje de Volder (eds), *Africa and the ICC: Perceptions of Justice* (Cambridge University Press 2016) 61, 63.

[13] See Rome Statute of the International Criminal Court (opened for signature 17 July 1998, entered into force 1 July 2002) 2187 UNTS 90.

[14] Geert-Jan Alexander Knoops, 'Introductory Note' in Giuliana Ziccardi Capaldo (ed), *The Global Community Yearbook of International Law and Jurisprudence 2016* (Oxford University Press 2017) 384.

[15] Dersso (n 12) 63.

[16] See Christopher Soler, *The Global Prosecution of Core Crimes under International Law* (Springer 2019) 258.

When looking at the ECCC, which was established in 2003, support, acquiescence, and dissent simultaneously exist as state responses to the Court, with the focus of these responses changing throughout the Court's mandate. Like the other hybrid courts, the ECCC was established with a view that it would be a collaborative venture.[17] The Cambodian government initially sought the assistance of the UN in establishing a court to prosecute crimes committed by the Khmer Rouge.[18] Despite this initial support, as time progressed the response of the Cambodian government turned to acquiescence and then dissent.[19] Negotiations between Cambodia and the UN were impeded and protracted because the Cambodian government pushed back against the UN.[20] This reflects the difficulty in establishing a hybrid court where there must be either agreement or concession between the two parties. Ultimately the ECCC was established within the Cambodian legal system but as an independent entity.[21]

A significant point of contention between the Cambodian government and the UN was the prosecution of more than two cases at the ECCC, with dissent expressed by the Cambodian government in relation to the prosecution of Cases 003 and 004.[22] Both the Cambodian Prime Minister Hun Sen and the Cambodian Co-Prosecutor at the ECCC have expressed dissent and have spoken out against further prosecutions, undermining the ability of the Court to fully respond to the crimes committed by the Khmer Rouge.[23] Hun Sen famously said that if international lawyers wanted to prosecute Cases 003 and 004 they should 'just pack their bags and return home'.[24]

There have been accusations that the Cambodian government has expressed dissent regarding Cases 003 and 004 because those individuals who are implicated have high positions within the current Cambodian political and social structure. These challenges highlight the difficulty in operating a collaborative justice venture and the role of state dissent in fostering a sense of conflict between the post conflict state and the authority they must work with to materialize the agreement.

17 ECCC Agreement (n 2).

18 Christian Tomuschat, *Human Rights: Between Idealism and Realism* (3rd edn, Oxford University Press 2014) 387.

19 The Aspen Institute, 'Trying Atrocity Crimes' (n 11).

20 Tomuschat (n 18).

21 *Kaing Guek Eav (Duch)* (Order of Provisional Detention) 001/18-07-2007/ECCC-C3 (31 July 2007) [20]; *Kaing Guek Eav (Duch)* (Decision on Request for Release) 001/18-07-2007/ECCC-E39/5 15 June 2009 [10].

22 Viviane E Dittrich, 'The Legacy of the ECCC' in Ignaz Stegmiller and Simon M. Meisenberg (eds), *The Extraordinary Chambers in the Courts of Cambodia: Assessing Their Contribution to International Criminal Law* (Springer 2016) 123, 146; Kirsten Ainley, 'Transitional Justice in Cambodia: The Coincidence of Power and Principle' in Renée Jeffery and Hun Joon Kim (eds), *Transitional Justice in the Asia-Pacific* (Cambridge University Press 2014) 136.

23 Ainley (n 22) 136.

24 Human Rights Watch, 'Cambodia: Stop Blocking Justice for Khmer Rouge Crimes: UN, Donors Should End Tribunal Support Unless Charges Pursued' (22 March 2015) <https://www.hrw.org/news/2015/03/22/cambodia-stop-blocking-justice-khmer-rouge-crimes> accessed 23 December 2023.

Continued dissent by the Cambodian government, particularly in the form of political interference, undermines the work of the ECCC, which affects both the internal resilience of the Court, but also its ability to foster external resilience in the community.[25] The dissent of the Cambodian government resulted in conflict between the Cambodian and international sides of the Court, which stalled the justice process, calling into question the integrity of the ECCC and its decisions. This arguably damaged the perception of the Court in the eyes of the Cambodian people and the international community more generally.

Another prominent hybrid court that was part of the initial wave of courts was the SCSL, which was established in 2002 by agreement between the UN and the government of Sierra Leone to prosecute those responsible for crimes committed during the Sierra Leone civil war.[26] Whilst technically a hybrid court, in practice, the SCSL was more akin to the UN ad hoc tribunals for the ICTY and ICTR. It operated more in terms of a UN directed court, as opposed to the more collaborative ECCC. When there was collaboration, the Sierra Leonean government cooperated more effectively with the SCSL than was illustrated in the ECCC context.[27] Despite this relatively easy relationship between Sierra Leone and the UN, there were significant impediments to the work of the SCSL, which caused commentators to question the Court's legitimacy and its effectiveness.[28] The SCSL is an example of insufficient dissent from the situation and host state in the face of the attempted influence from external Western states, which resulted in accusations such as that the Charles Taylor trial was a Western directed show trial.[29]

Also established as part of the original wave of hybrid courts, the Special Panels in the District Court in Dili were created in 2000, following Indonesia's twenty-four years of occupation of East Timor and its subsequent independence.[30] The Special

[25] Open Society Justice Initiative (OSJI), 'Political Interference at the Extraordinary Chambers in the Courts of Cambodia' (6 July 2010) <https://www.opensocietyfoundations.org/sites/default/files/political-interference-courts-cambodia-20100706.pdf> accessed 23 December 2023.

[26] Roger O'Keefe, *International Criminal Law* (Oxford University Press 2015) 92; SCSL Agreement (n 2).

[27] Linda E Carter, Mark S Ellis, and Charles Chernor Jalloh, *The International Criminal Court in an Effective Global Justice System* (Edward Elgar 2016) 108.

[28] See Adam Robert Green, 'Sierra Leone: Western Interests Undermined Integrity of Charles Taylor Trial - Interview with Courtenay Griffiths QC' (*All Africa*, 28 May 2012) <http://allafrica.com/stories/201205280815.html> accessed 20 January 2023; Sara Webb, 'Former Liberian President Taylor Should be a "Free Man": Judge' (*Reuters*, 26 November 2012) <https://www.reuters.com/article/us-sierraleone-taylor-judge-idUSBRE8AO09F20121125> accessed 23 December 2023; Wayne Jordash and Scott Martin, 'Due Process and Fair Trial Rights at the Special Court: How the Desire for Accountability Outweighed the Demands of Justice at the Special Court for Sierra Leone' (2010) 23 Leiden Journal of International Law 585.

[29] See regarding allegations against the Taylor prosecution in Webb (n 28).

[30] Francisco Forrest Martin and others, *International Human Rights and Humanitarian Law: Treaties, Cases, and Analysis* (Cambridge University Press 2006) 21; Suzannah Linton, 'Rising from the Ashes: The Creation of a Visible Criminal Justice System in East Timor' (2001) 25 Melbourne University Law Review 122, 126; Yves Beigbeder, *International Criminal Tribunals: Justice and Politics* (Palgrave Macmillan 2011) 109; David Cohen, 'Indifference and Accountability: The United Nations and the Politics of International Justice in East Timor' (*East-West Center*, 1 June 2006) <https://www.

Panels derived from the United Nations Transitional Administration in East Timor (UNTAET), which was established by the UN Security Council in 1999.[31] Dissent was exhibited at this court through the failure of the Indonesian government to cooperate with prosecutions.[32] There was also a lack of support for the Special Panels in East Timor.[33] As a result, this dissent affected the justice the court was able to disseminate. David Cohen has stated that: '[t]he Special Panels for Serious Crimes tried eighty-seven defendants. According to UN statistics, of these, 83 were convicted at trial of crimes against humanity or other charges ... This represents a 97.7 per cent conviction rate, a matter for some concern.'[34] Furthermore, the international judges on the Special Panels were criticized by the General Prosecutor, placing the hybrid court under stress.[35]

The Bosnia War Crimes Court, more formally known as the War Crimes Chamber in Bosnia and Herzegovina was established in Sarajevo on 9 March 2005 to prosecute crimes committed during the 1992–1995 conflict in Bosnia.[36] The Bosnia War Crimes Court is a collaboration between the ICTY and the Office of the High Representative for Bosnia and Herzegovina.[37] The Court is situated within the judiciary of Bosnia and resides under the auspices of the country's national law.[38] The ICTY was established to prosecute those most responsible for crimes committed in the Yugoslav wars, however this additional domestic hybrid court was thought to provide a more comprehensive justice response to the crimes that had been committed in the Balkans.[39] Human Rights Watch revealed that

eastwestcenter.org/publications/indifference-and-accountability-the-united-nations-and-the-politics-international> accessed 23 December 2023.

[31] ASPNet Policy Forum, 'Indonesia and East Timor: Against Impunity, For Justice' (24 April 2008) <https://nautilus.org/apsnet/indonesia-and-east-timor-against-impunity-for-justice/> accessed 23 December 2023; Suzannah Linton, 'Prosecuting Atrocities at the District Court of Dili' (2001) 2 Melbourne Journal of International Law 414, 415.

[32] Beigbeder (n 30) 109; Wayne Sandholtz, 'Creating Authority by the Council: The International Criminal Tribunals' in Bruce Cronin and Ian Hurd (eds), *The UN Security Council and the Politics of International Authority* (Routledge 2008) 131, 146.

[33] See David Cohen, '"Justice on the Cheap" Revisited: The Failure of the Serious Crimes Trials in East Timor' (*East-West Center*, 1 May 2006) <https://www.eastwestcenter.org/publications/justice-cheap-revisited-failure-serious-crimes-trials-east-timor> accessed 23 December 2023.

[34] Cohen, 'Indifference and Accountability' (n 30) 11–12.

[35] ASPNet Policy Forum, 'Indonesia and East Timor' (n 31); Cohen (n 33) 2.

[36] Faris Vehabović, 'Bosnia and Herzegovina: Impact of the Case Law of the European Court of Human Rights on Postconflict Society of Bosnia and Herzegovina' in Iulia Motoc and Ineta Ziemele (eds), *The Impact of the ECHR on Democratic Change in Central and Eastern Europe: Judicial Perspectives* (Cambridge University Press 2016) 80, 101; Avril McDonald, 'Bosnia's War Crimes Chamber and the Challenges of an Opening and Closure' in José Doria, Hans-Peter Gasser, and M Cherif Bassiouni (eds), *The Legal Regime of the International Criminal Court: Essays in Honour of Professor Igor Blishchenko: In Memoriam Professor Igor Pavlovich Blishchenko (1930-2000)* (Martinus Nijhoff 2009) 297.

[37] McDonald, 'Bosnia's War Crimes Chamber' (n 36).

[38] Human Rights Watch, 'Justice for Atrocity Crimes' (12 March 2012) <https://www.hrw.org/report/2012/03/12/justice-atrocity-crimes/lessons-international-support-trials-state-court-bosnia> accessed 23 December 2023.

[39] ibid.

through conducting interviews it found many individuals who believed that 'from the outset, the international community and the Bosnian authorities had no strategic vision to maximize the benefits of international staff'.[40] This reinforces the importance of the post-conflict state and the authority working together, rather than in opposition, to establish and operate hybrid courts.

The establishment of the STL is another example of state support and then dissent. The tribunal was established to prosecute those responsible for the 2005 assassination of the former Prime Minister of Lebanon, Rafik Hariri.[41] The Lebanese government sought international assistance to determine what would be required to prosecute these crimes with the resultant advice being that a hybrid court pursuant to an agreement between the UN and Lebanon should be established.[42] The UN Security Council requested that the Secretary-General 'negotiate an agreement with the Government of Lebanon aimed at establishing a tribunal of an international character based on the highest international standards of criminal justice'.[43] An agreement was signed by the UN and Lebanon in early 2007, however in order for the agreement to enter into force it was necessary for it to be ratified by the Lebanese government.[44] Exhibiting a move from support to dissent, the Speaker failed to convene the Lebanese parliament, therefore the agreement did not become law through domestic measures.[45] The UN then took decisive action pursuant to Chapter VII of the UN Charter, as had occurred with the establishment of the ICTY and ICTR and established the STL in 2007 through a UN Security Council Resolution.[46]

5.5.2 Second wave hybrid courts

Newer hybrids, which could be termed 'second wave' feature considerable state dissent in their establishment and in some circumstances this state dissent was pivotal to their failure to be established. Second wave hybrids are the result of state dissent in response to the ICC. Whilst it was thought that hybrid courts would no longer be a useful justice mechanism following the establishment and fully functioning of the ICC, we have now seen a resurgence in the establishment of hybrid courts, arguably as a turn back towards nationally driven justice mechanisms.

[40] ibid.

[41] Malcolm N Shaw, *International Law* (8th edn, Cambridge University Press 2017) 313.

[42] ibid.

[43] Nicolas Michel, 'The Creation of the Tribunal in Its Context' in Amal Alamuddin, Nidal Nabil Jurdi, and David Tolbert (eds), *The Special Tribunal for Lebanon: Law and Practice* (Oxford University Press 2014) 10, 17; UNSC Res 1664 (29 March 2006) UN Doc S/RES/1664.

[44] Sarah Williams, *Hybrid and Internationalised Criminal Tribunals: Selected Jurisdictional Issues* (Bloomsbury 2012) 76.

[45] ibid.

[46] Shaw (n 41) 313; UNSC Res 1757 (n 4).

Opening in 2013, the Extraordinary African Chambers (EAC) in Senegal was located within the domestic courts of Senegal to bring to justice international crimes committed in Chad between 1982 and 1990, specifically those committed by the former Chadian president Hessène Habré.[47] The Court was established by agreement between the AU and Senegal in 2012, rendering it a hybrid court.[48] The court was established with a view that it would be an example of African ownership of criminal justice processes. The Court could therefore be read as being inspired by African, and specifically AU, dissent over the ICC.[49]

In another example, following international pressure, to establish a court to prosecute international crimes committed by ethnic Albanian guerrillas during the 1998–1999 Kosovo War, the Kosovo Specialist Chambers (KSC) was established in 2015 by Kosovo's parliament.[50] The Court, which is located in The Hague, but established under Kosovo law, has a mandate to try crimes, including war crimes and crimes against humanity, committed during and in the aftermath of the Kosovo war.[51] The KSC became operational in 2017.[52]

The KSC is hearing cases against individuals, including those who were formerly members of the Kosovo Liberation Army (KLA).[53] Former members of the KLA have served in the Kosovo government, which presents an avenue for possible state dissent.[54] Also impeding trials in Kosovo and representing an avenue for potential dissent is that Kosovo is a largely ethnic Albanian country, therefore prosecuting crimes committed by Albanians is controversial.[55] In 2018, there were reports that members of the government of Kosovo had sought to repeal the law

[47] Human Rights Watch, 'Statute of the Extraordinary African Chambers' (2 September 2013) <https://www.hrw.org/news/2013/09/02/statute-extraordinary-african-chambers> accessed 23 December 2023. See also Kerstin Carlson, 'A New African Pluralism in International Criminal Law: Sovereign Immunity and the Trial of Hissène Habré' in this volume.

[48] Carlson (n 47).

[49] See BBC News, 'African Union Backs Mass Withdrawal from ICC' (1 February 2017) <https://www.bbc.com/news/world-africa-38826073> accessed 23 December 2023; The Guardian, 'African Leaders Plan Mass Withdrawal from International Criminal Court' (Addis Ababa, 1 February 2017) <https://www.theguardian.com/law/2017/jan/31/african-leaders-plan-mass-withdrawal-from-international-criminal-court> accessed 23 December 2023. See also Kamari M Clarke, Abel S Knottnerus, and Eefje de Volder, 'Africa and the ICC: An Introduction' in Kamari M Clarke, Abel S Knottnerus, and Eefje de Volder (eds), *Africa and the ICC: Perceptions of Justice* (Cambridge University Press 2016) 1, 1. See re: pushback in Africa regarding the prosecution of sitting leaders in Carlson, 'Hissène Habré' (n 47).

[50] Barbara Surk, 'World's Eyes on Kosovo Amid Push to Halt War Crimes Court' (*New York Times*, 13 January 2018) <https://www.nytimes.com/2018/01/13/world/europe/kosovo-war-crimes-court.html> accessed 23 December 2023.

[51] See Law on the Specialist Chambers and Specialist Prosecutor's Office (3 August 2015) Articles 13 and 14.

[52] Kosovo Specialist Chambers & Specialist Prosecutor's Office, 'Specialist Chambers Fully Operational' (5 July 2017) <https://www.scp-ks.org/en/specialist-chambers-fully-judicially-operational> accessed 23 December 2023.

[53] Caleb W Wheeler, *The Right to Be Present at Trial in International Criminal Law* (Brill Nijhoff 2018) 250; Surk (n 50).

[54] Surk (n 50).

[55] ibid.

that established the court, expressing obstructive state dissent.[56] The KSC undertook a protracted period of investigation[57] and only in 2020 was the first indictment issued.[58]

A peace agreement was signed in South Sudan in 2015 which included the establishment of a hybrid court to prosecute crimes that were committed during the civil war.[59] The establishment of this court was affirmed in the 2018 revitalization of the peace agreement.[60] Despite a hybrid court being mandated in the peace agreement, its establishment has been hindered through the dissent and opposition of the South Sudan government.[61] In a 2019 letter to the government of South Sudan and the African Union, Human Rights Watch urged that there should be a meeting on the issue with key stakeholders to 'chart a course forward'.[62] The South Sudan court would potentially prosecute current government officials, resulting in government opposition to the court. As of November 2022, Amnesty International and the South Sudanese Transitional Justice Working Group (TJWG) were calling on the AU to establish the court unilaterally in another African state with the option, if the situation improves on the ground in South Sudan, to hold hearings in or to establish the court in the country.[63]

Another new hybrid justice mechanism is the Special Criminal Court in the Central African Republic (SCC).[64] The SCC focuses on genocide, war crimes, and crimes against humanity committed since 2003.[65] In August 2014, the UN signed a memorandum of understanding with the transitional government of the CAR with

[56] ibid; United Nations, 'Attempts to Repeal Law on Kosovo Chambers a Grave Concern, Special Representative Tells Security Council Amid Calls for Continued High-Level Dialogue' (7 February 2018) <https://press.un.org/en/2018/sc13199.doc.htm> accessed 23 December 2023.

[57] Marija Ristic, 'Hague Prosecutors to Issue Kosovo War Crimes Indictments Soon' (*Balkan Transitional Justice*, 24 February 2020) <https://balkaninsight.com/2020/02/24/hague-prosecutor-soon-to-launch-kosovo-trials/> accessed 23 December 2023.

[58] Kosovo Specialist Chambers & Specialist Prosecutor's Office, 'Press Statement' (24 June 2020) <https://www.scp-ks.org/en/press-statement> accessed 23 December 2023.

[59] Rob Grace, 'Lessons from the Two Regional Missions: Fact-Finding in Georgia and South Sudan' in Christian Henderson (ed), *Commissions of Inquiry: Problems and Prospects* (Bloomsbury 2017) 65, 76.

[60] United Nations, 'Security Council Cautiously Commends South Sudan Revitalised Peace Agreement amid Concerns over Commitment of Signatories to Implementation' (18 September 2018) <https://press.un.org/en/2018/sc13510.doc.htm> accessed 23 December 2023.

[61] Human Rights Watch, 'South Sudan: Establish Hybrid Court and Facilitate Work of UN Rights Commission' (18 September 2017) <https://www.hrw.org/news/2017/09/18/south-sudan-establish-hybrid-court-and-facilitate-work-un-rights-commission> accessed 23 December 2023; Amnesty International, 'South Sudan: African Union Must Set Precedent for African-led Justice by Establishing Court for South Sudan' (23 November 2022) <https://www.amnesty.org/en/latest/news/2022/11/south-sudan-african-union-must-set-precedent-for-african-led-justice-by-establishing-court-for-south-sudan/> accessed 23 December 2023.

[62] Human Rights Watch, 'Re: Proposed Meeting between South Sudan and African Union Representatives to Address Hybrid Court for South Sudan' (30 September 2019) <https://www.hrw.org/sites/default/files/supporting_resources/hrw_letter_to_ss_authorities.pdf> accessed 23 December 2023.

[63] Amnesty International, 'South Sudan: African Union Must Set Precedent' (n 61).

[64] Patryk Labuda, 'The Special Criminal Court in the Central African Republic' (*ASIL*, 22 January 2018) <https://www.asil.org/insights/volume/22/issue/2/special-criminal-court-central-african-republic> accessed 23 December 2023.

[65] ibid.

a view to establishing a hybrid court.[66] In June 2015 a law was adopted by the CAR government to establish the court, which resides within the national judiciary of the country.[67] Dissent was exhibited when no investigations were possible until May 2018 when parliament finally adopted the Court's rules of procedure and evidence and then held its inaugural session in October 2018.[68] The first trial at the Court began in April 2022,[69] with the judgment delivered in October of that year.[70]

In other examples, a hybrid court may potentially be established through the collaboration of the UN and Ukraine to prosecute the crimes committed by Russia including the 2020 Russian invasion of Ukraine[71] and the shooting down of Malaysia Airlines flight MH17 in 2014.[72] The tense relationship between Ukraine and Russia and the probable dissent of the latter renders such a development uncertain.[73] There has however been the domestic prosecutions of the MH17 matter in The Netherlands,[74] and the ICC is investigating international crimes committed in Ukraine.[75] There have also been calls for a Special Tribunal for the Crime of Aggression as a response to the Russian invasion of Ukraine.[76]

Turning to Sri Lanka, the UN has repeatedly requested that Sri Lanka establish a hybrid court to prosecute crimes against humanity and war crimes in the country.[77] Despite this, Sri Lanka has repeatedly stalled the process and expressed open dissent, despite co-sponsoring UN Human Rights Council resolutions

66 ibid.

67 Human Rights Watch, 'Central African Republic: Support the Special Criminal Court' (16 November 2016) <https://www.hrw.org/news/2016/11/16/central-african-republic-support-special-criminal-court> accessed 23 December 2023.

68 Human Rights Watch, 'Central African Republic: New Court Should Step Up Effort' (24 July 2019) <https://www.hrw.org/news/2019/07/24/central-african-republic-new-court-should-step-effort> accessed 23 December 2023.

69 Human Rights Watch, 'Central African Republic: First Trial at the Special Criminal Court: Questions and Answers' (12 April 2022) <https://www.hrw.org/news/2022/04/12/central-african-republic-first-trial-special-criminal-court> accessed 23 December 2023.

70 Vianney Ingasso, 'Central African Republic: Special Criminal Court Hands Down First Judgment' (*Justiceinfo.net*, 1 November 2022) <https://www.justiceinfo.net/en/108356-central-african-republic-special-criminal-court-first-judgment.html> accessed 23 December 2023.

71 Matthew Mpoke Bigg, 'How Russia's War in Ukraine has Unfolded Month by Month' (*New York Times*, 24 February 2023) <https://www.nytimes.com/article/ukraine-russia-war-timeline.html> accessed 23 December 2023.

72 Monique Cormier, 'A Long Road Until Justice Served' (*Pursuit: University of Melbourne Law School*, 18 October 2015) <https://pursuit.unimelb.edu.au/articles/a-long-road-until-justice-served> accessed 23 December 2023.

73 ibid.

74 Anna Holligan and Kate Vandy, 'MH17: Three Guilty as Court Finds Russia-Controlled Group Downed Airliner' (*BBC News*, 17 November 2022) <https://www.bbc.com/news/world-europe-63637625> accessed 23 December 2023.

75 ICC, 'Ukraine' <https://www.icc-cpi.int/ukraine> accessed 23 December 2023.

76 Patrick Wintour, 'UK Offers Qualified Backing for Tribunal to Prosecute Russia's Leaders' (*The Guardian*, 21 January 2023) <https://www.theguardian.com/politics/2023/jan/20/uk-offers-qualified-backing-special-tribunal-to-prosecute-russia-leaders-putin-ukraine> accessed 23 December 2023.

77 UNHRC Res 30/1 'Promoting Reconciliation, Accountability and Human Rights in Sri Lanka' (adopted 1 October 2015) A/HRC/RES/30/1; Amnesty International, 'Sri Lanka: New Human Rights Council Resolution Must Lead to Faster Progress' (21 March 2019) <https://www.amnesty.org/en/latest/news/2019/03/sri-lanka-new-human-rights-council-resolution-must-lead-to-faster-progress/> accessed 23 December 2023.

asking the country to establish the court.[78] This situation is therefore indicative of dissent through stalling, as opposed to open dissent. In September 2022, four international human rights organizations, including Amnesty International and Human Rights Watch, called for the adoption of a 'strong resolution' by the Human Rights Council which would renew the commitment to establishing a hybrid court for Sri Lanka.[79]

The October 2022 resolution did not mention the establishment of a hybrid court specifically but does recall past commitments through resolutions to do so and emphasizes 'the importance of a comprehensive approach to dealing with the past, incorporating judicial and non-judicial measures, to ensure accountability, to serve justice, to provide remedies to victims, to avoid the recurrence of violations of human rights and to promote healing and reconciliation'. The resolution further extends and reinforces the capacity of the Office of the High Commissioner to collect and analyse evidence of human rights violations and related crimes in Sri Lanka.[80]

With the rise of ISIS and the crimes that have been committed in Syria and Iraq, there has been a movement to prosecute these crimes through a hybrid court.[81] Hybrid justice has been raised particularly because of the many challenges associated with prosecuting these crimes at the ICC and considerable political opposition by influential states in the UN Security Council, such as Russia and China.[82] Pursuant to Security Council Resolution 2379 (2017), the UN Secretary-General established the Investigative Team to Promote Accountability for Crimes Committed by Da'esh/ISIL (UNITAD).[83] While UNITAD, which began work in 2018, has assisted domestic prosecutions such as in Germany[84] and Sweden,[85] a hybrid court for ISIS has thus far not been established.[86]

[78] Amnesty International, 'Sri Lanka' (n 77).

[79] Human Rights Watch, 'Sri-Lanka—Adopt a Strong Resolution on Human Rights in Sri Lanka' (12 September 2022) <https://www.hrw.org/news/2022/09/13/sri-lanka-adopt-strong-resolution-human-rights-sri-lanka> accessed 23 December 2023.

[80] UNHRC Res 51/1 'Promoting Reconciliation, Accountability and Human Rights in Sri Lanka' (adopted 6 October 2022) A/HRC/RES/51/1.

[81] Amr Jomaa, 'Options on the Table: A Hybrid Tribunal to Prosecute ISIL Fighters' (*Justice in Conflict*, 18 September 2019) <https://justiceinconflict.org/2019/09/18/options-on-the-table-a-hybrid-tribunal-to-prosecute-isil-fighters/> accessed 23 December 2023.

[82] BBC News, 'Russia and China Veto UN Move to Refer Syria to ICC' (22 May 2014) <https://www.bbc.com/news/world-middle-east-27514256> accessed 23 December 2023.

[83] United Nations Investigative Team to Promote Accountability for Crimes Committed by Da'esh/ISIL, 'Home' <https://www.unitad.un.org> accessed 23 December 2023.

[84] United Nations Investigative Team to Promote Accountability for Crimes Committed by Da'esh/ISIL, 'UNITAD Special Adviser Christian Ritscher Welcomes Landmark Genocide Conviction of ISIL Member' (30 November 2021) <https://www.unitad.un.org/news/unitad-special-adviser-christian-ritscher-welcomes-landmark-genocide-conviction-isil-member> accessed 23 December 2023.

[85] United Nations Investigative Team to Promote Accountability for Crimes Committed by Da'esh/ISIL, 'UNITAD Welcomes Swedish Court Ruling of ISIL Woman Committing Grave Violations of International Law' <https://www.unitad.un.org/Swedish%20Conviction%20Press%20Release> accessed 23 December 2023.

[86] Anthony Dworkin, 'A Tribunal for ISIS Fighters?' (*European Council on Foreign Relations*, 31 May 2019) <https://www.ecfr.eu/article/commentary_a_tribunal_for_isis_fighters> accessed 23 December 2023.

In assessing the first and second wave hybrid courts, a number of patterns can be identified with regard to state dissent. State dissent is increasing in frequency over time and also in its ability to obstruct justice processes, both in hybrid justice mechanisms, but also in terms of international justice more generally. States currently dissent to such an extent, as has been evidenced in the most recent, second wave of hybrid courts, that there are barriers to the establishment of these courts or there is a protracted process towards establishment which hinders the justice process. On the face of it, this state dissent is in many respects an intention to protect those still in government and other high-ranking and affiliated individuals from being prosecuted. However, there is also an intention of states to want to use the justice process to their own benefit, such as to appear to be good global citizens and to appear to be pursuing justice domestically. What is also common with respect to state dissent is the belief that international justice processes can be neo-colonial and thus these states are seeking to assert state sovereignty through dissent in opposition to that perceived attempt to control the state.

5.6 Key Issues: Internal and External Resilience

In understanding dissent, how it occurs, and how it influences the creation of hybrid justice responses, it is possible to more accurately analyse the impact that hybrid justice has on external and internal resilience. External resilience is the beneficial impact the hybrid court has in the situation state. For example, to what extent the court has contributed to the strength, reconciliation, and healing of the local population through its prosecutions, trials, and judgments. An analysis of external resilience would question whether the existence of the hybrid court in a particular country contributed beneficially to the strengthening of the state both during and after the court's work.

Generally speaking, hybrid courts are designed to directly benefit the situation state. In contrast to the UN ad hoc tribunals and the ICC, hybrid courts embody an approach to international justice that is in theory more collaborative and inclusive, incorporating the views of both the international community and the host state. Hybrid courts are generally not enforced upon the situation state like the UN ad hoc tribunals, but rather they are an opportunity for cooperation. A hybrid court is said to not only benefit from, but also contribute to, capacity building in the host state. The value of hybrid justice is not generally opposed by states, but rather it has been the form and implementation of this justice that has been questioned.

In this context, the interaction between dissent and external resilience is particularly illustrative in analysing hybrid justice. When a state dissents against a domestic hybrid court, this reflects both the state's strength and resilience, but it also illustrates a lack of resilience. In theory, a state dissenting against international intervention, even when it is through collaboration, may be seen as a sign of strength and the reaffirming of the state's sovereignty. However, when a state dissents against the establishment and work of a court that they have agreed to co-create, this potentially illustrates a lack of state stability or integrity. It is incongruous, yet quite frequent for a state to express dissent against a justice mechanism they have agreed to establish as was illustrated in the previous section.

The notion of dissent is tied to the capacity and internal politics of situation states and their both open and veiled responses to hybrid justice. In terms of the original hybrid courts, there was initial support by the situation state, with both Sierra Leone and Cambodia, for example, requesting the assistance of the UN. However, as the mandates of the courts progressed, particularly with respect to the ECCC, opposition and dissent emerged which resulted in accusations that the Court had flawed justice outcomes and alleged judicial bias. There was not the same degree of opposition from the Sierra Leonean government to the SCSL, arguably because of the differences in the government's capacities when the respective courts were established.[87]

It could be said that the mere existence of the hybrid court and the state dissent that ensues actually contributes to external resilience because collaborating with an external authority to conceptualize what type of justice response the situation state deems to be appropriate and how it would like to proceed, is more collaborative rather than merely accepting an international vision of justice. As the state and the authority go through negotiations and then work together on the hybrid court, those wishes are further crystallized and redefined. Through a state being a part of the justice response and having its own views conflict at times with international opinion, this allows both the state and the authority to better understand the other.

Highlighting the connection between dissent, external resilience, and the local is that when there is an international or hybrid court established, there is also a rise in broader justice initiatives such as truth and reconciliation commissions. When a state dissents from the more formal justice process this can inspire and bolster local justice initiatives. For example, there were truth and reconciliation commissions in both Sierra Leone and East Timor and one was established in 2020 in the CAR.[88] The creation of these alternative justice processes illustrates a broader approach to justice in these countries than merely a court of law and also dissent from a solely international approach.

The tension between the host state and the external authority in establishing and operating a hybrid court raises issues of formation and law that are in

[87] See graphs and statistics on Cambodia and Sierra Leone in the early 2000s when the respective courts were established, especially GDP and GNI: World Bank, 'Cambodia' <https://data.worldbank.org/country/cambodia?view=chart> accessed 23 December 2023; World Bank, 'Sierra Leone' <https://data.worldbank.org/country/sierra-leone?view=chart> accessed 23 December 2023.

[88] Kirsten Ainley, Rebekka Friedman, and Chris Mahoney, 'Transitional justice in Sierra Leone: Theory, History and Evaluation' in Kirsten Ainley, Rebekka Friedman, and Chris Mahoney (eds), *Evaluating Transitional Justice: Accountability and Peacebuilding in Post-Conflict Sierra Leone*

contention. It publicizes these issues and forces the host state and also those who conceive of and work in hybrid justice to better understand points of contention and common areas of state dissent. This enables a better understanding of why these points of contention occur and how they can be worked through in future hybrid justice responses. In this way, understanding dissent in the area of hybrid justice, why it occurs, and how it is responded to by the external authority and the international community assists in facilitating reform in the establishment of future courts.

Disagreement between the intentions of the host state and the external authority also raises issues of power relations between states and external authorities. For example, it has been argued by numerous African leaders and also the AU that international criminal justice intervention in the African continent is excessive and disproportionate to the focus given to Western states.[89] It has been argued that responding to international crime is the responsibility of the situation state and regional actors, and that there would never be a court established to prosecute Western leaders in collaboration with an external authority, such as occurs with Africa because those Western states actually comprise and control the external authority through their influence in international and regional organizations.[90]

Internal resilience can be understood as the strength of the internal processes of a hybrid and its ability to pursue its mandate despite external pressure. State dissent is the most powerful challenge to the functioning of the court and its internal resilience. For example, the repeated interference of the Cambodian government in the workings of the ECCC resulted in delayed trials, truncated

(Palgrave Macmillan 2015) 1, 1–2; Patrick Burgess, 'Justice and Reconciliation in East Timor. The Relationship Between the Commission for Reception, Truth and Reconciliation and the Courts' in William A Schabas and Shane Darcy (eds), *Truth Commissions and Courts: The Tension Between Criminal Justice and the Search for Truth* (Kluwer 2004) 135; Eric Oteng, 'Central African Republic to set up Truth, Justice and Reconciliation Commission' (*Africa News*, 8 February 2019) <https://www.africanews.com/2019/02/08/central-african-republic-to-set-up-truth-justice-and-reconciliation-commission//> accessed 23 December 2023; Ephrem Rugiririza, 'Central African Republic: The Truth Commission with Feet of Clay' (*Justiceinfo.net*, 30 August 2021) <https://www.justiceinfo.net/en/81300-central-african-republic-truth-commission-feet-clay.html> accessed 23 December 2023.

89 BBC News, 'African Union Condemns "Unfair" ICC' (11 October 2013) <https://www.bbc.com/news/world-africa-24489059> accessed 23 December 2023. See also, eg, comments by Charles Taylor's Lead Defence Counsel Courtenay Griffiths in Anna Schecter, 'Playing the Race Card at War Crimes Trial' (*ABC News*, 27 October 2009) <https://abcnews.go.com/Blotter/defendant-calls-international-criminal-court-racist/story?id=8921725> accessed 23 December 2023.

90 See also Robert Fisk, 'From the Middle East to Northern Ireland, Western States Are All Too Happy to Avoid Culpability for War Crimes' (*The Independent*, 16 May 2019) <https://www.independent.co.uk/voices/amnesty-war-crime-britain-us-trump-michael-behenna-pardon-iraq-a8916346.html> accessed 23 December 2023; Twiggy Garcia, 'Tony Blair Should be Prosecuted for War Crimes— Not Just Judged by History' (*The Guardian*, 8 May 2014) <https://www.theguardian.com/commentisfree/2014/may/07/tony-blair-war-crimes-prosecuted-eel-like-boris-johnson> accessed 23 December 2023.

prosecutions, and even failure to prosecute individuals who should conceivably stand trial.[91] External dissent is also highly influential. This occurs when a state that is not the subject of a justice process, but rather the actual or potential facilitator dissents. For example, when a state who is responsible for financing the justice response dissents and threatens withdrawal from the process, such as occurred in the Cambodian and Sierra Leone contexts where there were funding shortages.[92] The decision to fund hybrid courts through voluntary contributions has therefore weakened their internal resilience.

However, state dissent can also be positive for internal resilience because when a court must deal with external dissent it can respond positively by further collaboration with the host state or internal reform. For example, in the Cambodian context, in 2007 the United Nations Development Programme commissioned an external audit into Cambodia's human resources practices at the court which was undertaken by an international accounting firm.[93] A review was carried out again in 2008 which found major improvements had been made based on the feedback from the original audit.[94]

Context and perspective are important when assessing state dissent. Western or external perceptions of state dissent are often different from how the state itself perceives its actions. This is because international justice is seen as being normative and dissent as being counter-normative, but it is possible to challenge these assumptions, particularly when viewing international criminal justice through a neo-colonial lens. Perceptions of justice and the characterization of the dissent also affect the perceived legitimacy of the court.

For example, perceptions of Cambodian dissent over the establishment and work of the ECCC are due to a belief that Cambodia is acting in a deviant manner

[91] Open Society Justice Initiative, 'Political Interference' (n 25).

[92] See Human Rights Watch, 'Bringing Justice: The Special Court for Sierra Leone: Accomplishments, Shortcomings, and Needed Support' (8 September 2004) <https://www.hrw.org/report/2004/09/08/bringing-justice-special-court-sierra-leone/accomplishments-shortcomings-and> accessed 23 December 2023; Radio Free Asia, *Cambodian War Tribunal Strikers Return to Work* (*Refworld*, 18 March 2013) <https://www.refworld.org/docid/5190dc8e3f.html> accessed 23 December 2023; OSJI, 'Recent Developments at the Extraordinary Chambers in the Courts of Cambodia: Threat to Permanently Stay Cases 003, 004 and 004/2A' (June 2007) <https://www.justiceinitiative.org/uploads/18f1be25-54b4-4e34-9bb5-a784cbeceadd/recent-developments-eccc-june-2017-20160614.pdf> accessed 23 December 2023, 2; Georgia Wilkins, 'ECCC Says No Pay for Nationals' (*Phnom Penh Post*, 3 March 2009) <http://www.phnompenhpost.com/national/eccc-says-no-pay-nationals> accessed 23 December 2023; Caitlin Reiger, 'Hybrid and Internationalized Tribunals' in Chiara Giorgetti (ed), *The Rules, Practice, and Jurisprudence of the International Courts and Tribunals* (Martinus Nijhoff 2012) 283, 291.

[93] OSJI, 'Corruption Allegations at Khmer Rouge Court Must Be Investigated Thoroughly' (14 February 2007) <https://www.justiceinitiative.org/newsroom/corruption-allegations-khmer-rouge-court-must-be-investigated-thoroughly> accessed 23 December 2023; John D Ciorciari and Anne Heindel, 'Experiments in International Criminal Justice: Lessons from the Khmer Rouge Tribunal' (2014) 35 Melbourne Journal of International Law 369, 409.

[94] Ciorciari and Heindel (n 93) 411.

and is dissenting from international norms. To take the opposing viewpoint, Cambodia and other states who similarly oppose international justice mechanisms would argue that they are not dissenting, but rather acting to preserve their own authority as a state and also to uphold their part of a collaborative agreement with the UN where the state has a legitimate say in the justice process. In defining Cambodia as deviant or dissenting, Western states are imposing their views on Cambodia. Such arguments constitute the origins of accusations that international criminal justice is neo-colonial.

The difficulty with making a general assumption that dissent from hybrid courts is negative and detrimental, is that it presupposes that hybrid courts have been established with legitimacy and that the agreements were in good faith. In this context, this chapter challenges what it means to 'dissent' from international justice norms and institutions such as a hybrid court. To dissent requires something authoritative or normative from which an entity can dissent. While there is stated and perceived authority in hybrid courts, whether there is actual authority and widespread perceived authority is contested. In this context, it is questionable whether it is possible to dissent from something that does not have legitimacy or whether a dissenting state is merely not taking part in a process that it does not believe is legitimate. The legitimacy of international criminal justice is increasingly disputed, which raises questions as to whether states are genuinely dissenting from international justice.

One could also argue that dissent is a necessary part of the creation of a hybrid court, because it is a collaborative agreement. There of course needs to be a constructive rather than destructive display of dissent, although that too is open to interpretation and perception, if one is to value dissent in the creation of hybrid courts.

5.7 Conclusion

State dissent has very much shaped and influenced both the creation and failure to create hybrid courts, in addition to their justice processes. There is an assumption that hybrid courts are a legitimate form of justice, which would mean that state dissent is counter-normative. However, dissent can be powerful and transformative; it can destabilize and rearrange outdated international and local power structures and monopolies and it can also contribute to reassessing and restructuring disenfranchising power dynamics and beliefs. There are therefore questions to be asked about whether dissent is actually negative, or rather whether it can be positive and part of the maturation of hybrid criminal justice. Despite this, in hybrid justice, dissent is not generally welcomed, but rather treated as being threatening to the project, its aims and integrity, when it could be seen as an opportunity for re-evaluation and reform. The assessment of what is a dissent and whether it is negative is of course subjective, and at times perceptions of hybrid justice, its value, and place are in opposition.

In explaining the existence and evolution of dissent that has taken place in the international criminal justice project both in terms of hybrid courts and more generally along the international criminal justice continuum, this chapter challenges the notion of being able to dissent from international criminal justice norms and institutions, due to the arguably fragile authority from which the international criminal justice project operates. To dissent from something suggests that the situation or issue that is being dissented from is the authoritative or authentic view, when this is arguably not the case in the international criminal justice project, particularly in light of accusations of neo-colonial and Western dominated power dynamics that are at play in the creation and implementation of international criminal courts and tribunals.

6

Institutional Design and (Non)-Complementarity

Regulating Relations between Hybrid Tribunals and other Judicial and Non-Judicial Institutions

Patryk I. Labuda[*]

6.1 Introduction

Hybrid tribunals usually operate alongside other judicial and non-judicial bodies with similar accountability functions. In particular, a hybrid tribunal can share jurisdictional powers with (ordinary) national courts, one or more international (criminal) tribunal(s), a truth commission, or other investigative and prosecutorial bodies. When the mandates of different institutions overlap, there is a need to identify and regulate relations between them. Ideally, legal rules embedded within each institution's mandate minimize a duplication of tasks, prevent unnecessary conflict, encourage cooperation, and maximize cross-fertilization of best practices. However, even sophisticated arrangements and dispute resolution mechanisms leave some questions unresolved, requiring ad hoc solutions when problems arise.

This chapter draws on examples from several conflict-affected countries to explore how relations can be regulated between hybrid tribunals and other judicial and non-judicial institutions with overlapping mandates, with a special focus on jurisdictional concurrence vis-à-vis the International Criminal Court (ICC). It argues that the term 'complementarity', which is used generically to describe questions of institutional design, is often unhelpful in conceptualizing relations between hybrid tribunals and other judicial and non-judicial institutions, as it generates confusion and uncertainty over jurisdictional priority and decision-making power. Other institutional frameworks and rules, for instance primacy and deferral, can delineate the powers and functions of different institutions more clearly, generating more principled interactions between accountability mechanisms in the long run.

[*] This chapter was drafted in 2020, with minor updates before publication.

Patryk I. Labuda, *Institutional Design and (Non)-Complementarity* In: *Hybrid Justice*. Edited by: Kirsten Ainley and Mark Kersten, Oxford University Press. © Patryk I. Labuda 2025.
DOI: 10.1093/oso/9780192893758.003.0006

6.2 Institutional Design: Regulating Jurisdictional Overlap

When a hybrid tribunal is established, it often operates alongside ordinary national justice institutions dealing with questions of (criminal) accountability, in particular domestic courts, prosecutors, and police. It may also share powers with other domestic mechanisms, for instance an investigative panel, a historical inquiry, or a truth commission. For instance, the Special Court for Sierra Leone (SCSL) and the Sierra Leone Truth and Reconciliation Commission operated in parallel from 2003 to 2004.

It has also become common for hybrid tribunals to operate alongside international mechanisms with analogous investigative or judicial powers, for instance a commission of inquiry or regional and international tribunals. For example, the War Crimes Chamber in Bosnia and Herzegovina (WCC) shared jurisdiction with the International Criminal Tribunal for the former Yugoslavia (ICTY). Relatedly, hybrid tribunals increasingly overlap with the ICC, the only permanent international criminal tribunal. As will be discussed in this chapter, the Special Criminal Court (SCC) in the Central African Republic (CAR) became the first hybrid court to share jurisdiction with the ICC, and hybrid tribunals have been proposed in at least three other—Sudan, the Democratic Republic of Congo (DRC), and Kenya—ICC situation countries.

Given the proliferation of these and other accountability mechanisms,[1] their architects should pro-actively consider how best to regulate relations between different bodies with analogous investigative, prosecutorial, and judicial powers. Yet the scholarship on institutional design, and jurisdictional design in particular, remains thin.[2] This chapter aims to advance this discussion by examining how hybrid tribunals regulate relationships vis-à-vis other accountability mechanisms with similar goals or mandates.

Before turning to specific examples of jurisdictional overlap and possible institutional design solutions, it is worth emphasizing that there is nothing wrong about overlapping mandates. Notwithstanding the rise of transitional justice and predictions of a 'justice cascade' since the end of the Cold War,[3] there remains a glaring impunity gap for serious crimes and human rights abuses. The vast majority of serious crimes still go unpunished and there is arguably a pressing need to create additional accountability mechanisms.

[1] Federica D'Alessandra, 'The Accountability Turn in Third Wave Human Rights Fact-Finding' (2017) 33 Utrecht Journal of International and European Law 59.

[2] For a descriptive account, see Steven D Roper and Lilian A Barria, *Designing Criminal Tribunals: Sovereignty and International Concerns in the Protection of Human Rights* (Ashgate 2006). See also Carsten Stahn, 'The Geometry of Transitional Justice: Choices of Institutional Design' (2005) 18 Leiden Journal of International Law 425; Erik Voeten, 'Making Sense of the Design of International Institutions' (2019) 22 Annual Review of Political Science 147.

[3] Kathryn Sikkink, *The Justice Cascade: How Human Rights Prosecutions Are Changing World Politics* (W W Norton & Co 2011).

That being said, the existence of an accountability gap should not be confused with the notion that 'more institutions' necessarily equals 'more justice'. There are operational, financial, and technical reasons to streamline relations between hybrid tribunals and other bodies with analogous accountability functions. Ideally, rules embedded within the mandate of each institution encourage cooperation, minimize a duplication of tasks, prevent unnecessary conflict, and maximize the cross-fertilization of best practices. Generally speaking, coordination and conflict resolution mechanisms can prevent ineffective practices and channel resources to areas which receive less attention.

A challenge that has emerged in recent years is the repeat questioning of victims and witnesses by multiple accountability mechanisms. For instance, concern about potential re-traumatization of victims subject to multiple questioning has arisen in countries like Myanmar or Ukraine.[4] If hybrid tribunals are to operate effectively and in an ethically responsible manner, testimony must be secured in ways that take into consideration the mandates of other accountability mechanisms.

Analogous considerations apply to the sharing of evidence, when, for instance, national courts are in possession of documents which may be relevant to investigations before a hybrid tribunal. As will be discussed later, the SCC has launched investigations on the basis of case files handed over by national prosecutors,[5] whereas prosecutors in the DRC have complained about the ICC's unwillingness to share evidence.[6] Similarly, analytical work on crime sites undertaken by, for instance, non-judicial inquiries may inform the prosecution strategies of hybrid tribunals, as in CAR, where the UN's Mapping Report served as a basis for the SCC's prosecutorial strategy and prioritization of cases.[7]

Aside from questions of cooperation, there are also *strategic* considerations regarding the synchronization of mandates of different accountability mechanisms. When should a hybrid tribunal decline prosecution in favour of a national court or an international tribunal? Conversely, when may a hybrid tribunal assert priority to try a suspect at the expense of another court? Answering these questions is difficult because one institution's mandate displaces or prevails over another. Similar challenges arise if a hybrid tribunal prospectively precludes the use of testimony

[4] Kingsley Abbott, 'Myanmar: Documentation Practices May Raise Challenges for Accountability' (*Opinio Juris*, 24 January 2019) <https://opiniojuris.org/2019/01/24/myanmar-documentation-practices-may-raise-challenges-for-accountability/> accessed 1 October 2024. Kateryna Busol and Rebecca Hamilton, 'Transitional Justice in Ukraine: Guidance to Policymakers' (*Just Security*, 2 June 2022) <https://justsecurity.org/81719/transitional-justice-in-ukraine-guidance-to-policymakers/> accessed 1 October 2024.

[5] AFP, 'Centrafrique: Les Auteurs Du Massacre de Paoua Seront Jugés Par La Cour Pénale Spéciale' (*VOA Afrique*, 30 July 2019) <https://voaafrique.com/a/les-auteurs-du-massacre-de-paoua-seront-jug%C3%A9s-par-la-cour-p%C3%A9nale-sp%C3%A9ciale/5022208.html> accessed 1 January 2023.

[6] Toussaint Muntazini Mukimapa, 'The Congolese Experience with the Complementary Role of the ICC' (*Justice Info*, 4 August 2016).

[7] Cour pénale spéciale, Stratégie d'enquêtes, de poursuites et d'instruction, December 2018. Interviews with SCC officials (New York, January 2019 and Bangui, CAR, June 2019).

elsewhere, for instance if such testimony would be useful to a truth commission but it imperils the effectiveness of an ongoing prosecution. Here, too, one institution achieves its goals at the expense of another institution.

Focusing on a set of strategic questions relating to institutional priority, this chapter explores how hybrid tribunals should regulate relations with concurrently operating accountability bodies. Answering questions about the relative importance of accountability mechanisms can be contentious, but institutions with overlapping mandates should avoid uncertainty or propose dispute resolution mechanisms that produce clear and definitive answers. As will be seen, this is not always the case in practice. Moreover, even sophisticated dispute resolution techniques leave some questions unaddressed, requiring ad hoc solutions from decision-makers. Although this chapter focuses on hybrid tribunals' institutional design at the strategic level, such choices indirectly influence the operational and financial context within which they operate.

6.3 Complementarity and its Drawbacks

The Rome Statute contains the best-known method of regulating relations between international criminal institutions with overlapping mandates. Known colloquially as complementarity, the ICC's jurisdictional framework gives national institutions priority to investigate, prosecute, and try perpetrators of serious crimes, with the ICC stepping in if states fail to perform their primary accountability role.[8] In theory, the Rome Statute establishes a simple rule of priority for national courts (national primacy) at the expense of the ICC (subsidiarity). Over time, however, the ICC has (re-)interpreted complementarity to suggest that there is parity or equality between the ICC, states, and other entities, where everyone works together to 'complement each other' and, in essence, no one enjoys priority over the others.[9]

In practice, complementarity thus re-interpreted has made it nigh-impossible for states to prevent the ICC from exercising jurisdiction if and when the Court wishes to assert priority. Carsten Stahn has even described the complementarity case law as 'quasi-primacy', referring to the opposite idea embedded in the statutes of the ad hoc tribunals, whereby international tribunals enjoy supremacy over national institutions.[10] Not only has the case law generated considerable confusion;

[8] The substance of what is referred to as 'complementarity' can be found in Articles 1 and 17–20. See Jann K Kleffner, *Complementarity in the Rome Statute and National Criminal Jurisdictions* (Oxford University Press 2008).

[9] For details of this evolution, see Patryk I Labuda, *International Criminal Tribunals and Domestic Accountability: In the Court's Shadow* (Oxford University Press 2023) 68-86.

[10] Carsten Stahn, 'Admissibility Challenges before the ICC. From Quasi-Primacy to Qualified Deference?' in Carsten Stahn (ed), *Law and Practice of the International Criminal Court* (Oxford University Press 2015).

the Prosecutor's oft-repeated claim that the ICC is mandated to try those most responsible, implicitly leaving other perpetrators to national courts, may further compound the confusion. In fact, under the Rome Statute, the ICC has secondary jurisdiction over all perpetrators, and states' priority to prosecute includes even those most responsible.[11]

This chapter is not the place to analyse the ICC's case law and how the Prosecutor and judges have de facto arrogated jurisdictional priority to themselves, turning the Rome Statute's jurisdictional framework upside down.[12] Suffice to say that one of the primary reasons for this state of affairs resides in various (re-)interpretations of complementarity. For instance, some advocates and scholars argue that there are multiple types of complementarity, some of which consist of legal rules (admissibility) while others are merely non-binding aspirational goals (eg positive complementarity).[13] It is often suggested also that, rather than the ICC (uni-directionally) *complementing* national courts in specific circumstances, more emphasis should be placed on the ordinary meaning of the word complementarity (which does not appear in the Rome Statute), implying parity and cooperation between institutions that *complement each other*. Accordingly, complementarity would mandate a horizontal relationship of co-equality, allowing the ICC to negotiate with states on an ad hoc basis who should exercise jurisdiction over a specific case or set of cases. Famously, this reading of complementarity enabled a series of uncontested self-referrals, with governments in countries like Uganda and the DRC 'delegating' the prosecution of political rivals to The Hague while the ICC Prosecutor de-prioritized those cases which should normally be admissible under the Rome Statute, namely against state agents whom national authorities are not prosecuting because they are unwilling or unable genuinely to do so.[14]

6.4 (Non-)Complementarity in Practice

Over time, complementarity's multiplicity of meanings has rendered it something of an 'empty vessel' for regulating relations between accountability bodies with overlapping mandates, including the ICC and other courts. For instance, by implying that there is a horizontal relationship of equality between

[11] Due to difficulties with investigations against high-ranking perpetrators, the Office of the Prosecutor adjusted its strategy in 2019. See ICC-OTP, 'Strategic Plan 2019-2021' (17 July 2019).

[12] For prominent critiques, see Kevin J Heller, 'Radical Complementarity' (2016) 14 Journal of International Criminal Justice 637; Padraig McAuliffe, 'From Watchdog to Workhorse: Explaining the Emergence of the ICC's Burden-Sharing Policy as an Example of Creeping Cosmopolitanism' (2014) 13 Chinese Journal of International Law 259.

[13] For a typology, see Carsten Stahn, *A Critical Introduction to International Criminal Law* (Cambridge University Press 2019) 222–26.

[14] For details, see Labuda, *International Criminal Tribunals and Domestic Accountability* (n 9) ch 2 and 3.

institutions—where neither has priority over the other—complementarity rarely offers meaningful guidance as to whether concurrently operating bodies should share evidence, or who has the authority to issue binding orders in jurisdictional matters. Nor can complementarity provide clear answers as to who has priority to investigate or prosecute suspects. Such questions are often negotiated on an ad hoc basis, with unpredictable results. Hybrid tribunals in DRC, CAR, and South Sudan illustrate the perils and confusion inherent in various iterations of complementarity.

6.4.1 Justice denied: the DRC Special Court

The DRC Special Court triggered the first sustained discussion of how to regulate jurisdictional relations between the ICC and a hybrid tribunal with a mandate to prosecute international crimes.[15] In late 2010, the Congolese Minister of Justice proposed the establishment of 'specialized chambers' (which then became known as a standalone 'Special Court').[16]

Comprising both national and international staff, the Special Court was expected to have jurisdiction over a range of violations, most notably genocide, crimes against humanity, and war crimes. Controversies included the Court's relative 'hybridity' (ratio of national to international staff), temporal jurisdiction (unlimited prospective vs mandated cut-off dates), and procedural rules (inclusion of international modes of liability).[17] However, one element of institutional design remained constant during months of negotiations in 2010–2011: the Special Court was to have exclusive primary jurisdiction over international crimes.[18] Magistrates would be able to refer cases back to national courts, in cases of 'lesser gravity', but

[15] A hybrid tribunal for Darfur was proposed in 2009 but no serious attempt to establish it ensued. See Human Rights Watch, 'AU: Back Mbeki Panel Call for Darfur Prosecutions' (29 October 2009) <https://hrw.org/news/2009/10/29/au-back-mbeki-panel-call-darfur-prosecutions> accessed 1 October 2024.

[16] This section is based on four draft bills that the author had access to as a justice advisor to the European Union in 2010–2011. Ministry of Justice, Avant-Projet de Loi portant création, organisation, fonctionnement, droit applicable, compétence et procédure des Chambres spécialisées pour la répression des violations graves du droit international humanitaire (November 2010) (Draft bill 1). Ministry of Justice, Avant-Projet de Loi relative aux Chambres spécialisées pour la répression des violations graves du droit international humanitaire: organisation, fonctionnement, droit applicable, compétence et procedure (January 2011) (Draft bill 2). Projet de Loi relative aux Chambres spécialisées pour la répression des violations graves du droit international humanitaire: organisation, fonctionnement, droit applicable, compétence et procedure (April 2011) (Draft bill 3). Projet de loi portant création, organisation et fonctionnement de la Cour spécialisée de la repression des crimes de génocide, crimes de guerre et des crimes contre l'humanité (August 2011) (Draft bill 4) (on file with author).

[17] For details, see Patryk I Labuda, 'Applying and "Misapplying" the Rome Statute in the Democratic Republic of Congo' in Christian M De Vos, Sara Kendall, and Carsten Stahn (eds), *Contested Justice: The Politics and Practice of International Criminal Court Interventions* (Cambridge University Press 2015).

[18] Draft bill 1, Article 14; Draft bill 2, Article 18; Draft bill 3, Article 18; Draft bill 4, Article 16.

draft legislation made no mention of the ICC in delineating the Special Court's jurisdictional powers.[19] Put differently, the Special Court and national courts had primary and secondary jurisdiction, respectively, while the ICC had only implicit tertiary jurisdiction.

This solution is in conformity with the Rome Statute. In line with the draft legislation, the ICC could still exercise tertiary jurisdiction, intervening as a backstop when the hybrid or ordinary national courts failed to assert jurisdiction, under the conditions enunciated in Articles 17–20 of the Rome Statute. However, the Special Court's robust re-affirmation of the primacy of national jurisdiction did not sit well with some international actors.

In practice, assumptions about the ICC and complementarity galvanized opposition to the hybrid tribunal. Notably, the ICC Prosecutor initially opposed the establishment of a Special Court, fearing it may jeopardize the ICC's freedom of action and forcing him to compete with Congolese prosecutors over cases.[20] This is not entirely surprising as the Special Court's jurisdictional design affirmed that the ICC was a subsidiary accountability forum, and that The Hague should respect the Congolese authorities' preferences.[21] In fact, in the DRC, the word 'subsidiarity' is often used interchangeably with 'complementarity' to describe national institutions' primacy vis-à-vis the ICC. According to this vision of complementarity, the DRC government has sole authority to decide when the ICC may assert jurisdiction over cases stemming from Congolese territory. This reading of complementarity was later enshrined in Rome Statute implementing legislation, adopted by Parliament in 2015, which re-affirmed the subsidiarity of ICC jurisdiction, and gave the Council of Ministers the power to 'defer' cases for prosecution at the ICC.[22]

But it was not just the ICC Prosecutor who saw the Special Court as a potential competitor. For many years, the European Union (EU) also opposed the hybrid tribunal on the grounds that international aid should strengthen the ordinary justice system rather than be used to set up temporary institutions. Embodying a vision of complementarity, where ordinary courts enjoy primacy of jurisdiction

19 However, the ICC would exercise priority in cases based on universal jurisdiction. Draft bill 1, Article 29; Draft bill 2, Article 18; Draft bill 3, Article 29; Draft bill 4, Article 49.

20 This has been confirmed in interviews and conversations with multiple sources in the DRC. Author interviews with civil society activists and former minister of justice, Kinshasa, DRC, April 2016. The OTP's reservations diminished over time. Some ICC officials denied later that the Prosecutor ever had reservations about the Special Court. Author interviews with ICC officials (The Hague, Netherlands, November 2015).

21 Draft bill 4, Exposé des motifs, Article 16. Draft bills 2 and 3 mention the ICC in the exposé des motifs, but note only the slow pace of its work and inability to handle most cases in the DRC.

22 Art 2 ajoutant art 21 octies CPC, Loi no 15/024 du 31 décembre 2015 modifiant et complétant le Décret du 6 août 1959 portant Code de procédure pénal. Initially one piece of legislation, the ICC implementation law was broken up into four bills to avoid legal obstacles: Loi no 15/022, Loi no 023-2002 and Loi no 15/024 of 31 December 2015. Loi organique no 17/003 of 10 March 2017.

and there is no space for ad hoc hybrid mechanisms,[23] the EU's support for purely domestic responses may be fiscally responsible, for instance by avoiding spending on international salaries that swallows the lion's share of aid. However, in this case, a somewhat dogmatic disagreement among international actors about which type of justice to prioritize—national or hybrid—contributed to the Special Court's failure.[24] Nearly ten years later, despite continued pleas from civil society and promises from Congolese politicians, no hybrid court has been established, with negative consequences for justice in the DRC.[25]

The Special Court is not the only example of complementarity channelling divergent ideas about accountability in the DRC. When mobile courts in eastern Congo are referred to as 'complementarity in action' or 'positive complementarity', the term is used generically to describe parallel accountability proceedings.[26] There is no evidence that the ICC has ever tried to exercise concurrent jurisdiction over the same cases (the jurisprudential standard for complementarity in the ICC's case law) as the mobile courts. While generalist usage of complementarity vocabulary abounds in human rights advocacy, it should not mask real disagreements among states, the ICC, and other actors over institutional priorities in cases of concurrent mandates, with the DRC's failed Special Court epitomizing how confusion over complementarity can have negative effects on advancing solutions to impunity.

6.4.2 Squaring the Circle: the SCC in CAR

The challenge of regulating jurisdictional relations between the ICC and hybrid tribunals resurfaced several years later in CAR. In 2014, a new UN peacekeeping mission, known by its French acronym MINUSCA, received a mandate from the UN Security Council to adopt 'urgent temporary measures' to restore law and order.[27] As part of this mandate, MINUSCA negotiated a memorandum of

[23] Technically, the Special Court would be a national court, integrated into the DRC justice system, but international participation makes its composition (as opposed to its legal basis) mixed.

[24] Interviews with civil society activists (Goma, DRC, September 2016 and Kinshasa, DRC, April 2016); Interviews with EU officials (Kinshasa and Goma, DRC, 2010–2011); Interviews with EU officials (Kinshasa, DRC, August 2016).

[25] On recent attempts to revive, inter alia, a hybrid court, see Ewelina Ochab, 'Dr Denis Mukwege: "The Time Has Come to Mobilize Real Political Will to Address CRSV in the DRC"' (*Forbes*, 29 November 2022) <https://forbes.com/sites/ewelinaochab/2022/11/29/dr-denis-mukwege-the-time-has-come-to-mobilize-real-political-will-to-address-crsv-in-the-drc/> accessed 1 January 2023. See also Valérie Arnould, 'Reflections on a Decentralized Approach to Transitional Justice in the DR Congo' (2021) Africa Policy Brief No 33.

[26] Daniele Perissi and Elsa Taquet, 'The Kavumu Trial: Complementarity in Action in the Democratic Republic of Congo' (*International Justice Monitor*, 5 February 2018) <https://ijmonitor.org/2018/02/the-kavumu-trial-complementarity-in-action-in-the-democratic-republic-of-congo/>.

[27] UNSC Res 2149 (2014) S/RES/2149, para 40.

understanding with CAR's transitional authorities to establish a specialized criminal tribunal.[28] In 2015, the transitional parliament adopted legislation to bring a new hybrid court into existence (SCC law).[29] After considerable delay, the SCC launched investigations in late 2018, with its first verdict announced four years later.[30]

For the purpose of this chapter, it is important to understand how the SCC's jurisdiction is regulated vis-à-vis other national courts and the ICC. In CAR, three jurisdictions share concurrent powers over perpetrators of international crimes, which requires coordination among different investigative, prosecutorial, and judicial authorities at national and international levels. Moreover, a Truth, Justice, Reparation and Reconciliation Commission (TJRRC) also received investigative powers over the same international crimes, further complicating the institutional landscape.[31]

Although CAR sought to devise a principled method of apportioning mandated powers between these institutions, beliefs and misunderstandings about complementarity in the Rome Statute produced confusion and even litigation. Acting under the influence of international advisors, Central African authorities inserted a provision into the 2015 SCC law that turned complementarity on its head.[32] Contrary to the Rome Statute, where national courts have jurisdictional priority and the ICC 'complements' them, Article 37 of the law suggests that the SCC should defer to the ICC if and when the ICC has 'seized itself of a case', which in turn implies that the ICC enjoys priority to choose cases for investigation.[33] While I and others have noted the problematic nature of this norm,[34] this is not the place

[28] Memorandum d'entente entre la Mission Multidimensionnelle intégré e des Nations Unies pour la stabilisation en République centrafricaine et le Gouvernement de la République centrafricaine (7 August 2014) (on file with author).

[29] Loi organique 15-003 portant création, organization et fonctionnement de la Cour pénale spéciale (3 June 2015) [SCC law].

[30] Vianney Ingasso, 'Central African Republic: Special Criminal Court Hands Down First Judgment' (*JusticeInfo.net*, 1 November 2022) <https://justiceinfo.net/en/108356-central-african-republic-special-criminal-court-first-judgment.html> accessed 1 October 2024.

[31] Loi portant création, organisation et fonctionnement de la Commission vérité, justice, réparation et réconciliation (7 April 2020) 20/009 (CVJRR).

[32] Interviewees suggested that the idea to 'reverse' the Rome Statute's jurisdictional scheme by giving the ICC primacy originated with international advisors in 2014–2015. The UN's Office of Legal Affairs and the ICC were informed about the future Article 37 but neither objected, and it raised no known objections in the Transitional Parliament. However, several judges of the CAR Constitutional Court, who verified the draft SCC law's constitutionality, expressed reservations about Article 37's compatibility with international and domestic law. Despite a split (internal) vote on the matter, the Constitutional Court decided not to invalidate Article 37. Author interviews with UN, MINUSCA, SCC officials, and Central African magistrates (Bangui, CAR, New York, NY, Dakar, Senegal, and by phone, 2016–2019).

[33] SCC law (n 29), Article 37.

[34] Patryk I Labuda, 'The Special Criminal Court in the Central African Republic: Failure or Vindication of Complementarity?' (2017) 15 Journal of International Criminal Justice 175, 191–95. Eugène Bakama Bope, 'The Surrender of Albert Yekatom to the ICC: An Infringement of the Positive Complementarity Principle?' (*International Criminal Justice in Africa Blog*, 27 November 2018). Downplaying the significance of Article 37, see Ignacio Tredici and Renaud Galand, 'Holding to Account the Commission of International Crimes in the Central African Republic: The Establishment of the Special Criminal Court' (2018) 21 Max Planck Yearbook of United Nations Law 1.

to revisit why Article 37 is arguably null and void, and should be severed from the SCC law when the tribunal's judges are presented with a challenge; suffice to say that the CAR legislator's re-allocation of jurisdictional powers stems from (re)-interpretations of complementarity qua horizontal relationship. It is quite ironic that human rights groups or the SCC insist that, despite relinquishing priority to the ICC, the SCC is nevertheless operationalizing complementarity.[35]

Legal controversies notwithstanding, three sets of courts with overlapping mandates have operated side by side over the past few years. According to the SCC law, national courts must defer to the SCC's jurisdictional primacy, and likewise the SCC must defer to the ICC's (purported) primacy. To date, interactions between the different justice actors in CAR have been mainly cooperative.[36] For instance, in June 2019, it was announced that ordinary courts had successfully referred several cases to the SCC, in line with the SCC's Rules of Procedure and Evidence (RPE).[37] A notable feature of the RPE is that the Special Prosecutor and investigative judges may compel unconditional case deferrals from CAR national magistrates, subject only to a general requirement of 'reasoned requests'.[38] By contrast, national magistrates may not refer cases to the SCC without the Special Prosecutor's prior agreement.[39] This procedural solution may help to avoid confusion over decision-making power, and alleviate disputes over who is responsible for prosecuting specific crimes.[40] Likewise, the SCC and ICC have partnered on issues such as training, forensic investigations, and case distribution.[41]

Practical challenges remain, however. First, it remains to be seen to what extent the ordinary courts are willing and able to prosecute international crimes,

35 Parliamentarians for Global Action, 'Mémorandum de PGA sur la création d'une Cour pénale spéciale en République centrafricaine' (February 2015); Elise Keppler and Lewis Mudge, 'En Quête de Justice': La Cour Pénale Spéciale, Une Nouvelle Opportunité Pour Les Victims En République Centrafricaine' (2018) Human Rights Watch 11; Cour pénale spéciale, Stratégie d'enquêtes, de poursuites et d'instruction (December 2018) paras 24–25 and 58 (concurrent complementarity).

36 Cour pénale spéciale, Stratégie d'enquêtes, de poursuites et d'instruction (December 2018) paras 29–30; ICC, 'Press Release: ICC holds training for Magistrates in Central African Republic' (22 March 2018) <https://icc-cpi.int/news/icc-holds-training-magistrates-central-african-republic> accessed 1 October 2024.

37 See Sikkink (n 3). Interview with SCC Special Prosecutor and Court of Appeals' Prosecutor General (Bangui, CAR, June 2019.) See also Communiqué du Bureau du Procureur près de la Cour pénale spéciale, (6 August 2019).

38 *Loi* No 18-010 portant règlement de procédure et de preuve devant la Cour pénale spéciale (2 July 2018) (SCC RPE) Articles 12 and 13, Article 12 (C), (E), and (F).

39 ibid Article 12 (H).

40 In theory, one aspect of the SCC RPE may create problems. If national courts defy a deferral order, such disputes are resolved by the Tribunal of Conflicts, in conformity with binding Central African law. Thus, the CAR hybrid court—given its status as a national court integrated into the national justice system—will not have the last say in jurisdictional disputes, contrary to the principle of Kompetenz-Kompetenz of international tribunals. See SCC RPE, Article 13 (D).

41 ICC, 'Press Release: ICC holds training for Magistrates in Central African Republic' (n 36); ICC, 'Press Release: Office of the Prosecutor of the International Criminal Court partners with national authorities and international experts in the forensic analysis of remains of victims in the Central African Republic' (23 June 2022) < https://icc-cpi.int/news/office-prosecutor-international-criminal-court-partners-national-authorities-and-international>. accessed 1 October 2024.

especially in politically sensitive cases. Despite an unprecedented conviction for war crimes in February 2020 before the Bangui Court of Appeals, domestic prosecutions remain difficult in light of the overall security situation, including the 2019 peace agreement, which brought several armed groups into the government.[42] While the Special Prosecutor concedes that the RPE provide no mechanism to compel national courts to prosecute crimes that the SCC is not handling,[43] Central African magistrates are likely to defer controversial cases to the SCC, which raises questions about the latter's operational capacity, its relationship to the ICC, and a possible impunity gap.[44]

The SCC's prosecutorial strategy, including the Special Prosecutor's case selection, has not been without controversy. For instance, many Central Africans and some analysts query why suspects like Alfred Yekatom and Patrice Ngaïssona are being tried in The Hague now that the SCC is fully operational.[45] Although Yekatom's complementarity challenge, arguing for his Hague case to be referred back to Central African courts, was rejected by the ICC judges,[46] the changing domestic politics of accountability—as seen in the DRC, Cote d'Ivoire, and other countries—suggest that the CAR government's deferential attitude vis-à-vis international actors may evolve over time and it may still try to re-assert primacy over other ICC cases, especially if trials in The Hague are seen as detrimental to the local peace process.[47] A vivid example of potential challenges in the future was Hassan Bouba's arrest on war crimes charges in 2021, pursuant to a request from the SCC Prosecutor, only for his case to grind to a halt after Central African security forces forcibly intervened and freed the militia leader-cum-government minister from detention.[48] Although Bouba's failed prosecution before the SCC seems like a paradigmatic case of state interference in the domestic justice process, the ICC Prosecutor has to date declined to assert jurisdiction over his case based

[42] Gaël Grilhot, 'National Court Gets Tough on Bangassou Crimes' (*Justiceinfo.net*, 10 February 2020) <https://justiceinfo.net/en/tribunals/national-tribunals/43747-central-african-republic-national-court-gets-tough-on-bangassou-crimes.html> accessed 1 January 2023.

[43] Interview with SCC Special Prosecutor (Bangui, CAR, June 2019).

[44] Interviews with SCC, MINUSCA staff and Court of Appeals' Prosecutor General (Bangui, CAR June 2019). For an update on investigations in CAR, see Julian Elderfield, 'The Rise and Rise of the Special Criminal Court, Part I and II' (*Opinio Juris*, 7 April 2021) <https://opiniojuris.org/2021/04/07/the-rise-and-rise-of-the-special-criminal-court-part-ii/> accessed 1 January 2023.

[45] Interviews and conversations with Central African and international staff (Bangui, CAR, June 2019). See also Bope (n 34).

[46] *Prosecutor v Yekatom et al* (Judgment on Mr Yekatom's appeal against Trial Chamber V's Decision on the Yekatom Defence's Admissibility Challenge) ICC-01/14-01/18-678-Conf (9 October 2020).

[47] Phil Clark, *Distant Justice: The Impact of the International Criminal Court on African Politics* (Cambridge University Press 2018). On Cote d'Ivoire, where Alassane Ouattara's government initially supported ICC trials of political opponents, only to later reassert domestic primacy, see Sophie T Rosenberg, 'The International Criminal Court in Côte d'Ivoire' (2017) 15 Journal of International Criminal Justice 471.

[48] Maxence Helen, 'The Long Bumpy Road Towards the Special Criminal Court' (*Justiceinfo.net*, 18 April 2022) < https://justiceinfo.net/en/90870-central-african-republic-long-bumpy-road-towards-special-criminal-court.html> accessed 1 January 2023.

on CAR's inability or unwillingness to genuinely prosecute, as foreseen by complementarity in the Rome Statute's Article 17.

At the time of writing, the SCC, the ICC, and CAR government officials have publicly emphasized cooperative partnership on issues such as case distribution, jurisdictional overlap and capacity building. Arguably, this emphasis on complementarity qua (horizontal) cooperation has obscured the tensions inherent in the SCC's relationship to the ICC (not to mention further complications that may arise if and when the TJRRC launches operations).[49] At the time of writing, relations between different accountability stakeholders are still routinely referred to as 'complementarity in action', but only time will tell whether the institutional design adopted in CAR—in particular, the SCC's attempted reversal of complementarity's prioritization scheme in the ICC's favour—will constitute a workable experiment and a model worth emulating in other countries.

6.4.3 Terminological vacuity: the hybrid court for South Sudan

South Sudan's accountability process is another example of how divergent and mutually unintelligible understandings of complementarity may create difficulties in practice. Adopted under international pressure, two successive peace agreements mandated prosecutions, alongside a truth commission, a reparations commission, and other transitional justice tools.[50] Although it is implicated in atrocities in the country's 2013–2018 civil war, the government led by Salva Kiir has nominally endorsed criminal accountability and the African Union (AU) with other partners have helped draft a statute for a proposed Hybrid Court for South Sudan (HCSS).[51] However, despite repeated promises, Kiir's government has not signed a memorandum of understanding, which would bring the HCSS into being.[52]

[49] The SCC's RPE postpones decisions on the future relationship with the TJRRC by noting that future 'protocols' will allow both institutions to function in a 'complementary' way. SCC RPE, Article 15. Given the considerable delay in operationalizing the Truth Commission, this chapter does not address complications (theoretical for the time being) likely to arise in light of the TJRRC law's non-regulation of relations with courts in CAR. On the challenges of regulating relations between hybrid courts and truth commissions, see the discussion of Sierra Leone in the following section.

[50] Agreement on the Resolution of the Conflict in the Republic of South Sudan (17 August 2015) (ARCSS). International pressure for the Court's establishment has abated since the signing of the revitalized peace agreement (R-ARCSS) in September 2018, as diplomats concentrate on preventing a collapse of the fragile transition. Revitalized Agreement on the Resolution of the Conflict in the Republic of South Sudan (12 September 2018) (R-ARCSS).

[51] Draft Statute of the Hybrid Court of South Sudan (August 2017). See AU, 'Press Release: African Union Commission and the Republic of South Sudan Successfully Conclude Working Session on the Draft Legal Instruments of the Hybrid Court for South Sudan' (14 August 2017) <https://au.int/en/pressreleases/20170814/african-union-commission-and-republic-south-sudan-successfully-conclude> accessed 1 August 2019.

[52] Human Rights Watch, 'South Sudan: Stop Delays on Hybrid Court' (14 December 2017) <https://hrw.org/news/2017/12/14/south-sudan-stop-delays-hybrid-court> accessed 1 January 2023. Since the signing of the 2018 R-ARCSS, international mediation has concentrated on setting up a transitional government. See International Crisis Group, 'A Critical Six Months for South Sudan' (8 May 2019)

According to Chapter V of both peace agreements (the R-ARCSS mostly replicated the ARCSS's institutional design on transitional justice), the HCSS is expected to have primacy over national courts in South Sudan.[53] The ICC is not part of the institutional landscape (there is no mention of the ICC in the peace agreement, although the UNSC could theoretically refer the situation in the future),[54] but this does not mean that complementarity is absent in South Sudan.[55] Echoing the experiences of CAR and the DRC, the term has been deployed unevenly and in often contradictory ways.

For instance, in 2016, shortly after the HCSS Statute had been drafted, the South Sudanese government seemed to backtrack on its recognition of the HCSS's primacy over national courts. It argued that the HCSS should:

> be seen as complementary to the national judicial responsibility for justice. In that connection, it must carefully balance the quest for justice and accountability with the promotion of peace and national reconciliation. For ... the Hybrid Court to succeed, cooperation and constructive partnership with the Government are critical.

Equating complementarity with the responsibility to protect one's own people, the government argued further that the key challenge facing international partners was:

> strengthening the capacity of the state to discharge [its] national obligations effectively, bearing in mind the principle that the international community has the complementary responsibility to provide a state in need with supplementary assistance to meet its national responsibility.[56]

<https://crisisgroup.org/africa/horn-africa/south-sudan/critical-six-months-south-sudan>. Most observers agree that the South Sudanese government is not likely to sign the memorandum; Interviews with UNMISS staff, foreign diplomats, and civil society activists (Juba, South Sudan, August 2019). See also Hereward Holland, 'South Sudan Hires U.S. Lobbyists to Help Block War Crimes Court: Contract' (*Reuters*, 29 April 2019) <https://reuters.com/article/us-southsudan-justice-idUSKCN1S51Z2>; Salva Kiir and Riek Machar, 'South Sudan Needs Truth, Not Trials' (*New York Times*, 7 June 2016) < https://nytimes.com/2016/06/08/opinion/south-sudan-needs-truth-not-trials.html> accessed 1 October 2024.

[53] ARCSS, Chapter V, Article 3.2.2; R-ARCSS, Chapter V, Article 5.3.2.2. The HCSS Statute is not publicly available.

[54] Patryk I Labuda, 'The Hybrid Court for South Sudan? Looking for a Way Forward ...' (*Justice in Conflict*, 23 February 2017) <https://justiceinconflict.org/2017/02/23/the-hybrid-court-for-south-sudan-looking-for-a-way-forward-part-1/> accessed 1 January 2023.

[55] David K Deng, 'Catalyzing Effects of Complementarity in South Sudan' in Ronald Slye (ed), *The Nuremberg Principles in Non-western Societies A Reflection on their Universality, Legitimacy and Application* (International Nuremberg Principles Academy 2017).

[56] 'Statement of South Sudanese Ambassador to the United Nations delivered to the UN Security Council' <http://africaintelligence.com/c/dc/ION/1439/Letter-Joseph-Moum-Majak-Ngor-Malok-Security-Council.pdf> accessed 1 August 2019.

While these arguments contradict the HCSS's proposed primacy, as required by the two peace agreements and the draft HCSS Statute, the UN reached the implausible conclusion that the HCSS's jurisdictional primacy is fully compatible with complementarity. According to a UNMISS/UNDP viability study:[57]

> [The HCSS] is intended to focus on high-level perpetrators and not displace the primary responsibility of South Sudan's national justice institutions to ensure accountability for other perpetrators. This approach reflects the principle of complementarity that underlies modern international law whereby the primary responsibility to prosecute conflict-related crimes rests with national authorities.

This statement is misleading. In fact, the HCSS is expected to have primacy over all perpetrators in South Sudan. While this does not mean that South Sudanese national courts cannot and should not play an important role in providing accountability (to date, only national institutions have dispensed some justice in a handful of cases),[58] the reality remains that South Sudanese institutions, as per the 2015 ARCSS, 2018 R-ARCSS, and the HCSS Draft Statute, have merely secondary jurisdiction. As far as institutional design is concerned, the HCSS's primacy over all crimes is the exact opposite of complementarity enshrined in the Rome Statute.

The point is not to criticize the UN staffers who wrote this and other unfortunate passages.[59] In fact, I would suggest that such statements illustrate what has become the norm in international criminal justice scholarship and advocacy, where even mutually exclusive positions, such as the South Sudanese government and the UN's views on the HCSS's institutional design, are shoehorned into the ambiguous vocabulary of complementarity. If a word can mean everything to all people, it no longer means anything. Most importantly, the multiple examples of confusion in the DRC, CAR, and South Sudan underscore why complementarity increasingly serves no meaningful legal purpose in delineating the powers of institutions with overlapping mandates. Even mutually contradictory positions are considered 'complementary', depending on how one chooses to define that term.

[57] UNMISS Rule of Law Advisory Section, UNMISS Human Rights Division and UNDP, 'Preliminary Viability Study on National Mechanisms to Promote Accountability for Serious Conflict-Related Crimes in South Sudan' (2017).

[58] UNMISS Rule of Law Advisory Section, 'Progress Report' (May 2019) (on file with author). See also Flora McCrone, 'War Crimes and Punishment: The Terrain Compound Attack and Military Accountability in South Sudan, 2016-18' (*Small Arms Survey*, 1 August 2019).

[59] UNMISS Rule of Law Advisory Section, UNMISS Human Rights Division, and UNDP (n 57) para 8.

6.5 Beyond Rhetoric: Regulating Relations and Avoiding Confusion

Complementarity's lack of fixed normative content can be contrasted with other rules of institutional design, in particular primacy which has been used on several occasions before international criminal tribunals and hybrid courts. For instance, the two ad hoc international tribunals had primacy over all national courts, including those from the former Yugoslavia and Rwanda.[60] The Sierra Leone Special Court and Bosnian WCC had primacy over the national courts of Sierra Leone and Bosnia and Herzegovina respectively.[61] In a nutshell, primacy means international and hybrid courts may, subject to pre-defined criteria, assert priority of jurisdiction over cases that national prosecutors and judges would normally handle in domestic proceedings.

Although primacy at international and hybrid courts sometimes produces contestation, it has the benefit of providing clearer procedural answers to questions of overlapping mandates and discourages manipulation based on the open-endedness of terms like complementarity. For instance, Sierra Leonean authorities attempted to contest the SCSL's primacy despite the SCSL Statute's requirement that '[a]t any stage of the procedure, the Special Court may formally request a national court to defer to its competence ...'[62] Adopted by the national legislature, the Ratification Agreement on the Special Court purported to give Sierra Leonean's Attorney General the power to decide whether to honour requests for deferral,[63] but the substance of primacy was clear and the country's leadership never challenged the hybrid court's jurisdictional supremacy. In practice, despite the Ratification Agreement's ambivalent terms, jurisdictional overlap was handled informally and suspects already under national investigation were handed over to the SCSL for prosecution.[64] To be sure, some factions within the Sierra Leonean government may have resented the SCSL's supremacy over national courts, but primacy left little doubt about the outcome of disputes.

The International Criminal Tribunal for Rwanda (ICTR)'s experience with domestic authorities offers different lessons. In the first years of the tribunal's existence, Rwandan authorities had reservations about the ICTR's primacy vis-à-vis Rwandan courts, prompting instances of competing jurisdictional claims over the

[60] UNSC, Statute of the International Criminal Tribunal for Yugoslavia (25 May 1993, as amended on 17 May 2002) Article 9; UNSC, Statute of the International Criminal Tribunal for Rwanda (8 November 1994, as amended on 13 October 2006) Article 8.

[61] UNSC, Statute of the Special Court for Sierra Leone (16 January 2002) Article 8.

[62] ibid.

[63] Special Court Agreement Ratification Act, Supplement to the Sierra Leone Gazette, Vol CXXXIII, No 22 (25 April 2002) Article 14.

[64] For details, see Labuda, *International Criminal Tribunals and Domestic Accountability* (n 9) 110–25.

same suspects.[65] With one exception, the ICTR relied on primacy to secure the custody of suspects, despite the Rwandan government's complaints, and eventually an unspoken *modus vivendi* emerged, whereby Rwanda settled for those cases that the tribunal did not want or could not handle due to resource constraints.[66]

However, the ad hoc tribunals illustrate not only how primacy encapsulates a clear(er) rule of priority but also that it is compatible with the opposite idea of giving domestic accountability mechanisms space to adjudicate international crimes. To facilitate domestic trials, the ICTR and ICTY enacted Rule 11*bis* to allow transfers of cases to national justice systems that met specific guarantees of due process. Importantly, both tribunals retained primacy to divest the national courts of such cases if domestic proceedings failed to meet international standards.[67]

While this chapter is not the place to describe and evaluate the impact of the rule 11*bis* case law, which led to dozens of referrals to Bosnia and Herzegovina's hybrid court and a specialized chamber in Rwanda,[68] it is worth pausing on the ICTR, whose judges initially declined to refer a series of cases in 2008 due to concerns over unfair domestic trials.[69] Although the Rwandan government sharply criticized these initial declinations and the ICTR later authorized referrals in a handful of other cases, the rule 11*bis* case law cast light on the difficult questions of where, when, and how trials should take place, and who gets to decide and according to which standards whether justice for international crimes is being served. Some criticize ICTR judges of double standards in declining to refer cases to Rwanda, while others regret that the tribunal eventually approved such referrals, pointing to the national justice system's flaws.[70] Lost in this controversy is that, whether one agrees or not with the referral decisions, Rule 11*bis* established a coherent framework to govern international–national relations. Grounded on primacy, Rule 11*bis* ensured that the ICTR remained responsible for the fairness of trials that it proposed to send back to Rwanda, producing a bilateral and iterative process of negotiation over case distribution and accountability standards, subject to human rights-based legal guarantees.[71] While the ICTR was tasked with making sure the

[65] Madeline Morris, 'The Trials of Concurrent Jurisdiction: The Case of Rwanda' (1997) 7 Duke Journal of Comparative & International Law 349.

[66] The one exception was Froduald Karamira, who was eventually deported to, tried, and executed in Rwanda. Interpretations differ as to why this happened. See Morris (n 65) 363–64.

[67] ICTR Rules of Procedure and Evidence, rule 11*bis* (adopted 6 July 2002).

[68] On the WCC, see Diane Orentlicher, *Some Kind of Justice: The ICTY's Impact in Bosnia and Serbia* (Oxford University Press 2018).

[69] For an overview of the case law, see Alhagi Marong and Charles Jalloh, 'Transfer of Cases under the Jurisprudence of the ICTR and Lessons Learnt for the ICC' in Charles C Jalloh and Alhagi BM Marong (eds), *Promoting Accountability under International Law for Gross Human Rights Violations in Africa: Essays in Honour of Prosecutor Hassan Bubacar Jallow* (Martinus Nijhoff 2015).

[70] Nicola Palmer, 'Transfer or Transformation?: A Review of the Rule 11 Bis Decisions of the International Criminal Tribunal for Rwanda' (2012) 20 African Journal of International and Comparative Law 1. See also Marong and Jalloh (n 69).

[71] Only if Rwanda met specific fair trial conditions would a case be sent back, and even then the ICTR—because it retained primacy—monitored whether Rwandan courts were meeting their obligations under the ICTR Statute.

referrals produced fair trials, producing high levels of dialogue with its domestic counterparts, Rwanda agreed to reform its justice system, resulting in enhanced capacity building.[72]

While the iterative process of negotiating case distribution before the ICTY and ICTR can be traced to certain institutional design features of primacy and rule 11*bis*, Sierra Leone's multi-actor transitional justice experiment provides another lesson, illustrating the risk of failing to sufficiently address inter-institutional relations. As explained above, the SCSL had primacy over Sierra Leonean courts, but neither the Special Court nor the Sierra Leonean Truth Commission's founding documents regulated issues of mutual interest, which then gave rise to disagreements over information-sharing and witness testimony.[73] Although the SCSL denied the Truth Commission's request for public testimony from a defendant awaiting trial, inter alia by adopting an expansive (and contested) interpretation of its primacy vis-à-vis the Truth Commission, the judges improvised by offering a mid-way solution to compensate for the lack of statutory guidance on competing requests for witness testimony.[74]

As this example shows, giving one institution 'primacy' does not in and of itself avoid conflict or ensure cooperation between different accountability mechanisms with overlapping mandates. Resolving competing jurisdictional claims and finding solutions to issues of mutual concern depends also on the procedural details of broad concepts such as primacy or complementarity, in addition to the good faith of decision-makers and other contextual factors. Ultimately, different stakeholders are likely to disagree about the merits of prosecuting a case internationally, referring cases (back) to a national court, or granting requests from a truth commission. It is worth acknowledging also that interpretative disagreements may arise under either primacy or complementarity, and that clashes are unavoidable no matter how detailed the normative framework.

Yet, while some disagreement over inherently contentious accountability priorities is unavoidable, this does not mean that institutional design is irrelevant. On the contrary, a few guiding principles are worth considering based on the experiences of conflict-affected countries examined in this chapter. First, the designers of

[72] For details, see Labuda, *International Criminal Tribunals and Domestic Accountability* (n 9) 147–65 and 200–18.

[73] The SCSL Prosecutor's decision not to use TRC-generated information avoided potential conflict. See further Elizabeth M Evenson, 'Truth and Justice in Sierra Leone: Coordination between Commission and Court' (2004) 104 Columbia Law Review 730, 744–47, 755–59.

[74] *Prosecutor v Sam Hinga Norman* (Decision on Appeal by the Truth and Reconciliation Commission for Sierra Leone and Chief Samuel Hinga Norman JP against the Decision of His Lordship, Mr Justice Bankole Thompson Delivered on 30th October 2003 to Deny the TRC's Request to Hold a Public Hearing with Chief Samuel Hinga Norman JP) SCSL-2003-08-PT (28 November 2003) [4]. On disputes over primacy, see Charles C Jalloh, 'Toward Greater Synergy between Courts and Truth Commissions in Post-Conflict Contexts' in William A Schabas, Margaret M DeGuzman and Diane M Amann (eds), *Arcs of Global Justice: Essays in Honour of William A Schabas* (Oxford University Press 2018).

hybrid tribunals should strive to prospectively delineate their powers with respect to case distribution, information-sharing, evidence collection, witness testimony, and other issues of mutual concern vis-à-vis concurrent accountability mechanisms. It may help to anticipate ICC intervention, even if its Prosecutor may not *yet* exercise jurisdiction at the time of a hybrid tribunal's establishment.

Second, while the label one attaches—complementarity, subsidiarity, or primacy—to regulate authority between hybrid tribunals and other institutions, including the ICC, does not pre-determine or guarantee specific outcomes, the experiences of the DRC, CAR, and South Sudan suggest that the vocabulary of complementarity often creates confusion or serves as a façade while leaving contentious questions unresolved. While primacy is not a procedural panacea for jurisdictional overlap or conflicting mandates, it has the benefit of prospectively signalling that one institution enjoys priority vis-à-vis other bodies, for instance national courts or a truth commission, and avoiding contentious debates further down the road.

Third, while conflict and disagreement cannot always be avoided, avoiding *unnecessary* disputes is facilitated if one institution enjoys clear decision-making authority in resolving competing claims in accordance with pre-defined criteria that are to be interpreted in a spirit of collaboration and good faith. A hybrid tribunal can perform this task vis-à-vis other accountability mechanisms, although alternative intermediary solutions, for instance an independent national or international body with interpretive authority, may be equally or better placed to perform dispute resolution functions, depending on the context.

It should be reiterated that opting for the label 'primacy' does not obviate challenges and disputes between institutions with overlapping accountability mandates. This chapter argues, however, that primacy and associated rules, for instance the power to order deferral or referral, may provide greater clarity as to concurrent powers, whereas an open-ended vocabulary of complementarity often breeds confusion between institutions who all consider themselves co-equal partners in contexts where difficult choices about accountability priorities must be made.

6.6 Conclusion

Some will likely observe that, for better or worse, the international criminal justice community is stuck with complementarity. Even if the word is nowhere to be found in the Rome Statute, the reality is that complementarity has, over the last twenty years, become a 'go-to' framework for regulating concurrent jurisdiction and relationships between accountability mechanisms with overlapping mandates. It is no coincidence that the Malabo Protocol, which the AU adopted in response to the ICC's track record in Africa yet conspicuously avoids any mention of the ICC, embraces the vocabulary of complementarity, implying a co-equal partnership between, inter alia, the ICC and the future African Court of Justice and Human Rights (ACJHR).[75] Yet, while the irony should not be lost on anyone, past practice suggests that disputes over the ACJHR and ICC's spheres of influence seem unavoidable. To take one example, because the Malabo Protocol enshrines the immunity of heads of state and senior officials, which contradicts the Rome Statute,[76] there cannot be any complementarity qua partnership between two co-equal institutions on this issue, and the ICC's case law makes it clear that immunity claims will not prevent the ICC from exercising jurisdiction.[77]

To be sure, from a diplomatic perspective, it may seem useful to couch future disputes in politically acceptable language. However, this does nothing to solve problems of case allocation when prosecutors and judges are required to make contentious decisions. Delaying difficult choices has pernicious effects down the line, including for hybrid courts. For instance, in countries like CAR, where five accountability mechanisms—the SCC, national courts, the ICC, the TJRRC, and the future ACJHR—may eventually operate side by side, it is apparent that appeals to 'complementarity' will not solve actual jurisdictional disputes or answer questions arising from overlapping mandates. In this context, complementarity simply means that issues will need to be decided later, on an ad hoc basis, and likely in a more arbitrary manner. Of the five institutions, each may plausibly argue that it is merely complementing the others, but this also creates the risk that responsibility for addressing impunity always lies with someone else. Put differently, when everyone is responsible for justice, no one really is.

While experience shows that there is no easy way to ensure effective coordination in the fight against impunity, institutional design is a good place to start if accountability advocates want to make a difference. An institutional framework that establishes a principled division of responsibilities and coherent prospective criteria for resolving competing (jurisdictional) claims will prevent confusion, a duplication of tasks, and unnecessary conflict. Although this chapter draws on comparative case studies to illustrate the risks of complementarity while emphasizing the benefits of primacy and referral mechanisms for hybrid tribunals, it does not exclude the possibility that other institutional frameworks will produce positive results as well. As seen in the divergent experiences of Rwanda, Sierra Leone, the DRC, and CAR, what matters most for institutional design is that coherent rules transparently address potential problems while ensuring workable solutions.

[75] Draft Protocol on Amendments to the Protocol on the Statute of the African Court of Justice and Human Rights (27 June 2014) EX.CL/846(XXV) Articles 27, 38, 46 (H).

[76] ibid, Article 46(A)*bis*; UNGA, Rome Statute of the International Criminal Court (17 July 1998, amended 2010) Article 27. See Dapo Akande, 'The Immunity of Heads of States of Nonparties in the Early Years of the ICC' (2018) 112 American Journal of International Law 172.

[77] *Prosecutor v Omar Hassan Ahmad Al Bashir* (Judgment in the Jordan Referral re Al-Bashir Appeal) ICC-02/05-01/09-397 (6 May 2019).

Conversely, it may not be enough for different judicial and non-judicial institutions to merely 'complement each other'. In fact, a risk exists that complementarity understood as co-equal partners operating side by side serves mainly to mask institutional divergences, cloak dilemmas in diplomatic language, and ultimately ensure that no one is responsible for ensuing impunity gaps.

PART II
PRACTICE

7

Valuing the Defence

A Comparative Analysis of the Hybrid Tribunals' Stumbling Efforts Towards Giving Meaning to Defence Rights

Sareta Ashraph

7.1 Introduction

Ever since the modern era of prosecutions for international crimes commenced at Nuremberg, there has been an underscoring of the importance of fair trials. Within this discourse, valuing the defence is oft referenced as a key aspect of conducting a trial that is both fair and seen to be fair.

Yet, for many of the earlier international criminal prosecutions held at international and hybrid courts and tribunals, these acknowledgements counted for little more than exquisite lip service, in contexts where there was either an absence of an institutional framework designed to safeguard the fair trial rights of the accused, or where those structures were so under-resourced as to call into question their efficacy. Within some justice mechanisms, the trial processes struggled to give meaning to the fundamental rights of the accused, as recognized under international human rights law.

This chapter traces the non-linear progress of the hybrid courts and tribunals[1] towards valuing defence rights, including but not solely through the eventual establishment of a structure dedicated to supporting those charged with the defence of the accused, and the subsequent movements towards rendering those structures viable. It briefly explores the importance attributed to fair trial rights from the post-World War II prosecutions to the present day. The chapter then follows the commitment to valuing the defence, as a core aspect of fair trial rights, in select hybrids established between 2000 and 2017. These include the Special Panels for Serious Crimes (SPSC, established in 2000); the Special Court for Sierra Leone (SCSL, 2003); the Iraqi High Criminal Court[2] (IHT, 2003); the Special Tribunal for Lebanon (STL, 2009); and the Kosovo Specialist Chambers (KSC, 2017).

[1] Hereinafter, the 'hybrids' or 'hybrid courts'.
[2] More commonly referred to as the Iraqi High Tribunal.

Sareta Ashraph, *Valuing the Defence* In: *Hybrid Justice*. Edited by: Kirsten Ainley and Mark Kersten, Oxford University Press. © Sareta Ashraph 2025. DOI: 10.1093/oso/9780192893758.003.0007

7.2 Fair Trial Rights as a Legitimating Tool

Since the inception of international criminal prosecutions in Nuremberg and Tokyo in the aftermath of World War II, prosecutors, other court officials, and supporting states have consistently emphasized that such efforts are exercises in justice, not vengeance. In his Opening Statement to the International Military Tribunal at Nuremberg (IMT), the chief American prosecutor, Associate Justice Robert H Jackson, held forth, '[t]hat four great nations, flushed with victory and stung with injury, stay the hand of vengeance and voluntarily submit their captive enemies to the judgment of the law is one of the most significant tributes that Power has ever paid to Reason.'[3] The distance between those giving and receiving the compliment was minute, to be sure; equally, however, in the novel context of those trials and against the backdrop of the atrocities of the Nazi regime, the compliment was not ill-deserved.

Rooting the fairness, and thus the legitimacy, of the trials in public consciousness is particularly acute for the hybrids, which take place with the consent and sometimes the substantive involvement of the government of the state where the crimes reportedly occurred. In the case of some hybrids—including the SCSL and the KSC—among the accused are senior members of the post-conflict government linked to earlier atrocity-era governments whose armed forces, militias, or agents are alleged to have perpetrated atrocities. Moreover, hybrids, such as the IHT in Iraq and the ongoing Special Criminal Court in the Central African Republic, are also more likely to be based in the countries where the crimes being prosecuted are alleged to have occurred, and where violence may still be taking place.[4]

The assertion that these trials are motivated by justice—sometimes also positioned as the need to combat impunity and to rebuild rule of law—is founded upon a commitment that the accused be given a fair trial. Absent this, the very legitimacy of the trials and the court is called into question. This was keenly stated by Associate Justice Jackson in his report on the 1945 negotiations of representatives of the United States, the United Kingdom, France, and the USSR culminating in Agreement and Charter of the IMT, where he averred that the procedural guarantees of fair trials sought to ensure that any punishment following judgment was

[3] Robert H Jackson, 'Opening Statement' in 'Second Day, Wednesday, 11/12/1945, Part 04' in *Trial of the Major War Criminals before the International Military Tribunal* (1947) vol II, 98. That said, there was a widespread view that the IMT had been created to convict: 'There is nothing more foreign to those proceedings than either the presumption that the defendants are innocent until proved guilty or the doctrine that any adverse public comment on the defendants before the verdict is prejudicial to their receiving a fair trial. The basic approach is that these men should not have a chance to go free.' Charles E Wyzanski, 'Nuremberg: A Fair Trial? A Dangerous Precedent' (*The Atlantic*, April 1946) <https://www.theatlantic.com/magazine/archive/1946/04/nuremberg-a-fair-trial-a-dangerous-precedent/306492/> accessed 29 December 2023.

[4] Human Rights Watch, 'The Former Iraqi Government on Trial' (16 October 2005) <https://www.hrw.org/legacy/backgrounder/mena/iraq1005/index.htm> accessed 30 December 2023.

meted out only to the 'right men and for the right reasons'.[5] Proponents and officials of later courts, including the hybrids, would similarly emphasize that the legitimacy of the institutions was inextricably tied to the meaningful provision and protection of due process rights to the accused.[6]

An explicit commitment to the rights of the accused is always to be found in the statutory instruments of the hybrids. Articles 16 and 17 of the Statutes of the STL and the SCSL, respectively, guarantee the fundamental fair trial rights of the accused; so too does Article 20 of the IHT. For the KSC, the most recently established of the hybrids, the rights of the accused are set out in Article 21 of the 2015 Law on the Specialist Chambers and Specialist Prosecutor's Office.[7]

Articles detailing the rights of the accused within the statutory and other founding instruments generally accord with international human rights law that protects an accused's right to an effective defence in respect of the charges brought against that person, by guaranteeing the accused: unrestricted and regular access to legal counsel of their own choice at all stages of criminal proceedings,[8] or to counsel appointed by the court in any case where the interests of justice so require, and without payment if the accused does not have sufficient means to pay for it;[9] adequate time and facilities to prepare a case in response to the particular charges against the defendant, including facilities to ensure the confidentiality of lawyer–client communications and the ability of the defendant to properly instruct their lawyer;[10] and the right to confront and examine witnesses against the defendant, and call witnesses on behalf of the defence under conditions equal to those of the prosecution.[11]

Despite the unambiguous language contained in the founding documents, however, the early international and hybrid courts and tribunals either failed to place in their frameworks structures designed to protect the much-publicized rights

[5] United States Department of State, 'Report of Robert H. Jackson, United States Representative to the International Conference on Military Trials' (1945) Publication 3080, section III, para 2 <https://avalon.law.yale.edu/imt/jack08.asp> accessed 30 December 2023.

[6] Among them, Charles Chernor Jalloh, 'Special Court for Sierra Leone: Achieving Justice?' (2010) Legal Studies Research Paper Series Working Paper No 2010-31, 396, who writes, at 437, 'the credibility and integrity of the SCSL depends, at least partially, on the accused party's access to fair trial rights'. See also, Human Rights Watch, 'The Former Iraqi Government on Trial' (n 4) 7, 'the legitimacy of prosecuting [international crimes] is inextricably linked to whether the prosecution meets international fair trial standards'.

[7] Law on Specialist Chambers and Specialist Prosecutor's Office (3 August 2015) Law No 05/L-053.

[8] Human Rights Committee 'Concluding Observations on Georgia' (9 April 1997) CCPR/C/79/Add 74, para 28; *Murray v United Kingdom* App no 18731/91 (ECtHR, 8 February 1996) [62]; UN Basic Principles on the Role of Lawyers (7 September 1990) principle 1.

[9] International Covenant on Civil and Political Rights (adopted 16 December 1996, entered into force 23 March 1976) 999 UNTS 171 (ICCPR), Article 14(3)(d); *Henry and Douglas v Jamaica* (26 July 1996) UN Doc CCPR/C/57/D/571/1994, [9.2].

[10] ICCPR, Article 14(3)(b); Human Rights Committee, General Comment 13, para 9; *D Wolf v Panama* (26 March 1992) UN Doc A/47/40, [6.6]; UN Basic Principles on the Role of Lawyers (7 September 1990) principle 22.

[11] ICCPR, Article 14(e).

of the accused or, more often, failed to ensure that what structures did exist were effective. This was to the chagrin of various defence counsel, charged with representing the accused in the proceedings while receiving little to no meaningful institutional support.

7.3 The Defence Office, as One Indicator of Progress

Realization of the fair trial rights of the accused has become keenly linked to the establishment of a structure within the hybrids to support those charged with representing the accused's rights at all stages of the justice process. Charles Chernor Jalloh writes about the STL:

> the Defense Office ... appears set to catapult the rights of the accused and the defense in international criminal proceedings to a new and unprecedented level. This will ultimately benefit not only the accused and the defense in that particular international court, but also the fledgling international criminal justice.[12]

It is perhaps surprising, therefore, at the time of their establishment that some of the early hybrids not only failed to create a structure within the institutions to safeguard those rights, but also failed to consider that such a structure might be desirable, if not necessary. In 2000, when the United Nations Transitional Administration in East Timor (UNTAET) established the SPSC, it made no provision for the defence.[13] Similarly, at the time of the 2002 decision to establish the SCSL, there was no mention of a defence office in any of the founding instruments.[14] That year saw the setting up of the SCSL's Office of the Prosecutor, the Registry, and the Judicial Chambers on the dedicated site in Sierra Leone's capital, Freetown. The decision to include a defence office in the SCSL's structure appears to have been made in early 2003, seemingly prompted by the realization that the first arrests were weeks away and that the detainees would require representation.

Increasingly, however, it has been accepted that an office dedicated to the defence should form part of the structure—though consensus around where it should be placed in the structure and the parameters of its role are not settled. The UN

[12] Charles Chernor Jalloh, 'The Special Tribunal for Lebanon: A Defense Perspective' (2014) 47 Vanderbilt Journal of Transnational Law 767, 773.

[13] Megan Hirst and Howard Varney, 'Justice Abandoned? An Assessment of the Serious Crimes Process in East Timor' (2005) International Center for Transitional Justice 20 <https://www.ictj.org/sites/default/files/ICTJ-TimorLeste-Justice-Abandoned-2005-English.pdf> accessed 29 December 2023.

[14] Article 17 of the SCSL's Statute set out recognized fair trial guarantees, but none of the court's founding documents envisaged how those rights would be realized within the institutional framework. In contrast, the same documents detailed the roles of the prosecution, the Registry, and the Judicial Chambers.

Secretary-General's 2006 'Report on the Establishment of the Lebanon Tribunal' stated that the creation of a defence office as an organ was now 'integral to the institutional fabric of these courts'.[15]

The gradual acceptance of a need for a Defence Office, in some form, was motivated by three separate impulses. The first was ideological in nature: the evolution of defence rights demanded an office within the institution specifically dedicated to ensuring the rights of the accused. Those committed to defence rights recalled the 'first generation' of the international tribunals in Nuremberg and Tokyo, where 'except for guaranteeing a right to counsel ... they paid very little attention to the rights of the accused'.[16] While the International Criminal Tribunal for the former Yugoslavia (ICTY) had the Lawyers and Detention Facility Management Section and the International Criminal Tribunal for Rwanda (ICTR), the Defence Counsel Management Section, these creations had come about in response to reports of fee-splitting and inflated fees and did not fulfil the role of providing legal support to defence counsel or of safeguarding defence rights more broadly. A Defence Office, within the modern era of international criminal justice represented by the hybrids, suggested a more serious commitment to ensuring the rights of the accused to a fair trial.

The second impulse, alluded to earlier, came from those concerned with the perception of the hybrids and the damage that would be done to the legitimacy of the institutions' work by the absence of a unit charged with protecting defence rights. A Defence Office would serve as a tangible reminder of the hybrids' adherence to the presumption of innocence, and to defence rights more broadly. For some hybrids, highlighting the existence of a Defence Office in outreach to local communities also served to convey to supporters of particular accused that they were not being subjected to a sham trial, thereby hopefully lowering the risk of political violence to which an in-country hybrid would be particularly vulnerable. At the SCSL, for example, the existence of the Defence Office underlined that the accused from the pro-government Civil Defence Forces militias—which a vocal part of the population believed to be, if not exactly innocent, then heroes—would be provided with a vigorous defence. In Baghdad, as the IHT trials took place amidst significant instability, it was deemed 'essential that the trials be fair and be seen to be fair so that accusations that the trials amount to "victors' justice" do not gain credence'.[17]

[15] Report of the Secretary-General, 'Establishment of a Special Tribunal for Lebanon' (2006) UN Doc S/2006/893.

[16] Kenneth Gallant, 'Politics, Theory and Institutions: Three Reasons Why International Criminal Defence is Hard and What Might Be Done About One of Them' (2003) 14 Criminal Law Forum 317, 318.

[17] Human Rights Watch, 'The Former Iraqi Government on Trial' (n 4). This was not to be with its first trial, the Dujail trial, referred to as 'a political spectacle, a new attempt at Iraqi justice, and, after the implementation of sentencing, an ill-fated symbol of sectarian revenge'. See Miranda Sissons and Ari S Bassin, 'Was the Dujail Trial Fair?' (2007) 5 Journal of International Criminal Justice 272.

The third, and arguably the most powerful, impulse motivating the creation of Defence Offices within the hybrids was financial. One of the draws of the hybrids in the post-2000 period was that the 1990s' ad hoc tribunals had been unsustainably expensive. In ten years of operation, the ICTY and ICTR respectively spent USD 1.2 billion and USD 1 billion, at the cost of between USD 10–15 million per accused.[18] One UN Report indicated that the two tribunals had more than 2,000 job posts and a combined annual budget of a quarter of a billion dollars—more than 15 per cent of the total UN budget.[19] Within the ballooning ad hocs, funding the defence had become unfeasibly expensive, with a 2003 Report finding that the cost of one defence team at the ICTY exceeded USD 360,000 a year.[20] The concern about defence spending had been compounded by a 2001 UN report that had found evidence of over-billing and fee-splitting, underlining the need to assess and supervise the payments to defence teams.[21] The limited budgets of the hybrids, some of which were funded through voluntary contributions of states, could not afford to spend large amounts on the defence teams. A Defence Office could assist in keeping costs down in two ways. First, the legal support provided by a Defence Office would justify the capped payments provided to the defence teams. Second, the Office could also supervise and assess the bills of the defence teams.

Valuing the defence, however, goes well beyond the question of the existence of a Defence Office and its place in the structure of a particular court (and particularly the question of whether it should operate as an independent 'fourth' pillar alongside the Prosecution, Chambers and Registry or as a sub-office within the Registry). The weight accorded to the valuing of the defence is less about the institutional structure, and more about the substance of how defence rights are recognized and protected. Undoubtedly the two are linked, but the establishment of the

[18] Rupert Skilbeck, 'Funding Justice: The Price of War Crimes Trials' (2008) 15 Human Rights Brief 6 <https://digitalcommons.wcl.american.edu/cgi/viewcontent.cgi?article=1028&context=hrbrief> accessed 29 December 2023. It should be noted, however, that it is not clear that the hybrids, while they are less expensive, are cost-effective given the lower number of accused tried. An analysis of the SCSL conducted by Charles Chernor Jalloh determined that 'even though [the SCSL's] total budget is much lower, given the relatively low number of persons it ultimately prosecuted over nine years, the Court turns out to not be significantly more cost effective' than the ad hoc tribunals. See Jalloh, 'Special Court for Sierra Leone: Achieving Justice?' (n 6). In his Independent Expert Report on the Special Court, 12 December 2006, Justice Antonio Cassese reached similar conclusions. At para 5, Cassese concluded that the overall level of efficiency of the SCSL trials 'is not a significant improvement on the record of the ICTR and ICTY'.

[19] Report of the Secretary-General, 'The Rule of Law and Transitional Justice in Conflict and Post-Conflict Societies' (2004) UN Doc S/2004/616 . See also David Wippman, 'The Costs of International Justice' (2006) 100 American Journal of International Law 861 <http://www.jstor.org/stable/4126321> accessed 29 December 2023.

[20] Report of the Secretary-General, 'Comprehensive Report on the Progress made by the International Criminal Tribunal for the Former Yugoslavia in Reforming its Legal Aid System' (2003) UN Doc A/58/288, para 31, cited in Sylvia de Bertadano, 'What Price Defence? Resourcing the Defence at the ICTY' (2004) 2 Journal of International Criminal Justice 503.

[21] UNGA, 'Report of the Office of Internal Oversight Services on the Investigation into Possible Fee-Splitting Arrangements between Defence Counsel and Indigent Detainees at the ICTY and ICTR' (2001) UN Doc A/55/759.

Defence Office as a fourth pillar should be regarded as only one possible indicator of progress. Valuing the defence more broadly encompasses the raising up of the rights of the accused at all stages of the trial, the proper resourcing of the defence and, significantly, the meaningful recognition of the substantively important role the defence plays, in a context where justice is not viewed as being synonymous with convictions.

7.4 Examining the Progress of Select Hybrids Towards Valuing the Defence

7.4.1 Special Panels of the Dili District Court (2000)

One of the earliest hybrid judicial mechanisms was the Special Panels of the Dili District Courts, a response by the international community to the mass atrocities—said to include genocide, war crimes, crimes against humanity, murder, torture, and crimes of sexual violence—committed between 1 January and 25 October 1999 by the Indonesian military and security forces, and by Timorese militia operating under their effective command.[22] In the immediate aftermath of the violence, the Security Council, through its Resolution 1272 (1999), established the United Nations Transitional Administration in East Timor (UNTAET). Under its mandate, UNTAET created four District Courts and a Court of Appeal in East Timor, with the Dili District Court having sole jurisdiction over 'serious crimes', such as those set out above. In 2000, and within that structure, UNTAET created the Special Panels for Serious Crimes (SPSC), with each panel presided over by two international judges and one Timorese judge.[23] The first panel was swiftly joined by a second, and then in late 2004, a third. A Court of Appeal, on which also sat two international and one Timorese judge, was established to hear appeals from the SPSC.[24] The panels were to apply the law of East Timor as well as international law.[25]

A number of problems plagued the SPSC, among them the inadequate resources provided to the court; the difficulty of recruiting Timorese judges with the requisite experience, given the exodus of legal professionals during the violence; and the fact that the SPSC, being in East Timor, was subject to attempts by the government to politically influence their policies and procedures. While these were

[22] UNTAET Regulation on the Organization of Courts in East Timor (6 March 2000) UNTAET/REG/2000/11, sections 10.1 and 10.2.

[23] UNTAET Regulation on the Establishment of Panels with Exclusive Jurisdiction over Serious Criminal Offence (6 June 2000) UNTAET/REG/2000/15, sections 22.1 and 22.2.

[24] ibid section 22.2 provided that, in cases of special importance or gravity, a panel of the Court of Appeal composed of five judges (three international and two national) could be established.

[25] ibid section 3.1.

extremely serious problems, they were dwarfed by the initial problem which faced the defence, which was that it did not exist.

When UNTAET established the SPSC, it made no provision for the defence.[26] One senior staff member, interviewed in early 2002, baldly stated that no budget had been provided for *any* defence functions within the SPSC.[27] There were no funds to set up an office, to conduct investigations, or pay for interpreters' or witnesses' travel. The defence teams had no access to a legal library, research resources, or a photocopier. Legal professionals in East Timor had largely fled during the violence of 1999 and the absence of experienced lawyers on the ground impacted on the recruitment of local judges, prosecutors, and those working in defence of the accused. This affected the defence more than any other, principally because the defence had no funds to recruit even less experienced lawyers. When defence lawyers were assigned, they often had little courtroom experience and no background in international criminal law (ICL).

The lack of interpreters proved particularly destructive to any semblance of a defence function as there was no way for local counsel to communicate with the international legal mentors who had been assigned to assist them with case preparation and to build their knowledge of the relevant law. The battle against impunity for the atrocities committed in East Timor had, as a primary assumption, that inexperienced defence counsel would learn what they needed to know during the course of cases in which the defendants were charged with international law's most serious crimes. One report would later note, 'the lack of capacity in the defence component was one of the most serious and troubling shortcomings of the trial and made itself vividly felt in the courtroom to the obvious disadvantage and detriment of the accused'.[28]

Concerns mounted and were forced into the open by inexperienced cross-examination by defence counsel and the fact that not a single defence witness was called in the first fourteen trials, almost a third of the total trials before the SPSC.[29] In September 2002, facing severe criticism and with the integrity of the fledgling justice project being called into question, the Defence Lawyers Unit (DLU) was established.

The very existence of the DLU was a step forward in safeguarding the rights of the defendants. The unit initially employed only one lawyer, though it expanded to three by November 2002 and six by April 2003.[30] Nevertheless questions

[26] Hirst and Varney (n 13) 20.

[27] David Cohen, 'Indifference and Accountability: The United Nations and the Politics of International Justice in East Timor' (2006) East-West Center 16 <https://www.eastwestcenter.org/publications/indifference-and-accountability-the-united-nations-and-the-politics-international> accessed 29 December 2023.

[28] ibid.

[29] David Cohen, 'Seeking Justice on the Cheap: Is the East Timor Tribunal Really a Model for the Future?' (2002) 61 Asia Pacific Issues 5.

[30] Hirst and Varney (n 13) 25.

persisted about how effective it was. It was brutally underfunded with a skeleton staff, no professional investigators, no online research facilities, and no law texts.[31] International counsel began to dominate the defence teams—by May 2005, the DLU only employed international staff and saw little or no collaboration with local lawyers.[32] For many of the international defence counsel, these trials constituted their first foray into the world of ICL and procedure.

By its closure in May 2005, the SPSC had tried eighty-seven accused in fifty-five trials. Eighty-three of these were convicted at first instance. One defendant had his acquittal reversed on appeal, with the consequence that all but three accused were convicted. David Cohen, having conducted interviews with eight of the nine SPSC judges serving in 2004–2005, stated that the majority expressed concerns about the fairness of some aspects of the proceedings, including the adequacy of the defence.[33] The failure to properly establish and then resource the accused's defence, whether via a Defence Office or directly to the defence teams, had a clear impact on the legitimacy of the hybrid: 'The perception that a conviction was more or less a fait accompli, in many cases as a result of the lack of adequate representation, constituted a serious setback for the serious crimes process.'[34]

More significant was the impact this had on the accused. As Cohen writes,

> it cannot be emphasized enough that what was at stake here is not bureaucratic efficiency, but the lives and liberty of individuals accused of the most serious crimes. Many of those individuals convicted in trials in which their rights were not adequately protected continue to serve out their sentences in Becora prison in Dili.[35]

7.4.2 Special Court for Sierra Leone (2003)

In 2000, during the dying embers of a brutal civil war, Sierra Leonean President Ahmad Kabbah requested that the United Nations form a court to try those responsible, following which the Security Council passed Resolution 1315 calling for the Secretary-General to begin discussions with the government of Sierra Leone to create a Special Court. The government of Sierra Leone and the United Nations signed an Agreement establishing the SCSL on 16 January 2002.[36] Based

[31] ibid.

[32] Siri Frigaard, Address (Domestic Prosecutions and Transitional Justice Conference, International Transitional Justice and the Foundation for Human Rights, Johannesburg, South Africa, 18 May 2005).

[33] Cohen, 'Seeking Justice on the Cheap' (n 29) 6.

[34] Hirst and Varney (n 13) 21.

[35] Cohen, 'Seeking Justice on the Cheap' (n 29) 5, 6.

[36] Agreement between the United Nations and the Government of Sierra Leone on the establishment of a Special Court for Sierra Leone (signed 16 January 2002, entered into force 12 April 2002) 2178 UNTS 138 ('the Agreement') <https://www.rscsl.org/Documents/scsl-agreement.pdf> accessed 30 December 2023.

in Freetown, Sierra Leone, the SCSL had the authority to prosecute 'those who bear the greatest responsibility' for crimes against humanity, war crimes, and violations of Sierra Leonean law committed in Sierra Leone since 30 November 1996. None of the ten indictments handed down contained charges based on Sierra Leonean law, however.

Although the SCSL Defence Office was later heralded as an innovation in defence rights,[37] there was little mention of it at the time of the Court's creation. Neither the Agreement nor the Court's own Statute (annexed to the Agreement) mentioned an office specifically dedicated to protecting defence rights. Article 17 of the Statute set out recognized fair trial guarantees, but none of the court's founding documents envisaged how those rights would be realized within the institutional framework.[38] While the Prosecution, the Registry, and the Chambers had been on the ground in Freetown since 2002, it was not until early February 2003, just over a month before the Court's first arrests took place, that discussions about establishing a Defence Office began in earnest.

The vision that prevailed was a model in which the SCSL would retain the services of independent defence counsel through a contract. The Defence Office would support the work of these contracted defence counsel, through the provision of legal research and administrative services. The role of the Principal Defender, the head of the Defence Office, was

> more as a behind the scenes administrator who would mediate between the defence teams, organise and facilitate the drafting of legal research and motions common to the defence, and who would have more of a limited advocacy within the Court's Outreach Program.[39]

The form of the Defence Office became thus: three lawyers employed by the Defence Office stood in as 'duty counsel' until defence counsel were assigned to each accused. Defence counsel were not staff but provided their services as per the terms of a Legal Services Contract. For all the defence teams, save for the Charles Taylor defence team, the contract allowed a quarterly lump sum to cover the fees of the entire legal team, flights, and associated travel costs. The relatively low quarterly sum was justified as legal research common to the defence teams was, in theory, conducted by the duty counsel.

[37] With William Schabas referring to it as one of the 'more significant innovations in this area'. William A Schabas, *UN International Criminal Tribunals: The Former Yugoslavia, Rwanda and Sierra Leone* (Cambridge University Press 2006) 615.

[38] In contrast, the same documents detailed the roles of the Prosecution, the Registry, and the Judicial Chambers.

[39] Sara Kendall and Michelle Staggs, 'Interim Report on the Special Court for Sierra Leone: The Special Court as a Model for "Hybrid Justice"' (2005) War Crimes Studies Center, UC Berkeley 19.

Recruitment of duty counsel happened rapidly, with the Defence Office becoming 'functional' on 17 February 2003.[40] The hasty creation of the Defence Office led to its being saddled with an unclear mandate and with duty counsel who had no experience in ICL or procedure and thus were unable to support the defence teams. These factors were the foundation of a relationship of profound friction with many of the defence teams.[41] One human rights advocate, who followed the SCSL closely throughout its lifetime, stated that when she visited the Court in 2006, she found the relationship between the Defence Office and many of the defence teams across all three ongoing trials 'so irretrievably broken down' that it raised serious questions as to the viability of this model for Defence Offices at future tribunals, despite such offices' theoretical advantages.[42]

While Jalloh considers the foremost issue to have been 'a fundamental structural problem: its lack of operational independence from the registrar', which is to say that the Defence Office was set up as a sub-office of the Registry and not as a fourth pillar akin to the Offices of the Prosecutor, Registry, or Chambers,[43] that view is not shared by this author. While the first three lawyers in the role of the Principal Defender saw their role as one of being of support to the defence teams representing the accused, the fourth Principal Defender, Vincent Nmehielle, imagined himself as head of an autonomous office, occupying the same position as the Prosecutor. He was quoted in one report as saying he believed that the Rules of Procedure and Evidence established 'that he leads the defence of the accused persons in front of the SCSL'.[44] This brought him into conflict, not only with defence counsel, but also with the Trial and Appeals Chamber which sought to correct his understanding of the Defence Office, and his role within it.[45] In the meantime, none of the genuine obstacles to valuing the defence at the SCSL were being addressed.

One significant obstacle was the poor staffing of the Office, which provided woefully inadequate support to the defence teams. None of the duty counsel employed had any background in ICL or procedure, and were unfamiliar with legal

[40] Position Paper on the Independence of the Office of the Principal Defender at the Special Court for Sierra Leone (OPCD Position Paper) 1 (Copy in author's possession). The first Acting Principal Defender was not appointed until April 2003, six weeks after the Defence Office started to function.

[41] Sareta Ashraph, 'The Naked Defense Office: How an Unclear Mandate, Poor Staffing, and Registry Disinterest Stripped the Office of the Principal Defender' in Christopher Jalloh (ed), *The Sierra Leone Special Court and its Legacy: The Impact for Africa and International Criminal Law* (Cambridge University Press 2013) 550–71.

[42] ibid 569.

[43] Charles Chernor Jalloh, 'The Contribution of the Special Court for Sierra Leone to the Development of International Law' (2007) 15 African Journal of International and Comparative Law 165, 180.

[44] Alison Thompson and Michelle Staggs, 'The Defence Office at the Special Court for Sierra Leone: A Critical Perspective' (2007) War Crimes Studies Center, UC Berkeley 37.

[45] Ashraph (n 41) 557–59.

databases and search engines. No training was ever provided to them by the Registry. Defence teams received little support despite, for example, multiple requests to put together a library of jurisprudence that defence counsel could draw upon.[46] As one commentator observed,

> [g]iven that the envisioned research support provided by the Office was cited as a key justification for the strict control over team budgets, the reality that substantial support has generally not been forthcoming has meant that the teams are often either (i) not carrying out the research or (ii) relying on underpaid interns or *pro bono* services to undertake it for them.[47]

In this way the lack of commitment to defence rights again became visible: it was unthinkable lawyers with no experience in ICL would have been hired to provide legal research support to the prosecution trial teams.

Defence teams were wildly under-resourced. Initially, in 2003, the three defence teams in each trial shared one office, with one three-drawer filing cabinet provided to each of them. Consequently, it was impossible to hold confidential meetings or house the confidential and often privileged material, which in the course of the trials spiralled to over 150,000 pages. By late 2004, after time-consuming entreaties by counsel, each team had its own office, measuring 15 metres by 7 metres —too small for all members of a defence team to fit in at one time—with one networked computer available for each team. Defence lawyers and legal assistants, armed with their personal laptops, commandeered tables in the canteen as workspaces.

While the Prosecution relied on skilled investigators, most with significant experience at the ad hoc tribunals, each defence team was permitted funding (at the rate of USD 600 per month) for a Sierra Leonean investigator, a job description which required only a background in policing. In the monthly stationery supplies, defence team members were allocated one pen each and three to four binders per team. Sitting in a sea of prosecution and defence papers and needing to make copies of the papers for the accused and for general team use, defence counsel who lived abroad began printing and binding papers and flying in with them.

The lack of resources had a particularly detrimental effect on defence investigations. While the Prosecution had investigators, drivers, interpreters, vehicles, and satellite phones on hand, a defence team had to apply for those resources and

46 In *Prosecutor v Sesay et al*, SCSL-04-T-672 (9 January 2007), the team indicated: 'The Defence Office ... does not—and has not—provided *any* assistance as regards other aspects of substantive defence preparation including legal research, evidential collation or any other aspects of case management.'

47 James Cockayne, 'The Fraying Shoestring: Thinking Hybrid War Crimes Tribunals' (2004) 28 Fordham International law Journal 616, 672.

obtain them in competition not only with the other nine defence teams, but also with the other Registry sub-offices including the Outreach Section which often needed these resources for events in rural Sierra Leone.[48] While professional prosecution investigators travelled into the provinces in white four-wheel drive SUVs, the local defence investigator together with legal assistants would climb into poda-podas of dubious roadworthiness and rumble along Sierra Leone's poorly maintained roads.[49]

Following one defence team's 2007 motion to compel the Registry to provide more resources—a motion that was opposed by both the Registry and the Defence Office—the Trial Chamber granted the defence team a second office, a second computer, a vehicle dedicated to investigations, and a witness management officer.[50] While an improvement, they did not radically alter the egregious inequality of arms under which the remaining defence teams worked, to the detriment of the trial and of the accused.

7.4.3 Iraqi High Tribunal (2003)

In the lead-up to the 2003 US-led invasion of Iraq, there were multiple public pronouncements about the need to hold Saddam Hussein and other Ba'ath party leaders accountable for their crimes.[51] Even prior to the fall of Baghdad, the US Ambassador for War Crimes announced that the United States intended to institute an 'Iraqi-led' justice process.[52]

The IHT, which had been earlier set up as the Iraqi Special Tribunal, was established by a Statute issued by the Coalition Provisional Authority and later reaffirmed under the jurisdiction of the interim Iraqi government.[53] Established

48 ibid 671, 672; Jalloh, 'Special Court for Sierra Leone: Achieving Justice?' (n 6) 441.

49 The term 'podas-podas' is used in Sierra Leone describes minibuses which operate as private taxis, usually along set routes in the capital or between provincial towns.

50 *Prosecutor v Sesay et al* (24 January 2007) SCSL-04-T-15-691.

51 See, eg, The White House, 'President's Remarks at the United Nations General Assembly' (12 September 2002) <https://georgewbush-whitehouse.archives.gov/news/releases/2002/09/20020912-1.html> accessed 28 December 2023. Also, President George W Bush, State of the Union (28 January 2003) <https://georgewbush-whitehouse.archives.gov/news/releases/2003/01/20030128-19.html> accessed 28 December 2023.

52 US Department of Defense, 'Briefing on Geneva Convention, EPW's and War Crimes' (7 April 2003) <https://documentafterlives.newmedialab.cuny.edu/content/cia-copy-dod-news-transcript-briefing-geneva-convention-epws-and-war-crimes> accessed 28 December 2023.

53 Between December 2003 and October 2005, the IHT was known as the Iraqi Special Tribunal, the Statute of which was promulgated as an Order of the Coalition Provisional Authority on 10 December 2003. In early August 2005, the Statute was revoked by Iraq's Transitional National Assembly, and replaced by an amended statute that renamed the Special Tribunal as the IHT. The August enactment proved legally defective, however, due to a failure to follow the proper legislative process, and was therefore re-debated and re-enacted in September 2005. The new law, Law No 10 of 2005, 20 was promulgated in the *Official Gazette* on 18 October 2005, only one day before the commencement of the IHT's first trial, the Dujail trial.

under Iraqi law, the IHT was mandated to try Iraqi nationals or residents accused of crimes listed in the Statute that were committed between 17 July 1968 and 1 May 2003.[54] The civil law foundations of the Iraqi Criminal Code provided the baseline for the de facto rules of procedure and evidence, which were then modified where appropriate to comply with relevant international norms.

In both the Statute and in some public pronouncements concerning the IHT, there was an emphasis on fair trial rights of the accused. This flowed from the desire on the part of the drafters of the Statute that the IHT's 'structure and operation be perceived in contradistinction to the corrosive effects of Ba'athist efforts to use a charade of justice as a tool for subverting the people's rights'.[55]

The first case began on 19 October 2005 and concerned the government's retaliations following an assassination attempt on Saddam Hussein in the village of al-Dujail. The retaliations included: detaining and torturing 800 men, women, and children; referring 148 male detainees to trial before the Revolutionary Court, where all were sentenced to death and most were executed; and confiscating and destroying land.[56] Saddam Hussein, three other senior former government officials, and four lower-level Ba'ath party members were all charged with crimes against humanity.

Maintaining adherence to the presumption of innocence proved challenging. In 2005, shortly before the trial opened, Iraqi President Talabani told the media that Saddam Hussein had confessed to crimes during his regime—including executions—and deserved to die, stating 'Saddam deserves a death sentence 20 times a day'.[57] This would eventually seep into courtroom, where, in August 2007, chief judge Mohammed Oreibi al-Khalifa shouted, 'Shut up, you dirty Baathist' at accused Abdul-Ghani Abdul-Ghafur, following the latter's courtroom outburst on his receiving a death sentence for committing crimes against humanity while crushing the 1991 Shiite uprising in southern Iraq.[58]

[54] Articles 11 to 13 of its Statute established the competence of the IHT to prosecute genocide, crimes against humanity, and war crimes committed during both international and non-international armed conflicts, while Article 14 of the IHT Statute established jurisdiction over a core group of crimes defined in the Iraqi criminal code.

[55] The costs of funding the defence at the ICTY and ICTR as compared with the lower costs of the funding the SCSL defence through the oversight provided by the Defence Office formed part of the discussions of building the IHT. See Laurel Miller, 'Building the Iraqi Special Tribunal: Lessons from Experiences in International Criminal Justice' (2004) US Institute of Peace <http://www.jstor.com/stable/resrep12307> accessed 28 December 2023.

[56] Human Rights Watch, 'Judging Dujail: The First Trial Before the Iraqi High Tribunal' (19 November 2006) <https://www.hrw.org/report/2006/11/19/judging-dujail/first-trial-iraqi-high-tribunal> accessed 30 December 2023.

[57] BBC, 'Saddam "confesses" says Iraq head, (7 September 2005) <http://news.bbc.co.uk/2/hi/middle_east/4221202.stm> accessed 30 December 2023.

[58] NBC, 'Second death sentence for Iraq's "Chemical Ali"' (2 December 2008) <https://www.nbcnews.com/id/wbna28011270> accessed 30 December 2023.

The IHT placed defendants at a profound disadvantage. Equality of arms—'[t]he most important criterion of a fair trial'[59]—was largely absent. Sissons and Bassin noted that the Tribunal:

> permitted ambiguous charging, limited access to important evidence and denied defendants the full opportunity to contest evidence presented against them. These problems were exemplified by insufficient charging documents, inadequate security arrangements, failure to gather and disclose exculpatory evidence, late or incomplete disclosure and an impaired opportunity to confront witnesses.[60]

Its Rules of Procedure and Evidence did provide for the establishment of a Defence Office, headed by a director and supported by the Administration of the IHT, to ensure adequate facilities for counsel in the preparation of defence cases. The hope was that the Defence Office would assist Iraqi defence lawyers with the preparation and presentation of legal arguments and facilitate the hiring of external experts if necessary. The anticipated complexity of the trials and the fact that Iraqi lawyers had been isolated from the rapid development of ICL since the 1990s underpinned a profound need for 'a robust and well-resourced Defense Office, with international advisors" capable of fulfilling these functions at the IHT'.[61] Unfortunately this did not occur.

The IHT Defence Office came into existence in September 2005, six weeks before the first trial started. Its director was appointed at the same time. Shortly afterwards, two Iraqi duty counsel were appointed prior to private counsel being retained by the accused. The quality of the duty counsel was troubling: one assigned to the accused Muhammad 'Azzawi in the Dujail trial did not meet with his client for at least a month after the opening of the trial.[62] While training in ICL and procedure was provided to Iraqi judges and prosecutors, defence lawyers were excluded. While an international advisor was hired in April 2006, the individual—although an experienced investigator—was not a lawyer. Human Rights Watch visited the Defence Office in November 2005 and found 'one office with three desks and two computers with no internet connection, shared among seven lawyers'.[63] When Human Rights Watch returned in July 2006, they found the facilities unaltered save for the fact that the computers were no longer there.

[59] Louise Arbour, 'In the matter of Sentencing of Taha Yassin Ramadan: Application for Leave to Intervene as Amicus Curiae and Application in Intervention as Amicus Curiae of United Nations High Commissioner for Human Rights' (8 February 2007) quoting M Nowak, *UN Covenant on Civil and Political Rights: CCPR Commentary* (2nd edn, Engel 2005) 321.

[60] Sissons and Bassin (n 17) 272. See also, Michael Newton, 'The Iraqi High Criminal Court: Controversy and Contributions' (2006) 88 International Review of the Red Cross 399.

[61] Human Rights Watch, 'Judging Dujail' (n 56) 14.

[62] ibid.

[63] ibid 15.

A split appeared between the duty counsel and the privately retained defence counsel. The Defence Office refused to provide logistical, administrative, or other support to privately retained defence lawyers. The director, in an interview with Human Rights Watch, was clear in his view that 'the Defence Office did not, and would not, have a role in supporting or assisting the private defense lawyers in the Dujail case'.[64] Duty counsel indicated that they preferred not to associate with the private lawyers due to safety concerns. This was not unwise: three defence lawyers were murdered in the course of the trial.[65] Amidst rising violence, the inadequate protection for defence counsel made it impossible for the defence to conduct its own investigations. The consequence was that the accused faced significant challenges in retaining counsel, regardless of whether they were privately arranged or court appointed.

Human Rights Watch, which monitored the entirety of the Dujail trial, said of the Defence Office, '[t]he picture is one of disarray in terms of recruitment and training, and fraught relations between private counsel and Defense Office lawyers, with the latter reluctant to provide any assistance or support to non-Defense Office defense lawyers'.

7.4.4 Special Tribunal for Lebanon (2009)

On 13 December 2005, the Lebanese prime minister, Fouad Siniora, sent a letter to UN Secretary-General Kofi Annan requesting the establishment of 'a tribunal of an international character to convene in or outside Lebanon, to try all those who are found responsible for the terrorist crime perpetrated against [former Lebanese Prime Minister] Hariri'.[66] In January and February 2007, the Secretary-General and the government of Lebanon signed an agreement on the establishment of a Special Tribunal for Lebanon. On 30 May 2007, the Security Council passed Resolution 1757 (2007) deciding that the provisions of the agreement between the UN and Lebanon on the establishment of a Special Tribunal for Lebanon would enter into force on 10 June 2007.[67]

The STL Statute had a number of distinct features, including its jurisdiction over the crime of terrorism and permitting trials in absentia.[68] Article 13 of the Statute

64 ibid.

65 Sissons and Bassin (n 17) 282.

66 UNSC, 'Letter dated 13 December 2005 from the Chargé d'Affaires of the Permanent Mission of Lebanon to the United Nations addressed to the Secretary-General' (13 December 2005) UN Doc S/2005/783.

67 UNSC Res 1757 (30 May 2007) UN Doc S/RES1757.

68 For discussion of the distinct features of the STL, see Cécile Aptel, 'Some Innovations in the Statute of the Special Tribunal for Lebanon' (2007) 5 Journal of International Criminal Justice 1107.

also provided, for the first time, an autonomous Defence Office charged with protecting the rights of the accused, 'and to make the exercise of these rights effective, which is an essential requirement for a fair trial'.[69] The Defence Office stood as a fourth pillar, with status equal to that of the Prosecutor. The Head of the Defence Office was appointed by the Secretary-General, in consultant with the President of the STL, and served for a term of three years.[70] The Office itself was much larger than its predecessors in earlier hybrids, and consisted of 'an Immediate Office, a Legal Advisory Section, an Operational Support Unit, and a Legal Aid Unit'.[71]

The role of the Defence Office was made clear at the outset: it would not represent, or take instructions from, any suspects or accused. Rather, independent defence counsel would represent the accused before the STL. The first Head of the Defence Office was French international criminal lawyer, Francois Roux. In a speech on 'The Evolving Defence Systems at the International Tribunals', Roux made his understanding of the Office's role clear, stating:

> The Defence Office does not speak on behalf of the Defence teams but it is the voice of the Defence both within and outside the institution ... [It] is not involved in the strategy of the defence teams or with the case file. We are there to provide legal, financial and logistic support to those teams. We offer regular training and monitoring if required. We provide them with suitable offices and the necessary equipment ... We strive for equal resources with the Office of the Prosecutor.[72]

The Defence Office, headed and staffed by experienced lawyers, provided significant support to the defence teams, including through research. It also produced compilations of best practices, including for example the Practitioner's Handbook on Defence Investigations in International Criminal Trials, for defence counsel practising before international and hybrid courts and tribunals, but useful to anyone whose work or mission is to gather evidence, to question witnesses, or to protect them.[73]

[69] STL, 'About the STL: Structure of the STL: Defence' <https://www.stl-tsl.org/en/about-the-stl/structure-of-the-stl/defence> accessed 30 December 2023.

[70] Statute of the Special Tribunal for Lebanon (2007) annexed to UNSC Res 1757 (30 May 2007) UN Doc S/RES/1757, Article 13(1).

[71] Colleen Rohan and Gentian Zyberi, 'The Role of the Defence in International Criminal Law' in Colleen Rohan and Gentian Zyberi (eds), *Defence Perspectives on International Criminal Justice* (Cambridge University Press 2017) 151.

[72] Francois Roux, 'Speech' (Panel on the Evolving Defence Systems at the International Tribunals) <https://unictr.irmct.org/sites/unictr.org/files/publications/compendium-documents/i%20-francois-roux-speech-stl-roux_0.pdf> accessed 30 December 2023.

[73] Defence Office of the STL, *Practitioner's Handbook on Defence Investigations in International Criminal Trials* (2017) <https://www.stl-tsl.org/sites/default/files/documents/guides/Practicioners-Handbook-on-Defence-Investigations-EN.pdf> accessed 30 December 2023.

Its Legal Aid Unit administered legal aid to accused who successfully applied to the Registrar. Legal Aid, under the Defence Office policy, covered all necessary and reasonable costs of legal representation. The Defence Office noted that a '"standard" defence team is composed of a lead counsel and a co-counsel, a junior lawyer, a case manager, an investigator, and a language assistant. In addition, the policy covered expenses for experts, and expenses related to defence investigations.'[74] Importantly the clear line between the work of the Defence Office and the defence teams, the Office being staffed by experience lawyers in the field of ICL, and its work to bolster defence interests within the framework of the STL, led to generally positive working relationships with the counsel assigned to the defence teams.[75]

7.4.5 Kosovo Specialist Chambers (2017)

On 3 August 2015, the Assembly of Kosovo amended its Constitution and passed the Law on the Specialist Chambers and the Specialist Prosecutor's Office.[76] The two judicial institutions were established within the Kosovan justice system to investigate; prosecute; and try crimes against humanity, war crimes, and other crimes under Kosovo law in relation to allegations reported in the Council of Europe Parliamentary Assembly Report of 7 January 2011.[77] Alleged crimes must have commenced or been committed in Kosovo between 1 January 1998 and 31 December 2000 by or against citizens of Kosovo or the Federal Republic of Yugoslavia. The KSC has its seat in The Hague. Its staff are international, as are the Judges, the Specialist Prosecutor, and the Registrar.

The KSC's first indictment was handed down on 24 June 2020. Since then, the court has handed down eight indictments, with cases against four persons in the pre-trial stage, one person currently on trial, a case in the appeals stage, and two persons serving sentences. The final trial, against four accused, commenced in April 2023, with 153 participating victims, and is expected to close in 2025..

At the KSC, the Defence Office has returned to being a sub-office of the Registry. Rule 23(6) sets out a vision of a limited mandate, stating '[t]he Defence Office in the Registry administers a list of Specialist Counsel eligible to practice before the

[74] Defence Office of the STL, 'Legal Aid Policy' (2011).

[75] Interview with Defence Counsel I (online, 23 February 2023); Defence Counsel IV (online, 1 March 2023); and Defence Counsel VI (online, 3 March 2023).

[76] Law on Specialist Chambers and Specialist Prosecutor's Office (3 August 2015) Law No 05/L-053.

[77] Council of Europe Parliamentary Assembly Report, 'Inhuman treatment of people and illicit trafficking in human organs in Kosovo' (7 January 2011) <https://www.scp-ks.org/en/documents/council-europe-parliamentary-assembly-report-inhuman-treatment-people-and-illicit> accessed 30 December 2023.

Specialist Chambers, as well as a system of legal aid for representation of indigent or partially indigent suspects or Accused before the Specialist Chambers'.[78] In practice, the role of the Defence Office was limited further due to a de facto alternative legal aid system set up by Kosovan government, which directly funds representation of all accused. With no suspects or accused declared indigent or partially indigent, the role of the Defence Office in administering a system of legal aid evaporated.

This was acknowledged by the Defence Office, who wrote in response to the author's questions:

> Due to the fact that there have been limited applications for legal aid, the focus of the work of the Defence Office is on the management of the List of Counsel. Furthermore, the Defence Office is the focal point for Defence teams in their contacts with the Registry on various topics, ranging from deontological issues to requests regarding office space, and from assistance in contacts with international organisations to requests for stationery and MFA-cards.[79]

This broadly accorded with the view of multiple defence counsel, who described the Defence Office's role as being purely administrative and limited to assigning counsel; supporting access to electronic work flow systems; and supporting communications with broader administrative work of the court, such as requesting letters to be signed and transmitted by the Registry to facilitate investigative missions.[80] One defence counsel described it thus: 'their job is to administer us, not to support us.'[81] Most described very little interaction with the Defence Office once assigned.

Who, then, advocates for defence rights within the institutional structure of the KSC? A partial answer may be found in Article 19(4) of establishing legislation, which envisaged the establishment of an independent representative body of Specialist Counsel (IRB).[82] The IRB's role, in theory, was to support the work of the Registrar in representing defence interests in discussions concerning amendments to the KSC's Rules of Procedure and Evidence.

[78] Rules of Procedure and Evidence before the Kosovo Specialist Chambers (adopted 17 March 2017, entered into force 5 July 2017) Rule 23(6) <https://www.scp-ks.org/sites/default/files/public/ksc-bd-03-rev1_rulesofprocedureandevidence.pdf> accessed 30 December 2023.

[79] Email from David Hein, Head of the KSC Defence Office to author (25 April 2023). On request, written questions by the author to Mr Hein were sent by email on 8 March 2023.

[80] Interviews were conducted, separately, with six defence counsels, operating across multiple cases, during February and March 2023.

[81] Interview with Defence Counsel V (online, 3 March 2023).

[82] Law on Specialist Chambers and Specialist Prosecutor's Office (3 August 2015) Law No.05/L-053.

The Registry appears to have done little to establish an IRB until the autumn of 2019, when the KSC hosted what it described as 'a working group of Counsel at its premises in The Hague in support of their efforts to establish an "Independent Representative Body of Counsel"'.[83] The ensuing press release further noted that '[t]he IRB would support the functions, efficiency and independence of Counsel practicing before the KSC and establish channels of communication and consultation between the body of Counsel and the KSC'. In early December 2019, the Court announced that the working group of seven practitioners—drawn from the list of counsel eligible to represent persons in proceedings before the KSC—had adopted the constitution of the IRB, drafted in consultation with the Registry.[84] The press release also stated that '[t]he Kosovo Specialist Chambers may consult with the IRB on amendments to the legal framework of the Kosovo Specialist Chambers and the IRB can also propose such changes'. In late 2019, an interim Executive Committee (EC) of the IRB was established, on the basis that the elections would shortly be held.

The Defence Office, in April 2023, underscored the importance of the IRB to the court, and affirmed that: 'The IRB is operational, and the Registry maintains contacts with the IRB.' All six of the defence counsel who were interviewed, however, emphasized how poorly they regarded the IRB's interim EC, none of whom practise before the KSC, and lamented what they saw as the lost opportunity of what could have been achieved by a functioning IRB. Their criticisms were multiple, often overlapping, and included the fact that the interim EC was 'unacceptably inactive';[85] had not taken any steps since December 2019 to organize elections for the IRB establishment, initially on the grounds that such elections would have to be held in person, an impossibility during the pandemic;[86] refused to respond to requests for updates on its work;[87] and refused repeated requests that its members step down.[88] The author reached out to the President of the IRB's interim EC on six separate occasions between March and May 2023 and did not receive any response.[89] In a short email exchange with a member of the interim EC, the

[83] Kosovo Specialist Chamber and Specialist Prosecutor's Office News, 'First IRB Working Group Meeting Facilitated by KSC' (4 November 2019) <https://www.scp-ks.org/en/first-irb-working-group-meeting-facilitated-ksc> accessed 30 December 2023.

[84] Kosovo Specialist Chamber and Specialist Prosecutor's Office News, 'Specialist Counsel Establish Independent Representative Body' (9 December 2019) <https://www.scp-ks.org/en/specialist-counsel-establish-independent-representative-body> accessed 30 December 2023.

[85] Interview with Defence Counsel IV (online, 1 March 2023).

[86] Interview with Defence Counsel II (online, 27 February 2023).

[87] Interviews with Defence Counsel I (online, 25 February 2023); Defence Counsel II (online, 27 February 2023); Defence Counsel III (online, 28 February 2023); Defence Counsel IV (online, 1 March 2023); and Defence Counsel VI (online, 3 March 2023).

[88] ibid.

[89] Emails were sent by the author to Mr Dodevski, President of the IRB's interim EC, on 5, 8, 16, 28 March; 23 April; and 22 May 2023.

committee member indicated that he was unable to provide much insight as he was not involved in cases before the KSC, and noted that the author had 'already found out that communication does not take place as it should be'.[90]

There have been no amendments to the KSC Rules of Procedure and Evidence since July 2017, and with the last trial having started in April 2023, it seems unlikely that the IRB will play its envisaged role, to the clear and immense frustration of multiple defence team members.

The KSC Defence Office represents a return to the initial concept of the Defence Office that came into being in the lifetime of the ICTY—a small administrative office, subsumed under the Registry. While the legal system set up by the Kosovan government has removed what is often a flashpoint between the court and defence teams, there remains a strong need for a robust Defence Office charged with representing the interests of the defence within the court. Between the limited mandate of the Defence Office and the IRB's lack of effective function, KSC unfortunately appears to lack any robust representation of defence interests within the structure and operations of the court. One Counsel referred to it as 'step backwards in the structural support given to the defence'.[91]

7.5 Conclusion

Over the last quarter century, the foundational importance of defence rights to the holding of fair trials remains a mantra for those advancing the need for justice in the form of criminal accountability.

Yet, as this chapter shows, in practice progress towards an effective valuing of defence rights in the hybrids has been stuttering and non-linear. The defence office is now an expected part of the court structure. Whether it is to play a substantive role, clearly delineated from the role of the defence teams, in the robust representation of defence rights remains unsettled. Beyond the question of the form and mandate of a defence office, the hybrids appear to continue to struggle with prioritizing resources that would ensure that each accused is represented by experienced counsel equipped with resources necessary to build and present their client's defence.

The lip service paid to defence rights must move beyond the rhetoric aimed at bolstering the legitimacy of the trials. A commitment to valuing the defence must imbue every aspect of the court, including, notably, its budgetary decisions; its

[90] Email from Mr Wamser, IRB EC member, to the author (10 March 2023).
[91] Interview with Defence Counsel V (online, 3 March 2023).

staffing choices; and its allocation of investigative, analytical, and legal resources. It requires that the metric of success in combatting impunity be measured not in the number of convictions handed down, but in a court process underpinned by a robust, resourced, and respected defence. In this way, the progress towards valuing the defence in the hybrids will chart the maturing of international criminal justice experiment.

8

Victim Participation in Hybrid International(ized) Tribunals

No Longer Just a Feature 'Nice to Have'

Philipp Ambach

8.1 Introduction

The fall of the Iron Curtain in 1989 has led to a new dynamic in the field of international criminal justice. In the mid-nineties the first tangible—and indeed revolutionary—steps were taken in this direction by the United Nations Security Council in establishing the International Criminal Tribunals for the former Yugoslavia (ICTY) and for Rwanda (ICTR).[1] Both tribunals served as judicial ad hoc solutions to immediate threats to international peace and security.[2] As an expression of a more durable justice solution for large-scale atrocities, the International Criminal Court[3] was established in 1998 through an international treaty, the Rome Statute.[4] In terms of its mandate and jurisdiction, the ICC follows the legacy of the international military tribunals in Nuremberg and Tokyo in 1946/1947 as well as the ICTY and ICTR to try the main perpetrators responsible for violent mass criminality in (armed) conflict—but as a *permanent* institution.[5] Yet, the ICC's mandate was 'enriched' by States Parties to the Rome Statute with a number of victim-centred features, amongst them, prominently, victim participation in the proceedings and the possibility for victims to get redress through reparations in

[1] For the ICTY: UNSC Res 837 (25 May 1993) UN Doc S/RES/827; for the ICTR: UNSC Res 955 (8 November 1994) UN Doc S/RES/955.

[2] Their jurisdiction entailed war crimes, crimes against humanity, and the crime of genocide.

[3] In the following: 'ICC' or 'Court'; general information on the ICC is available at <https://www.icc-cpi.int> accessed 15 January 2024.

[4] See Rome Statute of the International Criminal Court (opened for signature 17 July 1998, entered into force 1 July 2002) 2187 UNTS 90 <https://www.icc-cpi.int/resource-library/documents/rs-eng.pdf> accessed 15 January 2024.

[5] The International Military Tribunal (IMT) opened in Nuremberg, Germany, on 20 November 1945 with indictments against altogether twenty-four German political and military leaders of the NS regime for the cries of aggression, crimes against humanity, and war crimes. The judges delivered their verdict on 1 October 1946. The International Military Tribunal for the Far East (IMTFE) was a military trial also convened by the Allied powers on 29 April 1946 against twenty-eight Japanese military and political leaders. The tribunal was adjourned on 12 November 1948.

Philipp Ambach, *Victim Participation in Hybrid International(ized) Tribunals* In: *Hybrid Justice*. Edited by: Kirsten Ainley and Mark Kersten, Oxford University Press. © Philipp Ambach 2025.
DOI: 10.1093/oso/9780192893758.003.0008

case the accused is convicted. These features did not exist for the IMT and the IMTFE, or for the ICTY and ICTR.[6] For all these tribunals, the only way for a victim to participate in the criminal proceedings was as a witness—provided they could indeed testify to facts relevant to the case at hand. During negotiations in the mid-to-late nineties leading to the creation of the ICC through the Rome Statute in 1998, a majority of states underlined the fact that modern international criminal justice as exercised by the ICC does not only have a general-preventative and retributive character, but needs to be more inclusive of the idea of redress and restorative justice to victims.[7]

However, in the late nineties it also dawned on the international community that justice comes at a price, and more precisely, *international* justice comes at a *high* price. At the same time, both the ICTY and the ICTR started showing tangible results in this novel and sui generis international legal framework.[8] The need and indeed *usefulness* for international criminal justice mechanisms became more obvious to assist states in dealing with mass atrocities committed by their citizens and/or on their territories. Relevant state actors increasingly acknowledged this out of their own volition—as illustrated through a number of so-called 'self referrals' of states to the ICC of alleged international crime complexes within the ICC's jurisdiction.[9]

For non-ICC States Parties and/or where the relevant criminal conduct fell outside the temporal jurisdiction of the ICC (beginning on 1 July 2002 at the earliest), other solutions had to be found. This niche started to be filled increasingly with 'hybrid' judicial solutions, which at the outset consisted of international judges, prosecutors, and judicial support staff operating alongside their national colleagues (of the country in judicial need) in an internationalized court setting, preferably on the territory of the state where relevant crimes had been committed. Constituting parties are usually an international or regional organization

[6] For the ICTY: UNSC Res 837 (25 May 1993) UN Doc S/RES/827; for the ICTR: UNSC Res 955 (8 November 1994) UN Doc S/RES/95. In 2000, however, judges of the ICTY acknowledged the right of victims of crimes committed in the former Yugoslavia to seek compensation during their 22nd Plenary Session held in September 2000; see ICTY, 'The judges of the ICTY acknowledge the right of victims of crimes committed in the former Yugoslavia to seek compensation' (14 September 2000) <https://www.icty.org/en/press/judges-icty-acknowledge-right-victims-crimes-committed-former-yugoslavia-seek-compensation> accessed 15 January 2024.

[7] P Ambach in C Stahn *et al.* (ed), *The International Criminal Court in Its Third Decade* (Nijhoff 2024, vol. 109), Chapter 14 Victim Participation at the ICC—Putting the Concept in (Good) Practice, pp 253-296; D Donat-Cattin in Kai Ambos (ed), *The Rome Statute of the International Criminal Court: Article-by-Article Commentary* (4th edn, Hart 2021) Article 68, paras 3 and following.

[8] See, eg, *Prosecutor v Slobodan Milošević* IT-02-54; *Prosecutor v Jean Kambanda* ICTR-97-23; *Prosecutor v Bagosora et al.* (Military I) ICTR-98-41.

[9] Uganda: January 2004; DRC: April 2004 and again in spring 2023; CAR: December 2004, and again in 2014 (so-called CAR II); Mali: July 2012; Palestine: January 2015; then there are also state referrals under Article 14 of the Rome Statute by *other* states than the territory of commission of alleged crimes: see, eg, Venezuela I in September 2018 and most recently for Ukraine in March 2022; see generally ICC, 'Situations under investigations' <https://www.icc-cpi.int/Pages/Situations.aspx> accessed 15 January 2024.

on one side, and a state on the other: this may be United Nations missions in an effort to re-establish an administrative and governance structure in a given context (eg East Timor and Kosovo),[10] or even a more focused criminal justice portfolio (*Cour pénale spéciale de la Republique Centrafricaine*);[11] the United Nations Secretary-General at the request of the Security Council (Special Court for Sierra Leone; Special Tribunal for Lebanon);[12] the United Nations General Secretariat (Extraordinary Chambers in the Courts of Cambodia[13]); the UN Office of the High Representative (War Crimes Chamber in the state court of Bosnia-Herzegovina[14]); the African Union (*Chambres africaines extraordinaires*); and the European Union (Kosovo Specialist Chambers & Specialist Prosecutor's Office);[15] or the Council of Europe.[16]

Interestingly, almost all of these international(ized) justice mechanisms established subsequent to the ICC's creation include more or less comprehensive victim

[10] For the Special Panels of the Dili District Court, see UNTAET Regulation on the Establishment of Panels with Exclusive Jurisdiction over Serious Criminal Offence (6 June 2000) UNTAET/REG/2000/15 and UNTAET Regulation on Transitional Rules of Criminal Procedure (25 September 2000) UNTAET/REG/2000/30; for Kosovo, see UNMIK Regulation on the Appointment and Removal from Office of International Judges and International Prosecutors (14 February 2000) UNMIK/REG/2000/6 and UNMIK Regulation on Assignment of International Judges and Prosecutors and Change of Venue (15 December 2000) UNMIK/REG/2000/64—all of the aforesaid legal instruments dating the year 2000.

[11] *Loi organique* No 15.003 du 03 juin 2015, portant sur création, organisation et fonctionnement de la cour pénale spéciale (3 June 2015) following an agreement between the Central African authorities and the UN multidimensional peacekeeping mission MINUSCA, constituted by the UN Security Council in 2014: Memorandum d'Entente entre la Mission Multidimensionnelle integree des Nations Unies pour la stabilisation en Republique centrafricaine et le Gouvernement de la Republique centrafricaine (signed 5 and 7 August 2014) <https://www.fidh.org/IMG/pdf/mou_minusca_-_rca_concernant_la_cps.pdf> accessed 15 January 2024.

[12] For the SCSL, see Agreement between the United Nations and the Government of Sierra Leone on the establishment of a Special Court for Sierra Leone (signed 16 January 2002, entered into force 12 April 2002) 2178 UNTS 138 (SCSL Agreement) following UNSC Res 1315 (14 August 2000) UN Doc S/RES/1315; for the STL, see Agreement between the United Nations and the Lebanese Republic on the establishment of a Special Tribunal for Lebanon, Annex to UNSC Res 1757 (30 May 2007) UN Doc S/RES/1757 (STL Agreement)—the latter actually 'acting under Chapter VII of the Charter of the United Nations' per STL Agreement operational para 1.

[13] See Agreement between the United Nations and the Royal Government of Cambodia concerning the prosecution under Cambodian law of crimes committed during the period of Democratic Kampuchea (6 June 2003) (ECCC Agreement) <https://www.eccc.gov.kh/en/document/legal/agreement> accessed 15 January 2024.

[14] See Agreement between the High Representative for Bosnia and Herzegovina and Bosnia Herzegovina on the Establishment of a Registry for Section I for War Crimes and Section II for Organised Crime, Economic Crime and Corruption of the Criminal and Appellate Divisions of the Court of Bosnia and Herzegovina and the Special Department for War Crimes and the Special Department for Organised Crime, Economic Crime and Corruption of the Prosecutor's Office of Bosnia and Herzegovina (1 December 2004) <https://www.legal-tools.org/doc/27562c/pdf/> accessed 15 January 2024.

[15] Kosovo Law on Ratification of the International Agreement between the Republic of Kosovo and the European Union on the European Union Rule of Law Mission in Kosovo (23 April 2014) Law No 04/L-274 <https://www.scp-ks.org/sites/default/files/public/04-l-274_a.pdf> accessed 15 January 2024.

[16] See Parliamentary Assembly of the Council of Europe, 'PACE calls for the setting up of an ad hoc international criminal tribunal to hold to account perpetrators of the crime of aggression against Ukraine' (28 April 2022) <https://pace.coe.int/en/news/8699> accessed 15 January 2024.

participation regimes. The Extraordinary Chambers in the Courts of Cambodia, the Special Tribunal for Lebanon, the Kosovo Specialist Chambers, and the *Cour pénale spéciale Centrafricaine* (in English: Special Criminal Court (SCC)) all contain specific provisions on victim participation and, to varying degrees of detail, on reparations.[17] Similarly, the African Union-sponsored *Chambres africaines extraordinaires*,[18] established to try former Chadian dictator Hissèin Habré, provided for victim participation and a reparations regime subsequent to the accused's conviction.[19] Finally, the 'Transitional Rules of Criminal Procedure' of the Dili Special Panels also provided for some broad provisions recognizing victims in the process.[20]

It would thus seem that thanks to victims' advocates at the negotiation of the Rome Statute, the ICC pioneered a set of new victim-centred features that every subsequent internationalized justice mechanism for atrocity crimes has to some degree adopted since, at least regarding its main principles and premises. Yet, the ICC victim participation regime continues to pose challenges to the ICC in a number of aspects, including victims' access to the proceedings, procedural and budgetary challenges—particularly when it comes to the funding of reparation awards—and finally the impact of the system on victims and affected communities. At the same time it needs to be acknowledged that the ICC is presently the best-equipped international criminal justice mechanism in operation, with a budget of around 187 million Euros,[21] a number of field offices and presences in different countries where the ICC investigates/operates, and a Trust Fund for Victims,[22] which is designed to, inter alia, render the ICC's reparations mandate meaningful by supplementing the money available for reparations to victims mainly through

[17] All these courts and tribunals will be discussed in further detail regarding their victim participation and reparation regimes below.

[18] In English: Extraordinary African Chambers (in the following: EAC).

[19] See Statute of the Extraordinary African Chambers within the courts of Senegal created to prosecute international crimes committed in Chad between 7 June 1982 and 1 December 1990 (2013) 52 International Legal Materials 1028 (EAC Statute) Articles 14 (victim participation) and 27, 28 (reparations regime including the establishment of a trust fund) (unofficial translation of the French original) <https://www.hrw.org/news/2013/09/02/statute-extraordinary-african-chambers> accessed 15 January 2024; *Ministere Public c Hissein Habre* (Judgment) (30 Mai 2016) <http://www.chambresafricaines.org/pdf/Jugement_complet.pdf> accessed 15 January 2024.

[20] See Transitional Rules of Criminal Procedure of the Dili Special Panels (25 September 2000) UNTAET Regulation 2000/30, sections 12, 25, 49 <https://www.legal-tools.org/doc/f3e141/pdf/> accessed 15 January 2024.

[21] See the Assembly resolution approving the ICC's latest (2024) programme budget: Resolution of the Assembly of States Parties on the proposed programme budget for 2024, the Working Capital Fund for 2024, the scale of assessment for the apportionment of expenses of the International Criminal Court, financing appropriations for 2024 and the Contingency Fund (14 December 2023) ICC-ASP/22/Res.4 <https://asp.icc-cpi.int/sites/default/files/asp_docs/ICC-ASP-22-Res4-AV-ENG.pdf> accessed 22 October 2024.

[22] The Trust Fund for Victims (hereinafter TFV) is mentioned in Article 79 of the Rome Statute and has been established through Resolution of the Assembly of States Parties, 'Establishment of a fund for the benefit of victims of crimes within the jurisdiction of the Court, and of the families of such victims' (9 September 2002) ICC-ASP/1/Res.6; for general information on the TFV, see the Trust Fund for Victims, 'Home' <https://www.trustfundforvictims.org/en/home> accessed 15 January 2024.

states' and other funders' voluntary contributions. It may be even more difficult for internationalized ad hoc justice solutions operating in singular situations alongside the ICC particularly where the latter has no jurisdiction, to succeed with their victim participation and reparation systems absent a permanent structure and resulting stability.

This chapter will first provide an outline of the victim participation and reparation regimes as they are applied by the ICC and the more recent internationalized (hybrid) international criminal justice mechanisms. It will then identify a number of common key challenges in the application of these systems. The quantity and quality of these challenges will provide elements supporting the title of this contribution: that a more or less comprehensive victim participation regime has become a necessary part and parcel of a modern international criminal justice mechanism, and is no longer just an optional extra. Still, the reparation functions, particularly of hybrid ad hoc courts, should be carefully crafted with a view to there being sufficient funding and organizational stamina to render reparations meaningful.

8.2 The Different Victim Participation and Reparation Regimes in a Brief Overview

8.2.1 Victim participation

8.2.1.1 ICC

As a key novel feature of the ICC compared to its UN predecessors, the ICTY and the ICTR, victims have access and are allowed to participate in the proceedings. Article 68(3) of the Rome Statute is the key provision in the Rome Statute addressing this right particularly in proceedings following the arrest or appearance of a suspect ('case stage'),[23] and does so in rather open terms:

> Where the personal interests of the victims are affected, the Court shall permit their views and concerns to be presented and considered at stages of the proceedings determined to be appropriate by the Court and in a manner which is not prejudicial to or inconsistent with the rights of the accused and a fair and impartial trial.

[23] Articles 15(3) and 19(3) of the Rome Statute also stipulate important junctures at which victims' views and concerns are to be sought for the Chamber's appreciation—where the Prosecutor wants to open an investigation *proprio motu* and where the jurisdiction of the ICC or the admissibility of a case are being challenged. For a detailed overview, see Philipp Ambach, 'Victim Participation at the ICC—Putting the Concept in (Good) Practice' in Carsten Stahn (ed), *The International Criminal Court in Its Third Decade: Reflecting on Law and Practices* (Brill 2023).

Article 68(3) also stipulates that such views and concerns may be presented by legal representatives of victims as appropriate. For a more detailed determination, the Statute refers to the ICC Rules of Procedure and Evidence (ICC Rules). And indeed, the ICC Rules start off by properly defining the term 'victim' in Rule 85.[24] Rule 87 provides comprehensive protective measures for victims (not limited to victim-witnesses but extending to all victims recognized by the chamber). Rule 89 outlines the application process for participation of victims in the proceedings[25] and codifies the victims' right to make opening and closing statements, as appropriate.[26] Rule 90 provides a multi-step approach on the assignment of legal representation to victims.[27] A number of different approaches on victims' legal representation have been tested by the ICC Chambers to date, ranging from victim counsel external to the ICC and victim representation provided by ICC-internal counsel.[28] Finally and importantly, Rule 91 outlines to some degree the specific participatory rights of victims through their legal representatives in the proceedings.[29] Rule 131(2) adds to this in providing victims with access to the case record. Yet, the exact set of participatory rights remains in the prerogative of the respective chamber.[30] Jurisprudence in the different cases before the ICC has carved out a rather comprehensive set of victims' participatory rights, with minor differences between the cases.[31] As a fundamental premise, it is for the judges to find the just

[24] This term has been subsequently defined by various ICC trial chambers, see *Prosecutor v Thomas Lubanga Dyilo* (Trial Chamber I Decision on victims' participation) ICC-01/04-01/06-1119 (18 January 2008) [87]–[94] as well as the Appeals Chamber's findings at *Prosecutor v Thomas Lubanga Dyilo* (Judgment) ICC-01/04-01/06-1432 (11 July 2008); Redacted Version of *Prosecutor v Thomas Lubanga Dyilo* (Decision on 'indirect victims') ICC-01/04-01/06-1813 (8 April 2009). Regarding reparations, see *Prosecutor v Thomas Lubanga Dyilo* (Decision establishing the principles and procedures to be applied to reparations) ICC-01/04-01/06-2904 (7 August 2012) [194]–[201].

[25] For the standard 'A-B-C' approach applied across cases since 2015, see ICC, 'Chambers Practice Manual' (6th edn, 24 November 2022) <https://www.icc-cpi.int/sites/default/files/2022-11/chamber-manual-eng-v.6.pdf> accessed 15 January 2024; confirmed by the Appeals Chamber in *Prosecutor v Mahamat Said Abdel Kani* (Judgment on the appeal of Mr Mahamat Said Abdel Kani against the decision of Pre-Trial Chamber II of 16 April 2021 entitled 'Decision establishing the principles applicable to victims' applications for participation) ICC-01/14-01/21-171 OA2 (14 September 2021) (*Said* Appeals Judgment) [82]. For a detailed analysis, see Ambach, 'Victim Participation at the ICC' (n 23).

[26] Rule 89(1) of the ICC Rules.

[27] On the procedural regime encompassed in Rule 90 of the ICC Rules see the discussion *below*. See also Megan Hirst, 'Legal Representation of Participating Victims' in Kinga Tibori-Szabó and Megan Hirst (eds), *Victim Participation in International Criminal Justice* (TMC Asser Press 2017) 111 and following.

[28] Ambach, 'Victim Participation at the ICC' (n 23) chapter IV.

[29] For an early discussion of the applicable legal framework to victims before the ICC, see *Prosecutor v Thomas Lubanga Dyilo* (Trial Chamber I Decision on victims' participation) ICC-01/04-01/06-1119 (18 January 2008) [20] and following. Rule 91 grants legal representatives (i) participation in hearings; (ii) the right to make oral and written submissions; (iii) the questioning of witnesses, an expert, or the accused (upon application to the Chamber); and (iv) the introduction of documents.

[30] Pursuant to Rule 89(1) of the Rules, the Chamber shall specify 'the proceedings and manner in which participation is considered appropriate', in keeping with Article 68(3) of the Rome Statute (as 'determined to be appropriate by the Court'); see also similar language in Rule 91(3)(b) of the ICC Rules and Regulation 24(2) of the Regulations of the Court.

[31] See, eg, ICC, Appeals Chamber, *Prosecutor v Thomas Lubanga Dyilo* (Judgment on the appeals of the Prosecutor and the Defence against Trial Chamber I's Decision on Victims' Participation of 18 January 2008) ICC-01/04-01/06-1432 (11 July 2008); *Prosecutor v Francis Kirimi Muthaura and Uhuru*

equilibrium between giving the most meaningful rights to the participating victims and, on the other hand, avoiding prejudice to the rights of the accused or to the fair and impartial conduct of the proceedings.[32] The guiding principle throughout has been that the victims' personal interests have to be affected to invoke relevant participatory rights. Of note, judges have underlined that victims shall not take a 'Prosecutor *bis*' role: attempts by victims' legal representatives to elicit evidence which aims to prove the elements of the crimes charged or the accused's role in their commission are not acceptable.[33]

Due to the ICC's permanent nature and multitude of different situations and cases, victims' rights to participate in certain—early—stages of proceedings are somewhat special and do not necessarily find an equivalent in hybrid courts. For instance, when the ICC Prosecutor intends to open an investigation *proprio motu* pursuant to Article 15(3) of the Rome Statute, victims are provided with the right to report their 'views and concerns' to the Pre-Trial Chamber prior even to the commencement of an investigation.[34] Furthermore, Article 19(3) of the Rome Statute vests victims with a right to submit observations to the chamber where the jurisdiction of the ICC or the admissibility of a case has been challenged.[35] Recent jurisprudence of pre-trial chambers has extended this right of victims to submit their views and concerns to the chamber also to instances where a state has requested the deferral of the ICC Prosecutor's investigation (Article 18(2) of the Statute) and

Muigai Kenyatta (Trial Chamber V Decision on victims' representation and participation) ICC-01/09-02/11-498 (3 October 2012); *Prosecutor v Dominic Ongwen* (Pre-Trial Chamber II Decision on contested victims' applications for participation, legal representation of victims and their procedural rights) ICC-02/04-01/15-350 (27 November 2015) [27] and following; *Prosecutor v Dominic Ongwen* (Trial Chamber IX Public Redacted Version of Decision on the Legal Representatives for Victims Requests to Present Evidence and Views and Concerns and related requests) ICC-02/04-01/15-1199-Red (6 March 2018) footnote 22 and [17]–[23], [78]–[83]; *Prosecutor v Bosco Ntaganda* (Trial Chamber VI Decision on victims' participation in trial proceedings) ICC-01/04-02/06-449 (6 February 2015) (followed up by multiple decisions further qualifying the applicable regime of victim participation). For a recent decision, see *Prosecutor v Ali Muhammad Ali Abd-Al-Rahman* (Trial Chamber I, Decision on victims' participation and legal representation in trial proceedings) ICC-02/05-01/20-494 (19 October 2021) ('Ali Kushayb').

[32] See Rule 89(1), 91(2), (3)(b) of the ICC Rules; *Prosecutor v Dominic Ongwen* (Pre-Trial Chamber II, Decision on contested victims' applications for participation, legal representation of victims and their procedural rights) ICC-02/04-01/15-350 (27 November 2015) [28].

[33] *Prosecutor v Dominic Ongwen* (Trial Chamber IX, Transcript of hearing on 4 April 2017) ICC-02/04-01/15-T-65-Red-ENG, 56, lines 3–13 cited *The Prosecutor v Dominic Ongwen* (Public Redacted Version of Decision on the Legal Representatives for Victims Requests to Present Evidence and Views and Concerns and related requests) ICC-02/04-01/15-1199-Red (6 March 2018) footnote 27.

[34] See, most recently, in the Philippines situation: *Situation in the Republic of the Philippines* (Pre-Trial Chamber I, Decision on the 'Registry Request for Extension of Notice Period and Submissions on the Article 15(3) Process) ICC-01/21-9 (17 June 2021).

[35] See, eg, ICC, Pre-Trial Chamber I, *Prosecutor v Laurent Gbagbo* (Decision on the 'Corrigendum of the challenge to the jurisdiction of the International Criminal Court on the basis of articles 12(3), 19(2), 21(3), 55 and 59 of the Rome Statute filed by the Defence for President Gbagbo (ICC-02/11-01/11-129))' ICC-02/11-01/11-212 (15 August 2012).

the latter challenges the request under Article 18(3) of the Statute.[36] This right even extends into relevant appeal proceedings.[37]

8.2.1.2 Extraordinary Chambers in the Courts of Cambodia

The Extraordinary Chambers in the Courts of Cambodia (ECCC) were created by the Cambodian government and the United Nations as a national court with international participation, to try the most responsible perpetrators for alleged crimes committed between 17 April 1975 and 6 January 1979 during the leadership of the Khmer Rouge in Democratic Kampuchea.[38] The ECCC does not have an explicit provision allowing victim participation in its 'Law on the Establishment of the Extraordinary Chambers'.[39] However, the ECCC's 'Internal Rules'[40] provide a number of provisions regulating victims' access to the Court and participation in the proceedings. Inspired by the French legal tradition, Rule 23 of the Internal Rules stipulates that victims participate in the proceedings as 'civil parties'. Victims are indeed vested with far-reaching procedural rights: as per the Internal Rules they are even supposed to 'support[] the prosecution',[41] which suggests comprehensive participatory rights as a (quasi) party to the proceedings. During investigations and at the pre-trial stage, civil parties participate individually.[42] Civil parties at the trial stage and beyond (particularly on appeal) shall comprise a single, consolidated group, whose interests are represented in court by the so-called 'Civil Party Lead Co-Lawyers'.[43] The Co-Investigating Judges, and during trial the Chambers, may require civil parties to form a group and designate a common

[36] See *Situation in the Bolivarian Republic of Venezuela I* (Order inviting observations and views and concerns of victims) ICC-02/18-21 (18 November 2022); *Situation in the Republic of the Philippines* (Decision on submissions received and order to the Registry regarding the filing of documents in the proceedings pursuant to articles 18(2) and 68(3) of the Statute) ICC-02/17-171 (8 November 2021) [10]. At [9] the Chamber refers to its previous decision on the issue of 8 October 2021.

[37] *Situation in the Bolivarian Republic of Venezuela I*, Appeals Chamber (Decision on requests for victims' involvement) ICC-02/18-60 (24 August 2023).

[38] For general information on the ECCC, see the tribunal's official website at ECCC, 'Introduction to the ECCC' <https://www.eccc.gov.kh/en/introduction-eccc> accessed 15 January 2024; see also Philipp Ambach, 'Die "Extraordinary Chambers in the Courts of Cambodia'—endlich Gerechtigkeit?: das lange Tauziehen zwischen den Vereinten Nationen und Kambodscha um wirkungsvolle internationale Strafgerichtsbarkeit" (2006) 19 Informationsschriften Humanitäres Völkerrecht 168.

[39] The Law on the Establishment of the Extraordinary Chambers (amended 27 October 2004) ('ECCC Law') <https://www.eccc.gov.kh/en/documents/legal/law-establishment-extraordinary-chambers-amended> accessed 15 January 2024. Interestingly, the only procedural right of victims is encompassed in Article 36 of the ECCC Law, providing them with a right to appeal a first instance judgment. The only other explicit references to victims in the ECCC Law pertain to their protection (Article 32) and the Co-Investigating Judges' 'power to question suspects and victims' (Article 23 ECCC Law).

[40] ECCC Internal Rules, Rev 9 (16 January 2015).

[41] ibid Rule 23(1).

[42] ibid. Victims may also organize their civil party action by becoming members of a 'Victims' Association' and thus be represented before the ECCC by the association's lawyers, Rule 23*quater* of the Internal Rules.

[43] ibid Rules 23(3), 23*ter*(1), 106(3).

legal representative;[44] legal assistance is also provided by the institution in case the victim(s) do not have the necessary means to pay for a court-appointed counsel.[45] This procedure bears certain resemblance to the Rule 90 process at the ICC.

During the first trial, against Kaing Guek Eav alias Duch,[46] altogether four teams of Cambodian and international lawyers represented ninety-three civil parties.[47] At the time, the civil parties' procedural participatory rights were not regulated in much detail in the ECCC's Internal Rules. This lack of clarity and civil party lawyers' very active use of the procedural tools at hand led to an altogether challenging process. The Trial Chamber had to curtail civil parties' means to participate in order to preserve the fairness of trial for the defendant.[48] As a result, in 2010, the victim participation regime was substantially modified. As per Rule 12*bis* of the ECCC Internal Rules, a Victim Support Section (VSS)[49] facilitates victims' legal representation before the Chambers: it assists victims in submitting civil party applications and provides general support; it also administers the lists of (i) eligible civil party counsel and (ii) Victims' Associations approved to act on behalf of civil parties before the ECCC.[50] Rule 12 of the Internal Rules also establishes a 'Civil Party Lead Co-Lawyers Section' which remains autonomous from the Registry of the ECCC with regard to all substantive matters pertaining to civil parties. As such, this section bears strong resemblance to the ICC's 'Office of Public Counsel for Victims', which likewise carries out its substantive tasks in assisting

[44] ibid Rule 23*ter*(3); this also goes for the requirement that victims' distinct interests are appropriately represented and that conflicts of interests are avoided; see ICC Rules, Rule 90(4). At trial, the Civil Party Lead Co-Lawyers are in fact the civil parties' common legal representative *in court*.

[45] ECCC Internal Rules, Rule 23*ter*(3)(e); compare with Rule 90(5) of the ICC Rules: of note, the ICC provision spells out the possibility of financial assistance (as appropriate)—Rule 23*ter*(3)(e) of the Internal Rules stops short of this specification.

[46] Kaing Guel Eav, *alias* Duch, was the former Chairman of the Khmer Rouge S-21 Security Center in Phnom Penh; he was the sole defendant in Case 001 before the ECCC; see for more information at ECCC, 'Case 001' <https://www.eccc.gov.kh/en/case/topic/90> accessed 15 January 2024.

[47] See ECCC, *Prosecutor v Kaing Guel Eav* (Trial Chamber Judgment) Case File/Dossier No 001/18-07-2007/ECCC/TC (26 July 2010) [637], [645], and [650] <http://www.eccc.gov.kh/sites/default/files/documents/courtdoc/20100726_Judgement_Case_001_ENG_PUBLIC.pdf> accessed 22 October 2024.

[48] ibid [635] and footnote 1059, referring to revisions 4 and 5 of the Internal Rules; Johanna Herman, 'Realities of Victim Participation: The Civil Party System in Practice at the Extraordinary Chambers in the Courts of Cambodia (ECCC)' (2013) 16 Contemporary Justice Review 461; Brianne McGonigle Leyh, 'Strengthening the Participation of the Victims at the ECCC? A look at the revised legal framework for Civil Party participation' (2010) Oxford Transitional Justice Research Working Paper Series 2; Nadine Kirchenbauer and others, 'Victims Participation Before the Extraordinary Chambers in the Courts of Cambodia: Baseline Study of the Cambodian Human Rights and Development Association's Civil Party Scheme for Case 002' (2013) Cambodian Human Rights and Development Association (ADHOC) and Harvard University Humanitarian Initiative 4 <https://www.eccc.gov.kh/sites/default/files/Victims-participation-before-ECCC-Baseline-Study-Jan-2013.pdf> accessed 15 January 2024. For discussion about the participation of Case 001 civil parties at the ECCC, see Phuong N Pham and others 'Victim Participation in Duch's Trial at the Extraordinary Chambers in the Courts of Cambodia' (2011) 3 Journal of Human Rights Practice 264.

[49] See ECCC, 'Victims Support Section' <https://www.eccc.gov.kh/en/organs/victims-support-section> accessed 22 October 2024.

[50] ECCC Internal Rules, Rule 12*bis*(1).

and representing victim groups in the proceedings 'as a wholly independent office'.[51] The SCC in the Central African Republic (CAR) provides for a similar 'victims office' to facilitate victims' participatory rights.[52] Pursuant to Rule 12*ter* of the ECCC Internal Rules, Civil Party Lead Co-Lawyers 'shall ensure the effective organization of Civil Party representation during the trial stage and beyond'.[53] This entails representing the interests of the consolidated group of civil parties, and bearing the ultimate responsibility to the Court for their overall advocacy, strategy, and in-court presentation.[54]

Victims' rights entail the right to request the Co-Investigating Judges to take relevant investigative actions as appropriate for the conduct of the investigation.[55] Victims also have ample rights to appeal orders by the Co-Investigating Judges;[56] these rights would seem to be attached to the requirement that the victims' interests need to be affected by the relevant order—a qualifying criterion known also from ICC law and jurisprudence.[57] In turn, the Co-Investigating Judges may interview civil parties[58]—a feature shared with the SCC, the only other court featuring a 'civil party' participation system.[59] At trial, civil parties may take a broad array of procedural action through their Civil Party Lead Co-Lawyers, such as: question the parties' witnesses and the accused;[60] summon own witnesses;[61] request (additional) expert evidence;[62] present and specify the substance of the claim for collective and moral reparation;[63] be generally heard in court[64]—but also be summoned to appear before the Chamber and be questioned in court;[65] make closing

[51] ICC, Regulations of the Court (6 December 2016) ICC-BD/01-05-16, regulation 81(2) <https://www.icc-cpi.int/resourcelibrary/Documents/RegulationsCourtEng.pdf> accessed 15 January 2024.

[52] SCC, Loi no 18.010 du 02 juillet 2018, portan règlement de procédure et de preuve devant la cour pénale spéciale de la République Centrafricaine (SCC RPE) Article 75, <https://www.cpsrca.cf/bibliotheque/textes-juridiques/35/> accessed 15 January 2024.

[53] '[W]hilst balancing the rights of all parties and the need for an expeditious trial within the unique ECCC context', Rule 12*ter*(1) of the Internal Rules.

[54] ECCC, Internal Rules, Rule 12*ter* (1), (5). Rule 12*ter*(6) specifies that the Civil Party Lawyers shall endeavour to support the Civil Party Lead Co-Lawyers in their tasks; '[s]uch support may include oral and written submissions, examination of their clients and witnesses and other procedural actions'.

[55] ibid Rule 55(10). A rejection of such a request is subject to appeal.

[56] ibid Rule 74(4).

[57] *Prosecutor v Dominic Ongwen* (Trial Chamber IX, Public Redacted Version of Decision on the Legal Representatives for Victims Requests to Present Evidence and Views and Concerns and related requests) ICC-02/04-01/15-1199-Red (6 March 2018) [15]; *Prosecutor v Thomas Lubanga Dyilo* (Judgment on the appeals of the Prosecutor and the Defence against Trial Chamber I's Decision on Victims' Participation of 18 January 2008) ICC-01/04-01/06-1432 (11 July 2008) [92]–[98]; *Prosecutor v Germain Katanga and Mathieu Ngudjolo Chui* (Judgment on the Appeal of Mr Katanga Against the Decision of Trial Chamber II of 22 January 2010 Entitled 'Decision on the Modalities of Victim Participation at Trial') ICC01/04-01/07-2288 (16 July 2010) [1], [3].

[58] ECCC Internal Rules, Rule 59. A civil party may also be interviewed by the ECCC investigators, under certain conditions, see ibid Rule 59(6).

[59] Article 76 (investigation) and 88 (trial) SCC RPE.

[60] ECCC Internal Rules, Rule 90(2).

[61] ibid Rule 80*bis*(4), (5).

[62] ibid Rule 31(10).

[63] ibid Rule 80(2).

[64] ibid Rule 91(1).

[65] ibid Rules 41(5), 91*bis*.

statements;[66] and appeal the decision on reparations, as well as the verdict if the Co-Prosecutors have appealed as well.[67] The ECCC thus provides a very detailed regulatory framework in regards to victim-related matters; the far-reaching influence of victims potentially shaping the investigation stage is paralleled only by the SCC in CAR, the only other court featuring in a similar level of detail[68] the civil party concept derived chiefly from the French criminal procedure.[69]

8.2.1.3 Special Tribunal for Lebanon

The Special Tribunal for Lebanon (STL)[70] was established as an internationalized ad hoc tribunal with its seat in Leidschendam, The Netherlands, to try the alleged perpetrators of a terrorist attack on 14 February 2005 in Beirut which killed twenty-two people, including the former prime minister of Lebanon, Rafik Hariri.[71] It ceased its operations in late July 2021. Article 17 of the STL Statute in fact mirrored Article 68(3) of the Rome Statute, which resulted in victims' rights before the STL being comparable to those before the ICC.[72] Victims were entitled to participate once an indictment was confirmed by the Pre-Trial Judge, that is, once a suspect had been identified.[73] The definition of a victim as well as the application process to be accepted as such in the proceedings were somewhat similar to the ICC.[74] As for victims' procedural participatory rights, the ICC regime was mirrored for the largest part; however, as an advantage over the ICC regime, victims'

[66] ibid Rule 94(1)(a).

[67] ibid Rule 105(1)(c).

[68] The Extraordinary African Chambers also featured a 'civil party' victim participation scheme, albeit in much less regulatory elaboration than ECCC and SCC, see section 8.2.1.4.

[69] For a critical overview of the ECCC framework, see Elisa Hoven, 'Civil Party Participation in Trials of Mass Crimes: A Qualitative Study at the Extraordinary Chambers in the Courts of Cambodia' (2014) 12 Journal of International Criminal Justice 81.

[70] The STL was established by United Nations Security Council Resolution 1757 of 30 May 2007 following by an Agreement between the United Nations and the Lebanese Republic pursuant to Security Council Resolution 1664 (2006) of 29 March 2006; see S/RES/1757 with the STL's Statute at <https://www.onlinelibrary.iihl.org/wp-content/uploads/2021/04/Statute-ICTL-EN.pdf> accessed 15 January 2024.

[71] In terms of subject-matter jurisdiction, the STL applied provisions of the Lebanese Criminal Code, including the prosecution and punishment of acts of terrorism and crimes and offences against life and personal integrity.

[72] Statute of the Special Tribunal for Lebanon (2007) S/RES/1757.

[73] Rule 2 of the STL Rules of Procedure and Evidence (last amended April 2017) STL-BD-2009-01-Rev.9 (hereinafter 'STL Rules').

[74] See Rule 86(B) of the STL Rules, compared to Rule 89 of the ICC Rules and Regulation 86 of the ICC Regulations of the Court. As for the definition of 'victim', Rule 2 of the STL Rules requires that the victim's harm must be a 'direct' result of relevant criminal conduct; this requirement is not mirrored by the ICC Rules (*see* Rule 85) or the relevant ICC jurisprudence; see *Prosecutor v Thomas Lubanga Dyilo* (Trial Chamber I, Decision establishing the principles and procedures to be applied to reparations) ICC-01/04-01/06-2904 (7 August 2012) [194] and following, which also recognizes 'indirect victims' as long as the harm was *personal*, that is, 'there was a close personal relationship between the indirect and direct victim, for instance as exists between a child soldier and his or her parents' [195]; see also *Prosecutor v Thomas Lubanga Dyilo* (Judgment on the appeals of the Prosecutor and the Defence against Trial Chamber I's Decision on Victims' Participation of 18 January 2008) ICC-01/04-01/06-1432 (11 July 2008) [32].

procedural rights had been codified in the STL's Rules of Procedure and Evidence in a more comprehensive fashion, and arguably encompassed a much larger array of procedural rights—and duties.[75] The STL clarified that, as a rule, victims had to participate through a legal representative. The decision on common legal representation rested—akin to the ICC framework—with the judge.[76] Of note, the STL Rules obliged victims participating in the proceedings to file witness and exhibit lists of material they intend to use during the proceedings;[77] in addition, victims calling their own evidence were subject to corresponding disclosure obligations.[78] Furthermore, victims were vested with the right to (i) request the Pre-Trial Judge to exceptionally gather evidence which the victim was not in a position to collect;[79] (ii) have a role in the Pre-Trial Judge's potential questioning of an anonymous (protected) witness;[80] and (iii) request the Trial Chamber to call witnesses[81] and additional evidence after the parties' presentation of evidence.[82] These provisions are not mirrored by any other institution. Of note, at the ICC these issues are left to be determined by each trial chamber.

8.2.1.4 Extraordinary African Chambers

The Extraordinary African Chambers (EAC) were created pursuant to an agreement between Senegal and the African Union in February 2013 to prosecute the 'person or persons' most responsible for international crimes committed in Chad between 7 June 1982 and 1 December 1990, which correspond to the period when former Chadian President Hissène Habré was in office.[83] The EAC's Statute provided subject-matter jurisdiction over the crimes of genocide, crimes against humanity, war crimes, and torture. The definitions of these crimes generally align with those of the ICC and the UN ad hoc tribunals. The trial began on 20 July 2015 and ended on 11 February 2016 with a conviction and sentence for Mr Habré

[75] Rule 51(B)(iv) ensures that victims and their legal representatives receive parties' filings and files submitted by the Pre-Trial Judge; Rule 87 of the STL Rules lists further rights such as access to parties' filings, examination of witnesses, filing of motions and briefs, right to submissions (especially in sentencing, see Rule 87(C)); further relevant provisions are stipulated in Rules 91–93, 112*bis*-125 (including particular disclosure duties), 143–47 (including opening and closing statements, and the right to question the accused, albeit through the Chamber), 150, 155, 161, 165 of the STL Rules.

[76] STL Rules, Rule 86(D).

[77] ibid Rule 91(H).

[78] ibid Rule 112*bis*.These disclosure obligations also extend to exculpatory material (Rule 113(B)), and victim representatives are subject to corresponding sanctions if they fail to perform their disclosure obligations (Rule 114). Finally, victims can also claim grounds for non-disclosure akin to the parties, pursuant to Rule 116(E).

[79] ibid Rule 92.

[80] ibid Rule 93.

[81] ibid Rule 146.

[82] ibid Rule 165.

[83] See Human Rights Watch, 'Senegal: New Court to Try Chad Ex-Dictator in Senegal' (22 August 2014) <https://www.hrw.org/news/2012/08/22/senegal-new-court-try-chad-ex-dictator-senegal> accessed 15 January 2024.

to spend the rest of his life in prison.[84] On 27 April 2017, an appeals court confirmed the verdict and ordered Mr Habré to pay approximately 123 million Euros in victim compensation.[85] More than 4,000 victims were permitted to participate in proceedings as civil parties, represented through two teams of lawyers. On behalf of victims, the civil party lawyers questioned witnesses, presented evidence, and participated in the closing statements.[86]

Article 14 of the EAC's Statute (titled 'General Principles of Victims' Participation as Civil Parties') contained a victim participation provision which is very much akin to Rule 90 of the ICC Rules: civil parties may be formed at any stage during the investigative phase by submitting a request in writing to the Registry. Victims would be represented by a joint representative (who can be chosen by victims or appointed by the court if victims cannot reach agreement); victims' legal representation can be financially catered for by the court.[87] As default applicable law, the EAC Statute stipulated that in addition (and subject) to its own provisions, the participation of victims shall be governed by the Senegalese Code of Criminal Procedure.[88]

8.2.1.5 Kosovo Specialist Chambers

The 'Specialist Chambers and Specialist Prosecutor's Office' are embedded into the national court system of Kosovo, following an agreement on their establishment between the President of Kosovo and the High Representative of the European Union for Foreign Affairs and Security Policy in 2014.[89] They have jurisdiction over crimes against humanity, war crimes, and other crimes under Kosovo law committed between 1 January 1998 and 31 December 2000 in relation to allegations reported in the Council of Europe Parliamentary Assembly Report of 7 January 2011 on 'inhuman treatment of people and illicit trafficking in human

[84] See *Ministere Public c. Hissein Habre* (Judgement) (30 Mai 2016) <http://www.chambresafricaines.org/pdf/Jugement_complet.pdf> accessed 15 January 2024. For further background information, see Human Rights Watch, 'Q&A: The Case of Hissène Habré before the Extraordinary African Chambers in Senegal' (3 May 2016) <https://www.hrw.org/news/2016/05/03/qa-case-hissene-habre-extraordinary-african-chambers-senegal#3> accessed 15 January 2024.

[85] The EAC Appeals Chamber awarded 82 billion francs CFA (approximately USD 154 million) to 7,396 named victims. See Human Rights Watch, 'Hissène Habré Case: Trust Fund for Victims' (7 February 2018) <https://www.hrw.org/news/2018/02/07/hissene-habre-case-trust-fund-victims> accessed 15 January 2024.

[86] Human Rights Watch, 'Q&A: The Case of Hissène Habré before the Extraordinary African Chambers in Senegal' (3 May 2016) section 16.

[87] EAC Statute, Article 14(1).

[88] ibid Article 14(5).

[89] In the following: KSC; see Law on ratification of the international agreement (23 April 2014) 04/L-274 (Exchange of Letters) <https://www.scp-ks.org/en/documents/kosovo-law-ratification-exchange-letters-23-apr-2014> accessed 15 January 2024; regarding the KSC's integration into the Kosovo judicial system, see the Law on Specialist Chambers and Specialist Prosecutors Office Law (3 August 2015) Law No 05/L-053, Articles 1(2), 3(1) <https://www.scp-ks.org/en/documents/law-specialist-chambers-and-specialist-prosecutors-office-3-aug-2015> accessed 15 January 2024.

organs in Kosovo'.[90] The Law on Specialist Chambers and Specialist Prosecutors Office ('Law') clearly outlines the prominent position of victims in the proceedings. Article 22 of the Law adopts a definition of 'victim' akin to that of the STL and, to an extent, the ICC.[91] It also outlines that '[a] victim's personal interest and rights in the criminal proceedings before the Specialist Chambers are notification, acknowledgement and reparation'.[92] The Law further bundles victims in groups, assisted and represented by a Victims' Counsel provided *exclusively* through the KSC Registry's Victims Participation Office.[93] The application process (by filling in and submitting application forms) is similar to the regime applicable at the ICC.[94] Victims may make representations through their counsel during the pre-trial and trial proceedings as long as their personal interests are impacted and only when it is not prejudicial to, or inconsistent with, the rights of the accused[95]—a formulation common with the ICC and other hybrid courts.

Victim Counsel may file motions during pre-trial[96] and trial. Victim Counsel has a right to appeal a chamber's decision on victim status or a reparation order.[97] Victims may also make referrals to the Specialist Chamber of the Constitutional Court, within the subject-matter limits of their 'individual rights and freedoms guaranteed by the Constitution'.[98] Rule 114 of the Rules of Procedure and Evidence before the Kosovo Specialist Chambers outlines the modalities of

[90] Dick Marty, 'Inhuman Treatment of People and Illicit Trafficking in Human Organs in Kosovo' Council of Europe Parliamentary Assembly (7 January 2011) Doc 12462 <http://www.assembly.coe.int/committeedocs/2010/ajdoc462010prov.pdf> accessed 15 January 2024.

[91] According to Article 22(1) of the Law on Specialist Chambers and Specialist Prosecutors Office: '[a] Victim is a natural person who has personally suffered harm, including physical, mental or material harm, as a direct result of a crime within the jurisdiction of the Specialist Chambers. A Victim is a natural person who has personally suffered harm, including physical, mental or material harm, as a direct result of a crime within the jurisdiction of the [KSC].' Unlike the ICC definition, the definition applies the term '*direct* result' of a crime; furthermore, the definition does not encompass organizations or institutions; cf Rule 85(b) of the ICC Rules.

[92] Law on Specialist Chambers and Specialist Prosecutor's Office (3 August 2015) Law No 05/L-053, Article 22(3). Rules 113, 114 of the Rules of Procedure and Evidence before the Kosovo Specialist Chambers (KSC Rules) provide further specification, see below.

[93] ibid Articles 22(5), 24(1)(b), 34(6); the Victims' Participation Office administers the system of victims' participation before the KSC; it manages a list of specialized victim counsel; and it administers a system of payment for legal representation of victims; see also at KSC, 'Registry' <https://www.scp-ks.org/en/specialist-chambers/registry> accessed 15 January 2024, and regarding the general mandate of the Victims' Participation Office, Rule 23(5) of the KSC Rules.

[94] See at KSC, 'Victims' <https://www.scp-ks.org/en/victims> accessed 15 January 2024 and compare with the ICC system at ICC, 'Victims' <https://www.icc-cpi.int/about/victims> accessed 15 January 2024; Rule 113 of the KSC Rules.

[95] Law on Specialist Chambers and Specialist Prosecutor's Office (3 August 2015) Law No 05/L-053, Article 22(6).

[96] ibid Article 39(13).

[97] ibid Article 46(9). During those proceedings, all victim claimants shall be collectively represented as one group by Victims' Counsel assigned by the Registry—comparable to the system applied at the ECCC, STL, and SCC.

[98] Law on Specialist Chambers and Specialist Prosecutor's Office (3 August 2015) Law No 05/L-053, Article 49(3). It would appear that this right of referral indeed goes further than the right to appeal, which is limited to a question on a victim's status as beneficiary or a reparation order, see Article 46(9) of the Law.

victims' participation in the proceedings; participatory rights—and the chamber's possibility to restrict them—are comparable to those at the STL and ICC. Of note, Victims' Counsel may request to submit their own evidence, including witnesses, where the evidence on the record 'does not adequately address the impact the alleged crimes have on the personal interests of victims participating in the proceedings'.[99] In the four cases to date, Victim Counsel have held opening (and closing) statements, submitted written and oral submissions, and have questioned witnesses. In the case of the *Prosecutor v Salih Mustafa*, Victim Counsel had also proposed experts and made reparation requests to the Panel; in addition, one participating victim presented views and concerns to the Panel in the courtroom.[100] The participation regime is thus very similar to the ICC.

8.2.1.6 *Cour Penale Speciale Centrafricaine*

The Special Criminal Court for the Central African Republic (SCC)[101] is the most recent hybrid court to commence its judicial activities.[102] It was created through the *Loi Organique No 15.003 portant creation, organisation et fonctionnement de la cour penale special* of 3 June 2015. Its operationalization follows an agreement with the United Nations Mission for the Central African Republic.[103]Article 40(2) stipulates the '*constitution de partie civile*', that is, a civil party regime, which is further elaborated in Articles 74–76 of the SCC Rules of Procedure and Evidence.[104] As an important feature regarding victims' impact on the shaping of a potential case, at the SCC a civil party is entitled to request the investigation of alleged crimes before an investigative chamber, including a number of specific investigative acts.[105] In turn, civil parties can also be called to appear before the said investigative chamber for questioning (regarding the request)—comparable to the ECCC, as outlined above.[106] A number of provisions of the Central African code of criminal

[99] KSC Rules, Rule 114(5).

[100] See relevant decisions on victim participation in the *Salih Mustafa case* (KSC-BC-2020-05 and KSC-CA-2023-02)—and other cases—at KSC, 'List of important filings in relation to victims' participation in all the cases' <https://www.scp-ks.org/en/list-important-filings-relation-victims-participation-all-cases> accessed 22 October 2024.

[101] See Cour Pénale Spéciale de la République Centrafricaine <https://www.cpsrca.cf/> accessed 22 October 2024.

[102] See generally Patryk I Labuda, 'The Special Criminal Court in the Central African Republic—Failure or Vindication of Complementarity?' (2017) 15 Journal of International Criminal Justice 175; Patryk I Labuda, '"Open for Business": The Special Criminal Court Launches Investigations in the Central African Republic' (*EJIL: Talk!*, 8 February 2019) <https://www.ejiltalk.org/open-for-business-the-special-criminal-court-launches-investigations-in-the-central-african-republic/> accessed 22 October 2024.

[103] See MINUSCA, 'Signature d'un accord relatif à l'opérationnalisation de la Cour pénale spéciale de la RCA' (26 August 2016) <https://minusca.unmissions.org/signature-d%E2%80%99un-accord-relatif-%C3%A0-lop%C3%A9rationnalisation-de-la-cour-p%C3%A9nale-sp%C3%A9ciale-de-la-rca> accessed 15 January 2024.

[104] See SCC RPE (n 52).

[105] ibid Articles 75(A), 76(A).

[106] ibid Articles 74(C), 88 ('De l'audition des parties civiles').

procedure,[107] applicable by virtue of Article 5 of the *Loi Organique*, further outline the procedural rights of civil parties, alongside provisions of the SCC RPE.[108] In tune with the aforementioned international and hybrid courts, Article 64 of the *Loi Organique* provides that indigent victims before the SCC can benefit from court-appointed counsel.[109] In addition, Article 75(2) of the SCC RPE provides a common legal representation system where victim numbers per case are high. In the more recent past, judicial activity has picked up and following a first conviction,[110] reparation proceedings have ensued with submissions on behalf of victims in the courtroom, and a decision on reparations by the Appeals Chamber.[111]

8.2.1.7 Taking stock

It can be safely said from the above that the courts and tribunals under review here provide more or less comprehensive victim participation regimes with, to an extent, similar systems of allocation for participation, legal representation, and procedural rights.[112] All these justice mechanisms acknowledge the balancing act between meaningful victim participation and the accused's right to a fair and speedy trial, and the resulting general requirement that in order to exercise their rights, victims need to demonstrate that their personal interests are affected.[113] There seems to be no legitimate reason to curtail victims' rights for any hybrid court beyond these general reference points, quite the opposite: experience in all the aforementioned courts and tribunals to date demonstrates that victim participation has no detrimental impact on the speed of proceedings or the fair trial rights of the defence. Rather, victims' submissions have served to shed appropriate light on the impact that relevant crimes have had on victim communities—thus addressing the core of the transitional justice idea. The concept of purely punitive international(ized) criminal courts has been de facto abandoned for more

[107] *Loi* No 10.002 du 6 janvier 2010, code de procédure pénale centrafricain, in: Journal Officiel de la République Centrafricaine, JORCA (15 janvier 2010) <NATLEX - Central African Republic - Loi n° 10.002 du 6 janvier 2010 portant Code de procédure pénale. (ilo.org) > accessed 22 October 2024; see, eg, SCC RPE, Article 56 and following, 82, 100, 128, 133, 164, 194, 208.

[108] ibid Articles 76, 123(C), 150(E).

[109] Victims—or 'civil parties'—are represented before the SCC through counsel; see ibid Article 76(B).

[110] Cour Pénale Spéciale, *Le Parquet spécial Contre Issa Salet Adoum alias Bozize, Yaouba Ousmane, et Mahamat Tahir*, Reésumé Jugement N° 003-2022 (31 octobre 2022) Dossier No CPS/C.ASS/ISA/22-001.

[111] Cour Pénale Spéciale, *Le Parquet spécial Contre Issa Salet Adoum alias Bozize, Yaouba Ousmane, et Mahamat Tahir*, Décision de la Chambre d'appel sur les intérêts civils (reparation des victimes) (23 October 2023).

[112] Of special note is that civil parties at the ECCC and SCC have the ability to initiate a complaint procedure and thus shape a potentially forthcoming investigation; Rule 49 ECCC Internal Rules; Article 75 SCC RPE. In that sense, the civil party system puts victims slightly more at the centre of criminal proceedings (as a 'party') than other victim participation systems under review here (rather than as 'participants', eg at the ICC).

[113] The requirement to protect the independence of the Prosecutor's investigation is another important consideration—though it is less pronounced than the defence's rights and varies depending on whether the inquisitory or adversary procedural framework is applicable to the relevant court.

than two decades. In turn, the relevance of restorative, victim-centred elements in the international criminal justice context has steadily increased; the question 'if' victim participation is included in a tribunal's governing texts has been replaced by 'how', and even that question has been largely answered, as has been demonstrated above. This means that victim participation is indeed no longer optional or just a 'nice to have' feature. The question is therefore rather one of the most effective and efficient regime, and the main challenges in that regard. These shall be addressed further below.[114]

Yet, part and parcel of the novel victim-centred concept of international(ized) criminal justice is the inclusion of reparation features for victims. Consequently, in the following a brief analysis of the different reparations frameworks of the courts and tribunals under review shall be provided.

8.2.2 Reparations

8.2.2.1 Relevant provisions of the different courts and tribunals

The concept of reparations at the end of a criminal process and issued by the *same* court is alien to many national jurisdictions and surely a novelty on the international criminal justice platform.[115] The ICC has the most elaborate set of provisions in this regard; Article 75 of the Rome Statute provides the fundamental premise that in case of a conviction, a chamber may determine the scope and extent of any damage, loss, and injury to, or in respect of, victims as well as the principles on which it is acting. The ICC also differentiates explicitly between individual and collective reparation awards.[116] This approach is followed by the EAC, SCC, and the KSC.[117] Also, the ICC, SCC, and the KSC provide trial chambers with the possibility to 'appoint appropriate experts to assist [the judges] in determining the scope, extent of any damage, loss and injury to, or in respect of victims, and to suggest various options concerning the appropriate types and modalities of reparations'.[118] At the ICC a chamber, before issuing a reparations order, 'may invite and shall take account of representations from or on behalf of the convicted person, victims, other interested persons or interested States'.[119] The EAC Statute

[114] See Section 8.3.

[115] For an overview, see Carla Ferstman, 'Reparations, Assistance and Support' in Kinga Tibori-Szabó and Megan Hirst (eds), *Victim Participation in International Criminal Justice* (TMC Asser Press 2017) 385.

[116] ICC Rules, Rule 97(1).

[117] EAC Statute, Article 28(2); SCC RPE, Article 129(A); KSC Statute, Article 22(8); KSC Rules, Rule 168. The ECCC differentiates between 'collective and moral reparations', ECCC Law, Article 36(2) and Internal Rules, Rule 23*quinquies*(1).

[118] ICC Rules, Rule 97(2); KSC Rules, Rule 168; SCC RPE, Article 129(C). The ICC provision also obliges the chamber to invite observations from the convicted person, victims or their legal representatives, and other interested persons or states ('shall invite, as appropriate'). The KSC and SCC merely speak of '*may* invite/*peut* recueillir' (emphasis added).

[119] Rome Statute, Article 75(3).

entails a similar provision.[120] On a jurisprudential level, the ICC Appeals Chamber has set out a number of 'essential elements' for any order for reparations,[121] thus streamlining the fundamental quadrants of what trial chambers have to determine in any reparations order issued against a convicted person. Finally, the ICC system entertains a 'Trust Fund for Victims' (TFV), as provide for in Article 79 of the ICC Statute. Funded effectively through voluntary contributions for all its programmes,[122] the TFV provides important help in the implementation of chambers' reparation orders in particular where the convict lacks any means to afford reparations.[123]

The STL Statute recognized the institute of compensation to victims in its Article 25. Accordingly, the STL could identify victims who had suffered harm as a result of the convict's crimes and submit this information to national authorities so that a victim (or persons claiming through the victim) 'may bring an action in a national court or other competent body to obtain compensation'.[124] In other words, the STL framework did not provide for any direct judicial determination regarding individual claims for compensation and other forms of remedy.

At the ECCC, civil parties are vested with the right to seek collective and moral reparations in case of a conviction of an accused.[125] Pursuant to Rule *23quinquies* of the Internal Rules, such collective and moral reparations need to 'acknowledge the harm suffered by Civil Parties as a result of the commission of the crimes for which an Accused is convicted and ... provide benefits to the Civil Parties which address this harm'.[126] Any monetary payments to civil parties are explicitly excluded

[120] EAC Statute, Article 27(3); of note, the provision does not incorporate the more restrictive ICC language, that the Chamber '*shall take account of* representations, thus leaving more leeway to the Chamber in the exercise of its discretion.

[121] *Prosecutor v Thomas Lubanga Dyilo* (Appeals Chamber, Judgment on the appeals against the 'Decision establishing the principles and procedures to be applied to reparations' of 7 August 2012) ICC-01/04-01/06-3129 (3 March 2015) [32]: '(i) it must be directed against the convicted person; (ii) it must establish and inform the convicted person of his or her liability with respect to the reparations awarded in the order; (iii) it must specify, and provide reasons for, the type of reparations ordered, either collective, individual or both, pursuant to rules 97(1) and 98 of the RPE; (iv) it must define the harm caused to direct and indirect victims as a result of the crimes for which the person was convicted, as well as identify the modalities of reparations that the Trial Chamber considers appropriate based on the circumstances of the specific case before it; and (v) it must identify the victims eligible to benefit from the awards for reparations or set out the criteria of eligibility based on the link between the harm suffered by the victims and the crimes for which the person was convicted.'

[122] The Secretariat of the TFV, including its staff, travel, and other operational running costs are funded through the ICC's regular annual budget. The TFV Secretariat's annual budget for 2024 stands at 4,324 million Euros; see Resolution ICC-ASP/22/Res 4 (14 December 2023), para 1. The Fund may also receive 'money and other property collected through fines or forfeiture' as per Article 79(2) of the ICC Statute; in reality, however, the TFV's actionable funds have come almost exclusively out of voluntary contributions (by states).

[123] For more information, see <https://www.trustfundforvictims.org/> accessed 15 January 2024.

[124] STL Statute, Article 25(3). For the purpose of reparations in national proceedings STL Statute, Article 25(4) is to be considered as final and binding for national authorities. See also STL Rules, Rule 86(G).

[125] ECCC, Internal Rules, Rules 23(b), 23*quinquies*(1).

[126] ibid Rule 23*quinquies*(2).

by the Internal Rules.[127] One form of the aforesaid moral reparations is that the trial judgment at the ECCC 'shall include: ... the full names of the Civil Parties'.[128] Another may be publication of the judgment in appropriate media at the expense of the convicted person, or the funding of a non-profit activity or service to the benefit of victims.[129] In addition, the ECCC's Internal Rules ascribe an interesting competence to the Victim Support Section which is unparalleled by any other of the courts/tribunals presently assessed: the section is entrusted with 'the development and implementation of non-judicial programs and measures addressing the broader interests of victims. Such programs may, where appropriate, be developed and implemented in collaboration with governmental and non-governmental organisations external to the ECCC'.[130] In execution of this mandate, the VSS organizes, inter alia, mobile exhibitions, discussion forums on developments regarding reparations in ECCC proceedings, workshops, and radio programmes.[131] While these activities do not go to *individualized* victims in ECCC proceedings, they address larger victim communities, akin to activities of the ICC Trust Fund for Victims under its assistance mandate to the general benefit of victims of Rome Statute crimes.[132] In a somewhat comparable, albeit less elaborate fashion, the victims' office at the SCC in CAR is mandated to advise on potential reparation measures.[133]

For the KSC, the trial judgment may 'include a decision on the scope and extent of any damage, loss and injury to, or in respect of, Victims and will state the principles on which it is acting. Alternatively, if such a decision would unduly prolong the criminal proceedings, a Trial Panel may limit its decision to the identity of Victims of any crimes established in its judgment',[134] akin to the ECCC.[135] As at the ICC, where the KSC issues a guilty verdict, it may make an order directly against that accused specifying appropriate reparation to, or in respect of, victims collectively or individually.[136] However, '[w]here appropriate, the [KSC] may refer the

[127] ibid Rule 23*quinquies*(2).

[128] ibid Rule 101(6)(g).

[129] ibid Rule 23(11), (12); see also *Prosecutor v KAING Guek Eav* (Direction on Proceedings Relevant to Reparations and on the Filing of Final Written Submissions) Case No 001/18-07-2007-ECCC/TC, E-159 (27 August 2009).

[130] ECCC, Internal Rules, Rule 12*bis*(4).

[131] See relevant news clips on the VSS's website at ECCC, 'Victims Support Section' <https://www.eccc.gov.kh/en/organs/victims-support-section> accessed 15 January 2024.

[132] See Regulations of the Trust Fund for Victims, Regulation 47; for more information, see also the Trust Fund for Victims, 'Assistance Mandate' at <https://www.trustfundforvictims.org/en/about/two-mandates-tfv/assistance> accessed 15 January 2024.

[133] SCC RPE, Article 47(d).

[134] KSC Law, Article 22(7).

[135] ECCC, Internal Rules, Rule 101(6)(g).

[136] KSC Law, Article 22(8). See also ibid Article 44(6), speaking of a 'Reparation Order', comparable to Article 75(2) of the Rome Statute. As a practical example, see KSC Trial Panel I, *Specialist Prosecutor v Salih Mustafa*, Corrected version of Public redacted version of Reparation Order against Salih Mustafa, KSC-BC-2020-05 (6 April 2023). Pursuant to Rule 168 of the KSC Rules, the chamber may appoint experts to assist in determining the scope of any damage and suggest options of appropriate—individual or collective—reparations; this follows the relevant provision of Rule 97(2) of the ICC Rules.

Victims to civil litigation in the other courts of Kosovo'.[137] In order to enable victims to (also) seek reparations through relevant domestic civil litigation, a certified copy of the judgment as well as an indication of the damage caused to the victims may be transmitted, upon application of Victims' Counsel, to the competent authorities of any state, or directly to the victims affected.[138]

For the SCC, the RPE stipulates that the trial chamber is to issue a separate ruling on reparations after the judgement on the merits. In its ruling on reparations, the chamber is held to order reparations 'adapted to the nature and scale of damages suffered by the civil parties'.[139] In parallel, the national code of criminal procedure stipulates that reparation measures can be sought through civil action claims before national courts.[140] In case of an 'indigent' convict, the chamber can invite the Registry's victim service unit as well as the defence to seek external funding.[141] There already has been a first reparation ruling[142] and a very instructive decision on the matter by the CPS Appeals Chamber[143].

The EAC Statute provided that reparation measures awarded by the chambers are restitution, compensation, and rehabilitation.[144] Importantly, the Statute also provided that 'they are open to all victims, individually or collectively, whether or not they participated in the proceedings before the Extraordinary African Chambers'.[145] This provision shows that the EAC was heavily inspired by the ICC reparations regime which in its Rule 92 of the ICC Rules also provides for both individual and collective reparations. Of much greater importance however is the above statutory provision that the entitlement to reparations is independent from the participation at trial: this underlines a key principle that participation at trial is not—and should not be—a necessary precondition for reparations.

The EAC, along with the ICC, is the only court which in its governing text provides for a trust fund. Article 28 of the EAC Statute stipulates that

> [a] Trust Fund shall be established for the benefit of victims of crimes within the jurisdiction of the [EAC] ... The Trust Fund shall be financed by

137 KSC Law, Article 22(9).

138 ibid Article 22(10); KSC Rules, Rule 167. See in this regard the rather progressive stance of Trial Panel I in the *Salih Mustafa* case in paras 260 and following of the Corrected version of Public redacted version of Reparation Order against Salih Mustafa, KSC-BC-2020-05 (6 April 2023).

139 SCC RPE, Article 129(C). For a comprehensive report, see American University Washington College of Law, *Case-Based Reparations at the Central African Republic's Special Criminal Court*, Gender and International Criminal Law Project (December 2019).

140 Loi N°10.002 (6 January 2010), Article 2.

141 SCC RPE, Article 129(D).

142 CPS, Trial Chamber, 'Décision sur les intérêts civils' (16 June 2023).

143 CPS, Appeals Chamber, 'Décision de la Chambre d'appel sur les intérêts civils (réparation des victimes) dans l'affaire le Procureur contre Issa Sallet Adoum, Ousman Yaouba et Mahamat Tahir' (23 October 2023).

144 EAC Statute, Article 27(1).

145 ibid Article 28(2).

> voluntary contributions from foreign governments, international institutions, non-governmental organizations and other entities wishing to support the victims.[146]

On 28 and 29 January 2018, the African Union adopted the trust fund's statute during its summit in Addis Ababa, Ethiopia, and provided an initial monetary instalment for its activities.[147] However, sufficient fundraising remains a key challenge for the trust fund, compounded by high expectations of a victim community that largely surpasses those 4,000 victims that participated in the proceedings.[148] Still today, eight years after the conviction, the trust fund has not received any further funds, let alone initiated any implementation measures.[149] In the affected victims' eyes, the EAC reparations regime is thus viewed as a colossal failure.

8.2.2.2 Common features?

Unlike the victim participation regimes, the reparation frameworks of the different courts and tribunals differ quite visibly regarding (a) what types of reparations victims may claim; and (b) where they may do so. The ECCC importantly stops short of any *material* reparations for individual victims;[150] the STL referred exclusively to national courts for any compensation;[151] and the KSC does provide for the issuance of a reparations order (in addition to referring to the possibility of compensation claims before domestic courts), but does not explicitly regulate the situation where the convicted person has no funds to pay for a reparation award.[152] These different regimes point towards one of the fundamental challenges to any reparation regime, the question of funding. Where a court suggests through its governing texts that victims may benefit from reparations at the end of the process, the question of availability of funds becomes a core facet of the system. Experience from the UN ad hoc tribunals as well as the ICC and other hybrid courts has demonstrated that in most cases, a person convicted before an international(ized)

[146] ibid Article 28(1).

[147] See Statute of the Trust Fund for Victims, annexed to African Union Resolution EX.CL/1040(XXXI).

[148] Human Rights Watch reports that 7,396 named victims are direct reparation beneficiaries as per the EAC's verdict. An additional 3,489 victims who had not been registered at trial are also able to apply to the trust fund to determine their eligibility; Human Rights Watch, 'Hissène Habré Case' (n 85).

[149] Human Rights Watch, 'Chad: Still No Reparations for Hissène Habré's Victims' (26 May 2023) <https://www.hrw.org/news/2023/05/26/chad-still-no-reparations-hissene-habres-victims> accessed 15 January 2024.

[150] The Supreme Court Chamber clarified that the 'possibility to bring the civil action before civil courts, envisaged under domestic law' is not precluded for civil parties before the ECCC: *Prosecutor v KAING Guek Eav* (Appeals Chamber, Judgment) Case File/Dossier No 001/18-07-2007-ECCC/SC (3 February 2012), case file F-28 [643].

[151] STL Statute, Article 25(3); STL Rules, Rule 86(G).

[152] KSC Rules, Rule 168(1). As stated above, Trial Panel I in the *Salih Mustafa* case provided some insightful considerations in tackling this matter: Corrected version of Public redacted version of Reparation Order against Salih Mustafa, KSC-BC-2020-05 (6 April 2023), paras 260 and following.

court after many years of judicial proceedings will have no more funds available to fund any reparation awards to victims. A trust fund may be a solution, but, particularly in the case of ad hoc courts, will have enormous problems raising any funds. Even the ICC's—permanent—TFV is experiencing shortfalls of voluntary contributions. This is compounded by the potential reputational damage if and where a court promises reparations at the end of a trial but victims ultimately remain empty-handed—the EAC dilemma being a case in point. The issue of *sustainability* of any reparation regime is thus of utmost importance.

Unlike for the question of victim participation in the proceedings, it thus cannot be concluded without reservation that modern international(ized) criminal courts can—or maybe even should—regulate reparations beyond a mere reference to national courts and external compensation programmes. This translates into one of the main general challenges of hybrid courts in terms of their victim-related provisions, as shall be outlined in the following.

8.3 Challenges

Due to the ICC's permanent nature, its victim participation and reparations regime has been subject to constant review and critical comment from (the Assembly of) States Parties and civil society alike.[153] Key documents issued by the ICC in response to these calls are the 'Court strategy in relation to victims' of 2009[154] and updates in 2012 and 2013.[155] In 2020, the 'Independent Expert Review of the International Criminal Court' picked up on key victim-related topics in the ICC system and issued recommendations which are yet to be fully implemented.[156] The challenges identified for the ICC almost inevitably also apply to the hybrid courts previously assessed in one form or another.

[153] See resolutions of the Assembly of States Parties as well as the final report of the Independent Experts (of 30 September 2020) <https://asp.icc-cpi.int/Review-Court> accessed 15 January 2024. See also Gaelle Carayon and Jonathan O'Donohue, 'The International Criminal Court's Strategies in Relation to Victims' (2017) 15 Journal of International Criminal Justice 561.

[154] ICC, 'Report of the Court on the strategy in relation to victims' (10 November 2009) ICC-ASP/8/45.

[155] See ICC, 'Report of the Court on the Revised strategy in relation to victims: Past, present and future' (5 November 2012) ICC-ASP/11/40; ICC, 'Court's Revised strategy in relation to victims' (5 November 2012) ICC-ASP/11/38; ICC, 'Report of the Court on the implementation in 2013 of the revised strategy in relation to victims' (11 October 2013) ICC-ASP/12/41.

[156] See ICC, 'Independent Expert Review of the International Criminal Court and the Rome Statute System: Final Report' (30 September 2020) <https://asp.icc-cpi.int/iccdocs/asp_docs/ASP19/IER-Final-Report-ENG.pdf> accessed 15 January 2024. Regarding some advances of the ICC Registry to increase the efficiency of victims' access to judicial and reparation proceedings, see Ambach, 'Victim Participation at the ICC' (n 23).

8.3.1 Identification of and outreach to victims for the purpose of participation and/or reparations

In order to ensure meaningful participation of victims in judicial proceedings, it is fundamental that victims indeed have *effective access* to these proceedings. It is insufficient if a court or tribunal simply provides a legal framework allowing for the participation of victims, but remains inactive in terms of reaching out to affected communities on how they can best gain access. There needs to be a coherent outreach strategy for every institution to contact relevant victims and affected communities in order to explain what the court/tribunal is about, what victims' participatory rights are and, importantly, what they can expect quite concretely from their participation in the proceedings.[157]

There are a number of lessons learnt from the ICC and ECCC context, but also the UN ad hoc tribunals.[158] The effects of the absence of appropriate outreach by the ICTY into affected communities in the nineties and early 2000s—despite an increasingly convincing story to tell—has been painfully brought to the stakeholders' attention through a public survey study by the Berkeley Institute in 2000.[159] The amount of unawareness, misperceptions, and resulting suspicion was alarming and has led to a notable increase of the ICTY's attention to its outreach in the different field office locations and beyond. Probably having learnt from the ICTY's mistake, the ICC Registry created a Public Information and Outreach Section with its own strategic plan from the early days onwards.[160]

At the EAC, outreach was fully externalized to three non-governmental organizations (NGOs) that had credibility amongst victim communities on the ground, in Chad, in Senegal, and on the international level. The three organizations worked together as an 'Outreach Consortium'. The Consortium was charged with helping to relay the trial to a mostly untrusting audience in Chad.[161] It has been claimed

157 On this, see also Kirsten Ainley and Mark Kersten, 'Dakar Guidelines on the Establishment of Hybrid Courts' LSE and Wayamo Foundation (2019) <https://hybridjustice.com/dakar-guidelines/> accessed 19 March 2024 ('Dakar Guidelines') 40 and following; 78 and following <http://eprints.lse.ac.uk/101134/1/Dakar_Guidelines_print_version_corr_1_.pdf> accessed 15 January 2024.

158 See the relevant outreach strategy papers of the ICC at 'Background Materials: Outreach' <http://iccforum.com/background/outreach> accessed 15 January 2024; see also ECCC, 'Public Affairs Outreach Figures 2009 – 2017' (30 September 2017) <https://www.eccc.gov.kh/sites/default/files/Outreach%20statestics%20as%20of%20September%202017.pdf> accessed 15 January 2024.

159 Human Rights Center, International Human Rights Law Clinic, University of California, Berkeley; and Centre for Human Rights, University of Sarajevo, 'Justice, Accountability and Social Reconstruction—An Interview Study of Bosnian Judges and Prosecutors' (May 2000) <https://www.law.berkeley.edu/files/IHRLC/Justice_Accountability_and_Social_Reconstruction.pdf> accessed 15 January 2024.

160 ICC, 'Integrated Strategy for External Relations, Public Information and Outreach' <https://www.icc-cpi.int/NR/rdonlyres/425E80BA-1EBC-4423-85C6-D4F2B93C7506/185049/ICCPIDSWBOR0307070402_IS_En.pdf> accessed 15 January 2024.

161 Brian Obara, 'Outreach in the Hissène Habré Trial was an Exercise in Winning Hearts and Minds' (*Justice Hub*, 30 September 2017) <https://justicehub.org/article/outreach-hissene-habre-trial-was-exercise-winning-hearts-and-minds> accessed 15 January 2024.

that the EAC marked the first time in the history of international justice that a court gave so much importance from the very start to outreach by setting aside as much as 10 per cent of its budget.[162]

Similarly, in the—more focused—process of identifying victims to inform them of their procedural options to participate in proceedings (and potentially claim reparations), some hybrid courts have resorted to substantial help by the NGO community—be that voluntarily or involuntarily so. In the Cambodian context, rather than officials of the ECCC, for the most part it was a network of NGOs operating in Cambodia that went to victim communities and informed them of their option to become civil parties in ECCC proceedings. In a survey study carried out by the Cambodian Human Rights and Development Association (ADHOC) together with Harvard University, it was established that the majority of the respondents stated that ADHOC was their 'main source of information regarding the possibility of applying as Civil Party'.[163] Continued outreach activities by the ECCC through radio and television programmes and other public events by the Victims Support Section are essential.[164]

Providing victims with information about the possibility to access and partake in a justice process is crucial for the legitimacy of the relevant institution; regardless of which vehicle is chosen, the institution in question also needs to carefully measure its performance and impact on the target audience as these parameters directly link to its success.

8.3.2 Victims' choice of counsel and the provision of legal representation in the proceedings

Victims' choice of counsel with a view to their legal representation in the proceedings is important for their effective participation in the proceedings. The more effectively the victims' procedural rights are communicated and exercised, the more effective is how victims perceive and appreciate their access to justice. Yet, in the prosecution of mass crimes before an international(ized) court with finite resources, it seems unrealistic that many victims will be represented in the proceedings individually.[165] Rather, common legal representation will be the rule, also

[162] ibid.

[163] Kirchenbauer and others (n 48) 'Key findings', (ii).

[164] Regarding the latest activities at ECCC, see 'Victims Support Section' <https://www.eccc.gov.kh/en/organs/victims-support-section> accessed 15 January 2024.

[165] In the *Abd-Al-Rahman* proceedings in the Sudan situation, for example, the Common Legal Representative of Victims sought to introduce four participating victims to present their views and concerns directly to the Chamber, as well as one witness on specific harm to female victims, *Prosecutor v Ali Muhammad Ali Abd-Al-Rahman* (Public redacted version of 'Common Legal Representative of Victims' Request to present evidence and views and concerns') ICC-02/05-01/20-865-Red (6 February 2023). The Chamber granted the request. See also generally on legal representation: Human Rights

to enable the chamber to honour the accused's right to a fair and speedy trial.[166] Regulatory frameworks of the hybrid courts like the ECCC, KSC, SCC, and EAC have taken a clear position: victims at trial are organized in groups, represented by a common counsel in court; legal aid extends only to group representation.[167] Victims' choice of the common representative is limited to individuals accredited with the respective institutions.[168] In addition, with victims usually unable to pay for their (common) legal representative, such counsel will be in most cases court-appointed. Relevant courts have taken into account that certain victim groups within a case may have *distinct* needs, which has led to multiple *separate* victim groups where interests could be proven to differ.[169]

At the ICC, the applicable law (Rule 90 of the ICC RPE) and practice allow victims a certain degree of choice in selecting their common legal representative, provided relevant agreement can be facilitated by the Registry.[170] Still, budgetary constraints may force hybrid courts into simpler, in-house counsel regimes of common victim representation (as above). This is not in and of itself a deficit provided there are adequate facilities for these representatives to entertain a meaningful link to the represented victims, giving the latter satisfaction that their views and concerns are duly brought to the judges in the courtroom. The key is a

Watch, 'Who Will Stand for Us? Victims' Legal Representation at the ICC in the Ongwen Case and Beyond' (29 August 2017).

166 In *Lubanga*, in early 2008, Trial Chamber I still tried to take a flexible approach: *Prosecutor v Thomas Lubanga Dyilo* (Trial Chamber I, Decision on victims' participation) ICC-01/04-01/06-1119 (18 January 2008) [125]. Yet, later court practice at the ICC has exclusively opted for common legal representation. On this, see also *Prosecutor v Dominic Ongwen* (Trial Chamber IX, Decision on Registry's Request for Clarification on the Issue of Legal Assistance Paid by the Court for the Legal Representatives of Victims) ICC-02/04-01/15 (14 November 2016). The STL followed this approach: *Prosecutor v Ayyash et al* (Decision on Victims' Participation in the Proceedings) STL-11-01/PT/PTJ, F0236/20120508/R121249-R121291/EN/nc (5 August 2012) Disposition.

167 See, eg for the KSC: Registry Practice Direction KSC-BD-25/Rev1/2024/1 of 23, 'Legal Aid Regulations', Regulation 31; see further M Hirst, 'Legal Representation of Participating Victims' in K Tibori-Szabó and M Hirst (eds) *Victim Participation in International Criminal Justice*. International Criminal Justice Series, vol 11 (T.M.C. Asser Press 2017).

168 KSC: KSC Statute, Article 22(5); ECCC: Internal Rules, Rule 21(3); SCC: Article 47(c), 75, 76(B) of the SCC RPE; STL: Rule 51(C) of the STL RPE.

169 Think of a victim group of former child soldiers, and another group of victims of the crimes committed by child soldiers in the same case confines. See, eg, *Prosecutor v Jean-Bosco Ntaganda* ICC-01/04-02/06 or *Prosecutor v Alfred Yekatom and Patrice-Edouard Ngaïssona* ICC-01/14-01/18; see also KSC Rules, Rule 113(8); ECCC Internal Rules, Rule 23*ter*(3).

170 Most recently, see Pre-Trial Chamber II, *Prosecutor v Maxime Jeoffroy Eli Mokom Gawaka* (Decision on the legal representation of victims) ICC-01/14-01/22-182 (27 March 2023), following *Prosecutor v Maxime Jeoffroy Eli Mokom Gawaka* (Registry Report on Legal Representation of Victims) ICC-01/14-01/22-98 (7 October 2022); *Prosecutor v Ali Muhammad Ali Abd-Al-Rahman* (Decision on victims' participation and legal representation in trial proceedings) ICC-02/05-01/20-494 (19 October 2021) *('Ali Kushayb')*, following *Prosecutor v Ali Muhammad Ali Abd-Al-Rahman* (Registry Report on Common Legal Representation) ICC-02/05-01/20-477 (11 October 2021). In the *Al Hassan* proceedings, a team of external counsel is engaged; in the *Yekatom/Ngaissona* trial, a team of external counsel and counsel of the ICC's Office of Public Counsel for Victims is engaged as common legal representatives of victims, following Registry enquiries into victims' preferences and reports thereof to the relevant chambers.

meaningful communication between victims and their legal representative. It will be one of the essential tasks of relevant Registries to enable these connections and ensure their continuous good functioning.[171]

8.3.3 Procedural rights and obligations

Another challenge lies in the fact that the array of victims' procedural tools still differs across the courts under present scrutiny. At the ECCC, victims' submissions—despite victims being acknowledged as civil parties—have remained largely confined to issues around the equality of arms.[172] At the EAC, the Trial Chamber was more permissive regarding civil parties' submissions, allowing counsel to address the court and question witnesses for both the prosecution and the defence more inclusively.[173] At the KSC, the Rules limit the content of victims' submissions to 'submissions on legal grounds regarding admissibility and common representation';[174] they (only) allow for victim-led evidence where it addresses the 'impact the alleged crimes have on the personal interests of the [participating] victims'.[175]

ICC jurisprudence has been more permissive in this regard: in an early decision, the Appeals Chamber established the requirements to be met for victims to be allowed to present evidence: the Trial Chamber must assess whether the evidence proposed by the victims (i) affects their personal interests; (ii) is relevant to the issues of the case; (iii) is necessary for the determination of the truth; and (iv) its presentation would be consistent with the rights of the accused and a fair and impartial trial.[176] Importantly, victims' personal interests are generally affected when proposed evidence shows the nature and the specific types of the harm suffered

[171] This may arguably entail a monitoring role as to the effectiveness of the communication and victims' experience. See ICC, Registry, *Prosecutor v Maxime Jeoffroy Eli Mokom Gawaka*, Registry Observations pursuant to Pre-Trial Chamber II's 'Order seeking observations on matters related to the conduct of the confirmation Proceedings' (ICC-01/14-01/22-50), ICC-01/14-01/22-55 (25 May 2022), para 34; ICC, Trial Chamber VI, *Prosecutor v Mahamat Said Abdel Kani*, 'Decision on matters relating to the participation of victims during the trial' ICC-01/14-01/21-278 (13 April 2022), paras 30–31.

[172] Jeanne Elone, 'The Extraordinary African Chambers: A New Approach to Victim Participation in International Criminal Tribunals?' (*International Justice Monitor*, 28 October 2015) <https://www.ijmonitor.org/2015/10/the-extraordinary-african-chambers-a-new-approach-to-victim-participation-in-international-criminal-tribunals/> accessed 15 January 2024.

[173] ibid.

[174] KSC Rules, Rule 113(3).

[175] ibid, Rule 114(5).

[176] See in the *Katanga* case before the ICC, *Prosecutor v Germain Katanga* (Judgment on the Appeal of Mr Katanga Against the Decision of Trial Chamber II of 22 January 2010 Entitled 'Decision on the Modalities of Victim Participation at Trial') ICC-01/04-01/07-2288 OA11 (16 July 2010) [3] and [114]. See also, in the *Lubanga* case, *Prosecutor v Thomas Lubanga Dyilo* (Judgment on the appeals of The Prosecutor and The Defence against Trial Chamber I's Decision on Victims' Participation of 18 January 2008) ICC-01/04-01/06-1432 (11 July 2008) (n 7), [4] and in the *Bemba* case, *Prosecutor v Jean-Pierre Bemba Gombo* (Order regarding applications by victims to present their views and concerns or to present evidence) ICC-01/05-01/08-1935 (22 November 2011) [3].

by (groups of) victims or is illustrative of the victim population;[177] in addition, the Appeals Chamber also held that '[i]f victims were generally and under all circumstances precluded from tendering evidence relating to the guilt or innocence of the accused ... their right to participate in the trial would potentially become ineffectual'.[178] In the end, a case-by-case assessment of the relevant Chamber will best safeguard the delicate equilibrium between parties' and participants' rights.[179] The ICC's insofar inclusive interpretation of victims' participatory rights has not led to any finding of delay of the proceedings or any other prejudice to the defence.

Yet, absent a more uniform victim participation regime across institutions, the right balancing of parties' and participants' rights will remain subject to a 'court-by-court' approach. As a concrete step to solidify victims' rights across the different judicial institutions, one could envisage a comprehensive mapping of different victim participation schemes and procedural rights,[180] and create a model standard operating procedure—probably catering also for an analysis of key distinctions between the two 'major' approaches, namely the *partie civile* system and the victim participation scheme as embodied by the ICC. This standard operating procedure (SOP) could be a helpful template for future hybrid courts to adopt a victim participation scheme that is fair to the accused without having to re-invent the wheel. The benefits of this would be manifold, including time-gains through a speedier build-up phase of the system and more focused litigation during the proceedings; certainty and predictability of the applicable law (which goes to the benefit of all parties to the proceedings); and finally (as a result) notable monetary savings for stakeholders. Yet, differences in the current regimes (compare only the civil party systems of the ECCC and SCC with the frameworks at the ICC, STL, and KSC) also go back to relevant national legal systems which, in the case of hybrid tribunals, are part of their potential strengths to be anchored in national laws and traditions. This is where the SOP would have to address in sufficient depth key features of *different* regimes rather than attempting to construct a *one size fits all* solution. The idea of one or more template solution(s) has its appeal if it focuses

[177] See in the *Ntaganda* case, *Prosecutor v Bosco Ntaganda* (Public redacted version of 'Decision on the request by the Legal Representative of the Victims of the Attacks for leave to present evidence and victims' views and concerns') ICC-01/04-02/06-1780-Red (15 February 2017) (n 6) [10] and in the *Katanga* case, *Prosecutor v Germain Katanga* (Directions for the conduct of the proceedings and testimony in accordance with rule 140) ICC-01/04-01/07-1665 (20 November 2009) [30(c)].

[178] *Prosecutor v Thomas Lubanga Dyilo* (Judgment on the appeals of the Prosecutor and the Defence against Trial Chamber I's Decision on Victims' Participation of 18 January 2008) ICC-01/04-01/06-1432 OA9 OA10 (11 July 2008) [97].

[179] See, on the case-by-case assessment, *Prosecutor v Germain Katanga* (Judgment on the Appeal of Mr Katanga Against the Decision of Trial Chamber II of 22 January 2010 Entitled 'Decision on the Modalities of Victim Participation at Trial') ICC-01/04-01/07-2288 OA11 (16 July 2010) [112].

[180] The present contribution with its selection of assessed jurisprudence provides a mere starting point of a more comprehensive mapping exercise.

on overarching key principles and relevant—sufficiently general—suggestions of technical nature, and leaves space for contextual adaptation.[181]

8.3.4 Funds for reparation awards

Neither the ICC nor any of the hybrid courts have any powers binding states to co-operate financially when it comes to funding a reparations regime for victims. As outlined above, two general approaches have been taken by courts: first, there is the more inclusive reparations regime of the ICC, ECCC, KSC, SCC, and the EAC with their own statutory means to (a) issue a reparations order; and (b) award reparations *on paper*. For the ICC and the EAC,[182] this is being carried out through a trust fund for victims. Second, there are those internationalized court systems that merely refer to national courts and (potential) national compensation programmes, such as the STL and, to an extent, the KSC.[183] While in the latter cases victims may use a final judgment as an executable title ('final and binding'[184]) for compensation claims in national proceedings (before civil law courts), the relevant hybrid courts play no further role.

Both regimes have their challenges which relate back to states' willingness to make the system work. First, for hybrid courts which can issue reparation orders and even have their own trust fund, the main question will be where funds come from in the—likely—event of a convict without much wealth left for reparation awards. As an example, in the case of the EAC, it is highly improbable that the Chadian government—or any other state or organization for that matter—will adduce much to the altogether 123 million Euros of victim compensation ordered by the EAC. The EAC Trust Fund's fundraising efforts have had very limited success so far.[185] Looking at the fundraising challenges of the ICC Trust Fund for Victims with its much broader mandate and reach in terms of potential (state and private)

[181] While victims' rights may be defined differently, their technical access to relevant facilities follows rather similar best practice considerations. In a similar vein, see Ambach in Ainley and Kersten (n 157) 40 and following. Particularly the ICC victim admission and participation framework can be used as some sort of general template/yardstick as it embodies the best-tested system in practice, boasting a rich body of jurisprudence in its application; on this, see Ambach, 'Victim Participation at the ICC' (n 23).

[182] EAC Statute, Article 28 and ICC Statute, Arts 75, 79; see also section 8.2.1.4.

[183] STL: STL Statute, Article 25(3) and STL Rules, Rule 86(G); KSC, Article 22(8); as outlined earlier, the Rules of the KSC provide for (a) transmission of the judgment to national authorities for the purpose of a compensation claim (Rule 167 of the KSC Rules); and (b) a reparation order against the convicted person (KSC Rules, Rule 168).

[184] KSC Rules, Rule 167(2).

[185] To date, only the African Union has allocated USD 5 million to the Trust Fund. See Redress, 'Chad: Still No Reparations for Hissène Habré's Victims' (26 May 2023) <https://redress.org/news/chad-still-no-reparations-for-hissene-habres-victims/> accessed 15 January 2024; and previously Redress, 'Chad, the African Union and the International Community Must Not Abandon Hissène Habré's Victims Now' (30 May 2021) <https://redress.org/news/chad-the-african-union-and-the-international-community-must-not-abandon-hissene-habres-victims-now/> accessed 15 January 2024.

donors, sufficient funds may be hard to find in the present geopolitical climate where, particularly in the last two years, investments go into military spending rather than justice solutions.

For hybrid courts with no trust fund option, a simple statutory referral to national compensation programmes may be a dangerous path, too. The courts have no control over these programmes ever materializing. Even the statutory notion that victims may seek compensation before domestic jurisdictions with a guilty verdict as a recognized title may prove a source of frustration if any such redress eventually proves impossible to obtain. Victims' frustration may turn against the relevant court. A solution may be a memorandum of understanding with the relevant host state at the outset stating that national compensation programmes will be put in place and open to victims of the hybrid court in question. Yet, the court will have no control over this, and chances are that compensation programmes will be the first initiative falling by the wayside if competing government obligations materialize.

One option is to look into partnerships with international/regional relief organizations as implementing partners of reparation measures. It is important to establish such partnerships as early as at the creation of the relevant court itself, to have assurance that the system will function as a whole when it comes to reparation implementation. And again, the question needs to be answered as to where relevant funds will be taken from.

This points again to an active duty common to all international(ized) courts discussed here to manage potential beneficiaries' expectations from the very beginning of relevant proceedings. It is worse to tell victim communities that they will get reparations and then never fulfill that promise, than not to provide for the statutory option in the first place. Hybrid courts need to face up to the potential failure on this crucial issue.

8.4 Conclusion

Developments in the area of victim participation and reparations in the more recent hybrid criminal justice mechanisms have been remarkable. Different courts provide an array of solutions with broadly comparable regimes of victim participation, and more diverse solutions regarding reparations. It can be assumed that the following progressive view will prevail also for future hybrid courts: that international(ized) justice mechanisms not only serve the purpose of deterrence and prevention, but have a broader transitional justice mandate; they serve to bring satisfaction to victims (through participation in the proceedings) and, to some degree, reparative/restorative justice in the form of reparation regimes.[186]

[186] 'Reparations in the present case must—to the extent achievable—relieve the suffering caused by the serious crimes committed; afford justice to the victims by alleviating the consequences of the

Victim-centred justice providing for victim participation in the proceedings is no longer just a luxury feature of a comfortably funded ICC, but part of the modern standard for any present or future international(ized) criminal justice mechanism. A similar argument cannot be made about reparations, where a uniform regulatory pattern cannot be confirmed and the implementation of reparations depends on (f)actors external to the relevant court.

A number of key challenges persist: first, coherent outreach strategies need to be in place in order to (i) ensure victims' awareness of the respective court; and (ii) explain how victims can have access to the proceedings. Challenges here are manifold, reaching from security to societal tension if the strategy is not well equilibrated, to the issue of funding since proper outreach and victim admission mechanisms in judicial proceedings can be costly. Second, the choice of the victims' legal representative(s) in court proceedings needs to be handled wisely. Aspects of logistics, practicability, and funding will in most cases lead to common legal representation of (large) victim groups through counsel often appointed by the registry of the respective court. This system can be very capable of delivering victims the justice that they seek, if it is communicated properly, transparently, and in a timely manner. More broadly, as to the victim participation framework on a timescale and procedural tools at victim counsels' disposition, a plug-in solution with a broad standard list of rights may go a long way, as long as the differences in existing approaches are sufficiently recognized and conscious choices made. Finally, the issue of funding of reparations and related state support will remain a major challenge—and potential for failure in the restorative justice field if funds are not secured in a timely manner, no matter what reparation regime is being applied. An alternative may be to merely refer to a right to compensation before appropriate national jurisdictions, following the example of the UN ad hoc tribunals and the STL. Partnering with international/regional aid organizations may be a promising alley to explore. A final conclusion emerges as to what the new, more victim-centred approach to international(ized) justice for mass crimes is: work in progress.

wrongful acts; deter future violations; and contribute to the effective reintegration of former child soldiers. Reparations can assist in promoting reconciliation between the convicted person, the victims of the crimes and the affected communities.' *Prosecutor v Thomas Lubanga Dyilo* (Trial Chamber I, Order for Reparations) ICC-01/04-01/06-3129-AnxA (3 March 2015) [71].

9

Striking the Right Balance

Impact of the Nationality of Judges/Staff on the Legitimacy of Recent Hybrid Tribunals

Erica Bussey[*]

9.1 Introduction

The Special Criminal Court (SCC) in the Central African Republic (CAR), a 'hybrid' tribunal wholly grounded within the national justice system, has a majority of national judges and nationals in key staff positions. At the opposite end of the spectrum, the Kosovo Specialist Chambers (KSC), by design, has no national judges or staff. In the middle, there are various uneasy compromises—the proposed Hybrid Court for South Sudan (HCSS), with a majority of non-South Sudanese judges and key positions reserved for non-South Sudanese, as well as several of the first-wave of hybrids such as the Special Court for Sierra Leone (SCSL), with a majority of international staff and judges, and the Extraordinary Chambers in the Courts of Cambodia (ECCC), with a majority of national judges but a requirement that judicial decisions be unanimous or be made by a super-majority.

Against the backdrop of these two opposite models, this chapter examines the rationales for including or excluding national judges and staff in hybrid tribunals, focusing on the question of 'sociological' legitimacy and how this impacts on internal and external resilience. While commentators such as Hobbs have argued that the presence of national judges can enhance the sociological legitimacy of hybrid tribunals, the question of legitimacy can cut both ways—legitimacy underpins both the decision to include a majority of national judges in the SCC and to exclude or minimize their participation in the KSC and the proposed HCSS.

The chapter first considers definitions and indicators of sociological legitimacy, before examining the impact of decisions about composition on such legitimacy and on the ability of these tribunals to fulfil certain goals. The chapter then considers broader rationales for the inclusion or exclusion of international and

[*] The views expressed herein are those of the author and do not necessarily reflect the views of the United Nations. A shorter version of this article appeared as a blogpost: Erica Bussey, 'Striking the Right Balance—Blending International and National Components in Hybrid Courts' (*Justice in Conflict*, 14 March 2018) <https://justiceinconflict.org/2018/03/14/striking-the-right-balance-blending-international-and-national-components-in-hybrid-courts/> accessed 31 December 2023.

Erica Bussey, *Striking the Right Balance* In: *Hybrid Justice*. Edited by: Kirsten Ainley and Mark Kersten, Oxford University Press. © Erica Bussey 2025. DOI: 10.1093/oso/9780192893758.003.0009

national judges on hybrid tribunals, including the benefits that may arise as a result of a mixed composition. It then considers in detail the composition of a selected set of hybrid tribunals which demonstrate more concretely how these rationales have played out in various settings, as well as illustrating broader trends regarding legitimacy and resilience. Finally, the chapter unpacks the categories of 'national' and 'international' components of such tribunals, with an emphasis on the effects of the regionalization of the composition of judges and staff on the legitimacy of recently created tribunals, as well as on internal and external resilience.

As Hobbs, who has himself written extensively on this topic, has indicated, there has been little scholarship considering the composition of hybrid tribunals.[1] This chapter aims at an examination of emerging issues around composition that have become evident in the design of the 'second-wave' of hybrid tribunals that have been established in the last few years. While the focus will be on the newly created tribunals, the chapter will also consider the composition of other tribunals including those listed above as well as the Extraordinary African Chambers (EAC), the War Crimes Chambers in the courts of Bosnia and Herzegovina (BIH WCC), the Special Panels of the Dili District Court in East Timor (SPDDC), and the Special Tribunal for Lebanon (STL).

9.2 'Hybrid' Tribunals

There is no universally accepted definition of what constitutes a hybrid tribunal. However, as William indicates, 'such tribunals tend to apply a mix of national and international law (both procedural and substantive) and feature a blend of international and national elements, in particular international and national judges and personnel'.[2] Hybrid tribunals are often located in the country where the crimes were committed (the SCSL, the ECCC, the SCC), but can sometimes be located elsewhere for security or other reasons. Hybrids may be established by an agreement between the host government and an external entity such as the United Nations (UN) (as was the case for the SCSL and the ECCC), or the African Union (AU) (the EAC). They can also be established by a domestic law (the SCC and the KSC), or by means of a peace agreement (the HCSS). For the purposes of this chapter, a hybrid tribunal will be defined broadly as any tribunal having a mix of international and national elements, regardless of the means by which it was established.

[1] See Harry Hobbs, 'Hybrid Tribunals and the Composition of the Court: In Search of Sociological Legitimacy' (2016) 16 Chicago Journal of International Law 482, 486.

[2] Sarah Williams, 'Hybrid International Criminal Tribunals' (*Oxford Bibliographies*, 28 April 2014) <http://www.oxfordbibliographies.com/view/document/obo-9780199796953/obo-9780199796953-0069.xml> accessed 31 December 2023.

Over the past few years, there has been a resurgence in the establishment of hybrid tribunals, from the SCC in CAR to the KSC in the Hague, the EAC in Senegal, as well as several proposed tribunals, including the HCSS and in the Democratic Republic of Congo (DRC) (the so-called 'second wave of hybrid tribunals').[3] This follows a lull in the establishment of such tribunals after the so-called 'first wave of tribunals' over a decade ago, which included the SCSL and the ECCC, as well as the SPDDC and the STL. The composition of each of these tribunals reflects difficult choices about the appropriate balance between national and international judges and staff.[4]

9.3 Legitimacy

The central question considered in this chapter is whether the inclusion of national judges enhances or detracts from a hybrid tribunal's legitimacy. This will obviously have impacts on both the tribunal's internal resilience—insofar as the design and composition of such tribunals will affect their ability to function robustly and withstand pressures—and external resilience, since, as Ramji-Nogales argues, tribunals with greater legitimacy should enable such tribunals to better foster peace and reconciliation and support the re-establishment of the rule of law.[5]

Hobbs has defined legitimacy as the 'quality that leads people (or states) to accept authority—independent of coercion, self-interest, or rational persuasion—because of a general sense that the authority is justified', and has proposed that a tribunal has 'sociological legitimacy' (as opposed to normative legitimacy, which derives from the manner in which the court was created), 'because the people of the affected state accept or perceive it as justified'.[6] The question of the legitimacy of international tribunals,[7] and more specifically, international criminal tribunals,[8]

[3] For a discussion of this resurgence, see Mark Kersten, 'As the Pendulum Swings—the Revival of the Hybrid Tribunal' in Mikkel Jarle Christensen and Ron Levi (eds), *Internationalizing Criminal Law: Institutions, Elites and Practices* (Routledge 2017). See also Harry Hobbs, 'International Criminal Justice Redux: A New Wave of Hybrid Courts' (*Justice in Conflict*, 13 March 2018) <https://justiceinconflict.org/2018/03/13/international-criminal-justice-redux-a-new-wave-of-hybrid-courts/> accessed 31 December 2023.

[4] Throughout this chapter, judges and staff have been discussed together. However, the questions relating to each category may differ to some extent and certain issues only arise with respect to judges. Further, some of these considerations may be more acute in the case of judges or the principals appointed to positions in the prosecution, defence and registry rather than support staff. I have noted where this is the case.

[5] Jaya Ramji-Nogales, 'Designing Bespoke Transitional Justice; a Pluralist Process Approach' (2010) 32 Michigan Journal of International Law 1, 13.

[6] Hobbs, 'Hybrid Tribunals' (n 1) 494.

[7] See, eg, Harlan Grant Cohen and others (eds), *Legitimacy and International Courts—A Framework* (Cambridge University Press 2018) and other work by Pluricourts on questions surrounding the legitimacy of international tribunals <http://www.jus.uio.no/pluricourts/english/> accessed 31 December 2023.

[8] See, eg, Nobuo Hayashi and Cecilia Bailliet (eds), *The Legitimacy of International Criminal Tribunals* (Cambridge University Press 2017); Stuart Ford, 'A Social Psychology Model of the Perceived

has been extensively discussed in the literature. Indicators of legitimacy may include empirical measures of the degree or type of support that an institution enjoys, or by an assessment of the extent to which the population feels bound by, accepts, and implements judicial decisions rendered by these institutions.[9]

Legitimacy must also be considered in light of the myriad (and often over-ambitious) goals of hybrid tribunals. As Hobbs has said, 'hybrid courts were seen as more likely to heal, reconcile, strengthen and address the root causes of prior conflict—as well as embed the rule of law'.[10] In light of these purposes, it is particularly important for hybrid tribunals to be viewed as legitimate domestically. If they are not, there is little chance that they will achieve the goals of reconciliation and healing, nor will they be successful in achieving norm penetration and thus in embedding the rule of law.

The above discussion has primarily focused on domestic legitimacy rather than the international dimension of such legitimacy. However, similar considerations may apply in both contexts—hybrid tribunals are likely seen as more legitimate to both the domestic and the international community if they can ensure sufficient independence and capacity, as is the case with the KSC.[11] Increasingly, tribunals will also be seen as more legitimate to the international community if they ensure sufficient local ownership, something which will also in many cases lead to greater domestic legitimacy.[12] However, at times international and domestic legitimacy may pull in different directions—the international community may ultimately prefer, as it did with the SCSL, to privilege the judicial independence of the tribunal over local ownership by ensuring the appointment of a majority of international judges and staff, whereas a greater proportion of national staff and judges might have resulted in greater domestic legitimacy.

The composition of the court is, however, not alone in grounding the legitimacy of hybrid tribunals. Other features, such as its location in the country in which the crimes were committed, or the use of domestic law, may also contribute. In the case of the KSC, the Tribunal relies on its grounding in domestic law and status as a court within the Kosovo justice system to enhance a sense of domestic ownership of the Tribunal.[13]

Legitimacy of International Criminal Courts: Implications for the Success of Transitional Justice Mechanisms' (2012) 45 Vanderbilt Journal of Transnational Law 405.

[9] Cohen and others (n 7).

[10] Hobbs, 'Hybrid Tribunals' (n 1).

[11] Laura Dickinson, 'The Relationship between Hybrid Courts and International Courts: The Case of Kosovo' (2003) New England Law Review 1059, 1069.

[12] Ramji-Nogales (n 5) 20–21.

[13] Matthew Cross, 'Equipping the Specialist Chambers of Kosovo to Try Transnational Crimes: Remarks on Independence and Cooperation' (2016) 14 Journal of International Criminal Justice 73.

The question is then the degree to which the composition of the court, compared to other factors, impacts on the legitimacy of the tribunal. Such impact can be measured by means of the indicators relating to the tribunal's legitimacy, but also by the degree to which decisions about composition have impacted upon the tribunal's ability to achieve its stated or unstated goals, including the legacy of the tribunal once it is no longer operational.

The experience of international tribunals demonstrates that the impact of decisions regarding composition can be significant. The chapter next examines the rationales underlying such decisions.

9.4 Rationales—International v National Composition

9.4.1 National judges and staff

On the one hand, there are compelling reasons for including national judges and staff on hybrid tribunals. As the mandate of several hybrid tribunals such as the SCSL, the ECCC, the HCSS, and the SCC has provided, at least in the enabling legislation, for the prosecution of crimes under applicable domestic laws, it can be argued that there should be national judges on the court to interpret and apply these laws.[14] The STL, for example, has explicitly indicated that it is important to have Lebanese judges, as they are better placed to interpret Lebanese law and transfer this knowledge to the international judges.[15] However, given that at several of these tribunals, including the SCSL and the ECCC, there were in fact no charges laid for the domestic offences in the Statute, this rationale becomes less persuasive.

The appointment of national judges, like locating tribunals in the countries in which the crimes were committed, may also increase the hybrid judiciary's contextual, cultural, and historical understanding of cases. The lack of such an understanding has been the subject of critiques of the SCSL.[16] The presence of national

[14] At the SCSL, ECCC, and the STL, which were mandated to investigate and prosecute crimes under domestic law (see Statute of the Special Tribunal for Lebanon (2007) S/RES/1757, Article 2 <https://undocs.org/S/RES/1757(2007)> accessed 31 December 2023; Statute of SCSL, Article 5, annexed to the Agreement between the United Nations and the Government of Sierra Leone on the establishment of a Special Court for Sierra Leone (signed 16 January 2002, entered into force 12 April 2002) 2178 UNTS 138 (SCSL Agreement); Law on the Establishment of Extraordinary Chambers in the Courts of Cambodia for the Prosecution of Crimes Committed During the Period of Democratic Kampuchea (amended and promulgated on 27 October 2004) NS/RKM/1004/006, Article 3new. The statutes establishing these courts provided that national judges could be part of the bench (Statute of SCSL, Article 12; Statute of STL, Law Establishing ECCC, Article 8, Article 9new).

[15] See STL, 'Video: Why is it Important to Have Lebanese Judge' (2012) <https://www.youtube.com/watch?v=Enu_y-guITY> accessed 31 December 2023.

[16] See Tim Kelsall, *Culture under Cross-Examination: International Justice and the Special Criminal Court* (Cambridge University Press 2009).

judges also has the potential to contribute to capacity building and knowledge transfer both from international judges to national judges and vice versa, and in this way, contribute to the strengthening of the national justice system.[17] It may also increase the 'local ownership' of the tribunal, and thus contribute to local buy-in and acceptance of the tribunal and its decisions by the population.

The inclusion of a majority of national judges on the tribunal may also allay the concerns of states relating to sovereignty. Sovereignty is often cited as the rationale for having a majority of national judges on the ECCC. Moreover, as Labuda indicates, with respect to the SCC, '[t]he [complex rules of the SCC] reflect a tension between the demands of international actors, who pushed for a strong international presence, and the sovereignty concerns of CAR as an independent state with a primacy of criminal jurisdiction in its territory'.[18] This was also at issue for the proposed Specialized Mixed Chambers in the DRC, where concerns about sovereignty led to domestic opposition to the inclusion of international judges and ultimately derailed the Court's establishment.[19] However, considerations relating to sovereignty or calls for greater domestic ownership may be thinly veiled methods for the exertion of political control over the tribunal or interference with its processes.

One concern with including national judges and staff revolves around lack of capacity, particularly in investigating and trying crimes under international law. Perceptions of lack of capacity of national members of the court may reduce the legitimacy of the court. For example, the UN appointed to the SPDDC 'unqualified East Timorese individuals as judges, prosecutors and public defenders to respond to political pressure for integrating local actors into the legal system. Doing so achieved the goal of building local capacity, but undermined the effectiveness and legitimacy of the Tribunal, which, in the end, did not generate local significant support or participation.'[20]

Perhaps a greater concern, in the case of judges, is that of lack of independence and impartiality, and for all national staff, concerns about political interference. It

[17] Although this is often stated as a goal of hybrid tribunals, there is usually little funding or capacity to conduct formal training. While it may be the case that such skills 'trickle down' by the mere presence of internationals on the court, this is an assumption that has not been proven. Often international staff on the courts are unaware that this is part of their function, and what capacity building they may do is conducted on a personal and ad hoc basis, rather than being systematic or supported by the tribunal. See, eg, Kirsten Ainley and Mark Kersten, 'Dakar Guidelines on the Establishment of Hybrid Courts' LSE and Wayamo Foundation (2019) 26 and 80–82 <https://hybridjustice.com/dakar-guidelines/> accessed 31 December 2023.

[18] See Patryk Labuda, 'The Special Criminal Court in the Central African Republic: Failure or Vindication of Complementarity' (2016) 15 Journal of International Criminal Justice 190.

[19] Sophia Candeis and others, 'The Accountability Landscape in Eastern DRC: Analysis of the National Legislative and Judicial Response to International Crimes (2009-2014)' (2015) ICTJ Briefing 2.

[20] Debra Delaet, *The Global Struggle for Human Rights: Universal Principles in Human Rights* (2nd edn, Cengage Learning 2014) 174. See also Caitlin Reiger and Marieke Wierda, 'The Serious Crimes Process in Timor-Leste: In Retrospect' (2006) International Centre for Transitional Justice 2.

is often these concerns which led to the establishment of a hybrid tribunal in the first place, as purely domestic judicial processes were seen to be inadequate.

Another concern which has surfaced particularly in the context of the establishment of hybrid courts in states such as CAR or South Sudan, where the judiciary has already been weakened by conflict, is that the selection of the best national judges and staff to serve on the tribunal will deplete the national system of the most qualified individuals.[21]

9.4.1.1 Mitigating measures

Issues relating to lack of experience can to some extent be addressed by training, and mentorship by international judges.[22]

In some cases, it may be possible to mitigate concerns about independence and impartiality by various structural solutions such as those employed by the ECCC or the SCC, so that even with a numerical majority of national judges, final decisions can only be made by a majority or super-majority of international judges. Other ways to address concerns about real or perceived bias on the part of national judges is to ensure that national judges on hybrid tribunals represent different geographical areas and ethnic communities, and that adequate disciplinary mechanisms are put in place. Hobbs has also suggested the use of 'mechanisms designed to secure independence and impartiality, such as security of tenure and appropriate salary, [which] can minimize the need for local judges to think beyond the life of the hybrid court and reduce their incentives to curry favor with the domestic government'.[23]

An often-overlooked solution is reducing the size of the international component and phasing in more national judges and staff as the tribunal develops, as was proposed at the Specialized Mixed Chambers in DRC[24] and is being considered

[21] See Human Rights Watch, 'Killing without Consequences: War Crimes, Crimes against Humanity and the Special Criminal Court in the Central African Republic' (2017) 89.

[22] However, this should be a process that goes both ways—as international judges may also require training on national laws and procedure. See Hobbs, 'Hybrid Tribunals' (n 1) 519; Amnesty International, 'The Long Wait for Justice: Accountability in Central African Republic' (2017), 38 <https://www.amnesty.org/en/documents/afr19/5425/2017/en/> accessed 31 December 2023. Also, such training needs to be carefully designed, as there have been some instances, such as at the SCSL and in East Timor, where such training was seen as patronizing by domestic judicial actors. See Hobbs, 'Hybrid Tribunals' (n 1) 519.

[23] Hobbs, 'Hybrid Tribunals' (n 1) 512.

[24] Projet de *loi* modifiant et complétant la *loi* n°13/011-B du 11 avril 2013 organique portant sur l'organisation, le fonctionnement et les compétences des juridictions de l'ordre judiciaire en matière de répression des crimes de génocide, des crimes contre l'humanité et des crimes de guerre (2014), revised Article 91.12. The proposed Specialized Chambers were to consist of special sections within the Courts of Appeal, containing both international and national judges and staff, with the international staff to be gradually phased out. However, the draft legislation was rejected by Parliament in May 2014 on the basis of a technicality, and although a revised version was supposed to be submitted by the Ministry of Justice to Parliament, this has not yet occurred. There appears to be no political will to move forward with the establishment of these chambers.

for the proposed HCSS. This strategy was also employed by the BIH WCC.[25] This type of solution fits well within the framework of skills transfer and capacity building, as presumably after several years of international presence, national judges and staff will have acquired the necessary experience to be able to take over the relevant functions themselves, and will be more insulated from political pressures. Such a measure can also help to allay concerns about sovereignty, as in the case with the Specialized Mixed Chambers for the DRC, where the worries of the government that such internationalized chambers would infringe on its authority to prosecute crimes committed within its own borders were to some extent allayed by a proposal that the number of national judges on the Court would increase as the Court progressed.

Ultimately, however, despite the measures that can be put in place, sometimes the risks of political interference and lack of independence may be determinative—such as for the KSC, where it was deemed that there were no mitigating measures that could be put in place that would adequately guard against these threats. And there may be justifications for fearing that mitigating measures may not be sufficient. As Ciociari and Heindel have suggested regarding the ECCC, the mitigating measures put in place 'have proved inadequate to overcome political gridlock and strong indications of political interference'.[26] In these cases, perhaps the only solution is a fully internationalized tribunal.

Total internationalization, however, should be seen as the last resort, and comes at a cost. Many of the objectives often seen as positive features of hybrid tribunals—capacity building/skills transfer, strengthening of the national justice system—clearly will not be achieved by a tribunal that is purely international. As Williams suggests, 'there is therefore no pretence of capacity building for Kosovo . . . Capacity building and legacy creation are not stated aims of the SC and SPO and are unlikely to result from the proposed arrangements for internationalization'.[27]

9.4.2 International judges and staff

The rationale for the inclusion of international judges on hybrid tribunals is to counteract any weaknesses within the national judiciary as identified above, particularly in post-conflict contexts. International judges may have greater experience and capacity, particularly with respect to international crimes, and are considered to be disinterested and less prone to political interference.

[25] Sarah Williams, 'The Specialist Chambers of Kosovo: the Limits of Internationalization' (2016) 14 Journal of International Criminal Justice 25, 37, 70.

[26] John D Ciociari and Anne Heindel, 'Experiments in International Criminal Justice: Lessons from the Khmer Rouge Tribunal' (2014) 35 Michigan Journal of International Law 369, 393.

[27] See Williams, 'The Specialist Chambers' (n 25) 37.

However, international judges are unlikely to have a deep understanding of relevant domestic laws, or of the cultural and historical context in which the crimes took place.[28] This may be especially the case for tribunals which rely on national law, or national procedural systems (eg the STL) if international judges come from outside of this system. In addition, the presence of international judges may be resented by the states in which they work, as they may be viewed as an external imposition and a means by which to control domestic processes.

9.4.3 Mixed composition of tribunals

The rationale for having a mixed composition on hybrid tribunals is that the attributes of both groups will complement one another—national personnel with knowledge of local laws and context, and international personnel with a more in-depth understanding of international crimes and greater independence. In addition, it is hoped that by having international judges and staff on the court they will have a mentoring and capacity-building role vis-à-vis national judges.

Hobbs has argued that, as well as these pragmatic considerations, there is also a principled justification for the mixed composition of such tribunals—given the character of international crimes, which can be understood as both international and local crimes, a mixed composition best satisfies the principle of fair reflection as these crimes impact both the domestic and international communities.[29]

However, this delicate balancing act can backfire. As Cockayne has held 'the aim is to marry the best of two worlds: the expertise of the international community with the legitimacy of local actors, but the risk is to intermix the worst of both—the externality of international actors with the weakness of local institutions that produced the violence in question'.[30]

9.5 Composition of Hybrid Tribunals—SCC, KSC, HCSS, SCSL, ECCC

In light of these broader rationales, it is worth examining in detail the technical aspects of the composition of various tribunals including the SCC, the KSC, the HCSS, the SCSL, and the ECCC. This demonstrates how these rationales behind decisions on composition have played out in various settings, and also illustrates broader trends that have emerged in relation to legitimacy and resilience.

[28] See Kelsall, *Culture under Cross-Examination* (n 16).

[29] Harry Hobbs, 'Towards a Principled Justification for the Mixed Composition of Hybrid International Criminal Tribunals' (2017) 30 Leiden Journal of International Law 177.

[30] James Cockayne, 'The Fraying Shoestring: Rethinking Hybrid War Crimes Tribunals' (2005) 28 Fordham International Law Journal 616, 616–17, cited in Ramji-Nogales (n 5) 30.

The recently established SCC in CAR, created by an Organic Law in 2015, is a court entirely within the domestic judicial system of CAR, with mixed international and national judges and staff.[31] After several years of investigations, the Court began trying its first case in 2022. The law provides that the majority of the judges will be from CAR, and also reserves several important positions in the Court, including the Registrar, President, and Deputy Prosecutor for CAR nationals.[32]

However, the composition of the panels of judges effectively means that despite the numerical majority of national judges on the SCC, both the Pre-Trial Chamber and the Appeals Chamber have a majority of international judges.[33] As Labuda says '... the SCC law gives numerical priority to Central African staff, but—in cases of conflict—international experts appear to have the final word'.[34]

As Labuda points out, the composition of the Court was disputed throughout the process of its establishment, with earlier recommendations and drafts providing for a majority of international judges.[35] However, ultimately, the Organic Law provided for a majority of national judges, due in part to concerns about local ownership of the Tribunal by the Central African authorities, particularly as the SCC is a court entirely within the domestic jurisdiction of CAR, and will deal with crimes as defined in the CAR Penal Code. This decision is also consistent with the avowed goal of the Court of contributing to strengthening the capacity of the national judicial system.[36]

At the opposite end of the spectrum, the KSC, and the Specialist Investigative Task Force (SITF) that preceded it, have no national judges or key staff due to concerns about judicial independence, impartiality, and corruption.[37] The KSC, which was established in the Hague in 2015, and which is part of the judicial system of Kosovo, currently has six cases pending before it at various stages.[38] As Williams explains, the decision to include only international personnel was grounded in

[31] *Loi organique* No 15003 portant création, organisation et fonctionnement de la Cour Pénale Spéciale (3 June 2015) Article 3.

[32] ibid, Articles 6, 15, 18.

[33] ibid, Articles 11, 13, 14.

[34] Labuda, 'The Special Criminal Court' (n 18) 186.

[35] ibid 187 and 190, referring to the memorandum of understanding (MoU) between the government of CAR and the United Nations (MINUSCA) regarding the establishment of the court (7 August 2014); International Commission of Inquiry on the Central African Republic, 'Final Report' (22 December 2014) S/2014/928.

[36] See CAR government, MINUSCA, UNDP, *Projet conjoint d'Appui à la Cour Pénale Spéciale de la République centrafricaine* (August 2016) 14. For further discussion, see Amnesty International, 'The Long Wait' (n 22), 38.

[37] See Articles 26(1) and 33(1) of the Law on Specialist Chambers and Specialist Prosecutor's Office (3 August 2015) Law No 05/L-053, Republic of Kosovo (establishing a 'roster of independent international judges' for assignment). See also Article 31. See further Article 162(3) of the Constitution of the Republic of Kosovo (15 June 2008). See Williams, 'The Specialist Chambers' (n 25) 35. For further discussion, see Cross (n 13).

[38] See Kosovo Specialist Chambers and Specialist Prosecutor's Office, 'Cases' <https://www.scp-ks.org/en/cases> accessed 31 December 2023.

the past experience of internationalized tribunals in Kosovo, including the hybrid panels created by the United Nations Mission in Kosovo (UNMIK) as well as later attempts by EULEX to prosecute these crimes, where the presence of international judges was not sufficient to guard against bias. As Williams explains, '[t]hose accused of crimes are powerful figures in Kosovo and fully entrenched.... Only fully internationalized institutions would be sufficiently independent, impartial and immune to intimidation and pressure'.[39]

The first wave of hybrids left a mixed legacy for other tribunals to follow. The ECCC, like the SCC, includes a numerical majority of national judges for the court as a whole, but unlike the SCC, it also includes a majority of national judges on all panels, including the Appeal Chamber.[40] However, owing to concerns about potential political manipulation and judicial independence, decisions must be made by a super-majority of judges (in cases of impasse, one international judge must agree with national counterparts).[41] The ECCC also has both international and national Co-Prosecutors, Co-Investigating Judges, and co-lawyers for defence and victims. However, the enabling legislation allows for circumstances in which the International Co-Prosecutor and Co-Investigative Judge can act alone.[42] Despite these measures, the ECCC has been criticized for corruption, political interference in the conduct of investigations and trials, as well as a lack of judicial independence.[43]

The Statute of the SCSL provides for the majority of the judges,[44] the Prosecutor,[45] and the Registrar[46] to be appointed by the UN. In theory (and towards the later years of the Court, in practice), this allowed for the possibility that the UN could appoint Sierra Leonean nationals to these positions. However, for most of the Court's history, these positions were held by international judges. Three judges served on each Trial Chamber, one of whom was appointed by the government of Sierra Leone and two by the UN. On the Appeals Chamber, the Sierra Leonean government appointed two judges, and the UN appointed three.[47] De facto, the composition of the Court was at times even more international than this might suggest, as the government of Sierra Leone appointed several international,

[39] Williams, 'The Specialist Chambers' (n 25) 33.

[40] Law Establishing ECCC (n 14) Articles 9new and 20new; Article 3 of the Agreement between the United Nations and the Royal Government of Cambodia Concerning the Prosecution under Cambodian Law of Crimes Committed During the Period of Democratic Kampuchea (6 June 2003) (Agreement between the UN and the government of Cambodia).

[41] Law Establishing ECCC (n 14), Article 14new; Agreement between the UN and the government of Cambodia, Article 4.

[42] Law Establishing ECCC (n 14), Articles 20new and 23new; Agreement between the UN and the government of Cambodia, Article 6(4).

[43] For some of these critiques, see Ciociari and Heindel, 'Experiments in International Criminal Justice' (n 26), 369.

[44] Statute of the SCSL (n 14), Article 12.

[45] ibid, Article 15(3). The Deputy Prosecutor must be a Sierra Leonean, as per Article 15(4).

[46] ibid, Article 16 (3).

[47] ibid, Article 12.

rather than national judges. As a result, for much of the Tribunal's existence, only one of the Trial Chamber judges and one of the Appeals Chamber judges was a Sierra Leonean.[48]

Similarly, there was a lack of national staff appointed to the SCSL. As Kelsall indicates, 'although Sierra Leonean lawyers have been well represented in the defence teams, not until recently have they occupied the higher positions in the Office of the Prosecutor'.[49] One of the frequent criticisms of the SCSL is that this resulted in a lack of capacity building and transfer of legal skills to Sierra Leonean nationals as well as little contribution by the SCSL to strengthening the national justice system.[50] As Ramji-Nogales indicates, the design of the SCSL also alienated the local legal community, who were disappointed that half of the Court's positions were not, as they had expected, earmarked for locals and who 'would have preferred that the massive funds expended on the court be channeled into rebuilding the domestic legal system'.[51]

On the other hand, the Sierra Leonean judges appointed to the Court often took controversial positions on certain issues—the most notable being the dissenting opinion of Judge Thompson in the CDF case in which he would have acquitted the defendants on the basis that they had fought to restore a legitimate government, and that their actions were justified on the basis of necessity.[52] The Sierra Leonean judges in the Appeals Chamber in the same case also dissented on similar grounds, arguing that this should be taken into account as a mitigating factor in sentencing.[53] These dissenting opinions raised concerns about the impartiality of the Sierra Leonean judges.

More recently, the proposed HCSS is also attempting to achieve an appropriate balance. The HCSS is to be established by the AU and the government of South Sudan in accordance with the framework set out in the August 2015 Agreement on the Resolution of the Crisis in the Republic of South Sudan (ARCSS), which was adopted largely unchanged in the Revitalized ARCSS (R-ARCSS) signed in September 2018.[54] Despite the government's indication in January 2021 that it

[48] Tim Kelsall, 'Insufficiently Hybrid: Assessing the Special Court for Sierra Leone' (2009) 27 Law Context: A Socio-Legal Journal 132, 142.

[49] ibid 142.

[50] See, eg, Rachel Kerr and Jessica Lincoln, 'The Special Court for Sierra Leone: Outreach, Legacy and Impact' (2008) King's College London 29; Kelsall, 'Insufficiently Hybrid' (n 48) 142–43.

[51] Ramji-Nogales (n 5) 38.

[52] *Prosecutor v Fofana and Kondewa* (Dissenting Judgment of Justice Bankole Thompson) SCSL-04-14-T-785 (2007).

[53] *Prosecutor v Fofana and Kondewa* (Partially Dissenting Opinion of Justice George Gelaga King, Partially Dissenting Opinion of Justice Jon Kamanda) 04-14-A-829 (2008). For interesting discussions on the dissenting opinions at both trial and appeal, see Kelsall, *Culture under Cross-Examination* (n 16) 66–67; Thierry Cruvellier, *Terre Promise* (Gallimard 2018) 275–76.

[54] Agreement on the Resolution of the Conflict in the Republic of South Sudan (17 August 2015) (ARCSS); Revitalized Agreement on the Resolution of the Conflict in the Republic of South Sudan (12 September 2018) (R-ARCSS). Despite a draft MoU between the government of South Sudan and the AU as well as a draft statute for the Court, these have not yet been adopted by the government.

approved the establishment of the Court, there has been little to no progress towards its creation since then.[55]

The ARCSS provides that 'a majority of judges on all panels, whether trial or appellate, shall be composed of judges from African states other than the Republic of South Sudan'.[56] While this clearly allows for the possibility of South Sudanese judges on the bench, there have been some suggestions that the AU favours a bench composed solely of non-South Sudanese judges.[57] The ARCSS also does not specify the exact configuration of international to national judges on each panel, which is to be more clearly spelled out in the Statute to be agreed by the AU and the South Sudanese government. However, in the event that South Sudanese judges are appointed, the majority will still be 'international' (although of course 'international' in this context is limited to nationals of AU member states).

The ARCSS provides that prosecutors and duty defence counsel of the HCSS, as well as the Registrar, shall be personnel from African states other than South Sudan,[58] thus seemingly precluding the participation of South Sudanese nationals in many of the key functions of the Court.

The HCSS thus tends more towards the approach of the SCSL, with a majority of international judges and staff, likely due to concerns about capacity, and more importantly, concerns about the independence and impartiality of the judiciary, given the past experience of the domestic justice system in South Sudan.[59] However, if the HCSS does end up adopting the position that there should be no South Sudanese judges, it may then move closer towards the model of the purely international KSC.

[55] AU, 'Statement by H.E. Mr. Moussa Faki Mahamat, Chairperson of the African Union Commission, on African Union Hybrid Court of South Sudan' (31 January 2021) <https://au.int/en/pressreleases/20210130/statement-he-mr-moussa-faki-mahamat-chairperson-african-union-commission> accessed 31 December 2023; Nyagoah Tut Pur, 'A Glimmer of Hope for South Sudan's Victims: the Government Approves War Crimes Court, Other Measures' (*Human Rights Watch*, 31 January 2021) <https://www.hrw.org/news/2021/01/31/glimmer-hope-south-sudans-victims> accessed 31 December 2023. Several human rights organizations have continued to advocate for the AU to establish the Court even without the agreement of the government. See, eg, Elise Keppler, 'South Sudan's cynical bid to block war crimes court: African Union should step up on justice' (*Human Rights Watch*, 30 April 2019) <https://www.hrw.org/news/2019/04/30/south-sudans-cynical-bid-block-war-crimes-court> accessed 31 December 2023; Amnesty International, 'African Union must set precedent for African-led justice by establishing court for South Sudan' (23 November 2022) <https://www.amnesty.org/en/latest/news/2022/11/south-sudan-african-union-must-set-precedent-for-african-led-justice-by-establishing-court-for-south-sudan/> accessed 31 December 2023.

[56] ARCSS, Chapter V, Article 3.3.2; R-ARCSS, Chapter V, Article 5.3.3.2.

[57] Amnesty International and FIDH, 'Looking for justice: Recommendations for the establishment of the Hybrid Court for South Sudan' (2016), 22 <https://www.amnesty.org/en/documents/afr65/4742/2016/en/> accessed 31 December 2023.

[58] ARCSS, Chapter V, Article 3.3.3 and 3.3.4; R-ARCSS, Chapter V, Articles 5.3.3.3 and 5.3.3.4.

[59] See, eg, Amnesty International and FIDH, 'Looking for Justice' (n 57) and Elise Keppler, 'Ending the Era of Injustice, Advancing Prosecutions for Serious Crimes Committed in South Sudan's New War' (*Human Rights Watch*, 2014) <https://www.hrw.org/report/2014/12/10/ending-era-injustice/advancing-prosecutions-serious-crimes-committed-south-sudans> accessed 31 December 2023.

9.5.1 Considerations regarding legitimacy and resilience

The various models above demonstrate that the question of sociological legitimacy may ground decisions to both include and exclude national judges and staff. For example, legitimacy underpins both the decision to include a majority of national judges in the SCC and to exclude or minimize their participation in the KSC and the proposed HCSS.

These examples also illustrate that decisions regarding composition can have a profound impact on the legitimacy of the tribunal and on its resilience. In Sierra Leone, for example, the impact of the decision to include a preponderance of international judges and staff was significant, both because it reduced the legitimacy of the tribunal in the eyes of the population, and also because it ultimately limited the tribunal in achieving certain of its goals—that is, embedding rule of law norms within the country, strengthening the national justice system, and contributing to the healing and reconciliation process. This clearly affected the external resilience of the tribunal as its impact on the broader society was correspondingly limited. In addition, the composition of the SCSL also impacted on the internal resilience of this tribunal, insofar as it resulted in tensions between international and national staff and judges which weakened the functioning of the tribunal.

Similar tensions also emerged as a result of the composition of the ECCC, which clearly impacted on the tribunal's ability to function and thus on its internal resilience. However, contrary to the SCSL, at the ECCC, it was the very presence of national staff/judges and allegations of corruption/political interference that diminished its legitimacy, and also correspondingly its external resilience.

9.6 Breaking Down 'National' and 'International' Components

9.6.1 Composition of the national component

To understand the ways in which tribunals gain legitimacy, it is important to be more precise in analysing the inclusion of 'local' and 'international' staff. As Hobbs has argued, it is too simplistic to consider 'national' judges and staff as a monolithic bloc. A significant factor in contributing to the legitimacy of a tribunal is not only the inclusion of a 'national component' but the composition of that component and the extent to which it satisfies the principle of fair reflection.[60] That is, the extent to which the national composition of a hybrid tribunal reflects the ethnic and religious make-up of a country will contribute to its legitimacy.

60 Hobbs, 'Hybrid Tribunals' (n 1) 511.

These considerations may not be a factor for every tribunal—in situations where the basis for the conflict is not predominantly religious or ethnic, such as in Sierra Leone or Cambodia, these issues were not paramount.[61] However, particularly in contexts where conflicts have ethnic or religious dimensions, the need to have balanced representation on the bench and among staff becomes critical. This is clearly an issue for the SCC in CAR. Despite commitments to ensure that national judges and staff represent different geographical areas and religious communities, the first rounds of recruitment for judges and staff have not been very successful in this regard. To some extent, this is reflective of the limited representation of Muslims in the judiciary/legal profession in CAR.[62] Nonetheless, addressing this imbalance will be essential to ensure the fairness—and the perception of fairness—of the proceedings, particularly as there is already a perception in CAR that domestic proceedings are one-sided, and a corresponding lack of confidence in the judicial system.[63]

Similarly, given the roots of the conflict in South Sudan, the need to have an ethnic balance on the bench is critical.[64] The lack of such a balance within the judiciary, and the perception that national courts will therefore not be able to independently try cases of crimes committed by government forces, were factors which led to the call for the HCSS in the first place.[65]

What should be done when this balance cannot be achieved? In some cases, the presence of international staff—such as Muslim judges from other countries, which has been considered for the SCC to mitigate the lack of religious balance within the national personnel—might be enough to counteract this lack of national balance.[66] However, this type of solution might be harder to achieve if the balance required is an ethnic/tribal one. Arguably, in these cases, a purely international court is the only solution, as to establish a hybrid tribunal without the requisite balance runs the risk of replicating flaws in the national justice system.

[61] For a similar analysis, see ibid.

[62] Erica Bussey, 'Progress and Challenges in Establishing the Special Criminal Court for the Central African Republic, Human Rights in International Justice' (*Amnesty International*, 20 September 2017) <https://hrij.amnesty.nl/central-african-republic-scc/> accessed 31 December 2023.

[63] Amnesty International, 'The Long Wait' (n 22) 25–26.

[64] Amnesty International and FIDH, 'Looking for Justice' (n 57) 23, 32.

[65] ibid 9. Several prominent judges including the Chief Justice, resigned in 2016–2017, citing lack of judicial independence. See Denis Dumo and Jason Patinkin, 'South Sudan Supreme Court Judge Quits, Citing Lack of Independence' (*Reuters*, 14 November 2017) <https://www.reuters.com/article/us-southsudan-judiciary/south-sudan-supreme-court-judge-quits-citing-lack-of-independence-idUSKBN1DE20D> accessed 31 December 2023. Of course, concerns that the national system may not be best placed to judge members of the government who have committed international crimes may go beyond issues of representation.

[66] cf Section 9.6.2.

9.6.2 Composition of international component, and regionalization

Similarly, as Hobbs has indicated, there is also a tendency to view the international component as monolithic. He has argued that the concept of an 'international judge' can and should be particularized,[67] and suggests, among other factors, that prioritization should be given to selecting judges from regional states.[68]

In effect, whether intentional or otherwise, a regionalization of the international component is indeed what appears to be occurring in the establishment of the second wave of hybrid tribunals, in part because the impetus for the creation of several of these tribunals has come from regional institutions such as the AU and the EU rather than the UN.[69]

The EAC, for example, was established on the basis of an agreement between the AU and the government of Senegal. The Statute of the EAC provided for a majority of Senegalese judges but for the President of both the Trial and Appeal Chambers to be nationals of another AU member state.[70] The President of the Trial Chamber was from Burkina Faso and the President of the Appeals Chamber was from Mali, making the EAC truly a regional court, trying crimes committed in another country in the region—Chad. The AU will also be leading the process for the establishment of the proposed HCSS, where the 'international' positions on the HCSS can be filled only by nationals of AU member states.

The European Union (EU) was responsible for the establishment of the KSC, and for the SITF that preceded it.[71] While there is no requirement that members of the judiciary on the KSC are from states within the EU, in practice the majority of judges on the Court are from EU member states.[72]

Moreover, even in cases, such as that of the SCC, where the Tribunal was established by a process led largely by the UN, and where there is no presumption that the personnel of the Tribunal are from African or Central African countries,

[67] Hobbs, 'Hybrid Tribunals' (n 1) 513.

[68] ibid 514. Hobbs specifically focuses on judges, but many of the considerations that he invokes would be equally applicable to other staff members of tribunals.

[69] For a discussion of this phenomenon, see Williams, 'The Specialist Chambers' (n 25) 30.

[70] Statut des Chambres Africaines Extraordinaires au sein des juridictions senegalaises pour la poursuite des crimes graves commis au Tchad durant la periode du 7 juin 1982 au 1er Decembre 1990, annexed to Accord entre le Gouvernement de la République du Senegal et l'Union Africaine (12 August 2012), Articles 11(3) and (4), .

[71] For a discussion of issues relating to the regional aspects of the KSC, see Emanuele Cimiotta, 'The Specialist Chambers and the Specialist Prosecutor's Office in Kosovo: the Regionalization of International Criminal Justice in Context' (2016) 14 Journal of International Criminal Justice 53.

[72] See list of nationalities of judges appointed to the KSC at Kosovo Specialist Chambers and Specialist Prosecutor's Office, 'Chambers'<https://www.scp-ks.org/en/specialist-chambers/chambers> accessed 31 December 2023.

de facto, several of the international judges and staff appointed so far have been from African states, including from states in the region.[73] This derives in part from the need for French-speaking judges/staff from civil-law countries which will tend to be in West and Central Africa, as well as the realities of the salary scale and the distance from home which may make such posts more attractive to nationals of countries in the region. However, there may be other reasons—part of the rationale for the selection of the Special Prosecutor, who is from the DRC, was his expertise in conducting investigations and prosecutions in a context with similar challenges, although his selection was not couched explicitly in terms of regionalization.

Hobbs has suggested that prioritizing selection of judges from regional states offers the 'potential for enhanced awareness of the local *sui generis* situation, bringing additional legitimacy benefits for the court'.[74] Certainly, for some tribunals this has been the case—the EAC established by the AU has been widely lauded as having increased legitimacy, both because it was established by an African regional entity, and also because of the composition of the Court.[75] Such regionalization can thus also contribute to the tribunal's external resilience both at the local level, and within the broader regional context.

However, regional representation on the court can also result in potential complications given the involvement of neighbouring states or regional powers in the conflicts that led to their creation.[76] In the case of South Sudan, for example, several neighbouring states have been seen to be supporting one or the other of the government forces or the SPLM. The inclusion of judges/staff from any of these states may therefore be seen as favouring one side of the conflict over another, and may harm the legitimacy of the institution. As the pool of potential judges/staff is limited to nationals from AU member states, this may result in added complications in the nomination of judges and selection of staff.

Similarly, in CAR, several neighbouring states have been alleged to be involved in or supporting different parties to the conflict, both during the recent conflict and historically, including Chad and the DRC.[77] Through this lens, the selection of

[73] The Special Prosecutor is a national of DRC, and the Court includes magistrates and prosecutors from Burkina Faso, Togo and Madagascar. See SCC, 'Welcome' <https://www.cpsrca.cf> accessed 31 December 2023.

[74] Hobbs, 'Hybrid Tribunals' (n 1) 515.

[75] See, eg, Jason Burke, 'Hissene Habre trial provides model for international justice' (*Guardian*, 30 May 2016) <https://www.theguardian.com/world/2016/may/30/hissene-habre-trial-provides-model-for-international-justice> accessed 31 December 2023.

[76] Hobbs, 'Hybrid Tribunals' (n 1) 516.

[77] For a comprehensive overview of crimes committed in CAR from 2003–2015, including the involvement of neighbouring states, see UN, 'Report of the Mapping Project Documenting Serious Violations of International Human Rights Law and International Humanitarian Law Committed in the Central African Republic between January 2003 and December 2015' (2017) <http://www.ohchr.org/Documents/Countries/CF/Mapping2003-2015/2017CAR_Mapping_Report_EN.pdf> accessed 31 December 2023.

the Special Prosecutor of the SCC, a national of the DRC, might be viewed as problematic. This issue has not been raised with respect to his appointment, however, and he has in his public statements made clear that he is no longer representing his country—DRC—but the international community. However, no cases have yet been adjudicated by the Court and perhaps such objections may be raised at a later stage by defence counsel.

Even where regional states may not be involved in the conflict, prioritizing recruitment from countries in the region is not always an unqualified good. Individuals from countries in the region may lack skills, often for the same reason as nationals lack expertise in certain areas—that is, in forensic examination or investigation of complex crimes. In DRC, for example, the peacekeeping mission (MONUSCO), entered into an MoU with the government to deploy international experts, most from regional states, to assist the DRC authorities in investigating and prosecuting international crimes. However, many of these regional experts had never themselves investigated any international or complex crimes, and were often not viewed by the DRC authorities as providing the desired expertise. A report on lessons learned from this experience found that while

> the Government Provided Personnel (GPP) come predominantly from countries in the region and are often not only familiar with the cultural background and speak relevant local languages, they also serve in similar functions in their government service.…The GPP process may not be the best means for deploying certain types of expertise, particularly in the area [sic] international crimes.[78]

Finally, the international component itself may represent a way to balance out what is seen as an inadequately representative national component. At the SCC, for example, a reason for favouring judges and staff from certain Muslim countries is that this might help to counterbalance the lack of national judges from the Muslim community. This may, however, be difficult to implement in practice, and may be unique to this Tribunal.

These considerations demonstrate that while in some cases, such as at the EAC and SCC, regional representativity on the court may enhance its functioning and thus its internal resilience, in other situations, such as in DRC (and also potentially the HCSS), the opposite may be the case.

[78] UN Peacekeeping, 'Report of the Criminal Law and Judicial Advisory Section: Combatting Impunity in the Democratic Republic of Congo: Lessons Learned from the United Nations Prosecution Support Cell Programme' (2015). <https://peacekeeping.un.org/sites/default/files/2015_monusco_psc_lessons_learned.pdf> accessed 31 December 2023.

9.6.3 Between the national and the international

Interesting questions relating to legitimacy also arise regarding other categories of personnel who fall between the national and the international. For example, in some countries (often where is not a sufficient number of qualified national judges), foreign judges may already be present within the domestic judiciary. This was the case in Gambia during the Jammeh era, where several judges from other countries including Nigeria were appointed. These judges were widely viewed as controlled by the government and were not trusted. In this case, the presence of 'international' judges, appointed to the courts in order to enhance national capacity, (similarly to the rationale for appointing international judges to hybrid tribunals), detracted rather than contributed to the courts' legitimacy. To counter this, the new government under Barrow has appointed a greater number of Gambian judges.[79]

It is also unclear where judges from the diaspora fall on this spectrum. In response to concerns about lack of capacity within the South Sudanese judiciary, it has been suggested that judges from the diaspora might be a viable alternative for the HCSS.[80] However, it is not clear whether such judges would be able to bring to the Court the same qualities that purely 'national' judges possess, such as knowledge of the laws of the country and context, especially if they have been out of the country for a long time. On the other hand, they may have greater independence as they are less likely to be connected to existing power structures, which may enhance the legitimacy of the tribunal.

9.6.4 Quality control and gender representation

Ultimately, for both international and national judges and staff, many of these questions relate to issues of quality control. The fact that judges and staff are 'international' does not automatically mean that they possess the desired qualifications to serve on hybrid tribunals—there have been many examples where international judges have been appointed to international or hybrid courts, including the ICC, with little to no background in criminal or international law.[81] Similarly, national judges vary considerably in quality as well as in their ability to withstand political pressures. As discussed above with respect to the SPDDC in East Timor, the lack

[79] See Joshua Moses, 'Examining the Challenges Before Gambia and its Judiciary' (*Ventures*, 16 December 2017) <http://venturesafrica.com/examining-the-challenges-before-gambia-and-its-judiciary/> accessed 31 December 2023.

[80] Amnesty International and FIDH, 'Looking for Justice' (n 57) 23.

[81] See, eg, Asua Hirsch, 'System for appointing judges 'undermining international courts' (*Guardian*, 8 September 2010) <https://www.theguardian.com/law/2010/sep/08/law-international-court-justice-legal> accessed 31 December 2023. See also Ruth Mackenzie and others (eds), *Selecting International Judges: Principle, Process and Politics* (Oxford University Press 2010).

of qualified national personnel on the court can also impact on its legitimacy.[82] The importance of merit-based transparent selection processes for judges are thus critical.[83]

Another issue relating to both the national and international components is the question of gender. On the one hand, as Hobbs has argued, a court with a greater gender balance better satisfies the principle of fair reflection, and may thus enhance the legitimacy of the tribunal.[84] On the other hand, the promotion of gender balance may be seen as an international imposition and thus reduce a court's domestic legitimacy. This seems to be the case for the SCC, where it is international actors who have primarily pushed for greater gender equality on the Court.[85]

9.7 Conclusion

These reflections demonstrate that decisions about the composition of hybrid tribunals can have profound effects on the legitimacy of such tribunals as well as on their success in achieving their goals, but they also point to the complexities of the issues around composition. It is not clear, for instance, that the inclusion of a majority of national judges and staff will enhance the legitimacy of the tribunal in every case. In some situations—such as the SCSL and the SCC—this may indeed be the case. However, in others, such as the KSC, and arguably to some extent the ECCC, the inclusion of national staff or judges might undermine the legitimacy of the tribunal.

Similarly, in some cases, the balance of the composition of the national component is equally, if not more, important in contributing to or detracting from the legitimacy of the tribunal. Moreover, while regional representation in the composition of the international component may contribute to the legitimacy of the process, this is not always the case, and in many situations, may in fact undercut it. Interesting questions also arise about the role of judges/staff who fall between the categories of 'national' and 'international' including those from the diaspora.

In addition, decisions about the composition of hybrid tribunals may significantly impact on the resilience of the tribunal. They can affect a tribunal's ability to fulfil certain goals and thus its impact on the wider society (external resilience), as in the case of the SCSL and KSC. In addition, decisions about the composition of the tribunal may lead to internal tensions that may erode the internal resilience of the tribunal, as in the case of the SCSL and ECCC.

[82] cf Section 9.4.1.

[83] Amnesty International and FIDH, 'Looking for Justice' (n 57) 24, Amnesty International, 'The Long Wait' (n 22) 39.

[84] Hobbs, 'Hybrid Tribunals' (n 1) 497, and Hobbs, 'Towards a Principled Justification' (n 29) 181-182.

[85] See, eg, Human Rights Watch, 'Killing without Consequences' (n 21) 89.

It is too early to say how these considerations will play out with respect to recently established hybrid tribunals such as the KSC and the SCC, or for proposed tribunals such as the HCSS. However, the experiences of these tribunals, which have espoused diametrically opposite models regarding composition, will no doubt result in further lessons for tribunals that may follow.

10

Emerging Enforcement Practices of Hybrid Courts

Lessons Learned for Proposed Hybrid Mechanisms in Post-Conflict States

Philippa Greer

10.1 Introduction

An indispensable component of an effective international criminal justice mechanism is the enforcement of sentences. The modern international criminal justice system uses imprisonment as its primary sanction.[1] Yet it currently has no single entity tasked with overseeing the enforcement of prison sentences, nor does it have an international prison. Instead, hybrid criminal mechanisms, the UN ad hoc tribunals,[2] and the sole permanent international criminal institution, the International Criminal Court (ICC), enforce sentences by employing a domestic solution directly in local prisons (a model of local enforcement), or by adopting an ad hoc cooperating states model, which utilizes existing prison facilities in third states, relying on the cooperation of those states. There has been no discernable movement towards a permanent international prison.[3]

The sentencing options of hybrid courts, the UN ad hoc tribunals, and the ICC are primarily focused on incarceration, yet the implementation of penalties has often been treated as an afterthought when such institutions are established. While sentence enforcement is an integral part of the prosecution process, academics

[1] See, eg, Updated Statute of the International Criminal Tribunal for the Former Yugoslavia (ICTY) (September 2009), Article 24; Statute of the International Criminal Tribunal for Rwanda (ICTR) (January 2010), Article 23; Statute of the International Residual Mechanism for Criminal Tribunals (IRMCT) (December 2010), Article 22(1); Statute of the Special Court for Sierra Leone (SCSL) (August 2000), Article 19; Rome Statute of the International Criminal Court (opened for signature 17 July 1998, entered into force 1 July 2002) 2187 UNTS 90, Article 77.

[2] Namely, the ICTY, ICTR, and IRMCT, established by the UN Security Council, the latter having resumed the residual functions of the ICTY and ICTR.

[3] See Mary Margaret Penrose, 'Creating an International Prison' (2006) 38 Houston Journal of International Law 425.

Philippa Greer, *Emerging Enforcement Practices of Hybrid Courts* In: *Hybrid Justice*. Edited by: Kirsten Ainley and Mark Kersten, Oxford University Press. © Philippa Greer 2025.
DOI: 10.1093/oso/9780192893758.003.0010

have rightly observed that the focus to date appears to be on imprisonment for a term, rather than a purpose.[4]

Hybrid courts are often viewed as providing a more visible and culturally appropriate justice process that adheres to international human rights standards.[5] Yet, where the host state of the hybrid court is unable to enforce sentences locally, for reasons related to political instability, or compromised justice institutions, or the rule of law, it may be necessary to employ a decentralized enforcement model, despite the international penological recommendation that sentences should be served as close as possible to the prisoner's ordinary place of residence upon their request.[6]

This chapter addresses the enforcement practices of several hybrid criminal mechanisms, evaluating their ability to function robustly and legitimately in this crucial area. It reflects on broader questions related to capacity building and the synthesis between, and intersection of, international and domestic legal standards with respect to sentence enforcement, concluding with recommendations for future hybrid mechanisms.

The recent renaissance of hybrid courts in Senegal, Kosovo, the Central African Republic, and South Sudan; and proposed hybrid or quasi-hybrid courts for Colombia, the Democratic Republic of Congo, Syria, Sri Lanka, Ukraine, and the Islamic State of Iraq and Syria (ISIS), provides an opportune moment to examine the enforcement practices of hybrid courts.[7] As observed by Bryan Stevenson, Director of the Equal Justice Initiative in Alabama, United States, the strongest measure of a society and its commitment to justice and equality can arguably be assessed by how it treats those who have lost their liberty, including those incarcerated.[8]

[4] See Barbora Holá and Joris van Wijk, 'Life After Conviction at International Criminal Tribunals: An Empirical Review' (2014) 12 Journal of International Criminal Justice 109, 111–12, 125, noting the general lack of uniformity placed on the rehabilitation of international criminals and the generally long prison terms they serve. See also Penrose (n 3) 463; Richard Culp, 'Enforcement and Monitoring of Sentences in the Modern War Crimes Process: Equal Treatment before the Law?' (Human Rights Seminar Series 2010–2011, Centre for International Human Rights, John Jay College of Criminal Justice 2011).

[5] See Laura Dickinson, 'The Promise of Hybrid Courts' (2003) 97 American Journal of International Law 295. See also Elizabeth M Bruch, 'Hybrid Courts: Examining Hybridity Through a Post-Colonial Lens' (2010) 28 Boston University International Law Journal 1, 3.

[6] Body of Principles for the Protection of All Persons under Any Form of Detention or Imprisonment (adopted 9 December) 1988 UNGA Res 43/173, Principle 20.

[7] For a useful summary of such developments, see Beth Van Schaack, '"More than a Domestic Mechanism": Options for Hybrid Justice in Sri Lanka' (2005) Stanford Public Law Working Paper No 2705097 1, 10–11.

[8] Bryan Stevenson, *Just Mercy: A Story of Justice and Redemption* (Scribe 2014).

10.2 Enforcement Practices of Hybrid Courts

10.2.1 Special Court for Sierra Leone

The governance instruments of the former Special Court for Sierra Leone (SCSL), succeeded by the Residual Special Court for Sierra Leone (RSCSL), contain a statutory preference for imprisonment in Sierra Leone. However in practice the SCSL, and now the RSCSL, have replicated the enforcement practices of the UN ad hoc tribunals and the ICC for those convicted of atrocity crimes, by employing a decentralized ad hoc cooperating states model, amidst concerns that Sierra Leone lacked proper facilities and the capacity to enforce sentences locally.[9]

The RSCSL Registrar is responsible for negotiations with states to enter into cooperation agreements for sentence enforcement[10] and for overall detention matters, including supervising the enforcement of sentences.[11] The Office of the Principal Defender performs a supervisory role; addressing issues referred to it by either domestic prison authorities, or convicted persons.[12]

The SCSL built prison facilities for pre-trial detention, which were later used for the enforcement of contempt sentences, on land donated by the government of Sierra Leone in central Freetown.[13] In early March 2003, the SCSL constructed and opened a temporary Detention Facility, on Bonthe Island due to security concerns, carrying out extensive work on the compound and associated buildings to make them habitable.[14] A permanent Detention Facility was created by renovating the 'crumbling site' of the former New England prison at the SCSL's facility in Freetown.[15] It opened on 10 August 2003, at which time the detainees were transferred from the temporary Detention Facility.[16]

9 Statute of the Special Court for Sierra Leone (August 2000), Article 22(1); Rules of Procedure and Evidence of the Special Court for Sierra Leone (October 2004), Rule 103(A). See also Agreement between the United Nations and the Government of Sierra Leone on the Establishment of a Residual Special Court for Sierra Leone (adopted 11 August 2010). See further Roisin Mulgrew, 'On the Enforcement of Sentences Imposed by International Courts' (2009) 7 Journal of International Criminal Justice 376, 376–77.

10 Such functions have been assumed by the RSCSL pursuant to Article 1(1), Agreement between the United Nations and the Government of Sierra Leone on the Establishment of a Residual Special Court for Sierra Leone (adopted 11 August 2010). See SCSL, 'Eleventh and Final Report of the President of the Special Court for Sierra Leone' (2013), 29.

11 See ibid.

12 ibid. See also SCSL, 'Eighth Annual Report of the President of the Special Court for Sierra Leone: June 2010 to May 2011'.

13 International Centre for Transitional Justice, 'The Special Court For Sierra Leone: The First Eighteen Months' (2004) 2.

14 See RSCSL, 'Detention Unit' <https://rscsl.org/the-scsl/the-registry/detention-unit/#:~:text=The%20new%20Special%20Court%20Detention,of%20the%20Special%20Court%20complex.> accessed 15 January 2024.

15 ibid.

16 ibid.

The Detention Facility in Freetown was fully operational from 2003, until the transfer of eight convicted persons to serve their sentences in Rwanda in 2009.[17] Charles Ghankay Taylor was also held there for three months in 2006.[18] It was staffed in part by domestic correctional officers seconded from the Sierra Leone Prison Service (SLPS).[19] Such officers were expected to 'bring their training in international standards to the domestic penal system' when they returned there to work.[20] The Detention Section set up a training programme conducted by international trainers to increase the skills of national staff to an international standard. This was significant, and part of the capacity-building objectives of the SCSL, since seconded staff returned to the national system following their SCSL service.[21]

After the transfer of the majority of the SCSL-convicted persons to Rwanda on 31 October 2009, the Detention Facility fell vacant and the SCSL prepared for its use by national authorities. The SLPS took possession in May 2010 and has subsequently used it to house domestic female prisoners and their children born in custody.[22] However, a small number of sentences for contempt convictions have since been enforced in Sierra Leone in the Detention Facility.[23]

In August 2013, the SCSL signed a memorandum of understanding (MoU) with the government, transferring the Detention Facility, as well as the custody of the SCSL contempt prisoners and the responsibility for the enforcement of their sentences (subject to SCSL supervision), to the government.[24] Such sentences were to be enforced by the SLPS in accordance with international human rights standards, with costs to be borne by the SCSL and, thereafter, the RSCSL.[25] Yet, while sentences for contempt convictions have been enforced in Sierra Leone on this basis, such sentences relate to periods of imprisonment of eighteen to thirty months only.[26]

[17] SCSL, 'Eleventh and Final Report of the President of the Special Court for Sierra Leone' (2013), 33.
[18] ibid.
[19] RSCSL, 'Detention Unit' <https://rscsl.org/the-scsl/the-registry/detention-unit/#:~:text=The%20new%20Special%20Court%20Detention,of%20the%20Special%20Court%20complex> accessed 15 January 2024.
[20] Chandra Lekha Sriram, 'Wrong-Sizing International Justice? The Hybrid Tribunal in Sierra Leone' (2005) 29 Fordham International Law Journal 500, 500–01.
[21] RSCSL, 'Detention Unit' <https://rscsl.org/the-scsl/the-registry/detention-unit/#:~:text=The%20new%20Special%20Court%20Detention,of%20the%20Special%20Court%20complex> accessed 15 January 2024.
[22] SCSL, 'Eleventh and Final Report of the President of the Special Court for Sierra Leone' (2013) 33.
[23] SCSL, 'Press Release: Government of Sierra Leone to Enforce Sentences of Special Court Contempt Prisoners' (16 August 2013). See also SCSL, 'Eleventh and Final Report of the President of the Special Court for Sierra Leone' (2013), 33.
[24] SCSL, 'Press Release: Government of Sierra Leone to Enforce Sentences of Special Court Contempt Prisoners' (16 August 2013).
[25] ibid.
[26] RSCSL, 'Detention Unit' <https://rscsl.org/the-scsl/the-registry/detention-unit/#:~:text=The%20new%20Special%20Court%20Detention,of%20the%20Special%20Court%20complex.> accessed 15 January 2024.

With the exception of Charles Taylor, who was transferred to the United Kingdom to serve his sentence on 15 October 2013,[27] the majority of those convicted by the SCSL of atrocity crimes were transferred from the Detention Facility in Freetown for sentence enforcement in Mpanga Prison, Rwanda (given its relative proximity on the African continent) on 31 October 2010.[28] Sentence enforcement in third states followed security concerns that the local incarceration of high-profile prisoners would have a detrimental impact on local and regional stability.[29]

Sentences have been administered by the Rwandan Prison Services (RPS), through the RSCSL working with the RPS Commissioner-General's Office to ensure international standards of detention. Visits to prisoners from family members have been facilitated. For instance, in 2012, all eight prisoners received family visitation, with visits being partially funded by the Court.[30]

After the UN Security Council authorized the transfer of Mr Taylor's trial to The Hague on 30 June 2006 for security reasons and the UK offered its assistance, should he be convicted, Mr Taylor was transferred to the UK for sentence enforcement.[31] His presence in West Africa was viewed as an impediment to stability and a threat to the peace of Liberia and of Sierra Leone.[32] He challenged his imprisonment in the UK on the grounds, inter alia, that it violated his right to family life and cultural affinity; however the RSCL dismissed his application.[33]

The determination to transfer those convicted of atrocity crimes outside of Sierra Leone for sentence enforcement did not catalyze local efforts to establish rule of law institutions, nor foster the development of human rights norms within the emerging legal system. Building local capacity, which was achieved to a lesser extent through the transfer of the Detention Facility in Freetown to the government, could have perhaps been accomplished more broadly through the enforcement of sentences for atrocity crimes in Sierra Leone. However, following the deaths of two high-profile detainees under SCSL custody, the inability of the SLPS

[27] See Agreement between the Government of the United Kingdom of Great Britain and Northern Ireland and the Special Court for Sierra Leone on the Enforcement of Sentences for the Special Court for Sierra Leone, (adopted 10 July 2007, entered into force 9 August 2007) Treaty Series No 21.

[28] Charles Chernor Jalloh, 'The Law and Politics of the Charles Taylor Case' (2015) 43 Denver Journal of International Law and Policy 229, 235. See also RSCSL, 'Detention Unit' <https://rscsl.org/the-scsl/the-registry/detention-unit/#:~:text=The%20new%20Special%20Court%20Detention,of%20the%20Special%20Court%20complex> accessed 15 January 2024.

[29] See UNSC, 'Report of the Secretary-General on the Establishment of a Special Court for Sierra Leone' (2000) UN Doc S/2000/915, para 49.

[30] RSCSL, 'Detention Unit' <https://rscsl.org/the-scsl/the-registry/detention-unit/#:~:text=The%20new%20Special%20Court%20Detention,of%20the%20Special%20Court%20complex> accessed 15 January 2024. See also SCSL, 'Eleventh and Final Report of the President of the Special Court for Sierra Leone' (2013) 46.

[31] See UNSC Res 1688 (2006) UN Doc S/Res/1688.

[32] ibid.

[33] See *In the matter of Charles Ghankay Taylor* (Decision with Public and Confidential Annexes on Charles Ghankay Taylor's Motion for Enforcement of Sentence in the United Kingdom and for Transfer to Rwanda) SCSL-03-01-ES (30 January 2015).

to safeguard internationally convicted persons militated against sentence enforcement in Sierra Leone, in addition to the previously stated security concerns.

For instance, unprecedented security measures were taken by the SCSL following the arrest of Samuel Hinga Norman,[34] including holding his court appearances in closed session and attempting to facilitate his pre-trial detention outside of Sierra Leone.[35] The SCSL Registrar tried to negotiate his transfer to the International Criminal Tribunal for the Former Yugoslavia (ICTY) Detention Unit or the International Criminal Tribunal for Rwanda (ICTR) Detention Facility and Mr Norman's place of detention was not made public by the SCSL. According to the International Centre for Transitional Justice: '[t]here were regular rumors in Freetown about the Kamajors' plans to attack the prison and free their leader.'[36] While SCSL officials routinely assessed such threats, they ultimately did not materialize. However, Mr Norman died in Dakar, Senegal in 2007 while undergoing medical treatment involving routine procedures which were unavailable in Sierra Leone.[37]

Following imprisonment in Freetown Central Prison on murder charges, Foday Sankoh, a leader of the dominant rebel group, the Revolutionary United Front (RUF), initially appeared before the SCSL on 15 March 2003: 'slumped in a wheelchair, his hair and beard unkempt, his right leg trembling, and his head resting on his chest.'[38] A medical and psychiatric examination was ordered to determine whether he was fit to stand trial. It exposed that he was in a 'catatonic state and incapable of walking, talking, or feeding himself'.[39] After a further court order instructing an additional psychiatric examination, it became clear that Sierra Leone lacked the medical facilities required in order to carry out the examination.

Once his health began to further deteriorate, he was transferred to the medical facility of the UN Mission in Sierra Leone (UNAMSIL) on 29 March 2003 and the SCSL Registry determined that he should be transferred overseas for treatment. Yet despite the Registry's efforts to secure his transfer, and the SCSL stating that it was in 'urgent need' of assistance from a country which could properly treat Mr Sankoh, he died on 29 July 2003 from natural causes under the custody of the UN.[40]

[34] Mr Norman was the founder and leader of the Civil Defence Forces. Many reportedly objected to his indictment by the SCSL, believing that he had defended a democratically elected government. See Sriram (n 20) 489.

[35] International Centre for Transitional Justice, 'The Special Court For Sierra Leone: The First Eighteen Months' (2004) 3.

[36] ibid 6.

[37] *Norman* (Decision on Registrar's Submission on Evidence of Death of Accused Samuel Hinga Norman and Consequential Issues) SCSL-04-14-T-776)(21 May 2007).

[38] International Centre for Transitional Justice, 'The Special Court For Sierra Leone: The First Eighteen Months' (2004) 5.

[39] ibid.

[40] See *Prosecutor v Foday Saybana Sankoh* (Withdrawal of Indictment) SCSL-03-02-PT-054 (8 December 2003).

The death in custody of a key detainee while awaiting medical treatment overseas arguably struck at the legitimacy of the SCSL.

In the case of Sierra Leone, security concerns and the inability of a fragile state to carry out incarceration to international standards resulted in sentence enforcement in third states. Yet this did not increase the legitimacy of the SCSL and RSCSL, nor their impact on Sierra Leone's justice institutions and the development of human rights norms within itslegal system.

10.2.2 Serious Crimes Panels of the District Court of Dili in East Timor

The Special Crimes Panels of the District Court of Dili (East Timor Tribunal (ETT)), a hybrid international–East Timorese tribunal, was established by the UN Transitional Administration in East Timor (UNTAET) in 2000 in order to try cases of 'serious criminal offences' which took place in East Timor in 1999.[41]

Created as an internationalized regime of domestic prosecution within the District Court of Dili, the ETT sat from 2000 to 2005. Despite the indictment of Indonesian military officers, trials of such officers could not proceed given the Indonesian government's refusal to recognize the Court and extradite the accused. The ETT convicted eighty-four individuals,[42] over fifty-five trials, before ceasing operations on 20 May 2005 due to funding deficits.[43]

In 2006, the UN Security Council created the Serious Crimes Investigation Team (SCIT) in order to resume the investigative functions of the former Special Crimes Unit. On 25 August 2006, the UN Security Council established the UN Integrated Mission in East Timor (UNMIT).[44] The SCIT resumed investigations through the creation of a new investigative team in January 2007 through UNMIT.[45]

The sentences pronounced by the ETT were executed and supervised by District Courts.[46] The Presidency of each District Court was mandated to assign all matters related to the execution and supervision of prison sentences to a panel

[41] UNSC Res 1272 (1999) UN Doc S/RES/1272; UNTAET Regulation on the Establishment of Panels with Exclusive Jurisdiction over Serious Criminal Offences (6 June 2000) UNTAET/REG/2000/15; UNTAET Regulation on the Organization of Courts in East Timor (6 March 2000) UNTAET/REG/2000/11.

[42] Eighty-five convictions were rendered, with one person, Mr Gilberto Fernandes, being convicted on two separate occasions for two different crimes, as the ETT had jurisdiction over serious ordinary crimes as well as international crimes. See Mark A Drumbl, *Atrocity, Punishment and International Law* (Cambridge University Press 2007) 47.

[43] ibid 55. See also Benedict Kingsbury, 'Is the Proliferation of International Courts and Tribunals a Systemic Problem?' (1999) 31 NYU Journal of International Law and Policy 679, 688.

[44] UNSC Res 1704 (2006) UN Doc S/RES/1704.

[45] Agreement between the United Nations and the Democratic Republic of Timor-Leste Concerning Assistance to the Office of the Prosecutor-General of Timor-Leste (12 February 2008), section 1.5.

[46] UNTAET Regulation on the Establishment of Panels with Exclusive Jurisdiction over Serious Criminal Offences (6 June 2000) UNTAET/REG/2000/15, section 10.1(a).

of judges of that District Court. Prisoners could file complaints or requests related to the execution of their prison sentence to the panel, or, where applicable, the individual judge who pronounced their sentence.[47]

A Commission for Reception, Truth and Reconciliation was simultaneously established in 2002 to investigate the scope of historical human rights violations in East Timor and to facilitate the return and community acceptance of perpetrators of lesser crimes through amnesties.[48] A Commission of Truth and Friendship was also set up jointly by Indonesia and East Timor in 2005 to foster reconciliation.[49] The, then, UN Secretary-General, Ban Ki-moon, upheld the UN's policy that it cannot endorse or condone amnesties for genocide, crimes against humanity, war crimes, or gross violations of human rights and thereby determined that UN officials would not testify at such proceedings or otherwise further the possible grant of amnesties.[50]

The bifurcation of justice and reconciliation was compounded by the constraints under which UNTAET had to operate to achieve penal justice, including building a new judiciary and legal system almost entirely from scratch.[51] Jails were rebuilt, as a large number of people were held in detention on suspicion of committing atrocities and ongoing crimes.[52] Critiques that the Timor-Leste government failed to respect the human rights of those accused or convicted of crimes under its control were commonplace. These centred around the right to prompt access to legal counsel, judicial review of detention orders, trials conforming to international standards, humane conditions of detention or imprisonment, and the detention of suspects after their detention orders had expired.[53]

Yet, little attention has been paid to the enforcement of sentences of those convicted, including the impact of local enforcement on peace and reconciliation in East Timor. In part, this may relate to the desire to prevent a return to instability, over punitive justice. However, while the younger generation is reportedly finding

[47] UNTAET Regulation on the Organisation of Courts in East Timor (6 March 2000) UNTAET/REG/2000/11, section 13.

[48] UNTAET Regulation on the Establishment of a Commission for Reception, Truth and Reconciliation in East Timor (13 July 2001) UNTAET/REG/2001/10.

[49] UN News Centre, 'Timor-Leste: UN to Boycott Truth Panel Unless it Bars Amnesty for Gross Abuses' (26 July 2007).

[50] UN, 'Secretary-General says UN Officials will not Testify at Timor-Leste Commission, as Terms of Reference Include Possible Amnesty for Human Rights Violations' (26 July 2007) SG/SM/11101 <https://press.un.org/en/2007/sgsm11101.doc.htm>. See also UN News Centre, 'Timor-Leste: UN to Boycott Truth Panel Unless it Bars Amnesty for Gross Abuses' (26 July 2007).

[51] International Centre for Transitional Justice, 'Impunity in Timor-Leste: Can the Serious Crimes Investigation Team Make a Difference?' (2010) 10.

[52] UNTAET Regulation on the Organisation of the Public Prosecution Service in East Timor (6 June 2000) UNTAET/REG/2000/16.

[53] Joel C Beauvais, 'Benevolent Despotism: A Critique of UN State-Building in East Timor' (2001) 33 NYU Journal of International Law and Policy 1101, 1157–59. See also Amnesty International and Judicial System Monitoring Programme, 'Justice for Timor-Leste: The Way Forward' (ASA 21/006/2004, 2004).

its own ways of reconciliation through community groups,[54] 41.8 per cent of the population of East Timor lived below the national poverty line in 2014, while over 40 per cent remain illiterate.[55]

Grafting an internationalized justice process onto the fledgling criminal justice system of East Timor, without adequate resources being applied to ensure its proper functioning, struck at the legitimacy of the ETT.[56] Following the official closure of the UN peacekeeping operation, little information is available in the public domain concerning sentence enforcement at the ETT.

10.2.3 Special Tribunal for Lebanon

The Special Tribunal for Lebanon (STL) was a tribunal of 'international character', based in The Hague, which applied Lebanese criminal law to carry out the investigation and prosecution of those responsible for the 2005 assassination of former Lebanese Prime Minister, Rafic Hariri, the deaths of twenty-one others, and connected attacks.[57] While it shared many of the features of the SCSL, it was the first international tribunal that did not include core crimes against humanity in its jurisdiction, focusing instead on acts of terrorism.[58]

The government of Lebanon and the UN Security Council determined that the Tribunal should be located outside of Lebanon to ensure justice, fairness, and security.[59] Yet, the STL has been criticized for its failure to secure the approval of all political stakeholders, despite its promise to bolster the rule of law and strengthen state sovereignty in Lebanon.[60] The STL ceased operations on 31 December 2023.[61]

[54] Ali MC, 'East Timor: Between Hope and Unease 20 years After Referendum' (*AlJazeera*, 30 August 2019) <https://www.aljazeera.com/news/2019/8/30/east-timor-between-hope-and-unease-20-years-after-referendum> accessed 16 October 2024.

[55] Asian Development Bank, 'Basic Statistics 2019: Poverty Data: Timor-Leste' <https://www.adb.org/countries/timor-leste/poverty> accessed 16 October 2024; UNICEF, 'At a Glance: Timor-Leste Statistics' <https://www.unicef.org/infobycountry/Timorleste_statistics.html> accessed 28 March 2020.

[56] Beauvais (n 53) 1157–59.

[57] Statute of the Special Tribunal for Lebanon (30 May 2007), preamble and section 2.

[58] Jan Erik Wetzel and Yvonne Mitri, 'The Special Tribunal for Lebanon: A Court "Off the Shelf" for a Divided Country' (2008) 7 Law of Practice of International Courts and Tribunals 81, 81.

[59] STL, 'Why is the Tribunal Based in The Netherlands and not in Lebanon' (23 June 2011) <https://www.stl-tsl.org/en/ask-the-tribunal/477-why-is-the-tribunal-based-in-the-netherlands-and-not-in-lebanon> accessed 31 August 2019.

[60] Michael Humphrey, 'The Special Tribunal for Lebanon: Emergency Law, Trauma and Justice' (2001) 33 Arab Studies Quarterly 4, 19; Tamirace Fakhoury, 'Assessing the Political Acceptance of Hybrid Courts in Fractured States: The Case of the Special Tribunal for Lebanon' in Susanne Buckley-Zistel, Friederike Mieth, and Marjana Papa (eds), *After Nuremberg. Exploring Multiple Dimensions of the Acceptance of International Criminal Justice* (International Nuremberg Principles Academy 2016) 5.

[61] UN Secretary-General's Spokesperson–on the Closure of the Special Tribunal for Lebanon | UNSCOL (unmissions.org).

The STL provided for an ad hoc cooperating states model of enforcement, based on the designation of states by the STL President from a list of states which had indicated their willingness to accept convicted persons.[62] The ultimate decision regarding the pardon or commutation of sentences was made by the STL President, in consultation with the judges.[63]

The STL convicted Messrs Ayyash, Merhi, and Oneissi in absentia and sentenced them to five concurrent sentences of life imprisonment for their roles in the 14 February 2005 terrorist attack in Beirut that killed twenty-two people, including former Lebanese Prime Minister Rafik Hariri, and injured many others.[64] The Sentencing Judgments by the Appeals Chamber required enforcement, however all three convicted persons remain at large, including following the STL's closure .[65]

The STL sought to conclude cooperation agreements with states regarding the prospective enforcement of sentences.[66] It also concluded an agreement with the International Committee of the Red Cross (ICRC), similar to the practice of the UN International Residual Mechanism for Criminal Tribunals (UNIRMCT), providing the ICRC with authority to conduct visits to detainees held by the STL in the STL Detention Facility in the host state.[67] The purpose of such visits was to ensure that detainees were treated humanely and in conformity with widely accepted international standards governing the treatment of prisoners.

Given the contested acceptance of the STL within Lebanon's political landscape, it is unsurprising that it intended for sentences to be enforced based on an ad hoc cooperating states model. The reluctance of opponents of the STL to cooperate with its investigations affected its capacity to enforce arrest warrants, ultimately undermining its ability to enforce justice.[68] Given such disagreements among political leaders and related internal strife, facilitating a variety of options for sentence enforcement was the clear choice for the STL as it sought to operate amidst a multitude of challenges.

[62] Statute of the Special Tribunal for Lebanon (30 May 2007), Article 29.

[63] ibid Article 30.

[64] See Kosovo Specialist Chambers and Specialist Prosecutor's Office, 'Hysni Gucati & Nasim Haradinaj' <https://www.scp-ks.org/en/cases/hysni-gucati-nasim-haradinaj/en> accessed 26 November 2022.

[65] The STL has also issued contempt convictions, yet such convictions have resulted in monetary penalties rather than periods of imprisonment. See, eg, *Akhbar Beirut S.A.L. & Mr Al Amin* (STL-14-06).

[66] See STL, 'Tenth Annual Report (2018-2019)' 42.

[67] See Agreement between the Special Tribunal for Lebanon and the International Committee of the Red Cross on visits to persons deprived of liberty pursuant to the jurisdiction of the STL (12 June 2009). See also, eg, Agreement between the United Nations and the Government of the Republic of Mali on the Enforcement of Sentences Pronounced by the International Criminal Tribunal for Rwanda or the International Residual Mechanism for Criminal Tribunals, Article 6 (signed 13 May 2016, as amended on 30 June 2016), Article 6, in technical respects.

[68] Fakhoury (n 60) 6–7.

10.2.4 War Crime Chambers in Bosnia-Herzegovina

The War Crime Chambers in Bosnia-Herzegovina (BIH WCC) employed a local enforcement model. Long-term sentences of imprisonment were administered in closed facilities under strict control, after requests for funding to construct a state prison for use by the BIH WCC were not granted.[69] Bosnia and Herzegovina resorted to long prison sentences for serious crimes as an alternative form of punishment following the abolition of the death penalty. However, prison conditions fell short of international standards in terms of space, security, and health and safety. As observers have noted: 'underinvestment and a lack of willingness to impose such standards have led to the escape of some of the high-profile prisoners', which undermines the BIH WCC's operations.[70]

For instance, prior to the escape of Radovan Stanković from custody in Foča prison while being taken for dental treatment, BIH WCC officials had reportedly made numerous appeals for a new state-level prison to be built, to no avail.[71] In addition to the lack of funding for adequate facilities and deficient security measures, the exceptionally close nexus between the location of the atrocities and the enforcement of sentences generated critique with respect to the BIH WCC's local enforcement model. Questions arose regarding the fact that Mr Stanković was designated to have his lengthy sentence enforced in the exact town where he committed atrocities, Foča, which has become a local synonym for wartime rape, within a questionable political context.[72] Indeed, in 2009, a further nine prisoners escaped from the Ustikolina prison in Bosnia and Herzegovina.[73]

Only two prison facilities were suitable for convicts serving long sentences in the territory where the atrocity crimes occurred and consequently such prisons were typically located in the same Bosnian Entity from which the individual came. The exceptionally close proximity of the prison in Foča utilized by the BIH WCC for sentence enforcement highlights the potential problem of proximity to atrocity sites and the fact that security and impartiality may be better served by non-local personnel involvement. It has been noted that some of the convicted persons' friends and relatives work as guards in Foča in the same sections where the convicts serve their sentences.[74] Thus, any decision to enforce sentences domestically must take into account political and logistical realities.

[69] Bogdan Ivanišević, 'The War Crimes Chamber in Bosnia and Herzegovina: From Hybrid to Domestic Court' (International Centre for Transitional Justice 2008) 23.

[70] ibid.

[71] See Justice Report, 'War Crimes Convict Escapes from Foča Prison' (25 May 2007).

[72] Nada Davi, 'The Death Penalty and Post-Conflict Peace-Building in The Balkans: The Case of Bosnia and Herzegovina' in Madoka Futamura and Nadia Bernaz (eds), *The Politics of the Death Penalty in Countries in Transition* (Routledge 2014) 123.

[73] ibid.

[74] ibid.

10.2.5 Extraordinary Chambers in the Courts of Cambodia

With international assistance through the UN Assistance to the Khmer Rouge Trials (UNAKRT), the Extraordinary Chambers in the Courts of Cambodia (ECCC) was established within the Cambodian legal system in 2006 to seek justice for the crimes committed by the Khmer Rouge regime.[75] On 1 January 2023, after completing its judicial caseload, the ECCC commenced residual functions for an initial period of three years.[76] It applies a model of local sentence enforcement, whereby inquiries are made regarding the standards of imprisonment within the national penitentiary regime, prior to the Co-Prosecutors filing a specific request to the General Department of Prisons of the Ministry of Interior (GDP) to transfer a defendant to a Cambodian prison. Agreement must be obtained from the Government to facilitate the transfer of the convicted person from the ECCC Detention Unit to the specific national prison.[77]

To date, three individuals have been convicted and sentenced to life imprisonment by the ECCC,[78] with two such convicted persons passing away on 4 August 2019 and 2 September 2020, respectively.[79] The last surviving prisoner convicted by the ECCC, Khieu Samphan, is currently held at the ECCC Detention Unit, under the jurisdiction of the GDP.[80]

Enforcing sentences domestically, under the purview of the Cambodian authorities, provides a further opportunity for Cambodian society to confront the outcome of the international justice process. While the ECCC has been criticized regarding alleged corruption and political interference,[81] it employs broad programmes for public outreach and access. In addition to its extensive victim participation scheme, with thousands of Cambodians attending trials, the ECCC has

75 Law on the Establishment of Extraordinary Chambers in the Courts of Cambodia for the Prosecution of Crimes Committed During the Period of Democratic Kampuchea (amended and promulgated on 27 October 2004) NS/RKM/1004/006.

76 Extraordinary Chambers in the Courts of Cambodia (ECCC).

77 ECCC, Internal Rules (Rev 9) (16 January 2015) Rule 113,.

78 *Kaing Guek Eav alias Duch* (Case 001); *Nuon Chea and Khieu Samphan* (Case 002).

79 Nuon Chea passed away on 4 August 2019 in hospital at the age of 93. See ECCC, 'Press Release: Accused Person Noun Chea Dies' (4 August 2019) <https://www.eccc.gov.kh/en/articles/accused-person-nuon-chea-dies> accessed 26 November 2022. Kaing Guek Eav was serving his sentence at Kandal Provincial Prison, Cambodia, until he passed away on 2 September 2020 in hospital at the age of 77. See ECCC, 'Press Release by the National Co-Prosecutor on the Passing of the Convicted Person Kaing Guek Eav alias Duch' (2 September 2020) <https://www.eccc.gov.kh/en/articles/press-release-national-co-prosecutor-passing-convicted-person-kaing-guek-eav-alias-duch> accessed 26 November 2022.

80 ECCC, 'Khieu Samphan: Biography' <https://www.eccc.gov.kh/en/indicted-person/khieu-samphan> accessed 30 March 2020.

81 Human Rights Watch, 'Cambodia: Khmer Rouge Convictions "Too Little, Too Late"' (8 August 2014) <https://www.hrw.org/news/2014/08/08/cambodia-khmer-rouge-convictions-too-little-too-late#:~:text=Human%20Rights%20Watch%20expressed%20concern,based%20on%20the%20evidence%20and>.

engaged Cambodians through film screenings, study tours, school lectures, and daily live television broadcasts.[82]

While little public information is available regarding the impact of local sentence enforcement at the ECCC, enforcement overseas would likely have run counter to the role and impact of the ECCC in developing a sense of local ownership of the justice process.[83]

10.2.6 Extraordinary African Chambers

The Extraordinary African Chambers (EAC) was established in Senegal in 2012 by the African Union (AU) to prosecute the person or persons most responsible for international crimes committed in Chad from 7 June 1982 to 1 December 1990, including Hissène Habré, the former President of Chad.[84] Through execution by the AU and Senegal of an agreement establishing a special court with 'international elements' within the Senegalese judicial system, the EAC effectively applies a regionalized ad hoc cooperating states model of enforcement, whereby, if the circumstances so require, the convicted person may serve their prison sentence in one of the AU member states with which Senegal has signed an agreement for this purpose. The default provision is that such sentences: 'shall be executed in Senegal within existing penitentiaries and in accordance with Senegalese practices and law'.[85]

As the first internationalized tribunal established with the involvement of the AU, the EAC offers insight into a regionalized approach to sentence enforcement. The AU explicitly entrusted Senegal to prosecute Mr Habré 'on behalf of Africa'.[86] He could have been sentenced to death in absentia, if tried and convicted in Chad, where many observed he would not have been extended fair trial guarantees.[87] Indeed, the former President of Senegal, President Abdoulaye Wade, retracted his

[82] See Christoph Sperfeldt, 'Broadcasting Justice: Media Outreach at the Khmer Rouge Trials' (Asia Pacific: Analysis from the East-West Center 2014), 115.

[83] See Phuong Pham and others, 'After the First Trial: A Population-based Survey on Knowledge and Perception of Justice and the Extraordinary Chambers in the Courts of Cambodia' (Human Rights Center, University of California, Berkeley, School of Law 2011); Caitlin McCaffrie and others, '"So We Can Know What Happened": The Educational Potential of the ECCC' (WSD HANDA Center for Human Rights and International Justice at Stanford University and the East-West Center 2018).

[84] See Statute of the Extraordinary African Chambers within the Senegalese Judicial System for the Prosecution of International Crimes Committed on the Territory of the Republic of Chad during the Period from 7 June 1982 to 1 December 1990 (22 August 2012), Article 3(1).

[85] ibid Article 26.

[86] Assembly of the African Union, 'Decision on the Hissène Habré Case and the African Union' (2007) Doc ASSEMBLY/AU/3(VII), section 5(ii).

[87] Human Rights Watch, 'The Case of Hissène Habré before the Extraordinary African Chambers in Senegal' (3 May 2016) <https://www.hrw.org/news/2016/05/03/qa-case-hissene-habre-extraordinary-african-chambers-senegal>.

decision to transfer Mr Habré to Chad in July 2011, following international criticism regarding the risk of his mistreatment, or even death, in Chad.[88]

Mr Habré is currently serving his life sentence at Cape Manuel Prison in Dakar, Senegal, which was refurbished with funding from the AU and the international community. His conditions of detention have drawn mixed reactions, with some criticizing them for being too comfortable,[89] while Mr Habré's supporters have compared them to those of the infamous Guantánamo Bay Detention Camp in Cuba.[90]

Yet overall the regional model of sentence enforcement employed by the EAC in the case of Mr Habré enabled a degree of separation from the political context in Chad, while ensuring that justice was administered regionally and in accordance with international human rights standards. Given the history of the delay of Mr Habré's trial, which at one stage culminated in his extradition being sought from Senegal to Belgium four times,[91] sentence enforcement in Senegal became a key component of what many, including the AU itself, have referred to as an 'African solution' to mass atrocities.[92]

10.2.7 Kosovo Specialist Chambers

Following the 1999 Kosovo war, Kosovo moved beyond an immediate post-conflict state and began to undertake a long-term process of post-conflict legal redevelopment.[93] Yet, the international community has heavily criticized the continued weakness of the local judiciary, despite international involvement in the area of the administration of justice.[94]

The initial establishment of hybrid panels within a 'semi-internationalised court', the 'Regulation 64' Panels in the Courts of Kosovo, occurred in 2000 under the auspices of the UN Interim Administration Mission in Kosovo (UNMIK).[95] Embedded in Kosovo's domestic judicial structure, the 'Regulation 64' Panels opted for a local model of sentence enforcement. Yet, the local judicial system was

88 ibid.

89 Seneweb, 'Cap Manuel: In the Golden Prison of Hissène Habré' (6 October 2014).

90 Seneweb, 'Habré Prison: "Dakarnamo", the Senegalese Guantanamo?' (5 November 2013).

91 Human Rights Watch, 'Belgium/Senegal: World Court Should Order Habré Extradition Senegal Refuses to Prosecute Chad's ex-Dictator; Trial Should Move to Belgium' (8 March 2012). Belgium/Senegal: World Court Should Order Habré Extradition | Human Rights Watch (hrw.org) (accessed 16 October 2024).

92 See AU, 'Press Release: AU welcomes appeal outcome of the Hissene Habre case by the African Extraordinary Chambers' (2 May 2017).

93 Elena Baylis, 'Tribunal-Hopping with the Post-Conflict Justice Junkies' (2008) 10 Oregon Review of International Law 361.

94 Organisation for Security and Cooperation in Europe, 'Independence of the Judiciary in Kosovo: Institutional and Functional Dimensions' (24 January 2012).

95 UNSC Res 1244 (1999) UN Doc S/RES/1244.

in 'shambles'.[96] Physical infrastructure was highly damaged, and prisoners languished in overcrowded jails.[97] The internationalized panels failed to make significant progress towards ending impunity for international crimes in the region, with many Serb defendants having escaped from custody since 1999.[98]

By contrast, the more recently established Kosovo Specialist Chambers and Specialist Prosecutor's Office (KSC) are part of the judicial system of Kosovo, established by a Constitutional Amendment and a Law adopted by the Kosovo Assembly[99] to conduct trials for allegations stemming from the 2011 Council of Europe report, which alleges serious violations of international law.[100] They apply an ad hoc cooperating states model of sentence enforcement, whereby the President, having heard the accused, shall decide in which state the accused shall serve their sentence, from a list of states that have agreed to accept convicted persons, excluding the host state.[101]

The conditions of imprisonment, governed by the law of the enforcement state, while subject to the supervision of the KSC,[102] are not explicitly required to comply with international standards of imprisonment under the Court's governance framework, although such a proviso is arguably implicit.[103] The KSC has not yet publicly announced bilateral agreements on the enforcement of sentences.

As the KSC has only rendered two convictions in respect of atrocity crimes, namely: for the war crimes of arbitrary detention, torture and murder regarding Pjetër Shala, allegedly a member of the Kosovo Liberation Army (KLA); and for the war crimes of arbitrary detention, torture and murder regarding Salih Mustafa, the Commander of a BIA guerrilla unit, [104] with two atrocity crimes cases remaining at

[96] See ICTY, 'Statement by Carla Del Ponte Prosecutor of the International Criminal Tribunal for the Former Yugoslavia on the Investigation and Prosecution of Crimes Committed in Kosovo' (29 September 1999).

[97] ibid.

[98] See Sylvia de Bertodano, 'Current Developments in Internationalized Courts' (2003) 2 Journal of International Criminal Justice 910. See also Etelle R Higonnet, 'Restructuring Hybrid Courts: Local Empowerment and National Criminal Justice Reform' (2005) Yale Law School Legal Scholarship Repository, Paper 6, 31.

[99] Amendment of the Constitution of the Republic of Kosovo, Article 162: Specialist Chambers and the Specialist Prosecutor's Office (3 August 2015) 05-D39; Law on Specialist Chambers and Specialist Prosecutor's Office (3 August 2015) Law No 05/L-053, Republic of Kosovo.

[100] Council of Europe, 'Parliamentary Assembly Report: Inhuman Treatment of People and Illicit Trafficking in Human Organs in Kosovo' (2011).

[101] See Agreement between the Kingdom of the Netherlands and the Republic of Kosovo concerning the Hosting of the Kosovo Relocated Specialist Judicial Institution in the Netherlands (15 February 2016) Article 44: Enforcement of Sentences. See also Law on Specialist Chambers and Specialist Prosecutor's Office (3 August 2015) Law No 05/L-053, Republic of Kosovo, Article 50.

[102] See Law on Specialist Chambers and Specialist Prosecutor's Office (3 August 2015) Law No 05/L-053, Republic of Kosovo, Article 60.

[103] ibid Article 50.

[104] Pjetër Shala convicted of arbitrary detention, torture and murder | Kosovo Specialist Chambers & Specialist Prosecutor's Office (scp-ks.org); KSC Appeals Panel imposes new sentence of 15 years imprisonment in Salih Mustafa Case | Kosovo Specialist Chambers & Specialist Prosecutor's Office (scp-ks.org).

the Trial and Pre-Trial phases,[105] the international community should follow with great interest where, and under which conditions, the institution may proceed to enforce sentences. It is understood that those previously convicted of offences against the administration of justice remained in detention at the KSC Detention Unit, until their appeals against such convictions had concluded (resulting in conditional release and release under stict conditions, respectively) [106], in addition to both individuals convicted thus far of atrocity crimes.[107]

10.3 Recommendations for Future Hybrid Courts

International crimes are qualitatively different, cast as 'extraordinary in their nature', and understood not only as 'crimes against the victims in the camps or the helpless citizens in the invaded countries, but crimes in which everyone was a victim'.[108]

Incarceration alone cannot achieve reconciliation, while it is an important condition. For instance, despite sentence enforcement to international standards, the ICTY failed to achieve reconciliation in the former Yugoslavia, where many still view convicted war criminals as heroes while victims and survivors are silenced and dismissed.[109] Sentence enforcement forms part of a wider matrix of processes outside of the penal system which can foster reconciliation.

Additionally, it is important to note that the international community's commitment to a supranational legal process, through the establishment of the ICC, has not extended to a commitment to an international penal process centred on restorative justice. While the idea of retribution within the international criminal justice arena has evolved from the use of the death penalty by the International Military Tribunal at Nuremberg in 1945–1946, to the prohibition on its use by the ICC and UN ad hoc tribunals, the concept of rehabilitation is not yet adequately incorporated into international sentence enforcement practices.

The principles of retribution and deterrence primarily underlie international sentencing decisions rather than rehabilitation.[110] Yet rehabilitation should be

[105] Kosovo Specialist Chambers and Specialist Prosecutor's Office, 'Cases' <https://www.scp-ks.org/en/cases> accessed 26 November 2022.

[106] See Kosovo Specialist Chambers and Specialist Prosecutor's Office, 'Hysni Gucati & Nasim Haradinaj' <https://www.scp-ks.org/en/cases/hysni-gucati-nasim-haradinaj/en> accessed 26 November 2022. Cases | Kosovo Specialist Chambers & Specialist Prosecutor's Office (scp-ks.org).

[107] Public redacted version of Order to Transfer to Detention Facilities of the Specialist Chamber. (Annex 2 to F00008) | Kosovo Specialist Chambers & Specialist Prosecutor's Office (scp-ks.org); Annex 2-Public Redacted Version of Order for Transfer to Detention Facilities of the Specialist Chambers | Kosovo Specialist Chambers & Specialist Prosecutor's Office (scp-ks.org).

[108] Drumbl (n 42) 3.

[109] See Serge Brammertz Prosecutor, ICTY and IRMCT, 'Comments before the UN Security Council, ICTY' (ICTY24: Commemoration held at United Nations Headquarters, 5 December 2017).

[110] See analysis by Dirk van Zyl Smith, 'International Imprisonment' (2005) 54 International and Comparative Law Quarterly 357–86.

seen as a goal of incarceration.[111] The Mandela Rules, which detail UN minimum conditions for the enforcement of prison sentences, include the rehabilitation of prisoners and the preparation for their reintegration into society post-release as key objectives of imprisonment.[112] Such objectives are typically evaded by international sentence enforcement.

For instance, rehabilitative opportunities for prisoners are limited. They are usually incarcerated in high security prisons where rehabilitative programmes are not offered, or they may not fluently speak the language that programmes are conducted in, or there is an absence of suitably trained staff to provide programmes to them. Programmes aimed at rehabilitating domestic offenders are typically not suitable.[113] In addition, distance from their homeland often impedes the maintenance of family relationships and runs counter to rehabilitation and reintegration goals.[114] We must therefore be cognizant of the fact that the lack of rehabilitative opportunities provided to international prisoners does little to aid restorative justice goals.

With these realities in mind, this chapter concludes with recommendations for future hybrid courts with respect to sentence enforcement.

Prisons and jails, as total institutions, are notoriously closed to outside scrutiny.[115] They 'tend to consume their own smoke if they can'.[116] The fact that little attention has been paid to sentence enforcement practices at the ETT and ECCC is indicative of this.

Transparency might be better served in the international realm of imprisonment by applying a clear guiding principle for the exercise of sentence enforcement. Perhaps this might be referred to as a 'complementary principle' for the enforcement of sentences, based on the inability or unwillingness of a post-conflict state to locally enforce sentences.

It would dictate that states should have the first responsibility and right to enforce international sentences domestically. The principle of complementarity currently governs the exercise of the ICC's jurisdiction, recognizing that states have the first responsibility and right to prosecute international crimes,[117] based on

[111] See Roisin Mulgrew, 'On the Enforcement of Sentences Imposed by International Courts' (2009) 7 Journal of International Criminal Justice 373; and Richard Culp, 'Enforcement and Monitoring of Sentences in the Modern War Crimes Process: Equal Treatment before the Law?' (Human Rights Seminar Series 2010–2011, The Centre for International Human Rights, John Jay College of Criminal Justice 2011).

[112] United Nations Standard Minimum Rules for the Treatment of Prisoners (Mandela Rules) annexed to UNGA Res 70/175 annex (adopted 17 December 2015) Rules 4, 87–92 and 106–08.

[113] See Barbora Hola and Joris van Wijk, 'Life after Conviction at International Criminal Tribunals—Empirical Overview' unpublished manuscript (2013).

[114] Culp (n 111) 11.

[115] ibid 9.

[116] Jon Vagg, *Prison Systems: A Comparative Study of Accountability in England, France, Germany and the Netherlands* (Clarendon Press 1994) 250.

[117] Rome Statute of the International Criminal Court (opened for signature 17 July 1998, entered into force 1 July 2002) 2187 UNTS 90, para 10, preamble.

respect for the primary jurisdiction of states, as well as considerations of efficiency and effectiveness.[118] Such a principle in the sentence enforcement realm would build on the statutory preference for imprisonment in Sierra Leone employed by the SCSL and RSCSL.[119]

Prioritizing local enforcement under a complementarity principle could bolster the legitimacy of the domestic justice process, as demonstrated by the experience of the ECCC, as well as catalyzing local efforts to establish rule of law institutions, and fostering the development of human rights norms. For instance, pre-trial detention and the domestic enforcement of contempt sentences by the SCSL and RSCSL contributed to skills transfer and development, infusing international detention standards domestically and benefiting the national penitentiary sector to a certain extent through the transfer of the Detention Facility in Freetown to the government of Sierra Leone.

With international assistance through the hybrid system, prioritizing local enforcement could result in developing local capacity, as well as the 'internationalisation and interpenetration of [global] norms' through a process akin to osmosis.[120] This could extend the crucial link crafted by the hybrid process between the international community and the domestic legal order, generating institutional reform so that penitentiary institutions function more effectively. Additionally, the proximity of offenders to their family and ordinary place of residence provides cultural affinity and improved opportunities for rehabilitation and reintegration post-release. International involvement should be gradually tapered off, as it is with all other elements of the hybrid justice process, leaving the domestic system stronger for it.

The pivotal assessment as to when to utilize an ad hoc cooperating states model, which utilizes prison facilities in third states, could be made through a consultative process between the international side of the hybrid court (eg the UN, the AU, the European Union, or other regional or international organization, such as the Global Coalition to Defeat Daesh/ISIS), and the respective state.[121] The unwillingness or inability of a post-conflict state to enforce sentences domestically would centre on the capability of that state to carry out detention to international standards.

[118] See ICC Office of the Prosecutor, 'Informal Expert Paper: The Principle of Complementarity in Practice' (2003) 3.

[119] See Statute of the Special Court for Sierra Leone (August 2000) Article 22(1); Rules of Procedure and Evidence of the Special Court for Sierra Leone (October 2004), Rule 103(A). See also Statute of the International Criminal Tribunal for Rwanda annexed to UNSC Res 955 (1994) UN Doc S/Res/955, Article 26: Enforcement of Sentences.

[120] See Dickinson (n 5) 304.

[121] Considerations regarding the burden of proof fall outside the scope of this chapter, however it is of note that the Rome Statute and the ICC's Rules of Procedure and Evidence do not delineate the standard of proof that must be met for the ICC to render its complementarity-based admissibility determinations. See Megan Fairlie, 'Burdens and Standards of Proof for Complementarity Determinations' (2017) Florida International University Legal Studies Research Paper No 17-09.

Examples of unwillingness or inability to enforce sentences locally could include the lack of trust in public institutions, as observed through the experiences of the SCSL and RSCSL, STL, BIH WCC, ETT, and EAC (regarding Chad), or the capacity of local enforcement to negatively impact upon political stability (local or regional), or generate security concerns, as was seen most acutely in the case of the SCSL and RSCSL. Lack of infrastructure or inadequate resources also point to this, as seen in the case of the BIH WCC regarding the lack of funding to create a new facility resulting in poor security and health and safety standards.

Additionally, the lack of impartiality or corruptibility of local personnel or institutions may also point to such an assessment, along with the potential problem of proximity to atrocity sites reducing security standards and leading to potential prisoner escapes, as also seen through the BIH BWCC experience. New regimes may threaten to employ an overly zealous response to international crimes as a form of victors' justice,[122] as seen in certain respects through the EAC experience regarding Chad. This may also contribute to further instability and civil unrest. The inadequacy of available medical facilities domestically could similarly indicate inability or unwillingness, as demonstrated by the SCSL and RSCSL experience.

In practice, the inability to enforce sentences locally is typically attributed to a lack of funding available for local investment in post-conflict situations. In the immediate aftermath of conflict and mass atrocities, the inability of institutions to implement international standards is often due to exhausted resources and crippling damage sustained to physical infrastructure.[123] The vulnerabilities of devising a scheme for international justice without adequate material, human, and logistical resources being provided for its implementation have been exposed through the general experiences of the SCSL and RSCSL, ETT, and BIH WCC.

Thus, where a post-conflict state is unwilling or unable to enforce sentences, when applying the ad hoc cooperating states model, regional proximity to the location of the atrocities and to the convicted person's ordinary place of residence and family, as well as the rehabilitation programmes available within the prospective state should be considered.[124] Regional enforcement could cater to these factors where domestic enforcement is not possible. For instance, the degree of separation from the local political context in Chad, yet the regional proximity of Senegal to Chad, was considered to deliver justice 'on behalf of Africa' through the EAC. Similarly, in the case of the SCSL and RSCSL, imprisonment in Rwanda was embraced for the majority of persons convicted of atrocity crimes.

[122] Higonnet (n 98) 357.

[123] See Derek M Welski, 'Hybrid Court System in Kosovo: Has EULEX proven to be the device to strengthen the independence and effectiveness of the judiciary?' (2014) Group for Legal and Political Studies Police Report No 11.

[124] For instance, see IRMCT Practice Direction on the Procedure for the Designation of the State in which a Convicted Person is to Serve his or her Sentence of Imprisonment (24 April 2014) MICT/2/Rev 1, para 4(a).

Additionally, hybrid courts might avoid designating multiple states for decentralized enforcement. It is noted that while the UN ad hoc tribunals rely on a decentralized network of states to implement penal sanctions through an ad hoc cooperating states model, this has resulted in a regionalized approach to incarceration across states[125] which may be critiqued for its potential to create inequalities between international prisoners, including with respect to prison facilities, approaches to early release, and rehabilitation and reintegration programmes.[126]

In all cases, whether enforced locally or in third states, sentences should be administered in accordance with international human rights standards.[127] While the standard of prison conditions for international prisoners may attract scrutiny within a post-conflict setting, the criminal justice process cannot remedy the broad development needs of a post-conflict society, including with respect to access to shelter, food, medical treatment, and education for the liberated.

As the SCSL and RSCSL experience demonstrates, international standards should be supervised through collaboration between the international and domestic sides of the hybrid court. Appropriate independent monitoring mechanisms should be put in place to ensure accountability, for example by the ICRC (as employed by the STL), or the European Committee for the Prevention of Torture or Inhuman or Degrading Treatment or Punishment, in accordance with Rule 82(1)(b) of the Mandela Rules.

10.4 Conclusion

Critical theorist Bernard Harcourt has addressed the theme of the practical and theoretical invisibility of prisons in society and how this invisibility is a symptom of democracy's 'virtual reality', whereby it tends to operate without the full participation of its citizens.[128] Alluding to that of Albert Dzur, Harcourt's work reflects upon the invisibility of the problem of punishment within domestic societies. Collective disengagement within the international criminal justice sphere to the issue of the enforcement of sentences mirrors Harcourt's observations at the international level.

125 For instance, ICTR sentences are currently enforced in West Africa and ICTY sentences are currently enforced in Europe. See IRMCT, 'Enforcement of Sentences' <http://www.unmict.org/en/about/functions/enforcement-of-sentences> accessed 30 March 2020.

126 See Culp (n 111).

127 See UN Standard Minimum Rules for the Treatment of Prisoners (Mandela Rules), 2015; Body of Principles for the Protection of All Persons under Any Form of Detention or Imprisonment (adopted 9 December 1988) UNGA Res 43/173, Principle 20; Basic Principles for the Treatment of Prisoners (adopted 14 December 1990) UNGA Res 45/111; and UNGA, Universal Declaration of Human Rights (adopted 10 December 1948) UNGA Res 217 A (III).

128 Bernanrd E Harcourt, 'The Invisibility of the Prison in Democratic Theory: A Problem of "Virtual Democracy"' (2014) 23 Good Society 6.

Rigorous international engagement with the topic of sentence enforcement is long overdue. We must adopt a principled approach. As Bryan Stevenson, in the context of his work within the United States penal system, faultlessly puts it, one ultimately judges the character of society by how it treats the poor, the condemned, the incarcerated: '[b]ecause it's in that nexus that we actually begin to understand truly profound things about who we are'.[129] In the context of international criminal justice, including that administered by hybrid mechanisms, that society comprises us all.

[129] Bryan Stevenson, 'We need to talk about an Injustice' (*Ted Talks*, March 2012) <https://www.ted.com/talks/bryan_stevenson_we_need_to_talk_about_an_injustice?language=en> accessed 16 October 2024.

PART III
INNOVATION

11

A New African Pluralism in International Criminal Law

Sovereign Immunity and the Trial of Hissène Habré

Kerstin Bree Carlson

11.1 Introduction

There is an ongoing disagreement in international criminal law (ICL) regarding sovereign immunity. International humanitarian law takes the possibility of challenging impunity as a central element of its mandate, in part because a fundamental norm of rule of law practice is that no one is above the law, and in part because leaders are those who arguably bear the greatest responsibility for the types of collective harms international humanitarian law would criminalize. Thus ICL as practised by ad hoc tribunals, and the International Criminal Court (ICC) promises that sovereigns are not immune from prosecution for atrocity crimes, and suggests that violations of international humanitarian law by those in positions of power are more worthy of prosecution that low level offenders' infractions. This norm does not distinguish between sitting and former heads of state. Across Africa, however, there has been significant, organized pushback regarding prosecuting sitting leaders for atrocity crimes.[1] This pushback has arisen in many forms. One of the most public and contested was the 2015 refusal by South Africa and others to comply with the ICC's open arrest warrant against Sudan's then-president Al-Bashir when he travelled internationally representing Sudan. There is also the Malabo Protocol, the guiding document of the African Union's (AU) proposed African Court of Justice and Human Rights, which explicitly grants sitting heads of state immunity from prosecution (while also referencing norms that would limit sovereigns to two terms in office, thereby in principle making them available for prosecution when they leave office).[2] These examples demonstrate what is perhaps

[1] See discussion in Peter Brett and Line Engbo Gissel, *Africa and the Backlash Against International Courts* (Bloomsbury 2020).

[2] Protocol on Amendments to the Protocol on the Statute of the African Court of Justice and Human Rights (June 2014) (the Malabo Protocol), Article 46A*bis*.

Kerstin Bree Carlson, *A New African Pluralism in International Criminal Law* In: *Hybrid Justice*.
Edited by: Kirsten Ainley and Mark Kersten, Oxford University Press.
DOI: 10.1093/oso/9780192893758.003.0011

the central conflict defining ICL discourse today: a plurality of opinions regarding how sovereignty comports with state-sponsored atrocity crimes.

As hybrid tribunals grow in popularity, one area of their developing practice that merits particular attention is their treatment of immunity questions. A central element of how we measure the resilience of judicial systems is their capacity to act as a constraint on political actors, their 'speaking truth to power' function. At the same time, leaders accused of atrocity crimes are often at the centre of corrupted or failing states where dysfunction is too rampant to permit effective internal oversight, including by the judiciary. A central argument in favour of international criminal justice institutions concerns their status as outsiders to conflict situations, because this outsider status is in fact what permits them to speak truth—that is, justice—to power. Thus, one might expect that hybrid tribunals applying ICL content and local procedure will be caught between ICL's ideological commitment to ending impunity and the particularized and fraught question of judging the sovereign.

In this contested environment, the prosecution and conviction of former Chadian head of state Hissène Habré by an ad hoc, hybrid tribunal in Senegal was momentous. The Extraordinary African Chambers (EAC), a cooperative effort supported by Western governments, the AU, Chad, and Senegal, was a temporary tribunal nestled in Senegal's local juridical architecture that applied ICL to try Habré. The outcome of a twenty-five-year saga by Chadian victims groups and international non-governmental organizations (NGOs) to bring Habré to justice, the EAC was novel in several ways. It was the first court set up in one country to try the leader of another, and the first African application of universal jurisdiction. Despite these characteristics, the EAC's greatest acclaim came from being a deliberately African institution successfully prosecuting and convicting a former head of state. Other such attempts have always been the purview of institutions such as the Special Court for Sierra Leone (SCSL), in which the power was weighted to international actors, and the ICC.

The following sections explore the question of what the trial of the former Chadian President before the EAC reveals about current resistance to sovereign impunity on the African continent. Section 11.2 considers the question of pluralism, or fragmentation as its deterrents would have it, regarding questions of sovereign immunity and impunity in ICL. Section 11.3 traces the creation of the EAC as Habré's victims, human rights proponents, and sympathetic states worked to make Habré answer for the crimes committed under his regime. Section 11.4 considers the EAC's impact on the pluralist discourse surrounding sovereign immunity/impunity under ICL, and concludes with an examination of specific elements of the EAC's practice that should be considered in the ongoing discussion of how hybrid tribunals can identify best practices to resolving normative and political juridical conflicts.

11.2 Discourses on Sovereign Immunity

Carsten Stahn and Larissa van den Herik[3] have called ICL a 'jack in the box' based on its pluralism and dynamism, noting that ICL exists in a constantly developing confluence of international law, human rights, and criminal justice. International criminal law emerges from varying regimes, which include ad hoc courts, hybrid tribunals, and the ICC. It is in conversation with other legal regimes, including international, regional, and domestic judicial bodies. This multiplicity of sources and norms leads to diverse legal content and a near constant evolution. Given that predictability and transparency are central elements of legal regimes, ICL's dynamism risks challenging the legitimacy of its regime and the institutions applying it. Theorists concerned with what they identify as ICL's 'fragmentation' note that ICL's dynamism and diversity challenge distinctions between punishment and justice, further challenging legitimacy.[4]

The application of ideas regarding legal pluralism drawn from diverse domestic sources[5] has been applied to the debate regarding ICL's 'pluralism', 'fragmentation', 'heterogeneity',[6] or 'diversification' for over two decades, and many volumes.[7] Beyond the juridical discussion regarding how legitimacy in a dynamic judicial system is achieved, there are also normative concerns. International criminal law applies what Günther Teubner calls 'sociological natural law'.[8] Here natural law

[3] Carsten Stahn and Larissa van den Herik, 'Fragmentation, Diversification and '3D' Legal Pluralism: International Criminal Law as the Jack-in-the-Box?' in Larissa van den Herik and Carsten Stahn (eds), *The Diversification and Fragmentation of International Criminal Law* (Martinus Nijhoff 2012).

[4] Alexander KA Greenwalt, 'The Pluralism of International Criminal Law (2011) 86 Indiana Law Journal 1063.

[5] Sally Engle Merry, 'Legal Pluralism' (1988) 22 Law & Society Review 869; John Griffiths, 'What is Legal Pluralism?' (1986) 24 Journal of Legal Pluralism 1.

[6] Elies van Sliedregt, 'Pluralism in International Criminal Law' (2011) 25 Leiden Journal of International Law 847.

[7] See, eg, ILC, 'Fragmentation of International Law: Difficulties arising from the diversification and expansion of International Law: Report of the study group of the International Law Commission' (13 April 2006) UN Doc A/CN.4/L.682; Martti Koskenniemi and Paivi Leino, 'Fragmentation of International Law? Postmodern Anxieties' (2002) 15 Leiden Journal of International Law 553; Gerhard Hafner, 'Pros and Cons Ensuing From Fragmentation of International Law' (2004) 25 Michigan Journal of International Law 849; Bruno Simma, 'Fragmentation in a Positive Light' (2004) 25 Michigan Journal of International Law 845; Andreas Fischer-Lescano and Gunther Teubner, 'Regime-Collisions: The Vain Search for Legal Unity in the Fragmentation of Global Law' (2005) 25 Michigan Journal of International Law 999; Eyal Benvenisti and George W Downs, 'The Empire's New Clothes: Political Economy and the Fragmentation of International Law' (2007) 60 Stanford Law Review 595; Pierre Marie Dupuy, 'The Danger of Fragmentation or Unification of the International Legal System and the International Court of Justice' (1999) 31 New York University Journal of International Law and Politics 791; Georges Abi Saab, 'Fragmentation or Unification: Some Concluding Remarks' (1999) 31 NYU Journal of International Law and Politics 919; William A Schabas, 'Synergy or Fragmentation? International Criminal Law and the European Convention on Human Rights' (2011) 9 Journal of International Criminal Justice 609.

[8] Gunther Teubner, 'Exogenous Self-Binding: How National and International Courts Contribute to Transnational Constitutionalization' in Giancarlo Corsi, Elena Esposito, and Alberto Febbrajo (eds), *Transconstitutionalism* (Ashgate 2015).

can be contrasted against positive law, a jurisprudence grounded in legislative acts and answering to a legislatively determined *Grundnorm*. International criminal law appeals to natural-law grounded universalist notions of 'justice'.

The development of ICL has followed this 'sociological natural law' progression: ICL, first articulated at the Nuremberg and Tokyo tribunals following World War II, has sought to capture and define the limits of universally recognized state criminality. From the categories of war crimes, crimes against humanity, aggression, and (quickly following the first military tribunals) genocide, modern ICL, operationalized through multiple institutions, has developed a procedure and jurisprudence developing the content and limitations of those crimes. In its development, ICL has challenged two inter-related intellectual principles: the principle of legality, and the principle of sovereign rule.

The principle of legality looks backwards to establish law through articulated doctrine and rules. International criminal law's brand of sociological natural law looks forwards, however, to a universality we either share or we *should come to share*. International criminal law has developed a non-derogable jurisprudence, rooting its legitimacy in the progressive nature of its practice.[9] These non-derogable standards, when practised, in effect affix a strict liability standard to ICL's crime base.[10]

The problem of sovereign immunity versus sovereign impunity under ICL resides precisely in ICL's legitimation through non-derogability. International criminal law has not—and in truth cannot—draw sharp lines between conduct which is criminalized and that which is not. This is because some of what constitutes a 'legitimate state interest' (a standard explored in case law from the International Criminal Tribunal for the Former Yugoslavia (ICTY)[11]) will not be synonymous with good state behaviour. States continuously engage in what Brad Roth calls 'ruthless' behaviour,[12] and the distinction between 'ruthless' and 'criminal' behaviour is somewhat fluid, somewhat subjective, and almost always retroactive. International criminal law is replete with cases where individuals, performing their duties to sovereign states, have found themselves criminally liable for conduct that is criminal solely due to the illegality of the state purpose it serves. In other words, individuals whose acts are not per se criminal (unlike torture or murder or rape) but whose acts rather serve a state purpose that is, or comes to be seen as, illegitimate can find

[9] Kerstin Bree Carlson, 'International Criminal Law and Its Paradoxes: Implications for Institutions and Practice' [2017] Journal of Law and Courts 33.

[10] Kerstin Bree Carlson, *Model(ing) Justice: Perfecting the Promise of International Criminal Law* (Cambridge University Press 2018).

[11] See, eg, *Prosecutor v Blaškić* (Judgment on the request of the Republic of Croatia for review of the decision of Trial Chamber II of 18 July 1997) IT-94-14 (29 October 1997) [66] (discussing legitimate state 'sovereignty, security or national interests'); see also discussion in Sarah Williams, Hannah Woolaver, and Emma Palmer, *The Amicus Curiae in International Criminal Justice* (Bloomsbury 2020).

[12] Brad B Roth. 'Coming to Terms with Ruthlessness: Sovereign Equality, Global Pluralism, and the Limits of International Criminal Justice' (2010) 8 Santa Clara Journal of International Law 231.

themselves in violation of ICL. In this formulation, protecting state borders can be a legitimate interest, but East German border guards who shot defectors from the East German state were later found to have committed murder, because protecting the East German state from defectors was, at the end of the Cold War and upon German reunification, determined not to be a legitimate state interest.[13] Likewise as regards the planning of military operations: Croatian military operations designed to take back Croatian territory from rebel Croatian Serbs were legitimate military operations only in so far as those operations did not also encourage population movements. In this formulation, opening a corridor of non-military action through which civilians might escape hostilities can be criminal, as it foresees and enables ethnic cleansing.[14]

The tensions between ICL's progressive legitimation structure (wherein ICL contributes to building 'a more just world'[15]) and sovereign constraints on the content of legality are explored in the *Arrest Warrant Case* before the International Court of Justice (ICJ). In that case, Belgium had issued an international arrest warrant for the sitting Congolese Minister of Foreign Affairs in connection with atrocity crimes committed in Congo under its universal jurisdiction statute. The Court held that the minister enjoyed immunity from prosecution, and set out four situations in which a government official might be prosecuted: in domestic courts under domestic law; if immunity is waived by the state they serve; after leaving office; if prosecuted by recognized international tribunals such as the ICTY, the International Criminal Tribunal for Rwanda (ICTR), or the ICC.[16] In the latter instance, the specificity of the authority of the tribunal appears paramount: that UN tribunals are established through joint resolutions, and the Rome Statute specifically addresses the lifting of immunity in its Article 27, paragraph 2. In a joint separate opinion, Judges Higgens, Kooijman, and Buergenthal defined the 'balancing of interests' inherent in the tension between law as a constraint on state action and the rights inherent in sovereign order:

> On the one scale, we find the interest of the community of mankind to prevent and stop impunity for perpetrators of grave crimes against its members; on the other, there is the interest of the community of States to allow them to act freely on

[13] *Streletz, Kessler and Krenz v Germany* (Judgment) App nos 34044/96, 35532/97 and 44801/98 (ECtHR, 22 March 2001); see also Rudolf Geiger, 'The German Border Guard Cases and International Human Rights' (1998) 9 European Journal of International Law 540.

[14] *Prosecutor v Gotovina & Markač* (Judgment) IT-06-90 (16 November 2012): see also *Prosecutor v Popović et al* (Judgment) IT-05-88 AC (30 January 2015) (the Bosnian Serb commander who opened a column for Bosnian Muslims to escape, thereby saving them from genocide in the environs in Srebrenica, was found guilty of ethnic cleansing).

[15] This phrase is engraved on a plaque in the entrance to the ICC. See discussion in Kertsin Bree Carlson, *The Justice Laboratory: International Law in Africa* (Chatham House/Brookings Institution Press 2022).

[16] *Case Concerning the Arrest Warrant of 11 April 2000 (Democratic Republic of Congo v Belgium)* (Judgment) [2002] ICJ Rep 3 [65].

> the inter-State level without unwarranted interference... Moreover, a trend is discernible that in a world which increasingly rejects impunity for the most repugnant offences, the attribution of responsibility and accountability is becoming firmer, the possibility for the assertion of jurisdiction wider and the availability of immunity as a shield more limited. The law of privileges and immunities, however, retains its importance since immunities are granted to high State officials to guarantee the proper functioning of the network of mutual inter-State relations, which is of paramount importance for a well-ordered and harmonious international system.[17]

In this analysis, the balance is not between former and sitting representatives of state, but rather between the protection of core rights (through anti-impunity measures) and ordered governance (through preserving the immunity of the sovereign). It is not clear that distinguishing between former and current state representatives would impact the Court's analysis of 'the proper functioning of the network of mutual inter-State relations' when considered in light of the problem of 'ruthless' state behaviour, however. That is because, in the final analysis, the problem of sovereign immunity versus impunity under ICL confronts the age-old conundrum of international law's lack of sovereign authority. In domestic systems, the sovereign meets out justice, and through this action, comes to define what 'justice' is.[18] Within domestic systems, there is a final, irrefutable sovereign in a person, an office, or a principle. Outside the confines of domestic systems, this does not exist. International criminal law's reliance on principles of universality, sociological natural law, or non-derogable norms as a shortcut to an ultimate irrefutable sovereign ultimately fails because the legitimacy or illegitimacy of state action is itself pluralist.

The following sections consider elements of pluralism in the Habré trial, in order to analyse more fundamental questions of how developing ICL practices, in particular in hybrid courts, implicate the norms driving challenges to sovereign impunity.

11.3 The President on Trial: Hissène Habré Before the Extraordinary African Chambers

On 28 April 2017, the Appeals Chamber of the Extraordinary African Chambers upheld the Trial Chamber's judgment of the prior year sentencing former Chadian

[17] *Case Concerning the Arrest Warrant of 11 April 2000 (Democratic Republic of Congo v Belgium)* (Judgment) [2002] ICJ Rep 3 [65] (separate opinion of Judges Higgens, Kooijmans and Buergenthal [75]).

[18] Anne Sa'Adah, 'Regime Change: Lessons from Germany on Justice, Institution Building, and Democracy' (2006) 50 Journal of Conflict Resolution 303.

head of state Hissène Habré to life imprisonment. In what has been characterized as 'a milestone for justice in Africa',[19] the EAC harnessed local expertise and international criminal legal content to complete its work and reach judgment. A cooperative effort supported by the AU, Chad, Senegal, and several Western governments, the EAC has been celebrated as potentially modelling a 'third way' for international criminal justice between expensive, contested international processes and locally conceded immunity. Across Africa, leadership has remained an assurance of impunity, resisting global trends to the contrary.[20] Habré himself successfully avoided prosecution for more than two decades. Thus for some observers the EAC's capacity to put Habré on trial and convict him for atrocities committed during his reign represents a seminal African example of the 'revolution' of human rights in the twentieth century,[21] where the recognition of core human rights trumps political might.

Although charged with trying those 'most responsible'[22] for the commission of atrocities in Chad, the EAC was unable to secure the participation of the five other individuals named with Habré,[23] and was nearly dismantled when it attempted to explore questions which might have implicated Chad's then-president, Idriss Déby.[24] For his part, Déby—at one time a central supporter of the EAC—came to actively undermine the EAC's investigations after initially signing a cooperation agreement and providing the largest tranche of the EAC's financing. In other words, instead of representing a challenge to sovereign impunity, the EAC arguably reifies the capacity of the sovereign to define the content of justice,[25] as demonstrated by the Tribunal's incapacity to indict or try any defendants whose trial was not sanctioned by Chad's then president.[26]

The following section briefly lays out the history of the pursuit of Hissène Habré and the construction of the EAC, in preparation for Section 11.4, which considers some of the meaningful pluralities emerging from the EAC's practice.

[19] New York Times editorial board, 'A Milestone for Justice in Africa' (*New York Times*, 22 July 2015) <http://www.nytimes.com/2015/07/22/opinion/a-milestone-for-justice-in-africa.html?emc=edit_tnt_20150722&nlid=9510037&tntemail0=y&_r=1> accessed 25 January 2024.

[20] Ellen E Lutz and Caitlin Reiger (eds), *Prosecuting Heads of State* (Cambridge University Press 2009).

[21] Kathryn Sikkink, *The Justice Cascade: How Human Rights Prosecutions Are Changing World Politics* (WW Norton & Company 2011); Philip Allott, *Eunomia: New Order for a New World* (Oxford University Press 1990).

[22] *Habré Case* (Judgment) Chambres Africaines Extraordinaires (30 May 2016).

[23] See *Prosecutor v Habré* (Indictment) Extraordinary African Chambers (13 February 2015).

[24] Interview with EAC participant (Dakar, Senegal, March 2016); notes on file with author.

[25] Ruti Teitel, *Transitional justice* (Oxford University Press 2000); Sa'Adah (n 18).

[26] Julien Seroussi, 'L'internationalization de la justice trasitionnelle: l'affaire Hissene Habre' (2006) 30 Critique Internationale 83; Moriba Magassouba, *Tchad-Sénégal La Machination acte II* (Chaka 2015)

11.3.1 Getting to the EAC

The seeds of Habré's eventual 2017 conviction were sown in a report commissioned by Habré's one-time collaborator turned political rival and successor, Idriss Déby, in 1992. Upon ousting Habré in 1990, Déby made 'justice' a central piece of his ruling platform. As part of this pursuit, one of Déby's first acts of office was to appoint a truth commission to investigate Habré's misdeeds. Habré governed Chad from 1982 to 1990, coming to power as part of a continuous unrest that commenced with Chad's independence in 1960. His time in power coincided with the end of the Cold War and the re-configuration of global order. Habré was supplied with foreign money, equipment, and know-how, principally by the United States and France, in order to contain the Libyan threat on Chad's northern border. This containment was performed, in part, through a repressive state apparatus and secret police, which Habré also used to consolidate and retain power. Beginning in 1982, Habré's regime targeted individuals belonging to specific ethnic groups. The targeting shifted as considerations of the threat to the regime shifted. Individuals were arrested, tortured, and imprisoned for long periods in dire conditions: the most infamous Habré-era prison, 'la piscine', was a concrete covered former swimming pool, where inhuman temperatures, non-existent sanitation, and severe overcrowding killed many prisoners.

The truth commission Dèby constituted was under-equipped and precariously situated.[27] It nonetheless managed to produce a published report that found Habré guilty of several violations of international humanitarian law, including genocide.[28] Furthermore, the materials gathered by the Truth Commission in large part constituted the evidence against Habré. For example, the Truth Commission found that Habré's regime had killed 40,000 people. It made this determination based on 3,700 verified deaths, which the commission, without giving further detail or rationale, determined represented 'about 10 percent of Habré's actual damage' and then rounded up.[29] This estimation of the damage of Habré's regime has never been challenged or verified. Rather it was simply adopted as an estimate during Habré's trial before the EAC.[30]

[27] See discussion in Sharon Weill, Kim Thuy Seelinger, and Kerstin Bree Carlson (eds), *The President on Trial: Prosecuting Hissène Habré* (Oxford University Press 2020).

[28] *Les crimes et detournments de l'ex President Habré et de ses complices* (L'Harmattan 1993).

[29] The Commission's ultimate estimate of 40,000 dead is based on the 3,780 people it concretely determined were killed (69); its estimate that such number represented one-tenth of the actual damage done by Habré (69); and a rounding up from 37,000 to 40,000 (97). See *Les crimes et detournments de l'ex President Habré et de ses complices* (n 28) 13.

[30] Human Rights Watch and two judicial fact-finding missions found numbers far below the 40,000 figure. Human Rights Watch, for example, found that 1,208 people were killed or died in detention. Human Rights Watch, 'Chad: Alleged Habré Accomplices to Stand Trial' (10 November 2014) https://www.hrw.org/news/2014/11/10/chad-alleged-habre-accomplices-stand-trial accessed 25 January 2024.

In 2008, Dèby's regime again sought to bring Habré to justice when the criminal court in N'Djaména, Chad tried Habré in absentia and sentenced him to death for crimes against humanity.[31]

Outside of Chad, the history of the judicial case against Hissène Habré began in 2000, when Chadian victims, assisted by the international NGO Human Rights Watch, filed a complaint against Habré in Dakar District Court.[32] In the wake of the 1998 Pinochet case in the UK, Reed Brody of Human Rights Watch began speaking publicly about the value of trying a case under universal jurisdiction on the African continent. The case against Hissène Habré had all the makings for success, including an active, organized victims' association and a potentially sympathetic, and highly capable, state (Senegal). The case that Human Rights Watch and the victims attempted to bring in Senegal was dismissed on jurisdictional grounds, however.[33] In 2001, this decision was confirmed by Senegal's *Cour de Cassation*, which ruled that Senegal lacked jurisdiction over Habré because the crimes were not committed in Senegal.[34]

Although the legal reasoning in the Senegalese judgments is sound and predictable, politics certainly played a part in protecting Habré against early prosecution attempts. One of Habré's lawyers was also counsel to Senegal's President Wade, and also served as Wade's foreign minister for a time.[35] Wade was not indifferent to the possibility of holding Habré accountable for his crimes, he just nominated that it occur elsewhere, naming Belgium as a possible site.[36] In 2002, under its then-existing expansive universal jurisdiction statute,[37] Belgian *Juge d'Instruction* Daniel Fransen visited Chad with an investigative team on a *Commission Rogataire* to collect evidence. In 2005, after a four-year investigation, the Belgian court issued an international arrest warrant against Habré, who was subsequently arrested in Dakar. Ultimately, however, the Dakar Appeals Court found it had no jurisdiction to rule on the extradition request and Habré was released.[38]

Meanwhile, beginning in 2001, civil society groups applied to the Committee Against Torture (CAT) for recognition of crimes committed in Chad during

[31] International Crimes Database, 'Hisséne Habré' <http://www.internationalcrimesdatabase.org/Case/762> accessed 10 January 2017.

[32] See discussion in Weill, Seelinger, and Carlson (n 27).

[33] *Ministere Public v Hissene Habré*, Cour d'Appel Dakar, Chambre d'Accussation, Arret No 135 (7 April 2000).

[34] *Souleyman Guengueng v Hissène Habré*, Cour de Cassation, Criminal Arret No 14 (20 March 2001) (Sen).

[35] See Africa Confidential, 'Madické Niang' <http://www.africa-confidential.com/whos-who-profile/id/3232/Madick%C3%A9_Niang> accessed 10 January 2017.

[36] See Human Rights Watch, 'Senegal: Chad asks for the extradition of Hisséne Habré to Belgium' (22 July 2011) <https://www.hrw.org/news/2011/07/22/senegal-chad-asks-extradition-hissene-habre-belgium> accessed 10 January 2017.

[37] Steven R Ratner, 'Belgium's War Crimes Statute: A Postmortem' (2003) 97 American Journal of International Law 888.

[38] *Souleyman Guengueng v Hissène Habré*, Cour de Cassation, Criminal Arret No 14 (20 March 2001) (Sen).

Habré's rule. In 2006, the CAT released a decision granting the application and recommending that Senegal either prosecute Habré or extradite him.[39] Responding to this growing international judicial pressure, the AU in turn leaned on Senegal to deal with Habré[40] and in 2008, Senegal altered its constitution to permit the retroactive criminal punishment of core crimes (crimes against humanity, genocide, war crimes) with an eye to addressing the lacunae in Senegalese law that had precluded indicting Habré.[41] In turn, in 2008 Habré brought a complaint before the judicial arm of the Economic Community of West African States (ECOWAS), contesting retroactive application, which would violate the legality principle. In 2010, ECOWAS ruled that Habré could not be judged by a Senegalese court but rather that the court must be international in character.[42] Likewise, in 2009 the Habré case became the subject of the first judgment of the newly constituted African Court of Human and People's Rights[43] (ACtHPR). One of Habré's former ministers filed a case protesting Senegal's constitutional amendment 'authorizing retroactive application of its criminal laws, with a view to trying exclusively and solely Mr. Hissène Habré'; the application was rejected by the ACtHPR.

Ultimately, the critical push forward for the EAC consisted in two serendipitous events; the 2012 decision by the ICJ, following the claim brought by Belgium, which held that Senegal must either prosecute or extradite Habré,[44] and regime change in Senegal. Abdoulaye Wade, who had served two terms as president, attempted to challenge Senegalese and AU policy regarding term limits by seeking a third term. He was ultimately defeated by Mbacke Sall in April 2012. With Sall's election, obstacles preventing Habré's prosecution disappeared, and an agreement was signed between Senegal, Chad, and the AU creating the EAC,[45] an ad hoc, international tribunal situated in Senegal, applying international legal content and operating under local rules of procedure. The EAC's budget of 8.6 million euros was financed by a group including the AU, the EU, and Chad, which made the largest contribution (USD 3 million).

[39] CAT, 'Decisions of the Committee Against Torture under Article 22 of the Convention against Torture and Other Cruel, Inhuman or Degrading Treatment or Punishment' (19 May 2006) UN Doc CAT/C/36/D181/2001, paras 9.6–9.12.

[40] Specifically, in its 7th session July 2006.

[41] *loi* n° 2008–23 du 25 juillet 2008 de portant insertion d'un article 664 bis dans le Code de Procédure pénale (25 July 2008) (SEN); *loi* n° 2008–30 du 7 août 2008 de modifiant les articles 7, 63, 68, 71, et 82 de la Constitution (Sen).

[42] *Hissèin Habré v Republic of Senegal* (Judgment) ECW/CCJ/APP/07/08 (10 November 2010).

[43] *Michelot Yogogombaye v the Republic of Senegal* Application No 001/2008.

[44] *Questions relating to the Obligation to Prosecute or Extradite (Belgium v Senegal)* (Judgment) (20 July 2012) 51 ILM 706.

[45] Agreement of the Establishment of the Extraordinary African Chambers Within the Sengalese Judicial System Between the Government of the Republic of Senegal and the African Union (signed 22 August 2012) (2013) 52 ILM 1024.

11.3.2 The EAC as a hybrid tribunal

The EAC was a hybrid tribunal applying a mix of international and local law. It was not the first tribunal to mix local and international procedure or professionals: other experimental hybrids include the Special Tribunal for Lebanon (STL);[46] the Extraordinary Chambers in the Courts of Cambodia (ECCC);[47] the SCSL;[48] Special Panels and Serious Crimes Unit in East-Timor and Regulation 64 Panels in the Courts of Kosovo.[49] Hybrid tribunals typically imagine an informational flow from the international to the local, with international actors, legal content, and practices being locally transplanted.[50] The EAC, however, remained a local court, staffed almost entirely by local judicial professionals.

The EAC's *Chambre d'Instruction* was comprised of four working judges and two alternates, all Senegalese. The *Juges d'Instruction* completed nineteen months of work, which began in March 2013. They specifically declined external assistance, turning down offers from NGOs and Western governments to provide clerks or others with knowledge of ICL, based on a sense that the legitimacy of the EAC as a local Senegalese institution might be compromised by outside judicial assistance. Instead, in the early months, before receiving specific instructions from the prosecution, the *Juges d'Instruction* read widely ICL judgments, largely from the ICTY, to gain proficiency in the topic.[51] This proficiency is on display in the indictment eventually produced by the *Chambre d'Instruction*, which considers joint criminal enterprise and command responsibility at length.[52]

The main purpose of the *Chambre d'Instruction* was to investigate claims of crimes. This included four '*Commissions Rogatoires*', which were investigatory trips to Chad to collect evidence. Three were scheduled in advance, a fourth took place to answer outstanding questions, and a possible fifth trip was cancelled by Chad's determination to cease cooperating, due to the investigation's perceived threat to Chadian president Idriss Déby. Additionally, one *Commission Rogatoire* to France to interview one of Habré's lieutenants was also undertaken. The investigatory work that the judges accomplished in Chad was done with the assistance of

[46] See STL, 'Home' <https://www.stl-tsl.org/en/> accessed 25 January 2024.

[47] See Extraordinary Chambers in the Courts of Cambodia, 'Home' <https://www.eccc.gov.kh/en> accessed 25 January 2024.

[48] See Residual Special Court for Sierra Leone, 'Home' www.rscsl.org/ accessed 25 January 2024.

[49] See also summaries regarding hybridity at Hybrid Justice, 'The Hybrid Justice Project' <htttp://hybridustice.com> accessed 25 January 2024; International Crimes Database, 'Hybrid' <http://www.internationalcrimesdatabase.org/Courts/Hybrid> accessed 25 January 2024 and discussion in Laura Dickinson, 'The Promise of Hybrid Courts' (2003) 97 American Journal of International Law 295; see also Aaron Fichtelberg, *Hybrid Tribunals: A Comparative Examination* (Springer 2015).

[50] United Nations High Commissioner for Human Rights (OHCHR), 'Rule of Law Tools for Post-Conflict States: Maximizing the Legacy of Hybrid Courts' (2008) <http://www.ohchr.org/Documents/Publications/HybridCourts.pdf> accessed 25 January 2024.

[51] Interview with *Juge d'Instruction* (May 2016), notes on file with author.

[52] *Ordonnance de renvoi du Non-Lieu Partiel et de transmission des Pieces au Procureur General* (3 September 2014).

Chadian lawyers and intermediaries, who carried out interviews under the supervision of the *Juges d'Instruction*.[53] The appeals body for the Investigatory Chamber, the *Chambre d'Accusation*, heard a few limited appeals from the *Instruction* phase[54] and dissolved at the end of that phase, together with the *Chambre d'Instruction*.

From this point, the trial progressed to the *Chambre d'Assises*, the Trial Chamber. There were three judges assigned to the Trial Chamber: two from Senegal, and the third, the President of the Court, Kam, hailed from Burkina Faso and had spent more than a decade working for the ICTR. These judges were assisted by three clerks, two local Senegalese (both of whom were working towards or had received doctorates in ICL, but neither of whom had experience in its practice), and one French clerk with a decade of experience before international criminal tribunals. Following the Senegalese system, *parties civiles* (civil parties, ie victims) participated in the process through representation by counsel; at the EAC, victims appeared in two groups, represented by two different teams of attorneys.

The EAC began its second stage of work, opening the trial before the *Chambre d'Assises*, in July 2015. Habré had to be forced into the courtroom, carried bodily in the arms of a security agent. This spectacle caused several local attorneys present to quit the courtroom in protest;[55] trials in absentia are permissible under Senegalese procedure, so some felt that the enforcement of a defendant's presence in the courtroom was itself a violation of the defendant's rights.[56] At the opening of the trial, Habré's attorneys refused to address the Court, as they contested the EAC's legitimacy to try Habré. Apprised of this beforehand, the Trial Chamber judges had worked with the Dakar bar on a list of names of local attorneys who might be appointed by the EAC to represent the client. Thus the opening of the trial against Hissène Habré in July 2015 ended in a forty-five-day recess to allow the *Commis d'Office*, the court-appointed attorneys, to review materials.

After its forty-five-day recess, the trial re-opened in September 2015, and ran until February 2016. Witness testimony was heard between September and December, and final arguments were made in February.[57] The judges heard ninety-three fact witnesses. Testimony followed a timeline of persecution of ethnic groups over time, recounting the history of Habré's reign through waves of targeted attacks on certain Chadian populations. As regards Habré's targeting of

53 Interview with *Juge d'Instruction* (May 2016), notes on file with author.

54 These included procedure questions, such as whether Hissène Habré's turban could be forcibly removed (the determination was no), and whether the defence might be allowed to receive a copy of the dossier and not simply be allowed to review it as was typically the case under Senegalese procedure (the determination was yes).

55 Interview (Dakar, Senegal, May 2016), notes on file with author.

56 ibid.

57 Daily summaries of witness testimony are available in English on the website of Trust Africa, a local NGO monitoring the trial. Trust Africa, 'Hissène Habré Trial before the Extraordinary African Chambers: December hearings' (5 February 2016) <https://www.ijmonitor.org/2016/02/hissene-habre-trial-before-the-extraordinary-african-chambers-december-hearings/> accessed 25 January 2024.

Arabs and foreigners, this was not driven by particularized ethnic animus so much as by groups' imagined support of political opposition. The EAC also heard expert witness testimony relating to the political situation in Chad and the death rate in Habré-era jails.

Perhaps the most shocking testimony, or certainly the least expected, came from a victim participant who was testifying as a witness. While testifying about sexual violence in the dessert army camp Oudi-Doum, Khadija Hassan Zidane made an allegation she had not voiced before: she testified that Habré had personally raped her four times at the presidential palace before she was sent to the camp.[58] Kaltouma Deffala, another witness testifying to rape in the army camp, verified that Zidane had told her about Habré's rape when she arrived at the camp.

The judgment was pronounced on 30 May 2016.[59] Habré was found guilty of personally, and as a member of a joint criminal enterprise, committing crimes against humanity, torture, and war crimes. He was also found personally guilty of raping Khadija Hassan Zidane. In its judgment, the Trial Chamber found Zidane's testimony credible and, citing international criminal case law saying that corroborating evidence for rape is not necessary, determined that Habré bore personal guilt for rape.

Shortly after the judgment, the *Commis d'Office* announced its appeal. Habré's own personal lawyers also spoke out against the judgment, echoing challenges to legitimacy and judicial appointments in the EAC that comprised the substance of the appeal brought by the *Commis d'Office.*

In the fall of 2016 the Appellate Chamber began its work, comprised of Senegalese judges and headed by Ougadeye Wafi of Burkina Faso. Briefs were submitted and two days of hearings were held in January 2017; the judgment was rendered in April 2017.[60] The Appeals Chamber judgment upheld the life sentence delivered by the Trial Chamber in May 2016, reaffirming the Trial Chamber's legal findings with respect to all crimes except its conclusion that Habré had personally raped the prisoner, Khadja Hassan Zidane: this charge it overturned on procedural grounds, finding that charging Habré with direct commission of rape was an improper requalification of the charges. Under Senegalese procedure, charges are fixed at the end of the investigative phase prior to trial. Facts may be requalified as to their legal definition, but no new facts may be added.

The Habré trial was generally celebrated for its verdict and its means of working. Victims received their day in court, and the promise (if not the materiality) of

[58] Human Rights Watch, 'Senegal: At Hissène Habre Trial, Sexual Slavery Accounts' (10 October 2015) <https://www.hrw.org/news/2015/10/22/senegal-hissene-habre-trial-sexual-slavery-accounts> accessed 25 January 2024.

[59] *Ministère Public c Hissein Habré* (Judgment) (30 May 2016).

[60] *Le Proccureur General c Hissein Habre* (Arrêt) (27 Avril 2017).

reparations.[61] Habré himself was sentenced to life in prison (where, during the COVID-19 pandemic, he died). The EAC worked to deadline and within its budget, managing not to exhaust its funds and contributing its unspent monies, approximately USD 50,000,[62] to a nascent reparations fund for victims.

11.4 Analysis: The EAC and Sovereign Power

As a novel hybrid applying international legal content through local legal procedural rules, the EAC faced several greenfield questions, from how to proceed with the investigative phase after Chad ceased cooperating to whether Habré should be forced to attend his own trial. The EAC often departed from Senegalese criminal procedural rules in answering these questions, even though under the Statute, Senegalese procedure was always to apply in cases of silence. These moments of pluralism, particularly as regards the doctrinal construction of the case against Habré, are also instructive in an assessment of how the Habré trial might impact normative discourses regarding sovereign immunity.

11.4.1 Criminal law theory in ICL

Criminal law is theoretically divided between its 'general' and 'special' parts. The special part consists of specific criminal offenses, and categorizes them in families.[63] The general part is comprised of doctrines (insanity; necessity; provocation, etc) applicable to some or all of the special part. Theoretical scholarship on criminal law, following the work of HLA Hart in the mid-twentieth century,[64] has typically focused on the general part of criminal law. Recent theoretical criminal law scholarship, however, has advocated greater attention for criminal law's special part. In a 2005 edited volume, several authors explored movement between the categories describing the special part.[65] Nicola Lacey's work has critiqued organization and theorization more generally.[66] There has also been more consideration

[61] Nader Iskandar Diab, 'Challenges in the Implementation of the Reparation Award against Hissein Habré: Can the Spell of Unenforceable Awards across the Globe be Broken?' (2018) 16 Journal of International Criminal Justice 141.

[62] Interview, *greffier* (February 2018), notes on file with author.

[63] John Gardner, 'On the General Part of the Criminal Law' in RA Duff (ed), *Philosophy and the Criminal Law: Principle and Critique* (Cambridge University Press 1998).

[64] HLA Hart, *Punishment and Responsibility* (Oxford University Press 1968).

[65] RA Duff and Stuart Green (eds), *Defining Crimes: Essays on The Special Part of the Criminal Law* (Oxford University Press 2005).

[66] Nicola Lacey, 'Legal Constructions of Crime' in Mike Maguire, Rod Morgan and Robert Reiner (eds), *The Oxford Handbook of Criminology* (3rd edn, Oxford University Press 2002); Nicola Lacey, 'Contingency, Coherence and Conceptualism: Reflections on the Encounter between Critique and 'the Philosophy of the Criminal Law' in RA Duff (ed), *Philosophy and the Criminal Law* (Cambridge University Press 1998).

of the philosophical challenges occasioned by strict liability,[67] which is an important theoretical base in elements of ICL practice.[68]

At the same time that domestic criminal law theorists have been calling for new attention regarding the organization and normative legitimation of criminal law, the law and practice of ICL has been developing as a field.[69] Numerous volumes considering the theory and practice of international criminal tribunals have been produced in the past two decades, following the resurgence and explosive growth of ICL.[70]

Although the practice of the ad hoc tribunals for the former Yugoslavia and Rwanda, and the growing jurisprudence of the permanent ICC, have created rich and extensive materials regarding the doctrine and application of ICL, theoretical work regarding the doctrinal coherence of ICL is arguably still in its infancy. Although debates regarding the form and content of ICL accompanied the ICTs at Nuremberg and Tokyo and followed the historical considerations of these tribunals, it is only with the resurgence of ICL as a mechanism of transitional justice, that is, ICL as a global policy directive, that theoretical work regarding the socially constitutive potential of ICL has developed.[71]

ICL scholars have begun debating the necessity of establishing 'general' and 'special' parts of ICL. Proponents of developing an established distinction between the general and special part of ICL include Elies van Sliedregt, who advocated the distinction in a 2007 article,[72] and Kai Ambos, who published a three-volume

[67] Andrew Simester (ed), *Appraising Strict Liability* (Oxford University Press 2005).

[68] Carlson (n 10).

[69] MJ Christiansen, 'From Symbolic Surge to Closing Courts: The Transformation of International Criminal Justice and its Professional Practices' (2015) 42 Journal of International Criminal Justice 609.

[70] See, eg, Robert Cryer and others, *An Introduction to International Criminal Law and Procedure* (3rd edn, Cambridge University Press 2014); Vladimir Tochilovsky, *Jurisprudence of the International Criminal Courts and the European Court of Human Rights: Procedure and Evidence* (Brill 2007); Vladimir Tochilovsky, 'The Nature and Evolution of the Rules of Procedure and Evidence' in Karima AA Khan, Caroline Buisman and Christopher Gosnell (eds), *Principles of Evidence in International Criminal Justice* (Oxford University Press 2010); Mohamed Shahabuddeen, *International Criminal Justice at the Yugoslav Tribunal: A Judge's Recollection* (Oxford University Press 2012); Alex Whiting, 'The ICTY as a Laboratory for International Criminal Procedure' in Bert Swart, Alexander Zahar, and Göran Sluiter (eds), *The Legacy of the International Criminal Tribunal for the Former Yugoslavia* (Oxford University Press 2011); Richard May and Marieke Wierda, *International Criminal Evidence* (Brill 2002); John D Jackson and Sarah J Summers, *The Internationalization of Criminal Evidence: Beyond the Common Law and Civil Law Traditions* (Cambridge University Press 2012); M Cherif Bassiouni, *Introduction to International Criminal Law* (Martinus Nijhoff 2012); José Doria, Hans-Peter Gasser and M Cherif Bassiouni (eds), *The Legal Regime of the International Criminal Court: Essays in Honour of Professor Igor Blishchenko* (Brill 2009).

[71] See, eg, Gerry Simpson, *Law, War and Crime: War Crimes, Trials and the Reinvention of International Law* (Polity 2013); Immi Tallgren and Thome Skouteris, *The New Histories of International Criminal Law* (Oxford University Press 2019); Darryl Robinson, *Justice in Extreme Cases: Criminal Law Theory Meets International Criminal Law* (Cambridge University Press 2020); Kerstin Bree Carlson, 'Agents & Agency in International Criminal Law: Prison Guards, Intent, and the "Special Part" of International Criminal Law' in Marina Aksenova, Elies van Sliedregt, and Steven Parmentier (eds), *Breaking the Cycle of Mass Atrocities: Criminology and Socio-Legal Approaches in International Criminal Law* (Hart 2019).

[72] Elies van Sliedregt, 'Joint Criminal Enterprise as a Pathway to Convicting Individuals for Genocide' (2007) 5 Journal of International Criminal Justice 184.

treatise establishing the distinction.[73] Volume one of Ambos's set appeared in 2013. In it, Ambos situates ICL historically in order to define, over the course of several targeted chapters, concepts, sources, and functions of ICL.

11.4.2 Assessing Habré's criminality

As discussed in Section 11.3, Habré ran a repressive state. The Chadian Truth Commission found him liable for crimes that included 'genocide', though the EAC declined to make this charge. It is undisputed that Habré held political and other prisoners captive in horrible jails where they were tortured, afforded no due process, and died. We also know that Habré oversaw several military campaigns, the most violent of which was 'black September' in 1984. During these campaigns, there were massacres in villages and people were raped.

ICL recognizes the core crimes of crimes against humanity; war crimes; genocide; and aggression. Habré was prosecuted for crimes against humanity, war crimes, and torture. This still leaves the question of commission, however. How to connect Habré, the individual in his particular position as head of state, to the crimes committed by his subordinates and/or in furtherance of his regime?

Definitions of commission—how crime is 'done'—are approached differently by different international criminal justice institutions. All international criminal courts face the question of how to assign guilt to those who have not directly perpetrated crime (those 'without blood on their hands'). Two main rival approaches have been developed at ICL: joint criminal enterprise 'co-perpetration', developed by the ICTY, and 'control of the crime' developed by the ICC.[74] The EAC did not engage this debate, resting its juridical analysis largely in the ICTY's jurisprudence.

The EAC Trial and Appeals Chambers took a 'belt and braces' approach to the question of how Habré 'did' his crimes, charging him under joint criminal enterprise, command responsibility, and direct commission. For Habré's court-appointed lawyers (*Commis d'Office*), however, only direct commission was familiar. Early arguments put forth by Habré's court-appointed lawyers, for example, focused on questions of Habré's knowledge, intent, and participation; Habré's lawyers sought to distinguish the acts of Habré's subordinates from Habré himself. It was lawyers for the victims who clarified for the *Commis d'Office*—as a professional courtesy—that arguments regarding specific knowledge or intent were unlikely to

[73] Kai Ambos, *Treatise on International Criminal Law: Volume 1: Foundations and General Part* (Oxford University Press 2013). Opponents include Alexander Greenawalt, who argues against defining a 'general part' for ICL because it would too obviously conflict with domestic systems. Alexander Greenawalt, "Pluralism in International Criminal Law" (2012) 25 Leiden Journal of International Law 847.

[74] Jens David Ohlin, 'Joint Criminal Confusion' (2009) 12 New Criminal Law Review 406; Barbara Goy, 'Individual Criminal Responsibility before the International Criminal Court: A Comparison with the *Ad Hoc* Tribunals' (2012) 12 International Criminal Law Review 1.

assist in Habré's defence, because under ICL, individual liability can be assessed based on the simple *foreseeability* of crimes arising from a collective endeavour.[75] Thus, while questions regarding the possibility of a vigorous, effective defence are always fraught in ICL in ways they are not in domestic criminal law proceedings,[76] problems adhering to the construction of a defence were particularly acute in the *Habré* trial.

One clash of the 'belt and braces' approach occurred over the question of Habré's culpability for sexual violence. Crimes involving sexual violence formed part of the initial Habré indictment. The investigating judges found instances of sexual violence in the testimonies of victims of Habré's regime, and characterized this violence in the indictment as 'torture'. In the indictment, these charges were made against agents under Habré's control, and Habré's culpability was assessed under the international law norms of command responsibility and joint criminal enterprise.

As the Habré trial progressed, a group of US law professors filed an *amicus curae* brief with the EAC urging the Court to qualify evidence of sexual violence beyond the proposed 'torture' charge. They urged the EAC to requalify the ways in which sexual violence was defined as criminal in the judgment and to find these acts in violation of customary international law. In its May 2016 judgment, the Trial Chamber convicted Habré of rape and sexual slavery as crimes against humanity and torture. The Trial Chamber found Habré guilty of these crimes in two ways: first, as a senior official who ordered or was aware of the crimes, and second, as a direct perpetrator. The 27 April 2017 Appeals Judgment reverses only Habré's personal rape conviction and appears to leave other legal requalifications made by the Trial Chamber intact.

The question that these examples of legal pluralism leave unaddressed, however, is the critical question of sovereign immunity, or the flexibility the sovereign has with regard to the fate of his peoples. For some observers, Habré is best understood as a '*chef de guerre*'[77]. His repressive state, designed to protect against Libyan aggression, is the reason that Chad still is a state, this argument would submit. Thus while Habré's politics were 'rough' (read: 'ruthless') they were perhaps not out of keeping with other kinds of rough politics that ensure continuation of the body politic. Another way to ask the question would be to consider how different Habré's leadership was from that of his one-time second who became head of state, Déby. In answering this question, one might consider the reach and scale of Habré's

[75] This is the standard that arises from Joint Criminal Enterprise jurisprudence; see, eg, *Prosecutor v Tadić* (ICTY Appeals Chamber) IT-94-1 (7 May 1997); see discussion in Kerstin Bree Carlson, 'Punishment, Legality, and Other Challenges of International Criminal Law' (2022) 23(1) International Criminal Law Review 123.

[76] Michael G Karnavas, 'The ICTY Legacy: A Defense Counsel's Perspective' (2011) 3 Goettingen Journal of International Law 1053.

[77] Interview radio journalist (May 2016), notes on file with author.

violence: in such case, the curious disagreement regarding numbers of dead noted in Section 11.3 (the 1,200 identified by Human Rights Watch, 3,700 identified by the 1992 Truth Commission, and 'established' though never corroborated circulating number of 40,000 dead) might become important.

In the Habré trial, the critical question regarding how ICL might address 'ruthless' state behaviour is left unanswered. Instead, although ICL is employed to target the humanitarian law violating practices of the repressive state, the EAC seems only to have captured Hisséne Habré, the man. One indicator of this was the EAC's reliance on direct commission to shore up its other commission arguments, wherein for each of Habré's crimes, he was found directly and personally liable in addition to arguments regarding oversight, ordering, knowing, or credibly foreseeing the commission of such crimes. The capture of Habré the individual was possible precisely because Habré had become a private citizen: although once powerful, three decades of spending the spoils looted from Chad's treasury (reputedly USD 15 million) has rendered Habré, in the words of one local attorney, *inoffensive*.[78] Before the trial, the ex-dictator lived quietly between two homes in two posh Dakar neighborhoods[79] as a private citizen, and was primarily known as a family man who had contributed generously to local Muslim organizations. With minimal political salience, Habré made a relatively easy target, and his prosecution represented a nearly costless way for the three parties to the EAC (the AU, Chad, and Senegal) to appease persistent calls for justice from human rights groups and other interested international parties. From this perspective, Habré represented low hanging fruit tried at little cost with potentially significant political gain.

11.5 Conclusion

This chapter has explored the institutional and juridical outcome of the Habré trial as an innovative and important addition to ICL, identifying instances of how the EAC's practice and structure showcases the possibilities, and constraints, of hybrid international criminal justice. The chapter argues that although the Habré trial showcases pluralism within the field of ICL, it does not answer the most central question in heterogeneous ICL practice, which is the question of whether (and how) sovereigns may be prosecuted for atrocity crimes, as, in the end, Habré was effectively prosecuted as a private citizen not a (former) state agent. This question, in turn, is a question regarding how ICL might serve a role parallel to law's domestic purpose, which is to exact social control including over state actors.

[78] Interview with local attorney who participated in the case (Dakar, Senegal February 2017), notes on file with author.

[79] In Senegal, it is not uncommon for men with means to support several wives and therefore several households.

12
Innovations in Hybrid Justice
Comparative Opportunities and Challenges of the Central African Republic's Special Criminal Court and the Proposed Hybrid Court for South Sudan

Elise Keppler

12.1 Introduction

In 2015, two potential new hybrid accountability mechanisms to deliver a measure of justice for brutal crimes committed during conflicts in Africa emerged: the Special Criminal Court (SCC) in the Central African Republic (CAR) and the Hybrid Court for South Sudan (HCSS). The courts represent a resurgence of hybrid accountability mechanisms after a relative lull in their establishment and are innovative in their design.[1]

The two courts provide a study in contrasts as the institutions fall towards different ends of what can be described as a domestic–international spectrum of hybrid courts.[2] The SCC is a model characterized as being more a domestic court supported by an international organization, the United Nations (UN). The proposed HCSS framework is characterized more by its international—or in fact regional through the African Union (AU)—emphasis. The AU Commission even has the legal authority to create the HCSS unilaterally without the consent of the government of South Sudan, an unprecedented possibility among hybrid mechanisms.

In addition, the SCC and HCSS are among the only—if not the only—hybrid courts that are organized to operate while conflicts continue in the countries under their jurisdiction. Conflict has persisted in parts of both countries, and international crimes continue to be committed.[3]

[1] See Harry Hobbs, 'Towards a Principled Justification for the Mixed Composition of Hybrid International Criminal Tribunals' (2017) 30 Leiden Journal of International Law 177, 177–78; Padraig McAuliffe, 'Hybrid Tribunals at Ten: How International Criminal Justice's Golden Child Became an Orphan' (2011) 7 Journal of International Law and International Relations 1.

[2] See Cesare PR Romano, 'Mixed Criminal Tribunals' in *Max Planck Encyclopedia of Public International Law* (Oxford University Press 2006) 312; Harry Hobbs, 'Hybrid Tribunals and the Composition of the Court: In Search of Sociological Legitimacy' (2016) 16 Chicago Journal of International Law 482, 491–92.

[3] See Human Rights Watch, 'Killing Without Consequence: War Crimes, Crimes Against Humanity and the Special Criminal Court in the Central African Republic' (2017) <https://www.hrw.org/report/2017/07/05/killing-without-consequence/war-crimes-crimes-against-humanity-and-spec

Elise Keppler, *Innovations in Hybrid Justice* In: *Hybrid Justice*. Edited by: Kirsten Ainley and Mark Kersten, Oxford University Press. © Elise Keppler 2025. DOI: 10.1093/oso/9780192893758.003.0012

While established in 2015, the operationalization of the SCC only gained momentum in 2017, however, and the HCSS continues to exist on paper only due to major political blockages to its creation. Questions as to whether the HCSS will ever be established remain, and the Court may not materialize as an option to deliver justice for crimes committed in South Sudan.

This chapter assesses the comparative benefits and challenges of the creation, governance, staffing, and location features of the SCC and proposed HCSS in terms of their abilities to ensure justice for the crimes under their jurisdiction. The chapter's analysis is informed by the author's work experience conducting research and advocacy on South Sudan and the Central African Republic.[4]

12.2 Background

This section reviews the factors that motivated the establishment of hybrid courts generally and the circumstances that led to the creation of the SCC and the HCSS.

12.2.1 Why new hybrid courts?

As a general matter, hybrid courts provide an alternative to purely international or domestic accountability mechanisms by offering a combination of international and national features.[5] Hybrid courts have been lauded by some academics and practitioners as having the potential to offer certain benefits that international courts and national accountability efforts may lack with respect to efficiency, legitimacy, capacity building, and norm diffusion.[6]

While there are many differences between hybrid courts, the academic literature has established some common features. Hybrid courts are typically established as an ad-hoc response to a specific situation; have jurisdiction over a mix

ial> accessed 17 December 2023; Human Rights Watch, 'Soldiers Assume We Are Rebels: Escalating Violence and Abuses in South Sudan's Equatorias' (2017) <https://www.hrw.org/report/2017/08/01/soldiers-assume-we-are-rebels/escalating-violence-and-abuses-south-sudans> accessed 17 December 2023; Human Rights Watch, 'World Report 2020' (2020) <https://www.hrw.org/world-report/2020> accessed 17 December 2023.

[4] See, eg, Human Rights Watch, 'Central African Republic: New Court Should Step Up Effort' (24 July 2019) <https://www.hrw.org/news/2019/07/24/central-african-republic-new-court-should-step-effort> accessed 17 December 2023.

[5] See, eg, Laura Dickinson, 'The Promise of Hybrid Courts' (2003) 97 The American Journal of International Law 295, 295–96.

[6] See, eg, ibid 296, 305–08; Jane Stromseth, 'Pursuing Accountability for Atrocities After Conflict: What Impact on Building the Rule of Law?' (2007) 38 Georgetown Journal of International Law 251, 280–81; Human Rights Watch, 'Bringing Justice: The Special Court for Sierra Leone' (2004) 2, 36 <https://www.hrw.org/sites/default/files/reports/sierraleone0904.pdf> accessed 17 December 2023.

of international and national crimes; blend national and international judges; are partially financed by international actors; and involve partnership between the state where the crimes were committed and another party, 'whether the U.N., a regional organization, or another state'.[7]

Hybrid courts are sometimes able to operate more nimbly than international courts due to reduced bureaucracy and their narrowly focused mandates.[8] Hybrid courts generally require less resources than international tribunals and may be able to 'expedite prosecutions and trials without compromising respect for international standards on human rights and international criminal law'.[9]

Academics argue that hybrid courts build dual international and national legitimacy. The integration of international and national judges and staff mean that hybrid courts have the capacity to 'do domestic justice, while upholding international law and complying with international fair trial standards, and thus also doing international justice'.[10]

The literature emphasizes hybrid courts' positive effect on legitimacy as perceived by domestic stakeholders. Hybrid tribunals may be able to create a greater sense of local ownership of the justice process through their proximity to victims and their inclusion of local personnel and legal frameworks.[11] Hybrid courts based in-country are closer to witnesses and evidence than a distant international tribunal, while national staff can offer information on local customs, and legal culture.[12] Similarly, there are enhanced opportunities for outreach to local communities when a hybrid tribunal is located in-country.[13]

Hybrid courts can also strengthen respect for rule of law domestically through targeted capacity-building efforts by court staff, and spillover effects of their functioning. Some of the capacity-building effects of hybrids have been more

[7] See Sarah Williams, *Hybrid and Internationalized Criminal Tribunals: Selected Jurisdictional Issues* (Bloomsbury 2012) 252. An exception is the Extraordinary African Chambers where the partnership was with Senegal, as opposed to Chad where the crimes were committed. Senegal tried the crimes committed in Chad under the principle of universal jurisdiction. See Human Rights Watch, 'Q&A: The Case of Hissène Habré Before the Extraordinary African Chambers in Senegal' (3 May 2016) <https://www.hrw.org/news/2016/05/03/qa-case-hissene-habre-extraordinary-african-chambers-senegal> accessed 17 December 2023.

[8] Human Rights Watch, 'Bringing Justice' (n 6) 2 (acknowledging that the Special Court for Sierra Leone was set up to be 'leaner and meaner' to respond to criticisms that the ad hoc international criminal tribunals are too costly and slow).

[9] See Antonio Cassese, 'The Role of Internationalized Courts and Tribunals in the Fight Against International Criminality' in Cesare PR Romano, André Nollkaemper, and Jann K. Kleffner (eds), *Internationalized Criminal Courts and Tribunals: Sierra Leone, East Timor, Cambodia and Kosovo* (Oxford University Press 2004) 6.

[10] Mathias Holvoet and Paul de Hert, 'International Criminal Law as Global Law: An Assessment of the Hybrid Tribunals' (2012) 17 Tilburg Law Review 228, 230.

[11] See Phillip Rapoza, 'Hybrid Criminal Tribunals and the Concept of Ownership' (2006) 21 American University International Law Review 525, 526; Human Rights Watch, 'Bringing Justice' (n 6) 2.

[12] See Stromseth, 'Pursuing Accountability for Atrocities After Conflict' (n 6) 280–81.

[13] David Cohen, '"Hybrid" Justice in East Timor, Sierra Leone, and Cambodia: Lessons Learned and Prospects for the Future' (2007) 43 Stanford Journal of International Law 1, 5.

limited than might have been hoped for, such as at the Special Court for Sierra Leone (SCSL); they nevertheless have fostered national and international staff sharing best-practices, funding of new domestic judicial facilities and training programmes, and the opportunity for domestic staff to take their experience from working at the hybrid court back into their communities.[14]

In addition, hybrid courts can strengthen the idea of rule of law through diffusion of international human rights and international criminal law norms to the host population.[15] As Dickinson suggests, demonstrating that accountability is possible can spark progressive development of norms in the relevant domestic legal system.[16] These effects strengthen what is known as the external resilience of the institution, that is, its ability to promote domestic impacts in the affected country.[17]

The SCC and the HCSS are a second generation of hybrid courts, emerging more than a decade after hybrid courts such as the SCSL and the Extraordinary Chambers of the Courts of Cambodia (ECCC) were established. Both the SCC and HCSS came about as a result of country-specific developments. At the same time, international dynamics seem to have had some influence.

For the SCC, global increased attention to the importance of promoting national accountability initiatives wherever possible may have been a contributing factor. The principle of complementarity—which focuses on the role of the permanent International Criminal Court (ICC) only as a court of last resort—has over time become a greater focus within the international community.[18]

Even where the ICC has launched its own investigations, its officials and staff members can engage with national authorities to build capacity and political will to support additional prosecutions and investigations. This process, which has been known as 'positive complementarity', has been explicitly recognized by the ICC, and is reinforced by growing recognition that the ICC will only be able to

[14] See Human Rights Watch, 'Justice for Atrocity Crimes: Lessons of International Support for Trials Before the State Court of Bosnia and Herzegovina' (2012) <https://www.hrw.org/report/2012/03/12/justice-atrocity-crimes/lessons-international-support-trials-state-court-bosnia> accessed 18 December 2023 (noting the potential for international support to build institutional capacity and transfer knowledge to domestic staff); Human Rights Watch, 'Justice in Motion: The Trial Phase of the Special Court for Sierra Leone' (2005), <https://www.hrw.org/report/2005/11/02/justice-motion/trial-phase-special-court-sierra-leone> accessed 18 December 2023; Jane Stromseth, 'Justice on the Ground: Can International Criminal Courts Strengthen Domestic Rule of Law in Post-Conflict Societies?' (2009) 1 Hague Journal on the Rule of Law 87, 95.

[15] Stromseth, 'Pursuing Accountability for Atrocities After Conflict' (n 6) 281.

[16] Dickinson (n 5) 296.

[17] For a discussion of the concepts of internal resilience and external resilience with respect to hybrid courts, see the introduction to this volume.

[18] See Rome Statute of the International Criminal Court (opened for signature 17 July 1998, entered into force 1 July 2002) 2187 UNTS 90, Article 17(1)(a); 'Report of the Bureau on Stocktaking: Complementarity' (18 March 2010) ICC-ASP8/51, paras 16–18; Draft Resolution on Complementarity (adopted at Review Conference of the Rome Statute, 3 June 2010) Res ICC-ASP/8/Res 9, Ann VII, para 8.

pursue a small number of cases even in countries where the ICC is involved, as in the Central African Republic.[19]

At the same time, developing a hybrid mechanism that is deeply rooted in the domestic framework may have reflected an effort to surmount criticisms of some of the earlier hybrids for being too removed from the national justice system, thereby limiting domestic legitimacy and positive impacts.[20]

For the HCSS, backlash against the ICC by some African leaders since 2009, and the comparatively large number of African situations under investigation by the ICC may have fuelled interest in an accountability mechanism other than the ICC for South Sudan.[21] ICC intervention in South Sudan would require South Sudan's government to formally request the ICC to investigate or, in the absence of an invitation, the UN Security Council would have to refer the case to the ICC as South Sudan is not a party to the ICC.[22] A hybrid court for South Sudan also engendered support among members of civil society in South Sudan as a means to 'overcome capacity constraints and conduct trials that meet international standards', while also having the potential to 'stimulate much-needed reforms in the justice sector'.[23]

12.2.2 The Special Criminal Court

The Central African Republic's current crisis began in late 2012, when mainly Muslim Seleka rebels ousted President Francois Bozizé and seized power through a campaign of violence and terror.[24] In late 2013, Christian and animist militias known as anti-balaka also began to organize counter-attacks against the Seleka.[25]

[19] The ICC has opened two investigations in the Central African Republic, one focused on crimes committed during conflict in 2002 and 2003 and one focused on crimes committed since 2012. In the first investigation, there was only one case, of a former vice president from the Democratic Republic of Congo, Jean-Pierre Bemba. He was acquitted of charges of war crimes and crimes against humanity on appeal. In the second investigation, there are five suspects, three of whom were on trial, one whose trial is pending, and one who is a fugitive at the time of writing.

[20] McAuliffe (n 1) 34–40 (describing the criticisms of the dominating international elements of the Special Court for Sierra Leone, and hybrid accountability mechanisms in East Timor and Kosovo).

[21] See Jean-Baptiste Jeangène Vilmer, 'The African Union and the ICC: Counteracting the Crisis' (2016) 92 International Affairs 1319; S. Roach, 'South Sudan: A Volatile Dynamic of Accountability and Peace' (2016) 92 International Affairs 1343, 1359 ('the main purpose of the hybrid court is to ensure that the ICC does not get involved; that the judicial process remains an African solution').

[22] Rome Statute, Articles 12(3), 13(b). While some of South Sudan's leaders have suggested support for the ICC at points, they have never taken any steps to pursue a formal request for ICC intervention, suggesting such comments represent merely rhetoric. See Siobhán O'Grady, 'Talking Trump and War Crimes With South Sudan's Rebel Leader' (*Foreign Policy*, 25 May 2016) <http://foreignpolicy.com/2016/05/25/talking-trump-and-war-crimes-with-south-sudans-rebel-leader/> accessed 18 December 2023.

[23] See David K Deng, 'Special Court for Serious Crimes (SCSC): A Proposal for Justice and Accountability in South Sudan' (2014) South Sudan Law Society <https://www.cmi.no/file/2760-SSLS-SCSC-Proposal-for-a-Hybrid-Court.pdf> accessed 18 December 2023.

[24] For a more in-depth discussion of the recent conflict, see Human Rights Watch, 'Killing Without Consequence' (n 3).

[25] The term 'anti-balaka' means 'anti-balles', or bullet, from a Kalashnikov assault rifle.

The anti-balaka had its roots as local self-defence groups that existed under Bozizé. The group frequently targeted Muslim civilians, associating all Muslims with the Seleka.

As the Seleka and anti-balaka fought each other and carried out increasingly brutal tit-for-tat attacks on those who they perceived as supporting their enemies, civilians were caught in the middle. Many Muslims fled, and with the mass departure of the country's minority Muslim population, the anti-balaka turned on Christians and others they believed had opposed them or had sided with their Muslim neighbours. Over time, the anti-balaka turned on anyone in order to steal or loot.

In late 2013, the AU peacekeeping mission was joined by French soldiers to restore order. Violence continued despite the AU and French troops, and in April 2014 the UN Security Council authorized a new peacekeeping mission called the Multidimensional Integrated Stabilization Mission in the Central African Republic, known by its French acronym, MINUSCA. The mission has a multi-pronged mandate: protecting civilians; facilitating humanitarian access; monitoring, investigating, and reporting on human rights abuses; and supporting the political transition.[26]

In March 2016, after two years of an interim government, relatively peaceful elections were organized and Faustin-Archange Touadéra was sworn in as president. But violence and attacks against civilians have nevertheless continued, with Seleka factions and anti-balaka groups still controlling large swathes of the country, especially in the eastern and central regions.[27] In the second half of 2017, violence threatening civilians surged and has continued since then.[28]

In August 2014, the transitional government signed a memorandum of understanding with the peacekeeping mission that outlined a hybrid judicial mechanism. The Central African government requested the participation of international staff to bolster the capacities of the national justice system and to protect the Court's independence.[29] On 22 April 2015, the country's interim parliament, the National

26 UNSC Res 2217 (28 April 2015) UN Doc S/RES/2217.

27 See Human Rights Watch, 'Killing Without Consequence' (n 3).

28 Human Rights Watch documented killings by armed groups of at least 249 civilians between May 2017 and October 2017, mostly in the south-central and southeastern parts of the country. Human Rights Watch, 'Central African Republic: Civilians Targeted as Violence Surges' (27 October 2017) <https://www.hrw.org/news/2017/10/27/central-african-republic-civilians-targeted-violence-surges> accessed 18 December 2023. Human Rights Watch also documented twenty-five cases of rape by armed groups in Basse-Kotto province in May 2017, part of a pattern of systematic rape and sexual abuse of women and girls by armed groups over the past five years. Human Rights Watch, 'They Said We Are Their Slaves: Sexual Violence by Armed Groups in the Central African Republic' (2017) 64 <https://www.hrw.org/report/2017/10/05/they-said-we-are-their-slaves/sexual-violence-armed-groups-central-african> accessed 18 December 2023. For discussion of more recent violence, see UN Office for the Coordination of Humanitarian Affairs, 'UN Assistant-Secretary-General for Humanitarian Affairs and Deputy Emergency Relief Coordinator, Ursula Mueller, Remarks at Member States Briefing on the Central African Republic' (19 March 2018) <https://reliefweb.int/sites/reliefweb.int/files/resources/ASGCARBriefing031918AsDelivered.pdf> accessed 18 December 2023.

29 Human Rights Watch interview with staff member (Ministry of Justice, Bangui, 15 June 2016).

Transitional Council, adopted the law by a vast majority. On 3 June 2015, the transitional president, Catherine Samba-Panza, promulgated the law that created the SCC—a temporary hybrid court that is based in the national system but is staffed by both national and international personnel.

The SCC is mandated to investigate and prosecute 'grave violations of human rights and international humanitarian law committed on the territory of the Central African Republic since 1 January 2003, as defined by the Central African criminal code and its international law obligations, notably the crimes of genocide, crimes against humanity, and war crimes'.[30] The provisions in the Central African criminal code track the language of international law and include crimes such as murder, summary executions, torture, and sexual violence as crimes that may constitute crimes against humanity. They provide that war crimes are those set out in the 1949 Geneva Conventions and international customary law.[31]

The National Transitional Council tasked the new court with investigating not only crimes committed during the recent crisis, as had been proposed by the transitional government, but also those committed since 1 January 2003.The SCC has a mandate of five years, which can be renewed.[32]

The law establishing the SCC foresees that if the ICC and the SCC work on the same case, priority will go to the ICC.[33] In terms of jurisdiction over ordinary national courts, the SCC is given primary but not exclusive jurisdiction, meaning that the SCC has the authority to select cases, but ordinary courts can still try remaining cases of grave international crimes, in accordance with Central African law.[34]

Victims have an important role at the SCC. In addition to serving as potential witnesses, victims can join the criminal proceedings as civil parties (*partie civile*).[35] A feature of civil law systems, on which the Central African Republic system is based, civil parties serve as a formal party to the proceedings, alongside the Prosecutor and the defendant. Civil parties may take measures such as making submissions to the case file, requesting that an investigation be initiated and that steps be taken to advance the investigation, and examining witnesses.

Although progress on the SCC's establishment initially lagged after the law creating it was adopted, the SCC gained momentum in 2017 when many of the principal staff were appointed, including the Special Prosecutor, the Registrar, and judges.[36]

[30] Loi Organique portant création, organization et fonctionnement de la cour pénale spéciale, No 15.003 (3 June 2015) Article 3 <https://www.cpsrca.cf/bibliotheque/textes-juridiques/35/> accessed 18 December 2023.

[31] Loi portant code pénal centrafricain, No 10.001 (6 January 2010) Articles 154–157.

[32] *Loi Organique* No 15.003 (n 30) Article 71.

[33] ibid Article 37.

[34] ibid Articles 3, 36.

[35] For reference to civil parties in the proceedings, see ibid Article 40.

[36] Human Rights Watch, 'Looking for Justice: The Special Criminal Court, A New Opportunity for Victims in the Central African Republic' (2018) <https://www.hrw.org/report/2018/05/17/

In May 2018, parliament adopted the Court's Rules of Procedure and Evidence (RPE), which was a precondition for the Court to officially commence its work.[37] The Court then held its first official session in October 2018, and the Special Prosecutor released his prosecutorial strategy in December.[38]

Since then, more than a dozen investigations have been launched. The SCC's investigation process, which is consistent with the Central African Republic's civil law legal system, provides for two phases of investigation prior to cases going to trial. The first is conducted by the Prosecutor's office, to be completed within a six-month period, unless the judges approve an extension. The second is by a two-judge panel (*cabinet d'instruction*) consisting of one national judge and one international judge, which can last up to two years.[39] As of December 2020, the judges had also received twenty-two complaints from victims who wished to be considered civil parties, many of which related to ongoing investigations, but a small number of the cases were new.[40]

In April 2022, the SCC opened its first trial and on 31 October 2022, the Court issued its first judgment, convicting Issa Sallet Adoum, Ousman Yaouba, and Tahir Mahamat of the 3R rebel group for war crimes and crimes against humanity in May 2019 in the villages of Koundjili and Lemouna, northwest Central African Republic.[41]

12.2.3 The Hybrid Court for South Sudan

South Sudan's current crisis began in December 2013, only two and a half years after the country's independence, and dashed hopes for the country's positive progress as the world's newest state. Troops affiliated with President Salva Kiir, who is of Dinka ethnicity, clashed with troops loyal to Vice-President Riek Machar, who

looking-justice/special-criminal-court-new-opportunity-victims-central-african> accessed 18 December 2023.

37 Human Rights Watch, 'Central African Republic: Parliament Adopts Special Criminal Court Rules' (4 June 2018) <https://www.hrw.org/news/2018/06/04/central-african-republic-parliament-adopts-special-criminal-court-rules>.

38 'Stratégie d'enquêtes de poursuites et d'instructions', SCC workshop (4 December 2018) <https://www.cpsrca.cf/actualite/strategie-d-enquetes-de-poursuites-et-d-instructions/58/> accessed 18 December 2023.

39 Loi portant règlement de procédure et de preuve devant la cour pénale spéciale de la republique centrafricaine, *Loi* No 18.010 (2 July 2018) Articles 70, 106 <https://www.cpsrca.cf/bibliotheque/textes-juridiques/35/> accessed 18 December 2023.

40 Human Rights Watch, 'Central African Republic: First War Crimes Verdict Due' (28 October 2022) <https://www.hrw.org/news/2022/10/28/central-african-republic-first-war-crimes-verdict-due> accessed 18 December 2034; Human Rights Watch 'Central African Republic: First Trial at the Special Criminal Court' (12 April 2022) <https://www.hrw.org/news/2022/04/12/central-african-republic-first-trial-special-criminal-court> accessed 18 December 2023.

41 *Case Special Prosecutor v Issa-Salet, Yaouba et Mahamat* (Summary of Judgment No 003-2022) (31 October 2022).

is of Nuer ethnicity.[42] Within days, mainly Dinka government troops carried out large-scale targeted killings, detentions, and torture of mainly Nuer civilians in various parts of Juba, while thousands of Nuer soldiers defected to an opposition army.[43] The violence between the two sides escalated into a civil war between government and rebel forces, often along ethnic lines. Soldiers on both sides targeted victims based on ethnicity, killed thousands of civilians, committed acts of sexual violence, looted and destroyed civilian property, and unlawfully detained and tortured civilians.[44]

In August 2015, the parties signed the Agreement for the Resolution of Conflict in South Sudan (ARCSS), a power sharing peace agreement that established a transitional government of national unity.[45] Chapter V of the agreement provides for the creation of the Hybrid Court for South Sudan, to be established by the African Union Commission, and to be composed of South Sudanese and other African judges and staff.[46]

The HCSS is designed to have the authority to try genocide, war crimes, crimes against humanity, and other serious crimes that violate international law and Sudanese law committed since the current conflict began. It is designed to be distinct from the national system and have primacy over South Sudan's courts, and to have jurisdiction over anyone accused of the crimes within its jurisdiction irrespective of rank or whether the accused is a government official.[47] These are critical elements for ensuring that investigation and prosecution is independent, impartial, and effective.[48]

Following the accord, the AU Commission began to prepare a draft statute and other instruments to operationalize the HCSS. Further progress stalled when South Sudan failed to respond to AU Commission efforts to engage with the government on the substance of the Court's establishment.[49] On 24 March 2017, the AU Peace and Security Council called for the AU Commission 'to scale-up ongoing efforts towards establishing the Hybrid Court of South Sudan'.[50]

42 Human Rights Watch, 'Soldiers Assume We Are Rebels' (n 3) 13.

43 Human Rights Watch, 'South Sudan: Stop Delays on Hybrid Court' (14 December 2017) <https://www.hrw.org/news/2017/12/14/south-sudan-stop-delays-hybrid-court> accessed 18 December 2023.

44 See Human Rights Watch, 'South Sudan's New War' (2014) <https://www.hrw.org/report/2014/08/07/south-sudans-new-war/abuses-government-and-opposition-forces> accessed 18 December 2023; Human Rights Watch, 'Soldiers Assume We Are Rebels' (n 3) 14.

45 Human Rights Watch, 'Soldiers Assume We Are Rebels' (n 3) 15.

46 ibid 4; Agreement on the Resolution of the Conflict in the Republic of South Sudan (17 August 2015) (ARCSS), Chapter V, Article 3.2.1.

47 ARCSS (n 46), Chapter V, Articles 3.2.2, 3.5.5.

48 See Human Rights Watch, 'South Sudan—Ending the Era of Injustice: Advancing Prosecutions for Serious Crimes Committed in South Sudan' (2014) <https://www.hrw.org/sites/default/files/reports/southsudan1214_ForUpload_0.pdf> accessed 18 December 2023.

49 Human Rights Watch, 'Soldiers Assume We Are Rebels' (n 3) 47–48.

50 AU, 'Communiqué of the 667th meeting of the PSC on the Situation in South Sudan' (17 March 2017) <http://reliefweb.int/report/south-sudan/communiqu-667th-meeting-psc-situation-south-sudan> accessed 18 December 2023.

On 21 July 2017, South Sudanese officials met with AU Commission and UN officials for discussions on the creation of the HCSS in Juba. The meeting produced a joint roadmap for the Court's establishment, with finalization of the Court's statute and other legal instruments by 31 August 2017.[51] A more detailed follow-up meeting that was convened in Addis Ababa in August focused more on the technical details of the instruments. Both the draft statute and memorandum of understanding were submitted to the South Sudan council of ministers in August 2017, but the government took no further action until the council of ministers gave their approval in December 2017.[52] In March, South Sudanese officials suggested they were waiting on the AU Commission to move ahead, although discussions with interlocutors indicated the AU Commission was waiting on action by the government of South Sudan.[53]

Despite the August 2015 agreement, the conflict spread, armed groups proliferated, and abuses against civilians persisted. South Sudan's transitional government neither ended violations by its army nor provided accountability for serious crimes and abuses against civilians. Fighters continued to deliberately target civilians, often on the basis of ethnic identity, and to commit abuses including, as the UN found, 'killings, abductions, rape, and sexual violence, as well as the destruction of villages and looting'.[54]

In August 2018 the parties signed a new peace accord. The accord contained the same provisions as the 2015 accord on creation of a hybrid court.[55] But still further progress on the Court's establishment did not take place. In April 2019 news leaked that South Sudanese authorities had retained the services of US-based lobbyists to 'delay and ultimately block establishment of the hybrid court'.[56]

[51] Joint Roadmap for the Establishment of the Hybrid Court for South Sudan (21 July 2017), on file with the author.

[52] Human Rights Watch discussions with those involved with the negotiations on the documents (New York and Juba, October and November 2017).

[53] HE Gen Taban Deng Gai, Vice President of the Republic of South Sudan, 'Statement' (37th Session of the Human Rights Council, 27 February 2018), on file with the author (stating that 'the National Council of Ministers of the Republic of South Sudan has approved the draft Memorandum of Understanding on the Establishment of the Hybrid Court' and that South Sudan has formally written to the chairperson of the AU, inviting him to sign the memorandum); Tom Miles, 'Justice for Atrocities: South Sudan Just a Signature Away: U.N. Investigator' (*Reuters*, 13 March 2018) <https://www.reuters.com/article/idUSKCN1GP2J6/#:~:text=Sudan%20just%20a%20signature%20away%3A%20UN%20investigator,-By%20Tom%20Miles&text=GENEVA%20(Reuters)%20%2D%20U.N.,justice%20for%20millions%20of%20victims> accessed 18 December 2023.

[54] UN HRC, 'Report of the Commission on Human Rights in South Sudan' (2018) UN Doc A/HRC/37/71, para 101 <https://reliefweb.int/report/south-sudan/report-commission-human-rights-south-sudan-ahrc3771> accessed 18 December 2023.

[55] See also UN HRC, 'Report of the Commission on Human Rights in South Sudan, Human Rights Council' (12 March 2019) UN Doc A/HRC/40/69, para 115. The lobbyists removed reference to the hybrid court in an updated version of the contract provided after the language of the first contract attracted criticism.

[56] See Africa News, 'South Sudan Signs New Deal with US Lobby Firm' (9 May 2019) <https://www.africanews.com/2019/05/09/south-sudan-signs-new-deal-with-us-lobby-firm//> accessed 18 December 2023.

After years of relative silence, South Sudan's cabinet finally gave approval to the justice ministry to establish accountability mechanisms to address the country's conflict in January 2021, raising hopes that progress on the HCSS could at last be possible.[57] The AU Commission chairperson, Moussa Faki Mahamat, welcomed the statement and promised to work with the government to create the Court.[58]

But there has been no concrete action taken since then and in the face of inaction, the US government took the decision to end funding to the AU to support the Court's establishment.[59] At the time of writing, none of the core texts had been adopted, no key staff were appointed, and no decision had been taken on the Court's location.

Human Rights Watch has argued that given the stagnation, the AU Commission should unilaterally finalize the relevant documents needed to set up the Court, and the AU Peace and Security Council should ask to be kept abreast of preparations. Human Rights Watch has urged that if a credible, fair, and independent hybrid court does not progress, the option of the ICC remains and should be pursued.[60]

12.3 Comparative Strengths and Weaknesses of the SCC and HCSS

Hybrid accountability mechanisms can be seen to operate on a spectrum of internationalization.[61] On one end, for example, is the Special Court for Sierra Leone. Although the Court had a mixed bench and applied both international and domestic law, it was created as a distinct entity entirely outside the domestic legal system, by international treaty between the United Nations and Sierra Leone, was led by international staff, and held certain trials outside Sierra Leone.[62]

On the other end is the example of the State Court of Bosnia and Herzegovina. In March 2005, pursuant to a joint proposal by the International Criminal Tribunal for the Former Yugoslavia and the Office of the High Representative in Bosnia and Herzegovina, a War Crimes Chamber was established under domestic law as part of the State Court, and a Special Department for War Crimes was created within the Prosecutor's Office.[63] The State Court of Bosnia and Herzegovina initially had

[57] Jale Richard, 'Cabinet approves establishment of hybrid court', (*EyeRadio*, 30 January 2021) <https://www.eyeradio.org/cabinet-approves-establishment-of-hybrid-court/> accessed 18 December 2023.

[58] African Union, 'Statement by H.E. Mr. Moussa Faki Mahamat, Chairperson of the African Union Commission, on African Union Hybrid Court of South Sudan' (30 January 2021).

[59] Robbie Gramer and Colum Lynch, 'U.S. Quietly Gives Up on South Sudan War Crimes Court' (*Foreign Policy*, 20 July 2021) <https://foreignpolicy.com/2021/07/20/south-sudan-war-crimes-court-state-department-africa-biden-human-rights/> accessed 18 December 2023.

[60] See Human Rights Watch, 'South Sudan: Stop Delays on Hybrid Court' (n 43).

[61] See Hobbs (n 2) 491–92.

[62] See Human Rights Watch, 'Bringing Justice' (n 6) 10–11.

[63] See Human Rights Watch, 'Justice for Atrocity Crimes' (n 14) 9–12.

a majority of international judges, but the international judges were then phased out over time.[64]

The value of grounding hybrid mechanisms in domestic systems to maximize their positive impact has gained greater currency as attention to the importance of effective complementarity has increased. The SCC reflects this approach; domestic practitioners have leading roles at the SCC, are a majority on the bench, and the location of the Court is Bangui, the capital of the Central African Republic.

The proposed HCSS runs counter to this trend. Principal posts are required to be held by non-South Sudanese Africans and each Chamber is composed of a majority of non-South Sudanese African judges. Staff are selected by the AU Commission chair and the Court is actually to be created by the AU Commission. This may reflect anticipated difficulties the HCSS will encounter vis-à-vis the government of South Sudan, whose leaders are themselves implicated in crimes committed, in addition to major deficits in the domestic system in South Sudan.[65] The location of the HCSS will be decided by the chairperson of the AU Commission.

Having some level of international authority in the proceedings can help minimize the impact of a government's political will, or lack thereof, on the success of proceedings. The presence of international prosecutors and judges, for example, can bolster the confidence of domestic practitioners to act with independence.[66] Increasing the international presence in a hybrid mechanism can have trade-offs for its domestic legitimacy and resonance, however, as discussed below.

For the SCC and the HCSS, the particular features create significant opportunities, but also significant challenges to delivering meaningful justice for crimes committed in South Sudan and the Central African Republic.

12.3.1 Establishment

Government partnership has traditionally been an integral part of the set-up of hybrid tribunals. The main way hybrids were generally set up is through an agreement between a government and an international entity, following a request by the government.[67] The UN has often been the international partner, although the AU

[64] See ibid; Human Rights Watch, 'Looking for Justice: The War Crimes Chamber in Bosnia and Herzegovina' (2006) <https://www.hrw.org/report/2006/02/07/looking-justice/war-crimes-chamber-bosnia-and-herzegovina> accessed 18 December 2023.

[65] See Human Rights Watch, Soldiers Assume We Are Rebels (n 3); Elise Keppler, 'Giving Justice the Slip in South Sudan' (*Human Rights Watch*, 8 June 2016) <https://www.hrw.org/news/2016/06/08/dispatches-giving-justice-slip-south-sudan> accessed 18 December 2023; Human Rights Watch, 'South Sudan—Ending the Era of Injustice' (n 48).

[66] Human Rights Watch, Justice for Atrocity Crimes (n 14) 15; David Luban and others, 'Accountability for War Crimes: What Roles for National, International, and Hybrid Tribunals?' (2004) American Society of International Law: Proceedings of the Annual Meeting, 194.

[67] See UNSC, 'Letter Dated 9 August 2000 from the Permanent Representative of Sierra Leone to the President of the Security Council' (2000) UN Doc S/2000/786; UNSC and UNGA, 'Identical Letters Dated 21 June 1997 from the First and Second Prime Ministers of Cambodia Addressed to the

served as the international partner in the Extraordinary African Chambers, and the High Representative for Bosnia and Herzegovina was the international partner for the War Crimes Chamber in the State Court of Bosnia and Herzegovina.[68] The Special Tribunal for Lebanon was unique in that it was ultimately established by a Security Council resolution, but was nevertheless initiated as an agreement between the Lebanese government and the UN; the Security Council stepped in when the Lebanese legislature stalled in ratifying the agreement.[69]

For the HCSS, however, no government partnership is required. The AU Commission has the authority to establish the Court with, or without, the consent and engagement of the government of South Sudan. Chapter V, Section 3.1.1 of the 2015 peace agreement states: 'The Court shall be established by the African Union Commission.' Section 3.1.2 further indicates that the AU Commission shall provide 'broad guidelines' on the 'location of the HCSS, its infrastructure, funding mechanisms, enforcement mechanism, the applicable jurisprudence, number and composition of justice, privileges and immunities of Court personnel or any other related matters'. These provisions differ from those on truth telling and compensation, which give the transitional government, as opposed to any other entity, the responsibility to establish the relevant institutions.

Embarking on a hybrid court without the partnership of a government is in many respects counter to some of the traditional objectives that have fuelled the establishment of hybrid accountability mechanisms. Domestic norm diffusion and capacity building can be expected to be severely limited, if not entirely curtailed, in the absence of a government partnership. The opportunity to share lessons learned from the HCSS with the domestic justice system would be modest at best.

This arrangement also could undermine the Court's effective functioning in its core work. Investigating the alleged crimes is likely to be far more difficult if the government of South Sudan is not a partner to the Court's creation and staffing. Those close to the process point out that partnership with the government of South Sudan will be necessary for the HCSS to operate effectively. They also note that the peace agreement provides that a domestic law to implement the provisions of the HCSS be passed in South Sudan, even if the initial establishment of the HCSS falls

Secretary-General' (1997) UN Docs A/51/930 and S/1997/488; UNSC, 'Letter Dated 13 December 2005 from the Chargé d'Affaires of the Permanent Mission of Lebanon to the United Nations Addressed to the Secretary-General' (2005) UN Doc S/2005/783. The exception has been where there is no functioning government, such as Kovoso or East Timor. Office of the High Commissioner for Human Rights, 'Rule-of-Law Tools for Post-Conflict States: Maximizing the Legacy of Hybrid Courts' (2008) UN Doc HR/PUB/08/2, 3.

68 Agreement of the Establishment of the Extraordinary African Chambers Within the Senegalese Judicial System Between the Government of the Republic of Senegal and the African Union (signed 22 August 2012) (2013) 52 ILM 1024, Articles 1(1), 1(3); Agreement Between the High Representative for Bosnia and Herzegovina and Bosnia and Herzegovina (signed 1 December 2004) Article 1(1).

69 UNSC Res 1757 (2007) UN Doc S/RES/1757, para 1(a).

under the exclusive authority of the AU Commission, so partnership is in actuality necessary.[70]

These are legitimate concerns. Nevertheless, the language of the agreement clearly provides that the AU Commission may act unilaterally to establish the Court. Such provision may have foreseen the difficulty of securing consent from the government to establish the Court. Alternatively, the consent to the 2015 accord (and the updated 2018 agreement) between the warring parties arguably represents consent by the parties to the AU Commission moving ahead on the hybrid, or at least a delegation of authority by the parties to the AU Commission to establish the hybrid.

In the circumstances of South Sudan, awaiting consent may mean that the HCSS never comes to fruition. However, moving ahead in the absence of such consent may lead to extraordinary challenges to the Court's effective functioning. There are no easy answers to this dilemma.

While the SCC has been established, it has encountered and can be expected to continue to encounter different kinds of challenges to becoming operational due to its heavy reliance on domestic processes.[71] In order for the SCC to move ahead on investigations and prosecutions, it needed RPE by which to operate. It is debatable as a legal matter whether the rules could have been adopted by the SCC judges as opposed to adoption by parliament, but consensus on their adoption by parliament emerged among international and domestic players in 2017 and 2018.[72] Central African lawyers suggested that rules that are not adopted by parliament would lack credibility and legitimacy, thereby undermining the reputation of the SCC and its potential impact.[73]

But securing adoption of the rules by parliament was uncertain. Parliament needed to consider the rules and decide to adopt them, and there was a risk that

[70] Human Rights Watch discussions with close observers of the negotiations on the hybrid in 2017.

[71] For a different view on the whether the SCC has a greater international or domestic emphasis, see Patryk I Labuda, 'The Special Criminal Court in the Central African Republic: Failure or Vindication of Complementarity?' (2017) 15 Journal of International Criminal Justice 175, 205 ('The SCC is more reminiscent of large scale top-down interventions such as the SCSL or the ad-hoc tribunals. It is not the Central African authorities but international actors who will provide funding, technical expertise and operational resources. MINUSCA's role in crafting the SCC law, its lack of jurisdiction over peacekeepers, and the balance of power among the SCC's organs all reflect overwhelming international influence over this hybrid court'). But see also Godfrey M Musila, 'The Special Criminal Court and Other Options of Accountability in the Central African Republic: Legal and Policy Recommendations', International Nuremberg Principles Academy, Occasional Paper No 2, 15, <https://www.nurembergacademy.org/fileadmin/media/pdf/publications/car_publication.pdf> accessed 18 December 2023 ('The SCC, which is not a hybrid court but rather a special national court with participation of international actors, is established within the judiciary' of the Central African Republic).

[72] Discussions at Workshop on the Draft Rules of Procedure and Evidence, Bangui, 2–3 October 2017, attended by Human Rights Watch researcher; Human Rights Watch interview with SCC staff (Bangui, 5 October 2017). In addition, not all of the judges are appointed at this phase of the Court's operations. See Loi Organique No 15.003 (n 30) Article 71(1).

[73] Lawyers expressed these views at a workshop on the rules in October 2017 that the author attended, which took place in Bangui, Central African Republic.

members of parliament could alter their contents before adopting them, or block or delay their adoption. This set-up therefore posed challenges to the internal resilience of this mechanism to domestic political dynamics, while at the same time increasing the potential for domestic resonance should the Court be able to operate effectively. But in this instance, the rules fortunately were adopted in June 2018.

12.3.2 Staffing

The selection and composition of staff at the SCC and the HCSS reflect the different emphases of these two hybrid mechanisms.

The composition of the HCSS' judicial bench shows a predominately international—or rather regional—character. Indeed, there is no requirement that any of the staff be South Sudanese, although the language on staffing in the 2015 and 2018 agreements suggests South Sudanese jurists are envisioned to serve at the court alongside other African practitioners. The ARCSS provides that '[a] majority of judges on all panels, whether trial or appellate, shall be composed of judges from African states other than the Republic of South Sudan'.[74]

The president of the HCSS is to be elected by the judges of the hybrid court.[75] Moreover, the HCSS' judicial selection and appointment procedure is under the exclusive authority of the AU Commission.[76] The AU Commission chairperson will select all judges, whether they are South Sudanese or international.

As these provisions reveal, the ratio of the HCSS' bench will always be in favour of international judges, or rather regional judges. This approach can insulate the bench from attempted political interference, but increase the chance that the court is seen as something removed from the domestic context. The requirement that judges be from other African states, as opposed to any state around the world, is an innovation that seems geared to minimize any perception that the hybrid court is an imperialist or Western imposition. This reflects an effort at promoting a regional approach in the wake of the backlash against the ICC in Africa, and the AU Executive Council described the HCSS as an 'African-led and African-owned legal mechanism'.[77]

Beyond the judges, the prosecutors and the Registrar are required to be non-South Sudanese Africans. They are also to be selected by the AU Commission chairperson.[78]

[74] ARCSS (n 46) Chapter V, Article 3.3.2.
[75] ibid.
[76] ibid Article 3.3.5.
[77] AU Executive Council, 'Decision on the Supplementary Budget for the 2017 Financial Year' (27 January 2017) AU Doc EX.CL/Dec 940 (xxx) <https://au.int/sites/default/files/decisions/32521-sc19552_e_-_ex_cl_decisions_939-964-xxx_.pdf> accessed 18 December 2023.
[78] ARCSS (n 46) Chapter V, Articles 3.3.3, 3.3.5, 3.3.6.

At the SCC, the balancing of domestic and international judges can be seen as a careful response to the risks of structuring a hybrid court with a majority of local judges in a highly politicized environment, while also promoting the court's domestic character.

The initial plan for the SCC was for a majority of international judges at every level.[79] This, however, has changed and now the composition of the SCC's bench reflects its place on the domestic end of the internationalization spectrum. Central African judges consist of a numerical majority across all the Court's Chambers, and a Central African judge presides in every proceeding.

At the same time, the institutional structure attempts to strike a balance between international and domestic judge decision-making power. Article 9 of the SCC law provides that 'the composition of all decision-making bodies of the [SCC] and its Registry must include at least one international member nominated by MINUSCA', the UN mission in the Central African Republic.[80]

The Investigation Chamber is organized to have three cabinets, with one international and one national judge in each.[81] The Indictment Chamber's bench has two international judges and one national judge each, while each of the three sections of the Trial Chamber is to have two national judges and one international judge.[82]

Due to this structure, a majority of judges at the trial level will always be Central African. However, this ratio is reversed for the Appeals Chamber, which will consist of two international judges and one national judge.[83] The ratio skews in favour of domestic judges at the trial level, in favour of international judges at the indictment and appeals levels, and is equal at the pre-trial investigation level. This complex structure means that there is an international check on proceedings, but that the trial function retains a domestic majority.

As for other key positions, the SCC's Registrar is Central African, while the Special Prosecutor is mandated to be an international practitioner. Making the Registrar post reserved for a Central African creates challenges. Traditionally, Registrars in international and hybrid courts—including the SCC—have far more responsibility than Registrars in domestic courts. In the Central African Republic, Registrars are focused on organizing court papers and hearings, and have generally worked with proceedings that last a maximum of ten days. Registrars in international and hybrid war crimes courts however regularly oversee witness protection and support, defence representation, and outreach on the process for trials that last far longer, as will also be the case for the SCC. One way that this challenge

[79] See Labuda, (n 71) 201 (noting that the original memorandum required a clear majority of international staff in all the Court's organs).
[80] Loi Organique, No 15.003, (n 30) Article 9.
[81] ibid Article 11.
[82] ibid Articles 12–13.
[83] ibid Article 14.

is being managed is that the deputy Registrar post is reserved for an international practitioner, and that position holds responsibility for areas that are more novel in the Central African Republic system.

12.3.3 Location

To date, hybrid courts have generally been based in the country where the crimes were committed or in a country willing to act in partnership to try the crimes,[84] but not when conflict is ongoing.

The SCC is based in Bangui, the capital of the Central African Republic. But security is a major challenge. As a court located in a country where large parts remain under the control of armed groups, attacks persists, and abuses continue to be perpetrated, there are real questions as to how maintain security for investigations and trials. Staff working at the SCC have expressed concern about the challenges of conducting investigations in this environment.[85] Central African civil society members also identified security as a top challenge for the SCC.[86]

National forces are not well situated to provide security given the sensitivity of the court's work and the forces' lack of capacity. MINUSCA is currently responsible for security for the magistrates who comprise the judges and prosecutors.[87] Armoured vehicles provide security at the court's temporary premises, and all of the magistrates appointed to the SCC who have arrived in Bangui benefit from close protection by military escorts.[88]

These are important efforts, but it remains to be seen how the security situation for the court will be managed over time in the context of the country's continued instability.

A decision on the location of the HCSS has yet to be taken. The climate of insecurity that currently pervades much of South Sudan, including its capital, would create serious difficulties for holding trials in the country. Some hybrid courts, such as the Special Court for Sierra Leone, and now the SCC, utilized UN peacekeepers

[84] The Extraordinary African Chambers in Senegal reflects the latter approach. There are some exceptions to proceedings conducted in-country. The Special Tribunal for Lebanon, for example, is based in The Hague. The Special Court for Sierra Leone also conducted the trial of Charles Taylor in The Hague, although it conducted the rest of proceedings in Freetown, Sierra Leone's capital. Human Rights Watch, 'Charles Ghankay Taylor at the Special Court for Sierra Leone' (16 April 2012) <https://www.hrw.org/news/2012/04/16/charles-taylor-qa-case-prosecutor-v-charles-ghankay-taylor-special-court-sierra> accessed 18 December 2017.

[85] Human Rights Watch interview with SCC staff (Bangui, 5 October 2017).

[86] Human Rights Watch group interview with Central African civil society members (Bangui, 4 October 2017).

[87] Human Rights Watch group interview with SCC staff (Bangui, 6 October 2017). See also UNSC Res 2387 (2017) UN Doc S/RES/2387, para 43(e)(viii).

[88] Human Rights Watch interview with UN staff (Bangui, 4 October 2017); Human Rights Watch interview with SCC staff (Bangui, 5 October 2017).

to provide security.[89] This is unlikely to be adequate in South Sudan; in addition to concerns due to past insecurity for members of the judiciary, members of South Sudan's legal community have pointed out that civilians have faced attack even in the confines of UNMISS (the UN peacekeeping mission) bases in South Sudan.[90]

Court facilities in Arusha have been contemplated, which will require draft agreements on the use of facilities and infrastructure. Human Rights Watch has proposed that the HCSS be located outside South Sudan at the outset with the option to be relocated to the capital, Juba, should security permit at a later point. Some South Sudanese activists have raised concern about missed opportunities for the positive domestic impact of a hybrid court if it operates outside the country.[91] This is a legitimate argument, yet the court's impact will also be hamstrung if it constantly faces serious security threats.

12.3.4 Cooperation

Experience has generally shown that political support in practice by governments for prosecutions is an essential ingredient for cases moving ahead. Where such commitment is lacking, cases may never commence, or extensively lag. Overcoming a state's unwillingness to prosecute grave crimes is more difficult than addressing a state's inability to do so. Even the most robust efforts aimed at improving the capacity of states to prosecute serious international crimes can be stymied by a state's unwillingness to implement them.

The experience of the ECCC reinforces this.[92] In 1999, a UN Group of Experts recommended an international tribunal, warning of political interference, corruption, and a lack of competence in the Cambodian court system. But Hun Sen rejected the proposal, wanting to maintain control of the process. He also rejected a UN proposal for a mixed court with a majority of international judges and an independent, international prosecutor.

Ultimately, the UN negotiated an agreement with the Cambodian government that led to a hybrid court with government-installed Cambodian judges, co-prosecutors, and other court personnel, who have obstructed investigations and trials at the ECCC. The government did not require its members to provide

[89] UNSC, 'Seventeenth Report of the Secretary-General on UNAMSIL' (2003) UN Doc S/2003/321, para 50.

[90] Human Rights Watch interview with South Sudanese lawyer (Nairobi, 6 October 2014); Human Rights Watch interview with South Sudanese lawyer (Nairobi, 6 October 2014); Human Rights Watch interview with international expert (Juba, 7 October 2014).

[91] See Deng (n 23) 9.

[92] Human Rights Watch, 'Cambodia: Government Obstructs Khmer Rouge Court' (5 September 2013) <https://www.hrw.org/news/2013/09/05/cambodia-government-obstructs-khmer-rouge-court> accessed 18 December 2023; Human Rights Watch, 'Cambodia: Khmer Rouge Convictions Too Little Too Late' (8 August 2014) <https://www.hrw.org/news/2014/08/08/cambodia-khmer-rouge-convictions-too-little-too-late> accessed 18 December 2023.

evidence to the Tribunal's judicial investigation and trial proceedings. Serious corruption allegations affecting the proceedings have not been adequately investigated. Cambodian judges and prosecutors have successfully blocked the arrest and indictment of five additional suspects whom UN prosecutors have named as responsible for serious crimes during the Khmer Rouge period. Cambodia's prime minister, Hun Sen, has said that if efforts to expand the scope of prosecution persisted, he would 'pray for the court to run out of money' as a result of donor country dissatisfaction and would prefer the departure of the international co-prosecutor and international judges to trials of additional suspects.[93]

Even if the government of South Sudan ultimately consents on paper to the HCSS, it may obstruct the court's efforts in practice or take less overt measures to limit its effectiveness. This could be done through very slow responses to requests, among other steps. The same could be true for the SCC should the government of the Central African Republic shift what has been its supportive stance on the SCC over time. One incident has raised serious concerns in this regard, although it remains an isolated occurrence to date: in November 2021, Central African Republic gendarmes released an SCC suspect from detention without the SCC's notice and the suspect, who is a sitting minister, remains a fugitive at the time of writing.[94] Such considerations reinforce why hybrid courts are generally best pursued on the basis of an express government partnership or support in their creation, combined with adequate protections against government interference in court functioning.[95]

With respect to the SCC, human rights defenders and victims expressed strong concerns to Human Rights Watch in April 2019 that vague provisions on justice in a peace accord signed in February 2019 could limit the government's practical cooperation and support to the SCC.[96] The agreement makes no explicit reference to the court, but does provide for an Inclusive Commission, which is mandated to examine all aspects of the conflict, make proposals on justice, and produce a report to inform the work of a Truth, Justice Reparation and Reconciliation Commission. Human Rights Watch has argued that broader efforts to bring social healing are important, but they should not purport to negate or limit the crucial independent

[93] See Human Rights Watch, 'Cambodia: Khmer Rouge Convictions Too Little Too Late' (n 94). See also ECCC, 'Case 004' <https://www.eccc.gov.kh/en/case/topic/120> accessed 18 December 2023 (explaining that requests for investigations for Cases 003 and 004 were filed in 2009).

[94] Maxence Helen, 'Central African Republic: The Long Bumpy Road towards the Special Criminal Court' (*Justiceinfo.net*, 18 April 2022) <https://www.justiceinfo.net/en/90870-central-african-republic-long-bumpy-road-towards-special-criminal-court.html> accessed 18 2023.

[95] Of course, international criminal courts can face this problem with recalcitrant governments as well. See *Prosecutor v Ahmad Muhammad Harun and Ali Muhammad Ali Abd-Al-Rahman* (Decision Informing the United Nations Security Council about the Lack of Co-operation by the Republic of the Sudan) ICC-02/05-01/07-57 (25 May 2010).

[96] Human Rights Watch, 'Central African Republic: New Court Should Step Up Effort' (n 4).

role of judicial accountability for the most serious crimes.[97] Time will tell if support for the court diminishes as the accord is implemented.

12.4 Conclusion

The SCC and HCSS are new forms of hybrid accountability mechanisms that take very different paths to leverage the potential benefits of hybridity while seeking to ensure that justice is credibly delivered. Each of these mechanisms holds the potential to bring a measure of justice for horrific crimes committed in two countries where widespread impunity is a pervasive challenge. At the same time, whether the HCSS will ever even be established, or be effective if it is established, and whether the SCC will be able to conduct effective trials remain open questions.

The SCC continued to show signs of progress in 2019 and 2020. Investigations were underway by both the Prosecutor and the investigating judges,.[98] Meanwhile the HCSS remained at a standstill as South Sudanese authorities continued to resist signing the memorandum of understanding for its creation.[99] The Office of the Legal Counsel of the AU Commission, however, convened a conference on the Court's establishment in Tanzania in December 2019 raising the prospect that the commission may be considering steps to create the Court irrespective of the involvement of the South Sudanese authorities.[100]

It will be necessary to closely track the further development of these institutions to assess their progress and potential contributions to justice for crimes committed in South Sudan and the Central Africa Republic. Such efforts will be valuable to assess the extent to which their respective structures offer useful models to promote justice for atrocities in other countries. As serious crimes continue to be committed and the capacity of national courts to try these crimes remains uneven at best, additional viable tribunal models to increase access to accountability are vital. The utility of such mechanisms is only reinforced by the potential benefits of domestic involvement in the delivery of justice and the limited capacity of the ICC, whose docket is significantly overstretched.

97 Human Rights Watch, 'Central African Republic: Justice Vital to Peace' (22 February 2019) <https://www.hrw.org/news/2019/02/22/central-african-republic-justice-vital-peace> accessed 18 December 2023.

98 Human Rights Watch, 'Central African Republic: New Court Should Step Up Effort' (n 4).

99 Elise Keppler, 'South Sudan's Cynical Bid to Block War Crimes Court' (*Human Rights Watch*, 30 April 2019) <https://www.hrw.org/news/2019/04/30/south-sudans-cynical-bid-block-war-crimes-court> accessed 18 December 2023; Elise Keppler, 'Renew Commission on Human Rights in South Sudan' (*Human Rights Watch*, 5 March 2020) <https://www.hrw.org/news/2020/03/05/renew-commission-human-rights-south-sudan> accessed 18 December 2023.

100 See statement by the Office of Legal Counsel on 13 December 2019, on file with the author.

13

'Forced Marriage'

A Positive Development for International Criminal Law?

Rosemary Grey[*]

13.1 Introduction

Of all sexual and gender-based crimes that have been prosecuted by hybrid tribunals, forced marriage is among the most contentious. It is contentious because 'forced marriage' is not expressly enumerated in any treaty provision, but has nonetheless been recognized as a crime against humanity (namely, 'other inhumane acts' by two hybrids—the Special Court for Sierra Leone (SCSL) and Extraordinary Chambers in the Courts of Cambodia (ECCC)—and following those precedents, by the International Criminal Court (ICC) as well. It is also contentious because the prosecution of conflict-related forced marriage has brought scrutiny upon *arranged marriage* practices in the affected countries, raising uncomfortable questions about whether some of those practices might also constitute crimes under international law.

This chapter unpacks those legal and political controversies, which are expected to resonate in the ICC for many years to come. It does not look in-depth at the SCSL and ECCC's entire track record in prosecuting sexual and gender-based crimes; that has been done elsewhere.[1] However, a broad overview of each court's

[*] Senior Lecturer, Sydney Law School, University of Sydney (rosemary.grey@sydney.edu.au). The chapter was written in 2020, with 'postscripts' added where relevant. The author acknowledges collaborations with Amnesty International that influenced the chapter, while affirming that all views expressed here are her own.

[1] Regarding the SCSL, see: Valerie Oosterveld, 'Evaluating the Special Court for Sierra Leone's Gender Jurisprudence' in Charles Jalloh (ed), *The Sierra Leone Special Court and its Legacy: the impact for Africa and International Criminal Law* (Cambridge University Press 2014); Chiseche Salome Mibenge, *Sex and International Tribunals: The Erasure of Gender from the War Narrative* (University of Pennsylvania Press 2013); Jennifer Gong-Gershowitz, 'Forced Marriage: A "New" Crime Against Humanity?' (2009) 8 Northwestern Journal of International Human Rights 53. Regarding the ECCC, see Silke Studzinsky, 'Neglected Crimes: The Challenge of Raising Sexual and Gender-Based Crimes before the Extraordinary Chambers in the Courts of Cambodia' in Susanne Buckley-Zistel and Ruth Stanley (eds), *Gender in Transitional Justice* (Palgrave Macmillan 2012); Theresa de Langis, '"This Is Now the Most Important Trial In the World": A New Reading of Code #6, the Rule Against Immoral Offenses Under the Khmer Rouge Regime' (2014) 3 Cambodia Law and Policy Journal 61; Rachel Killean, 'An Incomplete Narrative: Prosecuting Sexual Violence Crimes at the Extraordinary Chambers in the Courts of Cambodia' (2015) 13 Journal of International Criminal Justice 331; Sarah Williams and Emma Palmer, 'The Extraordinary Chambers in the Courts of Cambodia: Developing the Law on Sexual Violence?' (2015) 15 International Criminal Law Review 452; Maria Elander, 'Prosecuting

Rosemary Grey, *'Forced Marriage'* In: *Hybrid Justice*. Edited by: Kirsten Ainley and Mark Kersten, Oxford University Press. © Rosemary Grey 2025. DOI: 10.1093/oso/9780192893758.003.0013

successes and failures in prosecuting sexual and gender-based crimes is provided at the start of the chapter, in order to bring readers up to date. The chapter then homes in on the crime of forced marriage, tracing its emergence in SCSL and ECCC case law, and its subsequent reception in the ICC. This discussion of case law focuses on conflict-related forced marriage, as committed by armed groups during Sierra Leone's civil war in the 1990s, and by the Khmer Rouge between 1975 and 1979. In the final part of the chapter, I examine each court's discussion of peacetime arranged marriage practices in Sierra Leone and Cambodia, respectively. I suggest that, in the process of differentiating those peacetime arranged marriages from the conduct charged as 'forced marriage', the SCSL and ECCC showed undue deference to traditions that can, in some instances, violate internationally recognized human rights. That detracted from both courts' otherwise salutary achievement in prosecuting conflict-related forced marriage as experienced in Sierra Leone and Cambodia.

Before proceeding, it is important to clarify that the term 'forced marriage' has different connotations in the SCSL and the ECCC. In the SCSL, it refers to situations in which armed groups abducted women and girls, who were then assigned as 'bush wives' to particular male fighters—a role which entailed submitting to the man's sexual demands and functioning as his domestic servant. These relationships were not recognized as marriages under domestic law or custom, but were described in such terms by the perpetrators. That label continued to haunt the affected women after the war, making reintegration difficult in communities where they were judged for having married 'the enemy'.[2]

In the ECCC, the term describes official marriages—that is, marriages orchestrated by the Communist Party of Kampuchea (CPK), better known in Cambodia as '*Angkar*' ('the Organisation') or the 'Khmer Rouge', which was in power between April 1975 and January 1979.,Tthese marriages were imposed upon men and women. in several parts of the country, especially towards the later end of the CPK's rule. Prospective spouses were directed into meeting halls after an exhausting day of forced labour, and then paired up by the authorities with their assigned husband or wife, who was often a total stranger. This was one of many ways that the CPK asserted its dominance over the Cambodian population, but it also served a more specific goal: married couples were required to produce children,

the Khmer Rouge Marriages' (2016) 42 Australian Feminist Law Journal 163; Valerie Oosterveld and Patricia Sellers, 'Issues of Sexual and Gender-Based Violence at the ECCC' in Simon Meisenberg and Ignaz Stegmiller (eds), *The Extraordinary Chambers in the Courts of Cambodia: Assessing Their Contribution to International Criminal Law* (Springer 2016); Emma Palmer and Sarah Williams, 'A "Shift in Attitude"? Institutional Change and Sexual and Gender-Based Crimes at the Extraordinary Chambers in the Courts of Cambodia' (2017) 19 International Feminist Journal of Politics 22; Rosemary Grey, 'Seen and Unseen: Sexual and Gender-Based Crimes in the Khmer Rouge Tribunal's Case 002/02 Judgment' (2019) 29 Australian Journal of Human Rights.

[2] See Oosterveld (n 1).

who would be the next generation of fighters and labourers for the state. This goal was pursued by making newlyweds vow to produce children 'for *Angkar*', monitoring couples at night to ensure that they had sex, asking invasive questions about whether the couple was 'getting along', and in some extreme instances, physically forcing men to rape their wives.[3]

Thus, the relationships described as 'forced marriages' in the SCSL and ECCC were unalike in many key ways, including that in Cambodia, both men and women were considered victims, although their respective experiences of forced marriage differed.[4] But in both conflicts, these 'forced marriages' departed from marriage practices that had existed for many generations, including the kinds of arranged marriages that were common in both Sierra Leone and Cambodia, as we will see in Section 13.4.

13.2 Overview of Sexual and Gender-Based Crimes in the SCSL and ECCC

In the SCSL, forced marriage was one of many sexual and gender-based crimes for which the defendants were held accountable: there were also convictions for raping civilians, forcing them to have sex with one another, and forced public nudity.[5] In *Taylor*, the SCSL also characterized the rape of a child soldier by another fighter in the same armed group as a war crime, which challenged the conventional wisdom that war crimes must be committed against 'the enemy'.[6] That precedent was later cited in a groundbreaking ICC decision confirming that the rape of child soldiers by their commanders is a war crime under the Rome Statute,[7] a decision that was upheld on appeal.[8]

In the ECCC, the prosecution of sexual and gender-based crimes was far more limited. The ECCC's first case (Case 001) concerned a man known by his alias 'Duch', who had headed the Khmer Rouge's most notorious prison, a former high school in Phnom Penh that the regime renamed S-21. Duch was not charged or convicted of any sexual crimes, save for one instance in which a male guard raped

[3] See Grey, 'Seen and Unseen' (n 1).

[4] On the different experiences of men and women in Khmer Rouge forced marriages, see Melanie O'Brien, 'Gender Dimensions of Forced Marriage in International Criminal Law' in Indira Rosenthal, Valerie Oosterveld, and Susana SáCouto (eds), *Gender and International Criminal Law* (Oxford University Press 2022).

[5] See Oosterveld (n 1).

[6] *Prosecutor v Charles Ghankay Taylor* (Judgment, Trial Chamber) SCSL-03-1-T (18 May 2012) [1179], [1206(vii)], [1207], [1451].

[7] *Prosecutor v Bosco Ntaganda* (Decision Pursuant to Article 61(7)(a) and (b) of the Rome Statute on the Charges, Pre-Trial Chamber II) ICC-01/04-02/-6 (9 June 2014) footnote 318.

[8] *Prosecutor v Bosco Ntaganda* (Judgment on the appeal of Mr Ntaganda against the 'Second decision on the Defence's challenge to the jurisdiction of the Court in respect of Counts 6 and 9', Appeals Chamber) ICC-01/04-02/06-1962 (15 June 2017).

a female prisoner with a stick during an interrogation in S-21.[9] In the second case (Case 002), four ex Khmer Rouge leaders were charged with crimes committed throughout Cambodia, including forcing people into marriages in order to control the population, and to encourage procreation.[10]

The Case 002 indictment also described numerous other sexual violence crimes committed by Khmer Rouge authorities. In addition to the prison rape described above, these included the rape of a second woman in S-21 while she was in chains, the rape and killing of a cook who stole food in North Zone security centre, three further rapes of women in the Sang security centre, the rape and killing of girls of Cham ethnicity in Kampong Cham Province, and an unspecified number of rapes in the Kraing Ta Chan prison, where the bodies of victims had been found naked with ammunition inserted into their genitals.[11] However, the investigating judges found that the CPK leadership could not be prosecuted for any of these acts of sexual violence because their official policy *prohibited* extra-marital sex, including rape, outside of marriage.[12] Hence, the acts of forcing people into marriages, and forcing them to consummate those marriages, were the only sexual and gender-based crimes to be charged in this case.

In both hybrids, there was a struggle to recognize sexual violence against men and boys. In the SCSL, defects in the prosecution's early submissions meant that, although evidence of sexual crimes against men and boys emerged in multiple cases, the defendants were only convicted for those crimes in the *RUF* case. In all other cases, the convictions for sexual violence pertained only to crimes committed against women and girls.[13] Male experiences of sexual violence were also largely overlooked in the ECCC. In Case 002, the prosecution did not elicit witness testimony from male survivors about their experience of forced sexual intercourse, and the lawyers representing putative victims (known as 'civil party lawyers') also contributed little in this respect. This oversight had serious consequences for the Case 002 judgment regarding forced marriage, as the chapter explains in more detail below.

13.3 Emergence of the Crime of 'Forced Marriage'

In the earliest international war crimes trials, namely the trials in the Nuremberg and Tokyo Tribunals after World War II, sexual and gender-based crimes were

[9] *Case 001(Kaing Guek Eav alias Duch)* (Judgment, Trial Chamber) 001/18-07-2007 (26 July 2010) [246], [366], [559].

[10] See Grey, 'Seen and Unseen' (n 1).

[11] Case 002 (Indictment) (15 September 2010) [457]–[459], [482], [504], [578], [785], [1426]–[1429].

[12] ibid [1429].

[13] Valerie Oosterveld, 'Sexual Violence Directed against Men and Boys in Armed Conflict or Mass Atrocity' (2014) 10 Journal of International Law and International Relations 107.

largely sidelined.[14] Hence, most of the leading precedents on sexual and gender-based crimes came later, in cases before the International Criminal Tribunal for the former Yugoslavia (ICTY) and the International Criminal Tribunal for Rwanda (ICTR). It was there that rape was first recognized as a method of torture and an act of genocide, for example.[15] The ICC has also started to make substantial contributions, particularly in relation to forced pregnancy and persecution on gender grounds.[16] But when it comes to the shaping the jurisprudence on forced marriage, the SCSL and ECCC represent 'ground zero'.

The idea of prosecuting forced marriage as a distinct crime was pioneered in the SCSL, in response to evidence that thousands of civilian women and girls had been abducted by male rebel fighters for use as 'bush wives' . The court first heard of this practice in May 2003, when the (then) SCSL Prosecutor David Crane brought indictments against leaders of three armed groups—the Armed Forces Revolutionary Council (AFRC), Revolutionary United Front (RUF) and Civil Defence Forces (CDF)—as well as Liberian president Charles Taylor. The *AFRC*, *RUF*, and *Taylor* indictments all referred to the abuse of 'bush wives', which was charged as rape and sexual slavery. However, the Prosecutor later added an additional charge to the *AFRC* and *RUF* indictments, namely: 'crimes against humanity— other inhumane acts (forced marriage)' in order to 'better reflec[t] the culpability of the accused'.[17] The rationale was that 'bush wives' suffered in ways unlike other victims of sexual violence in Sierra Leone. As explained by an investigator from the Prosecutor's office:

> I have found that the acts of sexual violence committed against women and girls within the temporal jurisdiction of the Special Court was not limited to rape and the use of women as sex slaves but also includes the abduction and forcing of women into conjugal-like relationships or forced 'marriages' by the AFRC/RUF leadership and their subordinates. These women were commonly referred to as

14 See Kelly D Askin, *War Crimes Against Women: Prosecution in International War Crimes Tribunals* (Martinus Nijhoff 1997); Rhonda Copelon, 'Gender Crimes as War Crimes: Integrating Crimes against Women into International Criminal Law' (2000) 46 McGill Law Journal 217.

15 Kelly D Askin, 'Prosecuting Wartime Rape and Other Gender Related Crimes: Extraordinary Advances, Enduring Obstacles' (2003) 21 Berkeley Journal of International Law 288; Helen Brady, 'The Power of Precedents: Using the Case Law of the Ad Hoc International Criminal Tribunals and Hybrid Courts in Adjudicating Sexual and Gender-Based Crimes at the ICC' (2012) 18 Australian Journal of Human Rights 75; Serge Brammertz and Michelle Jarvis (eds), *Prosecuting Conflict-Related Sexual Violence in the ICTY* (Oxford University Press 2016).

16 Rosemary Grey, 'The ICC's First "Forced Pregnancy" Case in Historical Perspective' (2017) 15 Journal of International Criminal Justice 905; Rosemary Grey and others, 'Gender-Based Persecution as a Crime Against Humanity: The Road Ahead' (2019) 17 Journal of International Criminal Justice.

17 *Prosecutor v Alex Tamba Brima et al ('AFRC case')* (Request for Leave to Amend the Indictment, Trial Chamber) SCSL-2004-16-PT (9 February 2004) [4]; *Prosecutor v Alex Tamba Brima et al ('AFRC case')* (Decision on Prosecution Request for Leave to Amend the Indictment, Trial Chamber) SCSL-04-16-PT-070 (6 May 2004); *Prosecutor v Issa Hassan Sesay et al* (*RUF* case) SCSL-04-15-PT (Decision on prosecution request for leave to amend the indictment, Trial Chamber) (6 May 2004).

> 'bush wives' and often kept for the exclusive use of their captors ... The 'wives' were forced not only to provide sexual services but also perform a range of conjugal duties including domestic chores, in some cases having children and taking care of the family—including their rebel 'husbands'. As a result of the stigma attached to their association with members of the AFRC/RUF forces, some of these women are still 'married' to their captors.[18]

The prosecution's portrayal of 'bush wives' as victims was challenged by Danish anthropologist Dorte Thorsen, a defence expert witness, who had conducted fieldwork on marriage practices in another West African country, Burkina Faso. Drawing on that experience, Thorsen argued that 'bush wives' may have made strategic choices to accept their marriages to rebel fighters because of the (relative) security and material prosperity afforded by that role. In her words, 'the position as a "bush wife" was not only drudgery and sexual abuse but also the base of power'.[19] Defence counsel also challenged the legality of the charge, given that 'forced marriage' was not enumerated in the SCSL Statute. They claimed that the prosecution had effectively invented this new crime, in violation of the principle of legality (the principle that a person cannot be prosecuted for acts that were not defined as crimes at the time of commission).[20]

It took five years, and multiple benches, before the matter was settled. In 2007, the *ARFC* Trial Chamber convicted the accused for their role in subjecting women and girls to forced marriage, although it held that this conduct amounted to 'sexual slavery' rather than 'other inhumane acts'.[21] The Chamber acknowledged that for some women, their status as a commander's 'wife' came with certain benefits, such as being exempt from chores.[22] However, it stressed that these benefits were 'relative only' and did not excuse the crimes committed against these women, including abducting them, labelling them as 'bush wives', and subjecting them to sexual abuse.[23] In a dissenting opinion, Judge Doherty held that the act of forcing women into so-called marriages was sufficiently distinct from sexual slavery, and sufficiently grave, to constitute the residual crime against humanity of 'other inhumane acts'.[24] She acknowledged that being a rebel wife could be strategic, stating: '[f]orced marriage became a means of survival for most girls in the bush.

[18] *Prosecutor v Alex Tamba Brima et al ('AFRC case')* (Request for Leave to Amend the Indictment, Trial Chamber) SCSL-2004-16-PT (9 February 2004), annex 2, Investigator's Statement, [5]–[7].

[19] *Prosecutor v Brima et al ('AFRC case')* (Joint Defence Disclosure of Expert Report on Forced Marriages By Dr. Dorte Thorsen, Trial Chamber II) (21 August 2006), 16–17.

[20] See *Prosecutor v Santigie Borbor Kanu* (Defence Response to the Prosecution's Request to Amend the Indictment) SCSL-2004-16-PT (17 February 2004) [3]–[4].

[21] *Prosecutor v Alex Tamba Brima et al ('AFRC case')* (Judgment, Trial Chamber II) SCSL-04-16-T (20 June 2007) [703]–[713].

[22] ibid [1160].

[23] ibid.

[24] *Prosecutor v Alex Tamba Brima et al ('AFRC case')* (Separate Opinion (Doherty) Trial Chamber II) (21 June 2007) [14]–[71].

"Bush wives' were spared gang rapes, were ensured regular meals and were protected by their 'husbands'".[25] However, Her Honour (quite properly) did not treat acquiescing to marriage in order to survive as legally meaningful consent.

The prosecution appealed the majority's rejection of the 'forced marriage' charge, and their appeal succeeded on that ground. Echoing the reasoning of Judge Doherty, in 2008 the SCSL Appeals Chamber held that the conduct charged as 'forced marriage' was distinguishable from sexual slavery, and was grave enough to amount to an 'other inhumane act' under the SCSL Statute.[26] As to the meaning of 'forced marriage', it stated:

> In the context of the Sierra Leone conflict, forced marriage describes a situation in which the perpetrator, through his words or conduct, or those of someone for whose actions he is responsible, compels a person by force, threat of force, or coercion to serve as a conjugal partner resulting in severe suffering, or physical, mental or psychological injury to the victim.[27]

The Appeals Chamber did not enter new convictions for 'forced marriage' in the *AFRC* case, reasoning that justice had been done by recognizing that the conduct was, in principle, a distinct crime.[28] However, the *RUF* Trial Chamber would later apply the Appeal Chamber's findings to render the SCSL's first conviction for 'forced marriage' as an 'other inhumane act'.[29]

The 2008 *AFRC* appeal judgment did not only have implications within the SCSL; it soon travelled 20,000 kilometres to Cambodia, where the ECCC investigating judges were gathering evidence of crimes committed by the Khmer Rouge. In line with the ECCC's procedural framework, this judicial investigation was not open-ended.[30] Rather, it was limited to the facts alleged in the prosecution's introductory submission: a 45,000-page document that had taken the Prosecutor's office twelve months to compile.[31] To date, that submission remains confidential. However, the press release issued by the Prosecutor's office on the day the submission was filed makes no reference to sexual crimes,[32] and although one former ECCC international Co-Prosecutor has confirmed that the submission did include

[25] ibid [29].
[26] *Prosecutor v Alex Tamba Brima et al ('AFRC case')* (Appeal Judgment) (3 March 2008) [157]–[202].
[27] ibid [196].
[28] ibid [202].
[29] *Prosecutor v Issa Hassan Sesay et al* (*'RUF case'*) (Judgment, Trial Chamber 1) SCSL-04-15-T (2 March 2009) [196].
[30] ECCC Rules, Rules 50 and 55(2).
[31] See Craig Etcheson, *Extraordinary Justice: Law, Politics, and the Khmer Rouge Tribunals* (Columbia University Press 2020) 219–24.
[32] ECCC, 'Statement of the Co-Prosecutors' (18 July 2007) <https://www.eccc.gov.kh/sites/default/files/media/Statement_of_Co-Prosecutors_18-July-2007_.pdf> accessed 22 January 2024.

a charge of rape as a crime against humanity,[33] that charge appears to have been based on just a single sentence about rape in one particular worksite.[34]

Seeking to remedy that perceived omission, the civil party lawyers pushed for the inclusion of charges of sexual and gender-based crimes, including forced marriage. This advocacy began in September 2008, when a *phet ti bey* (third gender) survivor named Sou Sotheavy became the first person to seek 'civil party' status in the ECCC. Although Sou Sotheavy identified and presented as female prior to 1975, the Khmer Rouge had forced them to live as a man, including forcing them to work in the men's unit, to cut their hair into the male style, and to marry a cisgender woman, which was not consistent with their sexual orientation or gender identity.[35] After encountering additional accounts of rape and forced marriage, the civil party lawyers requested investigations into forced marriage and sexual violence crimes, a request repeated in multiple filings between February and December 2009.[36] These filings cited the SCSL's jurisprudence to demonstrate that forced marriage could be prosecuted as an 'other inhumane act.'[37]

The subsequent judicial investigation revealed extensive evidence of sexual and gender-based crimes committed during the Khmer Rouge period. But as noted above, the investigating judges excluded most of these crimes from the indictment. Only the conduct of forcing people into marriages and forcing them to consummate those marriages were charged—both under the rubric of 'other inhumane acts'.[38] In November 2018, the ECCC Trial Chamber held that those charges had been established beyond reasonable doubt, and pronounced the two surviving defendants, Nuon Chea and Khieu Samphan, guilty of both rape and forced marriage as 'other inhumane acts'.[39] However, it held that although both men and women

[33] Andrew Cayley, 'KRouge's Female Victims Not Forgotten' (*Phnom Penh Post*, 1 June 2012) https://www.phnompenhpost.com/national/krouge%E2%80%99s-female-victims-not-forgotten accessed 22 January 2024.

[34] ECCC, 'Civil Parties' Co-Lawyers' Request for Supplementary Preliminary Investigations' 001/18-07-2007-ECCC/TC (9 February 2009) para 1; Sin Soworn and Silke Studzinsky, 'Tribunal Has Failed Victims of Sex Crimes' (*Phnom Penh Post*, 11 June 2012) <https://www.phnompenhpost.com/national/tribunal-has-failed-victims-sex-crimes> accessed 22 January 2024.

[35] ECCC, 'Press Statement by Civil Parties Lawyer Silke Stuzinsky: First Civil Party Application before the Extraordinary Chambers in the Courts of Cambodia (ECCC) on Gender-Based Violence under the Khmer Rouge Regime' (3 September 2008) <https://www.eccc.gov.kh/sites/default/files/media/PressRelease_1st_civil_party_on_Gender_Based_Violence.pdf> accessed 22 January 2024. See also Maria Elander, 'In Spite: Testifying to Sexual and Gender-Based Violence During the Khmer Rouge Period' in Dianne Otto (ed), *Queering International Law* (Routledge 2018); Rosemary Grey, 'Translating Gender Diversity In International Criminal Law: An Impossible But Necessary Goal' (2021) 47 Australian Feminist Law Journal 163.

[36] ECCC, 'Civil Parties' Co-Lawyers' Request for Supplementary Preliminary Investigations' (9 February 2009); ECCC, 'Second Request for Investigative Actions Concerning Forced Marriage and Forced Sexual Relations' (15 July 2009); ECCC, 'Co-Lawyers for the Civil Parties' Fourth Investigative Request Concerning Forced Marriage and Other Sexually Related Crimes' (4 December 2009).

[37] See, eg, ECCC, 'Civil Parties' Co-Lawyers' Request for Supplementary Preliminary Investigations' (9 February 2009) paras 11–12.

[38] ibid paras 1430–33, 1442–47.

[39] Case 002/02 (Summary of judgement in Case 002/02 against NUON Chea and KHIEU Samphan, Trial Chamber) (18 November 2018) [39]–[41].

were forced to consummate their marriages, only the *women's* experience was sufficiently grave to be an 'inhumane act'.[40] Nuon Chea (now deceased) and Khieu Samphan appealed their convictions, including those relating to forced marriage.[41] The prosecution also appealed, arguing that forcing men to rape their wives was an 'inhumane act'.[42] As no other sexual and gender-based crimes have been charged in the ECCC, save for a single rape in Case 001, the stakes of these appeals are especially high. [postscript: in 2022, the ECCC's Supreme Court Chamber confirmed Khieu Samphan's conviction and upheld the prosecution's appeal, with the result that both men and women who were forced to consummate their forced marriages were recognized as victims of the crime of sexual violence as an 'other inhumane act'.[43]]

Meanwhile, as the ECCC was busy prosecuting forced marriage as an 'other inhumane act', support for this charging strategy in the SCL had started to wane. In 2012, in the *Taylor* case, the Trial Chamber opined that 'the Prosecution erred in other Indictments by charging "forced marriage" as a crime that falls within the scope of the crime against humanity of other inhumane acts'.[44] In its view, the conduct was better captured by charges of rape and sexual slavery.[45] The Chamber added that the label 'marriage' was misplaced in this context, because 'what happened to the girls and women abducted in Sierra Leone and forced into this conjugal association was not marriage in the universally understood sense of a consensual and sacrosanct union'.[46] This decision was made by the full Trial Chamber, including Judge Doherty, who had supported the charge of 'forced marriage' as an 'other inhumane act' in the *AFRC* case.

Thus, in relation to forced marriage, the SCSL came full circle. Its Appeals Chamber held that the imposition of forced marriage was an 'other inhumane act', but three SCSL trial judges later distanced themselves from that approach, and reverted to describing the conduct as 'sexual slavery'. These two options for prosecuting forced marriage have been widely dissected by lawyers and commentators. Some support the SCSL Appeals Chamber's approach, arguing that being known as a rebel 'wife' exposed women to unique social and psychological consequences, which warrant a charge of 'forced marriage' as an 'other inhumane act'.[47] Others favour the 'sexual slavery' approach, arguing that forcing someone into marriage in order to control their body and labour amounts to asserting ownership over a

[40] See Grey, 'Seen and Unseen' (n 1).

[41] Case 002/02 (Nuon Chea's Appeal Against the Trial Judgment in Case 002/02, Trial Chamber) (1 July 2019); Case 002/02, (Khieu Samphan's Notice of Appeal (002/02), Trial Chamber) (1 July 2019).

[42] Case 002/02 (Co-Prosecutors' Appeal Against the Case 002/02 Trial Judgment, Trial Chamber) (20 August 2019).

[43] Case 002/02 (Appeal Judgment, Supreme Court Chamber) (23 December 2022).

[44] *Prosecutor v Charles Ghankay Taylor* (Judgment, Trial Chamber) (18 May 2012) [424].

[45] ibid [242]–[230].

[46] ibid [427].

[47] See, eg, Neha Jain, 'Forced Marriage as a Crime against Humanity: Problems of Definition and Prosecution' (2008) 6 Journal of International Criminal Justice 1013.

person (that being the defining feature of enslavement) but with an added sexual component, hence the crime of 'sexual slavery'.[48] Patricia Sellers, the (then) Gender Advisor to the ICC Prosecutor, has argued that the most appropriate charge is actually 'enslavement' because control over sexuality has *always* been part of the slave trade, making it artificial to separate 'sexual slavery' out from 'enslavement'.[49] The crime of enslavement also has another advantage: it has been expressly defined as a crime against humanity since the 1945 Nuremberg Charter, meaning that its prosecution in post-1945 settings complies unambiguously with the principle of legality.

Notwithstanding those debates among scholars, the SCSL Appeal Chamber's approach continues to find favour in international courts. In March 2016, a charge of 'forced marriage' as an 'other inhumane act' was confirmed in the ICC's *Ongwen* case, which concerns crimes allegedly committed by a rebel group in Uganda.[50] In September 2019, the ICC confirmed its second charge of 'forced marriage as an inhumane act' in the *Al Hassan* case, which focuses on crimes allegedly committed by Islamist fighters in Mali. [postscript: in 2022, the ICC Appeals Chamber confirmed Ongwen's conviction including for forced marriage as an 'other inhumane act', signalling that this charging strategy is legally acceptable in the ICC].[51] Yet as flagged by this chapter's introduction, this question of 'what crime to charge' was not the only contentious point raised by the SCSL and ECCC's dealings with forced marriage. A second issue that attracted much attention in both hybrid courts was whether the crime of 'forced marriage' can encompass 'arranged marriages'.

13.4 'Forced Marriage' and 'Arranged Marriage'

The practice of 'arranged marriage', whereby marriage is arranged by the families of the prospective spouses or a broker chosen by the families, was not the subject of charges in the SCSL or the ECCC. Nonetheless, that practice received attention in both courts as the benchmark against which the conduct charged as 'forced marriage' could be compared. There was no guidance from previous international criminal tribunals about how the SCSL and ECCC should approach this topic. However, the position in international human rights law was (and remains) fairly clear, and is thus a useful starting point for this discussion.

Under international human rights law, arranged marriage is not unlawful as a general rule; it is only unlawful if the marriage takes place without both spouse's

[48] Gong-Gershowitz (n 1).

[49] See, eg, Patricia Viseur Sellers, 'Wartime Female Slavery: Enslavement?' (2011) 44 Cornell International Law Journal 118. For a similar analysis, see Mibenge (n 1) chapter 4.

[50] *Prosecutor v Dominic Ongwen* (Decision on the confirmation of charges, Pre-Trial Chamber II) ICC-02/04-01/15-422-Red (23 March 2016) [87]–[95].

[51] *Prosecutor v Dominic Ongwen* (Appeal Judgment) (15 December 2022).

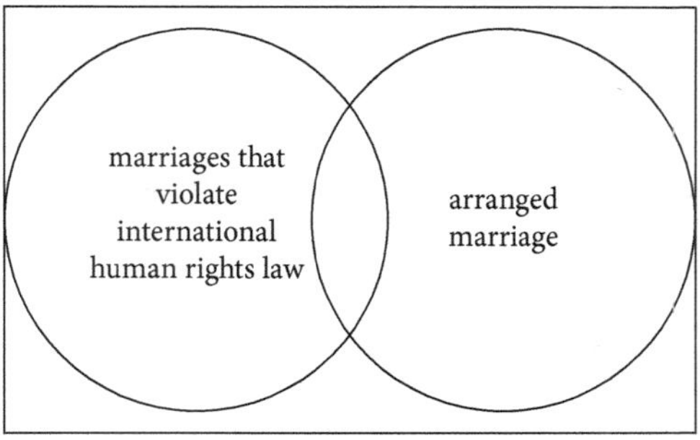

Figure 13.1 Forced and arranged marriage in international human rights law

'full and free consent'. Thus, if both spouses give full and free consent to delegating the matchmaking decision to a third party such as their parents, the arranged marriage is consistent with international human rights law. By contrast, arranged marriages that are imposed upon one or both spouses by force, threat, coercion, or deception will violate international human rights law (see Figure 13.1). This requirement was first set out in the 1948 Universal Declaration of Human Rights (UDHR),[52] and then given legal force in binding instruments including the 1956 Anti-Slavery Convention,[53] the 1966 International Covenant on Civil and Politics Rights (ICCPR),[54] the 1989 Convention on the Elimination of Discrimination Against Women (CEDAW),[55] and the 2003 Protocol to the African Charter on Human and Peoples' Rights.[56] This protection applies regardless of the persons' sex or gender identity.

The SCSL and ECCC could have mirrored that framework, by defining the term 'forced marriage' as any marriage—arranged or otherwise—that takes place without both spouses' 'full and free consent'. However, neither court took that position. Rather, they effectively isolated all arranged marriage practices from their definition of 'forced marriage', putting international criminal law out of sync with international human rights law (see Figure 13.2). An examination of the proceedings in both courts gives a sense of the politics behind this outcome.

[52] Universal Declaration of Human Rights (adopted 10 December 1948) UNGA Res 217 A (III) Article 16(2).

[53] Supplementary Convention on the Abolition of Slavery, the Slave Trade, and Institutions and Practices Similar to Slavery (adopted 7 September 1956, entered into force 30 April 1957) Article 1(c)(i).

[54] International Covenant on Civil and Political Rights (adopted 16 December 1966, entered into force 23 March 1976) 999 UNTS 171, Article 23(3).

[55] Convention on the Elimination of Discrimination Against Women (adopted 18 December 1979, entered into force 3 September 1981) Article 16(1)(b).

[56] Protocol to the African Charter on Human and People's Rights on the Rights of Women in Africa (adopted 1 July 2003, entered into force 25 November 2005) (Maputo Protocol) Article 6(a).

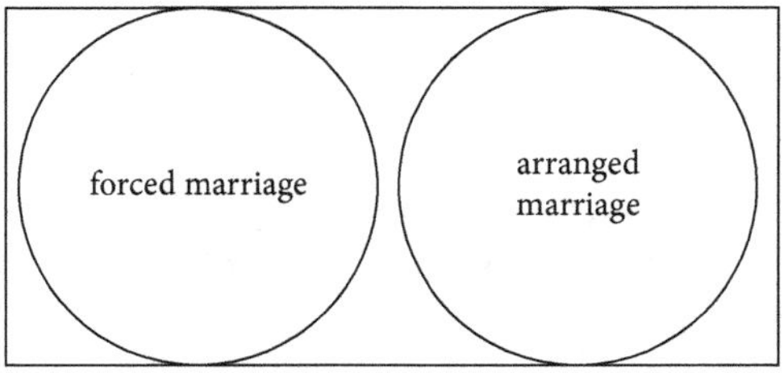

Figure 13.2 Forced and arranged marriage in international criminal law

In the SCSL, both parties called experts witnesses to describe the pre-war arranged marriage practices in Sierra Leone. In particular, both experts concentrated on arranged marriage involving child brides, which was relatively common practice before the war. The prosecution's expert was Zainab Bangura, a Sierra Leonean women's rights activist who had interviewed over 100 former 'bush wives', ex-combatants, and religious leaders in that country. In relation to pre-war marriages, Bangura stated that '[t]raditionally in Sierra Leone, young girls have been forced into early marriages by their parents. They have had no say in accepting or rejecting such marriages.'[57]

Dr Thorsen, the defence's expert, criticized that portrayal of child marriage. She argued that '[e]ven if girls were only asked symbolically at the very end of the courtship, they might well have had a chance to articulate their preferences directly or indirectly to some of their relatives at an earlier stage.'[58] Dr Thorsen also explained that when parents chose a husband for their daughter, their decision was shaped by poverty and other pressures, as well as what they perceived as best for their child.[59] This evidence did not directly contradict Bangura's point about girls' lack of choice, but it helped to contextualize and humanize the parents' decision-making process by explaining that often marrying off one's daughter when she is still a child may be the best economic and social option in the circumstances

Yet although these experts disagreed about the position of girls in child marriages, they agreed that those marriages were vastly different to the 'bush marriages' that occurred during the war. In those 'bush marriages', there was no process of seeking the family's consent and no wedding ceremony, and the wife could not turn to her family for support when the marriage became violent.[60] These distinctions between early marriages and 'bush marriages' were also emphasized

[57] *Prosecutor v Alex Tamba Brima et al ('AFRC case')* (Prosecution filing of expert report pursuant to rule 94(*bis*)) Annex 1, Trial Chamber II, 8 August 2005, 9.

[58] *Prosecutor v Brima et al ('AFRC case')* (Joint Defence Disclosure of Expert Report on Forced Marriages By Dr. Dorte Thorsen, Trial Chamber II) (21 August 2006) 9.

[59] ibid [6]–[7].

[60] *Prosecutor v Alex Tamba Brima et al ('AFRC case')* (Prosecution filing of expert report pursuant to rule 94(*bis*)) Annex 1 (8 August 2005) 13.

by the prosecution,[61] and in the separate opinions of Judge Doherty and Judge Sebutinde.[62] Judge Sebutinde also opined that:

> a clear distinction should be drawn between traditional or religious marital unions involving minors (early or arranged marriages), during times of peace; and the forceful abduction and holding in captivity of women and girls ('bush wives') against their will, for purposes of sexual gratification of their 'bush husbands' and for gender-specific forms of labour including cooking, cleaning, washing clothes (conjugal duties). In my view, while the former is proscribed as a violation of human rights under international human rights instruments or treaties like CEDAW, it is not recognised as a crime in International Humanitarian law. The latter conduct on the other hand, is clearly criminal in nature and is liable to attract prosecution.[63]

This comment on the legality or otherwise of 'traditional or religious marital unions involving minors... during times of peace' was not strictly necessary: those marriages were not at issue in the case. Yet evidently, Her Honour felt moved to address that politically sensitive issue.

The SCSL Appeals Chamber also elected to comment on this issue. It commended Judges Doherty and Sebutinde for drawing a 'clear and convincing distinction between forced marriages in a war context and the peacetime practice of "arranged marriages"'[64] and continued:

> [W]hile traditionally arranged marriages involving minors violate certain international human rights norms such as the Convention on the Elimination of all Forms of Discrimination Against Women (CEDAW), forced marriages which involve the abduction and detention of women and girls and their use for sexual and other purposes is clearly criminal in nature.[65]

This conclusion by the SCSL Appeals Chamber is concerning. It implies that the status of a practice as 'traditional' has a bearing on its criminality, which is an unacceptably vague test, and one that could excuse any number of violent practices with a sufficiently long lineage. The Appeals Chamber need not have taken that course. It could have affirmed that forcing someone into a marriage without their

61 *Prosecutor v Alex Tamba Brima et al ('AFRC case')* (Prosecution Final Trial Brief) (6 December 2006) [1884].

62 *Prosecutor v Alex Tamba Brima et al ('AFRC case')* (Separate Opinion (Doherty), Trial Chamber II) (21 June 2007) [36]; *Prosecutor v Alex Tamba Brima et al ('AFRC case')*, Separate Opinion (Sebutinde), Trial Chamber II, 21 June 2007 [12].

63 *Prosecutor v Alex Tamba Brima et al ('AFRC case')* (Separate Opinion (Sebutinde), Trial Chamber II) (21 June 2007) [12].

64 *Prosecutor v Alex Tamba Brima et al ('AFRC case')* (Appeal Judgment) (3 March 2008) [194].

65 ibid.

consent is an 'inhumane act' in *all* circumstances, because it violates that person's autonomy and personal dignity. This would not open the floodgates to prosecuting millions of arranged marriages as some might fear: to be a crime against humanity, the marriages would need to be 'part of a widespread and systematic attack on a civilian population', which would exclude most marriages arranged in a familial context.[66] However, it would bring international criminal law into line with international human rights law, and it would reinforce the message that gender-based violence is not excusable simply because it has been going on for centuries.

The issue of arranged marriage likewise proved contentious in the ECCC, because this practice was standard before Khmer Rouge times, and remains fairly common today.[67] Nuon Chea added fuel to the fire, claiming that, by charging him with 'forced marriage', the ECCC had 'effectively put the entire (and still widespread) practice of arranged marriage on trial here'.[68]

Both the prosecution and defence called expert witnesses to compare marriage during and prior to Khmer Rouge times. The prosecution's expert was Kasumi Nakagawa, a Japanese social scientist who had conducted interviews with Cambodian women about marriage and motherhood in Khmer Rouge times.[69] Nakagawa explained that in pre-Khmer Rouge times, marriage in Cambodia was arranged by each spouses' parents, 'so it's not a personal matter. It's a family matter between the two parties, two families, and also, it's a communal matters [sic], that the people in the village were invited to authorize such a marriage'.[70] The defence's expert, Australian-American anthropologist Peg Levine, affirmed that entire communities were involved.[71] Both experts stressed the importance of ceremony and rituals associated with marriage prior to Khmer Rouge times, and the grief caused by the regime's denial of these rites.[72]

Neither expert used the term 'forced' to describe arranged marriage in pre-Khmer Rouge times. However, Nakawaga's evidence indicated that in those times, young women generally had no option but to follow their parents' instructions. In her words:

> The traditional marriages in Cambodian society was arranged by the parents and agreed upon by the parents. In regard to the women's decision-making power,

66 See Rome Statute, Article 7(1); ILC, 'Crimes against humanity Texts and titles of the draft preamble, the draft articles and the draft annex provisionally adopted by the Drafting Committee on second reading' (15 May 2019) UN Doc A/CN.4/L.935, Article 2(1).

67 See Rosemary Grey, Yim Sotheary, and Kum Somaly, 'The Khmer Rouge Tribunal's First Reparation for Gender-Based Crimes: Where Art and Law Meet' (2020) 25 Australian Journal of Human Rights 488.

68 Case 002 (Nuon Chea's Closing Brief) (2 May 2017) [1136].

69 Nakagawa Kasumi, *Motherhood at War: Pregnancy during the Khmer Rouge regime* (2015).

70 Case 002/02 (Transcript of the hearing, Trial Chamber) (13 September 2016) 40, [16]–[19].

71 Case 002/02 (Transcript of the hearing, Trial Chamber) (10 October 2016) 53, lines [7]–[13].

72 Case 002/02 (Transcript of the hearing, Trial Chamber) (13 September 2016) 40, [1]–[15]; 69, line 10 to p 71, line 7; Case 002/02 (Transcript of the hearing, Trial Chamber) (10 October 2016) 53, [18]–[22].

> there was almost zero ... even though the single girls were consulted by her parents about her marriage, they blindly agreed to the marriage. So I don't think so it was a genuine consent that she really wanted to marry with that man from her own choice.[73]

Similarly, defendant Khieu Samphan argued that 'in Cambodian tradition marriage consisting of contract between two families whereby the consent of the prospective bride and groom is largely brushed aside or even ignored',[74] and added that disobeying one's parents 'had had far reaching consequences for *both* the young people concerned and their families, not least because it implied losing face' (emphasis added).[75] Several civil parties described their own pre-Khmer Rouge marriages in similar terms. For example, one woman recalled that 'we had to follow our parents' decision, so if our parents decided to marry us to that particular man or this man, we had to follow their decision'.[76] These statements indicate that marriage without both spouses' consent was fairly common prior to the Khmer Rouge period; it did not begin with the CPK's takeover in 1975. This is not to say that the Khmer Rouge marriages were *the same* as arranged marriages beforehand (there were significant differences, as explained above). However, it appears that even before 1975, young people's power in the marriage process was limited, and sometimes nil.

The Trial Chamber shied away from that point in its judgment. It emphasized the lavish nature of marriage ceremonies before the Khmer Rouge period, and the central role of family in the match-making process.[77] However, it enlarged the agency afforded to young people in those marriages, stating: 'while daughters were consulted about a prospective match and could refuse marriage, sons enjoyed more freedom in selecting a wife'.[78] The Chamber continued:

> In western culture, consent is given on the basis of an assessment and consequent choice of a partner made by the individual. In traditional Khmer culture, the making of this assessment and choice is delegated by the children to their parents on the basis of trust. Generally, arranged marriages do not include an element of force. There is no evidence that this delegation based on trust and the existence of a functional, caring family system was voluntarily transferred to the Party (*Angkar*).[79]

73 Case 002/02 (Transcript of the hearing, Trial Chamber) (13 September 2016) 39, [10]–[14], 47, [12]–[16].
74 Case 002 (Khieu Samphan's Closing Brief) (2 May 2017) (amended 2 October 2017) [2338].
75 ibid [2348].
76 Case 002 (Transcript, Trial Chamber) (23 August 2016) 26, [21] to page 27, [4].
77 Case 002/02 (Judgment, Trial Chamber) (27 March 2019) [3636]–[3640].
78 ibid [267].
79 ibid [3688].

The concept of 'delegation' seems misplaced here. Delegation suggests authorizing another person to exercise a power that one could otherwise exercise themselves. That was not the situation in pre-Khmer Rouge Cambodia, where young people generally lacked the authority to arrange their own marriage even prior to 1975. This revisionist history was not legally necessary: the Chamber's conclusion that CPK leaders were responsible for forced marriage did not depend on legitimizing marriage practices *before* the regime. However, the Chamber evidently felt compelled to recast those pre-1975 marriage practices in a positive light.

It was entirely appropriate that the SCSL and the ECCC drew distinctions between arranged marriages in peacetime and the conflict-related forced marriages that were the subject of prosecution. A failure to articulate those distinctions would be ignorant, and would unnecessarily demonize marriage practices in Cambodia and Sierra Leone. Indeed, that critique has been made of the Sierra Leone Truth Commission, which did not adequately distinguish 'bush marriages' from arranged marriage in that country.[80] However, when it came to analysing whether some arranged marriages in Sierra Leone and Cambodia were also *forced* marriages, according to international law, the SCSL and the ECCC obfuscated. Rather than acknowledging that 'arranged marriage' in peacetime spans a wide range of practices, some of which may be legally characterized as 'forced', both courts reserved the term 'forced marriage' for conflict-related marriages alone.

13.5 Conclusion

The recognition of the crime of forced marriage is an important, but controversial, part of the SCSL and the ECCC's legacies. It has been over ten years since the SCSL Appeals Chamber affirmed that forced marriage constitutes a crime against humanity, namely, an 'other inhumane act'. In the intervening years, three SCSL judges and many academic commentators have criticized that approach, but prosecutors at the ICC have nonetheless run with it, and have found favour with the Trial and Appeal Chambers.

Aside from that legal quandary, another problem that both the SCSL and the ECCC have struggled with is how to recognize the gravity and criminality of forced marriages that *disrupt* social norms, without appearing critical of local arranged marriage practices. This struggle is exacerbated by political undercurrents: international law is historically Euro-centric, and international courts bear the burden countering this image problem when they operate in other parts of the world. Hybrid courts may face additional pressures to be culturally sensitive, especially if they operate *in situ* and include national judges, as was the case with both

[80] See Mibenge (n 1) chapter 3.

the SCSL and the ECCC. These factors make criticism of local marriage practices especially impolitic. Reflecting on this challenge, ICC president Chile Eboe-Osuji has observed that:

> There is a certain anxiety surrounding this question [of forced marriage] ... That anxiety relates to the desire to exclude the practice of arranged marriages from the purview of international criminal law, noting, of course, that arranged marriages remain a sustained institution in much of the non-European world.[81]

It appears that both the SCSL and ECCC struggled with this anxiety, with the result that both courts blinded themselves to the reality that while many arranged marriages are consensual, some are not. This is particularly true for women and girls, who often have far less agency in the marriage process than their husbands-to-be.

A further concern is that, when speaking about arranged marriage, both courts tended to speak about local culture in static terms. In particular, the ECCC trial judgment made numerous references to 'Khmer culture', as if that is a unified and unchanging thing. The tendency to portray non-Western cultures in such terms is inaccurate: all cultures are multi-faceted and changable, none are preserved in amber. As a case in point, arranged marriage is becoming less common in Sierra Leone or Cambodia than it was one generation ago.[82] But the problem with presenting non-Western cultures as static is not just that it is inaccurate. The problem is also that it entrenches binary thinking, in which steps towards gender equality are perceived as steps *away* from culture, and local women's rights activists are seen to exist *outside* of culture rather than part of it. But these binaries are not inevitable: culture can also be seen as contested, and open to change. Embracing this more fluid understanding of culture means that universal human rights and culture need not be seen as competing values; the two can co-exist.[83]

As the ICC's jurisprudence on forced marriage continues to evolve, the Court can hopefully bring international criminal law closer to international human rights law in this respect. It can also avoid having to choose between internationally recognized human rights and local culture by recognizing that the right to consent to marriage is not only a top-down, international standard; it is also an aspiration for women and girls in many parts of the world, including those with firsthand

[81] Chile Eboe-Osuji, *International Law and Sexual Violence in Armed Conflicts* (Martinus Nijhoff 2012) 225.

[82] See, eg, *Prosecutor v Brima et al ('AFRC case')* (Prosecution filing of expert report pursuant to rule 94(*bis*)) Annex 1, Trial Chamber II (8 August 2005) 10; *Prosecutor v Brima et al ('AFRC case')* (Joint Defence Disclosure of Expert Report on Forced Marriages By Dr. Dorte Thorsen, Trial Chamber II) (21 August 2006) 9; Case 002 (Transcript, Trial Chamber) (23 August 2016) 26, [18] to 27, [4]. See also Grey, Yim, and Kum (n 65).

[83] Sally Engle Merry, *Human Rights and Gender Violence: Translating International Law into Local Justice* (University of Chicago Press 2005); Cyra Akila Choudhury, 'Beyond Culture: Human Rights Universalisms Versus Religious and Cultural Relativism in the Activism for Gender Justice' (2015) 30 Berkeley Journal of Gender, Law & Justice 226.

experience of being married without their 'full and free consent'. The experience of the SCSL and the ECCC also suggests that, for some victims/survivors, the inability to practice their religious and spiritual rituals around marriage may be felt as a particularly serious harm, perhaps more so than the inability to choose their own spouse. This form of cultural grief, where it is present in the evidence, ought to be addressed in prosecutions for 'forced marriage' in addition to the question as to the presence or absence of 'full and free consent'.

14

Hybrid Investigatory Mechanisms and Other Hybrid Justice Initiatives

Nelson Camilo Sánchez

Hybrid tribunals have not generally been used in Latin America. Typically, domestic ordinary criminal courts are favoured to provide accountability in transitions. However, in recent years, an innovative kind of hybrid investigatory mechanism has gained regional attention: the International Commission against Impunity in Guatemala (CICIG). CICIG was a United Nations (UN)-backed commission set up to support, strengthen, and assist Guatemalan institutions in investigating, prosecuting, and dismantling illegal groups and clandestine structures responsible for organized crime and human rights violations. It led the way to the creation of a similar commission in Honduras (MACCIH). In parallel, the Inter-American Commission on Human Rights (IACHR) launched an 'Interdisciplinary Group of Experts' to assist national authorities with the investigation of and search for forty-three disappeared students in Ayotzinapa, Mexico (Interdisciplinary Group of Independent Experts (IGIE)). The IACHR's effort in Mexico has since been replicated in Nicaragua and Bolivia.[1]

This chapter will focus on the aforementioned hybrid investigatory mechanisms and other innovative hybrid justice initiatives. The common feature underlying these mechanisms is the combination of domestic and international capacity applied to the investigation and prosecution of complex crimes in contexts characterized by gross and mass violence. Although this investigation is undertaken with the primary goal of bringing perpetrators to criminal trials—in contrast to other hybrids[2]—the trial and sanction of cases does not depend on the hybrid, nor the action of another international or internationalized tribunal. In most cases, domestic judicial authorities from the countries involved are those who use the work of documentation, investigation, and indictment of these hybrid mechanisms as the basis to criminally try those responsible.

[1] See IGIE Nicaragua, 'Report on the violent events that took place between April 18th and May 30th 2018' (December 2018).

[2] For other types of 'classic' hybrids, see Kirsten Ainley and Mark Kersten, 'Dakar Guidelines on the Establishment of Hybrid Courts' LSE and Wayamo Foundation (2019) <https://hybridjustice.com/dakar-guidelines/>.

Nelson Camilo Sánchez, *Hybrid Investigatory Mechanisms and Other Hybrid Justice Initiatives* In: *Hybrid Justice*. Edited by: Kirsten Ainley and Mark Kersten, Oxford University Press. © Nelson Camilo Sánchez 2025.
DOI: 10.1093/oso/9780192893758.003.0014

The chapter proceeds as follows. First, it distinguishes four types of modern hybrid justice mechanisms and summarizes their main traits. This assessment will include not only the aforementioned Latin American commissions, but also other arrangements of the type, such as the International Impartial Independence Mechanism to assist the investigation and prosecution of serious crimes in Syria (IIIM) and the Joint Investigation Team (JIT) established to conduct the criminal investigation of the Malaysia Airlines flight MH17 brought down over eastern Ukraine in 2014. Second, the chapter uses lessons from the Latin American hybrids and the context in which they operate to test some of the main questions of the book: how they are failing/succeeding in resisting political pressure, how they have increased their legitimacy, and how much we can expect them to contribute to delivering accountability.

14.1 Four Types of Investigatory Hybrids

The mechanisms this chapter analyses divide the process of accountability into two phases. The first phase concentrates on the tasks of investigation and prosecution. The second focuses on the trial and sanction. Although various versions of hybrids may result,[3] the trend is towards hybridization of the initial process, combined with a final phase governed above all by domestic judges and domestic law.

Within this trend, the chapter distinguishes four types of hybrids: (1) The Central American anti-corruption commissions (CICIG, in Guatemala; MACCIH in Honduras); (2) the IACHR interdisciplinary groups of independent experts (IGIE Ayotzinapa—Mexico; IGIE Nicaragua; IGIE Bolivia); (3) the UN International Impartial Independence Mechanisms (IIIMs) (Syria and Myanmar); (4) the Joint Investigation Teams (JITs) (Malaysia Airlines MH17 Flight JIT). This chapter will use, for its comparative analysis, emblematic examples from each category.

14.1.1 Anti-corruption commissions

The oldest of the mechanisms analysed is the CICIG, whose process of creation began in 2003. At the time, the UN, the government of Guatemala, the national ombudsman, and civil society organizations started discussing the establishment of a hybrid commission for combating the impunity of organized crime groups that had operated in Guatemala since the time of the internal armed conflict (they called it the Commission for the Investigation of Illegal Bodies and Clandestine

[3] Joint investigation and prosecution with solely domestic trial and sanction (or exclusively international), international (or domestic) investigation and prosecution and hybrid trial, or both phases may have hybrid characteristics.

Apparatus, CICIACS). Although the government and the UN signed an agreement for its creation, the Constitutional Court nullified the agreement, arguing the transfer of prosecutorial powers to a hybrid violated the state's constitutional sovereignty.[4] However, due to a progressive deterioration of the security conditions in the country, elite Guatemalans were forced to reopen the debate. The initial project was reformed and led to a signed agreement between the UN Secretary General and the government of Guatemala, creating a hybrid mechanism that would act completely within the Guatemalan legal system but would incorporate international staff and be financed completely by voluntary contributions from UN member states. The CICIG's primary task was to support the disarticulation of organized crime organizations and combat the impunity associated with their crimes. To fulfil this mandate, the CICIG had a series of powers that may be organized into two groups: powers related to promoting individual prosecutions and powers related to institutional reform.[5] The CICIG operated for over twelve years with mandates renewed every two years by different government administrations. As of September 2018, the CICIG estimated approximately 680 persons were being processed in cases initiated or assisted by the mechanism.[6] But beyond the statistics, the CICIG has generated interest due to the impact of various of its cases that have led to the disarticulation of illegal networks connected with very high-level state officials. The emblematic example of this impact is the investigation that forced then president and vice president, Otto Perez Molina and Roxana Baladetti, to resign, leading to their later investigation and conviction.[7] CICIG's mandate officially came to an end on 3 September 2019, after sitting Guatemalan president, Jimmy Morales, refused to renew its mandate and barred its chief from the country. However, the legacy of its work is still reverberating in Guatemalan society, as evidenced by the recent conviction of former president Otto Pérez Molina and his vice president, Roxana Baldetti. On 7 December 2022, a local court sentenced Pérez and Baldetti to sixteen years in prison after finding them guilty of two counts of corruption.

In 2015, during a time in which the CICIG was uncovering presidential corruption in Guatemala, allegations of public corruption to finance President Juan Orlando Hernández's campaign emerged in Honduras. At the top of the social demands for institutional reform was the creation of a CICIG for Honduras.[8] Given

[4] International Crisis Group, 'Learning to Walk without a Crutch: An Assessment of the International Commission against Impunity in Guatemala' (2011) Latin America Report No 36.

[5] To avoid the Constitutional Court from repeating the decision that prevented the entry into force of the CICIACS, the CICIG's mandate was more circumspect: in contrast to the mandate granted to the CICIACS, the CICIG did not have the authority to press charges independently of the judiciary and may only endorse them through the figure of '*querellante adhesivo*'/'complementary prosecutor').

[6] CICIG, 'Annual Work Report CICIG 2018' (2019) ¡Seguimos Trabajando!.

[7] Open Society Justice Initiative, 'Against the Odds: CICIG in Guatemala' (2016).

[8] Charles T Call, 'Avances y Desafíos: Informe sobre los primeros dos años de la Misión de Apoyo contra la Corrupción y la Impunidad en Honduras (MACCIH)' (2018) CLALS Working Paper Series No 16.

the magnitude of the political crisis, President Hernández had no option but to agree on an anti-corruption commission. But in order to avoid UN involvement in the process, he sought the assistance of the Organization of American States (OAS). This negotiation led to the establishment of the Support Mission against Impunity and Corruption in Honduras (MACCIH). Although there were similarities between the MACCIH and the CICIG, the former had a broader, more diffuse mandate, and fewer powers. The MACCIH had four lines of work: (i) to prevent and combat corruption through case processing; (ii) to review the criminal justice system and make recommendations for strengthening; (iii) to propose reforms to the political campaign finance system; and (iv) to propose reforms for the public security system. As in the case of the CICIG, the MACCIH worked with domestic institutions to strengthen them. However, in contrast to the Guatemalan commission, the MACCIH could not begin legal proceedings or receive complaints or investigate cases independently of the Public Prosecutor's Office. As a result, the MACCIH had to collaborate with Honduran prosecutors in their referral of cases to domestic courts. Since opening its doors in April 2016, the MACCIH faced a hostile domestic political context and had timid and ambivalent international support. In spite of this, the MACCIH worked with the Honduran Public Prosecutor's Office in eight cases of corruption, involving more than 400 people.[9] This work allowed the justice system to obtain, in the two first years of the MACCIH's existence, the conviction of twelve people, including two former ministers and a magistrate of the Council of the Judiciary. Additionally, the support of the MACCIH led to obtaining charges in two very high-profile cases against five legislators and the former first lady, Rosa Elena de Lobo.[10] Similarly to what happened in Guatemala, MACCIH's mandate came to an end in early 2020 when President Juan Orlando Hernandez decided not to renew its mandate.

14.1.2 The IACHR's Groups of Independent Experts (IGIEs)

The first IGIE was created in response to domestic and international indignation regarding the disappearance of forty-three students in Ayotzinapa, in the Guerrero State of Mexico in September 2014.[11] In the face of the lack of an appropriate response by Mexican authorities, the family members of the victims requested the IACHR adopt protection measures to guarantee the search for the students. As

[9] Center for Latin American and Latino Studies, American University, 'El Monitor de MACCIH. Análisis Independiente de la Misión de Apoyo contra la Corrupción y la Impunidad en Honduras (MACCIH) de la Organización de Estados Americanos' (2019) Special Edition, 1 August to 31 December 2018.

[10] Call, 'Avances y Desafíos' (n 8).

[11] OHCHR, 'Double Injustice: Report on Human Rights Violations in the Investigation of the Ayotzinapa Case' (15 March 2018).

part of the follow-up to these measures, the family members proposed the designation of a group of international specialists, selected independently by the IACHR, to supervise the actions of police and judicial authorities responsible for the search of the missing students. In November 2014, the IACHR, the Mexican government, and the families of the victims signed an agreement to create an Interdisciplinary Group of Independent Experts (IGIE) to provide technical follow-up and assistance on the case, such as to devise plans to search for the missing students, undertake a technical analysis of the lines of investigation to determine criminal liabilities, and perform a technical analysis of the Plan for Comprehensive Attention to Victims, among other related issues. The IGIE was comprised of five experts, including Claudia Paz y Paz, the former General Prosecutor of Guatemala, whose support was fundamental to the CICIG's work. The agreement established the group's six-month mandate that could be 'extended for as long as necessary in order to achieve its objective'.[12] The IGIE was authorized to undertake its own investigation of the facts independently, which included free access to detention centres to interrogate some of the accused being held in custody. However, in contrast to the commissions in Honduras and Guatemala, the Mexican Public Prosecutor's Office did not have a clear obligation to coordinate its actions with the IGIE or to follow its recommendations. Only six months after its conformation and after a rigorous process of technical investigation and the gathering of compelling scientific evidence, the IGIE published a report that refuted the narrative that other Mexican investigatory bodies defended. The report also contained a number of specific recommendations both for the Ayotzinapa case and for the more general context of disappearance in Mexico.[13] In 2016, the Mexican government did not endorse the renewal of the IGIE's mandate, but the IACHR continued to monitor compliance with its recommendations. Later, in 2019, President Miguel Lopez Obrador's administration requested the IACHR to set up a formal follow-up mechanism and welcomed two IACHR staff attorneys to support *in situ* local authorities.[14] Almost eight years after the enforced disappearance, the Mexican authorities made progress in the investigations. On 19 August 2022, at the request of the Attorney General's Office, arrest warrants were issued against the former Public Prosecutor in charge of the initial investigations, and against twenty military commanders and military personnel from the 27th and 41st battalions in the city of Iguala. Arrest

[12] United Mexican States, Inter-American Commission on Human Rights, Centro PRODH, 'Agreement for the incorporation of technical international assistance from a human rights perspective in the investigation of the forced disappearance of 43 students from the Normal Rural Raúl Isidro Burgos School of Ayotzinapa, Guerrero, within precautionary measures MC/409/2014 and in the framework of the monitoring powers the IACHR exercises regarding the human rights situation in the region' (2014).

[13] Mario Patrón and others, 'An Unprecedented Exercise of International Supervision: The Ayotzinapa Case and the Experience of the Interdisciplinary Group of Independent Experts (GIEI) in Mexico' (2017) 14 SUR International Journal on Human Rights.

[14] IACtHR, 'Third Report of the Special Follow-up Mechanism to the Ayotzinapa Case' (November 2022).

warrants were also issued against five administrative and judicial officials from the state of Guerrero; twenty-six police officials from Huitzuco; six from Iguala, and one from Cocula; plus eleven state police officials from Guerrero and fourteen members of the criminal group Guerreros Unidos.[15]

14.1.3 The UN International, Impartial and Independent Mechanisms (IIIMs)

The third model of hybrid investigation mechanisms this chapter analyses is represented by the United Nations International, Impartial, and Independent Mechanism to Assist in the Investigation and Prosecution of Those Responsible for the Most Serious Crimes Under International Law Committed in the Syrian Arab Republic since March 2011 (IIIM). Although the mechanism was created through a UN General Assembly resolution on 21 December 2016,[16] the head of the mechanism took up her duties on 8 August 2017. According to its own reports, the IIIM has been operational since April 2018.[17] Between the Mechanism's creation and the commencement of duties by its head, the UN High Commissioner for Human Rights oversaw the appointment of the start-up team that worked on structures and procedures for the IIIM's establishment. In the absence of UN Security Council action to ensure accountability for international crimes committed in Syria, fifty-five states represented in the General Assembly co-sponsored the creation of the IIIM, but not as a new criminal jurisdiction that can issue indictments, prosecute cases, or render judgments. Rather, the General Assembly created an office that would carry out preparatory work, grounded in criminal law methodologies, to advance the criminal process in 'available jurisdictions'.[18] Therefore, the legal work at the core of the IIIM's mandate has two main aspects. First, the IIIM has been mandated to collect, consolidate, preserve, and analyse evidence of violations. Second, the IIIM is mandated to prepare files in order to facilitate and expedite fair and independent criminal proceedings, in accordance with international law standards, in national, regional, or international courts or tribunals that have or may in the future have jurisdiction over these crimes. As of the IIIM's February 2022 report, the Mechanism is currently supporting the work of thirteen jurisdictions and has assisted ninety-one distinct national investigations.[19] However, the IIIM reported

[15] ibid.
[16] UNGA Res 71 (2016) UN Doc A/RES/71/248.
[17] UNGA, 'Report of the International, Impartial and Independent Mechanism to Assist in the Investigation and Prosecution of Persons Responsible for the Most Serious Crimes under International Law Committed in the Syrian Arab Republic since March 2011' (2019) UN Doc A/73/741.
[18] UNGA Res 71 (2016) UN Doc A/RES/71/248.
[19] UNGA, 'Report of the International, Impartial and Independent Mechanism to Assist in the Investigation and Prosecution of Persons Responsible for the Most Serious Crimes under International Law Committed in the Syrian Arab Republic since March 2011' (2022) UN Doc A/76/690, 3.

it had 'not received an acknowledgement of receipt or answer from authorities of the Syrian Arab Republic'.[20]

14.1.4 Joint Investigation Teams (JITs)

The last example of an investigation mechanism is the Joint Investigation Team of the Malaysia Airlines flight MH17 crash in 2014 (JIT). On 17 July 2014, Malaysia Airlines flight MH17, en route from Amsterdam to Kuala Lumpur, crashed in eastern Ukraine. Immediately after the crash, on 21 July 2014, the United Nations Security Council unanimously adopted a resolution supporting 'efforts to establish a full, thorough, and independent international investigation into the incident' in accordance with international civil aviation guidelines, and calling on all UN member states 'to provide any requested assistance to civil and criminal investigations'.[21] Dutch authorities took the lead in both the technical civil aviation and criminal investigations. For the latter, the Dutch government sought the assistance of Eurojust to promote cooperation from 'all countries that have lost nationals in the disaster'.[22] Ukrainian authorities were also invited to participate. A meeting held at Eurojust in July 2014 laid the groundwork for the establishment of a Joint Investigating Team (JIT) that comprised police officers and public prosecutors from Australia, Belgium, Malaysia, The Netherlands, and Ukraine. The Public Prosecutor from The Netherlands, in The Hague, coordinated the mechanism. A field office was established in Kiev, Ukraine.[23] The investigation focused on various components, including forensic investigation, finding and questioning witnesses and experts, analysing radar and satellite images, looking at huge quantities of telecommunications data such as wiretapped conversations, and analysing big data. However, the area of investigation in eastern Ukraine was inaccessible to the investigation team even before Russia's full-scale invasion of Ukraine. The technical report revealed the aircraft was shot down with a missile launched from a Buk-installation from the territory of Ukraine in an area that was under the effective control of separatists. Subsequent JIT investigations concluded that the weapon used to strike the aircraft had been brought into Ukraine from the territory of the Russian Federation and had been taken back to its territory after its deployment against flight MH17. Following the UN Security Council's refusal to establish an international tribunal to prosecute those responsible—prompted by Russia's

[20] ibid.

[21] UNSC Res 2166 (2014) UN Doc S/RES/2166.

[22] Letter of 24 July 2014 from the Minister of Foreign Affairs, the Minister of Security and Justice, and the Prime Minister to the President of the House of Representatives on the MH17 air disaster.

[23] However, since the February 2022 Russian Invasion of Ukraine, the team has been working from The Netherlands. See Netherlands Public Prosecution Service, 'The Criminal Investigation by the Joint Investigative Team' <https://www.prosecutionservice.nl/topics/mh17-plane-crash/criminal-investigation-jit-mh17> accessed 22 January 2024.

veto vote—in 2017, the five JIT countries decided prosecution under Dutch law and before a Dutch court was the best option. On 7 July 2017, Ukraine and The Netherlands concluded an agreement of international legal cooperation, allowing Dutch jurisdiction and the transfer of criminal proceedings; the extradition of suspects; conducting the trial via video-conferencing to enable defendant(s) to participate from outside The Netherlands; and the transfer of prison sentences. In June 2018, the Dutch senate approved new legislation to make it possible to charge suspects in The Netherlands. In June 2019, the JIT announced four suspects would be prosecuted for their alleged roles in the downing of flight MH17.[24] The JIT has sent out international arrest warrants for the four suspects. However, it has not requested their extradition as the constitutions of Ukraine and Russia do not allow the extradition of nationals. Criminal proceedings commenced before the district court in The Hague on 9 March 2020. The trial reconvened on 7 March 2022, and on 17 November 2022, the Court handed down life sentences to three defendants and acquitted a fourth. Presiding Judge Hendrik Steenhuis concluded, based on prosecutor evidence, that the plane was brought down by a Buk missile fired by pro-Moscow Ukrainian fighters.[25] Table 14.1 shows the hybrid investigatory mechanisms' main institutional features.

14.2 Institutional Design Choices

The options for institutional arrangements that derive from the creation and operation of these mechanisms are diverse. This section does not attempt to address each one in detail, but rather concentrates on two key aspects: the international/domestic balance in the hybrid, and the scope and nature of its mandate.

14.2.1 International–domestic trade-offs

Hybrid investigative mechanisms have a varied menu of options available to domestic policymakers in regard to its international component. In two of the five mechanisms, the international component stems from the United Nations, but through different bodies and forms of engagement. While the IIIM is the result of a General Assembly initiative, CICIG was under the wing of the UN Secretary General. Something similar occurs with the two mechanisms supported by

[24] According to information gathered by the JIT, three of the suspects have Russian citizenship and are currently residing in Russia. The remaining suspect is of Ukrainian nationality and the JIT believes he resides in eastern Ukraine, in an area not under the control of Ukrainian authorities.

[25] Mike Corder and Raf Casert, '3 convicted in 2014 downing of Malaysian jet over Ukraine' (*AP News* 18 November 2022) <https://apnews.com/article/russia-ukraine-business-kuala-lumpur-malaysia-netherlands-099084a82b49b77b116878e24fc63a18> accessed 22 January 2024.

Table 14.1 Hybrid investigatory mechanisms' main institutional features

Hybrid	Period of operation	Current status	Multilateral organization	Domestic jurisdiction	Headquarters	Source of funding	Annual budget
CICIG	2007 –2019 Mandate renewed every two years	Inactive	UN Secretary General	Guatemala	Guatemala	Voluntary contributions UN member states	Approx USD 15 million*
MACCIH	2016 –2020 Mandate renewed every four years	Inactive	Organization of American States Secretary General	Honduras	Honduras	Voluntary contributions from OAS state members and permanent observers	Approx. USD 9 million**
GIEI	2015 – 2016 Mandate renewed twice for an additional six months	Inactive	Inter-American Commission on Human Rights	Mexico	Washington, DC	Fully funded by Mexico	Approx. USD 2 million***
IIIM	2018 No term limit	Active	UN General Assembly	Syria	Geneva	UN regular budget	Approx. USD 18 million****
JIT	2014 No term limit	Active	None	Australia, Belgium, Malaysia, The Netherlands, Ukraine	The Hague/ Field office in Kiev	Prosecution proceedings jointly financed among all states. The Netherlands covers expenditures for its public prosecutors, the judiciary, and witness protection programmes	Unknown

* CICIG, 'Annual Work Report CICIG 2018'(n 6).

** MACCIH, 'Logros obtenidos de Abril de 2018 a marzo de 2019' (2019) <http://www.oas.org/es/sap/dsdme/maccih/new/docs/MACCIH.Logros-Abr2018-Mar2019..Actividades-Abr2019-Ene2020.pdf> accessed 22 January 2024.

*** OAS, 'Financial Reports' <https://www.oas.org/en/iachr/media_center/preleases/2019/067.asp> accessed 22 January 2024.

**** UN, 'In First Annual Budget Since 1973, Fifth Committee Approves $3.07 Billion for 2020, Concluding Main Part of Seventy-Fourth Session' (27 December 2019) <https://ww.un.org/press/en/2019/gaab4350.doc.htm> accessed 22 January 2024.

the OAS: while the MACCIH responds to a more political body (the Secretary General), the IGIE is supported by a technical human rights body—the Inter-American Commission on Human Rights. Finally, the outlier of the group is the JIT, which does not have a specific international connection, and thus is not a hybrid mechanism in the strict sense, but rather a system of cooperation between domestic jurisdictions.[26]

In the abstract, it is impossible to establish which of the two models prevails. On the one hand, international representation based on a more political body offers the high-level political support the hybrid requires. Yet, the political nature of the support body may lead to attempts of interference and politicization of the mechanism by the international institution, as demonstrated by the role played by the OAS Secretary General as regards the MACCIH.[27] On the other hand, although the IGIEs demonstrates how a technical and independent human rights body is a useful ally to avoid political interference, it also shows its intrinsic limitations. A vivid example is the IACHR's lack of political muscle to guarantee greater implementation of IGIE recommendations on the part of the Mexican Public Prosecutor's Office or to prevent the mechanism from having to abruptly end its work when its mandate was not renewed.

The type of relationship established between the international component and domestic authorities also presents interesting variations between mechanisms. The IIIM has a completely vertical relationship between the international and domestic components, as the General Assembly resolution did not negotiate the mechanism's mandate with Syria, the state involved.[28] The other mechanisms show a more negotiated process that ends in the adoption of an agreement between parties. This path opens the door not only to government participation, but also to the involvement of Congress and judicial review of the agreements by domestic courts, as occurred in Guatemala and Honduras. Buy-in from domestic stakeholders promotes greater legitimacy and better inclusion of the mechanism into the state's institutional fabric. At the same time, this model allows for the intervention of domestic powers that can completely veto the mechanism or substantially reduce its powers.

[26] However, the JIT MH17 is part of this selection for the specific internationalization needs of the context to be responded to, which makes it different from others of this type. In the context JIT operates, not only is there judicial cooperation between national jurisdictions, but also the facts involve the exercise of justice in a territory in which it is legally and factually unclear which authority has the obligation and capacity to exercise jurisdiction. Therefore, similarly to what the IIIM does, the JIT MH17 became as a judicial investigation project pending possible developments that allowed for an international court to have jurisdiction to process those responsible. As the Security Council denied this option, the alternative undertaken at the moment is processing in a single domestic jurisdiction by agreement of the five States involved.

[27] Call, 'Avances y Desafíos' (n 8).

[28] The Syrian government's official position is that it 'do(es) not recognize this mechanism', viewing it as 'counter to the UN Charter'. United Nations Budget 2020, Fifth Committee debate (27 December 2019).

The hybrids analysed demonstrate the need to balance the practical benefits and limitations of administrative and operational dependence on international bodies. Comparing the MACCIH with CICIG, for example, one can note how the relative administrative independence of CICIG with respect to the UN has meant that many of the bureaucratic obstacles derived from how the UN works were avoided. However, not being an official UN agency created problems regarding the benefits and stability of CICIG personnel, which made recruiting and retaining competent personnel extremely challenging. Additionally, greater independence from the international body generated doubts regarding the hybrid's ability to avoid overstepping or distorting its powers. Thus, a clear accountability mechanism is necessary.

Furthermore, the domestic/international dichotomy manifests through the ways the international community supports and legitimizes the hybrid to its domestic counterparts (prosecutors and judges) in the face of attacks from local elites, particularly when the interests of these elites are represented in the highest levels of government. The IIIM has a particular position; although the General Assembly mandate signals support from the international community, the lack of consensus among the powers represented in the Security Council prevents consistent backing to the prosecution of the crimes.[29] In the case of Latin American hybrids, beyond the multilateral organizations that support the international component of the hybrid, the support of the United States has really been the decisive factor in weathering the attacks of elites adversely affected by the work of the judiciary.[30]

14.2.2 Scope and nature of the mandate

One of the most important characteristics of these experiences of investigatory hybrids is their fluidity to adapt to the concrete needs and opportunities of their local context. It all starts with the negotiation of one of the most contentious issues in the existence of a hybrid: the scope of its mandate. The more limited a mandate is (a given case, or a group of specific cases), the greater the possibility of creating a realistic institution that the international community is more willing to finance. This model also makes it easier for monitoring its functions. Nevertheless, a more limited mandate may make it difficult for the hybrid to obtain long-term systemic impacts in the justice system. It may also become an undue intrusion in its capacity

[29] The Russian Federation, who sits on the UNSC, views the IIIM as 'an illegitimate mechanism' (followed by China, Iran, and others which disavow its existence). United Nations Budget 2020, Fifth Committee debate (27 December 2019).

[30] Michael Camilleri and Catharine Christie, 'How The "Art of the Deal" Hurt Latin America's Corruption Fight' (*Americas Quarterly*, 30 January 2020) <https://www.americasquarterly.org/content/how-trumps-art-deal-hurt-latin-americas-corruption-fight> accessed 22 January 2024.

to analyse patterns of violence and impunity and make the best determinations about which problems it should concentrate on in order to be more effective.

Regarding these criteria, the most expansive mandate is that of the IIIM, as its mandate extends, generically, to any international crime committed during the Syrian conflict. The IIIM thus has the jurisdiction, but also the great challenge, of determining what type of cases it will prioritize and select from the vast universe of the atrocious crimes committed over nearly a decade of conflict. CICIG and the MACCIH were given similar responsibilities, though with narrower aims. The CICIG's mandate, for example, does not include specific crimes, but rather a specific aim: investigate and dismantle 'illegal security bodies and clandestine security apparatus.'[31] For its part, the MACCIH's mandate gives it generic jurisdiction for 'cases of corruption.' The MACCIH decided to frame its work against impunity as dismantling 'corrupt networks.'[32]

By contrast, the JIT and IGIE are examples of investigatory hybrids whose objective is to support the investigation and prosecution of a high impact event. Thus, their mandates are restricted to those events. The JIT had a more limited mandate with respect to its scope, as its function has been to investigate the downing of Malaysian Airlines flight MHI7, without any additional connection to the armed conflict underway in Ukraine, even before the Russia's full-scale invasion of Ukraine. Although its work is limited to the search for the forty-three students who disappeared in Ayotzinapa, IGIE's mandate is broader as it sought to produce a systematic impact beyond the case (strengthening institutional capacities of the Mexican state for the search and localization of disappeared persons and the investigation of cases of forced disappearance). Table 14.2 lays out the mandates of the hybrid investigatory mechanisms.

Moreover, these hybrids have adopted different strategies to address the interplay between international crimes and other crimes usually committed in these contexts that tend to support the persistence of violence as well as its impunity. One option is to rely on the language of international criminal law (ICL). The resolution of the UN General Assembly that determines the sphere of intervention of the IIIM restricted its intervention to the 'investigation and prosecution of persons responsible for the most serious crimes under international law' committed in Syria.[33] Domestic law is not mentioned in the IIIM´s mandate, and its assessment

[31] Such bodies were defined as those that illegally undermine the ability of citizens to exercise political power and civil rights and that have links to state officials or generate impunity for their actions. Agreement between the United Nations and the State of Guatemala in the establishment of an International Commission Against Impunity in Guatemala, Article 1.

[32] According to a recent report, this narrow focus 'has frustrated some Hondurans who wish MACCIH to investigate important human rights cases with no apparent link to corrupt networks.' Charles T Call, 'International Anti-Impunity Missions in Guatemala and Honduras: What Lessons for El Salvador?' (2019) CLALS Working paper Series No 21.

[33] Thus, the IIIM was mandated to 'collect, consolidate, preserve, and analyse evidence of violations of international humanitarian law and human rights violations and abuses' and to 'prepare files in order

Table 14.2 Mandates of the hybrid investigatory mechanisms

Scope		Legal focus		Powers	
Limited	JIT IGIE	Strict ICL language	IIIM	Investigatory prosecutorial	IIIM IGIE MACCIH CICIG JIT
Broad	CICIG MACCIH IIIM	Human rights/ criminal law language	JIT IGIE		
		Anti-corruption impunity focus	MACCIH CICIG	Legal reform	IGIE CICIG MACCIH

seems to be subordinated to the needs of the mechanism in the valuation and application of international law.

By contrast, the JIT frames the problem mainly in the language of domestic criminal law of the countries involved. The downing of Flight MH17 potentially generated the activation of a series of normative statutes, from the point of view of international responsibility of the state, including criminal responsibility and individual civil liability.[34] The 1971 Montreal Convention for the Suppression of Unlawful Acts against the Safety of Civil Aviation is of particular relevance to this case. However, the substantive and procedural laws that have governed the investigation have been above all domestic (which has led to an act of legal filigree to adhere to the various laws and principles of the different countries). The trial has been carried out under Dutch criminal legislation.

For their part, Latin American hybrids present a more explicit opening to the combination of domestic and international law, as well as to the relationship between crimes exclusive to ICL and other types of crimes. The Ayotzinapa IGIE expressly determines the sphere of functions both in the view of international human right law, as well as that of domestic criminal law. As a result, the IGIE was responsible for analysing whether the state had 'correctly exhausted' all lines of investigation of the forced disappearance, 'in particular the ties between organized crime and state actors, using the appropriate legal figures for framing crimes and criminal liability'.[35]

The anti-corruption missions in Guatemala and Honduras are the most innovative. Both mechanisms were created in post-conflict societies confronting

to facilitate and expedite fair and independent criminal proceedings, in accordance with international law standards'. UNGA Res 71/248 (2017) UN Doc A/RES/71/248.

[34] Marieke de Hoon, 'Navigating the Legal Horizon: Lawyering the MH17 Disaster' (2017) 33 Utrecht Journal of International and European law 90.

[35] IGIE Agreement, Point 6.1.

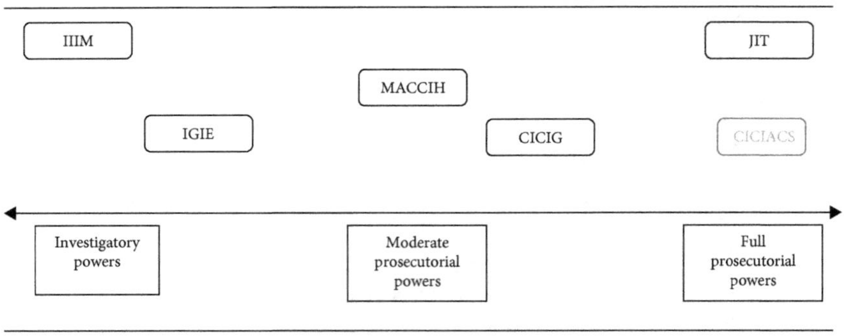

Figure 14.1

problems of severe impunity for past crimes; high lethal criminality in the present; little state capacity to judicially confront this criminality; and a perceived connection between public corruption, human rights crimes, and organized crimes. But neither of the mandates expressly address the issue of human rights or ICL. The approach adopted prioritizes the dismantlement of corruption networks as the central mandate of the hybrids. Because there are communication channels between corruption crimes and human rights violations, eventually the work of these mechanisms may promote accountability for these crimes, but this is not their specific function.

A third lesson is that the scope of the hybrids' mandate and functions influenced their overarching design. The most appealing characteristic of these mechanisms is the combination between hybrid investigation/prosecution and the adjudication of responsibility in an *unmixed tribunal* (which is generally entirely domestic in terms of personnel and the law it applies). But not all hybrids have enjoyed the same powers. Figure 14.1 presents the variations of the distinct mandates based on a spectrum that takes two reference points. The left side of the spectrum shows the mandates with the least expansive mandates, which are those that authorize powers of investigation, but do not act as legal prosecutors. On the right side of the spectrum are those mandates that grant full prosecutorial powers, which includes not only carrying out activities to investigate crimes, but also the capacity to decide to initiate processes and the authority to appear in court. The prosecutorial functions are divided into two groups. Prosecutorial functions may be moderate (where the hybrid accompanies or assists domestic prosecutors) or may extend to the authority to exercise these powers with complete independence and autonomy.

The IIIM is the mechanism with the most limited mandate in these terms. To the extent that its function is only 'to carry out essential preparatory work', its powers are limited to 'collect, consolidate, preserve, and analyse evidence of violations', and to 'prepare files' to facilitate and expedite future criminal proceedings. The mechanism has been described as having a 'quasi-prosecutorial function',[36] which is an apt description, as its functions go beyond being a mere information repository. The IIIM exercises functions that resemble the legal and strategic decisions of a prosecutor, including decisions regarding the selection and prioritization of cases.[37]

The Ayotzinapa mandate, for its part, is focused mainly on the 'technical analysis of investigatory lines to determine criminal responsibilities'. To this end, the IGIE acted as a specialized auditor of the work carried out by Mexican authorities. According to its mandate, if the IGIE found that not 'all lines of investigation' were 'correctly' exhausted, it had the authority to 'recommend what actions should be implemented to ensure the investigation is completely exhausted in the different levels of responsibility and lines of investigation'.[38] Regarding procedural initiative, the agreement also authorized the IGIE to act as an 'assistant in investigations', as well as 'to present criminal complaints for the prosecution of the crime' before relevant authorities. In practice, the independent labours of investigation (which radically contrasted to the investigatory activities of the Mexican judiciary) wound up being the main contribution of the IGIE. Given the lack of political willingness of the Attorney General to review the actions in the case and cooperate with the IGIE, the hybrid could not provide the support to domestic authorities envisaged in its mandate.

The MACCIH is located a step to the right on the spectrum. Although Honduran civil society expected the mandate to allow the mission to receive complaints directly, investigate cases of corruption, and file charges independently of the Public Prosecutor's Office and the Honduran Attorney General, the final agreement granted the MACCIH fewer powers. The mission was authorized to 'provide technical advice, supervise, evaluate, and actively collaborate' with Honduran institutions to investigate and try corruption cases. To do so, the MACCIH had the authority to select cases (something that goes beyond the mandate of the CICIG, which must coordinate the selection of cases with the Attorney General of Guatemala), but, in contrast to its Guatemalan sister, cannot directly receive complaints, nor present charges to judges. To exercise these tasks, the MACCIH created a special investigation unit against corruption (the UFECIC) comprised of local and international prosecutors selected and certified by the Mission. They

[36] See UNGA Res 71/755 (2016) UN Doc A/71/755, para 32.

[37] The IIIM has understood that its mandate requires it to 'collect the evidence, build a sophisticated understanding of the situation in Syrian Arab Republic and the relevant actors, map the crime patterns, identify those most responsible, craft appropriate legal frameworks and develop case files'. The mechanism has also proposed that its ultimate aim is 'to assure that the scope of the associated cases will be manageable, in terms of both cost and time'. UNGA, 'Report of the International, Impartial and Independent Mechanism to Assist in the Investigation and Prosecution of Persons Responsible for the Most Serious Crimes under International Law Committed in the Syrian Arab Republic since March 2011' (28 February 2018) UN Doc A/72/764 paras 10, 17.

[38] IGIE Agreements, Points 6.1 and 6.2.

investigated key corruption cases and networks in the country, through the establishment of integrated investigation and prosecution teams. This team worked together with a partner unit in the Honduran Attorney General Office, responsible for exercising prosecutorial functions per se.

CICIG is the mechanism with the most expansive powers regarding criminal prosecution.[39] However, as mentioned above, the initial agreement that granted 'complete authority to the CICIACS to exercise full independent prosecutorial functions' was abandoned as a result of a Guatemalan Constitutional Court decision that stated functions of filing criminal charges are exclusive to the national Public Prosecutor's Office.[40] According to its mandate, the CICIG served as a complementary prosecutor, working in close cooperation with domestic judicial institutions (the Public Prosecutor's Office, national civilian police, and law enforcement). CICIG could promote prosecutions by filing criminal complaints with national authorities, and it also had the authority to join criminal proceedings as a private prosecutor (acting as '*querellante adhesivo*'—complementary prosecutor).[41] According to many commentators, this authority was critical to the success of the CICIG throughout its mandate.[42]

Finally, the Latin American hybrids are characterized by having complementary powers to the criminal processing of cases. These powers generally focus on strengthening local capacities and promoting institutional reform. Anti-corruption missions like the IGIE have, at the basis of their mandate, the conception that the mechanisms promote systemic reforms that assist local powers in combatting violence and corruption more efficiently. Although this facet is generally considered critical in the functioning of these mechanisms, one must ask how much an agenda of technical advice for institutional reform diverts the mechanism from its prosecutorial functions.[43]

[39] Within the mechanisms under analysis, JIT MH 17 is the only example of full prosecutorial powers. However, as mentioned above, the JIT is not technically a hybrid mechanism for these effects, as prosecutors from the countries involved exercise their functions directly, in accordance with the constitutional and legal norms of each country.

[40] Lisbeth Zimmermann, 'On Our Terms! How Domestic Elites Localized the International Commission Against Impunity in Guatemala' (2018) 18 Conflict, Security & Development 347.

[41] Under this figure, in accordance with Guatemalan law, the CICIG may exercise criminal prosecution or adhere to that undertaken by the Public Prosecutor's Office. In such cases, the CICIC collaborates with the public prosecutor and assists in the investigation of the facts. It may also request the practice and reception of investigative procedures as provided for by Guatemalan law.

[42] International Crisis Group, 'Learning to Walk without a Crutch' (n 4).

[43] Thus, eg, in its two-year evaluation of the MACCIH, the report by CLALS of American University considered, 'these expansive mandates have not helped the mission have much impact, and by contrast, they have diverted resources and attention that could have been used to strongly hit corruption and impunity hard'. Call, 'Avances y Desafíos' (n 8).

14.3 Reflections on Impact and Legacy of the Latin American Investigatory Hybrids

This final section focuses on the experience of Latin American hybrids to provide some tentative answers to this volume's cross-cutting questions regarding the resilience, sustainability, and impact of hybrid mechanisms.[44] Variations among contexts and dates of establishment of the mechanisms make it impossible to give a single answer to these questions. CICIG has had more time to carry out its activities: twelve years, thanks to its initial mandate and five renewals. The MAACIH, by contrast, enjoyed a single four-year mandate. Finally, the IGIE of Ayotzinapa concluded its activities one year after formation and after its initial mandate of six months was renewed for an additional six months. Thus, given its longer history, much of the conversation regarding these mechanisms inevitably concentrates on the achievements, limitations, and challenges of the CICIG.

The Latin American hybrids have an excellent reputation, both within the specialized community and in the public opinion of some countries.[45] Within the specialized community, the CICIG has received greater interest and enthusiasm, but regional experts have also positively evaluated the progress of the MACCIH[46] and the innovation of the IGIE.[47] In fact, the word CICIG has become a symbol of anti-corruption in the community of justice activists.[48] The notion of hybrid

[44] The JIT and IIM are outside this analysis because to date they have not managed to produce concrete progress in the trial of those responsible for the crimes under investigation. This, at least in the case of the IIIM, is due to its short time of operation to date.

[45] Elizabeth J Zechmeister and Dinorah Azpuru, 'What does the public report on Corruption, The CICG, The Public Ministry and The Constitutional Court in Guatemala?' (2017) Latin American Public Opinion Project, Top Brief No 29. (Noting that 'the Guatemalan public has high levels of trust in the CICIG: in 2017, 70.6% of the population expressed some degree of trust in the institution').

[46] The two-year evaluation report on the MACCIH, published by the American University Project on Monitoring MACCIH and Anti-Impunity Efforts in Honduras states that, in spite of the limitations and critiques that one may make of the MACCIH, 'Ultimately, MACCIH and CICIG have shown that, with some minimal cooperation from the national authorities and institutions, hybrid missions can make a difference in helping anti-corruption investigations that touch high-level officials'. Charles Call, 'From Steady Progress to Severely Wounded: A Two-year Report on the performance of the OAS Mission in Support of the Fight against Corruption and Impunity in Honduras' (2018) CLALS Working Paper Series No 18.

[47] According to an expert report, the IGIE's main contributions to accountability for human rights violations in Mexico include: (i) greater visibility of the central role of the victims; (ii) the reconstruction of a complex criminal event based on a variety of voices and evidence; (iii) the prioritization of scientific and objective evidence; (iv) the identification of structures of macro-criminality underlying the facts; (v) the identification of a concrete and feasible path for establishing the whereabouts of the missing students; and (vi) the construction of a new model of international supervision to end impunity. See Patrón and others (n 13).

[48] As mentioned, the figure of CICIG was fundamental to the Indignant Movement in Honduras (Michael Lohmuller, 'Honduras Prosecutors Call for Own Version of CICIG' (*InSightCrime*, 9 June 2015). The Salvadorian government of Nayib Bukele used the creation of a CICIG for El Salvador as a campaign promise. (Luis Marroquin, 'Bukele reitera que creará comisión contra la impunidad' (*ElSalvador.Com*, 5 February 2019). Similar initiatives have extended beyond Central America, such as the case of Colombia, where a congresswoman recently proposed using this figure ('I think that for our country it is necessary to have a system, a very strong shock therapy, such as an international

mechanisms is not seen as a single panacea,[49] but rather as a possibly desirable option for an institutional arrangement to confront chronic impunity and corruption. The success of these mechanisms, in particular those that have involved high-level public officials, has generated expectations—in the hope that the tradition of absolute rejection of any type of international intervention and the absolute lack of a culture of judicial transparency has begun to crack, even if the enthronement of corruption, endogamy, and co-optation of regional judiciaries have not been fully eradicated.

These hybrids have adjusted to the circumstances to navigate the contexts in which they work. Given the contextual restrictions and existence of powerful spoilers, there is not a widespread culture or system of accountability. Rather, experience demonstrates that the strategic use of available resources to create small innovations allows for certain advances. The CICIG was the first innovative initiative, which stands out for its use of the 'complementary prosecutor' figure. In the MACCIH, justice activists did not find an environment for the use of a similar figure, and thus decided to strengthen the capacities of the hybrid to select its cases (something the CICIG cannot do) and deepen its role of institutional strengthening. For its part, the IGIE adopted the centrality of victims as a key aspect of its mandate and functions, not as an accessory service to its main functions. Additionally, IGIE stands out due to its extraordinary results in investigation that it carried out in only a few months.[50]

Nonetheless, each time an idea seems to work, there is a new wave of resistance that appears to limit its scope. This concentric pressure has left the feeling of 'sequels are never as good as the original'. This is seen in the comparison of the MACCIH with the CICIG, or between the Ayotzinapa IGIE and the IGIE created later to investigate the violence that occurred between 18 April and 30 May 2018, in Nicaragua. But this sensation does not take into account the differences in the context, moment, and needs of each case.

In fact, one of the lessons of the Latin American hybrids is the tremendous importance of translating legal mandates into investigative strategies. And, on this aspect, experience shows strategic battles are constant. The negotiation of the

commission of investigation and justice like that in Guatemala.'); Revista Semana, 'Interview: Comisión Internacional, propuesta de Angélica Lozano para el caso de Odebrecht' (20 November 2018).

[49] Peru is one of these exemplary experiences of exclusively domestic prosecution of both cases of human rights violations and corruption in the region. This is so, not only based on the emblematic trial of Alberto Fujimori, but also for the actions of the judiciary in the recent regional scandal regarding corruption promoted by the Brazilian company Odebrecht, which has resulted in the prosecution and detention of several former presidents. Sonia Goldenberg, 'Does Peru Need a Special Prison Just for Ex-Presidents?' (*New York Times*, 17 August 2017).

[50] This contrasts with the little progress the CICIG had made several years after beginning its work, or even with that of the MACCIH, which, although it achieved quicker investigatory results given its strategy of beginning with cases that had already been initiated by the domestic judiciary branch, did not do so in the record time the IGIE did.

international agreement has usually been the first, but not the definitive, hurdle, in the definition of the hybrid's functions. In some cases, this phase lasted years and various options were discussed (such as in Guatemala), while in others it was short and based mainly on a pre-existing format (such as the Nicaragua IGIE). A legal struggle carried out in the constitutional tribunals often follows, given the characteristics of the domestic legal systems. In Guatemala, this struggle led to the denial of independent prosecutorial powers to the hybrid; in Honduras, the Court left the MACCIH's mandate untouched, but struck down the Special Prosecutorial Unit against Corruption and Impunity (UFECIC), a unit created under the Attorney General to make MACCIH operative. Other battles occur in the political sphere (such as those related to the budget, renewal of the mandate, and national and international visibility), and obviously a final dispute occurs in domestic courts in each of the cases processed. The definition of the mandate in the installation agreement is therefore just the beginning of a road full of obstacles, clashes, and detours that gives few moments to accelerate and enjoy the view.

Manoeuvring in this minefield requires understanding domestic powers and creating strategic alliances that do not work against the basic principles the hybrid pursues. All the mechanisms have faced a lack of support, and in many cases hostility, from the government administrations, even when the same administration signed the international agreement.[51] Judiciaries have also been generally hostile. But key actors within these branches of government have opened the door for hybrids to develop. To the extent that their powers depend on the Public Prosecutor's Office, the successes of the hybrids are also successes of these institutions. What today are counted as successes of the CICIG, for example, were achieved only due to the participation of prosecutors like Claudia Paz y Paz and Thelma Aldana in Guatemala. Part of this strategic alliance also led to the creation of domestic structures that were extremely important for the processes: the creation of a series of specialized courts known as High Risk Courts and Tribunals.[52] For the creation of these bodies, usually the hybrids must go through the legislative branch, upon which they depend for the legal reforms that provide their counterparts in prosecutor's offices and specialized courts in order to do their work more efficiently. The paradox of this need, which was evident in Honduras, is that the structures of corruption the hybrids seek to investigate tend to have deep connections within these branches (and the power of the economic elites that underlie them), with which they may exercise an enormous veto power of the hybrids' work.

[51] Perhaps the tensest relationship that the CICIG experienced was when the Morales government declared persona non grata Commissioner Velásquez, prevented his entry into the country, and later denied the renewal of the mandate of the mechanism.

[52] Claudia Paz and Paz Bailey, 'Transformando la justicia en Guatemala: Estrategias y desafíos en la investigación de muertes violentas 2011-2014' (2018) Georgetown University—Open Society Foundations.

Indeed, this is an aspect that we must not lose sight of: the adverse context in which these mechanisms operate. The culture of prevailing impunity and the enthronement of corrupt powers in all decision-making arenas shape the environments in which these institutions move.[53] Thus, while expectations that hybrids can quickly and radically overcome the phenomena of corruption, violence, and impunity are understandable, they are unrealistic. Measuring the success or failure of the hybrids based on the eradication of these phenomena misses the mark. Rather, the hybrids must be understood as tools that, alongside other domestic and international processes, contribute to the dismantling of certain structures that promote conditions for these phenomena to perpetuate.

The judicial and institutional impact of these mechanisms is undeniable. Their unprecedented work made two important demonstrations to the citizenry of these countries. First, it showed that the most powerful people in the country can be held to account for criminal behaviour.[54] Second, it demonstrated that, given the political space, national judicial institutions could work.[55] The mechanisms also contributed to the legal framework for effective prosecution and to the institutional capacity of the Public Ministry and the courts. For instance, they have helped introduce and legitimize modern technical criminal investigation methods, including wiretapping conversations. Finally, compared to international tribunals, the anti-corruption commissions operated with remarkable efficiency.[56]

14.4 Conclusions

Promoting accountability for complex crimes in which sophisticated and powerful criminal networks participate is no easy task. Particularly when these crimes are committed in contexts plagued by violence and a culture of impunity. For this reason, the innovative measures analysed in this chapter are appealing to those who seek to promote institutional arrangements that support local efforts through technical, political, and financial support from the international community.

[53] For example, one must take into account that these contexts are highly violent and represent a high security risk for judicial authorities, victims, and witnesses. In fact, one of the saddest consequences of the success of these cases has been the exile into which, among others, Claudia Paz y Paz and Thelma Aldana, the two former general prosecutors of Guatemala that worked side by side with the CICIG, have been forced.

[54] Charles T Call and Jeffrey Hallock, 'Too Much Success? The Legacy and Lessons of the International Commission Against Impunity in Guatemala' (2020) CLALS Working Papers Series No 24 (noting that 'CICIG investigated and supported Public Ministry indictments of a sitting president, vice president, ministers, former generals and other military officers, and the country's powerful traditional economic families and non-traditional elites, as well as dozens of legislators and mayors.)

[55] In twelve years of work, CICIG contributed to 1,540 indictments in 120 cases involving over 100 illicit networks that were damaged if not dismantled.

[56] Call and Hallock, 'Too Much Success?' (n 54).

Miguel Zamora has wisely coined the term 'institutional grafting' to capture the delicate balance these mechanisms seek to achieve. In his words: '"grafting" refers to a system that is neither a surrogate for a national institution, such as an international tribunal or investigative commission, nor a transplant that creates a new institution, like a hybrid tribunal.'[57] In that sense, these mechanisms combine 'a discrete international element . . . with an existing national institution with the intention that together they will strengthen and develop the national institution.'[58]

This combination of features seems particularly promising for some contexts. For example, in cases in which there is not a local power with sufficient capacity or that can be trusted with the task of collecting and analysing information to support possible future trials (as is the case of Syria or Ukraine). Additionally, this model can make advances in situations in which cases do not reach justice due to local weaknesses in investigating facts, analysing responsibilities, and filing charges against alleged perpetrators. These are cases in which judges wait for cases to arrive to them, but whose public prosecutors do not have the tools to bring viable cases to court (as seen in Central America and Mexico).

These hybrid formats have other characteristics that make them preferable to completely internationalized mechanisms. First, they can be less expensive, as it is not necessary to create an entirely new system of judges, or to pay salaries and costs for international judges. Second, they can create greater legitimacy in decisions, as local, ordinary justices will decide regarding responsibility and sanctions, and not a temporary court or tribunal that will dissolve once the process is completed. Third, real incentives for cooperation between the international and domestic justice systems are created.

However, experience shows that these positive aspects must be evaluated against the limitations or risks that such hybrids bring or may bring. The combination of powers, models, and international and domestic norms brings opportunities and limitations. Additionally, in dividing responsibilities, there is always a latent risk of fragmenting the accountability of the mechanism. It is important that the hybrid is not constricted by local power nor by the international body, but that it is sufficiently responsible and accountable for its actions. Finally, those who design these mechanisms should, as far as possible, mitigate the risk that domestic spoilers obstruct justice and ensure that the investigatory and preparatory work of hybrids is not thrown out by an uncooperative domestic justice system. The experiences analysed in this chapter show strategies and alternatives that justice activists in the country studies have devised to confront these risks.

[57] Miguel Zamora, 'Institutional Inosculation: The International Commission Against Impunity in Guatemala (CICIG), International Rule of Law Mechanisms, and Creating Institutional Legitimacy in Post-Conflict Societies' (2019) 57 Columbia Journal of Transnational Law 535, 539.

[58] ibid.

15
Hybrid Tribunals as a Mechanism for Reparative Justice

*Sarah Williams**

15.1 Introduction

International human rights law recognizes that the state should endeavour to establish national reparations programmes and other assistance to victims where it is responsible for the harm or the party responsible for the harm is unable to (or will not) do so.[1] The choice of how to give effect to this obligation is left largely to the state, with no 'one size fits all' approach. Instead, when and how to provide reparations is a policy choice to be made taking into account the context including the legal, political, and resource constraints and whether reparations is to form part of a broader transitional justice and restructuring policy. This discretion is important in the context of mass atrocity, with potentially many victims,[2] limited resources and competing demands on the state.

International human rights law also recognizes that victims of serious violations of international law have a right to receive reparation for their harm.[3] Practice shows that the right to reparation can be realized by a number of mechanisms at the national level, including: constitutional provisions and petition via ordinary courts; human rights mechanisms (commissions, ombudsperson) linked to their mandate to determine violations of human rights and order (or recommend) reparations; civil claims processes, in particular claims for damages; national administrative processes, established as part of a peace or settlement agreement, including a link to a truth commission or an acceptance of responsibility on the part of the state; and establishing a fund for victims or funding reparations through the national budget or special taxation measures. States may also rely on their criminal

* Professor, Faculty of Law and Justice, UNSW Sydney.

[1] United Nations Basic Principles and Guidelines on the Right to a Remedy and Reparation for Victims of Gross Violations of International Human Rights Law and Serious Violations of International Humanitarian Law (adopted 15 December 2005) UNGA Res 60/147 (Basic Principles) Articles 15 and 16.

[2] This chapter uses the term victim, rather than survivor, as this is the term adopted by the instruments of the various tribunals studied.

[3] Basic Principles (n 1); Declaration of Basic Principles of Justice for Victims of Crime and Abuse of Power (adopted 29 November) 1985 UNGA Res 40/34.

Sarah Williams, *Hybrid Tribunals as a Mechanism for Reparative Justice* In: *Hybrid Justice*.
Edited by: Kirsten Ainley and Mark Kersten, Oxford University Press. © Sarah Williams 2025.
DOI: 10.1093/oso/9780192893758.003.0015

justice system to give effect—at least partially—to the right to reparation, including through the imposition of fines on the accused, restitution of property, orders for compensation to victims in specific cases, and separate criminal compensation or victims of crime processes.

International criminal law has been comparatively slow to link criminal processes to reparation. Instead, international criminal law has focused on its primary function, investigating and prosecuting international crimes. The Rome Statute for the International Criminal Court, adopted in 1998, was the first instrument for an international criminal tribunal to address victims' right to reparation. The Rome Statute links the order of reparations to the criminal trial process, with the International Criminal Court (ICC) able to order reparations only following a conviction, a model known as 'court-ordered reparation'. Linking reparation to the conviction of an individual recognizes that the victim has suffered harm as a result of a criminal act for which that individual is responsible and has a right to redress for that harm. However, the Rome Statute contains little detail and the principles on reparations and the process have been left to the judges to develop. Importantly, the ICC's reparative mandate is not directed at states, is not based on principles of state responsibility, and leaves domestic systems for reparations unaffected.

As explored below, the practice of the ICC shows that it has encountered significant challenges to realizing its reparative mandate. Given these challenges, this chapter explores whether hybrid tribunals—which are more closely interwoven with domestic systems—may be better placed to provide effective reparation to victims. It is not a comprehensive study; rather, it focuses on those tribunals considered in the Hybrid Justice Project:[4] the Special Panels for Serious Crimes in Timor Leste (SPSC); the Special Court for Sierra Leone (SCSL); the Special Tribunal for Lebanon (STL); the Extraordinary Chambers in the Courts of Cambodia (ECCC); the War Crimes Chamber of Bosnia and Herzegovina (BIH WCC); the Iraqi High Tribunal (IHT); the Extraordinary African Chambers (EAC); the Kosovo Specialist Chambers (KSC); and the Special Criminal Court in the Central African Republic (SCC).

Drafters of the legal frameworks for hybrid tribunals initially tended not to include a reparative mandate. Despite this, several hybrid criminal tribunals—in particular, those based in civil law systems—have extended their procedural rules to include reparations and have made orders for reparations. There now appears to be a trend towards including a reparative mandate, as seen in more recently established hybrid tribunals. However, the experience of the hybrid tribunals demonstrates that they face similar challenges to the ICC in giving effect to a reparative mandate within a criminal justice framework and the reliance on court-ordered reparation, and reparation linked only to a convicted person, without sufficient

[4] Kirsten Ainley and Mark Kersten, 'The Hybrid Justice Project' <https://hybridjustice.com> accessed 20 December 2023.

institutional or financial support is problematic and leads to 'empty' reparation awards that are not implemented.

This chapter thus explores the potential of hybrid tribunals to provide reparations. Section 15.2 considers the reparative mandate included in the Rome Statute and details briefly the challenges the ICC has encountered. Section 15.3 surveys existing practice, looking at how a range of hybrid tribunals have dealt with the issue of reparations. Finally, drawing largely on the experience of the ECCC and the EAC, the chapter demonstrates that hybrid tribunals will encounter many of the same challenges as the ICC in implementing their reparations mandates (Section 15.4). The chapter concludes that the decision to include a reparative mandate requires careful consideration of the context in which the tribunal is to operate; namely, legal, political, and resource constraints, as well as the relationship of the hybrid to other mechanisms, in particular national legal systems and mechanisms for compensation.

15.2 The Challenge of Reparation at the ICC

The Nuremberg and Tokyo Tribunals did not address the issue of reparations; in fact, victims barely featured in the proceedings of both tribunals. Similarly, the ad hoc tribunals for the former Yugoslavia and Rwanda lacked a reparative mandate,[5] although the rules allow the tribunals to forward a judgment convicting an accused for a crime to national authorities and for a victim to claim under national compensation processes.[6] The judges of both tribunals recognized that the legal framework did not give effect to the victims' right to compensation, referring to the inclusion of a reparative mandate in the Rome Statute (discussed below).[7] However, the judges advised against expanding the tribunals' mandates to include compensation, given the risk to the defendants' fair trial rights, the impact on the workload of the tribunals, and the challenge of securing funding for compensation given most accused were indigent. Instead, the judges suggested that the Security Council should establish a separate, international claims commission or other mechanism that would be an administrative, rather than judicial, scheme.

[5] For discussion as to proposals to include reparations in the International Criminal Tribunal for the Former Yugoslavia (ICTY) mandate and the arguments against, see Luke Moffett, *Justice for Victims before the International Criminal Court* (Routledge 2014) 65–67.

[6] Rules of Procedure and Evidence of the International Criminal Tribunal for the Former Yugoslavia (adopted 11 February 1994) UN Doc IT/32/Rev 50, Rule 106; International Criminal Tribunal for Rwanda, Rules of Procedure and Evidence (entered into force 29 June 1995) UN Doc ITR/3/REV.1, Rule 106.

[7] UNSC, 'Letter dated 2 November 2000 from the Secretary-General addressed to the President of the Security Council' (3 November 2000) UN Doc S/2000/1063; UNSC, 'Letter dated 14 December 2000 from the Secretary-General addressed to the President of the Security Council' (15 December 2000) UN Doc S/2000/1198.

The Council did not act on this suggestion, leaving victims to claim compensation through national processes.

While the question of reparations arose in negotiations for the ICC, reparation was not a key issue and proposals for reparations developed as negotiations progressed rather than having been an essential element of the court's design from the start.[8] During negotiations, it was clear that states had different conceptions of reparations based on their experiences in their own national jurisdictions, with a focus initially on restitution and compensation as seen in national systems.[9] A division was also evident between common law and civil law states, with France emerging as a leading driver of the reparations regime highlighting the role of civil parties and civil claims in its national system.[10]

States ultimately included a reparative mandate for the ICC in Article 75 of the Rome Statute, adopting an approach that directly links reparations to the criminal trial rather than a separate criminal compensation or administrative system. Therefore, unlike reparations in human rights law and international law generally, reparation orders at the ICC follow a determination of individual criminal responsibility after a criminal trial and are directed at a convicted person. Article 75 is brief and provides little guidance. While the Rules of Procedure and Evidence (RPE) provide further details, for example a definition of victim,[11] states have left the detail of ICC reparations—both in terms of process and the substance of reparations—to the judges to develop incrementally. The Rome Statute also created an independent Trust Fund for Victims (TFV) that has two distinct mandates: one to support implementation of court-ordered reparations and another to provide general assistance (not reparations) to victims of ICC crimes.[12] The emphasis on the link between reparations and the criminal responsibility of the accused has created three key challenges: the implications of linking reparations to a criminal trial, in particular the limited scope and number of charges, the time taken to reach implementation, and the risk that no reparations will eventuate; the absence of state responsibility and support for the reparations mandate; and challenges of funding and implementing reparations.

[8] Conor McCarthy, *Reparations and Victim Support in the International Criminal Court* (Cambridge University Press 2012) 36; Christoph Sperfeldt, 'Rome's Legacy: Negotiating the Reparations Mandate of the International Criminal Court' (2017) 17 International Community Law Review 351, 352. See also Christoph Sperfeldt, *Practices of Reparations in International Criminal Justice* (Cambridge University Press 2022).

[9] Sperfeldt, 'Rome's Legacy' (n 8) 358–61; Sperfeldt, *Practices* (n 8), chapter 2.

[10] Sperfeldt, 'Rome's Legacy' (n 8) 361; Sperfeldt, *Practices* (n 8), chapter 2.

[11] International Criminal Court, Rules of Procedure and Evidence (2002) ICC-ASP/1/3 and Corr 1, Rule 85.

[12] Rome Statute of the International Criminal Court (opened for signature 17 July 1998, entered into force 1 July 2002) 2187 UNTS 90, Article 79.

15.2.1 Link between criminal responsibility and reparations

Linking reparations to criminal responsibility provides recognition of both harm and culpability and distinguishes reparation from humanitarian assistance and development. The purpose of reparations is not to punish but to address the harm caused by the crimes for which the accused has been convicted. The Appeals Chamber in *Lubanga* reaffirmed the centrality of the convicted person to the ICC's reparations mandate, finding that reparations orders must be directed against the convicted person and may only follow a final conviction.[13] Reparations must be proportionate to the harm caused by the crimes for which the person is convicted.[14] Therefore, the first challenge for victims seeking reparations is securing a conviction: otherwise, there is no possibility of ordering reparations at the ICC.[15] The potential for reparations is therefore limited by the strategy adopted by the prosecution, in terms of the defendants, the victims, the geographical areas considered, the conduct examined, and the temporal scope of the investigation, as well as the extent to which harm can be connected to crimes for which the accused has been convicted. For example, criticism was directed at the Office of the Prosecutor's (OTP) failure to include charges of sexual violence against female child soldiers in the ICC's first case, *Lubanga*, which led to the trial Chamber finding that, as the accused had not been convicted for charges concerning sexual violence, it could not order reparations to the victims of sexual violence.[16] Similarly, in *Katanga*, the acquittal of the accused for charges relating to sexual and gender-based violence precluded reparations to address the harm caused by those crimes,[17] while in *Bemba*, the acquittal of the accused by the Appeal Chamber after a lengthy trial process left thousands of victims unable to seek reparations.[18]

The link to conviction also creates a hierarchy of victims, with only a small number of victims of a situation ultimately receiving reparations: those are victims

13 *Prosecutor v Lubanga* (Judgment on the appeals against 'Decision establishing the principles and procedures to be applied to reparations' of 7 August 2012) ICC-01/04-01/06-3129 (2015) (hereafter *Lubanga 2015 Decision*) [65]–[76]; see Carsten Stahn, 'Reparative Justice after the *Lubanga* Appeal Judgment' (2015) 13 Journal of International Criminal Justice 801. For a comprehensive study of the ICC's reparations jurisprudence, see Miriam Cohen, *The Politics of Reparations at the International Criminal Court* (Brill 2020).

14 *Lubanga 2015 Decision* (n 13) [118]–[119].

15 *Prosecutor v Bemba Gombo* (Final decision on the reparations proceedings) ICC-01/05-01/08-3653 (2018).

16 *Prosecutor v Lubanga* (Decision establishing the principles and procedures to be applied to reparations) ICC-01/04-01/06-2904 (2012) (hereafter *Lubanga 2012 Decision*); For criticism, see Louise Chappell, 'The Gender Injustice Cascade: 'Transformative' Reparations for Victims of Sexual and Gender-Based Crimes in the Lubanga Case at the International Criminal Court' (2017) 21 International Journal of Human Rights 1223.

17 *Prosecutor v Katanga* (Order for Reparations pursuant to Article 75 of the Statute) ICC-01/04-02/06 (2017) [146]–[152].

18 *Prosecutor v Bemba Gombo* (Judgment on the appeal of Mr Jean-Pierre Bemba Gombo against Trial Chamber III's 'Judgment pursuant to Article 74 of the Statute') ICC-01/05-01/08 A (2018); see also decision on reparations (n 15).

of a crime for which an individual is convicted.[19] The process significantly narrows the notion of victimhood in the context of mass atrocity and may result in few victims of the situation benefiting from court-ordered reparations. Chambers have grappled with the challenge of how to benefit the largest number of victims, with limited resources, and have expressed a preference for collective rather than individual compensation, and, where compensation is awarded, it tends to be symbolic rather that substantial.[20] The ICC's preference for collective awards was confirmed in the *Ntaganda* reparations order, with the Trial Chamber ordering collective reparations, albeit with individualized elements.[21] However, the Appeals Chamber clarified that Chambers relying on collective reparations must still indicate the number of actual and potential victims that may be eligible for reparations before setting the liability of the accused.[22] Relying on collective awards only has been somewhat controversial, as victims may prefer individual awards and seek compensation payments, or oppose reparations that are symbolic only. Collective awards also differ from the criminal compensation schemes adopted by many states. Using one form of reparation only is partly inconsistent with reparations 'best practice', which suggests that better outcomes for victims are realized through a combination of different forms of reparations, including both individual and collective, monetary and non-monetary.[23]

Where victims are unable to benefit from ICC court-ordered reparations, victims may rely upon assistance programmes offered by the TFV (which are not reparations) or may seek reparations, if available, under national law or in other fora. Even where victims do benefit from reparations, this is after a long and drawn-out process. As reparations are linked to a conviction, and due to concerns that early findings on reparations may prejudice the accused's right to a fair trial, reparations orders generally follow the—often lengthy—trial process and any appeals on conviction. This results in implementation of the reparations order many years after the crimes occurred and the harm was suffered. For example, in *Lubanga*, the accused was convicted in 2012, but implementation of the various aspects of the reparations award remains ongoing as of October 2024. This makes reparations at

[19] See Sara Kendall and Sarah Nouwen, 'Representational Practices at the International Criminal Court: the Gap between Juridified and Abstract Victimhood' (2014) 76 Law and Contemporary Problems 235; Stahn, 'Reparative Justice' (n 13).

[20] Rule 98(3) provides for collective reparations 'where the number of the victims and the scope, forms and modalities of reparations make a collective award more appropriate' and the Appeals Chamber has confirmed that a chamber may order only collective reparations: *Lubanga 2015 Decision* (n 13) [147]–[157].

[21] *Prosecutor v Ntaganda* (Reparations Order) ICC-01/04-02/06 (2021) [186]ff.

[22] *Prosecutor v Ntaganda* (Judgment on the appeals against the decision of Trial Chamber VI of 8 March 2021 entitled 'Reparations Order') ICC-01/04-02/06 A4-A5 (2022) [172]–[174].

[23] See, eg, Open Society Justice Initiative (OSJI), *Options for Justice: A Handbook for Designing Accountability Mechanisms for Grave Crimes* (Open Society Foundations 2018) <https://www.justiceinitiative.org/publications/options-justice-handbook-designing-accountability-mechanisms-grave-crimes> accessed 20 December 2023.

the ICC—with its link to the criminal process—not an effective way of responding in a timely fashion to the harm suffered by victims. An independent review of the ICC concluded that 'profound delays exhibit the whole process'.[24] While the challenge of implementing reparations is increased by the security situations that are often ongoing in the situation countries, and the COVID-19 pandemic also restricted the ability to develop and implement reparations, these alone do not account for such 'excessive' delays in implementation.[25]

15.2.2 State responsibility

To the limited focus of international criminal trials must be added the deliberate absence of state responsibility in the ICC reparations framework. Sperfeldt notes that the issue of state responsibility for reparations was a contentious issue during negotiations.[26] Proposals that ICC Chambers should be able to make reparations orders directly to states and/or require states to supplement reparations orders where the defendant was indigent were dropped.[27] Consequently, the Rome Statute says little regarding the intersection of individual criminal responsibility and the underlying obligation of states to make reparations. Article 75 indicates that 'Nothing in this article shall be interpreted as prejudicing the rights of victims under national or international law', which preserves the ability for victims to pursue other avenues for reparations, including against the state itself. The cooperation and complementarity frameworks of the ICC do not provide a basis to require states to make reparations or to supplement court-ordered reparations programmes.[28] Thus, at best, the Rome Statute preserves existing obligations of states to provide reparations mechanisms and the right of victims to claim under national law but does not integrate these obligations into the ICC regime.[29] The exclusion of orders directed at states effectively precludes any projects that would require state support, for example symbolic initiatives such as national memorial days, education reform, as well as many forms of guarantees of non-repetition that require legislative or police or security sector reform. There is some evidence of states voluntarily engaging in the implementation phase[30] and Mali benefited from a symbolic order

[24] ICC, 'Independent Expert Review of the International Criminal Court and the Rome Statute System: Final Report' (30 September 2020) (Expert Report) para 879.

[25] ibid para 880.

[26] Sperfeldt, *Rome's Legacy* (n 8) 371–73.

[27] ibid 371–73.

[28] States parties are required only to cooperate with the enforcement of the award, which is narrowly interpreted as seizing assets. For further discussion, see Luke Moffett, 'Reparative Complementarity: Ensuring an Effective Remedy for Victims in the Reparation Regime of the International Criminal Court' (2013) 17(3) International Journal of Human Rights 368.

[29] See *Lubanga 2012 Decision* (n 16) [257], recognizing that its order for reparation does not interfere with rights at the domestic level.

[30] The DRC and Mali have made submissions to the Trial Chamber as part of the implementation phase of the orders in *Lubanga* and *Al-Mahdi*, respectively.

for reparations for destruction of cultural heritage.[31] Trial Chambers have stressed the need for states to cooperate with the Court, including assisting the Court to give effect to reparations awards.[32] However, this is far removed from a system of reparative complementarity whereby states play an active role in supplementing ICC reparations proceedings through domestic legal systems.[33]

15.2.3 Funding

In the ICC system, the convicted person is liable for the cost of reparation orders, which should be funded by the assets of the convicted person.[34] Many—if not most—accused before the ICC are likely to be indigent, meaning there are no resources available to fund reparations. Even where a convicted person has assets—for example Mr Bemba—the ICC has not proved particularly capable of finding, seizing and managing the assets of the accused to support reparations. Without the ability to order a state to supplement reparations, this leaves a gap in funding. As noted above, the shortage of funding also impacts on the types of reparations a Chamber may order, with collective and symbolic reparations benefiting a greater number of victims. While the TFV has to an extent attempted to fill the funding gap by seeking donations from states and other actors, there often remains a significant gap between the value of the reparations ordered and the funds available to support victims in practice. The ICC independent review noted the impact of a lack of financial resources, together with limited implementation capacity and governance-related failings, on the ability of TFV to perform its role and to make reparations more than just 'numbers on paper'.[35]

In sum, the ICC's mandate, which is based on the link between reparations and a criminal conviction, has faced considerable challenges during the Court's first twenty years of operation. The ICC independent review concluded that: 'The Court's conceptual and procedural processes for reparations are laden with complexity and uncertainty'.[36] It continued:

> For victims, so far, the Court is not functioning and delivering as envisioned. Conceptually, the reparations process was regarded as seriously deficient also in that it (potentially) leads to inequality between victims, by anchoring Court-ordered reparations only on the crimes for which conviction against an accused

[31] *Prosecutor v Ahmad Al Faqi Al-Mahdi* (Reparations Order) ICC-01/12-01/15 (2017) [106]: a symbolic payment of one Euro was ordered.
[32] Ntaganda Reparations Order (n 21) [256].
[33] Moffett, 'Reparative complementarity' (n 28).
[34] *Lubanga 2015 Decision* (n 13).
[35] Expert Report (n 24) para 891.
[36] ibid para 879.

person has been entered, and not on the totality of the crimes charged or perpetrated in a situation.[37]

This has resulted in limited success in terms of the implementation of reparations orders and demands to reconsider the inclusion of the reparative mandate in the ICC.[38] At the very least, there is a need to provide accurate information to victims and to manage expectations, specifically that the process provides no guarantee of reparations. The ICC independent review recommended a range of measures, including improved data collection and management, enhanced procedures, clearer institutional roles and responsibilities, and proactively seeking support through partnerships.[39] More radically, there are calls to 'decouple' the reparations process from the criminal trial, including setting up a separate mechanism for reparations.[40] Other suggestions are to start reparations processes much sooner in the process to run parallel with the criminal trial (and any appeals) and/or to replace court-ordered reparations with a broader assistance mandate. Others have suggested greater reliance on national institutions or laws,[41] either instead of or as a complement to the ICC system, thus suggesting a potential role for hybrid tribunals with reparations mandates. Given this, this chapter now turns to consider the extent to which hybrid tribunals have incorporated a reparations mandate and, if so, in which form and whether they have adopted a similar approach to reparations.

15.3 Approaches to Reparations in Hybrid Tribunals

This section explores the practice of hybrid tribunals concerning reparations. There is no requirement that a hybrid tribunal include a mandate to provide reparations. Other institutions could fulfil this obligation at the national—or potentially international—level. Nor does the Rome Statute create an obligation on a state to create or utilize domestic/hybrid criminal mechanisms as part of the complementarity provisions. Therefore, whether or not to include a reparative mandate is a decision to be made when exploring whether to establish a hybrid tribunal and

[37] ibid para 885.

[38] Luke Moffett and Clara Sandoval, 'Tilting at Windmills: Reparations and the International Criminal Court' (2021) 34 Leiden Journal of International Law 749.

[39] Expert Report (n 24): The recommendations regarding reparations are set out in R342 to R353.

[40] For suggestions of a reparations chamber, see Luke Moffett, 'Reparations for Victims at the International Criminal Court: A New Way Forward?' (2017) 21 International Journal of Human Rights 1204. The Independent Review considered this option but did not endorse this suggestion: Expert Report (n 24) para 898.

[41] Tomas Hamilton and Göran Sluiter, 'Principles of Reparations at the International Criminal Court: Assessing Alternative Approaches' in Erika de Wet and Kathrin Maria Scherr (eds), *Max Planck Yearbook of United Nations Law* (Brill 2022) <https://brill.com/view/journals/mpyo/25/1/article-p272_12.xml> accessed 20 December 2023.

in determining its mandate, as recognized by the Dakar principles on the establishment of hybrid courts[42] and the OSJI handbook on designing accountability mechanisms.[43]

15.3.1 Tribunals without a reparative mandate

Despite the 'turn to reparative justice' in the Rome Statute, drafters of the legal frameworks for hybrid tribunals generally did not include a reparative mandate. The SCSL and STL adopt a similar approach to the ad hoc tribunals, despite their instruments having been adopted after the Rome Statute. The agreement between the UN and the government of Sierra Leone[44] did not address reparations, although the SCSL could order the forfeiture of property, proceeds, and assets unlawfully acquired and order restitution to the rightful owner or to the state of Sierra Leone.[45] Where a forfeiture order was made, the implementing legislation provided that where forfeited material is to be delivered to the state of Sierra Leone, the property must be used for the purpose specified in the order or—if no purpose is specified—to address the consequences of the armed conflict in Sierra Leone. Alternatively, the assets could be sold and any money contributed to the War Victims Fund established by the Lomé Peace Agreement.[46] The implementing legislation confirmed the role of national processes for victims to claim compensation, providing that victims of a crime within the jurisdiction of the SCSL may claim compensation under the Criminal Procedure Act 1965 where the SCSL has found a person guilty of that crime.[47] In practice, no claims for compensation arising from the conflict were made under this provision. The rules of procedure and evidence, similar again to the ICTY and ICTR, enabled the SCSL to transfer judgments to national authorities and preserved the right of victims to bring a claim under national processes, noting that the judgment of the SCSL is final and binding as to the responsibility of the accused.[48] The SCSL therefore played a limited role in relation to reparations, with reparations to be made pursuant either

[42] Kirsten Ainley and Mark Kersten, 'Dakar Guidelines on the Establishment of Hybrid Courts' LSE and Wayamo Foundation (2019) <https://hybridjustice.com/dakar-guidelines/> accessed 20 December 2023.

[43] OSJI, *Options for Justice* (n 23).

[44] Statute of SCSL, Article 5, annexed to the Agreement between the United Nations and the Government of Sierra Leone on the establishment of a Special Court for Sierra Leone (signed 16 January 2002, entered into force 12 April 2002) 2178 UNTS 138 (SCSL Statute).

[45] SCSL Statute (n 44) Article 19(3).

[46] Special Court Agreement 2002 (Ratification) Act No 9, section 22(1)(b)(ii) (SCA (Ratification).

[47] Ratification (n 46) section 45.

[48] Special Court for Sierra Leone, Rules of Procedure and Evidence as Amended (2012) (SCSL RPE), Rule 105.

to the truth and reconciliation commission established under the Lomé Peace Agreement or under national laws on compensation.[49]

The STL Statute similarly left the issue of compensation and reparations to national law, even though the Statute included provisions enabling victim participation. Article 25 of the STL Statute provided that the STL may identify those who have suffered harm as a result of the crimes for which the accused has been convicted. The Registry may then forward the judgment to the competent authorities of the state concerned, which suggests a role for states other than Lebanon. Victims may then apply for compensation under national laws from national courts or other competent bodies. The STL judgment is final and binding as regards criminal responsibility.[50] However, unlike the SCSL, ICTR, and ICTY, there is no provision on forfeiture in the STL Statute or the RPE. Therefore, even in a UN negotiated instrument adopted after the Rome Statute, the Statute does not incorporate a mandate for reparations, with drafters preferring to leave reparations—framed narrowly as compensation—to the national system.

The STL completed only one trial (excluding contempt proceedings). In the trial judgment, the Chamber acknowledged that it could not order reparations for victims.[51] Instead, the Chamber limited itself to recognizing the harm suffered by direct and indirect victims participating in the trial, as well as identifying non-participating victims who had suffered harm.[52] The Chamber declined the invitation of the victims' lawyers to make recommendations to the Lebanese government as to the modalities of awarding and calculating reparations, as this was beyond its mandate.[53] However, in the sentencing decision, the Chamber noted the challenges for victims in obtaining compensation under the national system and the inequity in support for victims.[54] It argued that it had 'a moral and legal duty to the victims of crimes found to fall within the Special Tribunal's jurisdiction to do anything it can to help them obtain redress'.[55] Recognizing that it did not have the power to make binding orders to the government of Lebanon, the Chamber made two recommendations: first, that the government establish a national compensation scheme, which should be free of political considerations;[56] and, second and independently of the first recommendation, the establishment by the international community of a special trust fund for victims to provide a 'just

[49] For discussion of reparations under the TRC, see Sarah Williams and Jasmine Opdam, 'The Unrealised Potential for Transformative Reparations for Sexual and Gender-Based Violence in Sierra Leone' (2017) 21 International Journal of Human Rights 1281.

[50] Statute of the Special Tribunal for Lebanon (2007) S/RES/1757 (STSL Statute) Article 25.

[51] *Prosecutor vs Ayyash et al* (Judgment) STL-11-01/T/TC (2020), eg [889], [957].

[52] ibid [889]–[897]. Part VI G—entitled Victim Harm—sets out the victims and details the harm suffered.

[53] *Prosecutor vs Ayyash et al* (Judgment) (n 51) [961].

[54] *Prosecutor vs Ayyash* (Sentencing Judgment) STL-11-01/S/TC (11 December 2020).

[55] ibid [294].

[56] Sentencing Judgment (n 54) [296]–[297], [308A].

and neutral mechanism' to compensate victims.[57] In a context where the STL ran out of funds and was forced to suspend permanently all remaining trials, neither recommendation has been implemented.

The SPSC, established under UN administration of Timor-Leste, had powers to impose fines as well as order forfeiture against a convicted person as a punishment.[58] The regulation also provided that a trust fund may be established to benefit victims, and that money or property obtained from fines, forfeiture, donations, or other means could be transferred to the fund.[59] A subsequent amendment addressed the issue of compensation, recognizing that a victim could file a civil claim in a national court and that a panel may include an order requiring the accused to pay compensation or reparations to the victim as part of the criminal judgment.[60] The provision was to be implemented by administrative directions;[61] however, in practice, the trust fund was never established and criminal panels did not make orders for compensation or reparations.

The UN was not involved in the establishment of the IHT, which also occurred after the Rome Statute. The Statute of the IHT addressed forfeiture and confiscation of goods[62] but there is no other provision relevant to reparations, including in the RPE. To the extent reparations were even considered, the issue was left to the national system. Similarly, nothing in the law establishing the BIH WCC refers to reparations,[63] leaving the issue of compensation to other national laws and procedures applicable to ordinary crimes. The Dayton Peace Agreement created two institutions to deal with reparations for post-war claims: the Human Rights Chamber and the Commission for Real Property Claims of Displaced Persons and Refugees.[64] Both institutions ended their operations in 2003, having administered thousands of applications. Since then, there has been no dedicated system for war reparations, with claims filed before Bosnian courts, and some international courts.[65] The Bosnian Criminal Code provides for courts to impose fines that contribute to the national budget, and allows a claim for compensation of material gain

57 ibid [301]–[02], [308B].

58 UNTAET Regulation On the Establishment of Panels with Exclusive Jurisdiction Over Serious Criminal Offences (2000) UNTAET/REG/2000/15 (UNTAET Reg 2000/15) sections 10.1(b)–(c).

59 ibid section 25.

60 UNTAET Regulation on the Organization of Courts in East Timor (2001) UNTAET/REG/2001/25 (UNTAET Reg 2001/25) section 50.

61 ibid section 50.3.

62 Iraqi High Criminal Court Law No 4006 (2005) (hereafter Iraqi High Criminal Court Law) Article 24(6); see also Statute of the Iraqi Special Tribunal (2003) Article 24(f).

63 Law on the Court of Bosnia and Herzegovina (Consolidated version) (2009) *Official Gazette* No 49/09 (hereafter Law on the Court of Bosnia).

64 See further Carla Ferstman and Sheri Rosenberg, 'Reparations in Dayton's Bosnia and Herzegovina' in Carla Ferstman, Marina Goetz, and Alan Stephens (eds), *Reparations for Victims of Genocide, War Crimes and Crimes Against Humanity: Systems in Place and Systems in the Making* (Brill 2009) 484.

65 Frederick de Vlaming and Kate Clark, 'War Reparations in Bosnia and Herzegovina: Individual States and Collective Interests' in Dubravka Zarkov and Marlies Glasius (eds), *Narratives of Justice In and Out of the Courtroom* (Springer 2014) 163.

from criminal activities, for example if property has been stolen.[66] Compensation to victims is generally claimed pursuant to the civil process, with a criminal court able to award a property claim to an injured party under the Criminal Procedure Code.[67] This property claim can cover both material and non-material loss suffered by a victim of crime, with the court to declare if the claim is upheld and assess the value of the harm. The WCC, as a court established under national law, should be able to rely on these provisions to order compensation in relation to a property claim, although for many years it did not do so.[68] However, in 2015 the WCC issued its first order for a property claim against two accused in connection with a conviction for the crime of rape.[69] To date, it does not appear that the compensation was paid.

For these five hybrid tribunals, drafters did not include a reparative mandate, deciding to leave reparations to other mechanisms, including truth commissions (Sierra Leone) or national court processes (in four instances). Even where the prospect of a reparations mandate was included (SPSC), the mandate was not implemented. However, it does not appear that relying on national legal processes has been successful, with either no awards being made or awards for compensation not being paid. As seen in the decision of the STL, judges at the hybrid tribunals are aware that national systems offer limited prospects for reparations. As a result, many victims have not benefited from reparations, including compensation, at either the hybrid or national levels.

15.3.2 Judicial borrowing from the national system: the Extraordinary Chambers in the Courts of Cambodia (ECCC)

The agreement between the UN and the government of Cambodia and the ECCC Law suggests that negotiators adopted a similar approach to the five hybrids discussed in the previous section: the instruments are silent as to reparations. This was despite the suggestion of the UN Group of Experts, based on the belief that the Khmer Rouge leaders had 'amassed vast amounts of wealth', that any tribunal established should 'provide for the possibility of reparations by the defendant to his

[66] Criminal Code of Bosnia and Herzegovina (2015) *Official Gazette* No 3/03 Chapter XII.

[67] Criminal Procedure Code of Bosnia and Herzegovina (2013) *Official Gazette* No 3/03, section 195.

[68] For discussion, see Adrijana Janusic, 'Enforcement of damage compensation claims of victims of war in criminal proceedings in Bosnia and Herzegovina: Situation, challenges and perspectives' (2015) <https://trial.ba/wp-content/uploads/2021/02/ENG_Ostvarivanje-zahtjeva-za-naknadu-stete-zrtava-ratnih-zlocina-u-okviru-krivicnih-postupaka-u-Bosni-i-Hercegovini-%E2%80%93-stanje-problemi-i-perspektive-.pdf> accessed 14 December 2023.

[69] *Prosecutor's Office of Bosnia and Herzegovina v Bosiljko Marković and Ostoja Marković* (Verdict) S1 1 K012024 14 Kri (2015). The panel ordered compensation against the accused for part of the claim, with the excess of the claim to be pursued through a civil action: see [234]–[245].

victims, including through a special trust fund'.[70] However, the ECCC Agreement and Law provide that the procedures of the ECCC shall be based on existing Cambodian procedural law, unless incompatible.[71] Cambodian law includes the concept of civil parties who can participate in proceedings and seek compensation and, when adopting the internal rules, the ECCC judges drew from local law to include the role of civil parties and the potential of court-ordered reparations, with the inclusion of reparations also reportedly influenced by the inclusion of a reparations mandate at the ICC.[72] As with the ICC, reparations are linked to the conviction of the accused and their liability for the harm arising from the crimes for which they have been convicted.[73] However, the approach adopted by the ECCC judges was limited: no trust fund was adopted, no resources for participation or reparations were allocated, and an administrative process was not set up.[74] Moreover, due to judges' concerns about the practicality of ordering compensation in a context with millions of potential victims, the internal rules restrict the ECCC to the award of 'moral and collective' reparations, thus precluding individual awards and/or financial compensation.[75] The ECCC model is thus different to the national model of compensation for civil parties and from the ICC regime.

In the ECCC's first case, Case 001 concerning the S-21 security prison, ninety-three civil parties participated, making several claims for reparations. The Trial Chamber rejected most of these claims based on the ECCC's limited mandate.[76] The Chamber distinguished the legal framework at the ECCC from those under national law.[77] As the accused was indigent, the Chamber could not order reparations against the accused and 'there is currently no mechanism allowing the ECCC to substitute or supplement awards made against them with funds provided

[70] UN, 'Report of the Group of Experts for Cambodia Established Pursuant to General Assembly Resolution 52/135' (18 February 1999) UN Doc A/53/850, paras 211–12.

[71] Agreement between the United Nations and the Royal Government of Cambodia concerning the prosecution under Cambodian law of crimes committed during the period of Democratic Kampuchea (6 June 2003) (ECCC Agreement) Article 12(1); Law on Amendments to the Law on the Establishment of the Extraordinary Chambers in the Courts of Cambodia for the Prosecution of Crimes Committed During the Period of Democratic Kampuchea (5 October 2004) (ECCC Law) Article 33new.

[72] For further discussion, see Christoph Sperfeldt, 'Reparations at the Extraordinary Chambers in the Courts of Cambodia' in Carla Ferstman and Mariana Goetz (eds), *Reparations for Victims of Genocide, War Crimes and Crimes Against Humanity: Systems in Place and Systems in the Making* (2nd edn, Brill Nijhoff 2020); Rachel Killean, '*Victims, Atrocity and International Criminal Justice: Lessons From Cambodia*' (Routledge 2019); and Christoph Sperfeldt, 'Collective Reparations at the Extraordinary Chambers in the Courts of Cambodia' (2012) 12 International Community Law Review 457; Sperfeldt, *Practices* (n 8).

[73] Extraordinary Chambers in the Courts of Cambodia Internal Rules (12 June 2007) (ECCC Internal Rules) Rule 23(11). Version 1 as originally adopted in June 2007 provided that reparations 'shall be awarded against, and borne by convicted persons'.

[74] See Sperfeldt, 'Reparations at the Extraordinary Chambers in the Courts of Cambodia' (n 72).

[75] ECCC Internal Rules (n 73) Rule 23(11).

[76] *KAING Guek Eav alias Duch* (Judgment) 001/18-07-2007/ECCC/TC (26 July 2010) (hereafter Case 001 Judgment). The Trial Chamber rejected several of the requests as the civil parties could not establish a link to the crimes for which the accused had been convicted.

[77] ibid [661].

by national authorities or other third parties'.[78] This differs from the approach adopted by ICC Chambers, outlined above, and reflected the ECCC judges' reluctance to order reparations that had no prospect of implementation.[79] As with the ICC, the ECCC has no jurisdiction to order reparations against Cambodia, even though Cambodia was a partner in establishing the Court itself.[80] Consequently, the Chamber ordered only symbolic reparations within the Court's own control, namely dissemination of the judgment and statements of remorse made by the accused during the trial.[81] This limited approach, which was largely confirmed by the Supreme Court Chamber on appeal, caused disappointment for the participating civil parties.[82] The Supreme Court Chamber specifically confirmed that reparations could only be ordered against and borne by the accused, could not be supplemented from other sources,[83] and, despite the Tribunal's hybrid nature, it was 'not vested with the authority to assess Cambodia's compliance with these international obligations [on reparations]'.[84]

The negative reaction to reparations in Case 001 led the judges to revise the reparations provisions ahead of Case 002,[85] in which more than 3,960 civil parties participated. The revisions created two avenues: first, judicial reparations against the accused (a traditional reparations claim); and second, judicial reparations implemented through the victim support section that are not linked to the assets of the accused.[86] Civil parties would have to decide which avenue to pursue and, as the remaining accused have been indigent, reparations have subsequently been ordered only under the second avenue. The amendments also introduced a process for 'non-judicial measures' separate from the formal reparations process and administered by the ECCC's Victim Support Section (VSS).[87] For judicial reparations, Chambers imposed a practice of approving reparations 'projects' requested by civil party lawyers in advance of the judgment. Chambers required that proposed projects be both specific and feasible (especially in terms of funding) before they will be recognized 'as giving effect to the award sought' on behalf of victims. This led to the outsourcing of the design and funding of reparations to civil parties and their lawyers, often in partnership with non-governmental organizations,

[78] ibid [664].

[79] ibid [666]–[668].

[80] ibid [663] and [671], noting that the ECCC can 'merely encourage national authorities'.

[81] ibid [667]–[669].

[82] *KAING Guek Eav alias Duch* (Appeal Judgement) 001/18-07-2007/ECCC/SC (3 February 2012) (hereafter Case 001 Appeal Judgement).

[83] ibid [656].

[84] ibid [654].

[85] ECCC, 'Eighth ECCC Plenary Session Concludes' (17 September 2010) <https://www.eccc.gov.kh/en/articles/eight-eccc-plenary-session-concludes> accessed 20 December 2023.

[86] ECCC Internal Rules (n 73), Rule 23*quinquies*, para 3 provides that these options are alternatives.

[87] Initially amended in Version 5 of the Internal Rules, this additional mandate of the Victims Support Section is currently Rule 12*bis*(4).

and with the support of the VSS.[88] This approach has been criticized for using the Court to 'rubber-stamp' projects and leaving reparations largely at the mercy of donors and their funding priorities. Moreover, the Chamber's focus has been on benefiting a wider category of victims than those directly affected by the crimes for which the accused is convicted, with a more flexible approach to reparations than seen at the ICC.[89] Cambodian authorities have also assisted in implementing some projects, for example the inclusion of material on the history of the Khmer Rouge in the national education syllabus and a national day of memory.

Does the approach adopted by the ECCC judges sever the link between the accused and reparations? Sperfeldt suggests that the ECCC approach is no longer accountability driven and is administrative in nature.[90] While this is certainly the case for non-judicial programmes, the ECCC judges have made clear that the projects recognized as judicial reparations remain linked to the criminal responsibility of the accused and the crimes for which they have been convicted. The ECCC legal framework has never provided for the compensation-based individual civil claim as seen in national systems, allowing only moral and collective reparations. The requirement underlying the traditional civil party claim that the accused is solely liable for reparations has been abandoned in the revisions to the rules, in favour of a more flexible approach to address challenges of reparations in mass violence context; an administrative approach that remains tied to the crimes. Therefore, at the ECCC, while only a limited number of collective reparations projects has been recognized, the projects have at least been implemented.

15.3.3 Inclusion in the Statute: Extraordinary African Chambers (EAC)

As with the other hybrids considered, the agreement on establishment of the EAC does not address reparations. The EAC was based in the legal system of Senegal and, like the ECCC, drew on the inclusion of civil party participation at the local level. The Tribunal was unusual in that it was based on the exercise of universal jurisdiction addressing crimes committed in Chad, and prosecuted one individual—Hissène Habré, the former President of Chad.[91] The EAC Statute included a provision on reparations, showing reliance on 'the Senegalese civil party system

[88] Sperfeldt, 'Reparations at the Extraordinary Chambers in the Courts of Cambodia' (n 72); Sperfeldt, *Practices* (n 8).

[89] Sperfeldt, 'Reparations at the Extraordinary Chambers in the Courts of Cambodia' (n 72); Sperfeldt, *Practices* (n 8)

[90] Sperfeldt, 'Reparations at the Extraordinary Chambers in the Courts of Cambodia' (n 72).

[91] For further discussion, see Sarah Williams, 'The Extraordinary African Chambers in Senegalese Courts: An African Solution to an African Problem?' (2013) 11 Journal of International Criminal Justice 1139–60; Emanuele Cimiotta, 'The First Steps of the Extraordinary African Chambers: A New Mixed Criminal Tribunal?' (2015) 13 Journal of International Criminal Justice 177–97.

with selective borrowing' from the Rome Statute regime.[92] In particular, Article 27 provided for reparations in the form of restitution, rehabilitation, and compensation, which is broader than the claims to compensation found under national law, and confirms that the EAC Statute is not to prejudice rights to reparations under national law. Article 28 provided for the establishment of a trust fund for victims, to be 'financed by voluntary contributions from foreign governments, international institutions, non-governmental organizations and other entities wishing to support the victims'. Unlike the Rome Statute and the ECCC, Article 27 did not appear to require specifically the order for reparations to the convicted person. Article 27 provided that the EAC may order the TFV to pay orders for compensation. The TFV is to be established for the 'benefit of victims of crimes within the jurisdiction of the Extraordinary African Chambers, and of the beneficiaries of such victims' and '[R]eparations shall be open to all victims, individually or collectively, whether or not they participated in the proceedings'. This suggests that reparations were not to be limited to the charges for which the accused is convicted and 'that the drafters were mindful of incorporating provisions into the Statute that allow for a more flexible approach to reparations beyond the strict boundaries of the criminal trial'.[93]

Following Habré's conviction in May 2016, the Trial Chamber issued its decision on civil party reparations claims in July 2016, ordering Habré to pay monetary compensation to victims on an individual basis, having calculated the amount of compensation appropriate for each category of victim based on the nature of the harm suffered.[94] As Sperfeldt notes, this reflects both the preference for financial compensation expressed by the civil parties as well as the compensation-based approach applied at the national level.[95] It also reflects that the parties, including the victims, had not given much thought to the reparations phase, focusing instead on the criminal trial.[96] The Trial Chamber rejected a number of claims by civil parties for collective reparations, which had included measures such as development projects in affected communities, inclusion of material on the Habré regime in the education curriculum, and declaration of a memorial day.[97] These requests were rejected as they lacked specifics that would enable the judges to assess their

[92] Christoph Sperfeldt, 'Reparations and the Habré Trial in Context' in Weill and others (eds), *Prosecuting the President: The Trial of Hissène Habré* (Oxford University Press 2020) 340.

[93] ibid 341.

[94] *Ministère Public c Hissein Habré* (Judgment) (29 July 2016) (hereafter *Habré Trial Judgment*) [59]–[68] <http://www.chambresafricaines.org/pdf/Jugement_complet.pdf> accessed 20 December 2023.

[95] Sperfeldt, 'Reparations and the Habré Trial in Context' (n 92) 347.

[96] Gaëlle Carayon and Jeanne Sulzer, 'The Real Fight Begins: Victims Struggle for and Effective Right to Reparation' in Weill and others (eds), *Prosecuting the President: The Trial of Hissène Habré* (Oxford University Press 2020) 165; Sperfeldt, 'Reparations and the Habré Trial in Context' (n 92) 343. See also Christoph Sperfeldt, 'The Trial against Hissène Habré: Networked Justice and Reparations at the Extraordinary African Chambers' (2017) 21 International Journal of Human Rights 1243.

[97] *Habré Trial Judgment* (n 94) [69]–[72]. For details of the reparations requests considered by victims, see Carayon and Sulzer (n 96).

feasibility. The Trial Chamber refused to approve any reparation that would require the involvement or consent of Chad, as Chad was not a party to proceedings.[98] The Trial Chamber also rejected, using similar reasoning, calls by civil parties to declare Chad to be responsible for reparations, including financing reparations payments.[99]

The Appeals Chamber largely confirmed the Trial Chamber's reliance on individual compensation payments, although it provided greater detail as to the number of beneficiaries and more detailed assessment of claims.[100] In addition, the Appeals Chamber determined the total amount of Habré's liability and ordered him to pay over CFA 82 billion to the civil parties.[101] This reaffirmed the connection between the liability of the accused and reparations and is similar to the approach adopted by the ICC, discussed above. However, though some assets had been seized,[102] there was a significant shortfall. The Appeals Chamber responded to victims' concerns as to how any reparations would be implemented, given that—while the African Union (AU) had formally established the TFV in 2016—little progress had been made in setting it up and the EAC would shut down following the appeal.[103] The Appeals Chamber confirmed that the TFV would be the implementing body for reparations, directed the TFV to make good any shortfall from the accused's assets, and urged the AU to set up the TFV urgently.[104] The Appeals Chamber sought the views of Chad on collective reparations, noting that the government 'did not respond favourably to the collective reparations solicited'.[105] It then confirmed the rejection of all requests for collective reparations, referencing the potential for such awards to infringe on the sovereignty of Chad.[106]

The EAC ceased its operations after finalizing the appeal, without the implementation of the reparations order. There has been some progress towards implementation. The AU adopted the Statute for the TFV[107] in 2018, signed a headquarters agreement with Chad in 2019, and allocated USD 5 million to the

[98] *Habré Trial Judgment* (n 94) [71]; see also Sperfeldt, 'Reparations and the Habré Trial in Context' (n 92) 347.

[99] *Habré Trial Judgment* (n 94) [75]–[76].

[100] *Le Procureur Général c Hissein Habré* (Appeal Judgment) (27 April 2017) (hereafter *Habré Appeal Judgment*) <http://www.chambresafricaines.org/pdf/Arr%C3%AAt_int%C3%A9gral.pdf> accessed 20 December 2023. For further discussion, see Sperfeldt, 'Reparations and the Habré Trial in Context' (n 92), 5–6.

[101] *Habré Appeal Judgment* (n 100) [938]–[939].

[102] The EAC could order forfeiture of assets based on Article 87 of the Senegalese Code of Criminal Procedure and assets were seized pursuant to an order for forfeiture issued on 29 October 2013: See *Habré Trial Judgment* (n 94) [77]–[79].

[103] Carayon and Sulzer (n 96) 176.

[104] *Habré Appeal Judgment* (n 100) [940].

[105] ibid [863]–[865], [843]; discussed in Sperfeldt, 'Reparations and the Habré Trial in Context' (n 92) 347–48.

[106] *Habré Appeal Judgment* (n 100) [848].

[107] See AU, 'Statute of the Trust Fund For Victims Of Hissène Habré's Crimes' (January 2018) EX.CL/1040(XXXI) <https://www.hrw.org/sites/default/files/supporting_resources/statute_trust_fund_victims_english.pdf> accessed 20 December 2023.

trust fund. Following the death of Habré in August 2021, the AU sent a delegation to Chad to take possession of a building for the TFV and announced its intent 'to render the Fund operational within the shortest possible time',[108] although little appears to have been done since. A further delegation was dispatched in August 2022, and in September 2022, Chad committed CFA 10 billion (USD 15 million) to the TFV, when it is operational.[109] Despite these developments, as of December 2023 the promised funds have not been received and victims have not received the reparations ordered.

15.3.4 A trend towards including reparations: The Kosovo Specialist Chambers and the Special Criminal Court in CAR

Two more recently established tribunals include a reparative mandate, suggesting perhaps that there is an emerging trend towards including reparations.[110] The law establishing the KSC sets out the personal interests and rights of victims, including reparation.[111] In particular, the rules of procedure must provide for 'the reasonable reparation to Victims from an accused who has pled or been adjudged guilty of a crime(s) which has directly resulted in harm to the Victims'.[112] Moreover, choosing not to participate in proceedings before the KSC will not impact rights to reparations under national law.[113] A Trial Chamber may on request or of its own motion make a decision on 'the scope and extent of any damage, loss and injury to, or in respect of, Victims and will state the principles on which it is acting'.[114]

The provision adopts a three-pronged approach to implementing reparations. First, following a conviction, a Trial Chamber 'may make an order directly against that accused specifying appropriate reparation to, or in respect of, Victims collectively or individually'.[115] The Chamber may also order the seizure of any property or assets used for or resulting from crime to be returned to the rightful owner or sold to finance a reparations order.[116] Second, where appropriate, the KSC may

[108] News Public Trust, 'African Union In Chad To Activate Fund For Hissène Habré's Victims' (6 August 2022) <https://newspublictrust.com/african-union-in-chad-to-activate-fund-for-hissene-habres-victims/> accessed 20 December 2023.

[109] Gerard Dawa, 'Chad: 10 billion CFA francs to be paid to victims of the Habré regime' (*Afro impact*, 22 September 2022) <https://www.afro-impact.com/en/chad-10-billion-cfa-francs-to-be-paid-to-victims-of-the-habre-regime/> accessed 20 December 2023.

[110] The International Crimes Division of the High Court of Uganda also has a reparative mandate under its RPE but is technically not a hybrid tribunal as it operates under national law with national personnel.

[111] In Specialist Chambers and Specialist Prosecutor's Office (2015) Law No 05/L-053 (hereafter KSC Law) Article 22.

[112] ibid Article 22(3).

[113] ibid Article 22(2).

[114] ibid Article 22(7).

[115] ibid Article 22(8).

[116] ibid Article 44(6).

refer victims to civil compensation before other courts in Kosovo.[117] Third, again following a conviction, the Registrar may transmit a copy of the judgment and any decision on victims, including any assessment of damage to victims, to 'the competent authorities of any State, or directly to Victims'.[118] This provision is not limited to the authorities of Kosovo, which suggests victims may be able to seek compensation or other forms of reparation from third states, including Serbia.[119] The KSC Law does not provide for the establishment of a trust fund, suggesting that where the accused is indigent the victims must rely on compensation at the national level. As Heinze notes, the KSC RPE 'combines the partie civile system of the civil law system, where victims have mainly used the process of initiating criminal complaints as a lever to obtain reparation, and of the common law tradition with its separation between criminal prosecution and civil litigation'.[120]

The KSC issued its first trial judgment on 16 December 2022, convicting the accused of war crimes.[121] The trial panel had earlier considered whether to refer claims for reparations to the civil litigation in the courts in Kosovo pursuant to Article 22(9) of the Law and Rule 167 of the Rules.[122] Having heard from three court appointed experts and received additional information from the Ministry of Justice of Kosovo, the Trial Panel concluded that 'that the national courts in Kosovo do not provide a realistic avenue for victims to claim reparations'.[123] This was primarily because the law in Kosovo did not have 'the ability to protect victims' identities, and consequently their and their families' safety and physical and psychological wellbeing'.[124] This was inconsistent with the panel's finding that it 'must ensure the protection of victims as provided for in Article 23 of the Law throughout the entirety of the judicial process, including the reparations proceedings, irrespective of the forum in which such reparations proceedings are conducted'.[125] In addition, the panel found that courts in Kosovo had no experience of granting civil claims for war crimes, with an expert advising that there had not been a single confirmed case of a victim initiating a claim for civil compensation following the rendering of a judgment in a war crimes case.[126] Accordingly, the trial panel decided

[117] ibid Article 22(9).

[118] ibid Article 22(10).

[119] This is confirmed by Rule 167 of the RPE before the KSC, which extends this provision to transfer of a separate reparation judgment to a third state. The rule also confirms that the decision 'shall be final and binding as to the criminal responsibility of the convicted person for such harm suffered'.

[120] Alexander Heinze, 'The Kosovo Specialist Chambers' Rules of Procedure and Evidence: A Diamond Made Under Pressure?' (2017) 15 Journal of International Criminal Justice 985, 999.

[121] *Prosecutor v Salih Mustafa* (Public redacted version of Trial Judgment) KSC-BC-2020-05 (16 December 2022) (Trial Judgment).

[122] *Prosecutor v Salih Mustafa* (Public redacted version of Decision on the application of Article 22(9) of the Law, setting further procedural steps in the case, and requesting information) KSC-BC-2020-05 (4 February 2022) (hereafter *February 2022 decision*).

[123] *February 2022 decision* (n 122) [39].

[124] ibid [39].

[125] ibid.

[126] ibid [37].

against referring reparations to the local system and indicated that it would instead issue a reparations order under Articles 22(8) and 44(6) of the Law.[127]

On 6 April 2023, the trial panel issued a reparation order in respect of the eight victims participating in the case, by which the trial panel ordered the accused to pay an overall sum of 207,000 Euros as compensation for the harm inflicted on the victims of the crimes for which he was convicted.[128] The reparations order sets out the principles that guide reparations at the KSC,[129] clearly influenced by the ICC framework and jurisprudence, together with other relevant human rights instruments and jurisprudence.[130] The reparations principles include recognizing direct and indirect victims (the family of the murdered detainees)[131] and confirm that a reparations order is to be made directly against the convicted person, regardless of their ability to pay.[132] The order refers to the possibility of both collective and individual reparations,[133] and forms of reparation including restitution and compensation, as well as rehabilitation and satisfaction, but makes no mention of guarantees of non-repetition.[134] The order reiterates the separate and distinct responsibility of the government of Kosovo to provide reparations[135] and that all entities in Kosovo have the obligation to cooperate during the reparations phase.[136] It recognizes that the judgment itself is a form of reparation, as it details the crimes and the harm suffered, while participation gave the victims the opportunity to be seen and heard, to demand justice, and to access to the truth of what happened.[137] The reparation order links back to the types of harm suffered by the victims and the panel's previous findings on the climate of fear and intimidation in Kosovo, recognizing the need to preserve the anonymity of victims and to avoid creating tensions within the community.[138]

The victims had sought individual compensation awards, arguing that collective forms of reparation of a non-pecuniary nature were not appropriate in the context of the case. The panel agreed, finding that individual compensation awards are the most appropriate in the context.[139] Noting that the liability of the convicted person for reparations must be proportionate to the nature and extent of the harm arising from the crimes convicted for, the panel set an amount for each type of harm.[140] As

[127] *Trial Judgment* (n 121) [40].
[128] *Specialist Prosecutor v Salih Mustafa* (Corrected version of Public redacted version of Reparation Order against Salih Mustafa) KSC-BC-2020-05 (2023) (Reparations order).
[129] ibid [62]. See generally Part B of the order, entitled 'Principles of Reparations: Overview'.
[130] Reparations order (n 128) [63]–[65].
[131] ibid [87].
[132] ibid [113].
[133] ibid [104].
[134] ibid [105]–[112].
[135] ibid [81].
[136] ibid [80].
[137] ibid [196]–[200].
[138] ibid [201].
[139] ibid [202].
[140] ibid [210], [214].

it found the ICC and other international jurisprudence to be too inconsistent to determine the amount of the award,[141] the panel decided to use Kosovo laws as a reference point and looked to various local laws giving amounts to wounded KLA veterans, wounded civilians at war, and their families when deceased.[142]

The implementation and enforcement of the reparations order is less clear than the award itself. The panel noted that its jurisdiction in relation to the case will cease with the issue of the order and that it is not empowered to monitor and oversee the implementation of the reparations award.[143] In this sense, the reparations framework at the KSC is different to the ICC, where the Trial Chamber is responsible for overseeing implementation of any reparations order. While the KSC Law and the RPE do not specify which body is to do so, the Trial Panel indicated that it considers it appropriate that a judicial body supervise implementation and Panel invited the president of the KSC to assign a judicial body to have responsibility for this role, supported by the Registry.[144] In relation to funding the order, the Panel noted that there are some assets that may be available and directed action towards seizing these assets, but also declared the defendant partly indigent for the purpose of reparations, and unable to pay the reparations award in full.[145] While he remains fully liable, the Panel noted that some other entity needed to advance the funds. The Panel considered the option of the state of Kosovo funding the reparations order, either via its existing victim compensation scheme or a new entity. However, as noted above, the panel had already decided that using the victim compensation scheme would involve revealing the identity of the victims and directed the registry instead to apply to the scheme on behalf of the victims to avoid this.[146] The panel also requested the victim compensation fund—which is required to cooperate with the KSC—give due consideration to the request, based on the trial judgment and the reparations order.[147] If awarded, the compensation would be given to the registry to allocate directly to victims.[148] Finally, the panel recognized that available compensation may not meet the extent of the order, so it urged consideration of other means of execution, particularly a new mechanism within Kosovo.[149] The panel noted that to do so would require new laws and, while it has no power to order Kosovo to do so, the panel reminded Kosovo of its obligations to provide an effective remedy under human rights law and the constitution.[150] It urged Kosovo to do so by establishing a new mechanism that is 'independent,

141 ibid [215].
142 ibid [216]–[226].
143 ibid [250].
144 ibid [250]–[253].
145 ibid [258].
146 ibid [266].
147 ibid [267].
148 ibid [268].
149 ibid [270]–[272].
150 ibid [274].

neutral and free from political consideration', would protect those cooperating with the KSC, and would be funded through the budget of Kosovo and/or donations from other states.[151] In the event that Kosovo failed to do so, the panel suggested the creation of a newly established trust fund at the KSC to be administered by the KSC registry and funded by donations from states.[152] As yet, there do not appear to have been any steps taken to implement either of these options and the order remains unimplemented.

The SCC was the first tribunal to operate concurrently with potential reparations in cases before the ICC.[153]The SCC was established in 2015 and has a wide temporal mandate (from 1 January 2003) and jurisdiction in respect of crimes beyond ICC core crimes.[154] This means the number of victims is large and the scope of reparations potentially vast. The law establishing the SCC contains an opaque provision requiring the Court to preserve its archives to the right to reparation.[155] Beyond this, the law does not address reparations. The CAR is a civil law system, which is reflected in the RPE of the SCC, adopted in 2018 after consultation with civil society.[156] Similar to the ECCC and the EAC, the RPE build upon the role of civil parties under national law, including recognizing the ability of the Trial Chamber to order individual or collective reparations.[157] Measures should be adapted to the nature of the harm suffered and may include financial compensation, as well as medical and psychological assistance, measures directed at occupational training or for the development of agriculture or industry, and education scholarships.[158] Reparations must follow a criminal conviction and be ordered in the first instance against the accused.[159] However, where the accused is indigent or there are insufficient assets, the victim support service is to assist civil parties and the defence to finance reparations from voluntary contributions.[160] No trust fund is established and there is no reference to state responsibility for reparations,

[151] ibid [275]–[277].

[152] ibid [280]–[272].

[153] The ICC OTP has brought four cases in relation to the CAR: the proceedings against Bemba, which resulted in an acquittal and no prospect of reparations; the proceedings in *Yakatom* and *Nagissona*, which are at the trial stage; proceedings in *Said*, also at the trial stage; and proceedings in *Mokom*, where charges were withdrawn in October 2023. The Prosecutor announced in December 2022 that investigations in the CAR had concluded and that no further cases would be forthcoming: <https://www.icc-cpi.int/news/prosecutor-international-criminal-court-karim-aa-khan-kc-announces-conclusion-investigation-0> accessed 15 January 2024.

[154] For an overview, see Patrick Labuda, '"Open for Business": The Special Criminal Court Launches Investigations in the Central African Republic' (*EJIL: Talk!*, 8 February 2019) <https://www.ejiltalk.org/open-for-business-the-special-criminal-court-launches-investigations-in-the-central-african-republic/> accessed 20 December 2023.

[155] On the creation, organization, and functioning of the Special Criminal Court (2015) Organic Law No 15-003 (SCC) Article 68.

[156] RPE (2018) Organic Law No 18-010 (SCC RPE).

[157] ibid Rule 129(A).

[158] ibid Rule 129(B).

[159] ibid Rule 129(A).

[160] ibid Rule 129(D).

with reports suggesting that the state 'has neither the capacity nor the willingness to pay reparations' and foreign donors unlikely to contribute.[161] The RPE call for a proactive approach to reparations from the Registry, which must develop guidelines for reparations for the benefit of judges and civil parties and to source funding for projects where the accused is indigent or lacks sufficient assets.[162] Thus the SCC appears to adopt a similar approach to the ECCC, requiring civil parties (and interestingly the defence) to source funding for reparations. After challenges finding sufficient funding for the criminal process, the Court issued its first trial judgment in October 2022, convicting three members of a non-state group for war crimes and crimes against humanity. The accused appealed the judgment and, after hearings in June 2023, the appeals judgment was delivered on 29 July 2023,[163] thus concluding the first case at the SCC. The Appeals Chamber found that the Trial Chamber had committed errors, both procedural and substantive. Rather than remit the case to the Trial Chamber, it substituted its own judgment, reversing a conviction for one charge and reducing the sentence for one accused to thirty years' imprisonment, rather than the life sentence originally imposed. The sentences for the other accused were confirmed at twenty years imprisonment.

Another first for the SCC was achieved earlier in 2023: the issue of the first reparations decision on 16 June 2023. The decision on reparations followed months of delay when it was not clear whether the Trial Chamber would issue a reparations decision at all.[164] No public explanation was forthcoming, although reports suggest that 'there was a fundamental disagreement between the two Central African judges who wanted to award more extensive compensation and the international judge who favoured a more realistic approach'.[165] Eventually a compromise appears to have been reached in early June, which allowed the decision on reparations to be delivered later that month.[166] The decision awarded individual compensation,

[161] Human Rights Watch, '"Looking for Justice": The Special Criminal Court, a New Opportunity for Victims in the Central African Republic' (2018) 19 <https://reliefweb.int/sites/reliefweb.int/files/resources/car0518_web.pdf> accessed February 2023.

[162] SCC RPE (n 156) Article 47(D); Nader I Diab, 'CAR's Special Criminal Court Should Start Preparing for Reparations Now' (*JusticeInfo.Net*, 2 July 2019) <https://www.justiceinfo.net/en/justiceinfo-comment-and-debate/opinion/41802-car-special-criminal-court-should-start-preparing-for-reparations-now.html> accessed 20 December 2023.

[163] The full judgment is Judgment No 9 on the appeals against judgment No 003-022 of 31 October 2022 of Trial Chamber I, 23 July 2023. It is available—in French—at <https://www.legal-tools.org/doc/f1s6pp/pdf/>. This discussion is based on the official English summary of the judgment, available here: <https://www.legal-tools.org/doc/bqm3v8/pdf/> (AJ Summary) accessed 20 December 2023.

[164] See Franck Petit and Jean-Fernand Koena, 'Central African Republic: Special Court hands down first reparations decision' (*Journalists for Justice*, 19 July 2023) <https://jfjustice.net/central-african-republic-special-court-hands-down-first-reparations-decision/> accessed 22 January 2024; and Jean-Fernand Koena, 'Special Court Faces Reparations Issue' (*Justiceinfo.net*, 2 February 2023) https://www.justiceinfo.net/en/111925-central-african-republic-special-court-faces-reparations-issue.html accessed 20 December 2023.

[165] Petit and Koena (n 164).

[166] *Special Prosecutor's Office Case Against Issa Sallet Adoum Et Al* (Judgment No 001-2023 on Civil Interests) 16 June 2023 (Civil interests).

requiring the three convicted persons to pay CFA 22.8 million (nearly 35,000 Euros) to twenty-six victims, including sixteen 'rightful claimants' representing their families.[167] The convicted persons were declared to be indigent[168] and the SCC Victims and Defence Aid Service requested to seek external funding for the reparations.[169] The decision also approved two requests for collective reparations: the construction of two wells for the two villages, 'which will enable the victims and survivors, who are still suffering from the trauma of the crimes, to have access to drinking water';[170] and the construction in the same villages of a historic monument to commemorate the attack.[171] The Chamber rejected several other requests for collective reparations.

The civil parties appealed the reparations decision and the Appeals Chamber issued its first appeal judgment on reparations in October 2023.[172] In its judgment, the Appeals Chamber first confirmed the requirements for admissibility of civil parties. It revisited the conclusions of the Trial Chamber on some civil party applications that had been dismissed before the reparations decision as having been filed too late, finding that applying to join proceedings at the trial phase is consistent with the rights of victims to participate and does not infringe upon the rights of the defence.[173] This resulted in the inclusion of a further twenty-two civil parties in the final reparations decision.[174] Second, the Appeals Chamber set out the general principles that should guide the SCC Chambers in relation to reparations awards, including the principles of dignity, non-discrimination, and non-stigmatization; the need to 'do no harm'; and to consider the needs of especially vulnerable groups.[175] The Appeals Chamber confirmed that awards are to be made against the convicted person[176] and that the SCC is not in a position to order the national authorities or international organizations to carry out any particular requests; third parties cooperate with reparations on a voluntary basis.[177] In relation to the awards made by the Trial Chamber, the civil parties had appealed the award of lump sum compensation to direct victims of the attacks, as well as the amount of the award, arguing that the Chamber had to consider individual harm. The Appeals Chamber rejected this argument, finding that the Trial Chamber had a margin of appreciation in determining individual compensation and could award

167 ibid [173]–[175].
168 ibid [176]–[177].
169 ibid [179].
170 ibid [172].
171 ibid [171].
172 Summary of the Appeals Chamber judgment of 16 June 2023, unofficial translation from the French. Original available at <https://www.cpsrca.cf/bibliotheque/ssmenu/resume-chambre-d-appel/53/> (Appeal judgment summary) accessed 20 December 2023.
173 ibid [11]–[20].
174 ibid [31].
175 ibid [25].
176 ibid [25].
177 ibid [25].

lump sum compensation.[178] Moreover, the amounts awarded were not unreasonable. The award was confirmed, although due to the decision on admissibility of additional civil parties, the total amount awarded increased. The civil parties also challenged the award of a lump sum to the families of direct victims. Again, the Appeals Chamber held that the Trial Chamber had discretion and—given this was a symbolic collective payment to families—and not individual compensation to direct victims, the award was appropriate. The amount awarded— CFA 350,000—was not unreasonable and so the award to families was confirmed (with the addition of further families due to the additional civil party requests admitted).[179] The Appeals Chamber included an additional award against the one accused convicted of sexual violence crimes, recognizing the participation of five rape victims (the sixth rape victim had died before the decision) in a project directed at survivors of sexual violence.[180]

In relation to the collective reparation requests, the Appeals Chamber confirmed the decision of the Trial Chamber not to award requests for construction of a health and training centre as this request lacked sufficient detail[181] and, while agreeing that a request for a civics and peaceful education programme would be within the scope of SCC reparations, found that this request also lacked sufficient detail.[182] It confirmed that the request to install security forces in the village was within the sovereign prerogative of CAR and could not be ordered by the SCC.[183] Similarly, the request to award the sum of CFA 15,000,000 to each of the two villages did not include sufficient detail as to the harm to be addressed and the beneficiaries and the Appeals Chamber found no error on the part of the Trial Chamber in rejecting it.[184] In relation to the collective reparations that the Trial Chamber had awarded—the drilling of the two wells in the villages—while the Appeals Chamber appreciated the importance of water to the inhabitants of the villages, there was no evidence showing how these wells would address the harm caused by the murders and no evidence as to the feasibility of the project. Accordingly, this request was also rejected.[185] The Appeals Chamber remained seized of the remaining request for a memorial or historical project. Thus, following the Appeals Chamber decision, the final award amount totalled CFA 13,800,000 and comprised CFA 6,100,000 in individual compensation to survivors of attempted murder and rape and 7,700,000 CFA paid as symbolic collective reparations to twenty-two families receiving CFA 350,000 per family. It is not clear as at early 2024 whether the reparations order has been implemented; however, the United States had contributed a voluntary

[178] ibid [40].
[179] ibid [48]–[59].
[180] ibid [45].
[181] ibid [64]–[66].
[182] ibid [69]–[71].
[183] ibid [67]–[68].
[184] ibid [72]–[73].
[185] ibid [74]–[79].

amount towards reparations at the SCC that could be applied towards the award, so there is at least some prospect that victims will receive some reparations.

15.4 Conclusion: Hybrids and Reparations

The practice of reparations mandates in hybrid tribunals remains limited and underwhelming, with four institutions—the EAC, the ECCC, the KSC, and the SCC—having issued awards as at December 2023. Victims have only realized reparations at the ECCC, and then only projects classed as 'collective and moral' in nature, although there remains some prospect of reparations being implemented at the SCC, depending on voluntary contributions from donor states. However, this overview leads to several findings. First, early hybrid tribunals left the issue of reparations exclusively to the national system, even though the Tribunal's judgment may be relied upon to establish responsibility or eligibility for reparations (often limited to compensation). In general, the domestic systems have not filled this need and many victims have not received any form of reparation. Those tribunals that included a specific reparations process tend to be based in a civil law system and incorporated a reparative mandate not due to the influence of the Rome Statute, but due to the rights victims are accorded as civil parties under national law.[186] Where the Rome Statute and the ICC practice do appear to have had some influence is on the principles that guide the award of reparations and the recognition of a wider range of forms of reparation beyond compensation. However, this too is modified to a local context, for example the ECCC's limited scope of collective and moral reparations. This is not surprising when one considers the divergent views and approaches to reparations that were reflected in the Rome negotiations for the ICC.

Second, for those hybrid tribunals that have incorporated a reparative mandate, all have linked the order of reparations to a criminal conviction. As a result, these tribunals have encountered the same challenges as the ICC: the limited number of victims that court-ordered reparations can assist due to the scope of the charges; the need for a conviction (and risk that the accused dies or is acquitted before an order is made); the link to the liability (and assets) of the accused; an absence of state responsibility and the ability to engage the state directly in the provision of reparations; and a lack of funding for reparations.

As with the ICC, hybrids have had to grapple with providing reparations to large numbers of victims. Consequently, hybrids have adopted different approaches to whether collective and symbolic reparations should be preferred over individual

[186] The one common law jurisdiction that has incorporated reparations—the Uganda's International Crimes Division—has adopted a narrow approach that reflects the focus on compensation in national law.

reparations, particularly compensation. The ECCC, like some Chambers in the ICC, has focused exclusively on collective and symbolic (moral) reparations that will benefit the greatest number of victims, including victims that chose not to participate in proceedings. With indigent accused and lacking a trust fund, the ECCC also transferred responsibility for funding reparations to civil parties and their lawyers, leading to projects funded by external donors and recognized by the Chamber as judicial reparations. The ECCC judges still require a connection between the crimes for which an accused is convicted and the reparations projects, so the element of recognition of criminal conduct is still arguably present, distinguishing these approved projects from others undertaken as non-judicial reparations. This approach has had the benefit that the projects have been undertaken and completed, with the judges clear that they did not want to endorse 'empty' reparations orders that had no prospect of realization. In contrast, the EAC favoured individual compensation payments to victims based on the national legal system, which in the absence of a functioning trust fund, have remained largely unenforceable. The SCC appeared to adopt initially a similar approach to the ECCC, placing an obligation on the registry to be proactive in terms of developing reparations projects and sources of funding. Judicial decisions awarded individual compensation, which given the link to the accused, seem likely to be paid only if sufficient contributions are received from external donors. These challenges—and diverging approaches—demonstrate the importance of managing expectations—both as to whether reparations are possible and, if so, which sorts of reparations are likely. It may also signal an acceptance of an approach—also visible at the ICC—that a criminal process may lead to reparations orders that are primarily symbolic rather than effective.

The tribunals have a similar approach to state responsibility. As with the ICC, with the possible exception of the KSC, none of the tribunals have been authorized to make orders directly binding on the state. This is striking, concerning, although perhaps predictable, and demonstrates the power that participating states have to reduce the scope of the reparative mandate in hybrid tribunals. The ECCC has confirmed it cannot issue orders to the Cambodian government but has instead chosen to involve the government, on a consensual basis, in specific projects. As the EAC is created by Senegal and the AU based on universal jurisdiction, it is alone in the hybrids studied as not having a strong link to the state with prima facie responsibility for reparations, although Chad did consent to its establishment and has offered to contribute funds to the trust fund when operational. This perhaps explains the deferential approach adopted by the EAC, which refused to order any symbolic or collective reparations as these would be inconsistent with Chad's sovereignty. Hybrid tribunals, like the ICC, have to consider the best way in which to engage the state—through a soft, cooperative approach such as applied by the ECCC, allowing states to make representations to the court on possible projects or on the challenges of implementation. Others, such as the STL, have made general recommendations to the government to establish a national compensation scheme. However, tribunals should not give the state a veto on projects or modes of reparation, as the EAC arguably did. Even the KSC, whose orders have binding effect within the local system, has realized the limits of forcing the state to act to realize reparations. The absence of state responsibility is therefore a major flaw in the design of hybrid tribunals. Moreover, the tribunals studied here do not show any success with linking into national reparative processes, which are themselves often only partially effective, as seen most recently by the decision of the KSC that local courts do not offer a realistic option for reparations for victims.

Funding to enable implementation of reparations is a challenge for all hybrids, as for the ICC. Hybrid tribunals tend to have no power to order seizure of assets in support of reparation and there may be no clear obligation on the state concerned to do so, which may have significant ramifications for funding. The maintenance of the link to the defendant's liability is important symbolically but leads to the defendant opposing more aspects of the process and presents challenges where an accused is indigent. Regardless of whether the link is retained, those designing a reparations mandate must accept that the defendant's resources will likely be inadequate and that other funds will be required. Commitments and arrangements for funding need to be made at the start, not left until after an order is made. They should be included in agreements with the government and provide for a clear administrative, financial, and planning structure. The two approaches appear to be seeking donors to fund individual projects (ECCC model) or establishing a trust fund (ICC, EAC). Both are problematic and will be impacted by the types of reparations likely to be ordered and the number of victims. Tribunals should avoid the 'unenforceable reparations orders' seen at the EAC and likely to be seen at other hybrid tribunals in future. There needs to be better awareness of the limited reparations emerging from a narrow criminal process and the need to supplement those reparations with state responsibility or other assistance programmes. Court-ordered reparations schemes in a hybrid tribunal 'cannot act as stand-alone reparations programmes in the aftermath of mass atrocities'[187] and state responsibility needs to be engaged.

Given these challenges, and the trend towards including reparations, should hybrids have a reparative mandate linked to the criminal trial? The tentative answer is possibly: however, the inclusion of reparations needs to be a context-driven decision, taking the national legal system, the political will to support reparations, and the financial resources available into account, as well as the wishes of victims' groups. Each context and institution is different. Before including a reparations mandate, it is essential to identify the frictions between the different ideas of reparative justice—narrow 'accountability' reparations focused on the accused and

[187] Sperfeldt, *Practices* (n 8) 307.

specific crimes or broader human rights awards linked to state responsibility—and how they should interact in a specific context.[188] These different notions of reparations impact on what can be expected from a tribunal. There has been a common failure to give early thought and planning to the purpose, design, and implementation of reparations, with the primary efforts of victims and their lawyers, as well as tribunal personnel, directed towards the criminal trial. Questions about reparations have been left 'until later'. Tribunals and those who design them should engage appropriate experts early in the design phase. There must be an early and realistic assessment as to what can be expected from a reparations process, what form it will take, who is responsible for reparations, and where the money is to come from. Moreover, the decision should be taken in the light of other actual or potential national and transitional justice processes. As Diab notes 'nationwide efforts for providing reparations can be designed to be more inclusive and provide reparations commensurate with the scale of the crimes committed' than court-ordered reparations.[189] That said, many national mechanisms with reparative mandates face similar challenges with funding and implementation. The connection to the accused in court-ordered reparations at least recognizes responsibility for international crimes and the right of the victim to reparation. That recognition is itself significant and a symbolic reparations order, even with no real prospect of implementation, may be of value itself. However, the limits of a reparations process linked to a criminal trial must be appreciated so that the tribunals do not create false expectations for victims or set themselves a task they have no hope of fulfilling.

188 ibid 305.
189 Diab, 'CAR's Special Criminal Court' (n 162).

PART IV
IMPACT

16
Hybrid Justice and the Promise and Expectations of Outreach

Olga Kavran

> Justice is an indispensable ingredient of the process of national reconciliation. It is essential to the restoration of peaceful and normal relations between people who have had to live under a reign of terror. It breaks the cycle of violence, hatred and extra-judicial retribution. Thus Peace and Justice go hand-in-hand.[1]

16.1 Introduction

The opening quotation is from a joint statement by the President and Prosecutor of what is considered as the first modern international criminal tribunal—the International Criminal Tribunal for the former Yugoslavia (ICTY)—in reaction to the signing of the Dayton Peace Agreement which ended the war in Bosnia and Herzegovina in 1995.[2] In their statement, they were reiterating the founding documents of the ICTY in which the United Nations (UN) asserted that the establishment of an international tribunal 'would contribute to the restoration and maintenance of peace'[3] as well as the ICTY's 1st Annual Report, which described the tribunal as '... a tool for promoting reconciliation'.[4]

In their *Handbook on Reconciliation after Violent Conflict*, the authors state that '[r]econciliation and justice are almost twin notions' and that '[m]any people argue that the search for peaceful coexistence, trust, empathy and democratic power sharing demands that 'justice be done ...'.[5]

[1] ICTY, 'The Tribunal welcomes the parties' commitment to justice: Joint statement by the President and the Prosecutor' (24 November 1995) <http://www.icty.org/sid/7220> accessed 13 December 2023.
[2] The General Framework Agreement for Peace in Bosnia and Herzegovina, General Assembly and Security Council (30 November 1995) UN Doc A/50/79C, S/1995/999.
[3] See UNSC Res 808 (1993) UN Doc S/RES/808; UNSC Res 827 (1993) UN Doc S/RES/827.
[4] 'Annual Report of the International Tribunal for the Prosecution of Persons Responsible for Serious Violations of International Humanitarian Law Committed in the Territory of the Fromer Yugoslavia since 1991 (29 August 1994) UN Doc A/49/342, S/1994/1007, para 16.
[5] David Bloomfield, Teresa Barnes, and Luc Huyse, *Reconciliation after Violent Conflict—A Handbook* (International Institute for Democracy and Electoral Assistance 2003) 97.

Olga Kavran, *Hybrid Justice and the Promise and Expectations of Outreach* In: *Hybrid Justice*.
Edited by: Kirsten Ainley and Mark Kersten, Oxford University Press. © Olga Kavran 2025.
DOI: 10.1093/oso/9780192893758.003.0016

The UN special rapporteur on the promotion of truth, justice, reparation, and guarantees of non-recurrence has stated that 'reconciliation should not be conceived as either an alternative to justice or an aim that can be achieved independently of the implementation of the comprehensive approach to the four measures' that form the basis of his mandate.[6]

The international community creates international and hybrid tribunals in response to great suffering. It never 'only' promises fair and public trials (which is the primary legal requirement of justice) but also sets other 'non-judicial goals', such as the restoration and maintenance of peace, contribution to reconciliation, strengthening the rule of law or capacity building aimed at the national legal system of the affected country.[7] The question that is rarely addressed by their creators is how these judicial institutions are meant to achieve their 'non-judicial' goals and what tools they have at their disposal to do so. This is equally true of fully international as well as hybrid courts. This chapter will argue that despite these challenges, international and hybrid courts should strive to achieve these non-judicial goals, and the international community must support them in this endeavour.

Section 16.2 of this chapter will show that the creators of international and hybrid criminal courts always assign them with non-judicial goals as evidenced through the various preparatory reports, UN Security Council resolutions, and other relevant documents. Section 16.3 will demonstrate that the courts and their creators have embraced outreach as one of the courts' important functions. Section 16.4 will look at the courts' contribution to the achievement of non-judicial goals through outreach efforts. The conclusion will demonstrate the need for a comprehensive approach and suggest a solution.

At the outset, a few clarifications are necessary. In this chapter, the term 'internationalized criminal courts' will be used to mean international and hybrid courts and tribunals, and 'outreach' will be used to mean any outreach and legacy activities conducted by the internationalized criminal courts. These usually include both information-sharing and capacity-building activities in their broadest sense.

Relying on UN terminology, the rule of law 'refers to a principle of governance in which all persons, institutions and entities, public and private, including the State itself, are accountable to laws that are publicly promulgated, equally enforced and independently adjudicated, and which are consistent with international human rights norms and standards'.[8] Justice 'is an ideal of accountability and fairness in

[6] UNHRC, 'Report of the Special Rapporteur on the promotion of truth, justice, reparation and guarantees of non-recurrence' (9 August 2012) UN Doc A/HRC/21/46, para 37.

[7] The term 'non-judicial goals' is borrowed from UN Human Rights Council terminology in the context of the Special Mandate and Special Rapporteur on the promotion of truth, justice, reparation, and guarantees of non-recurrence (see <https://www.ohchr.org/EN/Issues/TruthJusticeReparation/Pages/Index.aspx> accessed 13 December 2023) and refers to reconciliation, capacity building, enhancement of the rule of law, etc.

[8] UNSC, 'Report of the Secretary-General, The rule of law and transitional justice in conflict and post-conflict societies' (23 August 2004) UN Doc S/2004/616, para 6.

the protection and vindication of rights and the prevention and punishment of wrongs ... and implies regard for the rights of the accused, for the interests of victims and for the well-being of society at large'.[9] Transitional justice 'comprises the full range of processes and mechanisms associated with a society's attempts to come to terms with a legacy of large-scale past abuses, in order to ensure accountability, serve justice, and achieve reconciliation'.[10] They may 'include both judicial and non-judicial mechanisms, with or without differing levels of international involvement (or none at all) and individual prosecutions, reparations, truth-seeking, institutional reform, vetting and dismissals, or a combination thereof'.[11]

16.2 Internationalized Criminal Courts, their Non-Judicial Goals, and their Intended Legacy

Despite the fact that international and hybrid criminal courts and tribunals have been created as a result of different political compromises and have been given different mandates,[12] their challenges, especially when it comes to the fulfilment of their non-judicial goals, have, interestingly, been quite similar. International criminal trials have always been seen as part of a larger context. This is evident from the wide consensus among the founders of internationalized criminal courts that such institutions can and should contribute to the restoration and maintenance of peace, reconciliation, the rule of law, as well as capacity building. This view is reflected in many of the documents that preceded or accompanied their creation.

In its Resolution 827 establishing the ICTY, the United Nations Security Council (UNSC) stated that establishing a criminal tribunal would not only bring perpetrators to justice but would also ensure the cessation of violations of international humanitarian law and would contribute to the restoration and maintenance of peace in the former Yugoslavia.[13]

Reiterating the position expressed earlier in the UNSG Report on Establishing the Special Court for Sierra Leone (SCSL), UNSC Resolution 1315 states that 'a credible system of justice and accountability for the very serious crimes committed [in Sierra Leone] would end impunity and would contribute to the process of national reconciliation and to the restoration and maintenance of peace ...',[14] while Human Rights Watch considered it 'vital for the people of Sierra Leone to understand the purpose and operations of the Special Court and the principles by which

[9] ibid para 7.
[10] ibid para 8.
[11] ibid.
[12] James Cockayne, 'The Fraying Shoestring: Rethinking Hybrid War Crimes Tribunals' (2005) 28 Fordham International Law Journal) 616, 618.
[13] UNSC Res 827 (1993) UN Doc S/RES/827, 1.
[14] UNSC Res 1315 (2000) UN Doc S/RES/1315, 1.

it operates' and that 'the people of Sierra Leone should be left with a legacy of the court's work that goes beyond the decisions it issues or the new courthouse it has constructed' in hope that 'the Special Court will contribute to revitalizing Sierra Leoneans' belief in the rule of law . . .'[15]

In Cambodia, the Report of the Group of Experts stated that justice is a critical element for promoting internal peace and national reconciliation and that by having those who committed the abuses identified and punished, Cambodians can work together to build a peaceful and better future. It added that accountability and national reconciliation are complementary and inseparable[16] and referred to a statement by Cambodia's leading non-governmental organizations (NGOs) which called for trials 'for the reconciliation and healing of the Cambodian people'.[17] The UN General Assembly also saw accountability of individual perpetrators of grave human rights violations as one of the central elements of any effective remedy for victims of human rights violations and a key factor in ensuring a fair and equitable justice system and reconciliation and stability within a state.[18]

The report which preceded the creation of the Kosovo Specialist Chambers (KSC), currently the only internationalized criminal court established by the European Union, stated that '[k]nowing the truth and enabling victims' families to mourn at last is a vital precondition for reconciliation between the communities and a peaceful future in this region of the Balkans'[19] and added that '[i]t is a fundamental right of Kosovo's citizens to know the truth, the whole truth, and also an indispensable condition for reconciliation between the communities and the country's prosperous future'.[20]

The courts themselves have stated very specific ways in which their work may be said to contribute to reconciliation. For example, the International Criminal Tribunal for Rwanda (ICTR) stated it would do so:

> through creating a factual account of the genocide judicial history; issuing judicial notice confirming that there was genocide against the Tutsi ethnic group in Rwanda; establishing individual criminal responsibility, not group criminalization or stigmatization; giving voice to the victims to validate their experience of

[15] Human Rights Watch, 'Bringing Justice: the Special Court for Sierra Leone; Accomplishments, Shortcomings, and Needed Support' (2004), 32.

[16] UN, 'Report of the Group of Experts for Cambodia established pursuant to General Assembly resolution 52/135' (Group of Experts Report), transmitted by the Secretary-General along with his own report (Secretary-General Report) UN Doc A/53/850, S/199/231, paras 2–3.

[17] ibid para 94.

[18] UNGA Res 57/228 (2003) UN Doc A/RES/57/228, 1.

[19] Parliamentary Assembly of the Council of Europe, 'Inhuman treatment of people and illicit trafficking in human organs in Kosovo' (2011) 4.

[20] ibid 8.

suffering; and providing re-education and communication to promote respect for human rights and the rule of law in Rwanda.[21]

And according to the first president of the Special Tribunal for Lebanon (STL), the late Antonio Cassese: '... the STL pursues goals (to prosecute serious crimes of terrorism so as to contribute not only to putting a stop to impunity and to alleviating the suffering of the victims, but also to bringing about reconciliation and the establishment of peace and the rule of law) that are consonant with international legal standards prohibiting and penalizing terrorism'.[22]

The Office of the United Nations High Commissioner for Human Rights (OHCHR) stated that '[t]he rationales for creating hybrids are varied, complex and dependent on the national context.... in some situations, hybrid interventions have been intended to contribute to efforts to rebuild legal capacity ... Some argue that in the post-conflict context, trials should contribute to reconciliation.'[23]

In his report on the protection of civilians in armed conflict, the Secretary General of the United Nations (UNSG) stated that: '[t]he fair prosecution and trial of individual suspects can help significantly to build confidence and facilitate reconciliation in post-conflict societies, by removing collective attributions of guilt'[24] and that 'well publicized prosecutions can deter crimes in current and future conflicts'.[25]

Moreover, external observers also noted that, in the twelve years since the creation of the ICTY there had been a shift from a purely deterrent model for tribunals to one that prioritizes capacity building and efforts to build domestic rule of law.[26] Even a critic of one of the hybrid courts didn't appear to question whether the STL has 'broad goals of ending Lebanon's culture of impunity'[27] but rather how the tribunal might be able to achieve them.

This also formed part of the discussions on the courts' legacies. The OHCHR stated that legacy, the need for which is a part of UN policy, is defined 'as a hybrid court's lasting impact on bolstering the rule of law in a particular society, by conducting effective trials to contribute to ending impunity, while also strengthening

[21] Sara Kendall and Sarah Nouwen, 'Speaking of Legacy: Toward an Ethos of Modesty at the International Criminal Tribunal for Rwanda' (2016) University of Cambridge Faculty of Law Research Paper No 20/2016, 32, (footnote 152, quoting former ICTR Spokesperson Timothy Gallimore).

[22] Antonio Cassese, 'The Legitimacy of International Criminal Tribunals and the Current Prospects of International Criminal Justice' (2012) 25 Leiden Journal of International Law 491, 497.

[23] OHCHR, 'Rule-of-Law Tools for Post-Conflict States, Maximizing the Legacy of Hybrid Courts, Office of the United Nations High Commissioner for Human Rights' (2008) 3–4.

[24] Report of the Secretary-General to the Security Council on the protection of civilians in armed conflict (2001) UN Doc S/2001/331, para 11.

[25] ibid.

[26] Varda Hussain, 'Sustaining Judicial Rescues: The Role of Outreach and Capacity-Building Efforts in War Crimes Tribunals' (2005) 45 Virginia Journal of International Law 547, 551.

[27] Michelle Burgis-Kasthala, 'Defining Justice during Transition? International and Domestic Contestations over the Special Tribunal for Lebanon' (2013) 7 International Journal of Transitional Justice 497, 517.

domestic judicial capacity'[28] and that 'the aim is for this impact to continue even after the work of the hybrid court is complete'.[29]

Many observers have written on the topic of the role of courts in peace and reconciliation and asserted that this is not something the courts should aspire to do.[30] However, most do not provide a clear definition of 'reconciliation' describing it as a 'murky concept',[31] an imprecise term with multiple meanings,[32] or 'one of the most contested concepts in the scholarly debate on transitional justice, and arguably also the most difficult to measure empirically'.[33] Others see it as a finite end product with almost metaphysical qualities, stating that 'healing and national reconciliation cannot come into being with the stroke of a pen' and therefore cannot be undertaken by an international court or tribunal.[34] A detailed argument against that position is outside the scope of this chapter. However, the findings might well be different if reconciliation is seen as 'not simply an end state where enmity becomes amity' but a process that 'involves any incremental progress'[35] and that 'the ultimate purpose of both international law and international criminal justice is to contribute to a reconciled international society'.[36]

Capacity building and rule of law are arguably easier to define, and scholars have been more inclined to see a positive contribution. For example, Stromseth states that 'courts can make—and encourage—meaningful and direct contributions to improving the domestic justice systems in the societies affected by their work'[37] and lists different ways in which they have done so,[38] while Ainley and others concluded that while the SCSL 'was never the sole, or even the main, actor in prompting legislative change in Sierra Leone ... it was a contributing factor'.[39]

[28] OHCHR, Rule-of-Law Tools (n 23) 4–5.

[29] ibid.

[30] See, eg, the works of Stover and Weinstein, McMahon and Forsythe, Fletcher and others, Leila Nadya Sadat, David Tolbert, JN Clark, Bronwyn Anne Leebaw, and others.

[31] Eric Stover and Harvey M Weinstein (eds), *My Neighbor, My Enemy: Justice and Community in the Aftermath of Mass Atrocity* (Cambridge University Press 2004) 5.

[32] Harvey M Weinstein, 'Editorial Note: The Myth of Closure, the Illusion of Reconciliation: Final Thoughts on Five Years as Co-Editor-in-Chief' (2011) 5 International Journal of Transitional Justice 1, 6.

[33] Elin Skaar, 'Reconciliation in a Transitional Justice Perspective' (2013) 1 Transitional Justice Review 54, 54.

[34] Leila Nadya Sadat, 'The Legacy of the International Criminal Tribunal for Rwanda' (2013) Legal Studies Research Paper Series, Paper No 12-09-05, Washington University in St Louis School of Law, 17.

[35] Daniel Philpott, *Just and Unjust Peace, an Ethic of Political Reconciliation* (Oxford University Press 2012) 287.

[36] David Baragwanath, '"Reconciliation" as a Philosophical Foundational Concept in International Criminal Law' in Morten Bergsmo, Emiliano J Buis, and Song Tianying (eds), *Philosophical Foundations of International Criminal Law: Legally Protected Interests* (TOAEP 2019) 76.

[37] Jane E Stromseth, 'Justice on the Ground: Can International Criminal Courts Strengthen Domestic Rule of Law in Post-Conflict Societies?' (2009) 1 Hague Journal on the Rule of Law 87, 95.

[38] ibid 95–97.

[39] Kirsten Ainley, Rebekka Friedman, and Chris Mahoney (eds), *Evaluating Transitional Justice: Accountability and Peacebuilding in Post-Conflict Sierra Leone* (Palgrave Macmillan 2015) 142.

16.3 Internationalized Criminal Courts and the Need for Outreach

Despite these examples of non-judicial goals assigned to judicial institutions, the founding documents do not provide any guidance to the courts on how to achieve them. As expressed by an observer three years after the establishment of the SCSL: 'It remains unclear—even at this advanced stage of the Court's operation—how the Court is expected to prioritize "legacy" creation in relation to its other tasks, or, in other words, how to reconcile its justice mandate with its peace and reconciliation mandate.'[40]

Statutes and Rules of Procedure and Evidence (RPE) provide exclusively for those functions which support internationalized criminal courts' judicial functions as well as such additional functions as arise from the fact that institutions of international criminal justice often exist as standalone structures at the international level and cannot rely on a state structure to support their work. Internationalized criminal courts typically consist of three organs—Chambers, Office of the Prosecutor (OTP) and Registry—which are related in a variety of ways to their equivalents in relevant domestic systems.[41] The STL is an exception with the Defence Office as a fourth organ.[42]

In each of the courts, the OTP is typically staffed by a range of lawyers, investigators, analysts, and assistants, as well as other experts, such as, for example, demographers (as was the case in the ICTY) or telecommunications experts (at the STL). Chambers, for their part, consist of judges, legal clerks, and support staff. The Registry is typically the most diverse of all organs as it has both administrative (such as human resources, budget and finance, and facilities management) and judicial functions (eg court and records management). Very importantly, registries also typically include public information and outreach departments.[43] This will be discussed in greater detail in Section 16.4.

The judges and lawyers in internationalized criminal courts usually bring their own national experience, often from developed national systems and are unlikely to have previously encountered the courts' non-judicial functions. In addition, national systems do not encourage direct engagement by judges and prosecutors with the media. In fact, '[s]ome national codes of ethics require judges to refrain from

[40] James Cockayne, 'The Fraying Shoestring: Rethinking Hybrid War Crimes Tribunals' (2005) 28 Fordham International Law Journal 616, 659, footnotes omitted.

[41] Beth Van Schaack, 'The Building Blocks of Hybrid Justice' (2016) 44 Denver Journal of International Law and Policy 169, 225.

[42] STL, 'About the STL: Defence' <https://www.stl-tsl.org/en/about-the-stl/structure-of-the-stl/defenceaccessed 3 February 2023>.

[43] See, eg, the ICTY website at ICTY, 'Organisational Chart' <https://www.icty.org/en/about/tribunal/organisational-chart> accessed 13 December 2023; the ICC website at ICC, 'Outreach <https://www.icc-cpi.int/about/outreach> accessed 13 December 2023; the STL website at STL, 'Inter-University Programme' <https://www.stl-tsl.org/en/outreach/inter-university-programme> accessed 13 December 2023.

public comments on pending cases, in order not to make statements that might cause the public to question the judges' impartiality and to avoid violation of the presumption of innocence',[44] and advise the judges to 'express themselves above all through their decisions'.[45] And, although the attitude has been changing on this issue, with a growing number of national and international judges, prosecutors, and other decision-makers realizing the necessity of explaining judgments,[46] international judges and prosecutors who do engage also suffer criticism of their activities.[47]

At the same time, international trials have a vital demonstration effect which can either build or undermine public confidence in fair justice and convey crucial messages about justice and the rule of law.[48]

> By holding individual perpetrators accountable for their actions, these trials demonstrate that certain conduct is out of bounds … ; affirm that impunity for these crimes is being punctured [and that] perpetrators cannot presume on impunity … ; aim to demonstrate and to reassure people that justice can be fair—both procedurally in terms of due process and, substantively, in terms of even-handed treatment of comparable actions regardless of who committed them.[49]

In this context, it is worth remembering the lengths to which the Allies went following the Nuremberg trials to make sure ordinary Germans knew what kinds of crimes the defendants had been accused of, by broadcasting radio programmes, showing documentaries, and distributing pamphlets. 'The Allied information campaign made more Germans face up to the reality of the Holocaust and Germany's

[44] Bordeaux Declaration: 'Judges and Prosecutors in a Democratic Society' Opinion No 12 (2009) of the Consultative Council of European Judges (CCJE) and Opinion No 4 (2009) of the Consultative Council of European Prosecutors (CCPE) <https://search.coe.int/cm/Pages/result_details.aspx?ObjectID=09000016805cfebd#> para 75 accessed 13 December 2023.

[45] ibid.

[46] See, eg, the Dutch Council for the Judiciary's recommendations on dealing with the media which state: 'In the Netherlands judges generally do not explain their own judgments directly to journalists … That is based on the principle that the judge 'speaks through his judgment'. However, in practice that is not always sufficient to adequately respond to questions that arise with respect to the administration of justice. Therefore, each court has its own communications department, whose duties include ensuring that the press is informed properly.' De Rechtspraak, 'Press Guidelines 2013' (2013) <www.rechtspraak.nl/SiteCollectionDocuments/Press-Guidelines.pdf> accessed 13 December 2023.

[47] See, eg, Christine Schwobel-Patel's article 'The rule of law as a marketing tool: The International Criminal Court and the brand of global justice' and its scathing criticism of what she refers to as 'marketing efforts' by the ICC's President and Prosecutor. The critique from the political left appearing to be one of using neoliberal approaches to 'selling' international justice. '… [ICC's] key actors spend large amounts of time and energy on promoting and controlling its brand; disproportionately, it appears, to efforts of ensuring that justice is done in the courtroom'.

[48] Stromseth (n 37) 92.

[49] ibid.

responsibility for aggression. These efforts have helped build a powerful German culture of remembering and atoning.'[50]

As stated more recently by the OHCHR: '[t]rials involving serious and complex crimes, including war crimes and crimes against humanity, require dialogue with the public to be understood'.[51] This is based on the assumption that 'a well-informed public can contribute to guaranteeing lasting respect for and the enforcement of international justice'[52] or that the administration of justice 'serves the interests of the community at large and requires the co-operation of an enlightened public'.[53] Moreover, the OHCHR also warned that the dialogue with the public about complex trials is an important task that 'should not be left to the local or international media, which in the post-conflict era is often not able to responsibly deal with these issues, often requiring its own capacity-building'.[54]

Referring specifically to the ICTY, Janine Natalya Clark, critical of the Tribunal's ability to contribute to reconciliation emphasized that 'it is at least part of the Tribunal's responsibility to ensure that [members of the affected communities] are able to express *informed* opinions'[55] and added that if 'people on the ground are given only fragments of very minimal information about the ICTY's verdicts ... such truths cannot penetrate the group's own narrative'.[56]

The former UN Secretary General described ICTY and ICTR archives as 'tools for fostering reconciliation'[57] which 'have a secondary value for memory, education and research'[58] adding that, over time, this secondary value 'will progressively prevail'.[59] He went on to specify that the 'content of the Tribunals' archives is significant to victims, witnesses and their families and, more widely, the populations of the affected countries' and that 'Government officials, other international tribunals and courts, ... journalists, historians, legal researchers, political scientists and persons interested in memorializing an event or creating educational materials, may also seek access to the Tribunals' records'.[60] All this, of course, is on the

[50] Gary Jonathan Bass, *Stay the Hand of Vengeance: The Politics of War Crimes Tribunals* (Princeton University Press 2000) 200 (citations omitted).

[51] OHCHR, Rule-of-Law Tools (n 23) 19.

[52] ICC, 'Understanding the International Criminal Court' (2020) <www.icc-cpi.int/iccdocs/PIDS/publications/UICCEng.pdf> accessed 13 December 2023.

[53] *The Sunday Times v United Kingdom* App no 6538/74 (ECtHR, 26 April 1979) [65].

[54] OHCHR, Rule-of-Law Tools (n 23) 19.

[55] Janine Natalya Clark, *International Trials and Reconciliation: Assessing the Impact of the International Criminal Tribunal for the former Yugoslavia* (Routledge 2014) 81 (emphasis added).

[56] ibid 103.

[57] Report of the Secretary-General on the administrative and budgetary aspects of the options for possible locations for the archives of the International Tribunal for the Former Yugoslavia and the International Criminal Tribunal for Rwanda and the seat of the residual mechanism(s) for the Tribunals (2009) UN Doc S/2009/258, para 201.

[58] ibid para 42.

[59] ibid para 59.

[60] ibid para 59.

assumption that these records are available and intelligible—something the tribunals treat as part of their legacy.[61]

Indeed, a similar realization[62] led Judge Gabrielle Kirk McDonald, the former president of the ICTY to establish the first outreach programme.[63] All subsequently established internationalized courts have an outreach department within the Registry with a preference for significant engagement clearly evolving over the years.[64]

In his Report on the establishment of the Special Court for Sierra Leone, the UNSG called for 'a broad public information and education campaign ... as an integral part of the Court's activities'.[65] A later UN-commissioned expert report stated that effective outreach programmes are essential not only to ensure that people are aware of and understand prosecutions and why certain charges were brought, but also so that the judicial officials are aware of how human rights prosecutions are perceived by ordinary people and to ensure that public perceptions are not distorted due to a lack of information.[66]

Later that same year, in his Report on the rule of law and transitional justice in conflict and post-conflict societies, the UNSG referred to the importance of keeping the public informed: 'benefits [of locating tribunals inside the countries concerned], where combined with specially tailored measures for keeping the public informed and effective techniques for capacity-building, can help ensure a lasting legacy in the countries concerned'[67] and added that '[p]ublic expectations must be informed through an effective communications strategy'.[68]

[61] For an interesting broader discussion, see ICTY, 'Legacy Conferences' <https://www.icty.org/en/features/legacy-conferences> accessed 13 December 2023.

[62] 'We have a mandate at the ICTY... to help to bring about and maintain international peace and security. How are you going to do that if you cannot impress upon the people of the region, not the international legal community but people in the region—what happened; to give them a historical record of what happened?...

We have this ... judgement ... but it's not influencing people ... So I said to myself we've got to do something about it... How are we going to dispel these myths? If people in the region don't understand what we are doing, how we are doing it, and that we are doing it fairly to the best of our ability, how can they be influenced by our judgments? The Judgements are supposed to help bring about reconciliation. They can't, alone. But they can begin the process ...' Brandeis University, 'Gabrielle Kirk McDonald' <https://www.brandeis.edu/ethics/internationaljustice/oral-history/interviews/mcdonald.html> accessed 13 December 2023.

[63] See ICTY, 'Outreach Programme' <https://www.icty.org/en/outreach/outreach-programme> accessed 13 December 2023.

[64] The following overview is derived from one of the author's earlier publications: Olga Kavran, 'International Judicial Institutions (Re)Defining 'Public' Proceedings?' in Chrisje Brants and Susanne Karstedt (eds), *Transitional Justice and the Public Sphere: Engagement, Legitimacy and Contestation* (Hart 2017).

[65] Report of the Secretary-General on the establishment of a Special Court for Sierra Leone (2000) UN Doc S/2000/915, para 2.

[66] Diane Orentlicher, 'Independent study on best practices, including recommendations, to assist states in strengthening their domestic capacity to combat all aspects of impunity' UN ECOSOC, Commission on Human Rights (27 February 2004) UN Doc E/CN.4/2004/88, para 40.

[67] UNSC, 'The rule of law and transitional justice in conflict and post-conflict societies: Report of the Secretary-General' (2004) UN Doc S/2004/616, para 44.

[68] ibid para 46.

The UN report on the steps taken to establish the Special Tribunal for Lebanon emphasized that 'a key element for the success of the Special Tribunal is not only that justice be done but also that justice must be seen to be done'[69] and referred to 'the development of an effective and comprehensive outreach programme bringing the activities of the Special Tribunal closer to the population of Lebanon and the wider region' as 'a priority'.[70]

International NGOs have also weighed in on the issue, particularly in relation to the first permanent international criminal court—the ICC. Human Rights Watch stated that their field experience 'suggests that the ICC's mandate will not be fulfilled solely by conducting efficient, effective investigations with fair trials—however crucial those tasks are'.[71] According to Human Rights Watch, 'because none of the usual means for disseminating information about a national court are readily available to the ICC, the court needs to have an effective strategy for external relations, public information and outreach to popularize its work'. They further added that 'effective outreach and communications require meaningful engagement, dialogue and exchange with local communities and media'[72] and that such programmes must 'start early to be most effective'.[73]

According to the International Bar Association 'it is of key importance that extensive outreach campaigns are now initiated in all current situation countries, and provision made for adequate resources to be allocated to outreach when future investigations begin',[74] while the Coalition for the International Criminal Court (CICC) is of the view that 'lessons learned—including from the *ad hoc* tribunals—demonstrate that early, Court-led communications are essential for the meaningful delivery of fair and credible justice to victims as set out in the Rome Statute'.[75]

REDRESS has said that 'if the Court is to be relevant to communities most affected by the crimes within its jurisdiction, there is a need to go beyond simply notifying communities of certain decisions. Instead, a sustained capacity to respond and engage communities on new issues as they arise must be assured'.[76] And the Victims' Rights Working Group called for 'early and direct outreach' which would create 'conditions conducive to supporting the Court's operations

[69] Report of the Secretary-General submitted pursuant to Security Council resolution 1757 (2007) of 30 May 2007 (2007) UN Doc S/2007/525, para 33.

[70] ibid.

[71] Human Rights Watch, 'Human Rights Watch Memorandum for the 4th ICC Assembly of States Parties' (2005) 2–3.

[72] ibid.

[73] ibid.

[74] International Bar Association Human Rights Institute, 'ICC Monitoring and Outreach Programme First Outreach Report' (2006) 6.

[75] CICC, 'Comments and Recommendations to the 13th Session of the Assembly of States Parties' 1 <https://www.legal-tools.org/doc/173047/pdf/> accessed 13 December 2023.

[76] REDRESS, 'Making the ICC relevant to affected communities: Report prepared for the 6th Assembly of States Parties, New York, 28 November–14 December 2007' <www.redress.org/downloads/publications/REDRESS%20Making_the_ICC_relevant_3_Dec_07.pdf> accessed 13 December 2023.

by ensuring the necessary cooperation for conducting investigations in the field and carrying out trials; preventing or stemming the spread of misinformation; reinforcing complementarity initiatives; facilitating participation and legal representation of victims in ICC proceedings; explaining due process rights; facilitating redress for affected communities; and creating an enabling and supportive environment for field engagement and presence'.[77]

The courts and tribunals themselves have also continuously emphasized the necessity of outreach. The ICTY has stated that 'an Outreach Programme was established to improve understanding of the work of the Tribunal and its relevance in the territory of the former Yugoslavia',[78] and later expanded its outreach activities 'recognising the critical importance to the success of the Tribunal that populations in the region of the former Yugoslavia are informed about and understand the work and significance of the Tribunal'.[79]

The SCSL reported on an outreach programme 'established with the aim not only of ensuring that the purpose of the Special Court is understood across Sierra Leone, but also to grant to all sections of civil society in the country the opportunity to have their voice heard and their expectations of the Court identified'.[80] Its Prosecutor described how the 'outreach program assists in legacy building by teaching the importance of the rule of the law and facilitating modalities and opportunities for discussion of the role of the law in fostering an open and peaceful society'.[81]

The ICC issued a comprehensive strategy in 2006, which was presented and endorsed at the Assembly of States Parties. Addressing the Assembly, the then president of the ICC included outreach among the Court's core activities, along with the proceedings, securing cooperation, and responsibilities towards participants and stated that 'the fundamental priorities in the ICC Strategic Plan include ensuring the quality and effectiveness of such activities.[82] The then Prosecutor also emphasized 'the need for resources for outreach'.[83]

[77] Victims' Rights Working Group, 'International Criminal Court at 10: the implementation of victims' rights' (11th Session of the Assembly of States Parties, 2012) 4 <https://redress.org/wp-content/uploads/2018/01/Nov-12-Issues-and-Concerns-VRWG.pdf> accessed 13 December 2023.

[78] Report of the International Tribunal for the Prosecution of Persons Responsible for Serious Violations of International Humanitarian Law Committed in the Territory of the Former Yugoslavia since 1991 (7 August 2000) UN Doc A/55/273-S/2000/777, para 213.

[79] Report of the International Tribunal for the Prosecution of Persons Responsible for Serious Violations of International Humanitarian Law Committed in the Territory of the Former Yugoslavia since 1991 (17 September 2001) UN Doc A/56/352–S/2001/865, para 224.

[80] SCSL, 'First Annual Report of the President of the Special Court for Sierra Leone: 2 December 2002–1 December 2003' para 6.

[81] David M Crane, 'Dancing with the Devil: Prosecuting West Africa's Warlords: Building Initial Prosecutorial Strategy for an International Tribunal after Third World Armed Conflicts' (2005) 37 Case Western Reserve Journal of International Law 1, 8.

[82] Philippe Kirsch, 'Opening Remarks' (Fifth Session of the Assembly of States Parties, 23 November 2006) 2.

[83] Louis Moreno Ocampo, 'Opening Remarks' (Fifth Session of the Assembly of States Parties, 23 November 2006) 7.

In 2018, in an apparent agreement with the International Bar Association's position on the issue (see above) the ICC's Pre-Trial Chamber extended outreach and communication to the preliminary examination in the situation in Palestine, arguing that 'victims ... have the right to provide information to, receive information from and communicate with the Court, regardless and independently from judicial proceedings, including during the preliminary examination stage'.[84] Two years later, it did the same following the opening of the investigation in the situation of Bangladesh/Myanmar, stating that

> The Chamber considers that the need to be informed is equally applicable in the present situation, particularly in respect of victims of crimes that took place following the authorisation of the investigation. Likewise, outreach to victims should enable all the organs of the Court to better understand the concerns and expectations of victims, so that coordinated, effective and clear activities are organised in the context of the authorised investigation.[85]

In 2019, the Assembly of States Parties to the ICC commissioned a group of experts requesting them to identify ways to strengthen the ICC and the Rome Statute system and enhance their overall functioning and to make specific recommendations to enhance the performance, efficiency, and effectiveness of the ICC.[86] In 2021, the Experts published the 'Independent Expert Review of the International Criminal Court and the Rome Statute System Final Report', which included a number of specific recommendations in respect of outreach.[87]

Highlighting the importance of outreach activities, the experts stated that they 'should be built into the program budget of any new investigation',[88] and that 'Outreach programs and activities should be built into decisions to pursue particular investigative activities from the start, given the critical importance of winning the support of communities impacted by the events to be investigated'.[89] They added that '[a]n outreach plan, at least for every situation country, if not also per region, should be devised and then implemented from the preliminary examination stage of every situation'.[90]

[84] *Situation in the State of Palestine* (Decision on Information and Outreach for the Victims of the Situation) ICC-01/18-2 (13 July 2018) [10].

[85] *Situation in the People's Republic of Bangladesh/Republic of the Union of Myanmar* (Order on Information and Outreach for the Victims of the Situation) ICC-01/19 (20 January 2020) [7].

[86] ICCM, 'Independent Expert Review of the International Criminal Court and the Rome Statute System: Final Report' (30 September 2020) 7 <https://asp.icc-cpi.int/iccdocs/asp_docs/ASP19/IER-Final-Report-ENG.pdf> (citations omitted) accessed 13 December 2023.

[87] Olga Kavran, 'Communicating Justice: Lessons from International and National Courts and Prosecution Authorities Dealing with International Crimes' (2022) Asser Institute 18 <https://www.asser.nl/media/795748/communicating-justice-lessons-from-international-and-national-courts-and-prosecution-authorities-dealing-with-international-crimes.pdf> accessed 13 December 2023.

[88] 'Independent Expert Review' (n 86) 128.

[89] ibid.

[90] ibid 127–28.

From the foregoing, it is undeniable that a wide-ranging consensus has emerged on the necessity of an outreach programme in internationalized criminal courts.

Despite that fact, none of these institutions have included outreach in their Statutes. The judges at the STL took a step further than any before (or since) when they included outreach in the Tribunal's RPE, tasking the Registrar with setting up an outreach programme to 'disseminate accurate and timely information to the public, particularly in Lebanon, about the general role and functioning of the Tribunal, and ... carry out outreach activities related to victims'.[91] The STL Registry took that a step further when it established an Outreach and *Legacy* Unit.[92] The ICC has included outreach in its internal regulations of the Registry.[93]

16.4 Internationalized Criminal Courts and their Outreach Activities

Let us now turn to the actual outreach activities and how they may relate to the non-judicial goals of internationalized criminal courts, such as capacity building, enhancing the rule of law, and promoting reconciliation.

The public information and outreach departments at internationalized criminal courts closely monitor events in affected communities to identify issues that need to be addressed. In each new situation, they must carry out an initial assessment of political, cultural, historical, and sociological factors and map out the media environment.[94] In doing so, they identify target audiences, such as the media, victims, legal professionals, NGO representatives, the academic community and students, youth, members of the army or security services, and others and tailor

[91] Rule 52 of the STL Rules of Procedure and Evidence: Outreach Programme Unit: (A) The Registrar shall set up an Outreach Programme Unit within the Registry to (i) disseminate accurate and timely information to the public, particularly in Lebanon, about the general role and functioning of the Tribunal, and (ii) carry out outreach activities related to victims. (B) Due consideration shall be given, in the appointment of staff, to the employment of qualified Lebanese nationals. STL-BD-2009-01-Rev 6-Corr 1.

[92] STL, 'Outreach' <https://www.stl-tsl.org/en/outreachaccessed 13 December 2023.>

[93] ICC, 'Regulations of the Registry', Regulation 5*bis* Public information and outreach (adopted on 4 December 2013): 1. In fulfilment of the Registrar's mandate to provide information pursuant to rule 13, sub-rule 1 of the Rules of Procedure and Evidence, the Registry shall ensure the public dissemination of appropriate, neutral and timely information concerning the activities of the Court through public information and outreach programmes. 2. Public information programmes shall be aimed at fostering public understanding and support for the work of the Court. To this end, the Registry may employ various means of communication, including print and broadcast media, internet-based technologies, visits to the Court and public-speaking engagements by Court officials. 3. Outreach programmes shall be aimed at making the Court's judicial proceedings accessible to those communities affected by the situations and cases before the Court. To this end, the Registry shall develop appropriate communication tools and strategies, such as consultation and town-hall meetings, radio and television programmes, leaflets, booklets, posters and videos.

[94] Matias Hellman, 'Challenges and Limitations of Outreach' in Christian De Vos, Sara Kendall, and Carsten Stahn (eds), *Contested Justice: The Politics and Practice of International Criminal Court Interventions* (Cambridge University Press 2015) 268.

their activities to them. For this purpose, the courts have implemented a range of different projects: in addition to providing regular information through press releases and media advisories, the courts have also produced booklets, leaflets, audio-visual material, and other information materials. The courts' annual reports often list lectures and presentations; conferences; symposia; seminars; workshops; and roundtable discussions with judges, lawyers, and other practitioners, NGO representatives, academics and students. Such events address an array of topics related to the work of the institutions or the broader issues of international criminal justice.[95]

Some specific examples deserve highlighting.

In 2003, the UNSC specifically asked the ICTY to contribute to capacity-building efforts through its outreach programme.[96] To that end, the ICTY organized comprehensive training sessions on international criminal proceedings for legal professionals throughout the former Yugoslavia and contributed to the establishment of specialized organs for war crimes investigations and trials in Bosnia and Herzegovina, Serbia, and Croatia. These efforts are claimed to have significantly improved the capability of national judicial systems to battle impunity for war crimes.[97] The Tribunal also organized a series of 'Bridging the Gap' events in 2004 and 2005. The one-day events, held in towns where some of the most serious crimes took place, included presentations from tribunal staff who had been directly involved in the investigation, prosecution, and adjudication of crimes. Since the displaced victims and others were also brought to the venues from other areas of Bosnia and Herzegovina, the events provided a unique opportunity for local community leaders, victims, returnees, legal professionals, law enforcement personnel, journalists, scholars, and other members of the public to hear firsthand and ask questions about the Tribunal's work.[98] This interaction between different groups was of crucial importance for fostering understanding of different views.[99] And even a critic of the ICTY's ability to contribute to reconciliation lauded these events and regretted that there had not been more of them, stating that: '[a] strong focus on the grassroots level is crucial to the overall success of any outreach programme, and hence it is deeply regrettable that the Tribunal never built upon or repeated this "Bridging the Gap" series.'[100]

[95] See, eg, ICTY, 'Annual Reports' <www.icty.org/sid/31> accessed 13 December 2023; ICC, 'Outreach Reports' <https://www.icc-cpi.int/about/outreach/reports> accessed 13 December 2023; STL, 'Annual Reports' <https://www.stl-tsl.org/en/documents/annual-reports> accessed 13 December 2023.

[96] ICTY, 'Development of the Local Judiciaries' <www.icty.org/en/outreach/capacity-building/development-local-judiciaries> accessed 13 December 2023; UNSC Res 503 (2003) UN Doc S/RES/1503, para 1.

[97] ibid.

[98] ICTY, 'Bridging the Gap with Local Communities' <http://www.icty.org/en/outreach/bridging-the-gap-with-local-communities> accessed 13 December 2023.

[99] Refik Hodžić, 'Living the Legacy of Mass Atrocities: Victims' Perspectives on War Crimes Trials' (2010) 8 Journal of International Criminal Justice 113, 126.

[100] Clark (n 55) 81.

The SCLC distributed picture booklets explaining the work of the Court, produced radio and TV panel discussions, weekly summaries of court proceedings, poster campaigns, and theatre productions (some of which travelled to remote provinces), and organized screenings of trials. SCSL outreach activities resulted in the formation of Schools of Human Rights and Peace Clubs as well as 'Accountability Now' clubs at universities throughout the country which explored the broader issues of justice, accountability, and human rights.[101] The Court engaged with all levels of society—the national government, trade unions, local NGOs, the print and electronic media, the local bar association, and academia, from primary schools to universities.[102]

The Extraordinary Chambers in the Courts of Cambodia (ECCC) organized and funded transportation from remote areas of the country to the seat of the Court making it possible for ordinary people to attend the trials of the former Khmer Rouge.[103] Thousands have thus far benefited from these efforts and continue to do so.[104]

From 2014 to 2020, the STL organized annual training sessions for Lebanese lawyers on the conduct of international criminal proceedings so as to increase their understanding of the work of the Tribunal and other internationalized criminal courts.[105] A fifteen-minute video on international criminal proceedings, also produced by the STL and available on its YouTube channel,[106] features as an educational tool in each training session. The Tribunal also organized a training session for NGOs on how to monitor international criminal proceedings. Participating NGOs were thus provided with the tools necessary to conduct independent monitoring at the STL or any other internationalized criminal court.[107] In order to aid understanding and enhance knowledge of international criminal law (ICL), the Tribunal also published a glossary of legal terms in Arabic, English, and French and facilitated the translation of Antonio Cassese's 'International Criminal Law'

[101] Rachel Kerr and Jessica Lincoln, 'The Special Court for Sierra Leone: Outreach, Legacy and Impact, Final Report' (2008) War Crimes Research Group, Department of War Studies King's College, 11–12.

[102] Crane (n 81) 8.

[103] Cheryl White, 'Discursive Proceedings and the Transitional Trial: A View from the Extraordinary Chambers in the Courts of Cambodia' in Chrisje Brants and Susanne Karstedt (eds), *Transitional Justice and the Public Sphere: Engagement, Legitimacy and Contestation* (Hart 2017).

[104] ECCC, 'ECCC Hosts an Outreach Study Tour for 260 High School Students from Prey Veng province' <https://www.eccc.gov.kh/en/articles/eccc-hosts-outreach-study-tour-260-high-school-students-prey-veng-province> accessed 13 December 2023.

[105] STL, 'Outreach Activities' <https://www.stl-tsl.org/en/outreach/activities> accessed 13 December 2023.

[106] STL, 'International Criminal Proceedings (video)' (*YouTube*, 2013) <https://www.youtube.com/watch?v=2Mm29x9Gr1U> accessed 13 December 2023.

[107] STL, 'Representatives of Lebanese NGOs complete the training on monitoring international criminal proceedings' (30 November 2014) <https://www.stl-tsl.org/en/media/press-releases/3652-representatives-of-lebanese-ngos-complete-the-training-on-monitoring-international-criminal-proceedings> accessed 13 December 2023.

into Arabic. Published in 2015,[108] the translation became the first complete textbook on this topic in Arabic and is used by students throughout the Middle East.

The STL, uniquely, also initiated and implemented, together with the TMC Asser Institute in The Hague, the Netherlands and eleven universities in Lebanon, a course on International Criminal Law and Procedure (IUP-ICLP). The course brings students of the participating universities together to attend lectures which cover topics such as the history of the law of the international tribunals and sources of international criminal and procedural law; substantive law: genocide, crimes against humanity, war crimes, and terrorism; types of evidence used in international criminal proceedings; comparative international and Lebanese law; general principles: modes of liability, rights of the accused, role of victims; ICL, and sharia law; contempt proceedings in international criminal jurisdictions; and international criminal proceedings. The lectures are delivered from The Hague to students in Beirut, using video-conferencing equipment. For several years, while funding was available, the best students were rewarded with a three-day study visit to the STL and other internationalized criminal courts in The Netherlands. Professors at the participating universities also conducted working visits to the courts in The Hague as part of the programme. As a means to ensure the continuation of this important programme and other similar educational initiatives, the STL also supported the creation of the International and Transitional Justice Resource Center (ITJRC),[109] an NGO established by professors who connected through their participation in the IUP-ICLP, and from 2018, ITJRC began implementing parts of the IUP-ICLP. In 2020, the STL withdrew from the Inter-University Programme and handed its implementation over to ITJRC and the Asser Institute[110] who were later joined by La Sagesse University and IUSTICOM. More than 400 students have graduated from the course since then.[111] In 2024, the programme expanded to include students from universities in Jordan, Palestine, Egypt, Iraq, and Algeria.[112]

Following the closure of the ICTY at the end of 2017, the International Residual Mechanism for Criminal Tribunals (MICT) experimented without outreach in

108 ibid.

109 'International & Transitional Justice Resource Center – ITJRC' <https://www.facebook.com/pages/category/Education/International-Transitional-Justice-Resource-Center-ITJRC-1906460876347510/> accessed 13 December 2023.

110 STL, 'Handover Ceremony for the Inter-University Programme on International Law and Procedure' (7 December 2020) <https://www.stl-tsl.org/en/media/press-releases/handover-ceremony-for-the-inter-university-programme-on-international-law-and-procedure> accessed 13 December 2023.

111 Asser Institute, 'Inter-university programme in Lebanon' <https://www.asser.nl/education-events/inter-university-programme-in-lebanon/> accessed 13 December 2023.

112 Asser Institute, 'Universities across the MENA region join the inter-university programme on international criminal law and procedure' (17 January 2024) <https://www.asser.nl/about-the-asser-institute/news/universities-across-the-mena-region-join-the-inter-university-programme-on-international-criminal-law-and-procedure/> accessed 17 January 2024.

the former Yugoslavia for a year. In January 2019, it launched the 'Information Programme for Affected Communities' described by the then MICT president as a legacy project focused on informing affected communities and younger generations in the former Yugoslavia about the International Tribunal for the Former Yugoslavia and the ongoing work of the Mechanism and on facilitating access to the Tribunal and Mechanism archives.[113] The programme was also established '[t]o contribute to the creation of conditions for fact-based and sustainable education of young people in the former Yugoslavia about the crimes committed during the 1990s conflicts'[114] and to 'facilitate creation of a pool of educators, trained to deliver fact-based, engaging lectures on the topic'.[115] In a rather innovative approach in the area of international criminal justice, in July 2019, MICT launched a social media campaign on Facebook in English and the local languages commemorating some of the worst crimes committed during the war in the former Yugoslavia and the ICTY trials that addressed those crimes. The campaign, which continues as of 2024 features 'short informational videos, infographics and social media posts, using archival material that has been admitted into evidence in proceedings before the ICTY and the Mechanism, such as witness testimonies, original audio-visual material, military reports and forensic documents'.[116]

The Special Criminal Court (SCC) in the Central African Republic (CAR) has also organized several outreach events, for different target audiences. For example, the Court held workshops for journalists with the aim of informing them about the establishment, mandate, and work of the SCC so as to enable them to accurately report on the Court's activities.[117] They have also organized a competition for students of law with a view to increasing the students' knowledge both about ICL in general and the work of the Special Court more specifically. As explained by the Court on its website (originally in French, translated by the author below):

> The overall objective of the awareness program was to bring the Special Criminal Court (CPS) closer to students through a series of activities that involve interactive dialogue and constructive exchanges with them. The goal sought through

[113] UNSC, 'Assessment and progress report of the President of the International Residual Mechanism for Criminal Tribunals, Judge Carmel Agius, for the period from 16 November 2018 to 15 May 2019' (20 May 2019) UN Doc S/2019/417, para 112.

[114] UNIRMCT, 'Call for Interest: Individual Contractor—History Education Specialist' (5 July 2019) <https://www.irmct.org/sites/default/files/vacancy/190705-ic-hes-hague.pdf> accessed 13 December 2023.

[115] ibid.

[116] UNIRMCT, 'Mechanism launches media tool kit page and social media campaign commemorating the 24th anniversary of the Srebrenica genocide' (4 July 2019) <https://www.irmct.org/en/news/19-07-04-24-years-srebrenica?fbclid=IwAR1CZ5AQVSqYIKCXjn2JpS5uW0Yu2uqcZrAnHTPBBp_O7XvdVxniM2vz3ZE> accessed 13 December 2023.

[117] The Special Criminal Court, Central African Republic, 'Atelier de formation des journalistes du 20 au 24 juin 2019' (24 July 2019) https://www.cpsrca.cf/actualite/atelier-de-formation-des-journalistes-du-20-au-24-juin-2019-/33/ accessed 13 December 2023.

the implementation of this partnership was also to provide support to the Faculty of Legal and Political Sciences at the University of Bangui to strengthen and enhance students' knowledge of the Special Criminal Court and international criminal law. This initiative aims to inspire these young individuals to pursue careers as legal practitioners in the field of combating international crimes, as a guarantee of peace and sustainable development.[118]

The relevance of the preceding examples lies in the fact that they clearly show the diversity of activities conducted by outreach departments in the attempt to disseminate accurate information about the work of the internationalized courts and thus contribute to the achievement of the courts' non-judicial goals.

16.5 Conclusion

There is little doubt that the creators of international and hybrid criminal courts assign them with non-judicial goals and that the courts have made meaningful contributions to the achievement of these goals through their outreach programmes. But is that enough?

Numerous studies have been conducted on the impact of international and hybrid criminal courts.[119] They have generally found that outreach started too late (eg at the ICTY, where it started only six years after the establishment of the Court) or that it was insufficient, often due to underfunding. As per Stover and Weinstein, JN Clark, and others, the lack of accurate information about the work of the tribunals leads members of the affected communities to erroneous conclusions and

[118] SCC CAR, 'Concours d'éloquence" '(11 December 2019) <https://www.cpsrca.cf/actualite/concours-d-eloquence-/30/> accessed 13 December 2023.

[119] See, eg, Payam Akhavan, 'Justice in The Hague, Peace in the former Yugoslavia? A Commentary on the United Nations War Crimes Tribunal' (1998) 20 Human Rights Quarterly 737; Alexander Fatić, *Reconciliation via the War Crimes Tribunal?* (Ashgate 2000); Michael Humphrey, 'International Intervention, Justice, and National Reconciliation: The Role of the ICTY and ICTR in Bosnia and Rwanda' (2003) 2 Journal of Human Rights 495; Jean Marie Kamatali, 'The Challenge of Linking International Criminal Justice and National Reconciliation: The Case of the ICTR' (2003) 16 Leiden Journal of International Law 115; Rachel Kerr, 'The Road from Dayton to Brussels? The International Criminal Tribunal for the Former Yugoslavia and the Politics of War Crimes in Bosnia' (2005) 14 European Security 319; Rachel Kerr, 'Peace through Justice? The International Criminal Tribunal for the Former Yugoslavia' (2007) 7 Southeast European and Black Sea Studies 373; Diane F Orentlicher, 'Shrinking the Space for Denial: The Impact of the ICTY in Serbia' (2008) Open Society Justice Initiative; Jessica Lincoln, *Transitional Justice, Peace and Accountability: Outreach and the Role of International Courts after Conflict* (Routledge 2011); Kirsten Ainley, Rebekka Friedman, and Chris Mahoney (eds), *Evaluating Transitional Justice: Accountability and Peacebuilding in Post-Conflict Sierra Leone* (Palgrave Macmillan 2015); Simon M Meisenberg and Ignaz Stegmiller (eds), *The Extraordinary Chambers in the Courts of Cambodia: Assessing Their Contribution to International Criminal Law* (Asser Press & Springer 2016); Patrick Vinck and Phuong N Pham, 'Outreach Evaluation: The International Criminal Court in the Central African Republic' (2010) 4 International Journal of Transitional Justice 421; Tim Kelsall, 'Insufficiently Hybrid: Assessing the Special Court for Sierra Leone' (2009) 27 Law in Context 132; or the work of the Open Society Justice Initiative, among others.

biases about the institution and its work, which, in turn hinders reconciliation. For example, while acknowledging that the 'media, politicians and intellectuals have all contributed to undermining the ICTY's credibility',[120] Clark stated that 'this does not mean that the Tribunal could not have done more to improve its image and get its message across to the region'.[121] She also warned that '[t]he fact that many people remain ill-informed about the Tribunal ... is a serious problem, not least because a lack of information breeds misinformation, misinformation breeds mistrust'.[122]

In conducting a thorough analysis, however, researchers might also consider the following:

> causal relationships are extremely difficult, if not impossible, to establish; ... the change being sought through a transitional justice mechanism will be nonlinear, the result of multiple interactions by numerous actors; and ... these will be difficult to predict, let alone control ... This suggests that context-sensitive and systems approaches to evaluating transitional justice will be of much greater utility than the current linear approaches that dominate practice in the international development industry.[123]

A view expressed about the STL's Inter-University Programme is illustrative of this point. A Lebanese professor who had been involved in the programme's implementation since the outset described it as 'the best attempt towards reconciliation since the civil war in Lebanon, because it brings together universities and students from different backgrounds in a country where dialogue unfortunately lacks'.[124] In order to scientifically verify this claim, one would have to do a comprehensive study of what effects this programme has had on more than 2,000 students who have graduated since 2011; on more than twice that number of members of their families and friends who supported them and proudly attended the yearly graduation ceremonies; and on the study of ICL and international criminal justice in Lebanon more generally (some alumni have completed PhDs and begun teaching on the topic as a consequence of their participation in the programme).[125] To obtain a full picture of the broader societal impact of the STL (or any other internationalized court), one would have to analyse the effect not only of its trials, but also of the multiple and multilayered interactions achieved through its outreach

[120] Clark (n 55) 81 (citations omitted).
[121] ibid.
[122] ibid.
[123] Colleen Duggan, 'Editorial Note' (2010) 4 International Journal of Transitional Justice 315, 327.
[124] STL, 'Outreach: Inter-University Programme' <https://www.stl-tsl.org/en/outreach/inter-university-programme> accessed 13 December 2023.
[125] Internal report of the STL (on file with the author).

(and legacy) activities.[126] Regrettably, such a comprehensive study is lacking and long overdue.

In the meantime, it would appear reasonable to build upon the many achievements of outreach programmes and build upon their potential to better contribute to the non-judicial goals of restoration and maintenance of peace, reconciliation, strengthening the rule of law, and capacity building. Projects such as the ICTY Bridging the Gap series or youth outreach and high schools project[127] in the former Yugoslavia, the SCSL initiated School of Human Rights and Peace Clubs and 'Accountability Now' clubs, the Inter-University Programme on International Criminal Law and Proceedings in Lebanon, the numerous training programmes for the media, NGOs, and legal professionals are all examples of projects with long-term positive effects which can be built upon and adapted to ensure the legacy of these important institutions.

As explained by the ICTY Appeals Chamber—international law does not have a centralized structure or an integrated judicial system operating an orderly division of labour among different courts. Rather, each internationalized criminal court is a self-contained system, and this makes it incompatible with a narrow concept of jurisdiction.[128] For this and other reasons, international and hybrid courts should embrace the wider jurisdiction over their non-judicial goals; and the international community should fully support the courts in conducting activities that contribute to the restoration and maintenance of peace, reconciliation, strengthening the rule of law, and capacity building.

[126] It is also worth noting that the Inter-University Programme continues to be implemented despite the fact the STL has ceased to exist.

[127] ICTY, 'Youth Outreach' <http://www.icty.org/en/outreach/youth-outreach> accessed 13 December 2023.

[128] *Prosecutor v Duško Tadic* (Decision on The Defence Motion for Interlocutory Appeal on Jurisdiction) (2 October 1995) [11].

17

The Premise of Capacity Building in the Special Court for Sierra Leone, the Extraordinary Chambers in the Courts of Cambodia, and the Bosnian War Crimes Chamber

Ezequiel Jimenez Martinez

17.1 Introduction: Transitional Justice and Capacity Building

The legacy of the Nuremberg trials enabled the international community to creatively expand the reach of international criminal justice and the rule of law by establishing a network of international, hybrid, and internationalized criminal tribunals over the past twenty years.[1] The proliferation of international criminal law (ICL) legislation and advances in human rights and humanitarian law have paved the way for a set of principles that establish the legality of certain state behaviour.[2] As Sikkink would argue, there has been a justice cascade where human rights prosecutions have influenced international politics, raising the status of the fight against impunity worldwide.[3] The creation of the ad hoc tribunals for the former Yugoslavia and Rwanda as well as the establishment of the International Criminal Court (ICC), with jurisdiction over crimes against humanity, genocide, war crimes, and the crime of aggression illustrates this point. However, the application and safeguarding of the principles of ICL depend largely on the institutional capacity and the willingness of state actors that are mandated to ensure justice for serious violations of human rights.[4] Since early 2000, the human rights normative

[1] Beth van Schaack, 'The Building Blocks of Hybrid Justice' (2016) 44 Denver Journal of International Law and Policy 169.

[2] Antonio Cassese (ed), *Realizing Utopia: The Future of International Law* (Oxford University Press 2012).

[3] Kathryn Sikkink, *The Justice Cascade: How Human Rights Prosecutions Are Changing World Politics* (WW Norton & Company 2011); Kathryn Sikkink, *Evidence for Hope: Making Human Rights Work in the 21st Century* (Princeton University Press 2017).

[4] For example, Articles 14 and 16 of the International Covenant on Civil and Political Rights; Article 13 of Europe's Convention for the Protection of Human Rights and Fundamental Freedoms;

Ezequiel Jimenez Martinez, *The Premise of Capacity Building in the Special Court for Sierra Leone, the Extraordinary Chambers in the Courts of Cambodia, and the Bosnian War Crimes Chamber* In: *Hybrid Justice*.
Edited by: Kirsten Ainley and Mark Kersten, Oxford University Press. © Ezequiel Jimenez Martinez 2025.
DOI: 10.1093/oso/9780192893758.003.0017

framework has suffered a significant regression due to political[5] and capacity constraints at the international level as well as at the level of individual states, leaving an accountability gap in the international justice architecture.[6] The accountability gap widens in the context of post-conflict states that typically inherit judicial systems unfit for a process of transitional justice tasked with delivering accountability for past serious violations of human rights while rebuilding judicial capacity for compliance with international law.[7]

As the cases of post-conflict Sierra Leone, Cambodia, and Bosnia Herzegovina demonstrate, states emerging from complex political, legal, and socio-economic circumstances are unlikely to prosecute grave human rights violations if their judicial institutions cannot cope with the challenges of setting in motion a transitional justice process.[8] Therefore, as the United Nations Special Rapporteur for the Promotion of Truth, Justice and Reparations, Pablo De Greiff argued, 'in weakly institutionalized post-conflict settings, it is imperative to find ways of integrating the transitional justice agenda closely with institution-building and institution-strengthening processes'.[9] Within the field of transitional justice, the need to build judicial institutions that are resilient in the face of conflict involves reforming legislation, strengthening judicial processes, and investing in infrastructure, leading to developing a rule of law culture which prioritizes justice for victims of serious human rights violations. Recently, the recognition of the need to embed transitional justice mechanisms in larger state-building processes that prioritize investing in effective and resilient state institutions has been prioritized in the United Nations' (UN) peace and justice reform agenda under the Secretary-General António Guterres.[10]

In this context, the literature discussing hybrid tribunals recognizes the advantage of the hybrid model to capitalize on political will within and outside post-conflict states to reform and strengthen the domestic capacity of the judicial sector in order to ensure access to justice for victims of serious violations of human

Article 25 of the American Convention on Human Rights; Article 3 of the African Charter on Human and People's Rights; and Article 11 of the Arab Charter on Human Rights. See Thomas Risse, Stephen C Ropp, and Kathryn Sikkink, *The Persistent Power of Human Rights: From Commitment to Compliance* (Cambridge University Press 2013).

5 Sara L Ochs, 'A Renewed Call for Hybrid Tribunals' (2019) 52 New York University Journal of International Law and Politics 352.

6 Stephen Krasner and Thomas Risse, 'External Actors, State-Building, and Service Provision in Areas of Limited Statehood: Introduction' (2014) 27 International Journal of Policy, Administration, and Institutions 545.

7 Report of the Special Rapporteur on the Promotion of Truth, Justice, Reparation and Guarantees of Non-Recurrence (2017) UN Doc A/HRC/36/50.

8 Graeme Simpson, '"From the Normative to the Transformative": Defining and Promoting Justice and Human Rights as Part of Violent Conflict Prevention and Peacebuilding' (2017) 9 Journal of Human Rights Practice 379.

9 UNGA, 'Report of the Secretary General, Restructuring of the United Nations Peace and Security Pillar' (2017) UN Doc A/72/525, 11.

10 ibid.

rights.[11] This is true after a quiet period between 2008 and 2012 when the ICC took centre-stage in international justice.[12] However, persistent issues with the ICC have opened the door for a new generation of hybrid tribunals.[13] In this context, emerging literature on the link between hybrid tribunals and resilience is notable as a way of evaluating to what extent 'hybrids support the embedding and extension of the rule of law, democratization and the development of a human rights culture'.[14] However, if hybrid tribunals play a role in rebuilding judicial capacity at the national level, one must ask how they have delivered on their promise to strengthen domestic judicial institutions and the rule of law. To begin to answer this question, this chapter analyses the experiences of the Special Court for Sierra Leone (SCSL), the Extraordinary Chambers in the Courts of Cambodia (ECCC), and the unique judicial set up in the Bosnian War Crimes Chamber (BIH WCC).

17.2 Defining the Hybrid Tribunal Model

Hybrid tribunals 'blend the international and the domestic as a product of judicial accountability-sharing'[15] between a host state and international organizations. To date, hybrid tribunals have been used in the context of transitional justice in Sierra Leone, East Timor, Kosovo, Bosnia and Herzegovina, Cambodia, and Lebanon, with other countries recently considered,[16] notably Ukraine.[17] Indeed, the re-emergence of the hybrid tribunal model to deal with situations where an accountability gap persists is a topic of interest not only for academics, but for practitioners too.[18] Part of their appeal is their cost (compared to the ICC for example) and flexibility to adapt to political contexts.[19] Hybrid tribunals are typically the

[11] Rachel Kerr and Eirin Mobekk, *Peace and Justice* (Polity 2007); OHCHR, 'Rule of Law Tools for Post-Conflict States: Maximizing the Legacy of Hybrid Courts' (2008); van Schaack (n 1); Henrik Andersen, 'Hybrid Courts and Multilevel Rules of Law: Some Overall Considerations, Challenges and Opportunities' (2017) 6 International Journal of Criminology and Sociology 117; Daimeon Dean Shanks, 'From Aspirational to Prescriptive Capacity Building: Post-Conflict States, Rule of Law, and Hybrid International Justice Comments' (2019) 90 University of Colorado Law Review 1195.

[12] Juan-Pablo Pérez-Léon-Acevedo, 'UN-Backed Hybrid Criminal Tribunals (HCTS): Viable Options in International Criminal Justice?' (2022) 22 International Criminal Law Review 641.

[13] ibid 647–48.

[14] Kirsten Ainley and Mark Kersten, 'Resilience and the Impacts of Hybrid Courts' (2020) 33 Leiden Journal of International Law 971; Philipp Kastner, 'A Resilience Approach to Transitional Justice?' (2020) 14 Journal of Intervention and Statebuilding 368; Aaron Fichtelberg, 'Identity Politics and Hybrid Tribunals' (2020) 33 Leiden Journal of International Law 993.

[15] Mathias Holvoet and Paul de Hert, 'International Criminal Law as Global Law: An Assessment of the Hybrid Tribunals', (2012) 17 Tilburg Law Review: Journal of International and European Law 229.

[16] The Hybrid Justice Project, 'The Hybrids' <https://hybridjustice.com/hybrid-and-internationalised-mechanisms/> accessed 15 July 2019.

[17] Kevin Jon Heller, 'Options for Prosecuting Russian Aggression Against Ukraine: A Critical Analysis' [2022] Journal of Genocide Research 1.

[18] Kirsten Ainley and Mark Kersten, 'Dakar Guidelines on the Establishment of Hybrid Courts' LSE and Wayamo Foundation (2019) <https://hybridjustice.com/dakar-guidelines/>.

[19] Pérez-Léon-Acevedo (n 12) 665.

product of an agreement between the state where the crimes occurred and a branch of the UN. Because hybrids are negotiated between different entities, with different objectives, they might be severely limited to specific institutional frameworks.[20] These agreements, in theory, 'offer legitimacy by providing ownership without affecting independence and impartiality ... while also building domestic capacity'.[21] The model can be described in four distinct characteristics:[22] (1) their geographical proximity to victims; (2) the combined use of domestic and international law; (3) staffing the tribunal with international and domestic judicial personnel; and (4) the premise of capacity building.

Unlike the ICC located in The Hague, the advantage of hybrid tribunals is their proximity to victims and what this means for the effective exercise of their right of access to justice for victims of serious human rights violations. Attending and participating in court proceedings 'allow the affected population to better understand the conflict and can contribute to the social reconstruction process'.[23] In fact, witnessing the proceedings in a local language adjudicating international and domestic law may improve the perceived legitimacy of the tribunal, especially in the eyes of victims and affected communities.[24] In relation to hybrid tribunals' capacity-building premise, Costi points out that 'an international tribunal located far away from the affected country and operated by foreigners cannot train local actors in necessary skills'[25] for complex human rights prosecutions. Indeed, capacity building can only take place if the seat of the court is located in proximity to local judicial actors.[26] Even when the ICC has established offices in situation countries, their main objective has not focused on capacity building of the local judiciary.

A second core element of hybrid tribunals is the applicability of international and domestic laws. In practice, this means the combination of ICL covering atrocity crimes with domestic laws equally important for the adjudication of human rights abuses. In Cambodia, the Statute of the ECCC included genocide and crimes

[20] Sergey Vasiliev, 'Judicial Governance Entities as Power-Holders in International Criminal Justice: A Plea for a Socio-Legal Enquiry' in Morten Bergsmo (ed), *Power in International Criminal Justice* (Torkel Opsahl Academic EPublisher 2020) 490.

[21] Mathias Holvoet and Paul de Hert, 'International Criminal Law as Global Law: An Assessment of the Hybrid Tribunals', (2012) 17 Tilburg Law Review: Journal of International and European Law 229.

[22] van Schaack (n 1) 172; Michail Vagias, 'Other "Hybrid" Tribunals', in Sergey Sayapin (ed), *International Conflict and Security Law* (TMC Asser Press 2022) 633.

[23] Public International Law & Policy Group, 'Hybrid Tribunals: Core Elements' (2013) 6.

[24] Parinaz Kermani Mendez, 'The New Wave of Hybrid Tribunals: A Sophisticated Approach to Enforcing International Humanitarian Law or an Idealistic Solution with Empty Promises?' (2009) 20 Criminal Law Forum 63; Daimeon Dean Shanks, 'From Aspirational to Prescriptive Capacity Building: Post-Conflict States, Rule of Law, and Hybrid International Justice Comments' (2019) 90 University of Colorado Law Review 1195.

[25] Alberto Costi, 'Hybrid Tribunals as a Valid Alternative to International Tribunals for the Prosecution of International Crimes' (3rd Annual Victoria University Symposium on Human Rights, Wellington, Victoria University, 2005) 11.

[26] Ainley and Kersten, 'Dakar Guidelines' (n 18).

against humanity as well as homicide, torture, and religious persecution covered by the 1956 Penal Code of Cambodia.[27] In Sierra Leone, domestic laws included lowering the age of trial from 18 to 14 years old in response to the use of child soldiers during the civil war.[28] Advantages of combining international and domestic laws include the avoidance of *ex post facto* judgments and securing international trial standards to defend accusations of victor's justice by sceptical actors.[29] In terms of capacity building, this interaction offers the opportunity to develop domestic and international jurisprudence on atrocity crimes.[30]

Closely related to the interplay of international and domestic laws, hybrid tribunals mix international and domestic judicial personnel. All hybrid tribunals to date have followed this composition.[31] This corresponds to two main objectives: ensuring international procedural standards of transparency and impartiality, and achieving local fluency in domestic laws. The inclusion of international personnel safeguarding international trial standards offers protection from government interference for domestic personnel leading investigations.[32] In Cambodia, international judges have battled with the government in order to preserve impartiality and the appropriate application of international law.[33] Collaboration between local and international personnel enables a process of institutionalization of international norms within domestic judicial systems.[34] This, in turn, raises domestic standards to ensure impartiality and transparency for the accused and victims alike. In terms of capacity building, the interaction between domestic and international staff contributes to cross fertilization of legal expertise. Training manuals from the UN describe the interaction as a two-way process 'with internationals joining a hybrid initiative being required to learn about a country's history, culture and legal tradition',[35] and domestic personnel learning investigative and trial techniques. In sum, the premise of capacity building is a common theme across the

[27] Sarah Nouwen, 'Hybrid Courts-The Hybrid Category of a New Type of International Crimes Courts' (2006) 2 Utrecht Law Review 190, 206–07.

[28] Pérez-Léon-Acevedo (n 12) 656.

[29] James Cockayne, 'The Fraying Shoestring: Rethinking Hybrid War Crimes Tribunals' (2004) 28 Fordham International Law Journal 616; Costi (n 25).

[30] Laura A Dickinson, 'The Promise of Hybrid Courts' (2003) 97 American Journal of International Law 295; Kate Gibson, 'An Uneasy Co-existence: The Relationship Between Internationalised Criminal Courts and Their Domestic Counterparts' (2009) 9 International Criminal Law Review 275.

[31] The Hybrid Justice Project, 'The Hybrids' <https://hybridjustice.com/hybrid-and-internationalised-mechanisms/> accessed 15 July 2019.

[32] Public International Law & Policy Group (n 23); Rosalind Dixon and Vicki Jackson, 'Hybrid Constitutional Courts: Foreign Judges on National Constitutional Courts' (2018) 57 Columbia Journal of Transnational Law 283.

[33] Seeta Scully, 'Judging the Successes and Failures of the Extraordinary Chambers of the Courts of Cambodia' (2011) 13 Asian Pacific Law and Policy Journal 300; Harry Hobbs, 'Towards a Principled Justification for the Mixed Composition of Hybrid International Criminal Tribunals' (2017) 30 Leiden Journal of International Law 177.

[34] Rosalind Dixon and Vicki Jackson, 'Hybrid Constitutional Courts: Foreign Judges on National Constitutional Courts' (2018) 57 Columbia Journal of Transnational Law 283, 300.

[35] United Nations Office on Drugs and Crime and United States Institute of Peace, 'Criminal Justice Reform in Post-Conflict States' (2011) 35.

three core elements of the hybrid tribunal model aimed at long-term improvement of the domestic judiciary.[36]

17.3 The Fourth Dimension of Hybrid Tribunals: Delivering Capacity Building

The academic and practitioner-oriented literature offers multiple descriptions of the premise of capacity building of hybrid tribunals. Holvoet and de Hert talk about the ability of hybrid tribunals to 'impact ... local institutions [by] building capacity; rebuilding judicial systems and promoting international human rights standards throughout the local community'.[37] Stromseth argues that 'capacity-building is important ... to [prevent] future atrocities and to building a stable rule of law',[38] and van Schaack highlights the 'demonstration effect' from foreign to local judicial staff in the administration of justice.[39] Dixon and Jackson agree with van Schaack, arguing that 'if foreign judges engage in even quite micro-level efforts at capacity-building, this can help improve local judges' knowledge base'.[40] Ochs agrees, pointing out that international staff are best placed to develop skills of domestic counterparts 'in ways that are compatible with the local judicial system'.[41] In this regard, Fichtelberg warns of the need for 'training of criminal justice and legal professionals from all sides of a conflict'.[42] Shanks offers a description of the premise of capacity building assigning hybrid tribunals the responsibility to lead 'programmatic initiatives, such as monetary contributions, educational programs, and infrastructural works',[43] while Vagias argues that, ultimately, capacity building would materialize in 'the adoption of new domestic laws consistently with international standards'.[44] Thus, Pérez-Léon-Acevedo concludes that the legacy of capacity building provided by hybrid tribunals 'may be bigger and more lasting'[45] than other international criminal tribunals.

[36] Sara L Ochs, 'A Renewed Call for Hybrid Tribunals', (2019) 52 New York University Journal of International Law and Politics 351, 410.
[37] Mathias Holvoet and Paul de Hert, 'International Criminal Law as Global Law: An Assessment of the Hybrid Tribunals' (2012) 17 Tilburg Law Review: Journal of International and European Law 228, 230.
[38] Jane Stromseth, 'Justice on the Ground: Can International Criminal Courts Strengthen Domestic Rule of Law in Post-Conflict Societies?' (2009) 1 Hague Journal on the Rule of Law 87, 89.
[39] van Schaack (n 1) 173.
[40] Dixon and Jackson (n 34) 343.
[41] Ochs (n 36) 401.
[42] Aaron Fichtelberg, 'Identity Politics and Hybrid Tribunals' (2020) 33 Leiden Journal of International Law 1004.
[43] Daimeon Dean Shanks, 'From Aspirational to Prescriptive Capacity Building: Post-Conflict States, Rule of Law, and Hybrid International Justice Comments' (2019) 90 University of Colorado Law Review 1217.
[44] Vagias (n 22) 635–36.
[45] Pérez-Léon-Acevedo (n 12) 657.

While these authors mention capacity building in some ways, their definition and application is not consistent. The same finding applies to UN policy tools published to guide capacity building within hybrid tribunals.[46] As Ainley and Kersten, and Shanks warn, capacity-building initiatives cannot be understood as an inevitable by-product of the mix of international and domestic judicial personnel and the resources earmarked for infrastructure or legacy projects. Instead, the premise of capacity building deserves a clear and operational mandate from its constitutional statutes with the ability to support wider rule of law programming in post-conflict states. As Vagias argues, hybrid tribunals already suffer from the problem of goal-setting, including defining their role in capacity building.[47] Therefore, a more nuanced understanding of what constitutes capacity building within the hybrid tribunal model is worth developing.

To aide our understanding of what constitutes capacity building within hybrids, it is worth borrowing Risse, Ropp, and Sikkink's definition of capacity building as a 'highly institutionalized process of social interaction aiming towards education, training, and the building up of administrative capacities to implement and enforce human rights law'.[48] This definition is in line with earlier scholarship developed by Chayes and Chayes where issues of capacity have been infrequently recognized as the root cause for non-compliant behaviour of human rights norms.[49] In other words, as post-conflict states committed to transitional justice usually inherit a broken judiciary, involuntary non-compliance with human rights norms can be understood as the 'lack of administrative capacity to enforce decisions'[50] rather than their unwillingness to abide by such norms. Risse, Ropp, and Sikkink's definition of capacity building is particularly applicable to the hybrid tribunal model as it is located within human rights prosecutions analysis. In contrast to Risse, Ropp, and Sikkink's definition, the Organisation for Economic Co-operation and Development (OECD), which invests heavily in judicial capacity building in Bosnia Herzegovina,[51] merely defines it as 'the ability of people, organizations and society as a whole to manage their affairs successfully'.[52] The lack of specificity and actionable definitions of capacity building for hybrid tribunals complicates the ability to evaluate whether these tribunals are living up to their promise of re-building domestic judicial systems. To the greater detriment of citizens concerned with a judicial system resilient to conflict and victims expecting these expensive

[46] OHCHR, 'Rule of Law Tools for Post-Conflict States' (n 11) 2.

[47] Vagias (n 22) 636.

[48] Risse, Ropp and Sikkink (n 4) 15.

[49] Abram Chayes and Antonia Handler Chayes, 'On Compliance' (1993) 47 International Organization 175; Abram Chayes, Antonia Handler Chayes, and Ronald B Mitchell, 'Managing Compliance: A Comparative Perspective' in Edith Brown Weiss and Harold Jacobson (eds), *Engaging Countries: Strengthening Compliance with International Environmental Accords* (MIT Press 1998).

[50] Risse, Ropp, and Sikkink (n 4) 15.

[51] OECD, 'OECD Access to Justice' (17 January 2018) <http://www.oecd.org/gov/access-to-justice.htm> accessed 17 January 2018.

[52] OECD, 'The Challenge of Capacity Development: Working Towards Good Practice' (2006) 12.

justice processes to deliver accountability, the premise of capacity building in hybrid tribunals cannot be referred to as a by-product of their establishment, but rather there should be a tangible, intentional, and measurable standard of quality for the model. Therefore, defining capacity building in light of Risse, Ropp, and Sikkink's definition and dividing it into knowledge transfer (education, training) and investment in critical infrastructure (administrative capacities) can uncover the level of importance assigned to capacity building activities by the architects of these tribunals at the state and international level.

17.4 Capacity Building in Three Hybrid Tribunals

17.4.1 The Special Court for Sierra Leone

Between 1991 and 2002, Sierra Leone went through a destructive civil war. Fuelled by the invasion of the Revolutionary United Front (RUF) in 1991, commanded by Foday Sankoh, but de facto controlled by the now convicted Charles Taylor, it claimed the lives of more than 50,000 people.[53] Although there is disagreement over what started the civil war, Perriello and Wierda claim that competition over natural resources, namely diamonds, attracted different militias into the conflict.[54] Throughout the civil war, the various factions engaged in systematic war crimes and crimes against humanity. Crimes committed during the conflict include widespread and indiscriminate killing, the pervasive use of an estimated 7,000 child soldiers,[55] and horrific gender crimes.[56] International and regional pressure culminated in the Lomé Peace Agreement in 1999. Through Resolution 1315, the UN Security Council (UNSC) requested Secretary General Kofi Annan to negotiate the creation of a special court tasked with prosecuting human rights abuses. In 2002, an agreement created the Special Court for Sierra Leone,[57] tasked to prosecute those who bear the greatest responsibility for 'crimes against humanity, war crimes, and serious violations of international humanitarian law, as well as crimes under relevant Sierra Leonean law'.[58] The Special Court was established as an independent entity from the UN and outside the national court system.

[53] Lansana Gberie, *A Dirty War in West Africa: The RUF and the Destruction of Sierra Leone* (Indiana University Press 2005) 6.

[54] Tom Perriello and Marieke Wierda, 'The Special Court for Sierra Leone Under Scrutiny' (2006) International Center for Transitional Justice.

[55] ibid 9.

[56] Valerie Oosterveld, 'Sexual and Gender-Based Violence in Post-Conflict Sierra Leone: The Contribution of Transitional Justice Mechanisms to Domestic Law Reform' in Kirsten Ainley, Rebekka Friedman, and Chris Mahony (eds), *Evaluating Transitional Justice: Accountability and Peacebuilding in Post-Conflict Sierra Leone* (Palgrave Macmillan 2015).

[57] Perriello and Wierda (n 54).

[58] Etelle R Higonnet, 'Restructuring Hybrid Courts: Local Empowerment and National Criminal Justice Reform' (2005) 23 Arizona Journal of International and Comparative Law 347, 432.

Starting with an analysis of the agreement between the UN and the government, there is no mention of any specific capacity building objectives between the hybrid and the domestic judiciary. A thorough reading of the Court's Statute unveils the lack of any mandate for its organs to engage in judicial capacity building in terms of knowledge transfer or infrastructure investments.[59] The lack of such an operational mandate is at odds with Resolution 1315's 'pressing need for international cooperation to assist in strengthening the judicial system'[60] and the claim by the Court's first Registrar that the hybrid would improve the 'capacity of Sierra Leoneans working at the Court'.[61]

17.4.1.1 Knowledge transfer

Bearing in mind the particular relevance of the mix of international and domestic legal personnel for capacity building, according to the UN Development Programme (UNDP) and the International Centre for Transitional Justice, the Special Court was supposed to provide '(1) courses at the law school taught by the Chief Prosecutor; (2) court-based trainings in advocacy tools; and, (3) training for media, prison guards, and judges'.[62] Departing from these benchmarks, Perriello and Wierda argue that the delivery of knowledge transfer occurred mostly 'on the job' as incidental learning.[63] Lectures given by the Special Court's Prosecutor to local law students at the Fourah Bay College Law School, were given, at best, 'on an ad hoc basis rather than through a formal program'.[64] Although the defence and prosecution offices did recruit legal interns and volunteers, the lack of funding prevented taking advantage of the court's location 'because [local interns and volunteers] had to keep other [remunerated] jobs'.[65]

In regard to training for the Court's domestic legal personnel on international law and trial standards, several lectures were arranged on 'elements of war crimes, crimes against humanity and genocide'.[66] However, such training was not open to domestic legal personnel working in other courts in Sierra Leone.[67] Whenever training was offered, it was mostly available to judges and prosecutors, excluding

[59] Statute of SCSL annexed to the Agreement between the United Nations and the Government of Sierra Leone on the establishment of a Special Court for Sierra Leone (signed 16 January 2002, entered into force 12 April 2002) 2178 UNTS 138.

[60] UNSC Res 1315 (2000) UN Doc S/Res/1315.

[61] Varda Hussain, 'Sustaining Judicial Rescues: The Role of Outreach and Capacity-Building Efforts in War Crimes Tribunals', (2004) 45 Virginia Journal of International Law 570.

[62] International Center for Transitional Justice and United Nations Development Program, 'The "Legacy" of the Special Court for Sierra Leone' (2003) 5–7.

[63] Perriello and Wierda (n 54) 39–40.

[64] Sigall Horovitz, 'Sierra Leone: Interaction Between International and National Responses to The Mass Atrocities' (2009) DOMAC, 60.

[65] Alejandro Chehtman and Ruth Mackenzie, 'Capacity Development in International Criminal Justice: A Mapping Exercise of Existing Practice' (2009) DOMAC, 25.

[66] ibid 15.

[67] Giada Girelli, *The Hybrid Experiment: Assessing the Special Court for Sierra Leone* (Palgrave Macmillan 2017).

mid-level professionals.[68] Two years after the establishment of the Court, defence investigators had not received training on substantive matters of international criminal and humanitarian law, a skill needed for the delivery of justice in the Court and an asset for the local judiciary, taking advantage of the location of the Court.[69] In other words, only high-ranking judicial personnel such as judges and prosecutors, most of them foreigners[70] with the best paid packages,[71] benefited from the training. The only activities listed under the heading of 'legacy' for the Court were courses on information management for local staff at the national archival institutions and for interpretation teams.[72] This training was funded by the European Commission at the cost of USD 55,000, a mere 0.018 per cent of the total budget of USD 300 million by the time the Court concluded its mandate in 2013.[73]

Departing further from the premise of judicial capacity building by the mix of foreign and local judicial staff, field work undertaken by Cruvellier, Horovitz, and Girelli revealed that 'lessons and techniques learned in the international setting cannot necessarily be put to use when staff members return to the national system'[74] and that their 'approach was too foreign'[75] for the domestic judiciary system. These findings are confirmed by Cockayne's extensive interviews with members of the Court, concluding that capacity-building ambitions did not 'translate into a willingness to provide nuanced plans of action'.[76] In this context, Sierra Leonean staff trained in the Special Court emigrated to fill vacancies in other international justice mechanisms with better pay.[77] The drain of skills to other mechanisms defeats the entire purpose of the hybrid model. As a former member of the Prosecutor's office explains, the Court 'was expected to be an instrument for transforming the local judiciary, sadly, the impact ... has been minimal'.[78] The consequences of brain drain have also been noted in the Dakar Guidelines developed for policy choices when setting up new hybrid tribunals.[79]

68 Chehtman and Mackenzie (n 65).

69 ibid.

70 Kirsten Ainley, Rebekka Friedman, and Chris Mahony, *Evaluating Transitional Justice: Accountability and Peacebuilding in Post-Conflict Sierra Leone* (Palgrave Macmillan, 2015).

71 van Schaack (n 1) 243.

72 Residual Special Court for Sierra Leone, 'Legacy Projects' <http://www.rscsl.org/legacy.html> accessed 29 November 2019.

73 Daniel McLaughlin, 'International Criminal Tribunals: A Visual Overview' (2015) Leitner Center; van Schaack (n 1).

74 Thierry Cruvellier, 'From the Taylor Trial to a Lasting Legacy: Putting the Special Court Model to the Test' (2009) International Center for Transitional Justice and Sierra Leone Court Monitoring Programme 35–36; Horovitz (n 64); Girelli (n 67).

75 Sigall Horovitz, 'How International Courts Shape Domestic Justice: Lessons from Rwanda and Sierra Leone' (2013) 46 Israel Law Review 264.

76 James Cockayne, 'The Fraying Shoestring: Rethinking Hybrid War Crimes Tribunals' (2004) 28 Fordham International Law Journal 661.

77 Girelli (n 67).

78 Cruvellier (n 74) 33.

79 Ainley and Kersten, 'Dakar Guidelines' (n 18).

In relation to the relevance of the hybrid location for judicial capacity building for the domestic judiciary, the Special Court was established as a separate entity from the national judiciary. In fact, the government was entitled to nominate and appoint four nationals to three judgeships and to the influential position of Deputy Prosecutor.[80] Yet, the government chose to appoint a foreign Deputy Prosecutor, only two judges, and pushed for an amendment to the agreement granting the possibility to appoint foreign judicial staff over domestic ones in order to avoid any indication of ethnic or victor's justice.[81] As such, the inability by choice to influence the agenda of the Court further weakened the prospects of a capacity-building programme directed towards the domestic judiciary, tasked with rebuilding the rule of law after the civil war. In addition, the allocation of resources between the Court and the local judiciary created a tense relationship leaving the latter 'removed from the workings of the Special Court and resentful of the funds donated to it'.[82] In terms of the premise of the positive impact of the mix of international and domestic laws, the Sierra Leonean parliament was successful in repealing gender discriminatory laws and enacting gender justice laws expanding protection for children and women.[83] However, the Special Court was not directly involved in any of these improvements as it failed to deliver expert opinion on the matter.[84] Therefore, in the absence of a strong operational mandate to invest resources, political will, and expertise directed towards the Sierra Leonean judiciary, the promise of the Special Court as a mechanism to foster knowledge transfer to the domestic judiciary did not fully materialize.

17.4.1.2 Infrastructure investment

Given the in-country location of the hybrid tribunal, infrastructure investments can be significant for the whole of the domestic judiciary. In Sierra Leone, the agreement with the UN included the construction of a USD 3.5 million courthouse[85] fully equipped with furniture, computers, and electric generators.[86] In 2009, the government of Sierra Leone was unsure what to do with the modern building given that it cost USD 1,066,300 per year to maintain.[87] In 2011, a USD 195,000 grant from the UNDP turned several buildings of the old courthouse into the Sierra Leone peace museum and library.[88] However, as noted in the 2018

[80] Padraig McAuliffe, 'Hybrid Tribunals at Ten: How International Criminal Justice's Golden Child Became an Orphan' (2011) 7 Journal of International Law and International Relations 1.

[81] ibid.

[82] Perriello and Wierda (n 54) 40.

[83] Oosterveld (n 56).

[84] ibid.

[85] UN Africa Renewal, 'The Special Court for Sierra Leone Rests—for good' <http://www.un.org/africarenewal/magazine/april-2014/special-court-sierra-leone-rests---good> accessed 30 October 2014.

[86] Perriello and Wierda (n 54) 39.

[87] Cruvellier (n 74) 40.

[88] UN, 'PBF/SLE/B-10 Support to the Establishment of a Peace Museum' <http://mptf.undp.org/factsheet/project/00077001> accessed 2 March 2015.

report of the Residual Special Court for Sierra Leone, it appears that the original archives of the Court are actually hosted by the Dutch National Archives in The Hague,[89] diminishing their utility by domestic audiences and the wider judicial system of Sierra Leone. In addition, in 2018, the budget of the residual mechanism had a shortfall of USD 665,900. With such astronomical costs for a country still recovering from civil war, the infrastructure legacy failed to provide a sustainable gain for the domestic judicial system. Perriello and Wierda have called this 'the spaceship phenomenon' as the Court is seen by Sierra Leoneans 'as an alien anomaly',[90] despite its creation of an outreach and public affairs section.[91] Unfortunately, it appears that the only time the Court's Chambers have been used for a domestic purpose was during the 2015–2016 Ebola epidemic when the UN set up their 'situation room' in one of the Court's Chambers.[92]

17.4.2 The Extraordinary Chambers in the Courts of Cambodia

Between April 1975 and January 1979, the Khmer Rouge regime led by Pol Pot was responsible for the deaths of 1.7 million Cambodians by execution, starvation, or disease.[93] Although the regime suffered a military defeat in 1979, it was not until 1996 with a law granting amnesties in exchange for mass defections, that the Khmer Rouge regime finally perished. In 1997, then co-prime ministers Hun Sen and Norodom Ranariddh requested assistance from the UN to set up a transitional justice mechanism for atrocity crimes, including genocide.[94] The United States was particularly keen on creating a third ad hoc tribunal, but the alternative, to establish a hybrid, was chosen due to fears of China vetoing the proposal in the UNSC.[95] The negotiations between the government and the UN suffered a series of setbacks over substantial disagreement on the balance between the international and domestic component of the hybrid court.[96] In 2002, the UN withdrew from the negotiations claiming the Court's structure put forward by Cambodia 'would not guarantee the independence, impartiality, and objectivity that a court established with the support of the UN must have'.[97] However, pressure from the UN

[89] Residual Special Court for Sierra Leone, 'Fifth Annual Report of the President of the Residual Special Court for Sierra Leone' (2018).
[90] Perriello and Wierda (n 54) 2.
[91] Pérez-Léon-Acevedo (n 12) 664–65.
[92] Global Ebola Response, 'Sierra Leone: The Ebola Warriors in the Situation Room' <https://ebolaresponse.un.org/sierra-leone-ebola-warriors-situation-room> accessed 23 March 2015.
[93] Higonnet (n 58) 357.
[94] Extraordinary Chambers in the Courts of Cambodia, 'About the Extraordinary Chambers in the Courts of Cambodia' <http://www.eccc.gov.kh/en/about-eccc> accessed 22 January 2015.
[95] John D Ciorciari, *Sovereignty Sharing in Fragile States* (Stanford University Press 2021).
[96] Simon Meisenberg and Ignaz Stegmiller, *The Extraordinary Chambers in the Courts of Cambodia: Assessing Their Contribution to International Criminal Law* (Asser Press 2016).
[97] McAuliffe (n 80) 27.

General Assembly, and some changes in the structure, relaunched the negotiations in 2003.[98] Unlike the SCSL created by a UNSC resolution, the ECCC was the result of a bilateral agreement between the UN and the government. The agreement was signed in June 2003, and entered into force in 2005, paving the way for the Office of the Prosecutor to start work in 2006.[99] The hybrid tribunal mandate ended in 2022 after a total cost of USD 330 million since 1997,[100] with doubts about its impact on delivering justice.[101]

A close reading of the bilateral agreement and the Court's Statute reveals the absence of any specific capacity-building objective between the hybrid and the domestic judiciary despite a statement by the UN predicting that the ECCC would 'result in the transfer of skills and know-how to Cambodian court personnel'.[102] In fact, David Tolbert, who acted as a UN special advisor, characterized the ECCC structure as a flawed design for a hybrid court.[103] Despite the Court's website describing capacity-building roles for the Office of Co-Prosecutors and the Defence Support Section, the revised 2018–2019 budget reveals the absence of any staff post assigned to this function within the Court or with the local judiciary.[104] This is particularly problematic from an operational accountability perspective, as the 2019 budget[105] for the Defence Support Section alone is 17 per cent of the total budget. The absence of operational clarity and accountability vis-à-vis the portion of resources attached unveils the lack of a systematic approach to capacity building at the Chambers.[106]

17.4.2.1 Knowledge transfer

The role of the Office of the Co-Prosecutors and the Defence Support Section is particularly relevant for the premise of the mix of international and domestic legal personnel for capacity building. The Office of the Co-Prosecutors maintained an internal focus in their activities, while the Defence Support Section worked closely with the Bar Association of Cambodia to reach national legal professionals. According to court reports, one of the main goals of the Office of the Co-Prosecutors is to promote capacity building for national staff, international

[98] Diane Orentlicher, '"Worth the Effort"? Assessing the Khmer Rouge Tribunal' (2020) 18 Journal of International Criminal Justice 615, 623.

[99] ECCC, 'About the Extraordinary Chambers in the Courts of Cambodia' <http://www.eccc.gov.kh/en/about-eccc> accessed 22 January 2015.

[100] UN, 'Cambodia: UN-backed Tribunal Ends with Conviction Upheld for Last Living Khmer Rouge Leader' <https://news.un.org/en/story/2022/09/1127521> accessed 28 November 2022.

[101] Ciorciari (n 95).

[102] John D Ciorciari and Anne Heindel, 'Experiments in International Criminal Justice: Lessons from the Khmer Rouge Tribunal' (2014) 35 Michigan Journal of International Law 369.

[103] Ciorciari (n 95).

[104] ECCC, 'Revised Budget for 2018-2019' (2017).

[105] ECCC, 'Proposed Budget for the Biennium 2018-2019' (2017).

[106] Open Society Justice Initiative (OSJI), 'Performance and Perception: The Impact of the Extraordinary Chambers in the Court of Cambodia' (2016).

staff, and interns by having each group 'build each other's capacity in their areas of expertise, whether it be Cambodian or foreign legal traditions, technology, cross-cultural skills, or advocacy'.[107] As explained before, if we consider capacity building as a key premise of the hybrid tribunal model, then its design and policy implementation cannot be left as a mere by-product of the inclusion of international and domestic judicial personnel. Court documents do not offer a comprehensive report on how the Office of the Co-Prosecutors fulfils its goal of capacity building.

In addition, bearing in mind the relevance of the hybrid location for capacity building for the domestic judiciary, ECCC documents show several external facing activities undertaken by the Defence Support Section.[108] While the Court's reporting is far from robust, Chehtman and Mackenzie mapped fifteen training sessions on substantive ICL or case management techniques between 2006 and 2009.[109] In 2014, Ciorciari and Heindel confirmed the continuation of lectures and seminars, with the inclusion of internship opportunities for young Cambodian legal professionals although the internship scheme was effectively run by the UN.[110] In addition, the only available public information regarding the Defence Support Section mentions their close relationship with the Bar Association Cambodia to provide 'several one-week training courses to better equip Cambodian lawyers to defend cases at the ECCC'.[111] The number of people trained or the impact of this training (eg in terms of how many of these lawyers effectively appeared in front of the ECCC) is absent from the Court's public records. However, given that the Open Society Foundation participated in the development of training materials, they reported 'there was little systematic effort at capacity building and that the split nature of the national and the international sides of the court further undermined capacity-building opportunities for Cambodian staff'.[112] This is compounded by the fact that Cambodian staff went on strike twice in relation to pay inequalities compared to their international colleagues.[113]

Furthermore, as Martin-Ortega and Herman showed in 2010 and the Open Society Foundation confirmed in 2016, many of the successful capacity-building activities led by the ECCC were largely dependent on the leadership of individual people. While the Defence Support Section developed a programme of weekly briefings about international justice issues for both mid-level and high-level positions, the Office of the Co-Prosecutor did not offer a similar programme.[114] The absence of a systematic plan for capacity building, despite being noted as a core

[107] ECCC, 'Core Activities' <https://www.eccc.gov.kh/en/core-activities> accessed 3 August 2014.

[108] ECCC, 'Legacy' <https://www.eccc.gov.kh/en/legacy> accessed 11 December 2017.

[109] Chehtman and Mackenzie (n 65).

[110] Ciorciari and Heindel (n 102) 412.

[111] ECCC, 'Legacy' <https://www.eccc.gov.kh/en/legacy> accessed 11 December 2017.

[112] OSJI (n 106) 54.

[113] Rachel Hughes and Maria Elander, 'Scales of Justice: "International Standards" and "Local Ownership" at a Hybrid Tribunal' (2022) 54 Antipode 469.

[114] OSJI (n 106).

goal for at least two organs, means that the assertion made by the Defence Support Section that 'the skills and knowledge gained by lawyers may be also used in the regular Cambodian courts'[115] is unlikely to be true. Interviews with Cambodian legal professionals about the impact of the Court revealed that once they returned to the domestic legal system they did not succeed in adopting practices based on the ECCC.[116] This finding is at odds with the deputy prime minister's claims that '[ECCC] practices and procedures are being introduced in domestic courts'.[117] On the positive side, however, the mix of international and domestic laws and trial standards meant that lower national courts prioritized the defence counsel's role in the proceedings,[118] modelled after the ECCC's Defence Support Section.[119]

However, these advancements in the rule of law have been tightly controlled by political actors tolerating innovations in the domestic judicial system after the legacy of the ECCC.[120] The most eloquent example are the words of Prime Minister Hun Sen in 2009 stating: 'I would pray for this court to run out of money and for the foreign prosecutors and judges to walk out.'[121] In fact, issues of political interference have been identified as the main reason why ECCC innovations have not had a systemic impact on the rule of law in Cambodia.[122] As noted by the Open Society Foundation in 2016, there are minimal incentives for Cambodian judicial personnel to evoke the skills and knowledge acquired at the ECCC because of fear of retribution. Thus, beyond the location of the hybrid and mix of international and domestic personnel, even if capacity building at the ECCC were ultimately successful, the skills developed by domestic judicial personnel would represent a risk rather than an advantage in Cambodia.[123]

17.4.2.2 Infrastructure investment

Despite the positive impact that infrastructure investments in hybrid tribunals can have for the domestic judiciary, the newly built premises of the ECCC are occupied

[115] ECCC, 'Legacy' <https://www.eccc.gov.kh/en/legacy> accessed 11 December 2017.

[116] OSJI (n 106).

[117] Christoph Sperfeldt, 'From the Margins of Internationalized Criminal Justice Lessons Learned at the Extraordinary Chambers in the Courts of Cambodia' (2013) 11 Journal of International Criminal Justice 1125.

[118] OSJI (n 106).

[119] Mikkel Jarle Christensen and Astrid Kjeldgaard-Pedersen, 'Competing Perceptions of Hybrid Justice: International v. National in the Extraordinary Chambers of the Courts of Cambodia' (2018) 18 International Criminal Law Review 127.

[120] Alexander Hinton, *The Justice Facade: Trials of Transition in Cambodia* (Oxford University Press 2018); Paolo Lobba and Niccolò Pons, 'Rethinking the Legacy of the ECCC: Selectivity, Accountability, Ownership' (2020) 18 Journal of International Criminal Justice 599.

[121] Hannah Bertelman, 'International Standards and National Ownership? Judicial Independence in Hybrid Courts: The Extraordinary Chambers in the Courts of Cambodia' (2010) 79 Nordic Journal of International Law 341, 373.

[122] Diane Orentlicher, 'Worth the Effort' (n 98) 623.

[123] OSJI (n 106); Viviane E Dittrich, 'The Legacy of the ECCC' in Simon Meisenberg and Ignaz Stegmiller (eds), *The Extraordinary Chambers in the Courts of Cambodia: Assessing Their Contribution to International Criminal Law* (Asser Press 2016).

by the Royal Cambodian Armed Forces now that the Court's mandate has concluded.[124] The transfer of the Court's buildings took place in December 2022.[125] Similarly, the 2007 investment by Japan and India for a new detention facility, in line with Red Cross standards,[126] will become part of the armed forces compound rather than the local judiciary. The only infrastructure investment example benefiting the local judiciary is the USD 2.3 million building for the ECCC Legal Documentation Centre donated by the Japanese government and inaugurated in 2017.[127] The Legal Documentation Centre was established in 2015 as a repository to preserve and make accessible documentation of all cases from the ECCC, including judgments and proceedings, and other relevant books, magazines, newspapers, and electronic publications for educational and commemorative purposes.[128] The centre was prioritized by the Cambodian government in Case 002/02 as a reparations project for civil parties for memorial, rehabilitation, and educational purposes. McCaffrie agrees that these capacity-building interventions have played a positive role in educating young people about the Khmer Rouge regime.[129] The centre also houses the Bar Association of Cambodia.[130] In addition, investments in computerized systems for case management at the ECCC led the president of the national Court of Appeals, who was also the Cambodian co-investigating judge, to utilize the same system to dramatically reduce the backlog of domestic cases.[131]

17.4.3 The Bosnian War Crimes Chamber

Following the disintegration of the former Yugoslavia in 1991, a total of 100,000 people were killed, including 16,000 children; 2.2 million became refugees; and 1.3 million were internally displaced in Bosnia Herzegovina,[132] in what is considered the worst armed conflict in Europe since World War II.[133] The conflict

[124] Sperfeldt (n 117) 1117.

[125] ECCC, 'Handover Ceremony of the Former Khmer Rouge Tribunal Compound back to the Royal Cambodian Army' <https://www.eccc.gov.kh/en/articles/handover-ceremony-former-khmer-rouge-tribunal-compound-back-royal-cambodian-army> accessed 11 January 2023.

[126] Chehtman and Mackenzie (n 65).

[127] Embassy of Japan in the Kingdom of Cambodia, 'The Inauguration of the Legal Documentation Centre Relating to the Extraordinary Chambers in the Courts of Cambodia, No 14 PR-17/EoJ' (2017).

[128] Office of the Council of Ministers, 'The Formal Inauguration of the Legal Documentation Centre Relating to the Extraordinary Chambers in the Courts of Cambodia (LDC)' (2017).

[129] Caitlin McCaffrie, 'An Educational Legacy: Exploring the Links Between Education and Resilience at the ECCC' (2020) 33 Leiden Journal of International Law, 978.

[130] Office of the Council of Ministers, 'Speech by Chhin Bin Standing Deputy Prime Minister on the Occasion of Official Inauguration of Legal Documentation Center Relating to the Extraordinary Chambers in the Courts of Cambodia' (2017).

[131] OSJI (n 106).

[132] Bogdan Ivanisevic, 'The War Crimes Chamber in Bosnia and Herzegovina: From Hybrid to Domestic Court' (2008) International Center for Transitional Justice.

[133] James Gow, Rachel Kerr, and Zoran Pajic, *Prosecuting War Crimes: Lessons and Legacies of the International Criminal Tribunal for the Former Yugoslavia* (Routledge 2013).

is infamous for horrific human rights violations including widespread rape, imprisonment in concentration camps, ethnic cleansing, and—as ruled by the International ICTY—genocide.[134] After the establishment of the ICTY by the UNSC in 1993, violations of international criminal and humanitarian law were mainly prosecuted in The Hague. However, in 2003, the UNSC mandated the ICTY to develop an exit strategy commencing preparations to end all its operations by 2010.[135] Alleging donor fatigue, partially ineffective delivery of justice away from victims, and the conclusion of high-level trials, the UNSC resolution included 'transferring cases involving those who may not bear [the highest] level of responsibility to competent national jurisdictions'.[136] The establishment in 2005 of the BIH WCC within the Court of Bosnia Herzegovina (BiH) and the subsequent creation of the Special Department for War Crimes in the BiH Prosecutor's Office was the result of that exit strategy.[137] The Bosnian War Crimes Chamber, however, had not been the only domestic judicial institution investigating the crimes committed during the conflict. Abuses committed between 1992 and 1995 have also been investigated by ten cantonal (or municipal) courts.[138] Thus, with the creation of the BIH WCC, human rights abuses have been prosecuted at the international level with the ICTY, at the national or federal level by the BIH WCC, and at the local level with cantonal district courts.

An analysis of the law creating the Court of Bosnia and Herzegovina, and subsequently the Bosnian War Crimes Chamber does not include the mandate to conduct capacity building between the hybrid and the domestic judiciary. However, the ICTY exit strategy did create a multi-agency capacity building project to ensure the effective transfer of know-how and materials to the national judicial systems in the region of the former Yugoslavia.[139]

17.4.3.1 Knowledge transfer

The 4 million Euro War Crimes Justice Project, later renamed the War Crimes Capacity Building Project, was funded by the European Union (EU) and implemented between 2009 and 2017 jointly by the Organisation for Security and Co-operation in Europe's (OSCE) Office for Democratic Institutions and Human Rights (ODIHR), the ICTY, and the United Nations Interregional Crime and Justice Research Institute (UNICRI), together with OSCE field operations in the region. With an annual budget of 13 million Euros,[140] the BIH WCC has benefited from earmarked resources for capacity building via the EU as well as the OSCE's

[134] ibid.
[135] Ivanisevic (n 132).
[136] McAuliffe (n 80) 25–26.
[137] Ivanisevic (n 132); Gow, Kerr, and Zoran (n 133).
[138] Diane Orentlicher, *Some Kind of Justice: The ICTY's Impact in Bosnia and Serbia* (Oxford University Press 2018).
[139] ibid.
[140] van Schaack (n 1).

rule of law programming for Bosnia, totalling a sum of 5 million Euros in 2017 alone.[141] Brodersen agrees that the multi-agency support to the BIH WCC was critical for the transition of ICTY cases to Bosnia.[142] Compared to the other two examples examined in this chapter, the Bosnian hybrid offers an alternative institutional arrangement for capacity building by being the direct recipient of resources in rule of law programming via regional organizations with a strategic vision to stabilize the country for accession to the EU.[143]

Bearing in mind the particular relevance of the mix of international and domestic legal personnel for capacity building, in 2006 the BIH WCC established its own judicial education committee on the initiative of two foreign judges.[144] Comprised of six national and two international members, the committee organized training sessions on topics selected by national staff in an effort to foster national ownership.[145] In fact, some of the issues covered since 2006 correlate directly with the handover process from the ICTY to the hybrid, for example efficiency in proceedings, credibility of witnesses, and jurisdiction of the Court.[146] Beyond the judicial college, national and international judges, legal advisors, legal officers, and interns have benefited from seminars and professional development sessions organized by national Entity Centers for Judicial and Prosecutorial Training sponsored by the European Commission, the Norwegian Bar Association, and the Dutch government.[147] In addition to in-house training and external support, judges have benefited from study visits to the ICTY and other institutions such as the ICC. However, capacity building between national and international staff was hampered by the limited time for national counterparts to engage with international colleagues on identifying needs on 'how to transfer knowledge … and a formal briefing on cultural, professional and personal issues'[148] within the Court and the country. In addition, limited technical awareness of ICL among national staff created difficulties in delivering ICL and trial standards training.[149] The

[141] Organization for Security and Co-operation in Europe Permanent Council, 'Decision No.1252, Approval of the 2017 Unified Budget, PC.DEC/1252/Corr.1' (2017).

[142] Kei Hannah Brodersen, '"We Learnt that from The Hague": How the ICTY Influenced the Fairness of Criminal Trials in the Former Yugoslavia' in Carsten Stahn (ed), *Legacies of the International Criminal Tribunal for the Former Yugoslavia: A Multidisciplinary Approach* (Oxford University Press 2020) 514–15.

[143] Alejandro Chehtman, 'Developing Bosnia and Herzegovina's Capacity to Process War Crimes Cases Critical Notes on a "Success Story"' (2011) 9 Journal of International Criminal Justice; Orentlicher, Some Kind of Justice (n 138).

[144] Court of Bosnia Herzegovina, 'Court Brochure' <http://www.sudbih.gov.ba/files/docs/Brosura_o_Sudu_BiH_ENG_2012.pdf> accessed 12 May 2014.

[145] Almut Schröder, 'Strengthening the Rule of Law in Kosovo and Bosnia and Herzegovina: The Contribution of International Judges and Prosecutors' (2005) Zentrum für Internationale Friedenseinsätze.

[146] Court of Bosnia Herzegovina, 'Court Brochure' <http://www.sudbih.gov.ba/files/docs/Brosura_o_Sudu_BiH_ENG_2012.pdf> accessed 12 May 2014.

[147] Chehtman and Mackenzie (n 65) annex.

[148] Chehtman (n 143) 6.

[149] ibid 20.

barrier to improve capacity building on ICL and trial standards for domestic legal personnel were noted in the 2009 War Crimes Justice Project report.[150] The OSCE's Mission to Bosnia and Herzegovina responded by:

- Training 300 legal professionals through over 100 activities for judges, prosecutors, defence attorneys, and witness support providers on international humanitarian law.[151]
- Creating a curriculum on ICL for local training institutions, containing ICTY jurisprudence and the region's developing body of domestic war crimes jurisprudence.[152]
- Providing 60,000 pages of ICTY trial transcripts in local languages, to enhance the ability of local judiciaries to access and use testimonies given before the Tribunal.[153]
- Translating 200,000 words of the Appeals Chamber Case Law Research Tool into the regional language for professionals to conduct legal research using the same legal digest tool at the ICTY.[154]
- Launching a training and e-learning portal for legal practitioners on issues related to war crimes.[155]

When the project ended in 2017, the Director of the Federation of BIH Entity Centers for Judicial and Prosecutorial Training acknowledged that the transfer of skills and knowledge to legal professionals for processing war crimes at the cantonal level had been achieved.[156] Similarly, the acting Chief Prosecutor of the BIH Prosecutor's Office, which oversaw the War Crimes Chamber, explained that the improved quality of indictments and case management was partly achieved because prosecutors and staff had acquired knowledge from induction and specialized training.[157] In this regard, and in contrast with the Sierra Leone and Cambodian experiences, the Bosnian hybrid was able to outsource much of its domestic capacity building thanks to the strategic involvement of regional actors who wanted to stabilize the country for political reasons. Given that none of these

[150] OSCE, 'Supporting the Transition Process: Lessons Learned and Best Practices in Knowledge Transfer Final Report' (2009).

[151] OSCE Mission to Bosnia and Herzegovina, 'OSCE's War Crimes Capacity Building Project in Bosnia and Herzegovina Closes' <https://www.osce.org/mission-to-bosnia-and-herzegovina/362236> accessed 4 March 2018.

[152] UN Interregional Crime and Justice Research Institute, 'War Crimes Justice Project Strengthens National Capacities to Handle War Crimes Cases' <https://unicri.it/news/article/111027_post_wjp> accessed 3 February 2018.

[153] ibid.

[154] ibid.

[155] ibid.

[156] OSCE Mission to Bosnia and Herzegovina, 'OSCE's War Crimes Capacity Building Project in Bosnia and Herzegovina Closes' <https://www.osce.org/mission-to-bosnia-and-herzegovina/362236> accessed 4 March 2018.

[157] ibid.

hybrid tribunals have a clear mandate in their founding documents to deliver capacity building at the domestic level, the Bosnian experience offers an alternative model based on inter-agency cooperation and joint implementation.

In addition to the capacity-building initiatives between national and international staff on ICL and standards, the location in-country of the BIH WCC and its organizational design also contributed to increased domestic capacity. Created in 2004, the Court's Registry and the Criminal Defence Support Section (OKO) provided project management expertise to oversee the appropriate handover of cases from the ICTY to the hybrid court to cantonal districts. In order to maintain effective oversight, the Registry developed inductions, career development, and performance evaluations for the BIH WCC and domestic staff.[158] Professional development meant that the Registry was supported by the War Crimes Justice Project to deliver legal training and research support for judges and trial panels.[159] The Criminal Defence Support Section has been lauded as an example to follow in other tribunals.[160] Supported by the War Crimes Justice Project, OKO trained defence counsel inside and outside the BIH WCC with knowledge on substantive and procedural issues, case analysis, expert witness examination, strategies for effective advocacy, and the role of defence counsel in upholding fair trial standards.[161] Between 2005 and 2007, a critical time for the transfer of cases, OKO trained more than 350 defence lawyers.[162] Some of them have appeared in front of the BIH WCC while others have taken roles at the federal and cantonal level.[163]

However, the War Crimes Justice Project and internal efforts in the Chamber have not been enough to achieve the 2008 National War Crimes Strategy to conclude all war crimes cases by 2016.[164] A 2016 report by the OSCE, led by an independent reviewer, revealed that 672 war crimes cases remained unresolved at the BIH WCC.[165] As of December 2021, 495 war crimes cases remain in the dock of the Court waiting to be adjudicated within the new National War Crimes Strategy with a 2023 deadline.[166] The reasons for the failure to achieve the deadline were identified by the reviewer as: (1) lack of any strategic planning; (2) inadequate numbers of prosecutors and legal assistants, interpreters, and administrative staff; and

[158] Court of Bosnia Herzegovina, 'Court Brochure' <http://www.sudbih.gov.ba/files/docs/Brosura_o_Sudu_BiH_ENG_2012.pdf> accessed 12 May 2014.

[159] Orentlicher, *Some Kind of Justice* (n 138).

[160] Chehtman and Mackenzie (n 65).

[161] ibid 15.

[162] Lilian A Barria, and Steven D Roper, 'Judicial Capacity Building in Bosnia and Herzegovina: Understanding Legal Reform Beyond the Completion Strategy of the ICTY' (2008) 9 Human Rights Review 317, 327; McAuliffe (n 80) 38.

[163] Orentlicher, *Some Kind of Justice* (n 138).

[164] OSCE, Mission to Bosnia and Herzegovina, 'Processing of War Crimes at the State Level in Bosnia and Herzegovina, Her Honour Judge Joanna Korner CMG QC Report' (2016).

[165] ibid.

[166] OSCE, 'A Race Against Time: Successes and Challenges in the Implementation of the National War Crimes Processing Strategy of Bosnia and Herzegovina' (2022) 18.

(3) poorly trained investigators and poorly drafted indictments, in particular with regard to the legal characterization of the crimes.[167] A follow-up report in 2020 concluded that no substantial progress had been achieved since 2016, making it 'impossible'[168] to secure the 2023 deadline. These reasons question to what extent the War Crimes Justice Project managed to comply with its mandate to ensure the effective transfer of know-how and materials from the ICTY to the national judicial systems. Even with considerable multi-agency support for judicial capacity, the BIH WCC still faced considerable challenges. In fact, a visit by the UN Special Rapporteur on the Promotion of Truth, Justice and Reparation in December 2021 confirmed 'insufficient human and material resources ... continue to negatively affect war crimes prosecutions and delay progress'.[169]

17.4.3.2 Infrastructure investment

In relation to infrastructure investment in the domestic judiciary via the hybrid tribunal, the funding from the EU and OSCE went to new and redeveloped buildings.[170] The current buildings occupied by the BIH WCC will remain assigned to the BiH. The legacy aspect of infrastructure was planned at the same time proceedings were taking place in the ICTY, giving ample time for construction and refurbishment. Moreover, the BIH WCC invested in information technology for court proceedings and for administrative capacities.[171] Resources donated from European multilateral agencies enabled the modernization of the BiH with hopes to transform paper record keeping and document administration into digital archiving.[172] However, progress in infrastructure investment remains focused on the BIH WCC rather than on the cantonal district courts which are also engaged in prosecuting atrocity crimes.[173]

17.5 Conclusion

Capacity building is widely recognized in the literature as one of the main advantages of the hybrid tribunal model. This model has been deployed in the last twenty

[167] OSCE, Mission to Bosnia and Herzegovina, 'Processing of War Crimes at the State Level in Bosnia and Herzegovina, Her Honour Judge Joanna Korner CMG QC Report' (2016).

[168] OSCE, Mission to Bosnia and Herzegovina, 'Improving War Crimes Processing at the State Level in Bosnia and Herzegovina, a Follow-up Report by her Honour Judge Joanna Korner CMG QC' (2020) 54.

[169] Report of the Special Rapporteur on the Promotion of Truth, Justice, Reparation and Guarantees of non-Recurrence: Visit to Bosnia and Herzegovina (2022) UN Doc A/HRC/51/34/Add.2, 9.

[170] Court of Bosnia Herzegovina, 'Court Brochure' <http://www.sudbih.gov.ba/files/docs/Brosura_o_Sudu_BiH_ENG_2012.pdf> accessed 12 May 2014.

[171] Chehtman and Mackenzie (n 65); Orentlicher, *Some Kind of Justice* (n 138).

[172] OSCE, 'Mission to Bosnia Herzegovina' <http://www.oscebih.org/Default.aspx?id=70&lang=EN> accessed 15 January 2016.

[173] Barria and Roper (n 162).

years to reform and strengthen domestic judicial capacity in order to improve justice for victims of serious violations of human rights. However, as observed in this chapter, the lack of specificity of capacity-building efforts complicates the empirical exercise of evaluating whether these tribunals are living up to their promise of rebuilding the domestic judiciary. Risse, Ropp, and Sikkink's definition of capacity building as knowledge transfer and infrastructure investment was used to generate a comparative analysis of the SCSL, ECCC, and the BIH WCC. Using the definition, the analysis reveals significant gaps between the promises and the actual outcomes.

None of the three hybrids were mandated in their constitutional documents to deliver capacity building to the domestic judiciary. As expected, the statutes are only concerned with roles and responsibilities on the adjudication of atrocity crimes. The expectation that hybrids would provide capacity building is not documented in any of the three examples, including Sierra Leone and Cambodia where the UN, an early champion of domestic capacity building via hybrid tribunals, had influencing power over their mandates. In the absence of a clear mandate to deliver capacity building, the SCSL, ECCC, and the BIH WCC did not outline organizational priorities, strategic plans, or systematically earmarked resources to invest in the local judiciary. Instead, capacity-building activities were sporadic and unplanned.

In Sierra Leone, the missing institutional channels between the Special Court and the national judiciary meant that domestic staff, whether or not appropriately trained, could not use their expertise at the local level. This, in turn, damaged the legitimacy of the Court among legal professionals sceptical of the hybrid tribunal's purposes. Furthermore, the Court operated in the absence of a national rule of law reform plan, despite a few gains with regards to gender-based crime legislation. Removed from the domestic judiciary and tasked with a narrow mandate to prosecute human rights abuses, the main 'knowledge transfer' mechanism available for national staff was working with international legal staff. The premises of the Court—'the spaceship'—are an apt example of how legacy issues for the judicial system of the host state were not taken into consideration by the government and the UN.

In Cambodia, issues of political interference threatened the ability of the Court to fulfil even its most narrow mandate of human rights prosecutions. The absence of a systematic plan for capacity building, despite being noted as a core goal for at least two court organs, makes the transfer of skills to the domestic system unlikely. Interviews with Cambodian legal professionals on the impact of the Court revealed that once they returned to the domestic system, they did not succeed in influencing colleagues and superiors to draw on ECCC practice. Despite positive developments in infrastructure investment for the Legal Documentation Centre, the weak rule of law context in Cambodia mitigates against adopting innovations from the hybrid to the domestic judiciary.

Lastly, the BIH WCC stands out in comparison to both the Special Court and the Extraordinary Chambers. The capacity-building investments by the EU and the OSCE did benefit the War Crimes Chamber and the local judiciary. However, this was effectively an outsourcing of capacity building to international organizations. Despite considerable investment in judicial capacity building, the OSCE identified continuing gaps in the technical knowledge needed by local prosecutors to tackle atrocity crimes. These issues are reflected in the number of pending cases under the National War Crimes Strategy.

While this analysis shows the weak implementation of the capacity-building element of the hybrid tribunals in Sierra Leone, Bosnia and Herzegovina, and Cambodia, it should not be concluded that the model per se is at fault. These case studies demonstrate the need for clear mandates and operational plans to deliver capacity building linking the tribunal's creation with the local judiciary, supported by other actors engaged in rule of law initiatives. The BIH WCC is a promising example in this regard, though far from perfect. The creation of new hybrids should consider their relationship to wider efforts for rule of law reform making tactical investments across the domestic system, in partnership with key actors at the international and national level. For the hybrid tribunal model to render impact in the long term, the premise of capacity building should not only be an empty promise.

18

Beyond 'Fragmentation'

The Potential of Hybrid Courts to Restore Local Trust in International Justice through Prosecution of Economic, Social, and Cultural Rights Violations

Alice Dieci

18.1 Introduction

Scholars have identified ICL as a special branch of international law founded upon internal tensions between the 'universalist aspirations of public international law, the humanist dimensions of human rights law and the fairness-oriented foundations of criminal law'.[1] The fact that ICL is shaped by the interplay of different layers of jurisdictions, including domestic courts, and that it integrates principles from different legal traditions, has been considered by 'universalists' and general public international law practitioners a challenge to its authority and coherence, defining this branch of law as a paradigm of 'fragmentation fears'.[2] The debate over the fragmentation of international law (or its 'pluralism', for those who approve of this feature of international law), flourishing during the decade of ad hoc tribunals,[3] did not fade away with the creation of the International Criminal Court (ICC), which aimed at replacing 'a fragmented approach to international criminal justice with a permanent system of global accountability'.[4] Indeed, the recent resurgence of

[1] Carsten Stahn and Larissa van den Herik, 'Fragmentation, Diversification and 3D Legal Pluralism: International Criminal Law as the Jack-in-The-Box?' in Larissa van den Herik and Carsten Stahn (eds), *The Diversification and Fragmentation of International Criminal Law* (Martinus Nijhoff 2012), 3 <https://ssrn.com/abstract=2165001> accessed 28 December 2023. On the nature of ICL and its relationship to human rights law, see Andrew Clapham, 'Three Tribes Engage on the Future of International Criminal Law' (2011) 9 Journal of International Criminal Justice 689; Larissa van den Herik, 'Economic, Social and Cultural Rights—International Criminal Law's Blind Spot?' in Eibe Riedel, Christopher Golay, and Gilles Giacca (eds), *Economic, Social and Cultural Rights: Contemporary Issues and Challenges* (Oxford University Press 2013); Francoise Tulkens, 'The Paradoxical Relationship between Criminal Law and Human Rights' (2011) 9 Journal of International Criminal Justice 577.

[2] See Stahn (n 1) 3.

[3] ibid 1.

[4] Mark Kersten, 'As the Pendulum Swings—The Revival of the Hybrid Tribunal (New Paper!)' (*Justice in Conflict*, 26 April 2017) <https://justiceinconflict.org/2017/04/26/as-the-pendulum-swings-the-revival-of-the-hybrid-tribunal-new-paper/> accessed 28 December 2023

Alice Dieci, *Beyond 'Fragmentation'* In: *Hybrid Justice*. Edited by: Kirsten Ainley and Mark Kersten, Oxford University Press. © Alice Dieci 2025. DOI: 10.1093/oso/9780192893758.003.0018

hybrid courts demonstrates not only that a consolidated system of global justice is far from being achieved but also that fragmentation can be positively incarnated into the work of hybrid mechanisms, resulting in greater openness to diversification and specialization,[5] 'dynamic pluralism', and 'judicial creativity', which are increasingly perceived as essential features for the future of ICL.[6]

The chapter focuses on the scope of hybrid tribunals to reach beyond Rome Statute limitations, embrace pluralism, and bring accountability for economic, social and cultural rights' (ESCR) violations. Such violations have traditionally been excluded from the purview of ICL, yet are often critically important to victims and may underlie the causes of conflict. The chapter will explore the link between the fragmentation of ICL and ESCR violations through the lens of hybrid courts, attempting to identify their potential to fill the 'impunity gap' and restore local trust in international justice. After a discussion of the recent turn towards ESCR in transitional justice scholarship, the main—yet limited—jurisprudence of hybrid tribunals in prosecuting international crimes encompassing ESCR violations will be outlined. The chapter ends with an examination of the challenges and limitations exposed, and the potential the hybrids offer to bring a more complete accountability.

18.2 Marginalization of ESCR Violations in Transitional Justice and International Criminal Law

In the last decade, both scholars and practitioners have debated the inclusion of ESCR violations in transitional justice processes. While some scholars believe that expanding the scope of transitional justice to include ESCR violations would divert attention from the most heinous international crimes, others have progressively considered that the traditional notion of transitional justice—focusing, almost exclusively, on civil and political rights—is inadequate to capture the complexities of modern societies transitioning from conflicts or authoritarian regimes.[7] In this regard, the so-called 'Arab Spring' has largely nurtured the discussion as to whether transitional justice measures should address economic inequalities, corruption, and any other infringement on economic, social, and cultural rights.[8] Indeed, Mohammed Bouazizi, 'the man who set himself and Tunisia on fire' was not

[5] Gerhard Hafner, 'Pros and Cons Ensuing from Fragmentation of International Law' (2004) 25 Michigan Journal of International Law 849, 859.

[6] See Stahn (n 1) 4. See also Alexander Greenawalt, 'The Pluralism of International Criminal Law' (2011) 86 Indiana Law Journal 1064.

[7] See Ruben Carranza, 'Plunder and Pain: Should Transitional Justice Engage with Corruption and Economic Crimes?' (2008) 2 International Journal of Transitional Justice 310.

[8] Evelyne Schmidt and Aoife Nolan, 'Do Not Harm? Exploring the Scope of Economic and Social Rights in Transitional Justice' (2014) 8 International Journal of Transitional Justice 362, 363.

protesting against civil and political rights violations but against the infringement on his right to work and consequently to attain an adequate standard of living.[9] In Egypt, the motto of the 2011 uprising was 'Bread, Freedom, Social Justice', de facto upholding the indivisibility and interdependent nature of human rights and the importance of aspiring to a vision of mainstream justice that substantially includes social justice.[10] Most recently, Kenya, Nigeria, Lebanon, Sudan, Chile, Iran and India —among others—were the scene of austerity-driven protests mainly triggered by the lack of access to basic goods and services, such as bread, water, electricity, fuel, subway fares, and medical supplies, which further increased socio-economic inequalities. According to a 2022 Amnesty International Report, 1,484 out of 2,809 protests between 2006 and 2020 were focused on economic and social rights.[11]Yet, violations of ESCR have historically been neglected both in theory and in practice and have rarely been taken into account by judicial and non-judicial transitional justice measures.

Scholars researching in this field have identified some misconceptions in addressing ESCR violations in transitional societies. One of them relates to the so called 'structural argument', according to which there is a tendency to consider ESCR violations as structural, deep-rooted causes of conflicts and widespread violence rather than violations per se.[12] Such an approach not only falls short in accepting that even civil and political violations may have a structural component, but it also fails to recognize that ESCR violations deserve the same level of attention as civil and political rights violations, as they equally derive from states' failure to comply with both positive and negative obligations.

Despite the increased recognition of ESCR in international law, their justiciability still fails to be properly enforced. Practitioners have identified that the prejudices and misconceptions that have long discouraged judicial and quasi-judicial bodies from playing an active role in the protection of ESCR in cases of violations, relate both to the nature of these rights and to the ability and legitimacy of judicial and quasi-judicial bodies to adjudicate them.[13] For instance, ESCR are often considered too vague to be the subject of judicial review and, paradoxically,

[9] Rania Abouzeid, 'Bouazizi: The Man Who Set Himself and Tunisia on Fire' (*Time Magazine*, 20 January 2011) <https://content.time.com/time/magazine/article/0,9171,2044723,00.html> accessed 28 December 2023.

[10] Schmidt and Nolan (n 8) 363.

[11] Amnesty International, Rising Prices, Growing Protests: The Case for Universal Social Protection, 18, available at: <https://www.amnesty.org/en/wp-content/uploads/2023/05/POL4065892023ENGLISH.pdf. accessed on 7 October 2024

[12] ibid 371.

[13] See International Commission of Jurists, 'Courts and the legal enforcement of economic, social and cultural rights: comparative experiences of justiciability' (2008) Human Rights and Rule of Law Series No 2, 3 available at <https://www.refworld.org/docid/4a7840562.html> accessed 28 December 2023. See also UN Committee on Economic, Social and Cultural Rights (CESCR), General Comment n 9: the domestic application of the Covenant (1998) E/C.12/1998/24 para 10 <https://tbinternet.ohchr.org/_layouts/15/treatybodyexternal/Download.aspx?symbolno=E%2FC.12%2F1998%2F24&Lang=en> accessed 28 December 2023.

this has led to fewer efforts on the part of the judiciary to contribute to their interpretation and define principles for their construction.[14] As a consequence, some practitioners argue that a lack of specificity on their content and on the legal obligations stemming from them has traditionally hampered their judicial enforcement. While judicial and quasi-judicial protection should not be seen as the only way to fulfil ESCR, not ensuring their justiciability has severe repercussions in terms of victims' access to justice and the right to an effective remedy, such as reparations.

The polarization between civil and political and economic and social rights dates back to the adoption of the Universal Declaration of human rights and the related International Covenants on civil and political rights (ICCPR) and economic, social and cultural rights (ICESCR), which stemmed from embedded Cold War ideological differences.[15] Indeed, with regards to the Declaration, the Socialist Block abstained from the vote precisely because of the perceived predominance of the 'Western superior political model' and the lack of enforcement of economic and social rights;[16] similarly, the adoption of two different Covenants focusing on different categories of rights rather than of a single treaty encompassing all human rights, 'epitomizes the depth of these differences'.[17] A sign of the marginalization of ESCR in international human rights law can be seen in the creation and ratification of the Optional Protocols to the two Covenants: while ICCPR benefited from the concurrent adoption of an individual complaints mechanism—to which 115 states are currently parties—it was not until 2008 that a similar protection mechanism was adopted for ICESCR and not until 2013 that it entered into force, allowing the correspondent UN Committee to examine complaints and initiate inquiries in cases of alleged ESCR violations. This arguably reflects the assumption that international human rights law was created by—and according to the preferences of—the Western world, for which civil and political rights violations have traditionally been prioritized.

Similarly, practitioners have identified that the lack of jurisprudence in the area of ESCR is mainly ideological: during the eighteenth and nineteenth centuries, only in a few countries was priority given to developing a legal basis for the functions of the welfare state, and the designing and implementation of social policies were mainly left to the discretion of political branches.[18] The belief that ESCR should not be granted any kind of judicial or quasi-judicial protection, and should be left to the discretion of political branches of the state, has been identified as one of the main reasons why ESCR have been devalued within the legal hierarchy.[19]

[14] International Commission of Jurists, 'Courts and the legal enforcement of economic, social and cultural rights' (n 12) 15–16.

[15] Andrew Clapham, *Human Rights: A Very Short Introduction* (Oxford University Press 2007) 48.

[16] ibid 44.

[17] Louise Arbour, 'Economic and Social Justice for Societies in Transition' (2007) 40 International Law and Politics 1, 7.

[18] International Commission of Jurists, 'Courts and the legal enforcement of economic, social and cultural rights' (n 12) 13.

[19] ibid 5.

The lack of prioritization of ESCR—which arguably reflects the traditional approach of Western societies—also applies to other branches of international law, such as ICL. The Rome Statute of the ICC does not reflect the plurality of crimes that member states wished to see prosecuted at the Court. Rather than embracing the plurality of experiences in which international crimes can manifest themselves, the Rome Statute arguably reflects the preferences of global north states which advocated for criminalization of offences they had suffered, but sought to exclude some of those that they had perpetrated or supported.[20] For instance, the expansive approach to include colonialism and apartheid among international crimes was immediately dismissed by Western powers such as the United States, United Kingdom, Australia, Belgium, and The Netherlands, on the account that they were 'political novelties' that ceased to exist, rather than crimes, and therefore did not need to be criminalized.[21] Scholars have argued that many of the crimes in the Rome Statute are culturally biased, including in relation to ESCR violations, such as the war crime of pillage, defined as 'pillaging a town or place even when taken by assault', which clearly favours the 'European histories of siege warfare over the widespread experience of plunder in the Global South'.[22]

However, since the end of the Cold War, at least in the area of international human rights law, the international community has made concrete steps towards an increased recognition of ESCR, for instance through the work of United Nations (UN) Special Procedures,[23] and parallel regional initiatives further advocating for greater emphasis on these rights have also flourished.[24]

With regards to the relationship between ESCR and ICL, both academics and international jurisprudence have confirmed that most elements of international crimes indeed encompass ESCR violations.[25] However, as ESCR violations are often perceived as structural causes of conflicts and ICL deals with individual

[20] James G Stewart and Asad Kiyani, 'The Ahistoricism of Legal Pluralism in International Criminal Law' (2017) American Journal of Comparative Law 1, 79.

[21] ibid 78–80. See also United Nations International Convention on the Suppression and Punishment of the Crime of Apartheid, N 14861 (1976), at 245: Western domination of international law-making led to the exclusion of the crime of colonialism from the Rome Statute, while the crime of apartheid was eventually included in the final draft—following lobbying from Mexico, Ireland, and a group of African states, including South Africa—but only if committed in the context of a widespread or systematic attack directed against the civilian population, substantially reducing its scope and differing from what defined in the Apartheid Convention.

[22] Stewart and Kiyani (n 19) 74.

[23] Out of the forty-six Special Procedures' thematic mandates established by the UN Human Rights Council, at least 14 of them directly and exclusively pertain to ESCR.

[24] Notable is the jurisprudence of the Inter-American human rights system in this regard. As for regional initiatives, in December 2017, the first ever South-to-South Human Rights Forum was organized in China, resulting in the adoption of the 'Beijing Declaration', which strongly advocates for the prioritization of ESCR, such as the right to an adequate standard of living, the right to food, the right to housing, and, in particular, the right to development as a primary basic human right.

[25] For a comprehensive analysis on the definition of ESCR violations entailing individual criminal responsibility and on the overlapping between ESCR violations and ICL, see Evelyne Schmid, *Taking Economic, Social and Cultural Rights Seriously in International Criminal Law* (Cambridge University Press 2015).

responsibility, rather than structural inequalities and social justice, it is not surprising that, to date, there have been few international prosecutions related to ESCR violations.[26]

18.3 Hybrid Courts' Selected Jurisprudence on Prosecution of International Crimes related to ESCR Violations: A Step Forward or a Missed Opportunity?

18.3.1 The Special Court of Sierra Leone (SCSL) and the war crime of pillage

On 26 September 2013, the Appeals Chamber of the SCSL confirmed that former President of Liberia Charles Taylor assisted and planned numerous crimes committed during Sierra Leone's civil war. Accessory liability in the form of aiding and abetting was upheld for Charles Taylor for the war crime of pillage.[27]

Pillage is prohibited under customary international law, which does not restrict it to personal or private use.[28] On the contrary, the Rome Statute adopts a narrow definition of this war crime, requiring that: (a) the perpetrator appropriated certain property; (b) they intended to deprive the owner of the property and to appropriate it for private or personal use; and (c) the owner did not consent to the appropriation.[29] In the *Taylor* judgment, the Trial Chamber seemed to have adopted the narrow Rome Statute definition, stating that 'the perpetrator must have specifically intended to deprive the owner of the property and appropriate it for private or personal use' and basing its finding on the traditional looting of personal property rather than the more complex forms of pillaging diamonds and other natural resources.[30] Indeed, if one adopts the limited scope of the ICC definition of pillage, which limits it to private or personal use, perpetrators would more easily escape prosecution if they claim that they did not personally enrich themselves. In addition, when it comes to natural resources, concessions over them are often granted without the consent of the owner, making it a *probatio diabolica* to establish an intention to deprive the owner of the property.[31]

The issue of illegal resource exploitation was only raised indirectly before the SCSL as part of the joint criminal enterprise of which rebel groups were charged

[26] ibid 25.

[27] *Prosecutor v Charles Ghankay Taylor* (Judgment) SCSL-03-01-T (18 May 2012) [6948]–[6952].

[28] International Committee of the Red Cross (ICRC), 'Customary IHL Database', Rule 52.

[29] Rome Statute of the International Criminal Court (opened for signature 17 July 1998, entered into force 1 July 2002) 2187 UNTS 90, Article 8, paras 2(b)(xvi) and 2(e)(v). The pillage of cultural property is further criminalized by the second protocol to the 1954 Hague Convention on Cultural Property. See also *Bemba* (Decision on the Charges of the Prosecutor) ICC-01/05- 01/08- 424 (15 June 2009),76.

[30] Schmid (n 24) 192.

[31] ibid 206.

and that had as the objective 'gaining and exercising political power and control over the territory of Sierra Leone, in particular the diamond mining areas'. Despite having this possibility to do so, the Appeals Chamber did not qualify the objective as amounting to a crime within the Statute of the Court, with the result that resource exploitation was left unpunished.[32]

The SCSL's omission in making the link between pillage and exploitation of natural resources should be considered as a missed opportunity, which is in line with the lack of international prosecution in this regard so far. However, the flexibility of a hybrid tribunal in adopting a broader definition of a crime which could reach beyond the Rome Statute's limitations—such as in the case of pillage as a war crime—is a feature that could potentially make hybridity very useful in the amelioration of ESCR accountability and which deserves to be exploited, particularly where local populations place ESCR violations as a priority in their call for justice.

18.3.2 The Extraordinary Chamber of the Court of Cambodia (ECCC) and the crime against humanity of forcible transfer and extermination

In August 2014, the ECCC delivered the first trial judgment of Case 002, which confirms the importance of the possible overlap between crimes against humanity and ESCR violations. The accused, Nuon Chea and Khieu Samphan, were found guilty of the crimes against humanity of extermination, murder, persecution on political grounds, and other inhuman acts (forced transfer, enforced disappearances, and attacks against human dignity). In particular, they were convicted for forcible transfer of at least 2 million people, of which between 2,000 and 20,000 people died as they were already weakened from food shortage and 'forced to march to rural areas in the hottest time of the year and in the almost complete absence of food, water, medical care, accommodation or transportation'.[33] The transfer was qualified as forcible since most people were ordered to leave and were transferred under armed guard.[34] Moreover, the Court not only found that the pretext of food shortage was not a justification for forcible transfer but also highlighted the fact that it was the Khmer Rouge regime that had created the humanitarian situation of insufficient resources in which people found themselves during displacements between September 1975 and 1977.[35]

[32] *Prosecutor v Taylor*, SCSL-03- 1-T (26 April 2012) [1957]–[1962].

[33] Schmid (n 24) 109. *Noun Chea and Khieu Samphan* (Judgment) Case 002/19-09/2007/ECCC/TC (7 August 2014) [520].

[34] *Noun Chea and Khieu Samphan* (n 32) 632.

[35] ibid 634. See also Simon Meisenberg and Ignaz Stegmiller, *The Extraordinary Chambers in the Courts of Cambodia: Assessing their Contribution in International Criminal Law* (Asser Press 2016).

With regards to the crime of extermination, in Cambodia, the *actus reus* of extermination took place because perpetrators implemented 'a system of forced labour, state expropriation of foodstuffs and extreme restrictions on basic rights', and thereby subjected 'Cambodian civilians to famine conditions that would inevitably lead to death'.[36] The difficulty of obtaining a conviction for extermination based on the infliction of extreme living conditions, such as the creation of conditions conducive to malnutrition, disease, low life expectancy, and high infant mortality, is the requirement of *mens rea*, which was however proved by the ECCC.[37] Factual information showed that the regime was aware that their actions would have led to massive deaths and yet they used famine as a primary means to control the population.[38]

However, while the link with ESCR violations is present, it remains to be discussed why, for instance, the prosecution did not press charges to examine famine and the related violation of the right to food.[39] Indeed, according to some scholars, evidence exists proving that the Communist Party of Kampuchea (CPK) exported large quantities of rice without distributing it within the country, contributing to the starvation of the civilian population: for example, witnesses testified that only unmilled rice was eaten within the country and that there were several warehouses that often had to keep 'four to five' rice mills operating constantly to process sufficient rice to meet the CPK's demands for export.[40]

18.3.3 The East Timor Special Panels for Serious Crimes (SCU) and the right to housing

The SCU, in its six years of operation, tried fifty-five cases resulting in eighty-four individual convictions for crimes against humanity, of which twenty included violations of the right to adequate housing.[41] These crimes took place in the context of a widespread and systematic attack directed against the civilian population in East Timor in 1999 and were part of an organized campaign of violence that included

[36] Randle C DeFalco, 'Accounting for Famine at the Extraordinary Chambers in the Courts of Cambodia: The Crimes against Humanity of Extermination, Inhumane Acts and Persecution' (2011) 5 International Journal of Transitional Justice 142.

[37] Schmid (n 24) 154. Elias Davidsson, 'Economic Oppression' (2005) 23 Netherlands Quarterly of Human Rights 173, 195.

[38] DeFalco (n 35) 149–52. M Cherif Bassiouni, *Crimes against Humanity* (Martin Nijhouff 1999) 252. As Bassiouni points out, the elements of the crime of extermination are not only met through the action of directly killing someone with a weapon but also when the perpetrator creates 'conditions of life amenable to mass killing'.

[39] Schmid (n 24) 164.

[40] DeFalco (n 35).

[41] Joseph R Schechla, 'Reparation of Gross Violations of Economic, Social and Cultural Rights: A Work in Progress' (2011) 9 <https://www.academia.edu/7926424/Reparation_of_Gross_Violations_of_Economic_Social_and_Cultural_Rights_A_Work_in_Progress> accessed 28 December 2023.

intimidation; arson; plunder; and looting of homes, property, and livestock, as well as deportation and forcible transfer of civilians, including through abductions in Indonesian occupied territories.[42] The first major crimes against humanity case successfully prosecuted by the SCU was that of *Joni Marques et al*, where forced deportation and destruction of property were prosecuted as part of the underlying act of 'other inhumane acts'.[43] In the *Ena* case,[44] the SCU did not include, among acts constituting 'other inhumane acts', the stealing of a large number of cattle belonging to the villagers; however, scholars have argued that the panel missed an opportunity to further investigate the impact of such act on ESCR of the affected population, which could have constituted a violation of the right to be free from hunger. Indeed, no further analysis was carried out to determine, for instance, if the stealing of livestock resulted in the starvation of the victims, linking possible deprivation of food with crimes against humanity, and the conduct of the responsible militia was allegedly attributable to the state of Indonesia.[45]

In conclusion, while the early hybrid courts have the merit of having effectively prosecuted international crimes encompassing ESCR violations, overcoming some challenges related to justiciability of ESCR—such as proving the *mens rea* for extermination determined by imposition of extreme living conditions—they have largely followed the path of international tribunals. This arguably resulted in missed opportunities, such as that of prosecuting illegal exploitation of natural resources as a war crime, which would have offered an opportunity to also investigate the conduct of non-state actors, such as armed groups and corporations, whose violations of ESCR can amount to international crimes but are often perpetrated in a climate of complete impunity. Adopting a proactive approach in prosecuting ESCR violations would hence better reflect the extent of victimization on the ground and the complexity of conflict dynamics.

In order to fully explore the potential of hybrid courts in the area of ESCR, the common features of hybridity need to be unpacked to assess whether and how they can constitute an advantage in terms of accountability for ESCR violations amounting to international crimes.

18.4 The Inherent Features of Hybrid Courts and their Added Value in Relation to ESCR Violations

Hybrid courts or tribunals are at the crossroads of international and national justice and are considered by most scholars as the best of the two models: at least

[42] ibid. UNGA, 'Report of the International Commission of Inquiry on East Timor' (31 January 2000) A/54/726,S/2000/59 23 UNTAET, Case No (09/2000).
[43] Schechla (n 41) 9.
[44] *Prosecutor v Ena* (Special Panels for Serious Crimes) 05/2002 (23 March 2004) [42]–[46]; [92].
[45] Schmid (n 24) 162.

in principle, they should act with independence and impartiality while providing local ownership, prosecute a higher number of perpetrators in a shorter time span and with a lower budget, and improve the domestic justice system's capacity to comply with international standards.[46] While each hybrid tribunal has a different history and legal basis, they share some common elements, which will be analysed below to assess whether such inherent features could provide them with an advantage in prosecuting ESCR violations amounting to international crimes.

18.4.1 Mixed composition of international and national staff and additional expertise in the area of ESCR

While domestic courts usually employ national staff and international courts employ nationals of states other than the state/s where international crimes took place, hybrid courts, in their choice of judges, prosecutors, registrars, and support staff, employ a mixture of national and international staff. Overall it has been argued that the presence of national judges tends to increase the legitimacy of the court, but this is not necessarily the case for countries where the commission of international crimes largely implicates the ruling élite and where a majority of national judges could be accused of political interference, corruption, and lack of independence, as was the case for the ECCC.[47] However, given the adaptability of hybrid courts to a specific context, the nature of the conflict can be taken into account when defining the composition of the court, possibly resulting in greater legitimacy. Similarly to civil and political rights violations, prosecution of ESCR violations could also benefit from the mixed composition of hybrid courts. For instance, investigating crimes of land grabbing and forced eviction against indigenous communities by international corporations requires very specific linguistic, cultural, and legal knowledge of the functioning of that specific community and legal expertise in complex transnational human rights litigation cases, which might not be found locally and could be fulfilled by legal experts who have already dealt with similar cases in their domestic jurisdiction.

[46] It should be noted that, while this is true in theory, in practice, not all hybrid courts have lived up to such expectations in their operationalization. For instance, the Cambodian Court has been criticized for being too expensive and for lacking independence. Similarly, the Special Tribunal for Lebanon (STL) has been criticized for its excessive costs and lack of local ownership and impact on the domestic judicial system. Sarah MH Nouwen, 'Hybrid Courts: The Hybrid Category of a New Type of International Crimes Courts' (2006) 2 Utrecht Law Review 190.

[47] See Erica Bussey, 'Striking the Right Balance—Blending International and National Components in Hybrid Courts' (*Justice in Conflict*, 14 March 2018).

18.4.2 Increased flexibility in the mixed applicability of international and domestic law

Schmid has comprehensively demonstrated that ICL is intrinsically related to ESCR violations and can be used as an effective tool to prosecute those ESCR violations that overlap with international crimes.[48] However, in order to do so, the traditional elements of war crimes, crimes against humanity, and genocide have to be met. Since for hybrid tribunals the jurisdiction *rationae materiae* is set out by their respective statutes on a case-by-case basis, it can be better adjusted to the specific context so as to encompass violations that might not meet the requirements of international crimes but that nevertheless entail a particular seriousness for the domestic jurisdiction of the country at stake and whose lack of prosecution would, for instance, increase social tension and undermine national reconciliation. While it is true that most hybrid courts' statutes are drafted as to include the traditional international crimes, applicable law in the hybrid tribunal's statute can be modelled to cover ESCR violations of particular gravity or of particular relevance for the dynamics of that specific conflict as per domestic law. For instance, the ECCC has jurisdiction *rationae materiae* over 'serious violations of Cambodian penal law, international humanitarian law and custom and international conventions recognized in Cambodia'. The addition of 'international conventions' could be beneficial in the area of ESCR, which are protected by a series of international legal instruments that are not necessarily covered by the Rome Statute: for instance, forced labour and labour exploitation are disciplined by a series of International Labour Organization (ILO) Conventions.[49] Indeed, if the current gross human rights violations and abuses against migrants in Libya—which include trafficking in persons for the purpose of forced labour—will trigger the creation of an hybrid court, the mention of 'international conventions' in its statute could positively increase the chances of prosecuting the crime of forced labour as per the UN Protocol to Prevent, Suppress and Punish Trafficking in Persons, especially Women and Children and related ILO Conventions, even for lower threshold cases where the widespread or systematic nature of enslavement as a crime against humanity cannot be proven.

This argument is particularly relevant with regards to the war crime of pillage: as analysed above, the interpretation of the war crime of pillage under the Rome Statute is quite restrictive compared to customary international humanitarian law: the perpetrator needs to have the intention of depriving the owner of a certain property without their consent and do so for private or personal use. In

[48] Schmid (n 24).

[49] ILO Forced Labour Convention no 29 (1930); Protocol of 2014 to the Forced Labour Convention, 1930; ILO Abolition of Forced Labour Convention (1957) no 105; and ILO Convention on worst forms of child labour (1999) no 182.

addition, as per the interpretation followed in the *Bemba* decision, the ICC observed that a 'somewhat large-scale appropriation of property'—and not 'mere sporadic acts'—is required to apply Article 8, para 2 (e)(v) of the Rome Statute; moreover, without setting a certain monetary amount, the ICC excluded petty property expropriation from the definition.

The flexibility of hybrid tribunals in terms of applicable law allows for a broader interpretation, which could reduce the impunity gap and address cases where the Prosecutor could not prove that the perpetrator personally enriched themselves as a consequence of appropriation of property or where appropriation of property does not reach the level of large scale or is not of relevant monetary value but still significantly and adversely impacts the ESCR of the civilian population.[50] For instance, during the conflict in the Central African Republic, the Peuhl community has been progressively deprived of large quantities of livestock, which constituted the basis for their survival, by armed groups.[51] While such a violation might not be considered of 'relevant monetary value' as per the ICC's standards, one could argue that the deprivation of their main source of income largely contributed to their displacement, their complete dependence on humanitarian aid, and consequently their increased marginalization, further enhanced by ethnic persecution against them.

18.4.3 Proximity to affected communities and the issue of reparations

Proximity to affected communities has proven to be a key feature in increasing hybrid tribunals' legitimacy: indeed the choice of locating tribunals in the country or in the region where atrocities took place can effectively improve victims' access to justice and lead to a cathartic process within the society at large.[52] This feature of hybrid courts should not be read solely in terms of physical proximity in the choice of the location for the court but also in terms of meaningful inclusion and participation of victims and affected community and of their related grievances. For instance, conducting hearings in the local language increases victims' understanding of the proceedings and offers an immediate and unrestricted access to evidence and witnesses.[53]

50 See also the SCU *Ena* case analysed above.

51 See Association pour l'Intégration et le Développement Social des Peuhls de Centrafrique, 'Les Peuhls Mbororo de Centrafrique une communauté qui souffre' (2015).

52 This has not always been the case for all hybrid courts: both the STL and the Kosovo Special Chambers are located in The Hague. Indeed the location of the STL is part of the reason why it has been largely criticized for lack of local ownership.

53 Ezequiel Jimenez, 'Hybrid Tribunals as Capacity Buiding: Narrowing the Impunity Gap?' (Masters thesis, University of Gothenburg, University of Roehampton, University of Tromsø 2015) 19 <https://munin.uit.no/bitstream/handle/10037/8242/thesis.pdf?sequence=2> accessed 28 December 2023.

Early outreach programmes aimed at clarifying the mandate of hybrid courts and minimizing expectations, for example in relation to selectivity of prosecution or reparations, can play a pivotal role in the acceptance of international or hybrid courts within the affected population. In practice, however, outreach programs have often proven to be too narrow and to exclude relevant stakeholders, such as in the case of Sierra Leone with regards to victims' representatives and civil society groups, negatively impacting on the fruitful engagement of local actors but also on the accurate reflection of victims' grievances and needs into prosecutorial strategies.[54] The local acceptance and perceived legitimacy of hybrid courts can also be affected by lack of knowledge of the proceedings, excessively lengthy processes, political interference, selection of defendants, or perceived partiality in investigation and prosecution, leading to allegations of victor's justice. Empirical studies have confirmed that local ownership, and consequently greater acceptance and trust in international justice, can also be hampered by limiting the court's mandate or operations with regards to time spans, geographical areas, or crimes to be prosecuted.[55] In this regard, exclusion of ESCR violations can negatively affect victims' perceptions of justice if, for instance, addressing such violations was identified by civil society organizations and victims' representatives as a priority need for the affected communities, but does not end up properly reflected in the court's operations.

Several truth commissions have successfully taken up the demands and needs of affected communities in unveiling economic violations occurring during the periods they investigated: Chad's Truth Commission received an explicit mandate to shed light on allegations of former President Hissène Habré's illegal looting of the state's coffers; Sierra Leone's Truth Commission identified specific companies complicit in illegal trade of diamond and timber,[56] and the Truth Commission in Liberia had a specific mandate to include 'economic crimes, such as the exploitation of natural or public resources to perpetuate armed conflict', thereby linking pillage to the conflict and the possibility for it to be prosecuted as a war crime.[57] However,

[54] ibid 30. See also OHCHR, 'Rule of Law Tools for Post-Conflict States: Maximizing the Legacy of Hybrid Courts' (2008) UN Doc HR/PUB/08/2, 11 available at <https://www.ohchr.org/sites/default/files/Documents/Publications/HybridCourts.pdf> accessed 28 December 2023. For example, negotiations to establish the Special Court for Sierra Leone were held with a relatively small group, mainly including governmental actors, such as the Ministry of Justice, causing a sense of disengagement by legal professionals.

[55] Susanne Buckley-Zistel, 'After Nuremberg. Exploring Multiple Dimensions of the Acceptance of International Criminal Justice: An Introduction' (2017) International Nuremberg Principles Academy, 10 <https://www.nurembergacademy.org/fileadmin/user_upload/Introduction.pdf> accessed 28 December 2023.

[56] Kimberly Lanegran, 'Justice for Economic Crimes: Kenya's Truth Commission' (2015) 5 ASPJ Africa & Francophonie 63, 65. See also Sierra Leone Truth and Reconciliation Commission, 'Witness to Truth: Report of the Sierra Leone Truth & Reconciliation Commission' (2004) 2, 27 <http://www.sierra-leone.org/Other-Conflict/TRCVolume2.pdf> accessed 28 December 2023.

[57] Ministry of Foreign Affairs of Liberia, An Act to establish Truth and Reconciliation Commission (TRC) of Liberia (2005), Article IV, 4 <https://www.refworld.org/pdfid/473c6b3d2.pdf> accessed 28 December 2023.

for those countries where truth commissions were accompanied or followed by hybrid courts, such as Chad and Sierra Leone, the findings of the truth-seeking mechanisms were not adequately taken up by their respective judicial bodies. With regards to Sierra Leone, as mentioned above, Taylor was convicted for aiding and abetting pillage but only in relation to personal property and not for exploitation of natural resources. In the more recent case of Chad, the Extraordinary African Chambers (EAC) were only mandated with the power to try and prosecute those most responsible for genocide, crimes against humanity, war crimes, and torture. On 30 May 2016, Hissène Habré was convicted for crimes against humanity, war crimes, and torture, including sexual violence and rape, and sentenced to life in prison.

Questions arise as to why Habré was not charged with the war crime of pillage. The Investigative Chamber noted that the Prosecutor referred to the extensive destruction and appropriation of property, not justified by military necessity and carried out unlawfully and wantonly pursuant to Article 7(1)(c) of the EAC Statute in his opening submission but failed to refer to it in his final submission. As a consequence, the Investigative Chamber found that, if individuals were indeed victims of pillage of their property, 'the circumstances in which those acts were allegedly committed precluded the Chamber from considering the crime', because 'the conduct did not take place in the context of an armed conflict, as required by the elements of the war crime'.[58] As a consequence, no charge for pillage was brought to the attention of the Trial Chamber. However, the Appeals Chamber held that a substantial number of victims suffered from pillage—which could have been prosecuted pursuant to Article 7(2) of the EAC Statute —, concluding that the charges included in the indictment do not represent fairly the extent of the harm suffered by victims.[59]

On 27 April 2017, the Appeals Court confirmed the verdict and ordered Habré to pay approximately 123 million Euros in victim compensation, mandating a trust fund to trace, locate, and recover Habré's assets.[60] The EAC trial was considered a milestone for justice in Africa, being the first case in which an African Union (AU)-led process resulted in conviction for international crimes of a former head

[58] Daley J Birkett, 'Victims' Justice? Reparations and Asset Forfeiture at the Extraordinary African Chambers' (2019) 63 Journal of African Law 151, 159. See also Order for partial dismissal, indictment and remand to the Trial Chamber of the Extraordinary African Chambers, Investigative Chamber (Investigative Chamber order) (13 February 2015).

[59] Birkett (n 58) 159.

[60] See Nader Iskander Diab, 'Challenges in the Implementation of the Reparation Award against Hissein Habré: Can the Spell of Unenforceable Awards across the Globe be Broken?' (2018) 16 Journal of International Criminal Justice 141. See also Amnesty International and International Federation for Human Rights (FIDH), 'Looking for Justice: Recommendations for the Establishment of the Hybrid Court for South Sudan' (2016). See further Reed Brody, 'Victims Bring a Dictator to Justice: The Case of Hissène Habré' (2017) Bread for the World Analysis 70, 6 <https://www.brot-fuer-die-welt.de/fileadmin/mediapool/2_Downloads/Fachinformationen/Analyse/Analysis70-The_Habre_Case.pdf> accessed 28 December 2023.

of state through universal jurisdiction, and it was particularly praised for the centrality of a victim-centred approach and for the prominent role of civil society organizations in tirelessly pursuing the quest for justice for over twenty-five years.[61] However, ESCR violations originally reflected in the Truth Commission and sporadically mentioned by the investigative Chamber were not properly addressed by the Trial Chamber, neither in terms of prosecution nor in terms of reparations. As it was rightly pointed out, 'the Appeals Chamber's order that victims who experienced pillage are entitled to compensation is also difficult to reconcile with the Trial Chamber's earlier finding in its decision on reparations that victim status is tied to the crimes for which Habré was convicted'.[62]

Similarly, the final report of the Commission for Reception Truth and Reconciliation (CAVR) in East Timor provided a detailed analysis of ESCR violations, accusing Indonesia of repeatedly failing to abide by its international obligations to provide for the basic needs of the population, in terms of food, shelter, and basic healthcare, which were channelled in a discriminatory manner to favour certain groups.[63] It also found violations of the right to housing due to repeated displacements and non-recognition of customary land-ownership and land-use practices,[64] and violations of the right to education by using schools for propaganda and indoctrination.[65] Particularly interesting is the section on rights over natural resources, which makes quite a groundbreaking link between trading companies exploiting natural resources, the Indonesian government and military, and the violation of the right to an adequate standard of living, as well as of the right to self-determination, which includes disposal of natural wealth.[66] Once again, the SCU did not comprehensively bring to justice the extent of ESCR violations found by the Truth Commission.

While it is commendable that Truth Commissions highlighted ESCR violations in their final reports and some hybrid mechanisms successfully prosecuted such violations, upholding their justiciability under ICL, the extent of such allegations was not fully reflected in the prosecutorial strategy of hybrid mechanisms. Moreover, hybrid courts used the principle of prioritization of civil and political rights to single out reparations for ESCR violations, de facto perpetuating the existing impunity gap with regards to such violations.[67] Considering the importance

[61] Amnesty International and FIDH (n 60) 16.

[62] Birkett (n 58) 159.

[63] Truth and Reconciliation in Timor-Leste Commission for Reception, 'Chega!' (2005) CAVR, chapter 7.9, 131 <http://www.cavr-timorleste.org/en/chegaReport.htm> accessed 28 December 2023. With regards to the violation of the right to adequate food, CAVR found that the Indonesian authorities did not just neglect agriculture, they also took security measures that positively worsened the chances of the farming population making a living, primarily by forcibly settling them in infertile areas under conditions in which their movement was restricted.

[64] ibid 143.

[65] ibid 148.

[66] ibid 138–39.

[67] Schimd (n 24) 8–9.

of reparations to the affected population, ensuring the right to an effective remedy to victims of international crimes should be the final goal of ICL, whether the criminal conduct overlaps with ESCR or not. Hybrid tribunals should make efforts to attract external donors to reparations programmes, for instance through the establishment of trust funds, as in the case of the EAC, but ideally incorporating ESCR violations in reparation programmes, as well as in the prosecutorial strategy.

18.5 Complementarity of Hybrid Courts with Other Accountability Mechanisms

This chapter does not aim at blindly promoting hybrid courts, dismissing other international, national, or regional mechanisms that may prove to be equally suitable in prosecuting ESCR violations. Rather, it seeks to highlight the peculiarities of hybrid mechanisms. Hybrids are compared to other forms of accountability mechanisms in terms of their utility in prosecuting ESCR violations amounting to international crimes.

18.5.1 Hybrid courts vs the International Criminal Court (ICC)

Scholars have argued that the resurgence of hybrid courts is partially due to the realization that the ICC cannot deal with all the atrocities occurring on the planet.[68] In addition, failure to bring perpetrators to justice can indirectly perpetuate the cycle of impunity, which, coupled with the lack of adequate witness protection, can negatively affect the Court's legitimacy and contribute to revictimization of affected communities, as the ICC's role in the Kenyan case demonstrated.[69] Hence, complementary accountability mechanisms need to be put in place to bring international crimes to justice when, for instance, the political will for an ICC referral is lacking or when the Court's selectivity imposes the prioritization of certain situations or crimes over others.[70] Indeed, situations in the territories of non-member states can only come under an ICC investigation if the United Nations Security Council refers them to the Court or if the alleged perpetrators are citizens of ICC member states. Hybrid courts have the advantage that they do not necessarily

[68] Patryk Labuda, 'The Special Criminal Court in the Central African Republic: Failure or Vindication of Complementarity?' (2017) 15 Journal of International Criminal Law 175.

[69] See Geoffrey Lugano, 'Assessing the Acceptance of International Criminal Justice in Kenya' (2016) International Nuremberg Principles Academy, 14 <https://www.nurembergacademy.org/fileadmin/user_upload/Kenya.pdf> accessed 28 December 2023, whose empirical findings conclude, for instance, that the 'ICC's methods in conducting investigations and protecting its witnesses had an impact on its acceptance across all actor categories in Kenya.'

[70] Beth Van Schaack, 'The Building Blocks of Hybrid Justice' (2016) 44 Denver Journal of International Law and Policy 101, 101.

require the UN Security Council's intervention: the Extraordinary Chambers in Cambodia, for instance, were endorsed by the UN General Assembly. Moreover, the recent wave of hybrid courts has proven that they can also be set up without UN intervention: the EAC within the courts of Senegal and the Hybrid Court for South Sudan are the results of regional efforts at the AU level, while the Kosovo Specialist Chambers were negotiated by the European Union with the Kosovan authorities.

With regards to ESCR violations amounting to international crimes, in its policy paper on case selection and prioritization, the Office of the Prosecutor at the ICC stated that: 'it will also seek to cooperate and provide assistance to States, upon request, with respect to conduct which constitutes a serious crime under national law, such as the illegal exploitation of natural resources, arms trafficking, human trafficking, terrorism, financial crimes, land grabbing or the destruction of the environment.'[71]

Therefore, it will be interesting to see how such 'cooperation and assistance' will be implemented in practice, for example in cases like that of the CAR, where, for the first time, a hybrid tribunal has been created in a country concomitantly under investigation by the ICC and where ESCR violations, including illegal exploitation of natural resources, are allegedly widespread.[72] Indeed, the UN High Commissioner for Human Rights (OHCHR) Mapping Report, a fundamental tool for informing the prosecutorial strategy of the Central African Special Criminal Court, identified a pattern of gross violations of economic and social rights, further aggravated by poor infrastructure and extreme poverty, where 'development indicators and levels of attainment of economic and social rights have been chronically very low'.[73] The report also identified extensive campaigns of pillaging by armed groups, accompanied by widespread attacks on protected objects under international humanitarian law, such as schools, hospitals, and religious sites, the impact of which 'is often to deprive large segments of the conflict-affected population of humanitarian assistance, access to food, education, health care and places of worship'.[74] It remains to be seen how the hybrid court will cooperate with the ICC in relation to the ESCR violations identified and whether the Office of the Prosecutor policy paper will find its operationalization with regards to such violations, starting from the situation under investigation in CAR.

71 ICC Office of the Prosecutor, 'Policy Paper on Case Selection and Prioritization' (2016) 5.

72 See Global Witness, 'A Game of Stones and Blood Timber' (2017) <https://www.globalwitness.org/en/campaigns/central-african-republic-car/game-of-stones/> accessed 28 December 2023 and Kasper Agger, 'Warlord Business: CAR's violent Armed Groups and their Criminal Operations for Profit and Power' (2015) Enough Project.

73 OHCHR, 'Mapping Project documenting serious violations of international human rights law and international humanitarian law committed in the territory of Central African Republic between January 2003 and December 2015' (2017) 247.

74 ibid 258.

18.5.2 Hybrid courts vs national courts

Part of the legacy of hybrid courts is related to the idea that prosecution of gross and widespread human rights and humanitarian law violations cannot simply be delegated to existing domestic jurisdiction. This is not only because, following a conflict or an authoritarian regime, the domestic judicial system often suffers from systemic issues, such as lack of infrastructure and resources, poorly trained personnel, or endemic corruption, but also because justice—including through prosecution—is often perceived as a unique occasion for a society to make a transition to a culture of rule of law. Similar considerations should apply for ESCR violations. With regards to illegal exploitation of natural resources and other related abuses committed by international corporations, national courts of the country where these corporations are legally registered have so far demonstrated to be best suited at attempting to investigate such crimes. Some of the practical challenges identified by transnational human rights litigation are related to enforcement of legal claims against companies for complicity in human rights violations, which heavily relies on domestic systems: for instance, criminal complaints against both *Danzer* management in Germany and *Nestlé* in Switzerland were based on local investigations.[75] Nevertheless, domestic jurisdiction in the countries where violations are taking place often lack the capacity, independence, and expertise to conduct investigations and properly protect victims and witnesses.[76] Another major obstacle relates to the lack of corporate criminal liability, which has only been recently incorporated into the legal systems of a few European countries, such as Spain, Austria, and Switzerland.[77] The role of hybrid courts in this regard could be beneficial in terms of ensuring some international safeguards against national political interference, as well as bringing in international expertise, including with regards to transnational crimes, with the aim of strengthening weakened domestic legal systems, such as in the area of expert transnational investigation and witness protection.

18.5.3 Hybrid courts vs regional human rights courts

Finally, the role of regional human rights judicial mechanisms should also be explored in relation to prosecution and reparation for ESCR violations. For instance, reparations awarded by the Inter-American Court have incorporated the realization of ESCR in important and innovative ways: the case of the *Plan de Sánchez*

[75] European Centre for Constitutional and Human Rights (ECCHR), 'Holding Companies Accountable: Lessons from Transnational Human Rights Litigation', 15–16.
[76] ibid.
[77] ibid 21.

Massacre v Guatemala constitutes a landmark decision in this regard, leading the Guatemala state to recognize the massacre of over 260 indigenous people in 1982. In its ruling, the Court found that the massacre 'gravely affected the identity and values of the members of the Maya-Achí people', thus recognizing the infringement of cultural rights and issuing not only monetary compensation for the victims but also other types of reparations directly related to the violations of ESCR, in the form of development programmes which included 'a sewage system and potable water supply', adequate healthcare centres, and intercultural and bilingual teaching personnel for primary and secondary schools.[78] The contribution of a regional human rights mechanism should not be minimized but rather explored, including within the African system, which could draw from the wealth of jurisprudence of the Inter-American system in relation to ESCR violations.

Within the African context, recent developments with regards to hybrids, the ICC, and regional human rights courts deserve special attention in terms of their complementarity, especially in view of the adoption, in June 2014, of the Protocol on Amendments to the Protocol on the Statute of the African Court of Justice and Human Rights (Malabo Protocol) by the AU. The Protocol extends the jurisdiction of the proposed African Court of Justice and Human Rights (ACJHR) to include international crimes, including those covered by the Rome Statute, as well as transnational crimes, criminalizing trafficking with respect to persons (Article 28J), drugs (Article 28K), and hazardous waste (Article 28L), the illicit exploitation of natural resources (Article 28L Bis) and enumerating terrorism (Article 28G) and corruption (Article 28I) as distinct international crimes, among others.[79] On the one hand, the Malabo Protocol could potentially ensure a higher level of accountability for illegal exploitation of natural resources than that so far offered by international or hybrid courts, as it will exercise international criminal jurisdiction over corporate entities, which have consistently been excluded from the jurisdiction *rationae personae* of international courts.[80]

On the other hand, a hybrid court may be able to overcome certain limitations affecting the African regional system, for instance with regards immunity for sitting heads of state, as well as cooperation with the ICC. This is because the Malabo Protocol envisages immunities for heads of state, casting doubt on effective accountability in cases where ESCR violations are committed by the elite in power,

[78] OHCHR, 'Transitional Justice and Economic, Social and Cultural Rights' (2014) 38–40 <https://www.ohchr.org/sites/default/files/Documents/Publications/HR-PUB-13-05.pdf> accessed 28 December 2023.

[79] Sarah Nimigan, 'The Malabo Protocol, the ICC, and the Idea of "Regional Complementarity"' (2019) 17 Journal of International Criminal Justice <https://doi.org/10.1093/jicj/mqz040> accessed 28 December 2023.

[80] Barrie Sander, 'Addressing the Economic Dimensions of Mass Atrocities: International Criminal Law's Business or Blind Spot?' (*Justice in Conflict*, 8 June 2015) <https://justiceinconflict.org/2015/06/08/addressing-the-economic-dimensions-of-mass-atrocities-international-criminal-laws-business-or-blind-spot/> accessed 28 December 2023.

and it also does not mention any type of cooperation or complementarity with the international court.[81] While the Rome Statute contains a specific provision on cooperation with regional mechanisms, the AU has consistently called upon its members to refuse to cooperate with the ICC and has instead positively promoted hybrid courts for Chad and South Sudan. Therefore, future cooperation is more likely with a regional hybrid court than with the ICC.

Finally, while the Malabo Protocol seems to have a special interest—and probably less political interference—in prosecuting transnational crimes, such as human trafficking, or illegal exploitation of natural resources, a hybrid court could exercise a complementary role, filling the gap and covering those ESCR violations that amount to international crimes but are not properly addressed by the regional court, for instance when they entail state responsibility shielded by regional immunity.

18.6 Concluding Remarks

This chapter sought to argue that ESCR violations in conflict should be taken seriously and that hybrid courts can offer some advantages in prosecuting them. This is not to argue that hybrid courts should be considered as a panacea for the resolution of all challenges in the area of accountability for ESCR violations amounting to international crimes, but rather than they have some features which make them particularly well suited to prosecuting these crimes.

The chapter put forward three main arguments. The first is that the fragmented nature of ICL, understood positively in terms of the legal pluralism of hybrid courts, has the potential to more effectively reflect the needs and grievances of affected communities, including in the area of ESCR violations. The second is that long-lasting marginalization of ESCR violations should not solely be addressed in terms of transitional justice measures, such as truth commissions, but also through prosecution of ESCR violations amounting to international crimes, for which hybrid courts could play a pivotal role. Finally, by doing so, hybrid courts could fill the impunity gap derived from the lack of accountability for ESCR violations and positively contribute to the building or restoration of local trust in justice and the rule of law. By combining international principles and expertise with local ownership, expertise, and legitimacy, hybrid courts could positively reconcile the tension between purely international justice, increasingly perceived as Western dominated and excessively focused on civil and political rights, and growing local and regional accountability mechanisms striving for greater justiciability of ESCR violations but often lacking political will, independence, or impartiality.

[81] ibid 28.

19
Conclusion
The Design, Function, and Evaluation of Hybrid Courts

Kirsten Ainley and Mark Kersten

19.1 Plus ça Change, Plus c'est la Même Chose

This book was begun before the onset of the global COVID-19 pandemic. When the pandemic hit, the project stalled, both because professional and personal lives were thrown into disarray, but also because we could not imagine the world being the same again. The arguments and findings in the chapters of the book would surely, so our 2020 selves thought, soon be redundant. It was impossible to imagine that there would not be a rupture, a line that demarcated the world that was and the world that would now be. The early days of the pandemic signalled a permanent shift towards a more profound rendering of justice throughout societies. A glaring light was shone on not just those affected by or emerging from conflict, but all societies in which the injustices of unequal access to clean water, healthcare, and social support, as well as unequal contributions to basic services—the work that the poor do to enable the rich to stay rich. And yet here we are, in 2024, with the pandemic not being the portal that Arundhati Roy called for us to use as a gateway to a better world, but instead a temporary disruption to business as usual.[1] It is with some considerable sadness, therefore, that we have written a conclusion to this work on innovations in justice without reference to any of the innovations in justice we thought might appear during the pandemic. Hybrid justice is as relevant as it ever was, and while there may be little to celebrate in terms of structural change and broader justice achievements since 2020, the contributors to this volume offer reasons for optimism that incremental gains in justice for victims of egregious crimes, and in societal resilience more broadly, can be made through hybrid mechanisms.

To draw the findings of the chapters into conversation, this conclusion is structured around three themes: the design of hybrid courts; their function, in particular in relation to political actors; and their evaluation. As this is a book with both academic and practical ambition, we also draw here on the Dakar Guidelines

[1] Arundhati Roy, 'The Pandemic is a Portal' (*Financial Times*, 4 April 2020) <https://www.ft.com/content/10d8f5e8-74eb-11ea-95fe-fcd274e920ca> accessed 25 February 2024.

Kirsten Ainley and Mark Kersten, *Conclusion* In: *Hybrid Justice*. Edited by: Kirsten Ainley and Mark Kersten, Oxford University Press. © Kirsten Ainley and Mark Kersten 2025.
DOI: 10.1093/oso/9780192893758.003.0019

on the Establishment of Hybrid Courts (hereinafter Dakar Guidelines), another output of the Hybrid Justice project, to think through what the chapter findings mean for the applied work of establishing and operating hybrid mechanisms in the future.[2]

The Dakar Guidelines contain four Guiding Principles for establishing hybrid courts:

1. The design of the hybrid court should respond as much as possible to the particular needs and circumstances of the concerned state(s) and to the conflict or situation that gave rise to the crimes at issue.
2. Hybrid designers need to make choices about prioritizing certain aims or benefits over others, rather than attempting to achieve all of the potential goals or benefits of internationalized criminal justice.
3. The overriding objective of those who establish hybrid courts should be to design a genuinely independent institution, properly established in law, to maximize the integrity, effectiveness, and legitimacy of its organs.
4. Continuous evaluation should be planned from the outset of a hybrid court's creation, including by designing appropriate, and where possible measurable, aims, goals, and benchmarks by which to assess the tribunal.

These guidelines seek to provide a roadmap to build mechanisms that have high levels of internal resilience: the ability to withstand political and other pressures by virtue of their legitimacy, independence, appropriate scope, and resources. Doing so will enable them to contribute where possible to societal resilience in the form of stable peace, strong institutions, and adherence to the rule of law. The chapters in this book increase our understanding of why these principles matter and the ways in which hybrids do or, in some cases, do not exhibit internal resilience or reinforce societal resilience.

19.2 The Design of Hybrid Courts

To begin the book, Schmidt asks a deceptively simple question: how should we determine the ideal composition of a hybrid court? What is the right mix of international and domestic components? These are first-order questions which have been often overlooked in the history of establishing hybrid courts, with some courts enjoying lower levels of legitimacy as a consequence. According to Schmidt, we must ask whether a hybrid's authority is grounded in an appropriate constituent

[2] Kirsten Ainley and Mark Kersten, 'Dakar Guidelines on the Establishment of Hybrid Courts' LSE and Wayamo Foundation (2019) <https://hybridjustice.com/dakar-guidelines/> accessed 25 February 2024.

subject in order to judge whether it is constitutionally legitimate. Where a court serves primarily the interests of the international community or the ambiguous subject of 'humanity', as the international criminal tribunals and the early hybrid courts tended to, defendants appeared to be held accountable not to an amorphous international community, far less humanity, but instead to the powerful states who were seen to pull the strings. Schmidt thus argues that hybrid courts should primarily serve the interests of the societies in which the crimes they address were committed.

In order to discover the needs of societies in which crimes are alleged to have been committed, a needs assessment can help to determine what is desired by affected communities. It can also establish the resources available to create and support a hybrid justice mechanism. In the history of hybrid tribunals, it is striking that needs assessments have usually not been conducted, with interested publics, including victim communities, consulted only after a mechanism has been established.

The authors in this book differ in their assessments of the utility of hybrid mechanisms, but none would recommend them in every circumstance. Purely international courts can play a role when state power is so dominant that there is little to no hope of those alleged to have ordered atrocity crimes being brought before a hybrid court. The extraordinary, renewed interest in the International Criminal Court (ICC) generated by Russia's invasion of Ukraine in 2022 and Israel's attack on Gaza in 2023–2024 is illustrative here, though there is little indication yet that the ICC will be able to conduct trials of high-level offenders in either situation. But such courts can lack meaningful connections to local sites of crimes and be perceived as neo-colonial institutions as opposed to independent judicial bodies. In theory, hybrid courts can offer international funding and general expertise (assuming either would be useful in the context) alongside the grounded knowledge and specific expertise that domestic actors bring. However, as examples such as the Extraordinary Chambers in the Courts of Cambodia (ECCC) show, there are no guarantees that an international–domestic partnership will bring about justice that satisfies publics or victim groups (or that such a partnership can be maintained in the face of political pressure).

Whose needs should be prioritized when evaluating whether a hybrid tribunal should be established? Njeru and Masiya note the critical importance of consulting more than just the technocrats and elites who tend to hold local power within hybrid systems. They argue that peace and justice must also be owned by 'women, youth, and the marginalized; those most affected by the conflict and most in need of peace'. Depending on context, there may be a range of civil society actors, chiefs, religious figures, guilds, and the like which hold social power and organize for collective interests. Genuine deliberation (not after-the-fact consultation) should take place between and within all groups, facilitated but not dominated by external resources if needed.

Ambach argues that victims should play a central role in the design and practice of hybrid justice. Having a fully worked out scheme for the representation and participation of victims in the functions of the court, as well as for their protection and reparation, is now understood as being essential to any internationalized institution. Moreover, as Ambach reminds us, this originates from domestic legal practice; it is not a progressive innovation introduced by international actors, who have historically been content to run war crimes trials with only the minimal participation of victims, as witnesses. All of the second wave of hybrid courts, and many of the first, have comprehensive victim participation regimes.

Perhaps the most challenging and resource-intensive aspect of victim participation, an aspect that needs to be handled with the greatest care to avoid raising unrealistic expectations on behalf of victims, is reparations. The Extraordinary African Chambers (EAC) has followed the ICC in establishing a trust fund for victims—it is the only hybrid court to have done so. However, both the ICC and the EAC have faced significant challenges in raising money for these trust funds, let along satisfying the aspirations of victims and survivors. In cases in which it seems unlikely that funds for victim reparations can be raised to be dispensed by a hybrid court, there is precedent for referring victims to national courts to benefit from national compensation programmes, as has been established at the Kosovo Specialist Chambers (KSC) and the Special Tribunal for Lebanon (STL), although the possibility of individuals receiving reparations through these schemes has yet to be realized.

Williams, like Ambach, sees a trend towards reparative mandates in hybrid courts which exists alongside a variety of mechanisms that can be used to realize reparations, including ordinary domestic courts, human rights mechanisms, and national administrative processes. Still, Williams' chapter demonstrates that the record of hybrid courts over reparations has been largely unsatisfactory. In all hybrids with a reparative mandate, reparations have been linked to criminal convictions, meaning the only people who are entitled to reparation are those who can link their victimization directly to the crimes for which convictions have been achieved—usually a very small minority of the victims of a conflict. In hybrids such as the ECCC, a range of collective reparations awards have been implemented, which to some extent ameliorates the rigidity of the link between reparation and conviction; yet individuals have not received reparations. Where individual reparations are provided for, as at the EAC which has its own trust fund, they have not yet been dispensed. And, Williams reminds us, none of the hybrids established so far has had the power to order states (which are likely to have much greater resources than convicted persons) to fund reparations.

As Ambach and Williams demonstrate, hybrid courts (and the ICC) have not yet been able to adequately repair victims. As a result, making decisions over an inevitably imperfect system of victim participation, around which expectations will almost certainly be raised well beyond what a hybrid can deliver, is among the most challenging aspects in the design of hybrid courts. Williams therefore issues a plea for the design of this critical aspect of hybrids: 'There must be an early and realistic assessment as to what can be expected from a reparations process, what form it will take, who is responsible for reparations, and where the money will come from.'

Something which may emerge from a needs assessment, and which may be linked to the salience of reparations, is a desire among victim populations for economic, social and cultural wrongs to be repaired. Dieci argues that violations of economic, social, and cultural rights (ESCR) have generally been excluded from the jurisdiction of hybrid courts (although as Sánchez describes in this volume, hybrid investigatory mechanisms in Latin America have had some significant success in investigating corruption and other economic crimes). Dieci rejects the idea that violations of ESCR are inherently structural and therefore beyond the scope of criminal proceedings and documents the (relatively few) attempts made by hybrids to take seriously the economic harms involved in international crimes. She sees the hybrid form as particularly suited to the development of international law in this sphere, as hybrids are particularly able to innovate (as discussed also in relation to forced marriage, by Grey). For Dieci, prosecution of ESCR violations would 'better reflect the extent of victimization on the ground and the complexity of conflict dynamics' and, indeed, would be following the stated aims of the ICC in this regard. It would also increase the legitimacy of hybrids to victim communities and publics, reducing any perception of them as Western-dominated through their sole focus on violations of civil and political rights.

In the Dakar Guidelines, it is recommended that needs assessments are carried out early in the drafting process, by an advance team constituting qualified national actors, such as legal professionals, civil servants, and civil society leaders—particularly those from organizations that represent victim populations. Additionally, the team could include international experts, such as legal professionals who have worked in other international or hybrid criminal tribunals as well as international civil society representatives who have a longstanding presence and expertise in the region. Needs assessments should be carried out in two main stages. The first stage should determine whether a hybrid court is necessary and appropriate for the context (on the basis of victim preferences; the capacity of existing justice systems to deliver justice; resources available; and the political, legal, and security contexts in the affected country or proposed host country). A second stage, which should only proceed if it is determined that a hybrid court is appropriate and necessary, should assess the capacity of the national justice system and justice officials to contribute to the work of the hybrid court as well as the appropriate subject-matter jurisdictions. The needs assessment should help to distil what the various options for justice in any given context are—what can be achieved and what the trade-offs must be. Sánchez, for instance, notes that while victims and publics might want extensive and expensive justice processes, including reparations schemes, international partners are more likely to fund mechanisms with more limited mandates.

Once it has been established that a hybrid mechanism is an appropriate response to justice needs, and assuming the domestic partner is likely in most cases to be the state in which the alleged crimes took place, available international partners need to be identified. The contributions of Sánchez, Baylis, and Bussey each note the trend towards regional institutions acting as international partners in hybrids, as part of a longer-term trend towards the development of regional perspectives on, and instruments of, transitional justice and international criminal law (ICL). The African Union (AU), in particular, has strongly expressed its authority over transitional justice processes in Africa, in a purported attempt to reject interference from what is understood by some as a neo-colonial International Criminal Court.

Baylis argues that regional actors can offer significant benefits over more distant partners in terms of capacity building, as long as the regional and local actors share a common language and broadly similar legal systems. Additionally, they can be useful with respect to the integration of regional norms and crimes more relevant to the specific context and the greater localization of justice practices and access to financial and human resources (a point supported by Jiminez's findings on capacity building at the Bosnian War Crimes Chamber). Bussey describes the possible increase in legitimacy that a regional partner could bring, citing claims that AU involvement in the EAC enhanced its legitimacy as it was seen as an African project.

While a regional international partner might seem more appropriate than a more distant one, geographic or ideological closeness may also render a regional partner more troublesome. As Bussey notes, there can be complications if regional partners were involved in the conflict(s) that led to the creation of the hybrid. In the case of the Hybrid Court for South Sudan (HCSS), for instance, the involvement of judges from neighbouring states thought to support the government forces or the Sudan People's Liberation Movement (SPLM) could threaten the legitimacy of the proceedings. Aside from political influence, regional powers could also assert normative influence for instance over crimes charged. However, despite heightened international tension over head of state immunity, Baylis argues that we have not seen an assertion of authority over specific justice norms and their promotion from the AU through the EAC or the HCSS—the AU's position on head of state immunity is not evident in the Statute of either court.

Njery and Masiya also underscore the value of regional partners, arguing that the predominance of Western models and institutions in African justice practices have failed to provide genuine redress. Like Dieci, they note the particular importance of guaranteeing economic, social, and cultural rights within justice processes in states that have been impoverished through unequal global structures.

To return to Schmidt's original question, the nature of the domestic–international relationships should be established once the right partners are identified. Bussey examines the rationales for including or excluding national judges and staff in hybrid tribunals, focusing on the question of 'sociological' legitimacy and how it impacts on internal and external resilience. It has become expected that national judges will sit in hybrid courts, in particular where crimes may be prosecuted under applicable domestic law. However, Bussey argues that the inclusion of national judges can have costs, especially if the selection of the best national judges (and other staff) will deprive the domestic justice system. National judges are also thought to be more liable to political interference.

To evaluate the role of national judges, Bussey compares the Special Criminal Court (SCC) in the Central African Republic, a 'hybrid' tribunal which is within the national justice system, and which has a majority of national judges and nationals in key staff positions, but receives international support, with the KSC, which has no national judges or staff. Keppler also examines the SCC, which she compares to the proposed HCSS. Bussey reminds us that the question of legitimacy can cut both ways; legitimacy underpins both the decision to include a majority of national judges in the SCC and to exclude or minimize their participation in the KSC and the HCSS, in which the principal posts are all to be held by non-South Sudanese Africans and each Chamber will have a majority of non-South Sudanese African judges. Similarly, Keppler argues that members of South Sudan's civil society supported a hybrid court with only minimal domestic involvement as it had the potential to add much-needed capacity to the system and ensure a high standard of procedure. That being said, the lack of substantive connections between the South Sudanese justice system and the HCSS means that capacity is unlikely to be built domestically through the operation of the HCSS if it becomes operative—capacity is effectively just on loan (though there is some discussion of phasing national judges and staff into the HCSS over time, as was done at the Bosnian War Crimes Chamber). In the case of the SCC, the Central African government requested international staff, again to add capacity to the national system and also to protect the Court's independence.

Of course, it may be that a hybrid mechanism has no judges at all. As our understanding of both the potential and the limits of hybridity have increased, so have the variety of mechanisms that feature hybrid authority and staffing. Sánchez outlines the achievements of a number of hybrid investigatory mechanisms, arguing that such mechanisms may be valuable precursors to prosecutions if it is not yet possible for hybrid (or indeed national or international) courts to begin prosecutions. Hybrid investigatory mechanisms have proved extremely effective in the investigation of complex crimes, including those involving alleged perpetrators in positions of state power. These investigatory mechanisms may be particularly powerful in terms of their capacity-building potential. When well-designed, they take the best international resources available (funding and expertise) to document and investigate crimes (an extremely expensive element in any criminal justice process), before passing case files to relevant domestic systems so that prosecutions can proceed at a national level. Yet precisely because these mechanisms have begun to have significant purchase, they are less likely to be tolerated in the future by those whose actions may be targeted by them. As Sánchez explains, domestic involvement in hybrid institutions is a double-edged sword: 'Buy-in from domestic stakeholders promotes greater legitimacy, and better inclusion of the mechanism into the state's institutional fabric. However, at the same time, this model allows for the intervention of domestic powers that can completely veto the mechanism or substantially reduce its powers.'

The existence of hybrid investigatory mechanisms—as just one part of a larger justice project—highlights the importance of careful consideration of how hybrid mechanisms relate to other institutions with potentially overlapping jurisdictions. These institutions might be ordinary criminal courts, truth commissions, investigative bodies, international criminal courts, and the like. Hybrids sit among complex networks of accountability measures, and the relations between justice institutions operating in the same space can be productive, as Dieci argues in regard to reparations for victims in Guatemala, or more fraught, as Labuda shows in his chapter. He outlines arguments for the primacy of hybrid courts, which can reduce confusion and encourage cooperation, but concludes that the most important thing is that priority is established somewhere in the system—one specific institution needs to have clear primacy to avoid uncertainty and duplication.

Labuda notes that it is particularly important to establish the relationship of hybrids to the ICC clearly in contexts where both are active. The Rome Statute supposedly enshrines a rule of priority for national courts (national primacy) at the expense of the ICC (subsidiarity). Over time, however, Labuda argues that the ICC has reinterpreted the meaning of complementarity to suggest that there is parity or equality between the ICC, states, and other entities, with no clear primacy. In the context of criticism of the ICC as a neo-colonial institution, the stakes of primacy are high, especially in areas such as sovereign immunity. Head of state immunity is explicitly rejected in the Rome Statute of the ICC, yet supported for *sitting* heads of state within the African Union's Malabo Protocol. Carlson notes the minefield this presents for hybrid courts, which are usually internationalized precisely to challenge, sometimes even to prosecute, those with political power in the state in which crimes were committed and which do not wish to operate with the shadow of the ICC hanging over them. It is for the society in question to decide whether they can tolerate a mechanism that does not reach to the very top of those responsible. But as Carlson shows, the EAC is a useful example of a hybrid which was run by African states and the AU, yet created an extraordinary precedent for holding a (former) head of state accountable for atrocity crimes. She also makes clear that we still lack answers on how to hold state actors to account for 'ruthless' but perhaps not quite criminal behaviour.

The issue of primacy calls attention to one final area of hybrid design covered in the chapters. While good practice suggests that hybrids should be designed, as far as possible, according to the needs and preferences of the domestic publics that they are intended to serve, there are areas where there may be reasons for the imposition of standards understood as 'international'. Such areas include the provision of defence resources, including a dedicated and autonomous office for defence counsel, and the standard of prison conditions for convicted persons. Ashraph notes that hybrid and international courts are often claimed by their supporters to provide fair trials, but do not do so if they fail to provide sufficient resources for a comprehensive defence. It is not clear, and we are not aware of any research on, the extent to which the rights of the accused are more likely to be supported or institutionalized in domestic or internationalized contexts. Nevertheless, if there is little support in a specific context for these rights to be safeguarded, there is an argument, based on established good practices and the principles underlying the right to a fair trial, that the defence should be properly resourced anyway. The same is true of prison standards—Greer notes that hybrid courts primarily focus on incarceration when sentencing convicted persons, with the implementation of penalties often an afterthought when hybrids are established. There has been little thought given at the design stage of hybrids, or indeed while functioning, of *why* prison sentences are imposed and no consideration of whether rehabilitation is possible. Nor has there been a great deal of concern with prison standards, and again there is an argument from good practice that international prison standards should be upheld in internationalized courts regardless of whether there is public support for this.

19.3 Independence and Innovation

As David Luban argues, and Schmidt cites, legitimacy is something that is performed more than designed: 'The legitimacy of international tribunals comes not from the shaky political authority that creates them, but from the manifested fairness of their procedures and punishments. Tribunals bootstrap themselves into legitimacy by the quality of justice they deliver; their rightness depends on their fairness.'[3] This understanding of the critical importance of tribunal performance is the justification for the most important guiding principle in the Dakar Guidelines: that the overriding design objective of hybrid court founders be to build a genuinely independent institution, properly established in law, that maximizes the integrity, effectiveness, and legitimacy of its organs. It is the independence of a hybrid court (along with its resourcing) which contributes most to its internal resilience. Independence will also give a hybrid the best chance of contributing positively to societal resilience. But while independence is an overriding goal, it is impossible to achieve perfection. There is an art in deciding what can

[3] David Luban, 'Fairness to Rightness: Jurisdiction, Legality, and the Legitimacy of International Criminal Law' [2008] Georgetown Law Faculty Working Papers.

be tolerated in terms of political interference and what must be resisted. None of the hybrid tribunals, nor indeed the ICC or the International Criminal Tribunals for the Former Yugoslavia or Rwanda, have been free from political interference. Accountability mechanisms are an intervention into politics, and will be resisted by those actors who believe that their power will be threatened by justice, and supported by those who think that their power will be enhanced. Simply establishing a hybrid court can be a useful means of insulating the court from political manipulation given that multiple actors will have varying levels of authority and thus scrutiny over it. However, the hybrid nature of a court is not enough to protect it from interference, and every hybrid has faced political interference of one form or another.

Sánchez documents some of the many struggles that Latin American hybrids have faced when powerful domestic political actors have sought to challenge their constitutionality and functions. However, he also reminds us that it is not just domestic political actors who might seek to interfere with the processes of hybrids. Where the international partner to a court or investigatory mechanism is a political body, for instance the Secretary General of the Organisation of American States in the case of the Mission to Support the Fight Against Corruption and Impunity in Honduras (MACCIH), there is more likely to be high-level political will available to support the work of the hybrid, but this may well be coupled with political interference. More technical human rights bodies lack political interests (at least explicitly) but also lack power as partners in the face of resurgent domestic political power. Sánchez argues that the most influential factor of all in whether Latin American hybrid investigatory mechanisms have been able to weather challenges from domestic elites has been whether they have had the support of the United States.

Torrens emphasizes the importance of tracking hybrid performance over time. She shows that hybrids initially have some level of state support, but that it often turns into acquiescence and later dissent as the court operates over time. Torrens acknowledges the significant challenges that dissent can present to a hybrid, with state level dissent leading to delayed or failed trials, diminished funding, and a reduction in the legitimacy of the proceedings. Similarly to Sánchez, she also notes the challenge of dissent from the international partner, which can also lead to diminished funding and even the collapse of the hybrid. However, she reminds us that dissent is not inherently negative: 'dissent can be powerful and transformative; it can destabilize and rearrange outdated international and local power structures and monopolies and it can also contribute to reassessing and restructuring disenfranchising power dynamics and beliefs.' Ashraph's work on defence rights substantiates this point: dissent around the rights of the accused can (and in some cases has) led to the creation or strengthening of a defence counsel office, which works to demonstrate to those who support or are in community with a particular accused that the hybrid is not conducting sham trials or undertaking 'victor's justice'. Dissent and responses to it can increase the legitimacy of a court to domestic and international audiences. Schmidt underlines why legitimacy is important in practice as well as in principle: 'Courts will engender greater compliance among stakeholders—with regard to financial contributions, local cooperation, or the execution of international arrest warrants—when actors feel that they ought to follow their mandate and decisions.'

Alongside the independent administration of justice, one of the most important contributions that it is argued that hybrids can make is to build capacity in domestic justice systems. Capacity building should contribute to ongoing societal resilience by developing a domestic commitment to, and capacity to implement and enforce, the rule of law (if these things are not already present, as assumptions that capacity is lacking should be tested before work begins to build it). However, capacity building in practice has been weak. In his chapter, Jiminez examines the capacity building work of the SCSL, ECCC, and the Bosnian War Crimes Chamber (WCC). He argues that the UN has prioritized the embedding of transitional justice mechanisms in larger state-building processes effectively as capacity building projects post-conflict, with a view to preventing future conflict. However, he notes that, in practice, the work to strengthen domestic judicial institutions through knowledge transfer and investment in critical infrastructure has been relatively weak in the case of the three hybrids on which his contribution focuses. Too often capacity building has relied on the entrepreneurship of individuals rather than being embedded as a core function of the mechanisms.

Ashraph and Greer support Jimenez's findings. Ashraph notes the lack of training for the under-qualified duty counsel employed at the Defence Office at the Special Court for Sierra Leone (SCSL), while Greer argues that decisions to move convicted persons to foreign prisons make it hard for human rights norms to become embedded in domestic prison systems. The reasons for moving convicted persons abroad or not providing for their human rights in domestic prisons are usually the result of a lack of funding to support human rights compliant prisons in the state in which crimes took place—a reminder of the importance of securing sufficient funding at the outset of a hybrid process, and being clear-eyed about the priority of capacity building, an inherently resource-intensive process.

Kavran establishes the importance of outreach activities in the functioning of hybrid courts and the significant challenges to outreach in practice. Founders of internationalized courts, Kavran argues, have always seen trials as part of a broader project to support the achievement or maintenance of peace, reconciliation, and adherence to the rule of law. These are extremely ambitious goals and rely to some extent for their success on claims that in the long term, the archives of courts and trials will become tools for education and help ensure that the history of the conflict is accurately recorded so that false claims about the past cannot be used to justify future wars. Yet outreach has not generally been included in the design of past hybrids (the STL is an exception), but has developed as part of their functioning in attempts to ensure that justice is not just done but seen to be done. This work, like capacity-building work and reparations schemes, is often underfunded and initiated too late in the process, undermining the work and legitimacy of the mechanisms in practice.

Grey highlights the importance of the functioning of hybrid courts in terms of their legal innovation (or potential for it). She examines the crime of forced marriage, which is not included in the mandate or jurisdictional design of either of the hybrids it has been recognized as a crime within (the SCSL and the ECCC). Forced marriage and its treatment in ICL exemplifies one of the key tensions in the practice of hybrids. The two courts that delineated forced marriage as an international crime during conflict were so fearful of overstepping their bounds that they failed to challenge peacetime practices of forced marriage in both Sierra Leone and Cambodia that are counter to human rights standards. Both courts were also disappointingly regressive in terms of gender: Grey shows that neither court took seriously sexual violence against men and boys during conflict, despite significant evidence of such crimes and their impact.

19.4 Evaluating Hybrid Justice

Grey's work, alongside that of many others in the book, demonstrates why evaluation is so important to the success of hybrids. Only through the continuous evaluation of practice could, for instance, the failure to take seriously the sexual and gender-based violence against certain categories of victims be exposed and corrected. Ashraph also illustrates some of the ways in which the ambitions contained in the founding documents of hybrids are not achieved in practice. It may be, for instance, that the rights of the accused are fairly clearly set out in the mandate of a court, but when it comes to the practice of running trials, Registries fail to afford to defence staff the resources they need to mount a fair defence.

Most of the chapters in this book are inherently evaluative—commending some aspects of hybrid design and practice and noting where others fall short or are frustrated by external actors. But hybrids themselves have not generally undertaken systematic evaluation of their work, and the chapters, in their own ways, call for this to change.

The Dakar Guidelines recommend that hybrid courts establish continuous evaluation processes from their inception, including by designing appropriate and, where possible, measurable, aims, goals, and benchmarks by which to assess the tribunal. Ashraph's chapter also points to an element of hybrid mechanisms that should not be used as a yardstick of success: convictions. It might be tempting to count convictions as a key performance indicator in a state in which atrocity crimes have been committed, but an objective to secure convictions instead of fair trials can significantly bias the practices of a court. Donors have a responsibility here too, as they often want to see 'results', and results are, more often than not, understood to constitute the rate and number of convictions of perpetrators. The definition of appropriate goals and benchmarks is critically important for stakeholders to be able to track courts' progress, yet inherently controversial. As Sánchez notes, cultures of impunity, violence, and corruption cannot be overthrown, at least in the short term, by a hybrid investigative body or criminal court. Rather hybrids should be relatively modest in the goals they set out to achieve, and track progress towards achieving their specific mandates, alongside other goals such as capacity building in national justice systems (where relevant), victim protection and reparation, and modelling the very highest standards of fair criminal process by exhibiting values such as equality before the law and independence of decision-making.

19.5 Hybrid Futures

After a recent backlash against international and internationalized justice, we have seen significant interest in its response to Russia's invasion of Ukraine and Israel's war on Hamas in Gaza.[4] Through March and April 2022, forty-three mostly European states parties to the Rome Statute referred the situation in Ukraine to the ICC and when Prosecutor Karim Khan issued a call for financial support in March 2022, twenty states replied by mid-May (Office of the Prosecutor, 2022).[5] Even the United States, so historically ambivalent towards the Court, is exploring how it can support ICC prosecution of war crimes in Ukraine. There have also been calls for an international or internationalized tribunal specifically for Ukraine, from inside and outside the country, though less enthusiasm to consider whether Ukraine has fully complied with international humanitarian law.[6]

Between November 2023 and January 2024, seven states referred the situation in Palestine to the ICC (following Palestine's original self-referral in 2018): South Africa, Bangladesh, Bolivia, Comoros, Djibouti, Chile, and Mexico. A number of human rights organizations within and outside Palestine have also made representations to the Court, and some states, notably Belgium, have pledged funding for the ICC's investigation. Perhaps most significantly, in December 2024, South Africa filed an application at the International Court of Justice asking the Court to determine whether Israel was in breach of the Genocide Convention. A large

[4] Courtney Hillebrecht, *Saving the International Justice Regime: Beyond Backlash against International Courts* (Cambridge University Press, 2021).

[5] ICC, 'ICC Prosecutor Karim A.A. Khan QC announces deployment of forensics and investigative team to Ukraine, welcomes strong cooperation with the Government of the Netherlands' (17 May 2022) <https://www.icc-cpi.int/news/icc-prosecutor-karim-aa-khan-qc-announces-deployment-forensics-and-investigative-team-ukraine> accessed 25 February 2024.

[6] *The Guardian*, 'Amnesty regrets 'distress' caused by claims in Ukraine report' (8 August 2022) <https://www.theguardian.com/world/2022/aug/07/amnesty-international-ukraine-military-report-civilians> accessed 25 February 2024.

number of (mostly global south) states and more than a thousand organizations globally have declared their support for South Africa's case.[7] In addition, the slow speed at which the ICC moves and accusations of bias towards Israel have led for calls to establish an internationalized or hybrid tribunal to ensure accountability in the situation in Gaza.[8] However, despite the abundant resources that seem to be available to pursue justice in/for Ukraine, and the more limited resources but high level of international attention directed at Gaza, resources and will for other international justice projects are lacking and it remains possible, indeed likely, that the downstream costs of the pandemic will frustrate the adequate funding of courts and tribunals beyond those operating in Ukraine. Still, some hybrid courts remain active. The SCC began its first trial in April 2022. Others are being tentatively designed. For instance, plans have been announced to create a hybrid court in The Gambia. Elsewhere, the hope for hybrids is waning. Human rights abuses continue in South Sudan with no sign that the HCSS will become operative in the near future. Whether the second wave of hybrids ebbs or flows, the chapters here provide an important record of the history of this form of criminal justice, the challenges that hybrids have faced, and the standards they need to meet in future to ensure their effectiveness.

[7] Middle East Monitor, 'Over 1,000 organisations unite in support of South Africa's genocide case against Israel at ICJ' (11 January 2024) <https://www.middleeastmonitor.com/20240111-over-1000-organisations-unite-in-support-of-south-africas-genocide-case-against-israel-at-icj/> accessed 25 February 2024.

[8] UN Press, 'Underscoring Urgency for Ceasefire in Gaza, General Assembly Highlights Need to Protect Civilians, Grant Humanitarian Access, Free Hostages, Condemn Hamas' (15 December 2023) <https://press.un.org/en/2023/ga12573.doc.htm> accessed 25 February 2024; Henry Mance, 'UN aid chief Martin Griffiths: "The war in Gaza isn't halfway through"' (*Financial Times*, 17 December 2023) <https://www.ft.com/content/01b592be-47c7-4a20-9bbd-621aa40f7640> accessed 25 February 2024.

Index

For the benefit of digital users, indexed terms that span two pages (e.g., 52–53) may, on occasion, appear on only one of those pages.

Tables and figures are indicated by an italic *t* and *f* following the page number.